PENGUIN HANDBOOKS

THE PENGUIN CAREERS GUIDE

Anna Alston took a degree in English at Oxford and qualified as a careers officer. She was Senior Careers Officer in Waltham Forest for several years before becoming a freelance careers writer. She has co-authored several careers books and has written for the *Daily Telegraph*, *Woman*, *Good Housekeeping* and various other women's and family magazines. She was careers counsellor for *Company* magazine for three years and now edits the Independent Schools' Careers Organization's magazine, *CareerScope*. She has a teenage daughter.

Anne Daniel was born and educated in the USA. After taking a degree in English, which included a year in Oxford, she married an Englishman and returned to England. For many years she ran the Daily Telegraph Careers Information Service and edited six editions of *The Daily Telegraph Careers A–Z*. She also wrote and edited a special supplement on graduate careers for the *Daily Telegraph* and developed the Jobscope Service for the *Sunday Telegraph*. She lives with her husband and three children in Buckinghamshire.

As a freelance journalist in the fifties, Ruth Miller began to specialize in writing about careers because she had become fascinated by how and why the people she interviewed had chosen or drifted into their careers. Since then she has written about careers and related subjects for a wide variety of publications, including *The Times*, *Woman*, *Daily Telegraph*, *The Times Educational Supplement* and *Good Housekeeping* magazines, as well as for specialist publishers such as ISCO and CRAC.

All three collaborated on *Hours to Suit*, a guide to flexible patterns of work, are members of the Careers Writers Association and have served on its committee.

THE PENGUIN CAREERS GUIDE

Anna Alston
and
Anne Daniel

CONSULTANT EDITOR: RUTH MILLER

PENGUIN BOOKS

PENGUIN BOOKS

Published by the Penguin Group
Penguin Books Ltd, 27 Wrights Lane, London W8 5TZ, England
Penguin Books USA Inc., 375 Hudson Street, New York, New York 10014, USA
Penguin Books Australia Ltd, Ringwood, Victoria, Australia
Penguin Books Canada Ltd, 10 Alcorn Avenue, Toronto, Ontario, Canada M4V 3B2
Penguin Books (NZ) Ltd, 182–190 Wairau Road, Auckland 10, New Zealand

Penguin Books Ltd, Registered Offices: Harmondsworth, Middlesex, England

First published as *The Peacock Book of Careers for Girls* 1966
Second edition published as *Careers for Girls* 1970
Third edition 1973
Fourth edition 1975
Fifth edition published as *Equal Opportunities:
A Careers Guide for Women and Men* 1978
Sixth edition 1981
Reprinted with revisions 1982
Seventh edition 1984
Reprinted with revisions 1985
Eighth edition 1987
Ninth edition published as *The Penguin Careers Guide* 1992
Reprinted with updating material 1993
10 9 8 7 6 5 4 3 2

Copyright © Ruth Miller, 1966, 1970,
1973, 1975, 1978, 1981, 1982, 1984, 1985, 1987, 1992, 1993
Copyright © Anna Alston, 1984, 1985, 1987, 1992, 1993
Copyright © Anne Daniel, 1992, 1993
All rights reserved

The moral right of the authors has been asserted

Printed in England by Clays Ltd, St Ives plc
Filmset in Monophoto Times

Contents

iv   Contents

Europe and 1992   li

Sources of Help   liii

Some Useful Publications   lv

Main Careers in Alphabetical Order   1

(see index for specific careers)

v   Contents

vi   Contents

1993 General Note

Rapid change is a key feature of the world of education, training and careers. The problem for the writers is that so many current developments are progressive and their full implications not yet clear. For this revised reprint we have indicated where situations are 'under review' or qualifications, courses, titles, etc. being 'phased in' or 'phased out'. There are, however, two on-going developments which will, to a greater or lesser extent, affect virtually every chapter in the book:

1. All polytechnics are now universities. The sector as a whole offers a more diverse range of courses than ever before, and accepts a greater – and growing – range of qualifications for entry.

2. More and more national vocational qualifications, both job-specific (NVQs) and general (GNVQs), are becoming available. They will have an impact on professional membership, entry to higher courses and movement across the academic/vocational divide.

Acknowledgements

We would like to thank the statisticians in the Universities Central Council on Admissions, the Universities Statistical Record, the Polytechnics Central Admissions System, the Department of Education and Science, the Association of Graduate Careers Advisory Services, the Central Services Unit and the Department of Employment for letting us have up-to-date figures for the Sex Balance sections on pp. xl–xlvi and for their patience in explaining statistical method, and jargon, to a layperson.

We would also like to thank the 120-odd organizations who answered our many questions, especially about the details we wanted for the 'Position of women' paragraphs. Special thanks are due to John Jones and Malcolm Hudson of Thames Polytechnic for helping with the computing section. A special mention, also, to the Equal Opportunities Commission.

Finally we would like to thank careers and educational advisers for suggesting improvements in the presentation of the information.

Foreword

When this book was first published, in 1966, it was quite a trailblazer. Though called *Careers for Girls*, it covered careers generally, including such then male preserves as medicine and engineering. Its purpose was, unambiguously, to encourage girls to move off the tramlines and widen their career choice; squeeze through doors which were ajar (quite a few were, even then); hammer at those which were shut; and, where necessary, use the back door. The way into TV producing, for example, was as secretary. Equal opportunity legislation was nothing but a pious hope and a glint in feminists' eyes. Medical schools were allowed to impose quotas for women students (about 15%); barristers could bar women from their Chambers because, they said, there were no ladies' lavatories; draughtswomen and policewomen were still considered oddities. Even office managers in charge of rooms full of female typists were usually male. Interviewers could, and did, ask female job applicants about their marriage and child-bearing plans. Employers could be open about not training or promoting women in their twenties because they would soon leave to have children (no question of returners then), and not promoting women in their forties because they would soon reach 'a difficult age'. It really was like that, a generation ago. Nursing, teaching and secretarial work were still the main 'good jobs for a girl'.

Some Examples of Progress

Women as a percentage of total (home) applicants accepted for university:*

	1966	1991
Medicine	26	51
Law	13	58
Engineering and technology	2	15
Veterinary science	19	58
Total of students	30	49

* Figures for 1966 and 1991 are based on slightly different statistics, but UCCA says that for the subjects chosen the difference is insignificant.

Women as a percentage of:

	1966	1991
Solicitors on the roll	6	48 of new admissions
Called to the Bar	8	41 of new admissions
General practitioners	12 (1974 figure)	24
Hospital consultants	7	16
Chartered accountants	1	12 (35 student members)

I believe this book can take *some* credit for the changes since 1966.

In 1976 equal opportunities legislation was passed, and the book was retitled *Equal Opportunities: A Careers Guide for Women and Men*, but the emphasis on women's career considerations remained a special feature. The new, ninth, edition is simply *The Penguin Careers Guide* because *access* to virtually all courses and careers is now much the same for women and men. However, women's motivations and deliberations at the choosing stage and their subsequent career patterns and problems are, and will remain, different from men's. That is why the 'Position of women' paragraphs under each career heading will remain an essential ingredient of this *Guide*.

Residual constraints still affect women's choices. For example, what would be a perfectly ordinary choice for a boy may make added demands on a girl (though much less so than it used to): a boy who wants to be an engineer, say, needs only the right qualifications to train; a girl needs those, plus a modicum of assertiveness and self-confidence. That's why girls still need positive encouragement if they are to choose from the whole range of careers.

In some ways careers progression is still more difficult for women than for men. Take traditional career development: men's careers tend to have built-in training and promotion plans; most women still have to make it known to employers that they want a career, not just a job, even if they take a break to raise children just at the time men forge ahead. Entrenched assumptions don't stand up to being tested, e.g. that women aren't worth training because they do not repay the time and money invested in their training.

That may have been true in the past but it is not true today because the vast majority of women return to work within a few years, if not sooner. Other disproved assumptions are that women don't want responsibility; women aren't prepared to travel; and women are absent from work more often than men. The latter assumption is a misleading, sweeping statement. Women as a whole are absent from work more often than men. But the level of absenteeism for men, as for women, depends on the level of responsibility involved in the job; the lower down the ladder, the higher the absenteeism rate. Alas, far more women than men are on the lower rungs. In professional and management jobs absenteeism does not differ significantly between the sexes. That's a fact.

Few of us who in the 1960s were concerned with improving women's job prospects realized just how many intractable hurdles would have to be negotiated for the equal opportunities concept to be translated into reality. However, today's hurdles are different from those of a generation ago. The goalposts have shifted. Few women now feel badly disadvantaged at the job-getting stage. It's later, when it comes to balancing career and family, that problems start. It's a fact of life that in their thirties, when men (and determined women) concentrate on getting ahead, most women have other priorities: they are raising young families. That is why today's main equality concerns are:

1. *Poor childcare facilities.* Britain lags behind most other EC countries in this respect.

2. *Traditional, inflexible working patterns.* Part-time working is still far too often restricted to low or at best middle-level jobs, whatever the woman's qualifications and experience. Much female talent and training is wasted because women returners have to take jobs below their capabilities, unless they work full time. Job-sharing (see p. xxix) has proved itself efficient and cost-effective whenever it has been tried after careful preparation, but so far it's only in the public sector that professional and management-level jobs are being job-shared in any numbers. In the private sector it is still largely confined to low-level jobs.

However, help is on the way. It is rather ironic that what is bringing about a better deal for women has nothing to do with employers having seen the error of their ways. No, it's the 'demographic timebomb'. There is going to be large shortfall of school- and college-leavers over the next few years, but the workforce is expected to expand considerably, especially at professional and management level (once the recession is over). That's why women have suddenly become a 'valuable resource'. From having been a problem which employers had to cope with, women have become the solution to employers' problems. To judge by all the initiatives which have got off the ground, women are the flavour of the nineties.

First, the Hansard Society for Parliamentary Government, under the chairmanship of Lady Howe, produced a Report, *Women at the Top*. It lists lack of childcare provision and inflexible work structures as 2 of the 4 main barriers to equality (the others are outmoded attitudes about the role of women and direct and indirect discrimination). The Report's most important, and quite revolutionary, recommendation was that, under the Companies Act, annual reporting on equal opportunity policies and practices should become mandatory. *That* would cause a rumpus in a lot of boardrooms!

In October 1991 the Prime Minister launched 'Opportunity 2000', a 'business-led' campaign to 'increase the quality and quantity of women's participation in the workforce'. About 60 companies, including most household names, committed themselves to review their recruitment and employment practices and, broadly, become more woman-friendly. About 110 companies have now joined the campaign. However, unlike Lady Howe's Report, 'Opportunity 2000' prefers voluntary commitment; it does not want equal opportunity monitoring to become obligatory.

In February 1992 the London Business School, one of the most prestigious establishments of its kind in Europe, launched an award scheme jointly with British Gas and the *Independent*. Unlike other awards which go to individuals to reward their efforts, this award will go to 'the organization which has done the most to develop and promote women managers'. In March the Department of Employment launched *Equal Opportunities: 10 Point Plan for Employers*. It's an information pack which describes such measures as term-time working, job-sharing and monitoring equal opportunities implementation. The plan is sent to all employers with more than 50 staff and points out that 'equal opportunities practices are good business practice'. The list of encouraging happenings grows steadily: at the time of writing the choice of the next Director-General of the CBI is being discussed. Although names of contenders have not been published, the rumour is that headhunters have been asked to include women in their trawl. Such a rumour would not have seemed credible a few years ago.

Of course there are still lots of grumbles, many justified and some not. But I'm optimistic. Who would have thought, even a few years ago, that within a few weeks of each other, we would hear, as we did early this year, that the new Director of Public Prosecutions and the head of MI5 are both women?

It is true that women still have to be a bit better than men to get equally far – outstanding women have nothing to worry about anymore. But we won't have true equal opportunities until mediocre women get as far as mediocre men.

Ruth Miller
March 1992

Introduction to the Guide

What are Its Aims?

Firstly, to provide unbiased accurate careers information. Hard facts like entry and training requirements are checked with relevant organizations. Descriptions of the work involved – necessarily brief and only highlighting vital aspects – and descriptions of the sort of person likely to be good at/happy in the work are based on practitioners' experiences and views and on our own observations over many years of interviewing people at work. We believe this is the most important difference between this *Guide* and organizations' own careers literature.

Who is It For?

The *Guide* is likely to be used mainly by young people between 14 and 20. However, it is also valuable for the increasing number of people in their twenties, thirties or forties who want to, or have to, change their occupation. Some made the wrong choice the first time around or have developed new interests; others face lack of demand for their existing knowledge and skills, or redundancy. It is important to realize that most people could be happy in several different careers. What you enjoy at 40 may well be different from what you enjoyed at 21. Some people, in fact, take a long time to find out what they really want to do. For many occupations maturity is seen as an asset; education and training facilities may well be available; and standard entry requirements may be relaxed for older people (see individual entries, 'Late Start in Education and Training', pp. xxxvi–xxxix, and 'Higher Education', p. xxx).

More than ever before, individuals are expected to take charge of their own careers. This applies to everyone, from those working for large organizations to unemployed people on government training schemes. From time to time we all need to assess where we are in job terms, decide what we are aiming at, and what we need to achieve our aims. 'Buzz' phrases today are 'personal portfolio' – the individual's package of knowledge, skills and experience – and 'transferable skills' – those which can be put to good use in any work situation. The man or woman who is prepared to be flexible, to take advantage of (increasingly compulsory) continuing professional development (CPD), and who doesn't assume that any job is immune to change, is the one most likely to survive the present, and any future, recession.

How to Use This *Guide*

Careers in this *Guide* are listed alphabetically. However, many if not most careers are really 'areas of work'. Look at the index and you see how many more jobs than careers sections there are. Usually one kind of training leads to jobs in a variety of settings and you can normally mould training plus experience to the kind of job you will want to do when you know more about the whole spectrum and about your own likes, dislikes, strengths and weaknesses.

We could not hope to include all occupational areas in one book, so we have had to make arbitrary choices. Since the future demand is expected to be for more highly skilled, highly trained people, we have left out jobs requiring few, if any, educational qualifications, concentrating instead on those which need formal training or which lead to the widest range of options. School-leavers needing information on other jobs and training opportunities should contact their careers service. Adults should consult the Jobcentre or local guidance centre (see 'EGSAs', p. liii). Use this *Guide* in conjunction with 'Some Useful Publications' (p. lv), combined with discussions with careers advisers, family, friends who know you well and, if possible, with people doing the jobs you'd like to do.

Look at job advertisements. If you are a mature job-seeker you may be baffled by some of the newer or rarer job titles. Often it is only by reading the job specification that you discover it is something you know under a different name. Some are genuinely new occupations and you may need to dig more deeply to find out if your background and possible future training would make you a good candidate. Be adventurous, look at as wide a range as possible, using the 'Related Careers' sections as signposts.

Prospects

These are not, as in previous editions, singled out for special mention. The reasons are, firstly, within the book's lifetime the job market is likely to change – who would have forecast even 3 years ago that there would now be a surfeit of accountants? Secondly, there are always regional variations. Thirdly, and perhaps most importantly, it is frequently a mistake for a 16-year-old choosing A-levels or an 18-year-old choosing a degree subject to do so with the aim of entering a 'shortage' occupation 5 or 7 years later, as the marketplace may change dramatically meanwhile. Lastly, the term 'prospects' does not mean the same thing to all people – for some it means high salaries and/or early promotion, others link it with job security or the chance to follow the occupation anywhere in the country.

Equal Opportunities? Yes and No

Throughout the book's history, a main purpose has been to encourage girls to widen their career choices and speed their progress towards equality in the job market. Women now account for 44% of the total workforce. Within the EC the UK has the second highest proportion of married women who work. On average today's mothers take only 8 years out of their working lives for child-bearing and rearing. Growing numbers of single-parent families (nearly always headed by a woman), plus unemployment among men, mean that a career is very often a necessity rather than simply a choice.

Job segregation is still strong and there are still too many areas where women are noticeably under-represented. However, there *are* positive signs. The age profile is encouraging. Women aged 45-plus made their choices from a much narrower range of occupations than is available today. In many jobs there may be only a small proportion of women at senior level, and those have often had to be much abler than male colleagues to reach the top. However, a far higher proportion of *new* entrants to many occupations are women – determined, confident and expecting to find no real barriers to their progress – so in another 20 years the picture may look very different.

Changes in education (see 'Sex Balance in Education', p. xlv) should make girls keep their options open for longer than many have done up to now, particularly in the science/technological fields, where some of the best prospects are. At present, for a girl to choose surveying, engineering or building management (or, conversely, for a boy to choose nursery nursing, speech and language therapy, or secretarial work) is still unusual; it takes guts and self-confidence to differ from one's peers, to stand out in a crowd and to put up with sexist jokes and remarks.

Increasingly employers are having to acknowledge that they cannot move their male employees and expect the wives meekly to pack up and follow them; the wife's career may be as important to the family as the husband's and her prospects may be the better of the two.

A Word to Parents

It is likely that today's generation of mothers who value themselves and their own careers can, as they always have, influence their daughters' attitudes. Parents have always been the major influence on their children's choice of career: boys and girls who have followed non-traditional paths nearly always say that their parents' support has meant a great deal. Until the far-off day when all occupations are equally shared by men and women, parents will need to continue to encourage their sons and daughters to look for occupations in which they will be happy and successful, *regardless* of whether they are thought by others to be 'suitable' only for men or women.

Checklist

GCSE

The General Certificate of Secondary Education is the main qualification awarded at 16+ to pupils in England and Wales. Grades are on a scale from A to G; grades A, B and C are equivalent to the former O-level grades A, B and C (or CSE grade 1). Four or five GCSEs at grades A–C is a common starting point for most of the careers and courses in this book. (From 1994, in order to fit in with the National Curriculum, GCSEs will be graded on a scale from 4 to 10. The new grades will not be directly equivalent to the old: grades 10 and 9 will cover the levels of achievement covered by grade A and higher; 8 will be roughly equivalent to B; 7 and 6 will cover the same range as the current C, D and E.)

A-levels and AS-levels

A-levels are normally taken 2 years after GCSEs. Traditionally students have studied 2 or 3 complementary subjects (e.g. maths/physics/chemistry or English/history/French), but 'mixed' A-levels are becoming much more common and acceptable to higher education.

AS-levels were introduced to give A-level students the opportunity to broaden their education. An AS-level is studied to the same depth as an A-level but has only half the content. AS-levels may be chosen to complement or contrast with A-levels (for example, a science student can keep up a foreign language, or an arts student maths).

Normal entry to higher education (but see 'Higher Education', p. xxx) usually requires 2 or 3 A-levels, or 2 A- and 2 AS-levels. Some institutions may accept 1 A- and 4 AS-levels. Courses may require passes in specific subjects.

Scottish Certificate of Education

The Scottish equivalent to GCE O-level, the SCE Ordinary or O-grade, is being replaced by a new Standard grade. This examination caters for a much wider ability range, so far more pupils are able to gain a Certificate.

Grades are awarded on a scale from 1 to 7. Pupils take individual subjects at different levels, according to their ability in that subject. Grade 3 is considered to be the equivalent of C in the former O-grade and C in GCSE.

The SCE Higher grade is taken by the most able pupils after a further 1 year's study. Others take it after 2 years. For entry to degree courses in England and Wales candidates need passes in 4 or 5 H-grade subjects, 3 or 4 for entry to (4-year) Scottish degrees. Three Highers are equivalent to 2 A-levels, 5 Highers are equivalent to 3 A-levels.

The 1-year Certificate of Sixth Year Studies can be taken following a 1-year Higher course.

(Scottish secondary education is currently under review.)

National Vocational Qualifications (NVQs/ SVQs)

Job-specific NVQs

These (together with SVQs, the Scottish equivalent) make up a training revolution which will eventually affect employees at all levels of work. They are based on standards of competence agreed by industry. Each competence is made up of units setting out the standards of skill, knowledge and understanding that must be reached. For each unit the individual gains a credit and the NVQ certificate shows which unit credits have been collected.

Competence means the ability to perform tasks, and this is assessed 'on the job'. How or where you acquire this competence is immaterial. It may be through a full- or part-time course, by open learning (see p. xxxvi) while at work, or in your own time.

NVQs are awarded in 11 broad occupational areas and are at 5 levels. Level 1 is the most basic, while level 5 represents higher professional qualifications. By the end of 1992 levels 1–4 should be in position in all sectors. Because each NVQ fits into a framework it should now be possible to relate one qualification within an occupational area to another, regardless of what organization has awarded it, making it easier to move up the qualifications ladder. For example, an NVQ level 2 in retailing awarded by City and Guilds could be followed by an NVQ level 3 awarded by the National Retail Training Council.

NVQs are awarded by established awarding organizations, such as City and Guilds (see p. xxiii), BTEC (see p. xxi) and various professional bodies. In England and Wales these are approved by the National Council for Vocational Qualifications, in Scotland by SCOTVEC (which unlike NCVQ is also the awarding body).

People working towards NVQs/SVQs can obtain a National Record of Achievement (Record of Education and Training (RET) in Scotland): this is a personal record of achievement, experience, qualifications gained and plans for future training. It can help individuals to manage their own careers, while giving employers a good idea of what they can do.

People entering occupational areas as diverse as travel and tourism, engineering, retailing, publishing or building societies are almost certain to need NVQs in future.

General NVQs

The first General NVQs/SVQs are being piloted in 1992 and will be introduced widely from September 1993. They are intended for people studying full time at school or college who take GNVQs in 1 of 5 broad occupational areas (which differ slightly between England and Wales and Scotland). GNVQs/GSVQs will not be available at all levels to start with: in Scotland levels 2 and 3 should be introduced during 1992, with level 1 following in 1993; GNVQs are starting at level 3, with level 2 close behind. They will assess skills needed in a whole range of occupations, such as communication and problem-solving, languages and information technology. Students may go on to higher education or to courses leading to job-related NVQs. (See also 'BTEC', p. xxi, 'City and Guilds', p. xxiii.)

1993 NOTE: GNVQ levels 1, 2 and 3 are to be renamed Foundation, Intermediate and Advanced, with the Advanced known as 'vocational A-levels'.

BTEC (Business and Technology Education Council)

BTEC offers nationally recognized qualifications in a wide range of subjects. These include: agriculture, business and finance, caring, computing, construction, design, distribution, engineering, hotel and catering, leisure and science.

BTEC courses may be taken in colleges of further and higher education, polytechnics, some approved training centres and companies and, since September 1991, in schools. Courses are modular, with a range of compulsory 'core' and optional subjects so students can tailor-make programmes to suit their needs and interests. There are two types of qualification, Certificates and Diplomas. Certificates are usually studied on a part-time basis, Diplomas normally on a full-time basis. They are of the same standard, but Diplomas cover more ground.

There are several levels of course and qualification:

First awards
No minimum qualifications required, but some colleges may set some. Certificate courses last 1 year part time, Diploma courses 1 year full time or 2 years part time. Available in some schools.

National awards
Minimum 4 GCSEs (A–C) or acceptable pass in First Certificate/ Diploma or at the discretion of the college. National Certificate takes 2 years part time, National Diploma 2 years full time or 3 years part time or sandwich. Roughly equivalent to A-levels and acceptable (at the right standard of pass) for entry to degree courses.

Higher National award
Minimum 1 A-level plus supporting GCSEs (A–C) *or* BTEC National award. Higher National Certificate takes 2 years part time, Higher National Diploma 2 years full time or 3 years part time or sandwich. Generally accepted as equivalent of pass degree.

Continuing education
BTEC also offers a range of individual units and programmes for adults wishing to update and acquire new skills.

Many BTEC awards are NVQs (see p. xx). Many are also recognized by professional bodies for entry and/or exemption purposes.

1993 NOTE: As BTEC NVQs/GNVQs become available over the next few years, existing BTEC awards will be phased out.

Further information   BTEC, Central House, Upper Woburn Place, London WC1H 0HH

SCOTVEC (Scottish Vocational Education Council)

SCOTVEC administers a comprehensive and highly flexible system of vocational education. It is based on free-standing units, which can be taken on their own or built up to a group award.

National Certificate modules can be achieved by various modes of study, at school, college or place of work. A coherent group of modules at appropriate levels can lead to National Certificate

Group Awards; to Scottish Vocational Qualifications (SVQs, see p. xx); or entry to SCOTVEC Higher National Certificate and Diploma courses or entry to higher education; to recognition by professional bodies for entry and/or exemption purposes.

Higher National Certificates and Diplomas, which are broadly equivalent to BTEC HNC/D, have been reorganized on a unit or modular basis. Entry is with a relevant group of National Certificate modules, appropriate passes in S- or O- and H-grades, or at the discretion of the college.

Further information   SCOTVEC, Hanover House, 24 Douglas Street, Glasgow G2 7NQ

City and Guilds

Awards qualifications in around 400 different subjects for a wide range of industries, including hotels and catering, construction, engineering, printing, travel and tourism. City and Guilds does not run courses itself; these are held in centres such as colleges of further education, adult education institutes and training centres. Most are run as part-time day-release courses, but some full-time and evening courses are available. Some are also available through distance-learning (see p. xxxvi).

In the main, no specified time limits or entry requirements are laid down for qualifications. Many certificates are awarded jointly with an industry body and City and Guilds has been closely involved in developing NVQs (see p. xx). It has introduced a Diploma of Vocational Education at 3 levels: a broad Foundation for 14- to 16-year-olds and, for 16-year-olds upwards, an Intermediate and National. This replaces existing Foundation and CPVE awards and will eventually fit into the GNVQ framework (see p. xxi). Some students will combine this Diploma with A-levels.

All City and Guilds awards are available at several levels and individuals normally progress from one to the next. In addition, there are several senior awards which people can work for and which depend on experience and demonstrated ability, not on conventional academic study: Licentiateship (higher technician or master craftsman level); Graduateship (equivalent to first degree); Membership (Master's degree or full corporate membership of a professional body); Fellowship (outstanding at the highest level).

Further information   City and Guilds of London Institute, 46 Britannia Street, London WC1X 9RG

RSA (Royal Society of Arts) Examinations Board

The RSA Examinations Board provides pre-vocational and vocational schemes in a range of subjects, mainly, but not entirely, commercial. These include accounting, commercial law, computer literacy, modern languages. Students can take *groups* of subjects (for example in distribution or business studies) or *single* subjects. The RSA also administers some in-service training courses for teachers (e.g. teachers of health education and teachers of English as a foreign language). The RSA has links with a GCSE board to award joint RSA/GCSE certificates in a few subjects.

1993 NOTE: Many RSA awards are NVQs. GNVQs are being developed.

Further information
RSA Examinations Board, Westwood Way, Coventry CV4 8HS

Training and Enterprise Councils (TECs) and Local Enterprise Companies (lecs)

The first TECs (England and Wales) and lecs (Scotland) were created in 1991. These are independent companies which have been given responsibility for training and enterprise development in their own geographical areas. It includes several schemes previously run by the Training Agency.

They have an operating agreement with the Secretary of State for Employment which lays down how they are constituted and conditions they must meet to receive funding for their activities. At least two-thirds of the directors must come from local industry and commerce, with up to one-third being drawn from education, trade unions, public sector employers, voluntary organizations, etc. Within limits it is very much up to each TEC to decide how to spend its funds, as it is expected to respond to the needs of its local labour market. A TEC may provide a service itself or contract some or all services out to 'providers'.

From the job-seeker's point of view the most important schemes run by TECs and lecs are:

Youth Training and Employment Training (YT and ET)
Most of this is contracted out to approved training organizations. Training must meet certain criteria and some of the money the training providers receive depends on positive results. For youth

trainees a positive result is an NVQ (or equivalent), or credits towards an NVQ, at level 2 (level 1 for certain categories of trainee); this does not necessarily have to be gained within the training period, but must be within an agreed time. For adults on ET a result may be a job, self-employment, full-time education or other full-time training. Wherever possible, ET like YT should lead to an NVQ or NVQ credits.

High Technology National Training (HTNT) consists of short courses in IT, engineering, electronics, etc., run as part of ET.

For many 16- and 17-year-olds Youth Training is still the most likely way in to particular occupations, e.g. construction, horticulture and some retailing, and, as before, trainees may have employed or non-employed status. Unlike previous schemes, however, there is no set length for training; this depends on the individual's 'action plan'. Owing in part to the recession not every TEC has been able to meet the government's guarantee of a training place for eligible school-leavers or adults, although it has to 'use its best endeavours to do so'.

Training credits

These have been piloted in several TECs and lecs and are to be taken up by several more this year. They are a way of delivering Youth Training, but the actual system and money available varies from area to area. Basically each trainee is given credits with a monetary value which represent an entitlement to train. It is up to the trainee to 'spend' them as he or she wishes, by giving them to an employer, another training provider or a college (for a course or for open learning) in exchange for training.

Employment Action

This is a programme, separate from ET, of temporary work for people who have been out of work for 6 months or more and need work experience to prepare them for effective job-hunting.

Business and Enterprise Services

These include business advice and counselling for people wishing to become self-employed or to set up in business (see WORKING FOR ONESELF, p. 557). They also include the administration of the Enterprise Allowance which has replaced the old Enterprise Allowance Scheme which gave a fixed sum over a set period. The amounts given and for how long are now up to the TECs/lecs, subject to minimum and maximum sums laid down by government.

Training Access Points (TAPS)

Responsibility for providing information on training and educational opportunities for individuals and employers has been given to TECs. In some cases they maintain TAPS: these are user-friendly computer terminals linked to national databases such as ECCTIS (see p. liii) and PICKUP (see p. xxxvii) which may be located in libraries, careers centres, colleges, etc.

NOTE: It is still too early to know how effective TECs and lecs will prove. Also, all the schemes outlined are liable to change.

1993 NOTE: Training for Work will replace Employment Training, Employment Action, and High Technology National Training in 1993/94.

Degrees: See 'Higher Education' (p. xxx)

Diploma of Higher Education (Dip. H.E.) – England and Wales Only

Dip. H.E. courses take 2 years full time, some 3 years part time, and are held at colleges/institutes of higher education and poly-technics. Entry requirements for school-leavers: 2 A-levels (but A-level grades accepted are lower than for most degree students). Mature entrants account for a large proportion and are admitted according to 'suitability'.

Courses are comparable in standard and sometimes similar or identical in content to the first 2 years of an honours degree. Though intended as a qualification in its own right, the Dip. H.E. does not have a clear identity in the jobs market, and the vast majority of Diplomates go on to degree courses, towards which their Dip. H.E. may count.

Financing Your Studies

There are 2 main kinds of state financial awards: mandatory and discretionary. Mandatory ones are those to which students are legally entitled provided they are personally eligible and are attend-ing an eligible course. In Scotland there are no mandatory awards, but in practice the system is the same. The main difference is that in Scotland these awards are given by the Scottish Office Education Department, while in England and Wales they are the responsi-bility of local education authorities. Discretionary awards are those which an LEA (or, in Scotland, the education authority of the Regional or Islands Council) can choose whether or not to give.

Non-advanced courses

These include A-level, National Diplomas/Certificate, secretarial and art foundation courses. Generally they are free to those up to the age of 18 or 19 living in the area of the college. Any support for living expenses (maintenance) is discretionary and varies widely from area to area. Some LEAs will give Education and Maintenance Awards (depending on parents' income) to those under 19. In Scotland regional education authorities will give eligible students of all ages means-tested bursaries. To find out what might be available contact your LEA.

'Eligible' advanced courses

Full-time or sandwich first degree, Higher National, Diploma of Higher Education, PGCE and comparable courses are eligible or 'designated' courses for which eligible students are given mandatory awards. These cover fees (normally paid direct to the college) and the maintenance grant which is means-tested (i.e. the amount depends on your own and, in most cases, your parents' or spouse's income).

In 1990 a student loans system was introduced to make up the difference between the grant and what the student needs to live on. Loans are *not* means-tested. The existing level of grant was frozen as from 1991/2 and loans will be increased annually until they account for 50% of funding. Students (maximum age 50) decide at the start of each year how much they wish to borrow (up to a laid-down maximum) and have 5 or 7 years (depending on length of course) to pay the loan off, starting from the April following graduation. Loans are index-linked to inflation: the outstanding amount is adjusted annually in line with the Retail Prices Index. Repayments can be deferred for a year at a time if the individual's income is less than 85% of national average earnings.

'Non-eligible' advanced courses

Include post-graduate (except PGCE, see p. 526), articled teachers and part-time (except initial teacher training) courses. For these there is a decreasing supply of discretionary awards. The situation for post-graduate awards (except for teaching) is particularly complicated as a number of bodies are responsible for different kinds of courses. For information consult the college where you are studying or one of the publications listed below. In England and Wales students on courses for professions supplementary to medicine are funded separately by the National Health Service via health authorities. For details consult course organizers or the Department of Health (address below).

Access funds
These are distributed by government to colleges to pass on to some students who are in financial difficulties or who might not be able to take a further or higher education course without help. Further education students must be 19 or over. There is no upper age limit for higher education students. For information contact the college.

Career Development Loans
These are available for people wishing to take a vocational course – full or part time or by open learning (see p. xxxvi) – lasting at least a week and no more than a year, for which no other grant is available. The loans are made by 3 banks (Barclays, the Co-operative and the Clydesdale) in conjunction with the Department of Employment. No repayments are required for up to 3 months afterwards and the Department of Employment pays the interest during this time. At the end of this period the borrower repays the loan plus further interest within an agreed time limit, usually 3–5 years. For details contact the Jobcentre or one of the banks concerned.

NOTE: Some TECs/lecs (see p. xxiv) may introduce local training loans in the future.

Tax relief
As from April 1992 some tax relief is available for people who finance their own training through courses leading to level 4 NVQs/SVQs. Basic rate tax will be deducted automatically from the fees for qualifying courses, so non-tax-payers as well as tax-payers will benefit. Students should check when enrolling that fees quoted take this into account.

Further information

'Student grants and loans: a brief guide' from the Department of Education and Science, Corporation House, via Mowden Hall, Darlington DL3 9BG

'Post-graduate awards: State bursaries for post-graduate study on designated, professional and vocational courses' and 'Post-graduate awards: librarianship and information science student-ships and fellowships', both from the DES above

'A guide to undergraduate allowances' and 'A guide to postgraduate allowances' from the Scottish Office Education Department, Students' Awards Branch, Gyleview House, 3 Redheughs Rigg, Edinburgh EH12 9HH

Department of Health, Student Grants, Room 109, North Fylde, Central Office, Norcross, Blackpool FY5 3TA

Money to Study: The Complete Guide to Student Finance, from Educational Grants Advisory Service, 501/5 Kingsland Road, London E8 4AU, price £19.95 (inc. p. and p.)

Part Time and Job-Sharing

Many women and some men choose to work part time for at least some of their working lives, e.g. when their children are small or they are caring for an elderly relative. Part-time work now accounts for an increasing share of job vacancies. Yet the higher the position, the less likelihood there is that it is held by a part-timer. 'Conventional' part-timers are often perceived as less valuable than full-timers, and people going part time often have to accept a more routine job with less responsibility. According to a government survey, women in full-time employment are nearly twice as likely as part-timers to be given training.

Job-sharing is a different concept, of particular interest to people wanting to stay on the existing rung of the career ladder. In job-share schemes 2 people with the same qualifications and similar experience take full responsibility for one job. They share pay, holidays and fringe benefits on a pro rata basis. Job-sharers may work half a week each or alternate weeks or fortnights, according to the needs of the job and the people sharing it. In some cases the sharers overlap, either to cover busy periods or to 'hand over'. For the scheme to work, sharers have to be compatible, conscientious and flexible. They pay for the privilege of working part time in a job of their choice by giving a little extra time and commitment. Employers who have tried such a scheme tend to be enthusiastic, realizing the benefits of having 2 brains for virtually the price of one; higher productivity (energy levels drop towards the end of the working week) and little time lost through holidays, sickness, etc. Although there are many more examples of job-sharing than there were, especially in the public sector, the concept has not caught on as widely as many people hoped. The initiative still has often to come from job applicants themselves.

Further information

For more information on job-sharing contact:

New Ways to Work, 309 Upper Street, London N1 2TY

The Department of Employment has issued a useful 'Guide to Flexible Working' (March 1992). Available free from Jobcentres.

Higher Education

The traditional route to a degree is through a 3- or 4-year full-time or 4-year sandwich course. Students may specialize in a single subject, or in 2 major subjects in a 'joint' degree, or take various combinations of subjects in a 'combined' degree. Increasing numbers of institutions are organizing courses on a modular basis in order to allow students greater flexibility in developing a coherent course of study.

Degree courses are currently offered in universities, polytechnics and colleges or institutes of higher education. However, it is intended, in the very near future, that the distinctions between universities and polytechnics be ended. Polytechnics will be able to call themselves universities and to award their own degrees. Colleges will develop (or continue) arrangements to have their degrees validated by a new or existing university or polytechnic.

These changes will not mean an overnight change in the character of existing institutions. Institutions that are currently polytechnics, for example, are likely to retain their links with industry and to offer more vocationally orientated, sandwich and part-time courses than the universities do.

1993 NOTE: Following the Further and Higher Education Act, 39 institutions have become universities.

Entrance Requirements – Widening Access

Normally, to enter a degree course one needs 2 or 3 passes at A-level (or equivalent AS-levels, see p. xix) plus supporting GCSEs. However, an increasing proportion of students – in universities, 20% in 1991, up from under 12% in 1981 – enter with qualifications other than A/AS-level. Common acceptable alternatives are SCE (see p. xix), International Baccalaureate, European Baccalaureate and BTEC National (see p. xxii).

Many courses require that candidates have an adequate foundation in specific subjects, but there is increasing flexibility here too. For example, a number of universities and polytechnics run *conversion* courses to enable those without the usual maths and physics A-levels to study engineering.

Mature Entrants

There are increasing numbers of mature students studying for degrees: about 1 in 7 new university students is over 21, more in the public sector. This is a key group that needs to be attracted to increase national participation in higher education.

From the point of view of higher education institutions you are a mature candidate if you are over 21 (in a few cases 23 is the lower limit, in one or two it is 19). If you have the standard entry qualifications (see above), you will be considered in the same way as school-leavers. If not, institutions will look for evidence of your commitment, motivation and ability to study at a high level. That evidence might be, for example, an A/AS-level or two taken at evening classes or study for professional or vocational qualifications. Candidates who can present convincing evidence may be admitted as direct entrants. However, there is a range of developing schemes and initiatives to help smooth the way for mature candidates.

Access Courses

These are specially designed to prepare mature entrants for higher education. Courses may be full or part time and are offered by adult, further and higher education institutions. Many are designed to meet the needs of specific groups, e.g. women, ethnic minorities or the unemployed. Some are connected with a specific course and institution, guaranteeing a place on a degree course to those who successfully complete their access studies; others have wider applications.

Residential Courses

There are 7 adult residential colleges. They are intended for adults (over 21 usually, but many are in their thirties and forties, some even older) who missed out on educational opportunities and now want to catch up – either to go on to higher education or into professional training, or simply to stretch their minds. Courses are usually 1, occasionally 2 years. They may lead to a certificate or diploma but they are above all yet another type of 'access' course. (Colleges also run short 1- or 2-week courses, but these are usually 'special interest' ones.) Course content is varied; most courses cover liberal arts and/or social studies, but computing, languages and environmental subjects, etc. may be covered.

Once accepted, students qualify for grants to cover tuition and maintenance.

Further information

Details from individual colleges:

Coleg Harlech, Harlech, Gwynedd LL46 2PU

Co-operative College, Stanford Hall, Loughborough, Leicester-shire LE12 5QR

Fircroft College, 1018 Bristol Road, Selly Oak, Birmingham B29 6LH

Hillcroft College (women only), Surbiton, Surrey KT6 6DF

Northern College, Wentworth Castle, Stainborough, Barnsley S75 3ET

Plater College, Pullens Lane, Oxford OX3 0DT

Ruskin College, Walton Street, Oxford OX1 2HE

Other Preparatory Programmes

These range from courses which help students to improve A-level grades, to those which update special areas of knowledge, to those which deal with study skills.

Associate Student Schemes

Associate students are not formally enrolled on degree programmes but sample some units of degree courses. Assessment is optional. When associate students are assessed, the outcome can lead to formal admission.

Credit Accumulation and Transfer Schemes (CATS)

The *principle* behind credit accumulation and transfer is simple: students should be given 'portable' credit for all types of learning – on courses, at work or through 'life experiences' – which they can accumulate to enable them to move flexibly through further studies and achieve recognized academic awards. The *implementation* is quite complex, based as it is on individuals and on maximizing their flexibility and choice.

CATS schemes are run nationally, regionally and in individual institutions. The kinds of learning assessed include units of recognized courses, in-company training, professional studies and training, and experiential learning (provided the applicant can offer evidence of the learning, not just the experience). By transferring credits students may then be able to negotiate entry with alternative qualifications; admission with exemptions or advanced standing; transfer from one course or institution to another; additional or alternative courses at a different institution from the one the student has registered at.

As already mentioned, CATS schemes are many and varied, but the national CNAA scheme was a trailblazer and, while widely implemented itself, has also set the standard for many individual schemes. (When CNAA is wound up as planned, in the near future, a national CATS scheme will continue, though it has not yet been determined who will administer it.) CNAA has established a UK-wide system of credit-rating courses (known as the tariff) which assigns both a number and level of credits to courses or units. To give a simple example of application, to achieve an honours degree one must accumulate 360 credits with a maximum of 120 at level 1 and a minimum of 120 at level 3. It is not simply a numbers game, however, with students cobbling degrees together out of all their experiences: credits accumulated and transferred must represent a coherent programme of study. They are really a basis for negotiation; for example, a student may accumulate 120 credits, but only 60 may be transferable to the next stage of his or her programme of study.

Opportunities are also being developed for international credit transfer. For example, ECTS (European Community Course Credit Transfer System) was instigated on an experimental basis in 1989 by ERASMUS (European Community Action Scheme for the Mobility of University Students). It covers 5 subject areas: business administration, history, medicine, chemistry and mechanical engineering.

Further information   ECCTIS, see p. liii.

Assessment of Prior (Experiential) Learning (AP(E)L)

Integral to many initiatives to promote wider access and increasing flexibility are APL and APEL, which give people recognition and sometimes credit for learning already achieved. The titles and formality of this process vary. It is, in fact, the basis on which institutions of higher education have always considered mature candidates, but the development of CATS is extending its use. APL is generally regarded as a global term dealing with all sorts of prior knowledge and learning experiences; APEL normally excludes any certificated learning.

NOTE: CATS and APL principles are applied not just in higher education, but more widely throughout education and training.

Part-time Courses

The number of part-time students is increasing, but provision varies. Some institutions limit part-time opportunities to mature students and/or particular subjects; others are redesigning courses to provide the option of part-time study much more widely. Birkbeck College of the University of London specializes in part-time degrees.

The Open University

The Open University is Britain's largest institution of higher education. No academic qualifications are required for admission (except for higher degrees), but places are limited and students are admitted on a first-come basis. Students study at home in their own time, through a programme that includes specially prepared materials, set books, radio and television broadcasts, and other audiovisual materials. There are also residential summer schools.

Most students are undergraduates working for a BA degree (with or without honours). Courses are rated as full- or half-credit, depending on the amount of work involved, and are at various levels. The equivalent of 6 credits is needed for a BA, 8 credits, including 2 at higher levels, for Honours. It is possible to complete a degree in 3 years, but most people take 4–6 years.

Many people study as Associate Students, taking undergraduate courses but not registering for a degree. There are also facilities for research and higher degrees, courses for professional development, scientific and technological updating, family, community and personal interest, and, through the Open Business School, a range of management courses at different levels, culminating in an MBA (Master of Business Administration).

From 1992 the Open University will accept students from European Community countries and, at its discretion, other parts of Europe. It is also developing a programme of modern language courses for introduction in 1993.

Further information   The Open University, Walton Hall, Milton Keynes MK7 6AA

University of London External Degrees

Open University and London External degrees do not overlap. They serve different types of students and have fundamental differences. Whereas the Open University offers interdisciplinary courses, open entry and a paced system of support, London External degrees offer in-depth study in a single subject and set entry requirements. The University acts only as an examining body; tuition is offered by a number of correspondence colleges and a few other colleges, both maintained and private. Though it is possible for students to study totally independently, most receive tuition of some sort.

The basic entry requirement is 2 A-levels and 3 GCSE or O-levels (A–C); there may also be specific course requirements. Mature students are assessed on an individual basis. Most students are between the ages of 25 and 45.

Further information   Secretary for External Students, University of London, Senate House, Malet Street, London WC1E 7HU

NOTE: Flexibility invariably implies complexity. It is *vital* that mature and other non-traditional potential students seek help in finding their way through the maze of proliferating new opportunities to find the best way forward for them. The institutions themselves should be only too pleased to advise, but there are other sources of help (see p. liii).

Late Start and Return to Work

A Variety of Routes for Returners, Career Changers and Late Starters

There have never been as many or as flexible opportunities for catching up on missed educational and training opportunities as there are now. Adults who need educational or vocational qualifications – or simply more knowledge – for courses or careers they want to start or return to after a gap of some years can choose from an ever-increasing variety of courses and methods of study. For details of what is available nationally and locally see guides listed under 'Especially for Job-Changers and Late-Starters' on p. lvi.

Preparatory Courses

Most re-entry courses were started by women, for women wishing to return to work, but men are rarely excluded. These preparatory courses have various titles, such as 'Women into Work', 'Ready for Work' and 'New Opportunities for Women'.

Courses vary in content, organization, level and quantity of work expected. Some are mainly confidence-restoring and 'diagnostic': they help students to sort out their aims, motivation, level of confidence, circumstances, and then balance these with the available job opportunities, and the obstacles which may arise. Others include work experience or work-related skills training, introduction to new technology and job-hunting techniques.

Open Learning

(The terms *open learning* and *distance-learning* are often interchangeable.)

What is *open learning*? Essentially it is a system which enables more people to make use of educational and training facilities. Flexibility and accessibility are the key-words. All colleges are trying to attract more adults to their courses, whatever their chosen method of study. Open learning aims to remove traditional barriers to education and training, such as rigid entry requirements, the need for full-time attendance, fixed-length courses, and the need to live or work within daily travelling distance of college or training centre.

Flexibility is provided in 2 ways: by making entry requirements less rigid and by giving students a choice of study methods to fit in with their work or domestic commitments. For example, *distance-learning* courses have been steadily increasing in recent years. These are a kind of 'souped up' correspondence course with study by post being supplemented by audio and videotapes and/or computer programmes, plus personal or telephone contact with a tutor. One of the best-known providers is the National Extension College; over 60% of its students are women, studying because they need qualifications for career progression or to return to work or study.

Accessibility partly depends on where courses are held – some areas are much better provided for than others. Students can generally enrol on open-learning courses at any time and work at their own pace. Many courses require attendance on 1 or 2 days a week or even less, making it possible for many more people to participate than in the past.

Open learning is increasingly used to train people who are in work. PICKUP is a Department of Education and Science programme which has been running for 10 years and enables colleges of all kinds to provide updating courses for employees, in collaboration with employers. Many of its training packages are designed for open learning, since many users can only study at home. Some TECs and lecs (see p. xxiv) are introducing open-learning initiatives in response to local industry's needs.

The definition of the term 'open learning' is complicated by the fact that it refers both to a concept and to specific institutions and initiatives.

Open College Networks

These should not be confused with the Open University, the Open College or the Open Polytechnic. Open College Networks do not themselves run courses, but consist of groups of colleges which collaborate to provide accreditation for adult learning in their geographical area. This is carried out through a system of credits and levels (see CATS, p. xxxii). These can help individual learners plan their pathways through their local further and higher education system and, in many cases, enable them to have their achievements recognized by other Open College Networks. Although Networks differ in the way they work, it is hoped that they will all adopt the standards for 4 levels of award, ranging from basic skills to access to higher education, recently recommended by the National Open College Network.

The Educational Guidance Service for Adults (see p. liii) will have details of local Networks. Details are also given in the ECCTIS guide (see p. liii).

The Open College

This was set up in 1987 to provide and promote vocational training on the lines of the Open University, using open-learning materials. As from April 1992 it will be an independent, self-financing registered charity. Its main aims are to encourage employers to provide more effective training for their workforce and to help individuals, both in and out of work, to gain work-related skills. Courses focus on 5 main areas: management and supervisory management; education and training; health care and nursing; technical and personal development; basic work skills. Many courses lead to NVQs (see p. xx). Of particular interest to women returners and job-changers are the introductory courses 'Women – the Way Ahead' and 'Moving On – Career Change and Development'. There is a nationwide system of Open College Centres, mostly at further education colleges, providing advice and support and where students register for courses.

Further information

The Open College, FREEPOST, Warrington WA2 7BR. Inquirers are sent a brochure and details of their local centre.

The Open College of the Arts

This was set up in 1987 to provide training in the arts by open-learning methods to people wishing to develop their artistic and creative abilities at home. Courses currently available are in painting, sculpture, textiles, art and design, garden design, music, photography, writing and understanding Western art. The 2 main elements of a course are books and regular tutorial support: for some courses students attend a local centre about once every 3 weeks for a group tutorial, while other courses give tutorial support by post. There are over 300 OCA tutors, many based in colleges, art centres and studios, while others are practitioners with an interest in teaching. Optional summer schools, life classes, workshops, etc. are arranged by many tutors.

Courses do not at present lead to recognized qualifications, but students who wish to may be assessed for an OCA Award. Courses can be particularly useful for people who think they might want to work in the arts, but need to test their abilities and build up a portfolio, including those who have to study at home because of domestic circumstances.

Further information Open College of the Arts, Houndhill, Worsbrough, Barnsley, South Yorkshire S70 6TU

The Open Polytechnic

This does not enrol students, but provides a service to polytechnics (and, in future, to other higher education institutions). In 1990, 20 polytechnics set up the Open Polytechnic Foundation with the aim of increasing the accessibility of polytechnics and higher education generally to individuals, companies and public sector organizations by improving flexible learning. Through a wholly owned subsidiary, The Open Polytechnic Ltd, it is developing open-learning and teaching materials (the first ones – in languages, social work and business studies – will be available to polytechnics in autumn 1992); running staff development programmes to raise awareness of the potential of flexible learning; and helping institutions to manage the necessary organizational changes.

Further information The Secretary, The Open Polytechnic, 24 Angel Gate, Islington, London EC1V 2RS

NOTE: With the changes in higher education (see p. xxx) it will change its name to the Open Learning Foundation.

Mature Students in Higher Education: See p. xxxi

Employment Training: See p. xxiv

Sex Balance in Employment and Training

Women now account for about 44% (1991) of the total workforce. The proportion of women working (by work is meant 'economically active', i.e. includes those seeking work), and the extent of part-time work, varies with age and the ages of children. Overall about 71% of women aged between 16 and 60 work (1990). 72% of those aged 35–49 and 65% of those between 25 and 34 do so. Of the total about 46% work part time, compared with 10% of men. Married women increasingly work: between 1984 and 1990 the number of married women in employment rose by 20%, compared with 10% for those of 'other marital status'.

There are over a million lone-parent families in Britain, accounting for 14% of all families with children. 89% of these are headed by the mother. Lone mothers are as likely to work full time as those with partners, but significantly fewer work part time. 31% of all employees with children under 5 work fewer than 15 hours a week, compared with only 10% of those without dependent children. Only 30% of mothers with very young children work more than 30 hours.

Women working full and part time in main non-manual occupational groups (shown as a percentage of all employed women), 1990

	Full time	Part time
Managerial	5·7	1·4
Clerical & related	19·8	10·6
Professional & related in education, welfare and health	8·8	5·3
Literary, artistic, sport	0·8	0·5
Selling	2·8	6·1
Professional & related in science, engineering, technology, etc.	1·0	0·2
Other occupations	16·5	18·4

(*Source: Department of Employment 1990 Labour Force Survey*)

University graduates (first degree) entering different types of employment, 1990 (% of total home employment)

	Men	Women
Administration and operational management	7·3	9·1
Research, design, development	20·4	7·6
Environmental planning, construction	6·0	–
Sales, marketing, buying	5·3	9·6
Management services, computing	9·4	3·4
Financial work	19·9	16·1
Literary, entertainment and other creative work	–	3·2
Information, library, museum work	–	3·6
Health and social welfare	17·5	27·3
Teaching and lecturing	–	6·8
Others (including all categories with under 3%)	14·3	13·3

Polytechnic graduates (first degree) entering different types of employment, 1990 (% of total home employment)

	Men	Women
Administration and operational management	8·7	11·2
Research, design, development	19·1	4·4
Scientific support service	3·2	–
Environmental planning, construction	16·5	4·2
Sales, marketing, buying	6·3	10·1
Management services, computing	13·8	4·4
Financial work	10·8	9·0
Literary, entertainment and other creative work	5·2	8·9
Information, library, museum work	–	3·2
Health and social welfare	4·2	14·0
Teaching and lecturing	5·3	19·1
Others (including all categories with under 3%)	7·0	11·4

(*Source: Central Services Unit and Association of Graduate Careers Advisory Services*)

NOTE: These charts exclude graduates who have entered training, e.g. for the law (as solicitors or barristers), psychology, social

(NOTE – *cont*.)

work, architecture, town planning, librarianship, computing, other management services.

More men than women go straight into permanent employment and more go on to further academic study. More women go into training, including teacher training. More men than women are unemployed, probably because women are more likely to accept jobs not normally regarded as graduate-level (e.g. secretarial).

*

According to Department of Employment occupational groupings, women greatly outnumber men in catering, cleaning, hairdressing and other personal services, selling and clerical jobs. Roughly the same proportions of men and women are in manual jobs, but a far higher proportion of men are in craft or similar occupations. This is one reason why women overall still earn less than men – if they lack educational qualifications and training they tend to be concentrated in low-paid, low-skilled jobs. However, 28% of working women are in the managerial and professional groups compared with 36% of men; within these groups they greatly outnumber men in education, welfare and health and lag far behind in science, engineering and technology.

When and if the labour market expands again, women should be in a very good position to gain ground. According to 'Labour market and skills trends 1992/3', a Department of Employment publication, recent growth has been strongest in managerial and professional jobs. Between 1984 and 1990 numbers employed increased by 24% and are predicted to grow by another 15% by the year 2000. Clerical and related jobs grew by 19·5%; although 34,000 secretarial jobs are projected to disappear by the year 2000, this drop will be offset by a rise in other clerical posts. Professional scientific and engineering posts are expected to rise by 27% in the same period, with the female share projected to grow more rapidly (admittedly from a rather small base). As women increasingly gain professional-level qualifications, so they will benefit from the general growth in demand for highly skilled people.

Proportion of women in selected occupations

Institute of Chartered Accountants	Full members 12%	Student members 35%
Chartered Institute of Management Accountants	Full members 7%	Student members 25%

Proportion of women in selected occupations (cont.)

Institution of Civil Engineers	Full members below 1%	Student members 10·5%
Institution of Electrical Engineers	Full members below 1%	Student members 7·2%
Institution of Mechanical Engineers	Full members below 1%	Student members 6·6%
Medicine: general practitioners (principals)	23·5%	Entrants to medical school 1991
All consultants	15·5%	
All hospital doctors	26·9%	51%
Dentists, practising	30%	First-year students 46·7%
Ophthalmic opticians	30%	First-year students 56%
Law: solicitors with practising certificates	25%	Law Society Students 54%
Barristers, practising	18%	Called to the Bar 1991 41%
QCs	4·6%	
Circuit judges	4%	
Royal Institution of Chartered Surveyors	Full members 7%	Student members 16%
Society of Surveying Technicians	Below 1%	
Architects, practising	8%	Students 30%
Veterinary surgeons	24·3%	Students 58%
Advertising account executives	33%	
Air traffic control officers	10%	Trainees 19%
Driving examiners	10%	
Directors of social services	16%	
Health service management:		
Unit general managers	17%	
District and regional general managers	4%	
Local authority chief executives	1·4%	
Town planners: RTPI members	15%	Students 35%
Education:		
Professors in higher education	4·8%	
Lecturer Grade 1 in further education	32%	
Further education principals	4%	
Chief education officers	15%	
Primary heads	47%	
Secondary heads	18%	

Proportion of women in selected occupations (cont.)

Civil Service:	
Grades 1–3 (top grades)	6·5%
Grades 4–7 (senior grades)	12%
Administration trainees (high-flyer graduates)	43%

NOTE: Statistics on their own do not tell the whole story and can be misleading. These figures should be looked at in conjunction with the 'Position of women' sections in each chapter.

Sex Balance in Education

Absolute equality in education is essential if women are to be equal at work. For many years more girls than boys have achieved 5 or more A–C grades at O-level/GCSE, and a much greater proportion of girls goes on to further education. In recent years girls have caught up with boys at A-level, and in 1991 very nearly 50% of accepted entrants to university were girls. In terms of level and number of qualifications, girls are doing well.

However, if one looks at the subjects these new female undergraduates have opted for, the picture is anything but balanced.

Proportion of female students in various subjects

	University (1991)	*Polytechnic (1990)*
Medicine	50·7	–
Subjects allied to medicine	72·9	75·0
Biological sciences	57·2	58·9
Chemistry	35·8	29·7
Physics	17·6	13·1
Mathematics	34·0	36·5
Civil engineering	16·2	11·5
Mechanical engineering	10·3	5·7
Electronic engineering	8·0	4·7
Languages and related	68·9	72·6
Accountancy	36·0	34·6
Business and management	44·9	50·3
Sociology	70·8	68·6
Economics	26·7	25·8
Law	51·2	56·7

Girls still tend to opt for subjects which are much more competitive and/or much less vocationally relevant and in demand. Whatever subtle and insidious influences have been at work in terms of gender stereotyping, it is clear that many girls do not opt for courses in the physical sciences and engineering because they *cannot*: they do not have maths and physics at A-level, often because they did not lay the proper foundation at O-level/GCSE.

In 1990 only 10% of girls got GCSE higher grade passes in physics, compared with 22% of boys. For technology the figure for boys was 19%, and for girls 5%. (In both cases, though, a higher proportion of girl entrants was successful – girls are *not* inherently less able to do these subjects!)

Of those getting A-levels, 18% of girls got a pass in maths, compared with 32% of boys; 8% of girls got a pass in physics, compared with 26% of boys. At all levels, from GCSE through to degree, girls far outstrip boys in French, English and biology.

But perhaps this is all going to change. The implementation of the National Curriculum means that *all* pupils choosing their GCSEs from this year onwards must take maths, English and science. The science syllabus must include chemistry, physics and biology. No longer will girls be able to give up science altogether or settle for biology only. More girls studying more science can only lead to more awareness, more interest and more opportunities.

Sex Discrimination Legislation

Brief Summary of Main Provisions Relating to Employment and Education

The *Sex Discrimination Act* makes it unlawful to treat anyone on the grounds of sex (and, in the case of employment, on the grounds of marriage) less favourably than a person of the opposite sex.

Employment

The Act defines two kinds of discrimination:

Direct discrimination, e.g. sending boys but not girls on day-release courses when both are doing similar jobs; or *not* promoting the person next in line because she is a woman (or a man).

Indirect discrimination: applying the same conditions to both sexes which favour one sex rather than the other but are not justified. For example if an employer, when recruiting an *office* manager, demands that the candidate must have served a *technical* apprenticeship, he or she is discriminating against women because they are far less likely to have served an apprenticeship – which is irrelevant to the job to be done; or if an employer only recruits people aged 20–30, it indirectly discriminates against women who are likely to rear children during those years.

The Act's main exemptions – as amended by the Sex Discrimination Act 1986 – apply:

1. To employment in private households where the job involves living or working in a private house where there could be a reasonable objection to someone of the other sex having physical or social contact with a person living in the house, or knowledge of intimate details of that person's life.

2. Where sex is a genuine occupational qualification (known as a GOQ), e.g. in acting or modelling (neither strength nor stamina is a GOQ).

3. Where one sex is required for reasons of decency, e.g. in an Asian all-women's hostel.

4. In certain jobs providing care and/or supervision.

5. To jobs which genuinely involve work abroad in countries where women in such jobs are not acceptable. However, if, for example, an employer persistently employs men because he or she claims the job *might* take them to a country where women are unacceptable, but in fact few male employees are sent to such countries, the employer would be illegally discriminating.

6. To the Armed Forces, the Churches, competitive sport, charities, and work in the mines.

The SDA 1986 repealed restrictions on women's hours and times of work contained in the Factories Act 1961, as well as the exemption relating to firms employing no more than 5 people.

The Equal Pay Act

The Equal Pay Act stipulates equal treatment as well as equal pay for the same or broadly similar work where a woman's job has been rated as equivalent to a man's under an existing job evaluation scheme. It covers all conditions and benefits contained in a contract of employment, e.g. holiday entitlement, access to pension schemes and the payment of bonuses. Being able to claim your work is of equal value has only been allowed since 1 January 1984, when the government amended the original Act after the European Court of Justice decided it did not go far enough in awarding women genuine equal pay. Women's average earnings are still about three-quarters those of men; the change in the law may alter that by allowing a woman to claim her job is of equal value to any other job in the same firm being held by a man – for example, a woman secretary could ask for equal pay with a male clerk, a woman machinist in a textile factory with a male cutter or a woman checkout cashier at a supermarket with a male shelf filler.

The Equal Opportunities Commission and the TUC are two of the most outspoken critics of the amended Act, complaining, among other things, that it is too complex, time-consuming and costly to enforce. The experience of applicants bringing claims under the Act suggests that these criticisms are valid.

The Employment Protection Act

This says that a woman may not be dismissed because of pregnancy; she is entitled to 6 weeks' maternity pay and to reinstatement for up to 29 weeks after the birth of the baby. These provisions apply only if the employee works till 11 weeks before the baby is due and if she has worked for the same employer for at least 2 years full time or 5 years part time; if she wants to resume work, she must have told her employer so *in writing* before leaving.

Positive discrimination

The Sex Discrimination Act specifically permits 'positive action' to be taken by employers, employers' organizations, education and training establishments, in 2 kinds of situation:

1. Where in the past jobs (and training schemes) were available only or mainly to one sex, special training may be provided for the other sex, to redress the balance and improve job and promotion prospects for the hitherto under-represented sex.

2. Special training may also be provided to help women who wish to return to work after a gap.

Disappointingly little use has so far been made of the 'positive action' provision. Few women probably know that they could press for 'catching-up' courses and training.

Complaints concerned with employment matters are dealt with by Industrial Tribunals. (Leaflets setting out rights and procedures in full are available from Jobcentres.)

Education

Discrimination is unlawful in admission to and provision of education facilities in both the public and private sectors. A few exceptions relate to establishments which are single-sex. All other classes and establishments must be open to all pupils/students regardless of sex. Girls who want to take technical drawing, and boys who want to do cooking, must not be discouraged; medical schools may not operate a quota system, etc.

It is discriminatory not only to refuse entry, but also, for example, gently to persuade girls not to choose physics or craft, design and technology where laboratory and workshop facilities are restricted, and instead let them take biology, which is less useful later. It is also discriminatory to give boys more chance of work-experience schemes than girls, or to differentiate between the kind of schemes offered (e.g. to arrange that all girls work in hospitals once a week, all boys in engineering works).

To observe the spirit as well as the letter of the law, careers staff have a duty to widen the girls' careers horizons and to ensure that they are fully aware of all the opportunities, including the non-traditional ones, which are open to them.

As sex balance in education figures (see p. xlv) show, changes in boys' and girls' exam subject choices are not encouraging. While the letter of the law is observed, in many schools the spirit of the Act is ignored.

Complaints about discrimination in education must first be made to the appropriate Secretary of State (for England and Wales or Scotland) for Education. If no satisfactory conclusion has been reached within 2 months, cases may be taken before county courts in England and Wales, sheriff courts in Scotland.

Further information

Advice and information about all sex discrimination matters is available from:

Equal Opportunities Commission, Overseas House, Quay Street, Manchester M3 3HN

In Scotland: St Andrew House, 141 West Nile Street, Glasgow G1 2RU

Advice on employment matters is also available from the Advisory, Conciliation and Arbitration Service (addresses from local employment offices)

Also, local Citizens' Advice Bureaux, such women's organizations as Townswomen's Guilds and Rights of Women, 52–54 Featherstone Street, London EC1Y 8RT, will advise and/or provide leaflets

1993 NOTES:

To comply with EC directives, all women, regardless of length of service and hours worked, will be entitled to 14 weeks' maternity leave, after December 1994.

Details of maternity pay changes have not yet (August 1993) been decided.

Europe and 1992

The Treaty of Rome guarantees the freedom for every EC citizen to work, to seek work, to set up business or to provide services in any EC member state. Community citizens may not be discriminated against on grounds of nationality. The impression often given by the media is that this year's introduction of the Single European Market means that people from all member states will be free to work and practise their professions anywhere in Europe. In practice, the situation is rather more complicated. Undoubtedly, with the spread of multi-national companies, more people will spend part of their working lives with big companies abroad. Yet many professionals wishing to set themselves up in practice or to apply for comparable posts in other member states still face barriers. While 7 of the major professions – covering doctors, nurses, dentists, veterinary surgeons, midwives, architects and pharmacists – have agreed *'sectoral'* *Directives* making it easier for those covered to work anywhere in the EC, many more have not.

First General Directive

The sectoral approach is lengthy and difficult (it took 17 years for the architects to agree!), so the EC decided to tackle the remaining professions by means of a General Directive based on the principle of mutual recognition of qualifications. This was agreed in 1988 and came into force in January 1991. It covers those professions 'to which access is in some way restricted by the State and which require at least three years' university-level education or equivalent plus any appropriate job-related training'. In the UK there are very few professions regulated by law or public authority (state school teachers and lawyers are examples), but for the purpose of the Directive those controlled by their own Chartered bodies are included, e.g. chartered accountants, engineers, physiotherapists, psychologists, surveyors. Only the Irish Republic implemented it by the deadline, followed by the UK and Denmark and, more recently, Spain and Portugal. The remaining countries have not yet implemented the Directive, or are trying to do so sector by sector. However, legal pressure is being brought to bear, so implementation may be speeded up.

Second General Directive

This covers occupations for which qualifications are gained in under 3 years. This has reached the 'political agreement' stage (i.e. the content has been agreed), but it has still to be formally adopted. It is likely to be implemented in 1994. Among the UK qualifications recognized under this Directive are NVQs/SVQs.

CEDEFOP

The European Centre for the Development of Vocational Training has been undertaking a separate exercise to enable qualifications in member states to be more readily compared. This involves agreeing job descriptions against which each country lists its own national qualifications. Occupations already covered include hotels and catering, agriculture and textiles (clothing). Office work, transportation and tourism are in the pipeline.

Certificates of Experience

EC legislation already exists which mutually recognizes certain jobs and trades. People wishing to practise these in other member states have to apply for a Certificate of Experience (in the UK from the Department of Trade and Industry), which is then accepted by the other country in place of its own national qualifications. Included are those self-employed in wholesaling, retailing and food manufacturing, insurance agents and brokers, hairdressers and people providing various services.

This section is only a guide – interested individuals must make inquiries from the Department of Trade and Industry, Internal European Policy Division 1A, 6th Floor, Ashdown House, 123 Victoria Street, London SW1E 6RB. For a copy of a helpful booklet, 'Europe Open for Professions', which lists professions covered by the Directives, ring DTI's Hotline, 081-200 1992.

Sources of Help

Careers Advisory Services

Careers offices offer advice on career choice, course selection, employment and training opportunities to young people at school and college, school-leavers and, increasingly, to adults. The future of the Careers Service is under review, but there will continue to be a statutory service.

Higher education institutions have careers advisory services for their students and graduates (of any age).

EGSAs (Educational Guidance Services for Adults)

These are local independent advice centres aimed mainly at adults of all ages and from all educational backgrounds. They give free information on national and local educational and training opportunities and some also offer careers counselling. Although the number of EGSAs has been growing, provision is still patchy and in some cases under-funded. Some TECs (see p. xxiv) have already developed guidance networks which include the Careers Service and EGSAs. There is likely to be greater collaboration in future under the Gateways to Learning initiative starting this year, whereby TECs are invited to set up careers 'shops' and to issue adult guidance 'vouchers'.

Individuals should be able to find out the address of their local service from their local careers office, library, Jobcentre or Citizens' Advice Bureau. Services are also listed in the *Returning to Work* directory (see p. lvi).

ECCTIS

ECCTIS is a national computerized service providing information on nearly 80,000 courses at universities, polytechnics and colleges of further and higher education. Users are led through a sequence of questions to identify the type of course they are interested in – subject, type of course, type of institution, method of study, location. ECCTIS then displays the details of relevant courses.

Users can find ECCTIS, either on-line or on compact disc

(CD-ROM), in secondary schools, careers offices, adult guidance centres, libraries, TAPS (see p. xxvi), British Council offices and institutions of further and higher education.

ECCTIS also provides information on credit accumulation and transfer schemes (see p. xxxii) and on vacancies on first degree courses during the summer 'clearing' period.

ECCTIS produces handbooks on access to higher education and educational credit transfer and a student's guide to educational credit transfer. Reference copies should be available through advisers in the careers service, colleges and EGSAs (see p. liii).

TAPS: See TECs, p. xxvi

Some Useful Publications

Most of the following should be available in schools, careers offices and public libraries.

Higher and Further Education Information

Directory of Further Education, published annually by Hobsons. Lists full- and part-time vocational courses at all levels outside universities.

University and College Entrance: the Official Guide, published annually by the Universities and Colleges Admissions Service. Gives information on institutions and entry requirements for first degree, Dip.H.E. and HND courses.

Scottish Universities Entrance Guide, published annually by Scottish Universities Council on Entrance. Contains information about entry requirements and subjects of study and explains differences from other UK university courses.

Scottish Centrally Funded Colleges: *courses in Scotland*, published annually by the Committee of Principals of Scottish Centrally Funded Colleges. Lists courses, including post-graduate ones, and entry requirements.

A Compendium of Advanced Courses in Colleges of Further and Higher Education, published annually by London and South East Regional Advisory Council (LASER). Lists full-time and sandwich post-A-level courses outside universities. Similar information on part-time and fifth-form leavers' courses is published regionally.

The NATFHE Handbook, published annually for the National Association of Teachers in FE and HE. Lists B.Ed. and other degrees leading to qualified teacher status, post-graduate Certificate of Education as well as other degree and professional courses in those establishments. From 1993 it will be produced by PCAS.

Guide to the Colleges and Institutes of Higher Education, published annually by the Standing Conference of Principals and Directors of Colleges and Institutes of Higher Education.

Degree Course Guides, published (usually bi-annually) by Hobsons (for CRAC). Compares individual courses within disciplines.

Which Degree?, published annually by Hobsons. Gives course content and institution details.

The Student Book, published by Macmillan. Contains facts as well as opinion on subjects of study and institutions.

The Potter Universities Guide, published by Dalebank Books. Does not give course information, but has university profiles – size, location, facilities, etc.

British Universities' Guide to Graduate Study, published annually for the Committee of Vice-Chancellors and Principals.

Careers Information

Occupations, published annually by CO-IC (Careers and Occupational Information Centre).

'Working in' series of booklets on individual career areas, also published by CO-IC.

AGCAS (Association of Graduate Careers Advisory Services) publishes a series of regularly updated booklets covering most graduate career areas.

Working Abroad: Daily Telegraph Guide to Working and Living Overseas, by Godfrey Golzen, published by Kogan Page.

Especially for Job-Changers and Late-Starters

Second Chances, published by CO-IC and regularly updated. A comprehensive guide to education and training courses at all levels for adults.

Returning to Work: A Directory of Education and Training for Women, published annually by Kogan Page for Women Returners' Network. Includes county-by-county guide to information and advice contacts.

Manage Your Own Career: A Self-Help Guide to Career Choice and Change, by Ben Ball, published by The British Psychological Society and Kogan Page.

Making a Comeback, by Margaret Korving, published by Hutchinson Business Books.

The Kogan Page Mature Student's Handbook, by Margaret Korving, published by Kogan Page.

Major careers publishers include Cassells, Careers Consultants, CO-IC, Hobsons and Kogan Page. Check catalogues for current publications.

Free Leaflets

'Parents' Guide to HE'
'Mature Students' Guide to HE'

Available from UCAS, Fulton House, Jessop Avenue, Cheltenham GL50 3SH.

For various grants booklets see 'Financing Your Studies', p. xxvi.

For details of Scottish examination equivalents to GCSE and A-level, see p. xix.

1993 NOTE: All polytechnics are now universities. NVQs and GNVQs are becoming increasingly available; readers must check the up-to-date situation with the appropriate authorities.

Accountancy

Professional Accountant

Entry qualifications

At least 2 A-levels and 3 GCSEs (A–C) including maths and English language. Over half the total entrants (nearly 90% of chartered accountants, 30% certified and 60% public finance) are *graduates* (any discipline). (See also 'Accounting Technician' route below, p. 8.)

In Scotland, all entrants to chartered accountancy aged under 25 must be graduates.

The work

The image of accountants as deskbound figure-crunchers is quite wrong. An accountancy qualification leads to a vast variety of jobs, in virtually any environment: manufacturing industry or television; retail or merchant banking; professional consultancy; public service. There is scope for accountants interested in the intricacies of accounting procedures and their technological development, or in high finance, or as a way into general management, and also for people who intend to become entrepreneurs. (See WORKING FOR ONESELF, p. 557.)

There is a vast variety of jobs in all types and sizes of business and public enterprise. An accountancy qualification is also an excellent preparation for jobs in merchant and other banking, insurance and the City.

There are some opportunities for employment (but *not* in public practice) in the EC, and in most other countries.

Work falls broadly into three categories:

1. *Public* (illogically also called 'private') *practice*.
2. *Industrial/commercial accountancy*.
3. *Public sector accountancy*.

Public Practice Accountants

They work in firms of partners. They are consultants, and employ qualified assistants, trainees and technicians (see below). Firms vary in size from 1 to several thousand, and in type from high-powered international practices which deal mainly with large companies and are at the very centre of the country's commercial activities, to small suburban practices which function at a gentler pace and deal mainly with private clients and local 'small traders'. Normally each accountant deals with particular clients' affairs so that there is personal (at least written or telephone) contact with individuals.

As the financial scene becomes ever more complex, accountants now often specialize in one particular accountancy aspect; for example, computer systems, mergers, corporate finance. However, the bulk of public practice work is taxation and auditing. Auditing means analysing and verifying clients' books and ensuring that the annual balance sheet presents a 'true and fair' picture of the client's financial affairs. Auditing is done on clients' premises so it involves meeting people and possibly travelling. Audits take anything from a few hours to several months, depending on the client's size and type of business. Audits may be done in streamlined offices using the latest technologies, or it may mean having to create order out of chaos when, for example, a farmer's 'office' consists of a drawerful of bills. Auditing is largely desk-work (or desk-top computer work), but it also involves discussions with clients – anyone from clerk to managing director – if specific items in the books are not clear. Apart from auditing and making suggestions about how to improve their systems and procedures, accountants also advise their clients on personal and business financial matters, from how to invest a small legacy to setting up a business or liquidating one. Large accountancy firms provide *management consultancy* services (see MANAGEMENT CONSULTANCY, p. 288).

Industrial and Commercial Accountants

They work for an employer on a salaried basis. They can be divided into *financial* accountants, concerned largely with internal audits, taxation, wage and salary structure, financial record-keeping; and *management* accountants. This is a fast-growing accountancy specialization (and it overlaps with management consultancy). Management accountants assess the relative importance, value and cost of all aspects of a business (or public enterprise), labour, raw materials, transport, sites, administration, marketing, etc. Every person's, machine's, department's, vehicle's, etc., contribution to the effectiveness of an organization, and their interdependence, can, with the help of computer systems and mathematical models, be assessed separately and as part of the whole operation. Management accountants might, for example, compare the relative cost of using a cheap new raw material which would necessitate more expensive machine maintenance and require mounting a marketing campaign to launch the changed product, against the cost of going on using the more expensive traditional raw material – taking into account, among other factors, what the competition abroad might do, and how staff would feel about the change. Or they might assess the cost of moving a factory to a cheaper site, considering increased transport cost, recruiting and training new staff. Like management consultants, their work requires interviewing all the people whose work affects the efficiency of the organization concerned. Having compared the financial results of alternative courses of action, management accountants present the information to the decision-makers at the top of the organization.

Because management accountants take part in decision-making and business control they need a broader understanding of business organization in general and of the type of business with which they are concerned than do financial accountants. They often move into consultancy sections of auditing firms, or into *management consultancy* (see p. 288).

Public Sector Accountants

Accountants and auditors working in local and central government, the health service, and national audit and other public service bodies are, like industrial and commercial accountants, concerned with all aspects of financial management. The emphasis of their work is on the efficient and effective use of scarce resources and the need for public accountability.

In the 1990s public service organizations are becoming more commercially orientated. Involvement in the management of change, e.g. contracting out of services, and advising on alternative options for the use of limited funds are important aspects of the finance manager's job. Work in the national audit bodies involves auditing public income and expenditure, certifying accounts and carrying out value-for-money studies.

Companies providing services to the public sector increasingly seek to recruit public service accountants and auditors. Significant numbers of finance managers become top-level general managers.

Training   There are 6 main professional qualifications, each awarded by a different body:

1. Institute of Chartered Accountants in England and Wales.
2. Institute of Chartered Accountants of Scotland.
3. Institute of Chartered Accountants in Ireland.
4. Chartered Association of Certified Accountants.
5. Chartered Institute of Management Accountants.

6. Chartered Institute of Public Finance and Accountancy.

The differences between the syllabuses are small – there is a basic body of accountancy knowledge which all accountants must master – but emphasis varies.

Accountancy courses all cover economics; statistics; computer applications and systems; corporate finance; financial management; taxation; trustee work; share organization; management accounting; relevant law; EC accountancy implications; auditing. The emphasis on different aspects of accountancy differs in the various professional bodies' examinations; some syllabuses overlap more than others. The reason for the existence of several accountancy bodies is historical rather than logical and a merger has often been discussed.

It is generally believed that chartered accountants get all the best jobs, or indeed that all qualified accountants are 'chartered'. But that is not so at all. The various qualifications, with the exception of (6), are equally marketable. Choice of one qualification rather than another only partly depends on the ultimate career aim: it also depends on what training is available locally; and on the type of training method preferred.

Main differences in various qualifications' usefulness in the job-market

Only appropriately qualified *chartered* and *certified* accountants may, by law, audit limited companies' accounts. People who want to go into public practice must therefore choose one of these two qualifications. *Chartered* and *certified* accountants can also go into industry and commerce and the public sector so these two qualifications leave the widest range of options open. (More than half of all qualified accountants work in industry and commerce.)

Management accountants are the most commercial and profit-orientated. This training concentrates more on running a business and planning its future than do the others. So people who definitely want to go into industry/commerce might choose this qualification. They too can choose to work in the public sector.

The Chartered Institute of Public Finance and Accountancy qualification differs from the others in that it is specifically tailored to the very large amount of work in the public sector – public utilities; National Health Service; local and central government.

Training methods vary between the various bodies, and they are complicated. (Candidates should read carefully all the accountancy bodies' training literature.)

All non-graduates may, and students of the Institute of Chartered Accountants and Chartered Institute of Public Finance and

Accountancy must, take a 'foundation course', usually at a polytechnic. Candidates who are not sure which qualification they will ultimately want to take must ensure they take a 9-month full-time or 2-year part-time 'common' foundation course: most prepare students for any of the accountancy bodies' examinations, but some lead only to one or two bodies' exams. The Foundation course syllabus covers accountancy principles, law, economics, statistics, computer applications.

The essential differences between the various bodies' training methods are:

Institute of Chartered Accountants
Students enter a training contract (3 years for graduates, 4 for non-graduates, including BTEC/SCOTVEC HND/C holders) with a firm of chartered accountants or (a recent change) an approved (by the ICA) industrial or commercial organization (including some civil service departments). In England and Wales graduates with a relevant degree take 2 professional examinations; 'non-relevant' graduates first take a 'conversion' course (15 weeks full time, or 7–8 months combined block-release and evening classes or correspondence course) for a Foundation stage exam. A-level/BTEC/SCOTVEC entrants must take a 1-year full-time or longer part-time Foundation course before entering a 4-year training contract. Trainees are given broad practical training in all the main aspects of the work. Larger firms have their own in-house training scheme, smaller ones may join with others in a training consortium. Theoretical study is done mainly in the student's own time and is hard work. In Scotland trainees are given block release throughout training for classes. The Scottish Institute's qualification comprises a professional examination (with exemptions for those with fully accredited degrees) and 2 tests of professional competence.

Chartered Association of Certified Accountants
Training is the most flexible. Students do not have to enter into training contracts but can train while in salaried employment. Alternatively, they can study for the exams full time and get practical experience afterwards. They may change employers, and type of employer, during their training and thus can get varied experience. They need not make up their mind at the outset whether they wish to go into industry/commerce or into public practice. However, 30 months in public practice is obligatory for persons who ultimately want to go into public practice. Training – called 'relevant accountancy experience' – takes 3–4 years depending on educational qualifications and method of training. This

experience can be gained before, during or after passing the professional exams. Exams leading to Associate Membership (ACCA) are at 3 levels. Those with a relevant degree or a foundation course may be exempt from all or part of level 1 and some HND/HNC holders may have partial exemption. Some exemptions for certain graduates and SCOTVEC HNC/D holders are available at level 2. Study can be full time, by day- or block-release, evening classes or correspondence courses, or by the Association's own Open Learning system. Certified accountancy students are not automatically entitled to study leave, but many companies offer it. About 40% of all UK accountancy students now choose certified accountancy.

Chartered Institute of Management Accountants

Students do not enter into training contracts, but are required to gain relevant practical experience while in full-time employment. In addition to passing the CIMA exams, students need a minimum of 3 years' experience before applying for Associate membership. This experience can be in the industrial and commercial sectors or, increasingly, in the public sector, and they may change employers during this period. CIMA exams are in 3 stages, each covering 4 subjects. There is a strong bias towards the use and management of information systems; subjects include management, financial management, strategic planning and marketing. Exemption can be granted from parts of the exams to students who have covered topics in their own qualification to the same level. Partial exemptions are granted to BTEC/SCOTVEC HNC/D holders. Graduates of any discipline may sit two Graduate Exemption papers as an alternative to Stage 1. Some students are granted day- or block-release. Others take evening classes or correspondence courses. Some short (and revision) courses are also available.

Chartered Institute of Public Finance and Accountancy

Trainees must first have completed a Foundation stage by taking either a relevant degree or a non-relevant degree followed by a conversion course. Non-graduates need to take a Foundation course or an approved BTEC/SCOTVEC HND/C. CIPFA students must be employed in a public service finance post with an approved employer. They follow a structured practical experience scheme integrated with academic study, the whole scheme taking between 3 and 6 years to complete. Both the syllabus and work experience reflect the increasingly commercial focus of public service and the need for financial management skills.

Personal attributes   Academic ability; numeracy; ability to speak and write concisely; business sense; logical mind; ability to negotiate without self-consciousness with people at all levels within an organization; tact in dealing with employers and clients; a liking for desk work. Training demands determination, motivation and staying-power.

Accountants in public practice: A confidence-inspiring manner; ability to put things clearly to lay people.

Industrial/commercial accountancy: Ability to communicate with and extract information from people at all levels of intelligence and responsibility; enjoyment of decision-making.

Public sector accountancy: Ability to advise and explain financial matters to councillors and other public sector representatives.

Late start   No significant GCSE/A-level concessions, but individual cases judged on merit. It may be difficult to find training vacancies, but there are opportunities, particularly for people willing to undertake preparatory study (see 'Training', p. 3). Over 10% of the ICAEW student intake in 1989/90 was over 25.

Career-break   Should be no problem for ICA and ACCA members. There are lectures and journals which help to keep accountants up to date with developments. Some reduced professional membership subscriptions. It is possible to work in most parts of the country and also to run a small practice from home. More difficult with other two bodies but possible if well established first. CIPFA has a Career Break membership category and has helped promote equal opportunity policies among CIPFA employers.

Part time   Opportunities increasing especially in public practice. Job-sharing should be possible. Part-time training contracts may be possible.

Position of women   Proportions are still surprisingly low:

	Qualified Members	*Trainees*
Chartereds	12%	35%
Certifieds	10·5%	43%
CIMA	7%	25%
CIPFA	13%	37%

There is little prejudice in accountancy generally except perhaps in some City firms and at the top in local government (see LOCAL GOVERNMENT, p. 268). The reason for low proportions must be: (a) tradition (b) the image of accountancy as totally desk-bound work without contact with people and (c) the fact that fewer girls have taken GCSE maths. Yet accountancy training helps women to get into senior *management in industry* (see p. 272). A fair proportion have done extremely well in, for example, financial journalism, and some in *management consultancy* (see p. 288).

Further information

Institute of Chartered Accountants in England and Wales, PO Box 433, Chartered Accountants' Hall, Moorgate Place, London EC2P 2BJ

Institute of Chartered Accountants of Scotland, 27 Queen Street, Edinburgh EH2 1LA

Institute of Chartered Accountants in Ireland, 11 Donegal Square South, Belfast BT1 5JE

The Chartered Association of Certified Accountants, 29 Lincoln's Inn Fields, London WC2A 3EE

The Chartered Institute of Management Accountants, 63 Portland Place, London W1M 4AB

The Chartered Institute of Public Finance and Accountancy, 3 Robert Street, London WC2N 6BH

Related careers

ACTUARY – BANKING – CHARTERED SECRETARY – COMPUTING – INSURANCE – MANAGEMENT – PURCHASING AND SUPPLY – SCIENCE: *Statistics* – TAX INSPECTOR

Accounting Technician

Entry qualifications

For registration as a student member of the Association of Accounting Technicians: 4 GCSEs including an English and a numerate subject, and not more than one non-academic one; or BTEC First award in Business and Finance; or AAT's Certificate in Accounting. Requirements are relaxed for students over 21.

The work

There is no legal requirement for accountants to be professionally qualified; 'accountant' is not a 'protected title' in the way 'solicitor' or 'architect' is. This 'second tier' technician qualification was created because there is so much accountancy work which while being highly responsible and requiring expertise and training, does not require the breadth of *professional* accountancy education (see above, p. 3).

Broadly, professional accountants conduct audits (which technicians are not empowered to do) and deal with high-powered financial management and advice, etc.; accounting technicians collect the information on which professional accountants base their decisions, and deal with straightforward accountancy. This involves more desk-work than does professional accountancy, but it also involves contact with clients.

The vast majority of accounting technicians work in professional accountants' offices or under the direction of professional accountants in industry, commerce or the public sector. However, some are 'sole' or 'company' accountants in firms too small to warrant employing a professional accountant, and some accounting technicians set up on their own, dealing with private clients' (individuals, shopkeepers, etc.) VAT, income tax and similar matters. Some keep small firms' books and visit such clients at regular intervals on a contract basis. Others put advertisements in local papers and do 'one-off' jobs for people who need some straightforward accountancy advice, or help with tax returns. So accounting technicians can choose whether to take on secure employment and do mainly desk-work, or to have contact with a variety of clients and be their own boss (see WORKING FOR ONESELF, p. 557).

AAT members who want to become professional accountants (see above) normally get exemption from at least the professional accountancy bodies' (see above) Foundation examinations.

Training   The AAT is introducing a new 'competence-based' scheme in 3 stages: Foundation, Intermediate and Technician. (At Technician stage students will specialize in either accounting practice, central government, local government or the NHS.) These are likely to lead to NVQs/SVQs levels 2, 3 and 4 (see p. xx). The transition from existing AAT examinations will take 3 years: 1 stage will be introduced each year, starting in September 1992.

BTEC/SCOTVEC are preparing to introduce National and Higher National awards in Accounting (also leading to NVQs/SVQs) in line with these changes. As training is evolving it is essential to check the current situation with the AAT.

Personal attributes   A methodical approach; liking for figure, computer and desk-work. There is room in this work for those who prefer to work on their own but with limited responsibility as support staff to more highly qualified/experienced colleagues, and for those who, though unable to take the professional examination, wish to do responsible work and have contact with colleagues and clients. For AAT members who want to set up on their own: confidence-inspiring manner; self-confidence; ability not to worry as work may be sporadic rather than regular (see WORKING FOR ONESELF, p. 557).

Late start   Very good scope for various kinds of older entrants such as unqualified but experienced accountancy staff, returners to office occupations, mid-career changers. GCSE entry requirements waived for students over 21; older people with relevant experience or knowledge may be exempted from some AAT examinations.

Career-break

Unlikely to present any problems as long as people keep up with changes in taxation and other accountancy matters. Evening classes and correspondence courses (including Open University) can act as *refresher* training. Reduced membership subscriptions for those on maternity break.

Part time

Very good scope, both in employment and working on one's own. Job-sharing should be possible.

Position of women

Women are doing well as accounting technicians, both in employment and working on their own. In 1991 32% of Members and 59% of newly registered Student Members were women.

Further information

Association of Accounting Technicians, 154 Clerkenwell Road, London ECIR 5AD

Related careers

BANKING – INSURANCE – PURCHASING AND SUPPLY – SHIP-BROKING ... EXPORTING – STOCK EXCHANGE AND SECURITIES INDUSTRY

Actuary

Entry qualifications

Over 90% *graduate* entry, most graduates have degrees in a mathematical subject.

For school leavers:

England and Wales: 2 A-levels, one of which must be at least grade B in a maths subject, the other at least grade C, and 3 GCSEs (A–C) or equivalent including English.

Scotland: 3 H-grade passes including maths (grade A) and English plus Certificate in Sixth-Year studies with grade A and grade B in specified maths papers.

The work

Actuaries use the theory of probability and the theory of compound interest together with statistical techniques to highlight and solve financial problems; to suggest appropriate courses of action and to predict the financial implications of such actions. In other words, they 'work out the odds'. Their work has a strong mathematical bias and is essentially desk-work performed in a variety of settings. Some 60% of actuaries work for insurance offices, concentrating on the technical side of life assurance and pension funds, investigating such matters as relative life expectancies of various groups in the population, and assessing the effects of life-styles and characteristics on premiums and policies and investment. In other insurance branches – accident, fire, motor – actuaries assess risks and pin-point variables in the light of changing conditions and life-styles, and advise on reserves necessary to cover long-term liabilities. In government departments actuaries advise on public service pensions and insurance scheme. Though they are concerned with various aspects of people's lives and welfare (cushioning the effects of old age, accident, sickness which are the reasons for insurance schemes), actuaries do not usually have much contact with people outside their own office.

About 30% of actuaries work in consultancy. Much of their work involves advising clients, usually about pension funds, but they also advise insurance companies too small to have their own actuarial department, or give specialist advice to large insurance companies.

There are also openings in merchant banks, the Stock Exchange and other financial institutions, as well as some limited opportunities (usually to do with pensions) in industry and commerce.

Actuaries can go into middle and higher business management, especially in life assurance companies and pension funds.

Training   *For school-leavers*: On-the-job training (minimum 3 years) plus 6–7 years' part-time study (mainly by correspondence) and discussion classes for Institute of Actuaries' (England and Wales) or Faculty of Actuaries' (Scotland) examinations. Employers may give time off for daytime study, but considerable evening work is necessary too. The syllabus includes probability; statistics and compound interest; principles of actuarial treatment of statistical data; finance and investment; life offices; pension funds; general insurance (IOA only).

For graduates: On-the-job training and 3–5 years' (depending on degree subject) part-time study as above. A good degree in mathematics, statistics or economics qualifies a student for exemption from some early parts of IOA or FOA examinations. A first degree or post-graduate diploma (1 year full time, 2 years part time) in actuarial subjects can lead to further exemptions.

Personal attributes   Liking for concentrated desk-work; an analytical brain (actuaries tend to be good and devoted bridge-players); probing curiosity; pleasure in solving complicated problems; ability to interpret and express in clear English results of mathematical and statistical analysis; business sense.

Late start   Only advisable for very able mathematicians because of the long training; also difficulty in finding training posts.

Career-break   Possible for experienced actuaries who have kept up with developments, especially relevant legislation and data processing application (see p. 142). Temporarily retired members pay a reduced subscription which nevertheless entitles them to receive all journals and attend meetings. Correspondence courses can be adapted to form *refresher* courses.

Part time   In theory work could be done part time, and by job-sharers or freelances; in practice no concentrated attempts to organize this seem to have been made by prospective part-timers.

Position of women   Women comprise only 5% of fully qualified members of the Institute of Actuaries; but 26% of student members are women, so the proportion is going up. (The figures in Scotland are lower.) No special difficulties getting jobs and promotion.

Further information	Institute of Actuaries, Napier House, 4 Worcester Street, Gloucester Green, Oxford OX1 2AW
	The Faculty of Actuaries, 23 St Andrew Square, Edinburgh EH2 1AQ

Related careers	ACCOUNTANCY – BANKING – CIVIL SERVICE – INSURANCE – STOCK EXCHANGE AND SECURITIES INDUSTRY

Advertising

Entry qualifications

No rigid requirements; in practice usually at least A-level English. Most entrants are now *graduates*.

Graphic design, typography, etc., require art-school training (see ART AND DESIGN, p. 55).

The work

Advertising specialists work in:

1. Agencies.
2. Company advertising departments.
3. The media and for suppliers of advertising services (e.g. studios, film production, market research).

Agencies

Agencies plan, create and place advertisements on behalf of advertisers who appoint them to handle their 'account'. This may be a detergent, a package holiday, government information, or a nationalized industry. Only 40% of advertising expenditure is concerned with persuading people to *buy*; advertisements are also used to get money for charities, votes for political parties, support for legislation, to encourage energy saving or investment, to fill jobs.

Agencies vary in size and scope. A very few employ up to 500 people, most under 50. Some specialize: for example, in business-to-business or recruitment advertising. The largest agencies have a range of specialist services 'in house' such as package design (see p. 58), film production (see TELEVISION, FILM AND RADIO, p. 530), market research and marketing (see pp. 16, 294) and public relations (see p. 409). Others buy services in from outside suppliers.

Account Executive/Account Planner

Agency staff work in groups on individual accounts. Responsible for each account group of specialists are *account executives*. They are usually in charge of several accounts, each dealing with a different product, and are the link between clients and agency. They must acquaint themselves thoroughly with each client's product: this may involve asking Research (see below) to identify the 'target group' (the people at whom the advertisement is to be aimed); to investigate the competition's product; to ensure the client's claims for the product can be substantiated. After the initial research, the group decide on a 'campaign theme', then the account executive discusses it with the client. When the brief and the budget are agreed, work on 'creating the advertisements' starts.

The account executives coordinate the work, control the budget and present progress reports to the client. Their work involves travelling if clients are scattered over the country or abroad.

Some agencies split the job into *account executives* and *account planners*. The executives' main responsibility is liaison with the client; the planners' with organizing and interpreting research into consumer attitudes and developing the strategy on which the advertising will be based.

The executives' job requires self-confidence and diplomacy, as clients often have to be persuaded that the type and tone of a campaign suggested by the agency will be more effective than the client's own idea. Planners' jobs tend to be more academic in approach.

Media Executive and Buyer

Media planners' jobs are crucial to the success of any campaign. In consultation with account handlers and creative staff they work out how best to spend the available budget in order to generate most sales/influence. They choose the channels of communication – newspapers, magazines, radio, television, posters and so on – which are most appropriate for any particular campaign and reach the target group most economically. Media planning decisions are based on information and statistics provided by *media research*. Computers are widely used to compare effectiveness and costs, but creative requirements – for colour, movement or sound – require subjective judgement.

Media buyers are responsible for the purchase of advertisement space or air time.

Planning, research and buying are the three media functions; they may be carried out by different people within the department, or the whole media operation may be the responsibility of a group of individuals assigned to a particular campaign.

Market Research (see also p. 294)

Before an advertising campaign is planned, facts are compiled about the product's uses, its advantages and limitations, competitors' products, distribution and so on. Facts and opinions are also gathered about its potential users – the target group: not just in terms of who they are, how much money they have and where they live, but in terms of their attitudes and behaviour. Some facts come from desk research, collecting information from a variety of published sources and the client's own records. Others may need specially commissioned research, ranging from statistics compiled by part-time interviewers questioning members of the public, to sophisticated behavioural studies involving trained psychologists.

Creative Department

Once the account group has been briefed and a strategy agreed with the client, the creative team of *copywriter* and *art director* together develop the advertisement.

The advertising 'message' is translated into a 'communication' that makes an instant impact on the target group. Words and pictures must complement each other.

Copywriters must be literate and imaginative, but they must choose their words under considerable constraints – from the disciplines of the brief and the restrictions of the space or time available, to the obligations of the Code of Advertising Practice and legal requirements. An interest in commercial success and an understanding of people's ways of life and priorities are far more useful than literary leanings.

Television and cinema commercials may be created jointly by copywriters and producers, or written by specialist scriptwriters to the producer's brief. There is no hard and fast rule about who exactly does what, and whether the visual or verbal aspect is the more important.

The *art director* (see ART AND DESIGN, p. 55) is responsible for the visual appearance of advertisements, deciding whether to use photography, illustration, computer graphics or typography, and commissioning and supervising their production. The typographer chooses type which is easily readable, fits the layout and reflects the character of the product. The artist (only the larger agencies employ their own) may produce anything from a 'rough' to a finished 'visual' (see 'Graphics . . .', p. 58).

The atmosphere in agencies is often relaxed and informal, but the pace and pressure are very demanding indeed. The decline in the number of people in agencies means fierce competition for any openings. Considerable talent, the right kind of personality and commitment are needed to survive and succeed.

Advertisers

Many advertisers incorporate advertising into marketing (see p. 294). *Brand managers* are responsible for the marketing policy for a product, including its advertising. Others have their own advertising departments, which vary in size. If a manufacturer creates and places all the advertising directly, the department may be much like a small agency. There is less scope for employees to work on different types of products simultaneously, but there may be a broader range of work.

Retailers' advertisement departments may deal with store and window displays, exhibitions, fashion shows, promotions and public relations, for example, using an advertising agency only for display advertisements.

Advertising departments are useful training grounds, giving experience in a range of work. There are more opportunities for junior copywriters in advertising departments than within agencies.

Media

Advertising departments are responsible for selling space or air time to advertisers, directly or through agencies. The *research section* provides information about readers or viewers; it helps advertisers pin-point target groups. The *promotions section* may have its own creative department, which works in three areas: projecting the medium to advertisers, to distributors, and to retailers on behalf of advertisers. *Sales representatives* are responsible for selling advertisement space or air time; this may include telephone selling, trying to get classified advertisements (which may involve having to put up with being rebuffed, and trying again). *Media managers* are responsible for ensuring that advertisements comply with the Code of Advertising Practice, which may involve checking copy claims and possibly asking for changes to be made before accepting copy.

*

Training   Considerable persistence – apart from talent – is needed to get a job. Nearly three-quarters of the jobs are in London. Once in, training is a combination of practice and theory. Most examinations are set by the CAM (Communication Advertising and Marketing Education Foundation), but these are by no means compulsory. Agency policy varies concerning how far these vocational qualifications are looked for or encouraged.

1. CAM examinations

Study can be full time, part time, by correspondence or private.

Entry requirements for CAM Certificate: 3 GCSEs (A–C) or equivalent (including English language) and 2 A-levels; *or* BTEC or SCOTVEC Higher National award (see pp. xxi, xxii); *or* London Chamber of Commerce and Industry Third Group Diploma in Advertising, Marketing and Public Relations; *or* 1 year in full-time employment in the communication business and GCSEs (A–C) or equivalent, including English language.

The Certificate covers marketing; advertising; public relations; media; sales promotion and direct marketing; research and behavioural studies; communication practice; business and economic environment. It normally takes about 2 years' study, usually at evening classes, occasionally by day-release or distance learning.

Certificate holders can go on to take the CAM Diploma and specialize in a specific aspect of the communication business.

Partial exemption may be granted on a subject-for-subject basis from the Certificate stage to holders of related awards, e.g. certain BTEC awards (see p. xxi), or degrees in business studies or communication studies.

2. Other courses

(a) BTEC Higher National Diploma in Advertising Copywriting, Hounslow Borough College (2 years).

(b) College Certificate (2 years), Diplomas (1 year) and postgraduate Diploma (6 months) in Advertising at Watford College (1 year).

(c) An intensive 1-year course at the School of Communications Arts, an independent college that runs courses particularly geared to the needs of advertising agencies.

Qualifications are not obligatory in advertising, but increasing numbers of entrants are finding them useful. The larger agencies tend to run in-service training schemes, and some agencies take several graduates (any discipline) each year; many advertisers have management training schemes which can lead to advertising jobs.

The Institute of Practitioners in Advertising runs a phased programme of training courses designed to cater for the training needs of executives employed by IPA member agencies at each stage of their career development.

Secretaries occasionally progress to executive or copywriting positions; their chances are better with a small specialist agency (for example, a recruitment agency) or in an advertising department, but they are never great. Other ways into the industry are through production departments (see PUBLISHING, p. 412, and PRINTING, p. 393) and 'traffic control' (progress chasing – keeping the work flowing to schedule through all the different departments and processes).

Personal attributes   Business acumen; interest in social and economic trends; flair for salesmanship; numeracy; communication skills; ability to work in a team; ability to stand criticism whether justified or not; ability to work under pressure; stamina; resilience; persistence.

For creative people: Discipline; originality; strong feeling for uncomplicated images and 'messages'; willingness to produce the kind of words/artwork that are best for the campaign, whether artistically first-rate or not.

For research: Objectivity; a logical, analytical brain.

Late start   Little opportunity without previous relevant commercial experience.

Career-break   Prospects only reasonable for experienced researchers or for successful executives who have 'kept their hand in' with freelance work.

Part time   Little opportunity.

Position of women   Although the majority of advertisements are aimed at women, until very recently their share of account executive positions was small. However, this has been steadily growing and in 1989 was 33%. Overall, women make up nearly half of agency staff and do particularly well in account planning/research (52%) and media (42%). An increasing number of brand managers (see MARKETING, p. 294) are women. They fare much worse as copywriters and art directors. Although the Women's Advertising Club keeps an eye on women's promotion, they have not been able to do much about unequal promotion at senior level. It is an area where discrimination is difficult to prove, as there is no career structure; promotion does not depend on qualification and experience but on 'suitability' for any particular job.

Further information	CAM Foundation, Abford House, 15 Wilton Road, London SW1V 1NJ
	Institute of Practitioners in Advertising, 44 Belgrave Square, London SW1X 8QS

Related careers	MANAGEMENT – MARKETING AND SELLING – PUBLIC RELATIONS – RETAIL DISTRIBUTION

Agriculture and Horticulture

Entry qualifications
Entry at all levels, from no qualifications to degree.

The work
Agriculture and horticulture cover a wide range of land-based industries, both traditional and, increasingly, non-traditional. Pig and poultry rearing, fish and deer farming, fruit, vegetable and flower growing, shooting, nature trails, wine-growing – these and many other activities make up an industry that in the last few years has been going through one of its biggest ever changes, more particularly on the agricultural side. This is due to a number of factors: increased efficiency leading to over-production, which in turn has led to the imposition of quotas on what a farmer can produce. Farmers' incomes have been dropping, which means fewer staff can be employed and more farmers and their families work part rather than full time. Smaller units are disappearing, while larger ones survive by becoming even more efficient. Numbers employed in general farm work have dropped dramatically and anyone looking to a career in farming in future must be prepared to develop good management and/or specialist skills. Bad publicity about chemical pollution, intensive farming and several food scares, plus pressures from a more health-conscious public, mean more farmers have been switching to less intensive, organic methods of production. All farmers are having to find other ways to use their resources, for example by diversifying into the tourism or recreation industries (e.g. bed and breakfast, golf driving ranges). About 40% of agricultural holdings now have at least one non-farming activity. This may not mean a big increase in income, and many farms are not suitable for such developments, but somehow farmers have to find ways of 'adding value' to their products or activities – perhaps making ice cream from surplus milk, or encouraging the public to 'pick your own' fruit. Government schemes to pay farmers to 'set aside' land from production and to subsidize the planting of woodlands are part of a movement towards seeing farmers not just as producers of food, but as custodians of the countryside.

Management posts in agriculture and horticulture are often held by people who started out in practical work and then became supervisors. Increasingly, though, qualifications such as HNDs and degrees are essential for such jobs as farm manager, unit manager, manager of a country park. As farms and horticultural units grow in size, the range but not the number of management jobs is increasing. A manager of, for example, an animal unit needs scientific, technological, veterinary, accounting, even computer knowledge. Marketing skills are increasingly in demand.

Research is usually concerned with a particular aspect of crop production or of animal husbandry. This could be concerned with pest control, plant disease, soil chemistry, genetics, nutrition, taste preservation (researchers work closely with technologists in the food industry – see 'Food Science and Technology', p. 459). Work may be wholly or largely theoretical, involving study of scientific journals and papers as well as collaboration with scientists from other disciplines. It often involves experimental work in the laboratory or in trial growing areas. Researchers work for research establishments, for botanical gardens, in industry, in the Civil Service (mainly the Ministry of Agriculture, Fisheries and Food (MAFF)).

Advisory work is carried out by government (through MAFF) and by commercial firms which supply agricultural and horticultural goods and equipment. Advice may be given on pest control, selection of the best variety of crop, choice of feed, marketing, finance, diversification.

Agriculture

The main branches of 'traditional' practical farm work are:

Animal Husbandry

Beef cattle: work varies according to size and type of farm. Some farms only rear calves, others fatten cattle through to slaughter.

Dairy cattle: a 100-cow herd can be worth a large sum of money, so this is highly responsible work. Tasks involve feeding, milking and following strict hygiene maintenance routines.

Pigs: Farms breed pigs for sale, or buy young pigs and fatten them for sale as bacon or pork, or they do both. Extent of automation varies.

Poultry: highly specialized holdings concentrate either entirely on egg production or on hatching chicks – often in fully automatic giant incubators – or on rearing table birds. Some poultry units resemble a cross between a laboratory and a modern factory, with indoor, clean work. Increased demand for free-range eggs means more scope for alternative forms of egg production, but there are still few farms where looking after poultry means feeding birds in the farmyard.

Sheep: hill farms usually concentrate on large flocks; on lowland farms sheep may form part of a unit and shepherds also do other work. Shepherds work with, and may train, dogs.

Working in Arable Crops

The wide variety of crops grown on British farms tends to be concentrated in the east of the country. Most arable work is highly mechanized, but requires considerable skill in operating and maintaining sophisticated machinery.

On the whole, the larger and/or more mechanized the farm, the greater the degree of specialization. Individuals need not stick to one specialization throughout their career, though some prefer to do so. Livestock workers are expected to drive tractors.

General Farm Work

People who do not want to specialize can carry out general duties, driving tractors, helping with livestock, repairing buildings, clearing ditches, etc. The range of jobs depends on the type and size of farm.

Horticulture

There are two main divisions: commercial – growing plants for sale – and amenity – making and maintaining gardens as pleasant environments. Horticulturalists, therefore, may work in different settings – as sole employee or as one of a large team; in the depths of the country or in the middle of a town.

Commercial Horticulture

This includes the production of fruit, vegetables, flowers, plants of all kinds in market gardens, nurseries, garden centres, greenhouses and fruit farms. Some sell directly to the public, while others sell only to other horticultural concerns. Some specialize in, for example, bulb production, soft fruit, cut flowers or house-plants. Others grow a wide variety of plants. Many tasks are now mechanized, but some are still done by hand – some pollination, disbudding, collecting seed, grafting, for example. Much effort now goes into producing strains that are disease-resistant and/or have a longer growing season (e.g. through genetic engineering). Computer systems are often used to control the environment in order to produce exactly the right conditions for different plants. Garden centres are a feature of most towns, offering pot-grown plants which customers can plant in their gardens at any time of year, plus a huge range of garden tools and accessories. Jobs in these offer the most contact with members of the public, who expect them to be knowledgeable. Experienced horticultural workers can become plantation assistants on fruit stations or quality inspectors for commercial canning and quick-freezing stations, or manage 'pick your own' farms (weekend work).

Amenity Horticulture

Its purpose is to provide pleasant open-air environments in town and country. It includes town and country parks; picnic areas off motorways; National Trust and similar properties; nature trails; theme parks; bowling greens; golf courses. It frequently involves nursery work and arboriculture (see 'Forestry', below). Staff have to cope with the sometimes conflicting demands of the gardening programme and events held in the park (e.g. open-air concerts). A park manager may spend a large proportion of time on such non-horticultural activities as paperwork and rubbish disposal. Current reductions in staffing levels often affect types of planting, e.g. bedding plants may give way to grass and shrubs. Amenity gardeners are usually employed by public authorities rather than by commercial enterprises. The work involves contact with the public and often helping with recreational activities, such as sitting at cash-desks for open-air concerts, usher and patrol duty, although in some parks these duties are carried out by keepers with no horticultural training (see also Diploma in Management Studies, under LEISURE/RECREATION MANAGEMENT, 'Training', p. 266). There may be more of a career structure (and day-release) in this type of horticulture than in commercial concerns.

Landscape and Garden Contractors

The work overlaps with landscape architecture (see p. 244) and amenity horticulture. It includes design and construction of new gardens and regular maintenance of existing gardens. Increasingly, contractors are employed by local authorities (and in future even by the Royal Parks) to maintain public gardens and parks.

*

Training

Although it may still be possible to get a job in farming and horticulture without going to college, there is much more chance of a proper career for those with formal training. Expertise and management skills are of increasing importance. The main training routes are:

National Certificate route
National Certificate courses normally last 1 year full time. No set academic requirements, but students are required to have had 1 year's previous practical work, sometimes 2, on a farm or holding. (Youth Training, see p. xxv, may be available.) Also, as competition for places is keen, those with some good GCSE grades or with other certificates, e.g. City and Guilds, have more chance of acceptance. Most NCs are in general agriculture or horticulture, but a few are specialized, e.g. in dairy farming or greenkeeping.

Advanced National Certificate courses last 1 year and are specialized. Examples are agricultural mechanization, deer management, arable farm management, commercial fruit production. Some colleges offer a National Certificate in Farm Management – of a similar level to the ANC.

BTEC/SCOTVEC route (see pp. xxi, xxii)
BTEC National Diploma/SCOTVEC National Certificate courses can be in general agriculture or horticulture or specialized. Examples are game, wildlife and habitat management, fishery management, forestry, amenity horticulture. Entrants must normally have had 1 year's practical experience.

Post-Higher Diploma courses are also available, mainly in new technologies, in management and farm organization. These courses may be taken after some time at work.

Degrees
3 or 4 years. Entry requirements normally include 1 or 2 sciences at A-level. There is a wide variety of courses: examples of titles, apart from general agriculture or horticulture, are crop science, crop technology and resource management, agriculture and land management, agricultural botany, agricultural and food marketing, agroforestry, animal production science. Little actual farm work is included in degree courses, which are intended for future advisers, researchers, teachers or managers.

Kew Diploma

3-year, degree-level course in amenity horticulture. Entry requirements are minimum 5 GCSEs, including English, maths and a
science, plus 2 A-levels, preferably in science subjects, plus at least
2 years' work in a 'recognized' horticultural establishment. A
small number accepted straight from sixth form.

NOTE: NVQs (see p. xx), levels 1–4, are being introduced, but
National Certificates and Diplomas are likely to retain their titles
for the time being.

Fringe Specializations

Forestry

This is a small specialization, although until recent tax changes
made it less attractive, commercial conifer planting had been
increasing. The Farm Woodlands Scheme is encouraging farmers
to plant trees instead of crops; and environmentalists would like
to see the planting of more hardwoods (which take a long time to
grow and attract a wide range of wildlife) and fewer conifers. In
commercial forestry trees are grown as a renewable resource and
harvested like any other crop. Other woodlands are maintained
for sporting or recreational purposes. Urban forestry is growing
in importance; known also as arboriculture, it covers the establishment, care and maintenance of trees for amenity purposes (see
'Amenity Horticulture', above).

Employers include the Forestry Commission (though this is
selling off some of its forests), local authorities, commercial companies that own forests all over the country, co-operatives and
individual landowners. There are opportunities to work abroad.
Managers – senior forest officers – plan afforestation programmes
and may be in overall charge of a single plantation, a group of
forests or a whole district. Though an administrative job it involves driving and walking. It includes responsibility for fire
protection, wildlife protection, disease identification and control,
planning and control of recreational areas, possibly marketing.
Forest workers carry out practical tasks under supervision usually
of foresters or forest officers.

Training   Forest workers do not need formal qualifications, but may be given in-service training and/or sent on block-release for City and Guilds/SCOTVEC certificates.

Most foresters or forest officers train by taking *either* a BTEC National Diploma *or* SCOTVEC-based college diploma *or* a degree in a forestry-related subject or a post-graduate course. Diploma courses normally require a minimum 2 years' practical experience. Those seeking the highest level management posts may need to take the Professional Examination of the Institute of Chartered Forestry (forestry graduates take only part 2, ND holders take parts 1 and 2).

Traditionally, diploma-holders have been taken on as supervisors, responsible for overseeing day-to-day operations, and graduates as assistant or area managers. Graduates have more scientific knowledge than diplomates, but the distinction has become blurred and promotion is possible for both types of entrant.

Fish Farming and Fisheries Management

This is the breeding and rearing of various types of fish for food or sport. Most fish farms are small owner-run businesses, but there are larger ones employing several staff. Other employers of fisheries managers are water authorities, angling clubs, estate owners, fish processors. Like all animal husbandry this is usually a 7-day-a-week job and involves unsocial working hours.

Training   There is no prescribed entry and training route: the usual ways into this growing industry are through a BTEC/SCOTVEC National Award (see pp. xxi, xxii) in fish farming or fisheries management; or a BTEC sandwich Higher National Diploma; or the Institute of Fisheries Management correspondence course for its certificate and diploma (no entry requirements).

For research posts: degree in biological or agricultural science, usually followed by a post-graduate course.

It is possible to progress to management from a technician post.

Agricultural/Horticultural Engineering

Agricultural engineers apply engineering principles to all kinds of agriculture and horticulture. As the world's non-renewable and slowly renewable resources are being rapidly used up, it is essential to make the most efficient use of natural resources. This involves recycling processes; exploring and using new sources of energy; and, above all, incorporating new technologies in the design and manufacture of agricultural equipment. Agricultural engineers may be involved in the sales, marketing and servicing of equipment; in designing and constructing farm buildings; in product planning; mechanizing procedures; crop storage and processing. The work is related to food technology (see p. 459) and professional engineering (see p. 183). There is scope for work abroad, especially in developing countries.

Farm/Garden Mechanic

All farmworkers must be able to cope with running repairs; many arable units which use machinery worth thousands of pounds employ their own farm mechanics who are in charge of maintenance, repairs and adaptation of all types of mechanical gadgets. On large units there may be several mechanics; usually there is only one. However, the majority of mechanics are employed by agricultural and garden machinery dealers, carrying out servicing and repairs in a workshop or in the field where the machinery is being used.

Training For levels of engineering see ENGINEERING, p. 183.

Courses are available leading to City and Guilds, National Certificate or BTEC/SCOTVEC awards, as well as degrees in agricultural engineering. Holders of a Higher National Diploma or a degree in a related subject (geography, science, agriculture) can take a 1- or 2-year post-graduate course in agricultural engineering.

Farm or garden mechanics follow a formal training scheme laid down by the Agricultural and Garden Machinery Association.

Conservation

Concerned with the preservation of the country's plant and animal life and natural habitats. Conservationists are concerned mainly with environmental issues, the effects of various activities, such as farming, manufacturing and recreation, on our natural surroundings. Conservation takes in ecology: this is the study of how plants as well as animals exist together and act upon and react to each other in their natural surroundings, and what happens when the natural balance is disturbed through intervention by man in order to use land and resources for more immediate purposes. Conservationists work mainly for research organizations, including the Natural Environmental Research Council (see SCIENCE, p. 446).

Training Conservation is not a career as such. It is an activity and a concern for specialists in a number of relevant disciplines: horticulture, botany, zoology, geography. Some agricultural courses now have conservation or countryside management options.

Horticultural Therapy

This covers the use of horticulture and agriculture in the treatment of certain groups of patients. It may form part of a planned rehabilitation of a physically handicapped patient or it may provide education, recreation or vocational training for people suffering from mental handicap or other disabilities. Most therapists (who may be called a horticultural instructor/organizer or project worker) work in sheltered workshops, hospitals, residential homes, training centres or specialist colleges for people with a physical handicap.

Training   There is as yet no career structure, although the majority of the work is carried out by professional care staff and horticulturalists. Horticultural Therapy (a registered charity) launched a professional development Diploma in Therapeutic Horticulture in January 1992, consisting of a day-release course over 30 weeks for people with qualifications in either horticulture or occupational therapy. All will take a general horticultural therapy module and then, depending on background, choose the particular horticultural or therapy module.

*

Personal attributes   *For most jobs*: attention to detail; physical robustness and ability to cope with irregular hours; reliability; good powers of observation; ability to work without supervision.

For managers: ability to recruit and cope with permanent and seasonal staff; ability to take decisions, knowing that these may be subject to the vagaries of nature; enjoyment of responsibility.

Late start   On the whole this is not advisable as trainee vacancies tend to go to young applicants (partly because the pay structure is age-related), although there are no age limits on training schemes or courses. Some farmers' children return to farming as a second career when their parents wish to retire.

Career-break   There should be no problem for those in management jobs before the break, except that competition for jobs is fierce. The Forestry Commission has a 'keep-in-touch' scheme for men and women who retire temporarily for domestic reasons.

Part time Many more people than in the past are working part time, especially in agriculture.

Position of women The proportion of women employees in agriculture is still low. However, the proportion of women owners, partners and part-time family workers is about a third and many more are taking full-time college courses. With increased mechanization there is no reason why a healthy, fit woman should not do as well as a man, given that no one should be asked to lift exceptionally heavy loads. In horticulture, women do well at all levels. Women tend not to apply for forestry work, but some are employed, especially in the Forestry Commission.

Further information Careers, Education and Training Advice Centre, c/o Warwickshire Careers Service, 10 Northgate Street, Warwick CV34 4SR

Royal Botanic Gardens, Kew, Richmond, Surrey TW9 3AB

Forestry Training Council, 231 Corstorphine Road, Edinburgh EH12 7AT

Institute of Fisheries Management, 22 Rushworth Avenue, West Bridgford, Nottingham NG2 7LF

The Institution of Agricultural Engineers, West End Road, Silsoe, Bedford MK45 4DU

British Agricultural and Garden Machinery Association, 14–16 Church Street, Rickmansworth, Herts WD3 1RQ

Horticultural Therapy, Goulds Ground, Vallis Way, Frome, Somerset BA11 3DW

Related careers LANDSCAPE ARCHITECTURE – SCIENCE: *Scientist; Technician* – ANIMALS: *Veterinary Nurse/Surgeon*

Animals

Veterinary Surgeon

A-level chemistry plus 2 others normally chosen from physics, biology and maths. The subject not offered at A-level should be included among the GCSEs offered (usually at least 6). This is the most competitive of degree courses; very high A-level grades are required. Experience of handling animals, sometimes observing a veterinary surgeon in practice, is essential.

General practice

Some veterinary practices deal mainly or exclusively (except in cases of emergency) with small or 'companion' animals; others deal with farm animals or horses; some are mixed practices, but even here veterinary surgeons are likely to develop particular areas of interest and expertise. Veterinary surgeons must provide a 24-hour service, but most practices are organized so as to provide reasonable time off and holidays.

Veterinary surgeons treat animals both in their surgeries and at their owners' premises. It is important for them to be able to communicate effectively with animals' owners. This means a different approach for pet-owners, who have an emotional attachment to their 'companion animals', and for farmers to whom their animals are an investment. While always committed to the welfare of an animal, the veterinary surgeon must allow a farmer to balance an expensive new treatment against an economic return. In farm animal practice, veterinary surgeons are concerned not just with treating individual animals but with advising on the well-being and productivity of the entire stock.

Veterinary surgeons in practice often take on additional part-time appointments. Farm practitioners may be Local Veterinary Inspectors for the Ministry of Agriculture, testing cattle for tuberculosis or brucellosis or carrying on inspections at cattle markets. Some practices carry out supervision of meat hygiene in abattoirs or poultry slaughterhouses; others work at licensed greyhound tracks. District councils need veterinary surgeons to inspect the riding establishments, zoos, pet shops and dog-breeding and boarding kennels which they license.

Newly qualified veterinary surgeons normally start as assistants in established practices, moving on to a more senior assistantship and then to a partnership in an existing practice or setting up a new practice.

State Veterinary Service
The State Veterinary Service is concerned not with individual animals but with the 'common herd'. Its responsibilities include: the control and eradication of notifiable disease; diagnostic and consultancy work on notifiable and non-notifiable disease; epidemiological studies; disease monitoring and surveillance; special investigations and surveys; public health liaison and human diseases related to animals; red meat and poultry hygiene; the operation of animal health schemes; improved farm animal health.

Veterinary surgeons are employed as *Veterinary Field Officers* or *Veterinary Investigation Officers*. They work closely together, with the field officer generally carrying out a major part of the statutory work while the investigation officer provides diagnostic services based on laboratory tests. The Central Veterinary Laboratory contracts (as a Civil Service agency) to carry out research into conditions of economic importance to British farm livestock. Immediate practical farming problems as well as long-term applied and fundamental research projects are dealt with. It also provides services for the State Veterinary Service.

Other opportunities
Veterinary surgeons are also employed in research institutes of the Agricultural Research Service and Medical Research Council; animal welfare societies; the Royal Army Veterinary Corps; industry, mainly pharmaceutical companies and those making animal feeds and fertilizers; universities; the Animal Health Trust, a voluntary organization for veterinary research and the promotion of post-graduate veterinary education. There are also opportunities in developing countries, and British qualified veterinary surgeons may practise in any EC member state.

Training   Degree courses usually last 5 years (6 at Cambridge) and are divided into pre-clinical (anatomy, physiology, biochemistry, pharmacology) and clinical (animal husbandry, medicine and surgery, veterinary public health). During the vacations of the clinical years of the course students must spend 6 months gaining experience in aspects of veterinary work under the supervision of veterinary surgeons in practice, in veterinary laboratories and in other areas of veterinary work.

In some veterinary schools training is shortened by 1 year for science graduates.

Personal attributes   Scientific interest in animals and their behaviour and development, rather than sentimental fondness for pets; powers of observation; a firm hand; the ability to inspire confidence in animals (i.e. total absence of nervousness) and in their owners; self-reliance and adaptability; indifference to occasional physically disagreeable conditions of work.

For some posts: organizing ability and powers of leadership; for others, ability to work as one of a team.

Late start   As there is such stiff competition for degree course places, it is unlikely that anyone over 30 would be accepted, though there is no official upper age limit.

Career-break   In general practice, would have to be negotiated with partners. A retraining course has been organized every other year for those wishing to return to practice. Veterinary surgeons in the State Veterinary Service are civil servants (see p. 125).

Part time   Opportunities to work part time or as a locum.

Position of women   The proportion of female registered veterinary surgeons is 24%. In 1991, 58% of those accepted on to veterinary degree courses were women. It used to be thought that women, particularly small women, would have difficulty coping with some of the heavy work. The increasing numbers of women entering show that they cope well enough.

Further information   Royal College of Veterinary Surgeons, 32 Belgrave Square, London SW1X 8QP

Veterinary Nurse

Entry qualifications   4 GCSEs (A-C), including English language and a physical or biological science or mathematics.

The work   Veterinary nurses assist veterinary surgeons in their surgery and occasionally on visits. They hold and pacify animals during examination and treatment; in the surgery they also sterilize and look after instruments. They collect and analyse specimens, prepare medicines, take out stings and stitches, clean out cages, and clear up after operations. They may also assist in the reception of patients. They work mainly in 'small-animal' practices, i.e. those dealing with domestic animals, and for the RSPCA and other animal welfare and research organizations.

The hours are usually long and irregular. Animals have to be cared for at weekends which may mean going to work on Saturday and Sunday, perhaps just to feed them.

Some veterinary surgeons' practices employ only one veterinary nurse who may then have little companionship. Most of the working day will be spent with the employer.

Training

Minimum age for enrolment as trainee is 17; practical work may start earlier.

Training is on the job, plus study by correspondence or day- or block-release courses.

A potential trainee must first find a job with a veterinary practice or hospital approved by the RCVS as a training centre and must then enrol with the RCVS as a trainee. The syllabus covers anatomy and physiology, hygiene and feeding, first aid, side-room techniques (analysing specimens and preparing slides), and the theory and practice of breeding and nursing. Finals may be taken after at least 2 years' traineeship.

Trainee vacancies are sometimes advertised in the *Veterinary Record*, and prospective trainees may themselves advertise for jobs. Letters to local veterinary surgeons and animal research and welfare societies may also bring results; and the RCVS will provide a list of those veterinary practices and centres which are approved as training centres.

Personal attributes

A love of animals and a scientific interest in their development, behaviour, and welfare; lack of squeamishness; a willingness to take orders, and yet to act independently when necessary; readiness to work well both alone and with others; a sure, firm, but gentle grip; patience. Ability to type and drive is helpful.

Late start

There is no upper age limit, but most trainees are young. This is to some extent dictated by the low wages received during training.

Career-break

Any career-break would have to be negotiated with employer. However, this is basically a young person's job.

Part time

There are opportunities for part-time work. Trainees work full time.

Position of women

This is still a female preserve. The numbers of male veterinary nurses and students are barely in double figures.

Further   British Veterinary Nurses Association, Seedbed Centre, Coldhar-
informa-   bour Road, Harlow, Essex CM19 5AF
tion

Animal Technician

Entry   In theory, none required; in practice, 3 or 4 GCSEs, including
qualifica-   English, maths and a science, are preferred and may be essential
tions   for courses leading to recognized qualifications.

The work   Animal technicians look after animals used in laboratory experi-
                   ments concerned with medical, veterinary and pharmaceutical
                   research. They are concerned with their feeding, breeding, housing
                   and cleaning. The animals' conditions may have to be strictly
                   controlled for the purposes of the scientific research, and the
                   technicians may have to observe the animals closely and record
                   their observations for the scientists.

Training   Training is on the job, supplemented by day-release study for the
                   exams of the Institute of Animal Technology (4 levels taken over
                   5 or 6 years); *or* by a BTEC/SCOTVEC National award in a
                   relevant science and/or a Higher National Certificate in Science
                   (Animal Technology); *or* a 1-year full-time Certificate or 2-year
                   full-time Diploma in Animal Science of the Institute of Science
                   Technology.
                       NVQs are being introduced (see p. xx).

Personal   A mature, not sentimental, regard for animals; interest in scientific
attributes   research; good powers of observation; close attention to detail.

Late   Possible, but not common.
start

Career-   No reason why not. Depends on individual employers.
break

Part time   Possible in basic level jobs.

Position   More women are technicians; more men are trainees.
of
women

Further   Institute of Animal Technology, 5 South Parade, Summertown,
informa-   Oxford OX2 7JL
tion   Institute of Science Technology, Mansell House, 22 Bore Street,
                      Lichfield, Staffs. WS13 6LP

Horses

Entry qualifications

4 GCSEs, including an English subject, for riding instructors, but requirements waived for entrants over 19. None for grooms and stable managers. But see 'Training', below.

The work

Looking after horses nearly always means hard physical work that has to be carried out daily in all weathers. Hours tend to be long, especially in summer, and most people work a 6-day week. Most new entrants have had experience of working as unpaid helpers or have had their own pony/horse while at school, so they know what is involved. Staff may live in or out, but grooms and stable managers usually live on the premises because of the early-morning start. Meals may be provided.

Riding Instructors

They teach children and adults, both in private lessons and in classes, and accompany riders out on 'hacks'. Classes may be held early in the morning or late in the evening, to suit pupils coming before or after work. Some instructors work for one establishment full time, others work freelance or part time. Many combine teaching with general stable work. Setting up one's own riding school requires considerable capital, experience and business knowledge.

Groom/Stable Managers

They work in and may eventually manage a variety of establishments, e.g. hunt, racing, show jumping and eventing stables, livery yards (which look after other owners' horses), riding schools, studs. They clean stables, feed and water horses, watch out for and report any symptoms which indicate a horse may be sick, clean and maintain tack. They prepare horses for competition – eventing, showjumping, dressage, driving, polo, showing, etc. At a stud, grooms also look after the brood mares and care for their foals. They may also assist with breaking and training. This is highly skilled work. Opportunities are increasing for 'skilled' – not necessarily 'qualified' – workers. 'Plum' jobs like travelling with show horses are rare. However, British grooms are in great demand abroad.

Training

Instructors

The 2 main examining bodies in the horse industry are the British Horse Society and the Association of British Riding Schools. The

BHS exams consist of 2 parallel streams, riding, and horse knowledge and care. Intending instructors must take both, together with teaching tests. The route is:

Stage I (minimum age 16).

Stage II (can be taken after or at the same time as Stage I). Candidates for Stage II must first have passed the separate BHS Riding and Road Safety Test.

Stage III (minimum age 17). This together with the Preliminary Teaching Test (minimum age 17½) leads to the *Assistant Instructor* (AI) award.

Stage IV (minimum age 18). This together with the Intermediate Teaching Examination and a recognized First Aid Certificate leads to the *Intermediate Instructor* (II) award.

Stable Manager's Certificate (minimum age 22). Those who pass this plus the Equitation/Teaching exam gain the full *Instructor's Certificate*.

Grooms

People who want to become grooms and stable managers, but have no particular riding ambitions, can take either the BHS horse knowledge and care tests and Stable Manager's Certificate (without the riding tests) or the ABRS exams. These consist of *Preliminary Horse Care and Riding*, the *Assistant Groom's Certificate* (minimum age 17) and *Groom's Diploma* (minimum age 18). No educational qualifications are required for the ABRS exams.

The National Pony Society runs examinations for stud workers.

Training for horse exams is normally as a working pupil, an arrangement by which the pupil is given instruction and pocket money in exchange for work. Courses for Assistant Instructors last around 1 year. It is also possible to work for these exams while working as a groom. There are also some fee-charging schools. It is important to check that any training establishment is approved by the BHS and is a member of the ABRS. Increasingly, equestrian studies courses are being offered at colleges of agriculture and further education colleges, leading to BTEC National and Higher National awards and incorporating BHS qualifications. The first equestrian degree course started in October 1991. Youth training is also available. It is anticipated that in future people with academic qualifications will have the most opportunities in managing equestrian establishments of all kinds.

NVQs (see p. xx) are being introduced, awarded jointly by the Joint National Horse Education and Training Council and the examining bodies above.

Personal attributes   Physical stamina and ability to work outside in all weathers; indifference to getting dirty; willingness to work 'unsocial' hours and sometimes by oneself.

For instructors: authority; ability to express oneself clearly; patience; a liking for children.

Part time   There may be some part-time work for riding instructors at local riding establishments. Part-time work is on the increase.

Position of women   The proportion of women is probably around 80%. This is largely a young woman's field, as far as jobs are concerned, but quite a few women own their own riding schools or stables.

Further information   British Horse Society, The British Equestrian Centre, Kenilworth, Warwickshire CV8 2LR

Association of British Riding Schools, Old Brewery Yard, Penzance, Cornwall TR18 2SL

National Pony Society, Willingdon House, 102 High Street, Alton, Hants GU34 1EN

Other Work with Animals

There is a wide range of other opportunities to work with animals. They range from guide dog trainer to gamekeeper, pet shop assistant to RSPCA inspector, zookeeper to dog beautician. Some of these fields offer a very limited number of openings. Often no specific academic qualifications are needed and training is on the job. Most are essentially practical, manual occupations with limited prospects. (None is a suitable alternative for anyone who narrowly misses becoming a veterinary surgeon.)

Further information   Universities Federation for Animal Welfare, 8 Hamilton Close, South Mimms, Potters Bar, Herts. EN6 3QD. A very wide range of opportunities is covered in their leaflet *Careers with Animals* – send an s.a.e.

Archaeology

Entry qualifications

Degree course requirements. Maths or a science and modern language at GCSE normally required. For *classical archaeology*, Latin or Greek at either level. For *conservation*, chemistry at A-level.

The work

Excavation work is only one aspect of this science of gaining knowledge of the past from the study of ancient objects. Though archaeologists need a broad knowledge of the whole field they may specialize in one geographical area. For example there is Norse, Anglo-Saxon and classical archaeology. Most archaeologists also specialize in particular objects of study, for example coins, weapons, sculpture or deciphering inscriptions. Excavation technique is another, highly technical, specialization.

Many archaeologists work in museums (see MUSEUMS AND ART GALLERIES, p. 314). Others work for English Heritage, Welsh Ancient Monuments, Scottish Development Department, Historic Buildings and Ancient Monuments Directorate, the three Royal Commissions on Ancient and Historical Monuments, the archaeological section of the Ordnance Survey, for local authorities and full-time professional units or trusts.

Two archaeological specializations have developed: *environmental archaeology*, concerned with scientific examination of remains and artifacts and with changes in the environment as they affect previous cultures; and *archaeological surveying* which combines surveying (see p. 502) with archaeology. Archaeological surveyors use sophisticated instruments to locate and plot sites and to draw up maps. Most archaeological surveyors took land surveying training (see p. 508) and then a post-graduate course in archaeology or the CBA's Diploma (see 'Training', below). (A surveying qualification leaves rather more options open than an archaeology degree.)

There are many more archaeology graduates than jobs.

Training

BA in archaeology, ancient history, anthropology, or classics with archaeology, or any honours degree followed by a 2-year archaeology diploma; or, with A-level chemistry, B.Sc. in conservation of archaeological materials.

The Institute of Field Archaeologists was set up in 1983 as the professional institute for archaeologists.

Personal attributes   Deep curiosity about the past; intellectual ability well above average; artistic sensibility; patience; manual dexterity (for handling delicate and valuable objects). For excavation, physical stamina.

Late start   Advisable only for people who already have a relevant degree and/or hobby experience.

Career-break   Prospects for returners depend on previous experience.

Part time   Some posts for specialists and in adult education and heritage centres.

Position of women   The Institute of Field Archaeology set up an equal opportunities working party which reported in 1991. Its survey revealed a lack of opportunities for women as shown by various statistics. This cannot be explained by differences in physical strength, because increasingly the work requires organizational, negotiating and management skills, in which women can excel. Although women take up half of degree places, they form only 35% of the profession. Although women tend to have higher qualifications than male colleagues, many more women than men earn less than £12,000, while twice as many men as women earn over £12,000. Only 16% of top posts with salaries of £20,000 plus are held by women.

Men tend to dominate the areas of excavation, surveying, teaching, among others, while women do best in post-excavation, finds research and conservation. As finds research has lower status than field work in the profession, this affects many women's promotion prospects.

The report recommended a 5-year plan of equal opportunities initiatives.

Further information   The Council for British Archaeology, 112 Kennington Road, London SE11 6RE

The Institute of Field Archaeologists, Minerals Engineering Building, University of Birmingham, PO Box 363, Birmingham B15 2TT

Related careers   ARCHIVIST – MUSEUMS AND ART GALLERIES

Architecture

Architect

As for degree. Individual schools of architecture have widely
differing requirements, ranging from any 2 A-levels, and maths
merely as one of the 3 GCSEs, to 3 specified mixed science/arts
A-levels.

The work
Architecture is a multi-disciplinary profession requiring a combination of artistic, technological and sociological expertise. The
challenge of architecture is to produce, within a given budget, an
aesthetically pleasing design which will stand up to wear and tear
and is the kind of building in which people will want to live or
work. Architects must fully understand traditional and new
building methods and materials and appreciate their potential
and limitations. They must also understand and be interested in
contemporary society and changing lifestyles, the community's
expectations and needs, and social problems which may lead to
loneliness, mugging and vandalism. They need to question house-
holders, office workers, teachers, hospital staff, managers, social
workers, etc. to come up with a design for a building that is 'user
friendly' and which works. Some of the architectural disasters of
the post-war period are due to lack of consultation and lack of
imagination. For example, the design and layout of a housing
estate and its walkways can provide a haven for muggers; a
redesign can mean a dramatic drop in anti-social behaviour. This,
together with strict financial constraints, makes architecture today
a more demanding discipline than it has ever been. Tasks range
from converting houses into flats to designing hospitals, retirement homes or factory complexes.

Architects receive instructions (the 'brief') from their clients or
employers on the type, function, capacity and rough cost of the
building required. Then they do their research – and at that stage they
may question some assumptions on which the client based the brief.

When the type of the building has finally been decided upon,
the design work begins. This starts with producing, perhaps
jointly with colleagues, a sketch scheme of the floor plans, the
elevations, and perspective drawings. Several designs may have to
be produced before one is finally approved.

The next stage is to prepare contract documents, which will include detailed drawings and specifications; estimates of cost; and applications for necessary planning consents from the local authority. At this stage, especially if the scheme is a big one, consulting engineers (see p. 188) and quantity surveyors (see p. 505), may be appointed. When the contract for the work has been awarded to a building contractor, the architect is in overall charge of the project, with responsibility for certifying payment to contractors, and for inspecting the work in progress. This involves regular visits to the building site, issuing instructions to the contractor's agent or foreman and discussing any problems that might arise. Site visits may involve walking through mud and climbing scaffolding.

The architect is normally also responsible for the choice or design of fittings and the interior design of the buildings. (See ART AND DESIGN, p. 58.)

An architect can work in different *settings*: in private practice; in the architects' and planning departments of a local authority; in a cooperative; with a public body; with a ministry; or in the architect's department of a commercial firm large enough to have a continuous programme of building or maintenance work.

In private practice the client may be an individual, a commercial firm, a local authority or other public body. It is usual for private practices to specialize, but not exclusively, in houses, schools or offices, etc. In private practice architects normally work only on design and not, as in other categories, on design and maintenance.

In local authorities architects may work on a wide variety of buildings, such as one-family houses, blocks of flats, schools, sports centres and clinics. They also collaborate with private architects employed by the authority for specific schemes.

For other public bodies such as government departments, the architect's work is less varied and is largely confined to the organization's particular building concern: e.g. hospitals for the Department of Health.

The same applies to architects working for a commercial concern. Their work is confined to that organization's particular type of building: e.g. hotels and restaurants for a large catering organization; shops for a retail chain.

The majority of architects are salaried employees, but they may become junior partners and later principals in a firm, or set up on their own. But to start a firm requires a good deal of experience, capital and contacts. 70% of practices employ 5 or fewer full-time architects.

Since 1982, architects have been permitted, under RIBA rules, to become directors of building and development companies, so they can now combine professional work with running their own business. Architects' prospects can be badly affected by recessions and they have to be prepared to take on any work they can find. There are reasonable opportunities to work abroad.

Training The normal pattern of training is a 5-year full-time course, with 1 year of practical experience after the third year and a second year of practical experience at the end of the course, making a minimum of 7 years. There are a few part-time (day-release) courses, but this method of training is not suitable for everyone: it takes even longer than the normal training and the failure rate among part-time students is higher than among full-time students. Subjects studied include history of architecture, design and construction, town planning, environmental science, materials science, building control, some sociology, economics, law. The development of design skills through projects is central to an architect's education and increasingly involves CAD (computer-aided design).

For interior designers, architectural training need only be up to degree level. It must be followed by a specialized art-school course (part or full time) and practical experience.

NOTES: 1. Architecture, planning and landscape architecture are related disciplines. There are some courses which start with a combined studies year so that students can delay specialization until they know more about the whole field. But courses must be chosen with care: practising architects whether in private practice or public employment must be on the Register of the Architects Registration Council of the United Kingdom. Only recognized courses lead to Registration. Up-to-date lists of recognized courses are available from the RIBA (which recognizes courses on behalf of the ARCUK) and from the ARCUK. Course titles can be misleading, e.g. 'Architectural Studies' may or may not be a recognized course.

2. For candidates who are not quite certain whether to commit themselves to a 7-year training it is useful to know that the first 3-year stage of training, on most courses, leads to an honours degree in its own right, and therefore to all the graduate jobs for which no particular discipline is specified.

Personal attributes A practical as well as creative mind; an interest in people and their changing lifestyles; self-confidence to put over and justify new ideas; mathematical ability; drawing skills; the ability to deal with legal and financial questions; a reasonably authoritative personality; an aptitude for giving clear instructions and explanations.

Late start There are special provisions for members of allied professions and people with degrees in related fields to apply to the RIBA Special Entry Panel and then to take whatever training may be deemed necessary before sitting the RIBA's own examination. However, practical training and first jobs for people over about 35 are difficult to get.

Career-break Opportunities for those who have kept up by way of reading journals, attending occasional lectures and seminars. The RIBA's Women Architects' Group is helping to set up returners' courses. Architects are strongly advised to 'keep their hand in' and do *some* work throughout the break, however sporadic.

Updating courses are a feature of the profession under its CPD (Continual Professional Updating) scheme for all architects. There is currently one refresher course, but normally ad hoc arrangements are made for returners to work in architectural offices. Some returners take one of the post-graduate courses available and specialize in, for example, urban design, planning or conservation of historic buildings.

Part time A fair proportion of women architects work part time, virtually all of them in private practice. They predominate in 'agency' (temporary contract) work which may combine well with domestic responsibilities but rarely improves career prospects. There is little opportunity for part-time work in the public sector, but up to middle-level jobs it should be possible to organize job-sharing and other flexible working.

Position of women 8% of registered architects and 30% (higher in Scotland) of first-year students are women. Proportions have risen slowly in recent years. It seems that the image of architecture as being mainly concerned with building and technical matters generally keeps women from applying even to schools of architecture which do not require A-level maths.

At present, far fewer women than men are principals in private practice. Most women remain assistant architects; in public service women seem to progress further, but still the vast majority remain in middle-level jobs. However, this may change as more women qualify.

Further information The Director (Education and Practice), Royal Institute of British Architects, 66 Portland Place, London W1N 4AD

Royal Incorporation of Architects in Scotland, 15 Rutland Square, Edinburgh EH1 2BE

Society of Architects in Wales, 75a Llandennis Road, Rhydypennau, Cardiff CF2 6EE

Royal Society of Ulster Architects, 2 Mount Charles, Belfast, N.
Ireland BT7 1NZ

Architects Registration Council, 73 Hallam Street, London W1N
6EE

Related careers	*Architectural Technician* (*see below*) – ART AND DESIGN – ENGINEERING – LANDSCAPE ARCHITECTURE – SURVEYING – TOWN AND COUNTRY PLANNING

Architectural Technician

Entry qualifications

4 GCSEs (A–C) including maths, a science and a subject involving the use of written English. For membership of the British Institute of Architectural Technicians (BIAT), BTEC Higher National Award in Building Studies (or SCOTVEC Higher National award in Architectural Technology) or degree in building recognized by BIAT plus 2 years' practical experience.

The work

Architectural technicians work in architects' and planners' offices both in private practice and in public employment as well as with large firms of building contractors. Duties vary considerably according to the size and structure of the office. They may include any or all of the following: collecting, analysing and preparing technical information required for a design; preparing technical drawings for the builder and presentation drawings for the client; administration of contracts; liaison with clients and with specialists such as quantity surveyors; taking notes at site meetings; site supervision; collecting information on performance of finished buildings (which means contact with satisfied and possibly dissatisfied clients); office management. Technicians do responsible work but on the technical rather than the creative side. Those with a few years' experience in employment can set up on their own and, working for private clients or building contractors, design conversions; or help out in architectural firms which need occasional extra staff. Prospects vary according to economic climate but during the recession technicians suffered less than architects: many architectural technicians do much the same work as architects in junior positions but they are paid less than fully qualified architects. Contractors and individuals often now employ technicians rather than architects for the more routine type of work. Technicians who want to become architects must take the full architectural training; their BTEC award is normally accepted in lieu of A-levels. Few technicians, however, switch to architectural training: if they are good enough to take the architectural training, they usually do very well as technicians.

Training   Preferably full-time BTEC National Diploma in Building Studies
with architectural option followed by training on-the-job with
day-release for the BTEC/SCOTVEC Higher National Certificate (see pp. xxi, xxii). Alternatively, a traineeship with day-release
for BTEC National Certificate in Building Studies followed by
Higher award. The Higher award is required for associate membership of the BIAT. A further year's study for additional BTEC
units is recommended. Entrants with A-levels can take the one
degree in building studies (at Coventry Polytechnic) which is
currently approved by the BIAT for membership.

Personal   Accuracy; ability to draw; technical ability; interest in architecture
attributes   and environment; liking for teamwork; some design flair.

Late start   Not advisable because of low salary while training. Young trainees
tend to be preferred, but previous experience in construction is an
asset. BIAT offers a non-standard route for those aged 30 plus
who have a minimum of 10 years' experience.

Career-   Theoretically no reason why qualified technicians should not
break   return. BTEC training system can be adapted to help with updating skills in this fast-moving industry.

Part time   Not much opportunity in employment, but possible as self-employed technician.

Position   Only about 4% of BIAT members are women; figures for trainees
of   are about 5%. The job is highly suitable for women who are
women   interested in housing and the environment but are put off by the
long full architectural training (or have not got the necessary A-
levels). It is the image of architectural technicians' work as something highly technical (reinforced by the words 'Building Studies',
the title of the course trainees have to take) and the lack of role-
models (women technicians who can talk about their work) which
keeps the proportion of women so low. The few women who have
taken this training are doing very well, both in jobs and in their
own small practices. They had no special problems getting training
vacancies or places on full-time BTEC courses.

Further   The Registrar, British Institute of Architectural Technicians, 397
informa-   City Road, London EC1V 1NE
tion

Related   SURVEYING: *Surveying Technicians* – ENGINEERING: *Engineering*
careers   *Technicians*

Archivist

Entry qualifications   Good honours degree (usually in history). Preference given to applicants with A-level Latin.

The work   Archivists' work combines scholarly research with the selection, preservation, arrangement and description of documents, such as official records of central and local government and courts of law, or private documents such as title deeds, business records, family papers. Archivists assess the value for posterity of papers being currently produced and preserve and put in order, for reference purposes, all types of records which were produced in the past. They help members of the public with their research, whether they are professors of history, solicitors in search of evidence, students working on projects, or genealogists. They must understand methods of preservation and repair, of microfilming and new technologies.

Most archivists work in central and local government record offices. Other posts are in professional institutions, universities, and a wide variety of other establishments, including ecclesiastical foundations, hospitals, charitable organizations, specialist museums, libraries and research bodies. There is considerable scope for trained archivists who prefer to specialize in the management of current records, especially in business and industry. Some of these posts require scientific or other specialist knowledge, and computer technology is increasingly important in many areas of the work. The work involves contact with a vast variety of members of the public. The supply and demand for archivists are about even. It is usually necessary to go wherever there is a vacancy, both for the first job and later for promotion. Vacancies are very scarce in some parts of the country.

Training   Nearly all posts now require formal training: 1-year post-graduate full-time course for an MA or Diploma in Archives Administration. Subjects include palaeography, record office management, research methods, conservation methods, editing, some history and law. The Society of Archivists runs a correspondence course for graduates in professional archival posts. It is possible, but difficult, for a graduate to work up from an unqualified assistant post to a professional appointment.

Personal attributes A strong sense of history; liking for painstaking research; curiosity; ability to communicate with a wide variety of people.

Late start Probably difficult, for above reasons; see 'Career-break', below.

Career-break Return difficult, as there are always sufficient young job applicants and vacant posts may not occur in a particular area for several years. However, 'retired' members can pay reduced subscriptions to the Society of Archivists.

Part time Training: correspondence course normally available only to working archivists. Work: some part-time posts available, but with few promotion prospects. Job-sharing should be possible.

Position of women Just over half of Britain's archivists are women; but twice as many men as women are county archivists.

Further information Executive Secretary, Society of Archivists, Information House, 20–24 Old Street, London EC1V 9AP

Related careers ARCHAEOLOGY – INFORMATION WORK – MUSEUMS AND ART GALLERIES

Armed Forces (Officer Entry Only)

Entry qualifications
Minimum 5 GCSEs. See individual forces.

The work
The main purpose of the armed forces is the defence of the country. Following recent world events there have been, and probably will continue to be, cutbacks in defence spending and a reduction in the numbers required to serve throughout the forces. However, there will always be a demand for new entrants to ensure continuity, as many officers serve for only a few years. All the forces contribute to European defence through NATO and in addition may from time to time be involved in peace-keeping missions or disaster relief anywhere in the world.

Jobs are varied. As well as providing increasingly sophisticated technical expertise the three services have to be self-sufficient, i.e. they have to house, feed, clothe, equip, transport, select, train and provide medical and welfare services to servicemen and servicewomen at home and overseas. Many jobs are unique to the services, but some are also relevant to civilian life. Recruiters look for a particular mix of abilities and personal qualities to try to select people who will fit in and enjoy the way of life. Although the majority will spend their time without experiencing combat, nevertheless they can never forget that at any time they might have to take part in action against an enemy.

Most officers have a dual responsibility: as a leader and manager of a group of men and women, and as a specialist.

As jobs are so diverse, and training for them is so specific, it is not possible to give more than an outline of the various entry routes in this book. A great deal of information and help is available to people considering joining any one of the services; they should contact their school's or university liaison officer, or local recruiting office, or write to the addresses given below.

NOTE: Women are gradually being integrated into all three services, so a greater variety of jobs are open to them than in the past.

The Army

Regiments and corps are divided into Arms (those involved in battle) and Services (those providing many kinds of services to the Arms). Each has its own responsibilities, e.g. the Royal Army Ordnance Corps is in charge of provisions – anything from food to tanks; the Royal Signals handle communications (often using very advanced technology); the Royal Engineers handle engineering and construction, as well as running postal and mapping services for all three forces. Would-be officers apply to a corps or regiment, though not all are open to all entrants. Age limits vary, as do entry requirements. (Nearly half of recently commissioned officers are graduates.)

Main entry routes and types of commission
Regular commission (to age 55, but may apply to leave after 3 years' service):

Main school-leaver entry: for men and women aged 17¾–29 and with 5 GCSEs (A–C), including English language, maths and either a science or foreign language, and 2 A-levels.

Graduate entry (any subject) or with certain professional qualifications. Upper age limits vary.

Short-service commission (minimum usually 3 years and can be extended up to 8 years):

Minimum age 18 and up to 29, depending on regiment or corps. Minimum 5 GCSEs (A–C) including English and, for some regiments or corps, maths or science.

There are various scholarship schemes to give financial support to sixth formers and undergraduates; boys and girls are eligible for scholarships while doing A-levels, and there is a separate scheme for boys and girls to take science A-levels at the Army's own sixth-form college at Welbeck. Undergraduate cadetships and bursaries are available for men and women reading for a degree in any subject and lead to a Regular or Short Service Commission. Short Service Limited Commissions are available for men and women who want to spend time in the Army (4–18 months) before starting degree courses, i.e. in their 'gap' year.

Royal Navy

Over half the Navy's officers are graduates, who can be from almost any discipline. There are several branches, each providing a specialist service;

Seamen officers are responsible for the safe and efficient handling of a ship while on watch and they may also train to operate weapons systems. They can go on to 'sub-specialize' in aviation, either in aircraft control, as airborne observers or as helicopter pilots (a few are selected to fly the Sea Harrier jump-jet). Other specializations open to seamen officers are on submarines, as hydrographic surveyors (see SURVEYING, p. 508) and as divers (for mine clearance).

Engineer officers work with highly advanced technology and its complexity means that they specialize as one of the following: weapon engineer officers (surface ships), weapon engineers (submarines), marine engineers (surface ships), marine engineers (submarines) and air engineers.

Supply and secretariat officers work in ships and also at shore establishments. They are concerned with both the technical and the personnel aspects of a ship's organization. Their main duties are: administration; correspondence; welfare and personnel matters; naval stores; catering; pay and cash. While at sea, supply and secretariat officers also have quite separate operational duties.

Instructor officers are responsible for education and much of the training, from general academic studies to advanced technical training.

The Royal Marines are the Navy's amphibious infantry and they have their own entry and training requirements. The training is the physically hardest of all in the Forces and includes a very demanding commando course.

Main entry routes for men and women

Full career commissions (serve up to age 50). (1) *Seaman or Supply and Secretariat*: For direct entry to Naval College: aged 17 to under 23 with 2 A-levels and 3 GCSEs, including English and maths. Graduate entry for those with a degree (and GCSE (A–C) English and maths) aged under 26. (2) *Engineering*: Naval College entry: A-level maths and physics or BTEC National award in engineering (at specified level and with particular units). Graduate entry with a degree in mechanical, electrical, electronic or aeronautical engineering or acceptable equivalent. Age limits as in (1). (3) *Royal Marines*: Full career entry: 2 A-levels and 3 GCSEs (A–C), including English and maths, aged $17\frac{1}{2}$ to under 22. Graduate entry with a degree and with GCSE (A–C) in English and maths, aged under 25.

Short and Medium Commissions (from 8 to 16 years depending on specialization and personal choice). For *seaman* and *engineering officers* entry qualifications as above, but upper age limit 25. *Supply and Secretariat* direct entry to Naval College possible with 5 GCSEs (A–C), including English and maths, or as a graduate. *Pilots, observers* and *air traffic control*: with 5 GCSEs (including

English and maths) or as a graduate. *Instructor*: mainly with a degree or professional qualification in engineering, physics or maths. A few arts graduates taken each year. Must be aged under 34. *Royal Marines* (men only!): entry with 5 GCSEs (including English and maths), aged 17½ to under 23, or as a graduate aged under 25.

Women in the Navy

Entry and conditions of service are now mainly the same as for men. However, although they can become helicopter pilots and observers, they do not fly commando helicopters or Sea Harriers, or serve in submarines or in the Royal Marines.

Sixth-form scholarships, university cadetships and bursaries are available to male and female candidates.

Royal Air Force

As in the other forces, officers in the Royal Air Force are leaders, managers and specialists. Aircrew – pilots and navigators – provide the front line. Air traffic controllers are responsible for directing the movements of aircraft in the air and of aircraft and vehicles on the airfield. Fighter controllers report on radar pictures and control what goes on in the air by planning air operations and guiding aircraft to their targets. Intelligence officers gather and interpret data largely obtained from sensors in reconnaissance aircraft to help those planning operations. Engineers specialize in work either on aircraft or on communications and radar systems. Supply officers are responsible for provisions of all kinds and the movement of cargo and personnel by all means of transport. In the administrative branch, officers work in accountancy, estates management, personnel and welfare services. Others work as education and training officers, station catering managers and physical education officers. There are two types of commission in the RAF: *permanent* (up to age 38 or for 16 years, whichever is the longer, with possible extension to age 55) and *short service* (3–6 years, varying from branch to branch; for pilots and navigators it lasts 12 years, with the option to leave after 6 years' 'productive service'). For most branches both types of commission are available.

Main entry routes

For all commissions the minimum academic standard is 5 GCSEs (A–C) or equivalent, including English and maths, unless otherwise stated. A-levels are preferred and there is a large graduate intake (38% of officers have degrees).

Aircrew: aged 17½ to under 24 (pilots) or under 26 (navigators). *Air traffic control, fighter control* and *intelligence officers*: aged 17½ (men) or 18 (women) to under 30. *Engineering Officer*: aged under 39 and must have an acceptable engineering degree or Higher National award. *Supply Officer*: aged under 30 (exceptionally under 39) with degree or Higher National award in business studies, public administration or computer studies prefered. *Catering Officer*: aged under 39 with Higher National award, degree or professional qualification in catering. *Education Officer*: aged under 30 (exceptionally 39) with a degree (occasionally Higher National) in science, engineering or similar subject. *Administration Officer*: aged under 30 (exceptionally 39), needs a degree or Higher National award in business studies or relevant professional qualifications, e.g. accountancy. *Physical Education Officer*: aged under 27 (exceptionally 39) and must be qualified PE teacher.

Sixth-form and flying scholarships are available, as well as university cadetships and bursaries.

Personal attributes
Depend very much on the branch or job, but all officers need certain qualities of leadership, initiative, ability to get on with people from all kinds of background, liking for teamwork, adaptability, physical fitness. Must enjoy and be willing to contribute to community life.

Further information
(Army) The Ministry of Defence, Officer Entry DAR 1 (d), Empress State Building, Lillie Road, London SW6 1TR, or any Army Careers Information Office

Officer Enquiry Section, Ministry of Defence (Navy), Old Admiralty Building, Spring Gardens, London SW1A 2BE, or any Royal Navy and Royal Marines Careers Information Office

RAF Officer Careers, Freepost 4335, Bristol BS1 3YZ, or any RAF Careers Information Office

Art and Design

Entry qualifications	See 'Training', below.
The work	Covers 2 distinct fields: art, which is largely painting and sculpture and is not a career in the usual sense; and design, which could be called applied art: it covers design for industrial and commercial application and industrial engineering. The terminology can be confusing. For example *industrial design* (engineering) is also called *product design*, and comes under the broader heading *3-dimensional design*. Similarly, *graphic design*, with all its sub-categories – illustration, typography, photography, etc. – is also called *visual communication* or *communication design*.

In the Art and Design degree (see below), the areas of specialization are: (1) fine art; (2) graphic design; (3) 3-dimensional design; (4) textiles/fashion. Within these broad categories there are many specializations.

Fine Art

An extremely small number of artists are talented enough to make a living by painting and sculpting alone. Anyone determined to paint or sculpt for a living must have a private income, a second string to their bow, or be prepared for a precarious existence.

Commissions for murals and sculptures for public buildings are extremely rare, and private commissions even more so.

The majority of painters and sculptors also teach, and for that they need art teacher training. Part-time teaching is now *very* difficult to get. Others combine fine art with design in overlapping areas, for example, studio-based craft, or such graphics specialization as book illustration or advertising. But in these areas opportunities are also rare. A few artists do picture-restoring or copying, but again there are few openings.

Design
(see also ENGINEERING, 'Design', p. 185)

The function of the designer, who is, broadly, a specialist combining artistic talent and training with sufficient technical and business knowledge to appreciate the requirements of an industry, is still evolving. Design careers tend not to be structured, although the last 20 years have shown that there are certain employment patterns that new entrants can aspire to. Most designers start as assistants and work first in the area of specialization in which they trained. Later, with experience and evolving interests, they can switch specializations, or at least sub-specializations. For example, a 3-dimensional designer might switch from light engineering to furniture or interior design; a graphic designer from typography to photography; a fashion/textile designer from fashion (see p. 61) to floor-covering or wallpaper, etc. Sometimes 3-dimensional-trained designers switch to visual communication – but the switch the other way round is less likely. A few later combine several design categories.

Titles in industry are arbitrary and mean little; an assistant designer may have more scope for creativity and decision-making than a designer or even design director. Many industrial employers are not yet used to working with designers; the contribution the designer is expected or indeed allowed to make varies from one job to another. For example, sometimes the bias is towards technical expertise: the designer is expected to state, through design, exactly how a product is to be manufactured or printed. Sometimes the bias is towards creativity, and the designer is expected to put forward ideas for totally new products. Usually, the visual appearance of the product is the most important aspect of the designer's brief.

Designers usually work with a team of experts from different disciplines, both technical (engineers, printing technologists, etc.) and business (buyers, marketing people, etc.). This teamwork is one of the important differences between artists and designers. Designers cannot just please themselves: their ideas on what is good design and what is not have to be adapted to fit in with commercial and technical requirements.

Though the designer's work varies from one field of design to another, the end-product always has to fulfil at least 3 demands: it must look up-to-date, perform its function adequately, and be economically produced so that it is profitable. For example, a poster must attract attention and be easily readable; a tin-opener or a fridge must work well, look good and last; a biscuit pack must attract attention, fit into shelf-displays, keep its contents fresh, and open easily; a machine tool must serve the engineer's stated purpose, be easy and safe to handle and clean; and all these products must be manufacturable within given cost-limits. Designers must fully understand the purpose of the product they are designing and its marketing and manufacturing problems. They must know the limitations and potentialities of materials and machines available for production. Sometimes a change in technology allows the designer to develop a revolutionary design: e.g. the removal of buffers from the high-speed train allowed the design of a totally different engine shape.

Starting as design assistant, the trained designer gains useful experience when carrying out simple 'design-technician' rather than design tasks. For example, the beginner may translate a designer's idea for a product into detailed working drawings: this requires technical know-how rather than creativity. In furniture design, for example, the task might be specifying how to fix A satisfactorily to B in manufacturing terms without spoiling the appearance.

One designer is usually responsible for several design assistants (now sometimes called design technicians); the size of design teams varies greatly. Designers and design assistants work in various settings: in advertising agencies; manufacturing concerns' design departments; architects' offices; interior design studios; design consultancies, and many others. Organizing freelance work either on one's own or with colleagues on a design consultancy basis is complex and requires experience: newly trained designers should try and gain experience as staff designers first. They need to know a lot not only about production problems and organization, but also about how to deal with clients and finance.

The ratio of opportunities to qualified applicants is more favourable in the less glamorous and more technical field of *product design* than in *interior, set,* or *textiles* and *fashion design*.

There will never be as many creative top-level jobs as there are aspiring designers, but there is scope for design assistants or 'technicians' whose work varies in creativity and responsibility; for example, making working drawings from designers' scribbled outlines; model-making; or, in communication design, trying to get as near the designer's intended effect as possible with a restricted number of colours and within printing constraints. There is a vast range of jobs in product design which require technical competence, an appreciation of what constitutes good design and *some* creativity rather than creative genius.

Prospects are reasonable for people who *want* to design for industry and appreciate that it is teamwork, but *not* for failed artists. Many of the best product and fashion designers go abroad where British training is greatly appreciated.

Graphics or Graphic Design or Visual Communication

This is concerned with lettering; illustration, including photography; the design of symbols or 'logos'. It ranges from the design of books, book jackets, all kinds of advertisements (posters, packaging, etc.), to the visual corporate identity symbol of organizations, i.e. presenting the image of that organization in visual, instant-impact-making terms. For example, a logo might be required for use on all of an airline's, hotel chain's, local authority's or company's equipment and property; from planes to cutlery, letter-heads to delivery vans and perhaps even items of clothing.

Visual communication includes 'visual aids' for industrial and educational application. This is an expanding area: instructions and/or information are put over in non-verbal language, with symbols taking the place of words. Symbols are used as teaching aids in industrial training; as user-instructions in drug and textile labelling; as warning or information signs on machinery; on road signs. Symbols may be in wall-chart or film-strip form, or on tiny labels as on medicine and detergent packages, or on textile labels, or on huge posters. Symbol design, whether single or in series, requires great imagination, social awareness, logical thinking.

Visual communication also includes TV graphics: captions, programme titles, all non-verbal TV presentation of information, such as election results, trade-figure trends, etc.; packaging, publicity and advertising; stamp and letter-head design. Computers are being used increasingly to produce graphics. Graphic designers work in advertising agencies, in design units, or in manufacturing firms and other organizations' design departments. Television absorbs only a tiny proportion.

There are few openings in general book and magazine illustration and design, but there is considerable scope in technical and medical graphics, which require meticulous accuracy rather than creative imagination. There is also some scope in the greeting-card trade and in catalogue illustration. Much of this is considered hackwork by creative artists.

3-Dimensional Design

This can be divided conveniently into *product design* and *interior design*.

Product design

This covers the design of all kinds of consumer goods (e.g. domestic appliances, or suitcases) and of machine tools, mechanical equipment, cars, as well as pottery, furniture, etc.

There is pressure on manufacturing industry to pay more attention to design than it has in the past. But there is no general agreement on how this is to be brought about. Many engineers and manufacturers still believe that with a bit more design training, engineers can cope with the aesthetics and ergonomics (ease of handling and cleaning, convenience in use, legibility of instructions). But most progressive manufacturers now agree that engineers must work *with* design specialists who, for their part, must have a thorough understanding of engineering principles and production constraints.

The proportion of 'design input' and 'engineering input' varies from product to product. Designers talk about a 'spectrum' – for example, in the manufacture of a plastic cup the 'engineering input' is very small, the 'design input' large; at the other end of the spectrum is a gas turbine, where the design input may be confined to the lettering of the instructions and the colour (which is, however, important, as it affects the 'work environment', which affects industrial efficiency). In between the two extremes are appliances such as food processors and CD players. The engineer designs the components and says how they must be arranged to do the job; the industrial designer is primarily concerned with the appearance and ergonomics of the product.

Between the first sketch and the final product there may be many joint discussions, drawings, modifications, working models and prototypes. The designer negotiates with the engineer; design technicians develop the product through the various stages. Designers and engineers work in teams – whether the team leader is an engineer or a designer varies according to the type of product, the firm's policy and, last but by no means least, the engineer's and designer's personalities.

Product designers need such extensive knowledge of relevant engineering and manufacturing processes that they tend to stay within a particular manufacturing area. The greatest scope is in plastics, which cover a wide range of products, from toys to complex appliances and equipment.

Interior design

Interior designers work in specialized or general design consultants' studios; large stores; for a group of hotels or supermarkets; in private practice or local authority architects' offices. A considerable knowledge of architecture is required in order to know how to divert drains, move walls safely, or enlarge a shop window satisfactorily. The job of the interior designer, besides being responsible for such things as the management of contracts, is to specify the nature of an interior – how it is made, built and finished – as well as selecting the finishes and fixtures and fittings.

Planning interiors for a hotel, shop, aircraft, etc., needs research before designing starts. Beginners often spend all their time on fact-finding: the different items of goods to be displayed; the number of assistants required in a new shop; the kind of materials suitable and safe for furnishing a plane. They also search for suitable light fittings, heating equipment, furnishing materials, and they may design fixtures and fittings.

The term 'interior design' is often interpreted rather loosely, and some jobs require less training and creativity. This applies particularly to work done by assistants in the design studios of stores or architects' offices; in showrooms of manufacturers of paint, furniture, furnishings, light fittings, wallpaper, etc.; in the furnishing departments of retail stores, and in specialist shops. In these settings, interior designers may advise customers or clients on the choice and assembly of the items needed. This may mean suggesting colour schemes, matching wallpaper and curtains, sketching plans for room decoration, or advising on the most suitable synthetic fabric for a particular furnishing purpose. As stores estimators and home advisers, they may go to customers' houses to give advice or even only to measure up for loose covers and curtains. Some stores and specialist shops employ interior designers as buyers in furniture and furnishing departments, and paint, wallpaper and furnishing fabric manufacturers may employ them as sales representatives. In these jobs 'interior designer' is a courtesy title rather than a job description.

Set design

The work requires a knowledge of period styles, structures and lighting techniques, and a wide range of interests, to help visualize the right kind of set for any particular play or TV programme. Limited scope.

Design for exhibitions and display

Combines some of the work of interior and set designer with model-making and graphic design. Exhibition design is usually done by specialist firms. Exhibitions are often rush jobs, and designers may help put up stands and work through the night before opening. Exhibition designers also work in museums (see p. 314). Limited scope. See also TELEVISION, FILM AND RADIO, p. 533.

Display design

Closely allied to exhibition design, but can be a specialization on its own. The essence of window and 'point-of-sale' design is communication: the display designer must present the store's or shop's image, attract attention and persuade the passer-by to buy. Window display can consist of merely putting a few goods in the window or a show case, or it can be a highly sophisticated exercise in marketing, using specially designed models (see 'Model-making', below) and specially chosen merchandise to convey a 'theme' and marketing policy. In stores there may be a *display manager*, a *display designer* and several *display assistants* or *technicians* who make/arrange the props and merchandise. Reasonable scope.

Studio-based design (*glass, jewellery, silverware, stained glass, etc.*)

Design and production by designer-craftspeople who run their own small-scale studios or workshops where each article is made individually. This is a fairly precarious way of making a living. However, some studios survive, especially in tourist areas, selling to local shops and individual customers. They have 'studied the market', and perhaps compromised, producing designs which sell rather than those which they would ideally like to produce.

Model-making

This includes the design and/or making up of models for window and exhibition display, and the making of scale models for architects, planners, and interior-design and product-design studios. Many designers, architects, etc., find that their clients are better able to judge a design if they see it in 3-dimensional model form rather than as drawings.

Model-makers use the traditional materials – wood, plaster, fabric, etc. – and also the new synthetics. They usually work in specialist studios and firms, but some work in other types of design studio. There is more scope here for manual work requiring some creative ability than for pure artistic design. It is an expanding field.

Textiles/Fashion
(see also FASHION AND CLOTHING, p. 209)

Textile design includes printed and woven textiles, carpets, lino, wallpapers, and plastic surface coverings and decoration. There are few openings in manufacturing firms. One of the difficulties is that thorough knowledge of manufacturing methods is essential, but it is difficult to get a job with suitable firms.

Textile designers work on their own more frequently than do other designers. They usually work through agents who show their designs to manufacturers. Fashion collections are held two or more times a year, furnishing collections usually twice.

Training

No particular level of qualification is indispensable for, or guarantees access to, any particular level or type of job. Course choice needs very thorough research: no 2 courses, even at equal level, have exactly the same aim and content, whatever their title. A BTEC award (see below) plus experience may lead to as good a job as a degree – in some cases even to a wider choice of job. It depends on whether employers want as many people with exceptional creativity as people with thorough industrial training and technical skills – people who put the end-product's marketability above aesthetic considerations. What matters in the job-market above all is the portfolio of work, and experience. To get the first job – i.e. experience – *some* systematic full-time training is essential in all but exceptional cases.

Methods of training:

4-year sandwich, 3-year full-time (4-year in Scotland) or 4–5 year part-time Degree in Art and Design at colleges of art, polytechnics, colleges of higher education
1993 NOTE: The majority of foundation courses are now validated by BTEC.
Entry requirements: Either 5 GCSEs (A–C) plus Foundation course lasting 1 or 2 years; or 1 A-level and 3 GCSEs (A–C) plus – normally but not invariably – a 1-year Foundation course; or BTEC Certificate or Diploma (see below). Individual colleges vary in their precise requirements; some demand, for example, GCSE (A–C) maths or craft design and technology and English. Acceptance also very much depends on applicant's portfolio, i.e. on proof of creative ability.

Degrees are normally awarded in 4 separate areas of specialization: fine art, graphic design, 3-dimensional design, and textiles/fashion. Within their specialization, students normally study 1 principal and 1 or 2 subsidiary subjects. In graphic design, for example, typography may be the principal subject, with photography and lettering as subsidiaries. In 3-dimensional design, product design may be the principal, with ceramics and/or silversmithing as subsidiaries.

Students sometimes work for some weeks in a studio or design department in industry. Contact with whatever branch of design they hope to take up should play a vital part throughout the course. All students spend 15% of their time on complementary studies which may include history of art and/or management.

Within these broad outlines, individual courses vary greatly. Courses are normally preceded by a full-time Foundation course (not in Scotland) which should be 'diagnostic' to help students decide on the specialization in which to qualify. There are many aspects of design which school-leavers cannot know about, and this course is expected to lead many students to one of the less well-known design fields. However, not all Foundation courses give such broad training and candidates should find out something about the courses. Acceptance for the Foundation course is no guarantee of acceptance for the degree course itself. A BTEC National Diploma is normally acceptable for entry to a degree course (see p. xxi). Over a quarter of those accepted on to degree courses in 1990 had done a BTEC course.

There are some art/technology, art/management, creative arts and similar 'mixed' degree courses (2 A-level entry) but they are not intended for potential designers.

Post-graduate training is almost always required for designers who aim at top jobs. There are post-graduate full-time courses (1–3 years) in most design specializations, for example, in film, in TV graphics or in graphic information for technical, scientific and educational application. The highest qualification is the Royal College of Art Master's Degree (M. Des. RCA).

University courses

Very few universities offer degree courses in design, but there are plenty of university courses in fine art, history of art and, for students with arts degrees, post-graduate courses in history of art. Fine arts and history of art qualifications may lead to work in museums and art galleries, in art publishing, in research and teaching. Prospects are severely limited.

Vocational courses – most leading to BTEC/SCOTVEC awards (see pp. xxi, xxii)

These vary considerably. Some are almost indistinguishable from degree courses, but they do not necessarily contain so many complementary studies, and can therefore devote more time to professional design studies. Many vocational courses are approved by the Chartered Society of Designers (the professional association for designers), and they may be as useful in career terms as degree courses (possibly even more so). The Society approves only courses which have up-to-date equipment at their disposal and which include 'professional practice'.

Other vocational courses are chosen for their relevance to the student's objectives. Some are suitable for the student who wishes to concentrate on, for example, lettering or typography, costume jewellery, glass decoration, photography, model-making, interior decoration, window display, book-binding, picture restoring, etc., but who does not aim to be a designer responsible for the creative conception of projects and products. Some degree courses – for example, ceramics in Stoke-on-Trent, contour design in Leicester – are geared to local industries. They cover a particular design field in depth and may lead to top jobs in those fields. In some specializations – for example, model-making, window display, picture restoring – it is also possible to learn on the job as trainee, sometimes but rarely with day-release. It is essential, when taking such a post, to make sure that it includes some kind of training and is not a dead-end unskilled job.

BTEC/SCOTVEC courses (see pp. xxi, xxii)

BTEC General Art and Design Diploma for people who are not sure which aspect of design attracts them (this is essentially diagnostic like a Foundation course), and the *National Diploma in Design* for those already committed to an area of work. In some cases students with A-level art (or mature entrants) may enrol for the second year of these courses. (There are very few National Certificate courses.)

SCOTVEC National Certificate Diploma in Art and Design

Higher National Certificate: there are only a handful of BTEC HNCs.

Higher National Diploma: HND holders compete in the design job-market on equal terms with art and design graduates. Admission to all these courses depends partly on the quality of the portfolio.

National Certificates and Higher National Certificates, and National Diplomas and Higher National Diplomas, are intended to lead to the same level of achievement, but the two types of award emphasize different design aspects. Certificate and Higher National Certificate courses teach technical skills and procedures within one, or possibly two, sub-specializations. For example, within graphic design, typography and photography; within 3-dimensional design, model-making and window display. A Higher National Certificate holder who specialized in photography, for example, would be able to brief photographers to carry out work required for a mail-order catalogue, as requested by the chief designer, but would not be a top-rank photographer.

National Diploma and Higher Diploma courses are more broadly based than Certificates, and they place more emphasis on creative aspects and design problem-solving. A Higher National Diploma holder in graphic design would be expected, for example, to see through the production of a mail-order catalogue from the marketing manager's brief right up to the finished product.

Some National award students get 'design-related' jobs immediately after the course, i.e. clerical work in a studio; or simple lettering or model-making, etc.

In job-getting terms, Certificate courses at both levels may be more useful than same-level Diploma courses, because there are more jobs for technically skilled than for creative design-management people.

BTEC courses are usually industry-orientated. Students are taught by staff with industrial experience (though how recent that experience is varies from one course to another). All courses include 'professional practice'. That covers 'client-contact', i.e. communication with people who want work done (and who do not necessarily understand art course jargon); business administration; design management. Colleges which cannot guarantee work experience in a commercial studio must simulate such real world-of-work pressures as working to absolute deadlines; coping with late or non-delivery of materials; absence of vital colleagues; last-minute changes in design-brief; working to stringent cost-limits.

In future there are probably going to be more courses which integrate business and design practice, and courses which move across the traditional design specialisms, training 'multi-skilled' designers who can adapt to changing industrial demands. Students will also all have to learn to work with the many new visual-communication technologies.

Choosing the right course is difficult, terminology is very vague and course-titles can be misleading. For example, a graphic design and a visual communication course could both cover exactly the same ground. Equally, graphic design could be much narrower, or indeed much broader, than visual communication; also the approach to the work and sub-specializations and options within courses vary enormously. Candidates must study one of the guides to courses and then send for prospectuses of likely sounding courses. If at all possible, colleges should be visited before deciding on any particular course (although for 16+ Certificate and Diploma courses choice will be restricted to what is available locally; no grants are normally paid to students on these courses). Competition for many courses is extremely tough.

The Open College of the Arts

This was set up in 1986 as a charitable trust to offer distance-learning courses in various art-related subjects. While not leading to vocational qualifications, this form of studying can be a useful introduction.

Subjects in which courses can be taken (not usually at all levels) full time or by part-time day-release or evening classes

Antique restoration
Audio-visual
Book design and production and bookbinding
Book illustration
Ceramics
Communications
Conservation
Crafts
Decorating and sign-writing
Display and exhibition design
Dress design and manufacture
Embroidery – hand and machine
Enamelling
Etching
Exhibitions
Fashion
Film and TV
Fine art
Footwear
Furniture design
Glass design and decoration
Interior design
Jewellery
Lettering and illumination
Lithography

Media design
Metalwork
Millinery
Modelling and sculpture
Model-making
Mosaic
Packaging
Painting
Paper conservation
Photography
Picture restoring
Product design or industrial design (engineering)
Sculpture
Set design
Shoe design
Silversmithing
Stained glass
Technical graphics
Technical illustration
Textile conservation
Textile design (including carpets and lino, synthetic surface coverings)
Toys
TV graphics
Typography

Art Therapy

Work and training

This is a growing field. Its purpose is twofold: painting and other art forms help withdrawn patients to express themselves and relieve tension, and seeing patients' work helps psychiatrists pinpoint patients' thoughts and problems. The majority of art therapists work – usually on a sessional basis – in psychiatric and mental handicap hospitals with children and with adults, individually and in groups; some work with children with special needs. Art therapy is not so much a career in itself as a field in which practising artists with the necessary human qualities can do useful work. Post-graduate 1-year full-time or 2-year part-time courses are essential.

*

Personal attributes

All careers in art and design require resilience, self-confidence and exceptional talent.

Especially for design: Ability to work as one of a team; creative sensibility and imagination coupled with a logical analytical mind; an interest in science and technology; curiosity and a desire to solve technical problems; perseverance; an interest in the social environment and in the community's needs, tastes and customs; the ability to take responsibility and criticism; willingness at times to lower one's artistic standards in the interests of economic necessity or technical efficiency.

For freelances and senior staff jobs: Business sense (see Design Enterprise Programme, p. 68); the ability to communicate with employers and clients who commission the work but are possibly not themselves interested in art.

For 'technician' jobs: Considerable manual dexterity, technical ability and some creativity.

Late start

The largest group accepted on to degree courses are aged 20–24. Over 11% are aged 25 plus; on HNDs 18–19-year-olds predominate, though 8% are aged 25 plus.

Career-break

If experienced and established, designers can set up on their own; some return to outside employment, but competition from recent art-school leavers is likely to be stiff.

Part time

As freelance.

Position of women

In 1990 more women than men applied for degree courses, more men than women for HNDs. However, a higher proportion of women than men were accepted for both. Women painters and sculptors are these days doing as well as men, but fewer have made it to the top in design. This is due less to discrimination than to the fact that they still tend to shy away from the most promising specializations, especially industrial/product design. Although they are becoming more realistic they still far outnumber men on degrees in glass and ceramics, textiles, jewellery and fashion, and on HNDs in conservation, crafts and theatre. Men far outnumber women on product and furniture design degrees and on HNDs in graphics, illustration, and film and video.

In the Chartered Society of Designers women form 50% of diploma members (those with design qualifications and within 5 years of leaving college) and 20% of full members (practising designers accepted for membership after their work has been assessed).

Further information

National Society for Education in Art and Design (NSEAD), 7A High Street, Corsham, Wilts SN13 0ES

Design Council, 28 Haymarket, London SW1Y 4SU

Chartered Society of Designers (formerly SIAD), 12 Carlton House Terrace, London SW1Y 5AH

British Institute of Interior Design, 1C Devonshire Avenue, Beeston, Notts NG9 1BS

Art and design degrees and BTEC HNDs: Art and Design Admissions Registry, Penn House, 9 Broad Street, Hereford HR4 9AP

British Association of Art Therapists, 11A Richmond Road, Brighton, Sussex BN2 3RL

British Display Society, 92–94 Foxberry Road, London SE4 2SH

BTEC and SCOTVEC (see pp. xxi, xxii)

The Design Enterprise Programme, London Enterprise Agency, 4 Snow Hill, London EC1A 2DL (offers small business course with training grant for qualified artists/designers, see WORKING FOR ONESELF, p. 557)

Open College of the Arts, Houndhill, Worsborough, Barnsley, South Yorks S70 6TU

Related careers

ADVERTISING – ARCHITECTURE – CARTOGRAPHY – ENGINEERING – FASHION AND CLOTHING – LANDSCAPE ARCHITECTURE – MUSEUMS AND ART GALLERIES – PHOTOGRAPHY – TEACHING – TELEVISION, FILM AND RADIO

Banking

Banking has gone through a period of rapid and dramatic change. Competition has intensified, spurred on by new technology and legislation. Distinctions between different institutions have blurred with activities and services formerly offered by one particular kind of institution now being offered by others. For example, banks offer mortgages and insurance, while building societies (see p. 85) offer cheque accounts. The clearing banks have merchant banking divisions or subsidiaries, while the merchant banks (as well as the clearers) have bought stockbroking firms. More and more one hears the term 'financial services group' to convey the range of financial activity.

Banking can be broken down into services to individuals and services to companies, though there may be overlap (especially in the clearing banks) in terms of both activity and career opportunity. For example, a high street branch manager may be involved with individuals and with corporate clients; a trainee might have a spell in a department marketing corporate services and then move into a role as a personal accounts executive.

Retail/Personal Banking

Entry qualifications

Most banks do not now set minimum academic requirements. Those with A-levels, a BTEC National award or a degree can slot in higher up the training ladder if recruited to an accelerated training programme. In Scotland, three Highers at grades A–C are required.

The work

Banks provide a wide range of financial services to personal customers, largely through their branch networks. They take deposits and make loans, transmit money from one account to another, exchange foreign currency and travellers' cheques, offer mortgages, insurance policies, pensions and investment schemes. They also offer financial advice on a range of matters.

Staff at all levels in a branch deal with people as well as money and figures. From an early stage in training considerable emphasis is placed on the ability to relate to customers, identify their needs and promote the bank's services.

Trainees normally start in the general office, where they learn basic procedures such as sorting and listing cheques so that they can be 'read' electronically and operating the terminal linked to the central computer on which customers' accounts are updated. First promotion is usually to cashier. Cashiers are in the front line of the intensifying battle for customers so they must make a good impression. Courtesy, efficiency and helpfulness are important.

After a spell at the counter, trainees undertake other customer service duties, for example, setting up standing orders/direct debits and opening accounts. Promotion to senior clerical duties involves the development of supervisory skills and the more specialized technical knowledge needed to deal with, for example: customers' investments; the sanction of small personal loans and analysis, with the management team, of more detailed lending propositions; or executor and trust work, dealing with trusts and wills in which the bank may look after customers' or their dependants' interests, advise people who have been left money on investment, or explain complex money matters to bewildered heirs. As clerical officers are promoted to junior management grades they take on increased responsibility for customer service and the smooth running of the branch.

Managers may be responsible for one branch or several. Within policy laid down by the bank, they have considerable responsibility for approving loans, dealing with business customers from the small to, sometimes, the very large, overseeing the smooth running of their branches and marketing the bank's growing range of services and 'products'.

Those on accelerated management training programmes might spend only very short periods in the clerical functions. They are not necessarily expected to master the tasks but need to appreciate their importance in the overall service the bank offers its customers. There are also opportunities in regional and head offices where, for example, specialist advice is available and new 'products' are developed. A career with a bank can also develop into non-banking functions, e.g. personnel.

The combination of recession and new technology has led to large cuts in staff among the banks. The impact is more marked in lower-level jobs; in an intensely competitive climate, the banks continue to recruit and train those who have the potential to become middle managers. The banks all have well-developed graduate recruitment and training programmes, but in theory it is still possible to reach senior levels from a modest start. (Many graduates also opt to develop their careers on the corporate side of the business.)

Training   Largely on the job, with residential courses at more senior levels.

Day-release may be available for those preparing for the exams of the Chartered Institute of Bankers, but it is often restricted to Stage II candidates and those on accelerated programmes. There are evening and correspondence courses for other candidates.

Personal attributes Meticulous accuracy; the interpersonal skills to deal with customers; a clear, logical mind; tact; courtesy; a feeling for figures and interest in work with data-processing equipment.

Late start No precise figures are available for the profession overall. In the past the proportion of full-time late entrants has been small, but banks are now looking very seriously at mature applicants in view of demographic trends and predicted shortages of school-leavers.

Career-break Most of the major banks operate a career-break/return-to-work scheme. They vary in detail but, broadly speaking, are open to male and female staff, for a period of 2–5 years. Some guarantee a return to the organization at one's previous grade. Normally the member of staff is expected to undertake refresher training for 2–4 weeks a year and to keep abreast of developments.

Position of women About 60% of staff employed are female. About 25% of junior managers, 6% of middle managers and 3% of senior managers are women. Nevertheless, it is estimated that the figure has probably doubled in the last 5 years. Approximately 50% of graduate trainees are women. Though, according to Women in Banking, 'theory is well ahead of practice', all the banks are concentrating on the barriers to promotion for women and looking into childcare, flexible hours, job-sharing and so on. Some banks run special management development courses for female staff which deal with such issues as assertiveness and women's expectations. Approximately 20% of female staff work part time; at present these are mainly at clerical and secretarial level.

Wholesale/Corporate Banking

Entry qualifications There are some opportunities for GCSE or A-level school-leavers, but their prospects may be limited. Most banks recruit mainly graduate trainees.

The work Companies and governments require financial services broadly equivalent to those offered to individuals, but the scale and complexity are much greater. Among the services offered by the banks to their corporate customers are: banking, which is basically taking deposits, transferring funds and lending money; corporate finance, which includes advising on mergers and acquisitions, raising capital, business strategy, competitors and outside factors; and treasury, which involves buying and selling foreign currency to protect against disadvantageous currency movements. The banks are also involved in investment management on behalf of institutional investors of large sums of money, such as pension funds and investment trusts, and the securities business (see p. 498) – making issues and buying and selling shares. Government work on the privatization of nationalized industries has been a feature of recent years.

Corporate banking can start with the local branch manager, but the more complex work will be done in the corporate divisions of the clearing banks, their merchant banking subsidiaries, the merchant banks and investment banks. Not all banks offer the same range of services. Staff are required for a range of tasks from analysis through sales. In most jobs staff should be capable of analysing, researching and selling the results, but team work is a common feature of this area of banking.

An important related activity is dealing – in currencies and various financial 'products' designed to help firms finance their businesses. Banks may deal speculatively on their own account to make a profit, or on behalf of clients to help them manage financial risks.

After the rapid expansion of the mid-1980s, numbers have been steadily declining, affected by both fierce competition and recession. However, though the level varies, the larger banks will maintain some regular recruitment as a long-term investment. For those who are successful, the financial rewards are high, but, as recent years have shown, high rewards are often balanced by high risks, especially on the dealing side. It is not a business that carries 'passengers'.

Most 'bankers' and corporate financiers will be graduates, but dealers are often non-graduates who start in a support function. Specialist staff, e.g. experts in a particular industry, have good opportunities to move between banks.

Training   Largely on the job with the opportunity and encouragement to obtain relevant qualifications.

Personal attributes   High intelligence; ability to work as a member of a team and to relate to clients at a high level; flexibility; competitive drive; ability to think analytically and practically. *For dealers*: confidence, quick wits, entrepreneurial flair, independence.

Late start   Some 20% of entrants are over 30, with relevant industrial/professional experience. A 'fresh' start for job changers without such experience is unlikely.

Career-break

Most of the major high street banking groups operate a career-break/return-to-work scheme (see p. 71). Formal schemes are rare, if not non-existent, among the other banks.

Position of women

Women are not yet seen in large numbers in top positions. However, at the entry level they have been very successful in recent years, with some banks reporting a higher success rate among women graduate applicants. Job-sharing and part-time work are not widespread and mainly confined to clerical/secretarial areas and possibly support functions like personnel. Employers claim resistance from clients who want continuity of service from their bankers.

Further information

Banking Information Service, Education and Careers, 10 Lombard Street, London EC3V 9AT

Chartered Institute of Bankers, 10 Lombard Street, London EC3V 9AS

Institute of Bankers in Scotland, 19/20 Rutland Square, Edinburgh EH1 2DE

British Merchant Banking and Security Houses Association, 6 Frederick's Place, London EC2R 8BT

Related careers

ACCOUNTANCY – ACTUARY – BUILDING SOCIETY WORK – INSURANCE

Beauty Specialist

Entry qualifications

For school-leavers, 2 or more GCSEs depending on course, but some schools ask for biology or chemistry; see 'Training', below. Minimum age for employment as beauty therapist, 18 + ; as consultant, usually about 24.

The work

Practitioners may use one of several job-titles, but the two most common terms are *beauty therapist* and *beauty consultant*.

Beauty Therapist

Most *beauty therapists* use the full range of available treatments on the face and body. These extend from make-up, facials and wax or electric depilation (removal of superfluous hair) to massage, saunas, diet and exercise. They know when to deal with a skin complaint themselves or when to advise the client to see a doctor. It is possible to learn one or two techniques only, e.g. a *beautician* works on the face and neck only; a *manicurist/pedicurist* on the hands/feet; the *electrologist* (or *epilationist*) uses various means to remove unwanted hair; a *masseur/masseuse* performs face/body massage. (*Aromatherapists* massage with aromatic oils.)

Beauty therapists work in private high street salons (sometimes combined with hairdressers), in their own, or clients' homes, in health farms or cosmetic firms' salons. Clients may be of all ages, male or female.

It is not always easy for students to find jobs, but generally beauty and fitness treatments are becoming more popular. Some beauty specialists set up on their own: the initial financial outlay on equipment depends on the treatments offered. The town hall will advise on necessary licences (see WORKING FOR ONESELF, p. 557). For those trained in hairdressing there are some opportunities in television (see p. 535) and with psychiatric and other patients for whom beauty care can be part of their rehabilitation.

Beauty Consultants (Sales Consultants, Sales Representatives)

Usually work in the perfumery department of large stores,

occasionally in luxury hotels (at home or abroad), on liners, or at airports. They are usually under contract to a cosmetics firm and travel round the country, working for a week or two each in a succession of stores or shops.

They sell and promote the firm's products and try to win regular customers. They answer questions on skin-care and make-up problems, and may give talks and demonstrations.

Top jobs are as cosmetic buyers for stores, at the head offices of cosmetic firms, and as training consultants.

Training   *Professional training*

For jobs in a reputable salon or health farm, it is important to take a course leading to one of the mainstream qualifications. NVQs (see p. xx) are being introduced and students should make sure that courses lead to these qualifications, as they are likely to become very important in the future (e.g. for getting insurance cover). Courses are available in both local education authority colleges and private schools. The advantage of main-tained college courses is that they are free for younger students, although they generally last longer than private ones. Most good private courses last from 5 to 12 months (some are longer). Fees for private colleges range from a few hundred pounds to several thousand, depending on range of skills taught. Syllabus includes theory – anatomy, physiology, diets, salesmanship, salon organiza-tion – and practical work: giving facials, different types of mas-sage, make-up, sometimes electrical treatments, etc.

Main courses are:

1. 2-year (1-year for over-21s) full-time course for City and Guilds Beauty Therapist's Certificate. *Entry requirements*: 3 GCSEs (A-C), preferably including a science. (Separate Certifi-cate in Electrical Epilation may be available as part of the course.)

2. BTEC National Diploma in Beauty Therapy. *Entry require-ments*: 4 GCSEs, including biology (some students may need to take First Level courses in chemistry or physics) or SCOTVEC National Certificate.

3. BTEC Higher National Diploma in Beauty Therapy. Courses last 2 years full time; special emphasis on TV make-up requirements, and remedial aspects. *Entry requirements*: 4 GCSEs and 1 A-level in approved subjects which must include at least 1 science subject (some colleges ask for A-level science). There is also a BTEC HNC.

4. Courses leading to awards of one of the national or inter-national beauty therapy examining bodies, for example the Inter-national Health and Beauty Council, the British Association of

Beauty Therapy and Cosmetology and ITEC (International Therapy Examination Council). Minimum age usually 18.

NOTE: It is important to check the usefulness of courses not included above with one of the organizations mentioned under 'Further information'.

Courses given by cosmetics houses for sales consultants
Minimum age depends on age range at which product is aimed, e.g. teenagers or mature people. Majority need to be 24+ and must have several years' selling experience and must be good salespeople. Training is mainly in-store and lasts a few weeks. Subjects dealt with are facials, simple massage, eyebrow shaping and make-up, for both day and evening. These courses qualify students as sales consultants, but not as beauty therapist.

It is useful to take a hairdressing training as well as beauty training. It widens the choice of jobs later

Personal attributes
A liking for people of all ages; a friendly, confident manner; tact; courtesy; an attractive, well-groomed appearance; naturally good skin; cool, dry hands; good health; business sense; ability to express oneself easily; foreign language sometimes an asset.

Late start
Beauty specialists' work is very suitable for late entrants. Many salons prefer women who are nearer in age to the majority of clients than young school-leavers are. Nurses and physiotherapists sometimes choose this work as a second career.

Career-break
No special problem, except for need to find new clients.

Part time
Fairly easy for experienced people.

Position of women
Up to now this has been a 100% female occupation, but some male students are now on courses.

Further information
City and Guilds of London Institute (see p. xxiii)
BTEC and SCOTVEC (see pp. xxi, xxii)
IHBC, 109 Felpham Road, Felpham, West Sussex PO22 7PW
ITEC, James House, Oakelbrook Mill, Newent, Glos GL18 1HD

Related careers
TELEVISION, FILM AND RADIO: *Make-up artists/Designers*

Bookselling

Entry qualifica-tions
None laid down, but good general education essential.

The work
All bookselling is a branch of retailing, but there is a difference between a specialist bookshop, where customers expect to find knowledgeable staff, and non-specialist bookshops with a limited range of titles and various non-book products on sale. The latter are more suitable for people interested more in a retailing career than in books. Specialist bookshop staff must be well read in order to be able to advise customers and answer queries. Reading should cover a wide field rather than only one's own interests, but in large bookshops staff usually specialize in one or two subjects. Customers are often left to browse undisturbed amongst the stock and are offered help and advice only when they want it.

Assistants' duties include daily dusting and filling and tidying shelves and display-tables. This also helps them to learn the stock and remember where titles are shelved. Assistants also write out orders, keep records and may do some book-keeping. In many bookshops, ordering, stock control, etc. is now computerized. Assistants may pack and unpack parcels and carry them to the post; bookshop work is physically quite hard.

One of the most interesting and most skilled parts of the job is helping customers who have only a vague idea of what they want or cannot explain what they have in mind. It may involve tracing titles in bibliographies and catalogues.

Book-buying – selecting a small proportion of the vast number of new titles published each month – is a highly skilled and often tricky task. Several members of staff may be responsible for buying within one or more subject areas. They have to be able to judge what will interest their particular customers, whether to buy a new title at all and how many copies to order. New titles are ordered before reviews have appeared so staff must trust their own judgement. They must also judge how much reliance to place on the recommendation of publishers' representatives.

Managers may take part in or do all the buying – it depends on how experienced their staff and how large the shop. Above all, the manager tries to give the shop an 'image' to attract a nucleus of regular customers. This is done partly by the choice of books in stock and partly by the method and type of display and arrangement of the shop as a whole. The manager is also responsible for the stock-control system (as would be the case in any other kind of shop).

Far more people want to work in bookshops than there are vacancies. Bookshops thrive only at Christmas; nevertheless some owner-managers of small bookshops do reasonably well if they have researched the market thoroughly before setting up shop (see WORKING FOR ONESELF, p. 557).

Training Staff learn mainly on the job, although some large shops and chains have formal training schemes. Good bookshops and departments encourage staff to take the Booksellers' Association's qualification, the Certificate in Bookselling Skills. The syllabus includes computerized ordering and cataloguing systems, up-to-date marketing and customer-relations principles. It therefore contains 'transferable skills' which may be useful in other retail spheres. On-the-job training is complemented by distance-learning packages. Students may have a tutor, seminars and tutorials; self-help groups complement the training. An outside examiner assesses students' work before the Certificate is awarded.

Personal attributes An excellent memory; commercial sense; wide interests and extensive general knowledge; pleasure in reading and handling books; a liking for meeting people with various interests; a helpful friendly manner and the knack of making diffident customers who are not well-read feel they are welcome; the ability to work well in a large team or in a very small shop or department; a calm temperament.

Late start No greater problem than young entrants.

Career-break Should not present any problems.

Part time Good scope.

Position of women A large proportion of staff and managers, but not of owners, are women. The proportion of part-time staff – mainly women – has increased recently, but their pay is low.

Further information The Booksellers' Association of Great Britain and Ireland, 272 Vauxhall Bridge Road, London SW1V 1BA

**Related
careers**   INFORMATION WORK – RETAIL DISTRIBUTION

Building

Entry qualifications

For degree in building: 2–3 A-levels, to include maths/science for some courses. *For technician training*: see BTEC/SCOTVEC National and Higher National, pp. xxi, xxii. *For craft training*: none specified.

The work

The building industry is made up of companies ('contractors') of all sizes, from international giants employing thousands of skilled craft workers and professional staff, including architects, chartered builders, surveyors and chartered engineers, to small 'jobbing builders' employing one or two craftsmen/women and taking on additional people as required. Many small builders work part of the time on their own and part of the time as sub-contractors to larger firms, sometimes providing a specialist skill which the main contractor may not be able to offer. Large companies have their own design departments and execute large-scale projects such as housing estates, large office blocks, hospitals, etc. Smaller firms – and often large ones too – work to plans drawn up by the client's architect and may sub-contract work to specialist firms of plumbers, tilers, smaller general builders, etc. On large projects the client, or the client's architect, appoints a *clerk of works* (see p. 82).

The building trade (particularly, but not only, firms concerned with large projects) is very dependent on the economic climate. Traditionally, when there is plenty of work, especially large-scale projects, there is a shortage of skilled, trained people at all levels. There are still too few building graduates, so experienced managers are usually in demand.

Levels and organization of work are very much less well-defined than, for example, in the engineering industry. Many contractors start at craft level and build up their own business, but they need to understand the new technologies and materials, know how to work to given standards and how to organize work efficiently (i.e. ensuring that workforce, plant and materials are at the right place at the right time and that there is a regular flow of work). There is, therefore, increasing scope for people with specialist and management qualifications, but there will always be scope for craftsmen and craftswomen who are good at their job and also have organizing ability to build up their own business. Knowledge of basic crafts like bricklaying, carpentry and plumbing is useful even for managers; knowledge of new materials and technologies is essential in all parts of the industry.

Building Managers

Managers are responsible for co-ordinating the wide variety of activities and processes involved on a project. They must see that work is carried out in the right sequence with the right materials – which must be available at the right time – and at the right cost. They organize the labour force, so must understand the work of bricklayers, carpenters, etc. Depending on the size of the firm, work may include organizing the financial side (paying wages, paying for materials, etc.). Some building management jobs are site-based (there may be a site office), some are office-based; nearly all jobs involve some site visits; and many jobs, at least for large firms, involve working away from home at times, occasionally overseas.

Usual job titles and specializations (which vary very much between firms) are:

1. *Buyer* (*purchasing officer*): Selects from the design drawings the materials and services needed; contacts suppliers and subcontractors to obtain the most competitive prices; ensures materials are available at the right time.

2. *Estimator*: Calculates the likely cost of materials (from door handles to concrete), labour and plant, and the time needed for the project when the firm is tendering for a contract. Also analyses costs of existing projects to provide guide to future estimates.

3. *Planner*: At pre-tender stage is involved in the decision about how the tender can be adjusted. When tender is accepted, produces charts showing sequence of operations. Works closely with contract manager. In large companies will use computer for this. Planners need experience of estimating, buying or contracts management.

4. *Site engineer*: In charge of technical side of an individual project. Sets out the positions and levels of the building to ensure it is placed in the correct position in accordance with the designs. Oversees all the work on site, including quality control (see 'Civil Engineering' and 'Structural Engineering', p. 190).

5. *Site manager/site agent* (used to be called 'general foreman'): In charge of the contract. Ensures the designs and specifications are understood by the foremen/women; plans and coordinates materials and labour. Sees that building keeps to the plan and time schedule (see 'Building Technicians', below, and 'Surveying Technicians', p. 512). May control work of young engineers.

6. *Production controller*: Works on incentive schemes; measures work done by operatives as part of productivity control; takes part in construction planning at site level. Some specialize in work study and/or industrial relations.

7. *Contract manager*: Oversees several projects. Moves from site to site ensuring that work is progressing according to plan. Plans movement of machines and labour to minimize delays and time-wasting. Has overall responsibility for completion of projects to correct standard at the right time.

8. *Clerk of works*: Other building management specialists work for the contractor; the clerk of works is employed by the client (or client's architect). May be employed full-time by a local authority or, in the private sector, on a contract basis. Works from an office on site and is responsible for seeing that the work is carried out according to the architect's specifications. As the only person on site not working for the contractor the clerk can be rather isolated, so needs to be confident and self-sufficient. On large schemes duties may include supervising several other clerks of works specializing in, for example, heating and ventilating or electrical installation.

9. *Building control officers*: They are responsible for checking sites to see that work complies with building regulations. In certain circumstances they may advise contractors on alternative methods of construction. Up until recently they worked only for local and other public authorities, but they can now work in the private sector.

Building Technicians

The work of technicians overlaps with that of managers and, in fact, many managers start as technicians (see 'Training') and do not gain any higher qualification. Technicians may be involved in any of the specializations mentioned above. They do many of the detailed costings, work out quantities and prepare drawings. On site they may be involved in surveying, measuring and detailed planning of the work.

The work of building managers and technicians overlaps and both overlap very much with that of chartered surveyors/surveying technicians and civil/structural engineers/technicians.

Building crafts

Craftsmen and craftswomen are skilled in one, occasionally more than one, occupation or trade: the most common are bricklaying, carpentry, joinery, plastering, plumbing and electrical installation, tiling and roofing.

Training   *Manager*
Either on the job by training first as a technician (see below) and
then taking BTEC/SCOTVEC Higher National awards. Successful completion plus appropriate experience leads to exemptions
from various examinations of the Chartered Institute of Building.

Or (for jobs with big organizations) 3-year full-time or 4-year
sandwich degree in building/building technology/building construction and management. Most give full exemption from Chartered Institute of Building's Final examination.

Clerk of works: As above followed by evening or correspondence course for Institute of Clerk of Works' Intermediate and
Final examinations. (BTEC National awards give some exemptions.) Membership of the Institute is compulsory before sitting
the examinations. Some local authorities give day-release.

Building control officers qualify in building, surveying or
relevant engineering subjects at BTEC/SCOTVEC or degree
level.

Technician
Either via the Construction Industry Training Board's youth
training programme (see below) *or* as a trainee with a company
and day- or block-release (both may lead to BTEC/SCOTVEC
National awards) *or* by studying full time for BTEC National
Diploma (or SCOTVEC equivalent) (see pp. xxi, xxii). Courses
can be in building studies, construction or building services
engineering (see ENGINEERING, p. 190).

Craft
In recent years most school-leaver entrants have *either* been
trained by a company with on-site practical training and day- or
block-release for City and Guilds certificates *or* followed the
CITB youth training programme which included a minimum 20
weeks' full-time training.

At the time of writing (September 1991) CITB youth training
is being revised and NVQs (see p. xx) are being introduced. For
up-to-date information contact the CITB.

Training for *electricians* is run separately: in England and
Wales by JTL (Joint Training Ltd) and in Scotland by the
Scottish Electrical Charitable Training Trust.

Personal   *Building crafts*: Some manual dexterity; an inquiring and logical
attributes   mind; willingness to work with the minimum of or no supervision
with potentially dangerous equipment; a reasonably careful nature
or at least awareness of dangers unless basic rules are observed.

Building management: Ability to work with all kinds of people and help them work as a team; technical and practical aptitudes; good at organization; willing to work outdoors in all weathers; commercial sense.

Late start
No age limit for traineeships as there used to be for apprenticeships, but in practice young school-leavers are given preference. There are training and retraining schemes for adults (see p. xxiv) with or without related experience and/or qualifications, e.g. as surveying technician, p. 512.

**Career-
break**
Probably difficult without retraining. So far nothing is known about returners (see WORKING FOR ONESELF, p. 557).

Part time
Possible if working for small contractor or shop or for oneself.

**Position
of
women**
There are as yet few craftswomen; more women have entered building management (10% of first-year building degree students are women) and are proving very successful. There is no reason why there should not be many more at all levels. Some women-only craft courses are available for late entrants.

**Further
informa-
tion**
Construction Careers Service, Construction Industry Training Board, Bircham Newton, King's Lynn, Norfolk PE31 6RH (for England and Wales) or 4 Edison Street, Hillington, Glasgow G52 4XN (for Scotland)

Chartered Institute of Building, Englemere, King's Drive, Ascot, Berks SL5 8BJ

Institute of Clerks of Works, 41 The Mall, London W5 3TJ

Institute of Building Control, 21 High Street, Ewell, Epsom, Surrey KT17 1SB

JTL, Head Office, South Block, Central Court, Knool Rise, Orpington, Kent BR6 0JA

Scottish Electrical Charitable Training Trust, Bush House, Bush Estate, Midlothian, Edinburgh EH26 0SB

Women and Manual Trades, 52–54 Featherstone Street, London EC1Y 8RT

**Related
careers**
AGRICULTURE AND HORTICULTURE – ARCHITECTURE – ENGINEERING. CIVIL ENGINEERING – SURVEYING

Building Society Work

The traditional function of building societies has been, on the one hand, to encourage people to save and invest with them, and, on the other, to use this money to lend out as mortgages to house-buyers. However, since 1986 building societies have been widening their activities and have become more directly competitive with the banks. Many now operate bank-type cheque accounts, make unsecured loans, offer estate agency services, insurance services, pension plans, stock market investment schemes. Not all societies have developed all options but most have diversified in some way. Some societies are likely to follow the lead of the Abbey National and become public limited companies to enable them further to develop as 'personal financial services' groups.

Entry qualifications
For *clerical staff*, who take the Chartered Building Societies Institute Certificate in Building Society Practice, normally 4 GCSEs; for *trainee managers*, who take the CBSI Associateship examination, 2 A-levels and 4 GCSEs (A–C), including English and a subject proving numeracy, *or* BTEC National Award in Business or Financial Studies *or* high-level pass in CBSI Certificate. There is also graduate and professional level entry.

The work
In the past, most managers started as clerks and were promoted within the society. It is still possible to reach a management position from a humble start, especially in a small society, but in practice most large and medium-size organizations now have 2-tier entry.

Clerical staff carry out routine office tasks such as filing, accounting and data-processing. *Cashiers* or *customer advisers* deal with clients at the counter, handling routine transactions and giving advice and information. They have a key role in promoting new services and 'products'. Some may be promoted to a management development programme.

Trainee managers, who must have the minimum qualifications for the Associateship examination (see above), do some counter work to learn how to deal with customers, but most of their time is spent on such work as mortgage principles and processing, assessing applicants' suitability for mortgages, and liaising with surveyors, estate agents, conveyancers and investment specialists. Some time may be spent in head office functions. After 2–3 years trainee managers are expected to be fully fledged managers of small branches or assistant managers of larger branches.

Much of *managers'* time may be spent on routine mortgage processing or on some of the new activities, but marketing is one of their key functions. Not only are managers responsible for selling *their* society and branch to the local community, but they have an important role in talking and listening to customers about their needs and feeding this information back to head office, where new products are developed. Managers may be promoted through a succession of larger branches, to an area or regional office management role, or to a head office function such as marketing or systems development.

To compete in the highly competitive financial services market, there is a growing need for people with specialized skills and knowledge in, for example, accountancy, law, marketing, economic planning. Most of the major societies now run graduate-training schemes.

Building societies vary in size, structure and the kind of career they offer. There are still small local societies without organized management and training structures. People interested in a more varied career in personal financial services should try for a job in one of the large or medium-size organizations.

Training

Largely on the job. Clerical staff can study part time for the CBSI Certificate in Building Society Practice. Trainee managers work for the Associateship examination, which can take up to 4 years. The big societies run their own in-house courses, and there are some CBSI residential courses. Day-release may be available, but the bulk of exam preparation has to be done by private study.

Some societies help staff to gain other relevant professional qualifications, for example in accountancy.

Personal attributes

Communication skills; flexibility; ability to learn quickly; organizing ability; numeracy; liking for routine desk work; good business sense.

Late start

Trainee managers may be taken on up to about 30, branch staff later. Retail banking, office or retail experience may be useful. Academic entry requirements may be waived.

Career-break

Not as common as in the banks, but schemes do operate in some organizations and are likely to grow over the next few years. Rapidly developing technology, services and products can make a return more difficult.

Position of women

80% of staff in the industry are women, but at higher levels and in management, males predominate. Most students for the CBSI Associateship exam are male, for the Certificate female.

Societies vary greatly in their policies. Some are introducing parental breaks, term-time working, part-time and job-sharing opportunities, though these innovations are not common at management level. Some organizations are running assertiveness courses to encourage female staff to be more career-minded. Career-minded girls should shop around for a good employer.

Further information

Chartered Building Societies Institute, 19 Baldock Street, Ware, Herts. SG12 9DH

Building Societies Association (for member societies), 3 Savile Row, London W1X 1AF

Individual societies (and the Abbey National plc)

Related careers

BANKING – INSURANCE – MANAGEMENT

Careers Work

Careers Officer

Entry qualifications

Degree, Dip. H.E., teaching qualification or acceptable alternative of comparable standard.

The work

The traditional role of careers officers is to help young people to make sound and realistic career choices and to implement those choices. This covers a wide range of activities from helping an unemployed school-leaver find a job to helping a school to plan an on-going programme to suit various age and ability groups. Recent developments in education and training have broadened the scope of careers officers' work so that they have a more active role in, for example, helping to plan work-related areas of the school curriculum and liaising with training organizations on the provision of appropriate training. In addition, work with adults has increased; a growing number of careers services throughout the country have become all-age guidance services, developing their work with adults who might be unemployed, looking for a change of career, or returning to education or work after a break.

Interviewing individuals at various points in their education is an important part of careers officers' work. They must be objective and impartial in helping the clients come to understand their own interests, abilities and personalities and how these relate to career opportunities; they must not push or favour one particular option or route. This demands both guidance and counselling skills and a sound knowledge of all the opportunities.

Careers officers work closely with schools and their role is expanding. They work with careers teachers to plan and implement a programme of careers education and guidance which can span several age groups and decision points. This work in schools can include work with individuals or groups; helping with the careers library; arranging for people to come in and talk about their work; arranging visits to work places; or work experience for pupils. Careers officers also have a key role in promoting and establishing closer links between education and industry. For example, they might arrange courses and conferences which bring teachers into industry, liaising with schools to select suitable teachers, helping employers to develop appropriate programmes, assisting both sides in the evaluation of the exercise and helping teachers to relate what they have learned to the curriculum.

A good deal of careers officers' time is spent gathering information. They need to keep up to date with developments, trends and impending changes in education, training and the jobs market. They visit employers, talking both to training and personnel officers about their needs and to people actually doing jobs about the nature, demands and satisfactions of their work. They contact colleges and other educational institutions to keep themselves informed about courses, entry qualifications and employment prospects.

Much of this work takes careers officers out and about, but there is a certain amount of essential office-based administrative work. Good record-keeping is very important, and the information collected must be made accessible to colleagues and clients. Often this involves writing brief summaries or more detailed information sheets on, for example, a particular occupational area or topics like choosing a course.

After a period of general experience careers officers may specialize. Opportunities include work with ethnic minorities, with special-needs pupils, with adults or with more academically able pupils.

1993 NOTE: New legislation transfers the duty to provide a statutory careers service from local education authorities to the Secretary of State for Employment. Over the next couple of years, the Department of Employment will seek bids, through open competitive tendering, from organizations wishing to deliver the careers service in their areas. It is expected that LEAs and TECs will be among the bidders, but it is too early to foretell the effect on careers officers.

Training   1-year full-time (2-year part-time) course plus a probationary year in service leading to the Diploma in Careers Guidance. Courses are offered by polytechnics, a few universities and Kent College for the Careers Service (which can also offer distance learning).Trainee careers officers may be seconded on a course by a local education authority. The syllabus includes organization of education services; occupational and social psychology; public and social administration; organization of industry; counselling aims and methods; practical work with pupils; visits to a variety of places of work and talks with/by employers.

Personal attributes   Ability to get on with and understand people of all levels of intelligence and temperament; interest in industrial and other employment trends and problems; sympathy with rather than critical attitude towards other people's points of view; organizing ability; willingness to work in a team; ability to put facts across clearly and helpfully; ability to gain young people's confidence and to put them at ease however shy and worried; insight and imagination to see how young people might develop; ability to communicate with individuals, with groups and in writing.

Late start   Those over 25 with 5 years' relevant work experience are exempted from normal entry requirements, but must demonstrate ability to cope with post-graduate level course. Relevant jobs are those which involve dealing with a variety of people, preferably in a work situation. Maturity and variety of experience can be an asset: approximately a quarter of students are 'mature'.

Career-break   Should not present any problems.

Part time   Some opportunities. Job-sharing is also possible.

Position of women   Women careers officers outnumber men, but a very much smaller proportion are in senior jobs. As in many other professions, women have felt that they have had to be better qualified and experienced than men for the same type of promotion. Recent years have seen more women making it to more senior roles.

Further information   Institute of Careers Guidance (formerly Institute of Careers Officers), 27A Lower High Street, Stourbridge, West Midlands DY8 1TA

Careers Service Training Committee, Local Government Management Board, 4th floor, Arndale House, The Arndale Centre, Luton LU1 2TS

Other Careers Work

There are opportunities for careers work in a number of other organizations, but they are limited in number and the entry qualifications of practitioners are very varied. In some cases careers officers have diversified into another area; in most cases previous employment experience is a prerequisite.

In *higher education*, careers advisers carry out a range of activities similar to those of careers officers but at a level appropriate to the age, maturity, sophistication and educational level of their clients. A degree and employment experience are essential; beyond that, backgrounds vary enormously. There is no pre-entry training; in-service training may be arranged by the employer or by the Association of Graduate Careers Advisory Services.

Other employers of careers advisory staff include *professional bodies, charities* and *vocational guidance organizations*. Again, backgrounds vary widely. Some people have experience in the Careers Service, in teaching, in personnel or in the relevant profession. Vocational guidance organizations often look for psychology graduates.

A related and growing (though small) area is that of *educational guidance* for adults. As mentioned elsewhere in this book, flexibility in education at all levels is increasing. Educational guidance for adults aims to help them to understand and take advantage of the full range of opportunities available. The work includes information, assessment, advice, counselling and promotion so, again, a wide variety of backgrounds may be appropriate.

| **Related careers** | PERSONNEL/HUMAN RESOURCES MANAGEMENT – TEACHING – YOUTH AND COMMUNITY WORK |

Cartography (Map Making)

Entry qualifications

Depends on type of work – from 3 GCSEs (A–C) to degree. See 'The work' and 'Training', below.

The work

Cartography is concerned with the evaluation, compilation, design, editing, reproduction and draughting of maps. A map in this context covers any type of chart, plan or 3-dimensional model representing the whole or sections of the earth or of other parts of the universe.

Both cartographic data collection and map reproduction methods have changed drastically in the last few years. Apart from traditional land survey techniques and aerial photography, such advanced technologies as satellite photography, seismic sensing and electrostatic mapping are being used. But cartography does not involve exploring uncharted territory, taking photographs from helicopters or setting up satellite photography. It is an indoor desk job, though very occasionally cartographers may accompany the information gatherers. While the cartographer determines what data are needed for any particular map and may discuss which type of data collection is best in any particular case, the actual collection is done by specialists such as *surveyors* (see p. 508), *specialist photographers* (see p. 376), *computing people* (see p. 142) or by historical or archaeological researchers. *Cartographers* interpret the information collected by other specialists, *cartographic draughtsmen/women/technicians* represent the information in graphic form. Apart from tracing and drawing, draughtsmen/women use highly sophisticated reproduction methods and materials and are increasingly involved in applying computer-assisted map production methods.

The largest single employer is the Ordnance Survey. Other employers include various Ministries (Defence and Environment particularly), nationalized industries, local authorities, commercial map-publishing houses, motoring organizations and exploration departments of oil companies.

The varieties of maps which are produced can include: cartographic portrayals of airfield approaches with landing charts for pilots; maps showing traffic flow or the distribution of population, housing, employment and industry for planning purposes; maps for the Forestry Commission showing planting, thinning and felling; maps of the surface of the moon and maps of ancient Rome. Jobs are mainly in London and Southampton (Ordnance Survey). At the time of writing (1991) the Ordnance Survey is not recruiting non-graduates, following a restructuring of the department, and is unlikely to do so for the next couple of years. The grade of Cartographic Assistant no longer exists and any future posts will be for trainee or experienced cartographic draughtsmen/women and surveyors.

Training   *Cartographer*: Degree in cartography with related subject, or degree in geography or topographic science or mapping sciences, or a post-graduate diploma in cartography. Minimum entry requirements: 2 A-levels normally in geography and a science subject.

The Ordnance Survey has occasional openings for graduates in the above subjects, or in computer science, who go on to specialize in geodosy, land surveying, photogrammetry, digital cartography or geographic information systems. After 2 years they become Higher Mapping and Charting Officers.

Cartographic draughtsman/woman or surveyor: BTEC National award in Cartography or Surveying. Preferred GCSEs: English, maths, geography, a science, art or a technical-drawing subject.

Personal attributes   Patience; great accuracy; good colour vision; keen interest in physical surroundings; powers of observation.

Late start   Very few opportunities – only about 5% of entrants.

Career-break   Should be no problem for qualified cartographers who keep up with technological changes.

Part time   Possible, but promotion for part-timers unlikely. Graduate cartographers might be able to get sporadic rather than part-time project work. Job-sharing should be possible. Part-time courses are under consideration.

Position of women   *Cartographers*: Comparatively few women have qualified, but those who have had no special problems.
Cartographic draughtspeople: about 1 in 5 are women.

| **Further information** | British Cartographic Society, R. W. Anson, Department of Civil Engineering, Building and Cartography, Oxford Polytechnic, Headington, Oxford OX3 0BP |

| **Related careers** | ARCHITECTURE: *Architectural Technician* – ART AND DESIGN |

Catering

Entry qualifications

All educational levels. Considerable *graduate* entry: See 'Training', below.

The work

Catering is the umbrella term for providing accommodation and/ or food and drink services. It overlaps with LEISURE/RECREA-TION MANAGEMENT (see p. 264) and TRAVEL AGENT/TOUR OPERATOR (see p. 552) and is sometimes referred to as the 'hospitality industry'. It covers an enormous array of totally different types of concern. The main branches are: *hotels* – vast number of small ones, small number of large and/or luxury ones, motels, pubs; *restaurants* – all types and sizes; *industrial and institutional catering* – for example, staff canteens, restaurants, halls of residence, meals-on-wheels (all of which are increasingly provided by contract caterers). Institutional catering is also called '*institutional management*' (see p. 105). There is not necessarily any greater difference between jobs in commercial and in institutional (i.e. non-profit-making) catering than there is between individual jobs *within* commercial and *within* institutional catering. The difference is in emphasis on various aspects rather than in operation and management methods.

Catering skills are highly transferable and there is considerable overlap between the different sectors. But for senior hotel management, experience in food and drink services as well as in accommodation services is necessary; for non-residential catering, experience of accommodation services is *not* necessary.

Job titles often mean very little: 2 jobs with the same title may involve totally different tasks and levels of responsibility. Much depends on the size of establishment and the level of service it provides. It is an industry in which it is still possible to start at the bottom and, with aptitude, hard work and willingness to gain qualifications, reach the top, particularly for those who are able to become self-employed.

In senior management, work often overlaps with other managerial jobs and does not necessarily involve any contact with the public (the reason which brings most entrants into this industry). Senior managers in a fast food chain may, for example, work entirely at head office; in industrial catering they may be responsible for a group of catering units, visiting individual managers and liaising with head office; or they may investigate latest 'catering systems' (see below).

The majority of catering jobs involve working when customers are at leisure, as do so many jobs in service industries. This can make a 'normal' social life difficult at times, but there are compensations to be had in being able to shop, play sport, etc. at less crowded times.

Success in most jobs depends largely on motivating others to do their jobs well, and on efficient utilization of equipment and deployment of staff.

As in other industries, technology is 'de-skilling' many jobs and introducing new skills in others. Large industrial and institutional catering concerns and speciality restaurants increasingly use *systems catering* or *catering systems* instead of letting the chef decide what is for dinner and then getting the staff to prepare the meal. There are variations on the catering systems theme, but broadly this is how it works. Market research (see pp. 16, 294) identifies the most popular dishes within given price-ranges for given consumer-groups. Dishes are part- or fully prepared, and often even 'trayed up' in vast production kitchens. Then they are transported, frozen or chilled, to the 'point of consumption', which may be many miles away. Finally, at the point of consumption, food is 'reconstituted', perhaps in a microwave oven. An example of this new technology is in a large hospital: here patients' food is put into covered trays similar to those on an aircraft; different materials are used in different sections of the tray so that when they have been transported from the kitchens and placed in large ovens in corridors outside the wards the hot food is heated up while the cold food, such as salad, stays chilled.

Managers must understand the technologies involved and their effects on ingredients, and they must be good organizers.

Hotels

Manager

The work   The manager's work varies enormously according to size and type of hotel. In large hotels, the general manager is co-ordinator and administrator, responsible for staff management, financial control, provision of services, quality control and customer care. Departmental managers are in charge of specialist services: reception, sales, food and bar service, housekeeping, banqueting, etc. The manager deals with correspondence, has daily meetings with departmental managers and may be in touch daily or weekly with head office. Although managers try to be around to talk to guests (not only when they have complaints), most of their time is spent dealing with running the business side, making decisions based on information obtained from the accountant, personnel manager, sales manager, accommodation manager, etc.

Managers do not normally have to live in, though they may have a bedroom or flat on the premises. Working hours are long, and often busiest at weekends and during holidays. They must be able to switch from one task to another instantly, and change their daily routine when necessary – which it often is.

Among managers' most important tasks: creating and maintaining good staff relations, as success depends entirely on the work done by others under their overall direction; giving the hotel the personality and the character which either the manager, or more often the employer, intends it to have; and being able to make a constantly changing clientele feel as though each of them mattered individually. However, the extent of emphasis on personal service varies according to the type of hotel.

In small hotels the manager may have a staff of about 15 to 30, and instead of several departmental managers, possibly 1 general assistant. Living in may be necessary, and off-duty time may be less generous than in large hotels. There are *far* more small (and unpretentious) hotels than large or small luxury ones. Many small and medium-sized country hotels are owned by companies and run by couples.

General Assistant – Assistant Manager

The work   This varies according to the size and type of hotel. In small hotels, assistant managers help wherever help is needed most – in the kitchen, in the bar, in housekeeping. Although the work is extremely hard, it is the best possible experience – some hotel managers say the only valuable experience – better than theoretical training (though the ideal is a sound basis of technical training complemented by experience).

In large hotels, assistant managers may be the same as departmental managers (see above). They may take turns at being 'duty manager' available to deal with any problem that occurs on a particular shift. Trainee managers may spend some time as assistants in different departments before deciding to specialize.

An assistant departmental manager may be as responsible and

as well paid as a general manager: it depends on size and type of hotel.

Personal *For top jobs*: Exceptional organizing ability and business acumen;
attributes outgoing personality; the wish to please people, however unreasonable customers' demands may seem; an interest in all the practical skills – cooking, bar-management, housekeeping, etc.; willingness to work while others play; ability to shoulder responsibility and handle staff; tact.

For assistants/managers of small hotels: Partly as for managers, but exceptional organizing ability is not necessary; instead, a liking for practical work is essential, and willingness to work hard and get things done without taking the credit.

Receptionist/'Front Office'

The work Receptionists work in or near the entrance hall, and are always at the centre of activities. Since they are usually the first contact guests have with the hotel on arrival it is essential that they make a good impression.

Head receptionists are assisted in large and medium-sized hotels by junior receptionists. They take advance bookings over the telephone or by post and keep the chart or 'bedroom-book', which shows at a glance provisional and definite bookings. To steer a course between unnecessary refusal of bookings and overbooking is skilled work. Receptionists deal with correspondence; they must be able to do straightforward book-keeping, type and compose their own letters: they notify other hotel departments of arrivals and departures, and keep the customers' accounts up to date by collating chits handed to them by the kitchen, hall porter, bar, etc., and entering them on to guests' accounts. Almost all large and most medium-sized hotels have computerized reservations and accounts systems, which give instant information on a whole hotel group's vacancies, on guests' accounts, and possibly on the supply position regarding clean linen, beverages, etc. Reception also acts as general information office: staff answer guests' queries about, for example, train times, local tourist attractions or the address of a good hairdresser.

Receptionists work shifts. Especially in country hotels, they may live in; meals on duty are supplied free.

In motels guests 'buy keys' as they arrive to rent a suite with garage for one night at a time. Receptionists explain the procedure and hand over the keys.

Head receptionists are usually responsible directly to the manager; theirs is considered one of the most important posts in the hotel business and can be a stepping stone to general management.

Personal attributes A friendly, helpful personality; an uncritical liking for people of all types; a good memory for faces – visitors appreciate recognition; ability to take responsibility and to work well with others; considerable self-confidence; a methodical approach; a liking for figures; meticulous accuracy. *For top jobs*: business acumen; good judgement of people; leadership.

Housekeeper

The work Except in small hotels, housekeepers do not do housework, but supervise domestic staff (mainly room-service attendants, formerly called chambermaids). Other duties include: checking rooms, seeing that they are clean, comfortable and that all the amenities are working (e.g. tea-makers and fridges); supervising laundry; pass-key control; room-service organization and supervision; discussions with heads of other departments; training and engaging staff and arranging work schedules. In a large hotel a head housekeeper may be in charge of a staff of 200.

In small and medium-sized hotels the housekeeper may be responsible for choosing and maintaining the furnishings, decoration and general appearance of bedrooms and lounges. In large hotels there may be one assistant or floor housekeeper to every floor, or every two floors; the head housekeeper, who is immediately responsible to the manager, therefore has considerable overall responsibility.

Personal attributes Organizing ability; practical approach; an eye for detail; ability to handle and train staff.

Hotel Sales Management

A fringe hotel management career. Hotel sales managers work for large hotels and hotel groups. They sell 'hotel facilities' – efficiency, service, atmosphere, as well as conference and banqueting facilities. A hotel sales manager working for a group may approach large business concerns and try to fix contracts for business executives to stay regularly at the group's hotels. Jointly with tour operators (see TRAVEL AGENT/TOUR OPERATOR, p. 552) and airlines, etc., they build package tours.

No career structure or definite way in yet. Hotel sales managers come either via hotel management, or marketing (p. 294) or any other type of business experience. (BTEC diplomas with tourism specialization are useful preparation.)

Personal attributes   Business acumen; numeracy; extrovert, friendly personality.

*

Restaurant Management

Eating places range from wine bars to large 'popular' and to exclusive *haute cuisine* restaurants. Restaurant managers must know how to attract and keep customers. Budgeting is often not as tight as in industrial and institutional catering. Menu-planning complexity depends on type of restaurants, with special scope for culinary creativity, for example, in vegetarian and in luxury restaurants; for management skills in narrow-range large or chain restaurants.

Catering for fluctuating numbers of customers with the minimum of waste is a highly skilled job, as is arranging staffing rosters to cope with busy periods without being over-staffed in slack ones.

Managers' responsibilities vary greatly according to type and size of restaurant. For example, if the restaurant is one of a chain, overall planning and ordering may be done at head office; in other places the manager may be given a very free hand to 'give the restaurant that personal touch', as long as menus keep within a given price-range and reach the profit target.

According to type of restaurant, managers spend varying amounts of time on 'customer contact'. Except in lunch-only restaurants, working hours, though not necessarily longer, are more spread out, with some evening and weekend work.

Professional Cooks

Cooking always involves some physically hard work – the larger the kitchens, the tougher the job often is. Even with modern design and equipment, kitchens still tend to be hot, noisy and damp, and at times very hectic.

There are a variety of openings at various levels of skill and responsibility. For example, in large-scale *haute cuisine*, a chef heads a hierarchy of assistant chefs, each responsible for one type of cooking – meat, vegetables, pastry, etc. The chef may be responsible for budgeting, buying, planning – or this may all be done by a food and beverage manager, or at head office; responsibilities depend on type and size of organization worked for. In small restaurants, 2 or 3 cooks may do all the work. In simpler restaurants, convenience foods are used extensively and cooks' ability to produce palatable, inexpensive yet reasonably varied menus is the most important aspect of the work. It is no easier than, but very different from, *haute cuisine*. Production kitchens (see p. 96) leave little scope for creative cooking; every dish is prepared to recipes specifying such details as the size, weight, colour and often even the position on the plate of meat or cucumber slices, of sprouts or strawberries. But in experimental kitchens where new dishes and technologies are tried out, the work combines creative cooking skills, an understanding of the effects on the ingredients of being prepared in these unorthodox ways and, above all, managerial skills.

In large kitchens there are many cooking jobs without managerial responsibilities, but anyone who wants to progress beyond the kitchen-hand stage must take systematic training; home-cooking experience is not enough.

It is important to distinguish between courses for professional cooks and for *haute cuisine* for home cooking. Cookery classes and schools do not always make this difference quite clear.

Freelance Cooks

Many people, both those professionally trained and gifted amateurs, make a living by freelance cooking. Clients range from company directors hosting lunches for a dozen clients to individuals wanting someone to cook for dinner or cocktail parties. Some cooks specialize in party food for large or small gatherings. They need their own car to transport equipment and shopping. They must be able to budget and cook within various price-ranges.

Sometimes they cook for families on holidays abroad, or for travel agents' chalet-party package tours, working in ski resorts all winter, at the seaside all summer. This type of work usually includes general housekeeping.

Food and Drink Service – 'Waiting'

Food service can range from working behind a self-service food counter to highly skilled 'silver service' in a directors' dining-room or luxury hotel. *Beverage service* includes working behind a bar in a hotel or public house and, as *wine waiter*, helping a customer choose a suitable wine. Like cooking, waiting is at times physically hard, although the working environment is less hot and noisy than in many kitchens. In a restaurant the quality of the meal service is often as important to the customer as the quality of the food and can help to make or break its reputation.

Fast Foods

The products of this expanding part of the industry range from fish and chips to curry, pizzas to hamburgers. Outlets may be independent businesses, part of a large chain or franchises (the parent company, or franchisor, supplies materials and services and the right to use a trade name, in return for which the franchisee invests capital and pays a levy). Some sell takeaway food only, others also provide table service; all resemble small factories with a retail counter. All operations can be learnt quickly; most chains train 'on the job' and in their own training centres. In what is very much a young person's environment, promotion from school-leaver entrant to supervisor level can be rapid. Management posts are filled either by very successful supervisors or by people with degrees or diplomas in catering, business studies or even arts subjects. The latter have to learn all the basic operations at first hand before undergoing management training. The fast food industry is highly competitive and requires considerable business expertise in order to maintain cash flow and to control stock. Success depends on high turnover, which in turn involves very long hours, but there are real opportunities for people to run their own business.

Pub ('Licensed House') Management

There are over 65,000 pubs in Britain, of which nearly three-quarters are owned by brewers, the rest being 'free houses'. Although the typical British pub has a traditional image, many now offer the additional facilities of cocktail bar, restaurant, café, even theatre. Children are now allowed in parts of many pubs, especially in the country, while the loosening of licensing hours restrictions means that some pubs are open all day. Those who run pubs are either managers or tenants. A manager works for the pub owner for a salary. A tenant rents the pub from the owner on agreed terms and lives off the profits. There are many more tenants than managers. The work is best suited to couples, many of whom take up the work in middle age. It is a way of life rather than a job, as it means being tied to the bar during licensing hours, 7 days a week. Work involves purchasing, stock-keeping and record-keeping as well as bar service. Thorough knowledge of licensing laws is essential. Interest in entertainment trends and more than just a 'liking for people' of all kinds are essential. Specialist training and experience in bar and cellar work is required by anyone hoping eventually to become a licensee.

In some leisure centres, as well as holiday camps, race courses, etc., bar staff are the licensees and have their own 'franchise' – they run their own bars, i.e. instead of working for a salary they 'rent' the bar on the premises.

Industrial Catering

This covers the provision of meals at places of work and is often called 'employee feeding'. Service is provided either by staff employed by the organization itself, or, increasingly, by *catering contractors*. These run 'catering units' on clients' premises in factories, offices, old people's homes, leisure centres, motorway restaurants, at airports, and, with mobile units, on racecourses, agricultural shows, etc. They may also operate vending machines. Contractors' staff can change the setting in which they work without having to change employers. Middle and senior managers are in charge of a number of units; junior staff work on the same premises regularly for a period.

Unit managers themselves usually only cook if fewer than about 20 meals are being served. Their main task normally is trying to achieve as even a flow of work as possible. Other tasks include: *menu-planning* – the complexity of this varies according to the range of meals to be provided, from a narrow range of unexciting standard dishes to a wide selection including directors' dining-room 'specials', and according to the importance attached to nutritional values and tight budget control. Expertise includes being able to provide at least 2 weeks' changing menus within several given price-ranges and at different grades of sophistication; *costing* – ingredients, labour costs, etc.; *purchasing*, which includes negotiating with suppliers and specifying, for example, the uniform size and weight of each lamb chop in an order of several hundreds.

Managers normally attend meetings with directors and/or personnel managers and also discuss improvements or complaints with staff representatives. They must keep up with technological developments and are usually responsible for, or for advising on, types of service, and purchase and maintenance of equipment. (That work may also be done by specialists.)

There is a wide choice of jobs: from preparing sophisticated snacks for a West End showroom, or a dozen *haute cuisine* lunches in a managing director's office with 1 or 2 assistants, to feeding 2,000 a day with a staff of 50 including 2 or 3 assistant managers.

School Catering Service

This has undergone big changes in the last few years. Compulsory competitive tendering by local education authorities has meant that in many areas contract caterers, not the local authority itself, provide the service and, therefore, employ the school meals staff. Schools catering is basically the same as industrial catering, with special emphasis on catering for children's tastes, nutritional values and strict budget control. In some areas, only snacks are provided, in others much effort has gone into improving the standard and image of the service. The future of the service is currently uncertain.

After training, caterers supervise the preparation of dinners, either at school kitchens or at centres from which up to 1,000 meals are distributed to a number of schools.

Promotion depends on the employing organization. Senior staff (who may be called school meals organizers) advise on buying, planning, staffing, kitchen management, nutrition, etc. They are also concerned with contract compliance, specifications and marketing. Cost control is very important. Organizers are responsible for geographical areas and do a good deal of travelling.

Hospital Catering

Hospital catering officers organize provision of meals for patients and staff, which means meals for between 200 and 3,000 people, many of whom need meals round the clock. They usually prepare diets under the overall direction but not day-to-day supervision of *dietitians*. Unlike other catering managers who may have learnt largely on the job, hospital catering staffs (management level) invariably have had systematic specialist training. This is the only catering specialization with a formal career structure (apart from school meals). At the top, *catering advisers* work as National Health Service Regional Officers (see HEALTH SERVICES MANAGEMENT, p. 217), i.e. not actually in hospitals. They advise on planning kitchens, catering technologies (see systems catering, p. 96), staff training and staffing requirements, etc. *Catering managers* are responsible for the catering arrangements in a group of hospitals. *Catering officers* are responsible for provision of meals in individual hospitals. (See DIETETICS, p. 168, for dietitian catering officers.)

Assistant and *deputy catering officers* are steps on the ladder to catering officer. In small hospitals, *catering supervisors* may be in charge of the whole catering operation; in larger hospitals they are responsible for a section.

Experience in hospital catering is very useful training for other specializations.

Increasingly hospital catering is contracted out to industrial caterers.

Transport Catering

This is often done by contractors using *catering systems* (see p. 96) Menu planning in airlines involves taking into account climatic conditions at point of consumption; commercial facts such as air commuters' 'menu-fatigue' (business people travel the same routes regularly; frequent menu changes must be made or customers are lost to the competition); research into which dishes and wines 'travel well'. Occasional food poisoning scares mean that food handling and hygiene must have high priority.

Airline catering is very tightly cost-controlled; but in *marine catering* priorities are different: for passengers and crews at sea, meals are the highlight of the day. Proportionately more money is spent on food at sea than in the air, so sea-cooks and chefs have greater opportunities for creative cooking, and therefore for getting good shore-based jobs later.

Victualling ships – ordering supplies for trips sometimes several months long – is another catering specialization. Work is done in shipping companies' offices. Previous large-scale catering experience is essential.

Institutional Management

The work This is management in non-profit-making, mainly residential establishments: halls of residence, hostels; the domestic side of hospitals; as well as, increasingly, in commercial conference and training centres. It also includes non-residential work: private school catering; meals-on-wheels; social service departments' day centres.

Managers may be called bursar, warden, domestic superintendent, institutional manager. Titles are arbitrary and do not indicate any particular level of responsibility, status or duties.

There are almost as many different types of 'institutions' as there are of hotels, and there is considerable overlap between catering and institutional management. The difference is one of emphasis and setting in which the work is done. Some jobs in institutional management have more in common with running a hotel – for example, running a large conference or management training centre – than with other institutional management jobs, in which residents' general well-being and emotional needs as well as their creature comforts have to be considered (such as old people's homes, where the job is part catering, part social work).

An *institutional manager* may be wholly or partly responsible for all or some of the following aspects of community life: meals service; budgeting; purchase and maintenance of kitchen equipment; planning additional building; furnishings and decoration;

the use of the buildings for conferences or vacation courses; dealing with residents' and staff's suggestions and complaints; helping to establish a friendly atmosphere both among staff and among residents; in small establishments, first aid and home-nursing (but *not* responsibility for sick residents); acting as host and as general information bureau; dealing with committees.

Most jobs are entirely administrative, but in small institutions the manager occasionally has to help out with housework or cooking. Many (by no means all) jobs are residential; accommodation varies from bedsitter to self-contained flat for couples (with partner not necessarily working in the organization concerned).

Assistant institutional managers – often means housekeepers – are usually beginners seeking experience or those unwilling or unable to take the more responsible jobs, but in large organizations, especially hospitals, it is a step on the ladder.

*

Training

The main choice is between a full-time pre-entry course and training on the job with or without part-time study. What used to be a somewhat haphazard training scene has been restructured to provide a continuum of qualifications from practical and craft skills through to management. Most are divided up into units or modules which can be studied or trained for one at a time and eventually built up into a whole qualification. Most qualifications can be studied for in a variety of ways – full time, part time, by distance-learning – although availability of particular courses varies from district to district.

Pre-entry courses

For general information on City and Guilds and BTEC/SCOTVEC see pp. xxi, xxii.

City and Guilds General Catering Certificate (1 year full time).

City and Guilds specialist craft courses in food or beverage service, accommodation services, hotel reception, cooking. No set entry requirements. The City and Guilds Specific Skills Scheme is for people not wishing to take a full craft course.

BTEC First courses in Hotel and Catering Studies. Compulsory core subjects: introduction to the industry, introduction to food preparation and service; the clean environment.

BTEC National Diploma in Hotel, Catering and Institutional Operations. The core subjects are: the hotel and catering industry; hotel and catering in context; administration; people at work; applied science; purchasing, costing and finance. Students also learn practical skills in accommodation operations, food and drink service, food preparation and front office. They then choose options (as available) from the above, plus modern languages, marketing and tourism.

BTEC Higher National Diploma in Hotel, Catering and Institutional Management. The core subjects are: work organizations; the external environment; operational techniques and procedures; physical resource management; human resource management. Options (which vary from college to college) include accommodation management; applied nutrition; conference and banqueting management; licensed trade management; modern languages; sales and marketing; small business enterprise.

Degree courses: 3 years full time or a 4-year sandwich course. These vary in emphasis on differing catering aspects but include supervision of food and beverage preparation (and some practical work); catering management principles and practices; catering technologies (e.g. equipment and processes used in 'fast food' restaurants, 'systems catering'); specialist work such as airline catering; sales management and marketing; accounting; computer application; the various aspects of tourism; the implications of the growing recreation and leisure industries; international catering with an emphasis on languages.

HND and degree courses recognized by the Hotel, Catering and Institutional Management Associaiation (HCIMA) lead to membership of the Association without the need to take further examinations.

For graduates with either a relevant degree or comparable qualification, or any degree plus proof of interest in/experience of catering: 1-year full-time courses for post-graduate qualifications, including the HCIMA Professional Diploma (see below) for which a minimum of 1 year's relevant employment or work experience is required. There are also a few HCIMA Diploma courses for non-relevant degree holders.

Courses for people in relevant employment
City and Guilds and SCOTVEC courses (see above) by part-time study or block-release.

BTEC First Certificate or Diploma in Hotel and Catering Studies (see above).

BTEC National Certificate or Diploma (see above).

BTEC Higher National Certificate. Subjects covered as for Higher National Diploma above but with fewer options.

BTEC Continuing Education Certificate in Hospitality Management.

HCIMA Professional Certificate. Courses normally take 2 years part time or with block-release. Subjects studied are: food

and beverage operations, accommodation operations, human resource organization; business, accounting and introduction to
law; sales and marketing. Students need to be either currently
working in appropriate employment or have had 2 years' employment in the industry previously, including some supervisory experience. They need to show they are capable of succeeding on the
course by having either 4 GCSEs A–C (or equivalent) or other
catering qualifications.

HCIMA Professional Diploma. Mainly for those currently
holding a responsible post in the industry. Students should hold
either the HCIMA Professional Certificate or BTEC National
Diploma/SCOTVEC National Certificate or other recognized
qualification. Courses normally take 2 years part time or with
block-release. (Some full-time courses available, see above.) The
management subjects covered are: food and beverages; accommodation; human resources; finance; marketing and operations.

It is also possible to gain nationally recognized qualifications
for practical skills as they are learnt by being tested in the
workplace through the Caterbase Scheme. The combination of
Caterbase assessment and the relevant City and Guilds Specific
Skills test adds up to an NVQ (see p. xx).

Licensed trade: in addition to relevant City and Guilds and
BTEC awards, training and qualifications are also offered by the
Brewers Society and the British Institute of Innkeeping (for staff
of public houses) and the Wine and Spirit Education Trust (for
those in the wine and spirit trade).

Personal attributes

For all catering (in varying degrees): organizing and administrative
ability; outgoing personality; ability to motivate staff and to
communicate with all types of people – from kitchen porters to
managing directors, from salespeople to a coachload of pensioners; interest in people and in their creature comforts; some practical skills; ability to work under pressure; stamina; flexibility; tact
when dealing with 'difficult' customers; sense of humour. *For
freelance cooks*: as above, plus business acumen. See also 'Hotels'.

Late start

No problem. Admission to courses depends on experience and
motivation rather than age and GCSEs.

Career-break

No problem in institutional management for people who can live
in and/or work irregular hours; nor in industrial and schools
catering. Many women set up their own small-scale catering
businesses: for example, providing local firms with midday snacks,
etc. (see WORKING FOR ONESELF, p. 557). Refresher training is possible.

Part time   Half the workforce is part time, but there are still very limited opportunities at management level. Opportunities exist in cooking, housekeeping and junior reception, and freelance catering offers possibilities.

Position of women   Although hotel management has traditionally been a man's world, women are steadily coming through the ranks and there is currently a woman manager of one of Britain's top hotels. But to do really well women must, like men, be mobile: companies say that the reason for not promoting more women is that more women than men are unwilling to gain varied experience by moving around the country.

Women chefs are still rare in certain kinds of upmarket restaurants, but some highly talented women chefs own and run their own establishments. Elsewhere women have similar opportunities to men.

In industrial catering, women have equal chances at all management levels and are, in fact, encouraged to move up the management ladder. Just over half of managers are women. In hospitals, institutional-management-trained women have top jobs in domestic management, but top catering officers – concerned with food and drink, not housekeeping – are more frequently men. About 70% of schools and institutional catering managers are women. The fact that women do hold large-scale catering management jobs in some areas shows that it is only tradition which has kept them out of other catering management areas.

Further information   The Hotel, Catering and Institutional Management Association, 191 Trinity Road, Tooting, London SW17 7HN

Hotel and Catering Training Board, International House, High Street, Ealing, London W5 5DB

Brewers Society Training Centres Ltd, 42 Portman Square, London W1R 0BB

Scottish Licensed Trade Association, 10 Walker Street, Edinburgh EH3 7LA

British Institute of Innkeeping, 121 London Road, Camberley, Surrey GU15 3LF

Wine and Spirit Education Trust Ltd, Thames House, Queen Street Place, London EC4V 3AJ

Related careers   DIETETICS – SCIENCE: *Food Science and Technology* – HOME ECONOMICS – TEACHING – TRAVEL AGENT/TOUR OPERATOR

Chartered Secretary and Administrator

Entry qualifications

None laid down for entry to Foundation Programme of Institute of Chartered Secretaries and Administrators, but must be 17 or over. Exemptions for graduates and BTEC Higher award holders (see 'Training', below).

The work

This has nothing to do with personal secretarial work (see SECRETARIAL AND CLERICAL WORK, p. 462). Instead, it is general administration and management in both public and private sectors. In the past general managers were generally called administrators in local government and other public service organizations, while their counterparts in industry and commerce were called managers. Now that 'management' has become a crucial function in public service, titles are often interchangeable. Professional administration can be one of the specialist activities carried out in the public service or in industry and commerce. The largest proportions of students are in local government, financial services and service industries.

The main element in professional administration, wherever it is carried out, is coordinating (and possibly also controlling) various individuals and/or departments within an organization. Administrators are generalists who co-ordinate the activities of specialists. They form a link between people and their separate activities; they make sure that different sections or departments dovetail, and fit into the whole. Increased use of information technology in all organizations means they need a good grasp of information systems – how they work and what they can do. At senior level, administrators have an 'overview' over whatever their organization does; at junior level, they may, for example, co-ordinate the work of the accounts department; at middle level they ensure that, for example, production, distribution and personnel departments are informed of each other's needs. Professional administrators often work for a time in the various departments, to find out how each works and where it fits into the whole. Like other professional qualifications, professional administration can lead to the top in whatever the type of organization. The work is immensely varied, and so are the top jobs. Senior administrators may be involved in the choice and design of complicated computer systems aimed at improved decision-taking by top managers.

Qualified chartered secretaries can become company secretaries: public companies are by law required to have company secretaries, i.e. people who have either a legal, an accountancy or the ICSA qualification. According to type and size of company, company secretaries can be chief executives – possibly called director, or secretary-general – responsible only to the Board or whoever are the policy-makers; or they can be the chief administrative officer responsible to the director or chief executive. The ICSA examination is now the professional qualification for administrators in local government (see p. 268).

As it is an adaptable qualification, chartered secretaries have a wide choice of jobs.

Training The Institute's examinations consist of 3 programmes; Foundation, Pre-professional and Professional, all made up of modules. The first two programmes give a broad business education, covering law, accounting, information systems, organizations and personnel. The Professional Programme includes more practical and applied studies, with modules on principles and policy of management, meetings, company law and management of systems. In addition students choose a job-related stream (4 modules): financial, company secretarial, pension fund, or local government administration and management.

Study can be full time or part time, by correspondence course or distance learning. Typically, students take 4 modules a year. Graduates in any discipline are exempt from the first 2 programmes, so can qualify in 2 years. All students are expected to complete the examinations within 5 years. Holders of BTEC/ SCOTVEC Higher National awards start with the Pre-professional Programme or, in some cases, with the Professional Programme.

People with other professional qualifications may also be given some exemptions.

There is also a technician level course (30 weeks part time) for those employed in more junior positions, e.g. company secretarial assistants and share registration officers. Successful completion may lead to exemption from ICSA's Foundation Programme.

Personal attributes A flair for administration; common sense and good judgement; numeracy; interest in current affairs; tact; discretion.

Late start Good opportunities, especially now that access to ICSA examinations is 'open'. Over 70% of students are aged 21–35.

**Career-
break**   Should be no problem for people who had responsible jobs before
                 the break. Because of the flexible examination structure it is
                 possible for people to study while on a break. Reduced member-
                 ship rates are offered to mothers on a break. The 5-year qualifying
                 rule could be waived for women starting a family.

Part time   Fair possibilities, particularly in small firms. The Institute main-
                 tains a file for members wanting part-time or temporary jobs.

**Position
of
women**   Women are doing very well. About 30% of all Institute members
                 and 58% of its students are women. Many women who feel
                 trapped in secretarial roles are gaining this qualification as a
                 means of climbing the career ladder.

**Further
informa-
tion**   The Institute of Chartered Secretaries and Administrators, 16
                     Park Crescent, London W1N 4AH

**Related
careers**   ACCOUNTANCY – HEALTH SERVICES MANAGEMENT – SECRE-
                 TARIAL AND CLERICAL WORK

Chiropody
(Podology, Podiatry, Podiatric Medicine)

The profession is in the process of changing its title. The professional body, the Society of Chiropodists, remains the same for the time being because its title change requires Privy Council approval and that is a lengthy and expensive procedure. Relevant courses are, however, in Podology, Podiatry, Podiatric Medicine or Chiropody.

Entry qualifications
Minimum age 18. 2 A-levels and 3 GCSEs (A–C) (or equivalent), including at least 1 science at either level, or Access course (see p. xxxi).

The work
Chiropodists diagnose and treat foot diseases and functional and constitutional foot disorders; they inspect children's and adults' feet to prevent minor ailments from growing into major ones. When patients need their shoes adapted, chiropodists give the necessary instructions to surgical shoemakers or shoe-repairers; they also construct special appliances themselves. Chiropodists can choose the environment in which to work:

1. *Private practice*: This is the most remunerative work and scope is growing. Chiropodists may practise in their own homes and, occasionally, visit patients in their homes. Private practice can be lonely work (even though patients are seen all day) but group practices are now being set up in some areas, partners renting premises jointly or using rooms in one of the partners' homes as a surgery.

2. *Hospitals and health authority clinics*: Chiropodists are employed on a session (3-hourly) basis, part or full time.

3. *Industry*: Firms where staff are on their feet all day often employ full-time or part-time chiropodists.

In both (2) and (3) chiropodists enjoy the companionship and social facilities of a large organization. Some combine part-time work with private practice, to have a small regular income which supplements private practice income.

There is a shortage of chiropodists in some areas, largely because of the increased numbers of elderly people needing treatment. For opportunities in the EC see p. li.

Training   This is changing. Traditional diplomas are being replaced by degrees (last diploma courses started in 1991). Only graduates will in future be eligible for State Registration, which is essential for all public and most private sector jobs, and for membership of the Society of Chiropodists. All courses are inspected by the Board of Chiropodists of the Council for Professions Supplementary to Medicine. Two-thirds of the course must be practical and include treatment of patients under supervision. Theory includes the life sciences, anatomy, physiology, some basic medicine and surgery, and local anaesthesia. Courses are at schools attached to higher education institutions.

Courses which, as from 1992, do not lead to degrees, do not lead to State Registration and Membership of the Society of Chiropodists. All recognized courses last at least 3 years, full time. In contrast to diploma courses which qualified students only for discretionary grants (see p. xxvi), degree courses now qualify students for mandatory grants.

Personal attributes   A high degree of manual dexterity; ability to get on with people greatly enhances chances of promotion and of having a flourishing private practice. However, unlike many other careers with patients, shy, retiring people may get on well, providing they are even-tempered.

Late start   Good opportunities, with some relaxations in entry requirements. 20% of entrants are over 25.

Career-break   No problem if kept up with developments. *Ad hoc* arrangements with 1 month *refresher* courses can be made.

Part time   Ample scope for work (although not for promotion), no part-time training. Job-sharing possible.

Position of women   At present, 65% of practising chiropodists and 75% of students are women. Proportionately there are more men than women in senior jobs and in private practice.

Further information   The Society of Chiropodists, 53 Welbeck Street, London W1M 7HE

Related careers   NURSING – PHYSIOTHERAPY

Civil Aviation

Air Traffic Control Officer

Entry qualifications

Study to A-level standard of 2 subjects (preferably maths, geography or science) and 3 GCSEs (A–C). Must include English language and maths at either level. Graduates or people with other qualifications welcomed.

The work

Teams of ATCOs control and monitor the movements of aircraft taking off, landing and when *en route* in designated controlled airspace. An aircraft leaving a controller's area of responsibility is co-ordinated with the next ATC unit, which may be an airfield or an air traffic control centre in the UK or in Europe. Pilots of aircraft are, in fact, in 2-way radio communication with controllers from the time they request permission to start engines until the engines stop at their destination.

The work is responsible and highly skilled: it may involve the safe 'stacking' of aircraft in an airfield's 'holding area' while awaiting approach; the 'sequencing' of aircraft using radar to maintain a safe distance between them, and ensuring that aircraft flying the same routes at varying speeds, heights and directions are always safely separated horizontally and vertically. ATCOs use computers in their calculations. After gaining operational experience, a small proportion of ATCOs specialize in ATC computer work.

ATCOs spend most of their time – normally wearing earphones – monitoring data about relevant aircraft, either looking at a radar display unit or out over an airfield. The international language of ATC is English, so UK ATCOs talk and are talked to in their own language. Foreign pilots sometimes have problems expressing themselves clearly, especially when under pressure. Although ATCOs must make quick decisions, they can ask pilots to repeat anything which is not quite clear.

The great majority of operational ATCOs work shift duties, and all ATCOs must be prepared to do so; as far as possible shifts are planned well in advance, but last-minute changes are sometimes necessary.

Training Cadets (trainee ATCOs) follow an initial 72 week course for their air traffic control licence. This consists of periods of academic and simulation training at the College of Air Traffic Control near Bournemouth, with some periods of practical training at operational units. Training is given in all aspects of ATC, and in basic meteorology, navigation, telecommunications and principles of radar and associated techniques; an 'introduction to flying' course is also given in which cadets normally reach 'solo' standard.

Personal attributes Good eyesight (including normal colour vision) and high level of physical fitness; a calm cool temperament; ability to conceal and control excitement in emergencies; ability to concentrate both in busy and in quiet periods; a good quick brain, with quick reactions and the ability to be decisive; the ability to work as part of a team.

Late start Normal maximum age 26; with substantial relevant experience, this is raised to 34. Suitable applicants may be offered deferred entry so that they can complete a professional training or a degree course before joining the service.

Career-break Re-training could in theory be given to people who have left ATC and wish to return; the number who have done so is tiny.

Part time None.

Position of women The number of women who apply for ATCO posts is increasing. In 1991, 10% of qualified ATCOs, but 19% of new cadets, were women.

Further information Civil Aviation Authority Personnel Services, Room T1, Gate 3, CAA House, 45–59 Kingsway, London WC2B 6TE

NOTE: Air Traffic Control Assistants (ATCAs) assist ATCOs in their tasks by undertaking certain routine functions, particularly with data preparation and display, at both airfields and airways control centres. In the past they have been recruited at minimum age 17 with 4 GCSEs (A–C) or substantial flying experience. However, since many of their tasks have been automated, fewer ATCAs are now needed. Recruitment is done as required. Some cadets who fail their training are offered posts as ATCAs.

Air Traffic Engineering Cadetships
About 30 cadets with entry qualifications of at least BTEC/
SCOTVEC National Diploma in Electronics and Communications and preferably GCSE (A–C) in English undertake a 1-year
full-time training course at the Authority's College of Telecommunications Engineering, Bletchley, Bucks, on sophisticated electronic navigational aids and radar equipment. Successful completion of training leads to a career as an Air Traffic Engineer at the
CAA's National Air Traffic Service units throughout the United
Kingdom.

Cabin Crew (Stewardess and Steward)

Entry qualifications

Minimum age usually 20. Upper age limit for trainees about 34.
Minimum height requirements vary between airlines. No set educational qualifications, but good GCSE standard, preferably including English and maths, and conversational ability in a foreign
language. Some catering or nursing experience, or minimum 1
year in a responsible job which involved dealing with people, e.g.
in a travel agency.

The work

The cabin crew welcome passengers, supervise seating and safety-belt arrangements, and look after air-sick travellers, babies, and
children travelling alone. Stewards and stewardesses serve meals
(but do not cook them), and sell drinks, cigarettes, etc. in a
variety of currencies.

They 'dress the plane' to see that blankets, head-rests, magazines, cosmetics, etc. are available and in good order, and make
necessary announcements over the public-address system. They
deal with any emergencies and write reports after each flight, with
comments, for instance, on the behaviour of unaccompanied children.

Most of the time cabin crews are airborne waiters and waitresses. From the moment the plane is airborne they are continuously busy, working at great speed in a confined space.

Duty hours vary from one airline to another and are likely to
be changed at the last minute because of weather and other
'exigencies of the service'. Normally on European routes cabin
crews are 'on' for 4–6 days with a good deal of night duty; they
are then off-duty for 2–4 days. On long-distance trips they may be
away from home for 3 weeks, but that would include several days'
rest at a foreign airport.

The farther the destination, the more chance of sightseeing. On
short routes cabin crews may fly backwards and forwards for a
month without seeing more than the airport at their destination.

On long-distance trips crews often change planes at 'slip-points' and stay for a few days' rest, living in luxury hotels at their airline's expense.

British-trained crews are in demand by American and other foreign airlines if they speak the appropriate language.

Training   About 6 weeks with Europe-only airlines to about 8 with transatlantic ones. Subjects include meal-service, first aid, documentation, airborne procedure, foreign currency exchange, emergency drill with swimming-pool lesson in the use of the inflatable dinghy and life-jacket, practical fire drills, customer service, grooming and deportment.

Personal attributes   A likeable personality; calmness in crises; common sense; efficiency; sensitivity to anxious passengers' needs; well-groomed appearance.

Position of women   See p. 121.

Further information   Individual airlines.

Ground Staff
(some examples)

Passenger Service Assistant/Agent
(titles vary)

Entry qualifications   Usually good GCSE-standard English, maths, geography and foreign language. Minimum age usually 18.

The work   Passenger service assistants see that passengers and luggage get on to the right plane, with the minimum of fuss. They check-in luggage, which involves checking travel documents, and check-out passengers at boarding gates. They answer passengers' questions on travel connections and similar matters.

Other duties carried out by experienced PSAs include: load-control – preparing information for aircraft loaders on luggage weight; cargo documentation for customs clearance; checking that planes leave with the right meals, cargo, baggage.

PSAs work in uniform, and do shift work. They move about the airport all day, rarely sit down.

Training   Several weeks' induction and on-the-job training.

Sales Staff
(titles vary)

Entry qualifications   Usually good GCSE-standard English, maths, geography, a foreign language.

The work   Sales staff sit in airport and city offices and answer questions on international flight connections; make fare calculations (in various currencies); sell tickets over the counter and over the phone. Bookings are made to and from all over the world; each reservation must be related to reservations made elsewhere and reservation vacancies available for any particular flight at any given moment. This is called 'space control'. Reservations staff use computerized information systems: at the push of a button they can see, on their computer terminal, exactly what the present reservation situation is on any flight of their airline.

Senior sales staff may call on travel agents, business houses and other important customers to explain ancillary services such as car hire, hotel accommodation, package holidays, and 'sell' their own particular airline, both passenger and cargo services.

Sales staff may do shift work, though less so in senior positions.

Training   Short on-the-job training with some lectures.

Personal attributes   For all 'public contact' jobs: an orderly mind; communication skills; a liking for meeting many people very briefly; a calm, helpful manner; good speech and appearance.

Position of women   See p. 121.

Commercial Management, Flight Operations and Flight Planning

Entry qualifications

Vary with different airlines and according to supply and demand. Some promotion from sales staff; most entrants have A-levels; many have degrees or BTEC/SCOTVEC HND in Business Studies (see pp. xxi, xxii).

The work

The administration of flight programmes, which cover many thousands of flight-miles, millions of tons of freight and ever-growing 'passenger throughput', is a highly complex undertaking. Staff organize the airline's fleet of planes over its network, making the most efficient use of each aircraft, e.g. ensuring that as far as possible outgoing freight is replaced with return-flight freight, and that the 'turn-round' time in airports is as short as possible, while allowing time for maintenance, loading, etc. 'Aircrew management' involves arranging individual crew members' schedules, taking into consideration maximum flying hours allowed; rest-days ('stop overs') abroad, etc.

Apart from this planning work, staff are also responsible for ensuring that at all times aircrew have all the information they need before each take-off, throughout the planned itinerary. This involves discussions with a variety of departments and individuals; keeping detailed records; being prepared for emergencies.

Training

Through airlines' own training schemes, lasting 2 to 3 years, or BTEC/SCOTVEC Higher awards or degree, followed by shorter airline training. Schemes vary between companies and according to expansion or contraction of airline industry.

Personal attributes

Drive; organizing ability; liking for working under pressure.

Late start

Good opportunities for cabin crew, passenger service assistants and sales staff (see 'Entry qualifications', above).

Career-break

Possible, but depends on vacancy situation. Also, returners have to start again with basic training.

Part time

Possible in some jobs, for example cabin crew, passenger services, but this affects promotion. Also some short-term contracts with 'package tour' companies for cabin crews.

**Position
of
women**

Air stewardesses and stewards are all 'cabin crew'; a woman is quite often in charge of an aircraft's cabin crew. *Ground staff* examples: traditionally mainly women, but more men joining. *Commercial management*: so far very few women have tried. Equal chances of promotion.

**Further
informa-
tion**

Individual airlines.

**Related
careers**

CATERING – LANGUAGES – TRAVEL AGENT / TOUR OPERATOR

Pilot

**Entry
qualifica-
tions**

None is laid down by the Civil Aviation Authority for the Commercial Pilot's licence, but 5 GCSEs (A–C) including English, maths and a science are preferred. Sponsoring organizations normally specify higher qualifications: for example, British Airways Cadet Scheme requires 5 GCSEs (A–C), including English language, maths and a science, and 2 A-levels (preferably maths and physics).

The work

The pilot's most taxing task is assimilating a mass of separate bits of information presented by an array of indicators on the instrument panel and by colleagues, to 'process' all this in the mind, and to take whatever action may be necessary. Procedures during the flight and specially during take-off and landing are complex enough, but what makes pilots' jobs so arduous is the fact that they must at all times be prepared for the unexpected. Instrument failure may require the pilot instantly to override the computerized equipment's instructions and perhaps take evasive action to avoid a mid-air collision. Though individual pilots may never have to cope with such 'incidents', they must be ready and able to do so.

In an airline, the first job is as *co-pilot*. Promotion to *captain*, which is not automatic, would come about half-way through a pilot's career. The captain has total responsibility for the aircraft, crew and passengers. *Navigators* are no longer employed, and *flight engineers* not on all aircraft: the pilot must in any case be able to perform navigating and engineering tasks.

Work starts at least an hour before take-off, studying the detailed flight plan. This gives such information as exact height at various stages on the precisely defined route; meteorological information; take-off and landing weights which are vital data in case of emergency action.

On 'short hauls' (in Europe) pilot and crew are busy all the time. On long hauls there can be long hours with only routine checks to go through. This can be difficult in an unexpected way: pilots get bored, because there is no real work to do, yet the need for alertness is as great as ever.

UK pilots are increasingly working in Europe. There is some small demand for other types of pilots (plane or helicopter): on air taxis; crop spraying; aerial photography; oil rig supplying; weather and traffic observation; flying privately- or company-owned planes and helicopters, and especially for instructors in flying clubs.

Training

Fixed wing – i.e. planes

The overwhelming majority of students at the recognized air training schools are sponsored; the major sponsor of pilots in the UK at present is British Airways.

Basic training lasts at least 12 months (the BA scheme lasts 16 months). The syllabus includes aerodynamics, meteorology, electrical engineering and electronics, aircraft design and systems, flight procedures and aviation law. Flight training is carried out both in aircraft and in simulators.

The first qualification is the Commercial Pilot's Licence (CPL), but to fly in an airliner as co-pilot the basic requirement is the CPL plus Instrument Rating. Ratings are qualifications in particular aspects of flying and in flying particular types of aircraft; the type of aircraft a CPL holder may co-pilot depends on individual Ratings. To become qualified as captain of an airliner a pilot must have the Airline Transport Pilot's Licence (ATPL) and many thousands of flying hours.

Full-time, non-sponsored training to CPL costs about £42,000 but many people now qualify by first getting a Private Pilot's Licence (PPL). They then gain sufficient hours to take an Instructor's Course; as Instructors they are paid and they can accumulate the 700 hours' flying-time necessary to qualify for exemption from the full-length, full-time CPL training. This roundabout way of qualifying is very much cheaper and can be done while, most of the time, earning a living in part-time employment.

Helicopter

At present most commercial helicopter pilots are recruited from the Services, where they are trained while holding a short service or similar commission. Commercial operators run sponsorship schemes from time to time to provide co-pilots, because a current worldwide pilot shortage is attracting many experienced ones to the airlines. It is difficult to predict how long this, or any, pilot-recruiting situation will last.

Personal attributes   Above-average intelligence; ability to fight boredom and be alert at all times; mental agility; high standard of fitness; self-confidence; leadership qualities; ability to take instant decisions; total unflappability; very well-balanced personality.

Late start   30% of newly qualified pilots are late entrants (see 'Training', above), but there are upper age limits to airline sponsorship schemes.

Career-break   Should be possible as all pilots need retraining throughout their career.

Part time   Should be possible, but hours often irregular.

Position of women   Only about 1% of pilots are women. Once trained they have no greater difficulty getting work (outside large airlines) than men. The recent shortage of trained pilots has provided better opportunities for women; for example, the sponsorship schemes are open to women as well as men. British Airways employs about 30 women pilots. The British Women Pilots Association has over 300 members and helps with advice and (small) scholarships.

There are now one or two women helicopter pilots: up until now, as the Services have not trained them, their only avenue has been through commercial sponsorships or by paying for the training themselves (current cost around £40,000).

NOTE: The RAF (see p. 53) is now training women pilots.

Further information   Aviation Training Association, 125 London Road, High Wycombe, Bucks HP11 1BT

British Helicopter Advisory Board, Building C2, West Entrance, Fairoaks Airport, Chobham, Woking, Surrey GU24 8HX

British Women Pilots Association, Rochester Airport, Rochester, Kent ME5 9SD

Civil Aviation Authority, Flight Crew Licensing, Aviation House, South Area, Gatwick Airport, Gatwick, West Sussex RH6 0YR (licensing inquiries only)

| **Related careers** | *Air Traffic Control Officer* (*see above*) – ENGINEERING – SUR- VEYING |

Civil Service

The Civil Service exists to administer the business of the government. This covers a vast range of activity from defence procurement to the issue of driving licences, and the Civil Service is one of the largest employers in the country with more than half a million staff. Staff work in about 60 government departments and executive agencies throughout the country; about 20% of civil servants work in London.

Opportunities exist at all educational levels. There is a strong tradition of and commitment to training to enable staff to function effectively and progress up a well-defined career structure. Training may be on the job, at the Civil Service College or on outside courses as appropriate, and may cover anything from time management to print buying to the most up-to-the-minute computer techniques.

Over the last few years the Civil Service has been undergoing major changes with far-reaching developments still taking place. The aim is to make the Civil Service more efficient, businesslike and responsive.

Although by definition the Civil Service is an administrative organization and its careers in administration are well recognized, within its vast and varied structure it offers opportunities in virtually every career area. Approaching half of its staff are specialists, some of whom were recruited after their specialist training, while others were given the opportunity to acquire specialist qualifications after joining the Civil Service. There are also increasing opportunities for mature entrants and job changers, at all levels.

The work of government departments – and their staff at all levels – is immensely varied. It affects virtually every aspect of modern life – health, education, the environment, transport, agriculture, defence, foreign affairs, social security, energy policy, taxation and so on. These broad headings cover a vast and complex range of activities and concerns of which it is possible here to give only a few examples.

The Ministry of Agriculture, Fisheries and Food offers opportunities for senior staff to participate in meetings in Brussels on the development, negotiation and implementation of EC agricultural policy, but it is also responsible for the management of sea fisheries and consumer protection. The Department of Trade and Industry has had a key role in preparing British business and industry for the opening of European markets in 1992. The Ministry of Defence is one of the largest consumers of the products of British industry with vast annual expenditure to manage. In the Gulf War of 1991 it had the awesome task of supplying and arming tens of thousands of British troops, thousands of miles from the UK. It is also responsible for the Meteorological Office. In the Home Office staff might be concerned with the administration of prison management and reform or with how the Data Protection Act is working. The Scottish and Welsh Offices, with their regional responsibilities, embrace a range of activities handled by different departments elsewhere, e.g. education, agriculture and fisheries, transport, health.

Across all departments and levels there is a broad spectrum of functions, both strategic and operational. Some civil servants advise ministers; others deal direct with members of the public; some research the implications of policy options; others provide support services in, for example, computer operations, personnel, finance or general support work.

Civil servants face similar pressures to those in industry, and the work is no less stimulating. Efforts continue to make the Civil Service more 'businesslike' with all the demands and satisfactions for its staff which that implies. Management is increasingly decentralized, allowing more flexibility in decision-making and managing budgets and staff. Increasing numbers of civil servants now find themselves working in 'executive agencies' which operate like businesses under a Chief Executive who is set financial and quality of service targets and given the financial and management freedom to pursue them. The idea is to make managers more accountable and visible and for the new ethos to filter down through the staff, with financial rewards for outstanding performance.

Administration

Administration Trainees
(The Fast Stream)

Maximum age 26, but older candidates with appropriate qualifications and experience can enter the fast stream as Higher Executive Officers (Development).

Entry qualifications

A first- or second-class honours degree in any subject. Arts graduates have traditionally predominated in the higher grades of the Civil Service, but science, technology and business graduates are particularly welcome as the Civil Service recognizes the need for relevant, expert knowledge in high-level administration. There is a shortage of top-quality applicants, especially those with science and technology degrees.

Method of entry and training

An annual recruitment scheme is organized by the Recruitment and Assessment Services Agency. Candidates undergo a qualifying test and 2 days of written tests, group exercises and interviews conducted by the Civil Service Selection Board in London. Successful candidates are told the initial estimate of their potential at the time of selection; this assessment is progressvely revised. (Unsuccessful candidates may be offered a post as an Executive Officer without further interview.)

Applicants can state their preferences for particular departments or agencies during the selection process.

Successful Administration Trainees (and newly appointed HEO (D)s) spend 2–4 years (the first 2 of which are probationary) in this grade. During this time they will have several carefully selected 'postings' involving different types of work and 4–5 months of formal training at the Civil Service College. Throughout the trainee period ATs are supervised and their progress monitored.

Some ATs are given the opportunity to gain accountancy qualifications. Others, in the 'European Fast Stream', are helped to prepare for competitions for posts in European Community institutions.

The work

Senior civil servants are responsible, under ministers, for formulating and implementing the policy of the government of the day. As indicated above, the subject matter of the work varies considerably, but the work of civil servants at this level falls into several broad categories. It includes researching and analysing policy options; developing the organization and procedures necessary to translate policy objectives into practice; dealing with parliamentary business, including briefing ministers and drafting replies to Parliamentary questions; drafting legislation; dealing with operational matters affecting the day-to-day responsibilities of a department; working in a minister's Private Office. There is scope for liaison and negotiation at a senior level within and between departments, with outside organizations, and with foreign governments. The balance of tasks varies between different postings.

As mentioned above, the Civil Service is moving towards greater accountability and responsibility for individual managers. Ultimately, however, ministers make final decisions. These decisions (including the nuts and bolts of legislation) are made on the advice and recommendations of their civil servants, so there is a real opportunity to contribute to matters of national and international importance from an early stage of a fast-stream career. There is also considerable intellectual challenge in mastering complex issues and giving impartial advice, whatever one's own politics or those of the government of the day.

Fast-stream administrators are selected for their potential to reach the top grades of the Civil Service. For both ATs and HEO (D)s there is a probationary period of 2 years. After the successful completion of this period, ATs are normally promoted to Higher Executive Officer (Development). Further promotion is based on performance, which is regularly assessed against objectives; an HEO (D) performing to expectations could expect further promotion in 2–4 years. Fast-streamers who do not perform satisfactorily may have their appointments terminated or be offered an appointment in the main stream. Though those in the fast stream are recruited and trained for accelerated career development, they compete for promotion on merit against those who joined the Civil Service through other routes.

Personal attributes   High intelligence; capacity to grasp all issues involved in a problem, to weigh up facts, conflicting opinions and advice and to make a decision; ability to extract the main points from a mass of detail and to write balanced and concise reports; ability to hold and delegate authority; enjoyment of responsibility; the ability to manage both people and resources; the ability to communicate and work well with other people at all levels – junior staff, colleagues, outside organizations and ministers.

Executive Officers

Entry qualifications   2 A-levels and 3 GCSEs (A–C), including English language; *or* acceptable Scottish equivalents; *or* a good BTEC/SCOTVEC National award; *or* a degree. About 50% of entrants are graduates or have BTEC Higher awards.

Method of entry and training   Entry is by competitive tests and interview. Recruitment schemes may be organized individually by departments or agencies, or on their behalf by the Recruitment and Assessment Services Agency. For the latter candidates may state preferences for departments and/or location; these are met as far as possible.

The majority of training for executive officers is given on the job and may be supplemented by courses at the Civil Service College. There are also opportunities for more specialized training leading to external qualifications as appropriate (e.g. in account-ancy and computing). Many departments organize their own management development programmes for EOs.

The work   Executive officers are the first line of management in the Civil Service. Their role is more operational than strategic and is generally concerned with applying policy. The subject matter obviously varies a great deal from one department or agency to another, but executive officers may be involved in several broad types of work. In carrying out their duties EOs *manage staff and resources*, allocating, monitoring and controlling the team's work, motivating them and helping them to develop their potential. Many EOs *handle casework*, making decisions on the basis of often complex law, regulations and precedent. A major part of the work of many EOs involves *dealing with the public*; EOs are the civil servants who often have a public face and sometimes specific job title – as customs officers, immigration officers, rev-enue executives, in the Department of Employment or Department of Social Security. *General administrative duties* are an essential part of EOs' work and essential to the smooth running of a department or agency; they may include finance, personnel, estate management, purchasing and support for senior colleagues, includ-ing arranging meetings and writing reports.

Some EOs have more specialized responsibilities and are re-cruited and trained accordingly. Examples are the Immigration Service, Inland Revenue, Customs and Excise and the Diplomatic Service (see p. 131). There are also opportunities for EOs to train in accountancy (see p. 1) or information technology (see p. 142).

Successful EOs (there is annual appraisal) are promoted to Higher Executive Officer and Senior Executive Officer. After 2 years, however, EOs may be considered, along with graduate entrants, for selection to the 'fast stream' with prospects for accelerated promotion to the higher grades.

Personal attributes   Practical intelligence; organizing ability; enjoyment of a measure of responsibility; a liking for paper work and for dealing with people; ability to manage staff.

Administrative Officer

Entry qualifications

5 approved GCSEs (A–C), including English language; *or* a written test; *or* relevant previous experience. Many candidates have A-levels or a BTEC/SCOTVEC National award. Recruitment is usually carried out by departments or agencies advertising posts locally and at Jobcentres. The Recruitment and Assessment Services Agency also undertakes some recruitment on behalf of agencies and departments.

The work

Administrative officers are employed in most government departments and executive agencies. They do much the same wide range of jobs as office staff and administrative assistants in industry and commerce. They deal with incoming correspondence, see that it is distributed to those concerned, write letters or draft them for their manager, handle correspondence with and telephone inquiries from the public, assemble statistics and keep records, often on computer.

There is often more variety of work than in comparable jobs in a private firm. For example, in the Immigration Department of the Home Office, an administrative officer may deal with students visiting this country, with permits for employment, and with aliens whose residence permits have expired. Administrative officers may also interview the general public who call in for information or papers.

There are opportunities for promotion to executive officer. Administrative officers may be given day-release to study for appropriate examinations.

Personal attributes

Accuracy; reliability; a liking for desk work and for meeting the public. There is room both for good mixers and for those who prefer to work on their own.

Administrative Assistants

Entry qualifications

Either GCSE (A–C) in English language and one other subject; *or* a short test; *or* relevant previous experience. In practice most entrants have several GCSEs (A–C) or a BTEC/SCOTVEC National award. Recruitment is local.

The work

Administrative assistants do routine clerical work for administrative officers: filing, sorting, keeping records. They may also deal with inquiries from the public, and they may learn to use computers or electronic mail equipment. They are encouraged to take appropriate day-release classes and examinations. There are good prospects for promotion to administrative officer.

The Diplomatic Service

1. For Grade 8/7D, the fast stream, as for administration trainee. Any degree subject welcome. Linguistic aptitude is assessed as part of the selection process, but will not necessarily be the deciding factor, except possibly in borderline cases.

2. For Grade 9, mainstream entry, as for executive officer. The majority of successful applicants at this grade are graduates.

3. For Grade 10, clerical entry, as for administrative officer. Entrants must be at least 17 and under 20 on 1 January in the year in which they apply.

4. There is also a secretarial branch as well as occasional openings for research officers, economists, legal advisers, architects, surveyors, engineers and other specialist staff.

Staff spend about a third to a half of their career working at the Foreign and Commonwealth Office in London. For the remainder of their time they are serving overseas in any of the more than 160 countries with which the UK maintains diplomatic relations. During a working lifetime anything from 6 to 10 'tours' of 2–4 years each are spent working at British embassies, high commissions and other missions in a variety of countries. The willingness to serve anywhere in the world is, therefore, vital.

Work is very varied. In the course of their careers staff may work on trade promotion, political reporting and analysis (especially in the fast stream), consular services to British nationals living or travelling overseas, immigration work, aid administration, or personnel and financial management.

Promotion is generally on the basis of performance on the job. There are special competitions involving written tests and interviews to secure accelerated promotion or to transfer to the fast stream, where promotion is most rapid (though opportunities for promotion to senior levels exist for all entrants, including school-leavers).

The Diplomatic Service attaches great importance to proper training. New entrants at all levels usually undertake a short induction course which acquaints them with the organization and working of the service and its place in the machinery of government. Specialized job-related courses are arranged for staff who are going to take up jobs in, for example, commercial or consular work, and there are also courses designed to develop individual skills and potential, for example in management, effective speaking or international economics. The Diplomatic Service, not surprisingly, attaches great importance to language training. For some jobs full-time language training for up to 2 years is provided; all staff, even when it is not essential for their jobs, are encouraged to learn something of the local language and are entitled to at least 100 hours of free tuition. Language allowances are paid to staff who reach a certain level of proficiency. Diplomats can master several languages during their careers.

Personal attributes   Members of the Diplomatic Service must combine the skills of salespeople, political analysts and public relations officers. They must have a calm and reliable personality; a persuasive, confidence-inspiring manner; the ability to make friends easily and put down roots instantly; and the adaptability and resourcefulness to cope with the constant upheaval of moving from one place to another. The Diplomatic Service is not so much a job as a way of life. It demands balance, staying power, curiosity about the way other nations live and the confidence to put forward the British point of view.

Specialists and Professionals in the Civil Service

The Civil Service employs a wide range and substantial number of specialists and professionals. There are opportunities for those with considerable previous experience outside the Civil Service; the newly qualified; and those seeking opportunities to obtain professional qualifications.

The basic entry and training structures of these careers and their different functions and applications are discussed in detail in other sections of this book. This section looks at their roles within the Civil Service.

Scientists
(see SCIENCE, p. 435)

Scientists in the Civil Service may be involved in research and development; providing scientific services; statutory advisory and inspection duties; scientific contributions to the formulation of government policies. Within these broad areas of work is a vast range of activity and interest covering aspects of life as diverse as the food we eat, the air we breathe and the weapons that defend us.

For example, scientists in the Ministry of Agriculture study problems caused by animals, from insect damage to stored food-stuffs to bird collisions with aircraft. Others are concerned with food additives and the evaluation of new food products and processes, especially biotechnology. The Ministry of Defence's Chemical Defence Establishment carries out research to evaluate the hazard to the armed services of biological and chemical agents, work which gained widespread attention during the Gulf War. At the Royal Mint metallurgists and chemists control the composition of the coinage alloys at a number of stages in the manufacturing process. The Home Office maintains the Forensic Science Service, which provides the scientific backing to the search for criminal evidence, using sophisticated techniques to analyse a wide range of materials such as blood, fibres, glass, paint and soil. The National Physical Laboratory of the Department of Trade and Industry has developed spectroscopic techniques for the analysis of the atmosphere and carries on investigation into noise and its effect on hearing.

There are opportunities in most scientific disciplines, both major areas like chemistry, physics and computer science, and smaller, more specialized fields like animal nutrition, meteorology and plant pathology.

Entry qualifications

1. Science Management Training Scheme: first- or upper-second-class degree in relevant subject plus interest in and aptitude for senior science management. This is an accelerated promotion scheme to groom high-calibre scientists for a role in complex policy formulation and the management and implementation of those policies. Selection is by written and group exercises, tests and interviews.

2. Scientific Officer: a degree or BTEC/SCOTVEC Higher award in a relevant subject. Recruitment is carried out centrally and departmentally, regularly and as vacancies arise. All posts are advertised nationally, usually in *New Scientist*. Some departments offer sponsorship and sandwich placements to students.

3. Assistant Scientific Officer: 4 GCSEs (A–C) (or acceptable Scottish alternative), including English language and maths or a science. Preference may be given to those with a science *and* maths or with a relevant A-level. Recruitment is carried out locally as vacancies arise. There are opportunities for further study and promotion.

Engineers
(see ENGINEERING, p. 183)

There are opportunities for every type of engineer in the Civil Service. The Ministry of Defence has the greatest requirement, and for example needs engineers to design test software for combat simulators and develop improved helicopter rotor blades. At the Department of Transport, while civil engineers might design new roads and bridges and manage huge projects, electrical engineers develop computer-based traffic control systems. Department of the Environment engineers work in multi-disciplinary teams seeking an integrated approach to pollution control over a range of industries. Recent projects for the Property Services Agency's engineers have included the new British Library and the renovation of the Palm House at Kew Gardens.

Entry qualifications

1. Defence Engineering Service Fast Stream: a first- or upper-second-class degree in a relevant subject plus aptitude for management. This is an accelerated training and promotion scheme run by the Ministry of Defence to groom good graduates for the most senior posts in both engineering and general management. Selection is by written and group exercises, tests and interviews.

2. Graduate Engineer: honours degree in relevant subject. Relevant training leads to chartered status.

3. There are also opportunities for those with A-levels or Scottish Highers to be sponsored on a degree course, and for those with technician and craft qualifications to join an appropriate grade and obtain training for further qualifications and promotion.

Surveyors
(see SURVEYING, p. 502)

The majority of opportunities for surveyors in the Civil Service lie with four main departments. The Valuation Office is concerned with acquisitions and disposals, renewals, and rent reviews and valuations for capital gains tax. The Property Services Agency is the largest design and construction organization in the country with responsibility for conservation and restoration as well as new building. Surveyors in the Defence Estate Service are responsible for all the property owned by the Ministry of Defence, one of the largest landowners in the UK; there are also overseas projects to be managed. The Agricultural Development and Advisory Service offers advice, often as a chargeable service, to farmers, growers and landowners on all aspects of land and estate management. Smaller numbers of openings are available in other departments including the Department of Health, the Department of Education and Science, Ordnance Survey and National Museums. All types of surveyor are needed, but different departments have different requirements.

Entry qualifications
There are opportunities for qualified professionals; for graduate trainees; and, in the Property Services Agency, for *Cadet Valuers*. The latter must have at least 3 GCSEs (A–C) and 2 A-levels (subjects at either level to include English and maths) *or* a noncognate degree. Distance-learning and day-release courses plus practical training lead to professional qualification.

Economists
(see ECONOMICS, p. 180)

Economists work in about 20 government departments, analysing the economic implications of virtually every aspect of government policy. A key part of this work is the interpretation of economic and other statistics. In some departments, for example the Treasury, economists specialize; in others they apply economic principles to a variety of different situations.

Entry qualifications
A first- or second-class honours degree in economics or agricultural economics, or in a subject including major elements of these. There are also opportunities for graduates in other subjects to undertake post-graduate courses in economics.

Statisticians
(see SCIENCE, p. 448)

Across the range of government activity statisticians collect, analyse and interpret data on a variety of subjects and for a variety of purposes. Statistics on subjects as diverse as transport, health, education, trade and household expenditure are used both to shape and reflect policy and to inform industry, the academic world and the general public on aspects of modern life.

Entry qualifications
A good degree. Those who have at least a second-class degree which includes formal training in statistics are appointed as assistant statisticians. There is a special trainee scheme for those whose degrees are not in maths or statistics.

Press and Publicity

The Civil Service is one of the largest employers of press and public relations specialists. Overall their job is to explain government policies and measures to the public. This might involve advising a minister on dealing with the news media; planning a publicity and information campaign on, for example, drink-driving; organizing an exhibition to promote British trade overseas; working on a range of publications dealing with subjects as diverse as recruitment, overseas aid or detailed statistics on social trends. The Central Office of Information offers the greatest number of opportunities, but there are openings in most departments.

Entry qualifications There are openings both for new graduates and for experienced professionals.

Lawyers
(see LAW, p. 253)

Lawyers in government service have a great number of roles, many of which mirror work done in private practice and industry, some of which are unique to government. Lawyers have a key role in drafting legislation and assisting ministers in steering it through Parliament. They are also advisers on the formulation and implementation of policy. Many are involved in prosecution and litigation over, for example, serious VAT fraud. Lawyers working on the administration of justice might be advising on the discipline, conduct and welfare of the judiciary or settling cases before the European Court. There are also opportunities to advise on a range of matters concerning the Civil Service as a large organization – employment legislation, employee accidents at work, conveyancing and pay agreements.

Entry qualifications There are opportunities for both qualified lawyers and for graduates who wish to qualify through government service.

Architects
(see ARCHITECTURE, p. 42)

There are 2 main areas of work: advising ministers on the building aspects of policy and then putting policy into effect; and designing new buildings or project-managing the work of private contractors. Work embraces schools, hospitals, historic buildings and defence establishments.

Entry qualifications

There are opportunities both for fully qualified architects and for graduate trainees.

Accountants
(see ACCOUNTANCY, p. 1)

Accountants in the Civil Service are at the forefront of many developments designed to promote accountability and introduce financial management disciplines. They are also involved with government's dealings with industry and commerce and with tax matters.

Entry qualifications

There are openings for those with a professional accountancy qualification and opportunities for some administration trainees and executive officers to train and qualify as accountants.

Research Officers

Research officers study the impact of government policies and provide information on which policy is based. Most opportunities are with the Resource and Planning Research Group and the Social Sciences Research Group.

Entry qualifications

A first- or upper-second-class honours degree or post-graduate degree in an appropriate subject, e.g. geography, economics, social anthropology, psychology.

Information Systems and Technology

Computers are in widespread use throughout the Civil Service. Applications range from sophisticated weather forecasting and research into climatic change, through a new Home Office electronic photofit system to help catch offenders, to the Department of Education and Science's administration of the country's largest and most complex pension scheme (for teachers).

Entry qualifications

All levels and types of computer personnel are needed. Specialists are recruited, but there are also opportunities for executive officers to train in administrative computing.

*

Late start (Civil Service generally)

There is no upper age limit (except for a few schemes which involve long-term training). There are increasing opportunities for mature candidates, especially those with managerial, professional, technical or scientific qualifications and/or experience. There is a fast-stream administrators' recruitment scheme for experienced managers and professionals.

Career-break

Formal career-break schemes of up to 5 years are available to all staff. Many include 'keep in touch' programmes. It is also possible for former staff with a good track record to apply at any time after resigning for reinstatement in the same grade and at the same salary level as when they left.

Part time

See 'Position of women'.

Position of women

Since 1984 the Civil Service has had a programme of action to promote equality of opportunity for women. It has been a pioneer among employers in developing a range of measures such as career-breaks, part-time working, job-share, childcare and keep-in-touch schemes. (These are not exclusive to women employees.)

In 1989/90 women represented 58% of all new entrants to the Civil Service. The majority are in the administrative grades; 66% of administrative officers and 73% of administrative assistants are women. The percentages of women at middle and senior management grade levels seem still to be relatively small, but must be looked at in the context of the rate of improvement and the age profile of the grades. In the last 6 years the percentage of women at the most senior levels (grades 1–3), where the pyramid really narrows, has increased from 4% to $6\frac{1}{2}$%. Civil servants are normally well into their forties by the time they reach this stage, so will have embarked on their careers *before* equal opportunities legislation, initiatives to help women take advantage of the opportunities, and high education and career expectations for girls. The women who reach these grades at present actually do so earlier than do men: 20% of women in grades 1–3 are under 45, while only $14\frac{1}{2}$% of men are.

Slightly lower down the career structure, where younger women can be expected to have been more influenced by the factors mentioned above, the percentages are higher. In the same period, in grades 4–7 the percentage of women went up from 7% to nearly 12%, i.e. more than 60%. Administration trainees, who are selected and groomed for rapid promotion to senior levels, show an encouraging trend: in 1980 only 20% of ATs were women; in 1986 the figure was 27%, and in 1989 it had increased to 43%.

The Civil Service is continuing to look at other, perhaps less immediately obvious, barriers to women. Some years ago it did away with upper age limits for most categories of entrants; these were seen to discriminate against women who had given time to domestic commitments. Now it is reducing the 'seniority' (the term used to indicate how long a member of staff has remained in a particular grade) needed to get promotion. Women are also encouraged to be more assertive and career-minded by, for example, asking for 'hard'or 'crunchy' (Civil Service jargon) jobs, e.g. finance rather than personnel. Getting as wide a range of experience as men is bound to stand them in good stead at promotion boards.

The number of staff working part time has more than doubled in the last 6 years: 6% of all staff, 12% of women, work part time. This includes staff at all levels. The highest-graded job-share, at the time of going to press, was at grade 5, and the highest-level part-timers at grade 3. 12% of women at grade 7, and 10% at grade 5, work part time.

| **Further information** | Graduate and Schools Liaison Section, Room 1003, Office of the Civil Service Commissioners, Alencon Link, Basingstoke, Hants. RG21 1JB |

| **Related careers** | *See those mentioned in the text* – LOCAL GOVERNMENT |

Commodity Markets

Entry qualifications

None rigidly laid down, but at least GCSEs (A–C) in English and maths normally expected. Graduates also compete for jobs.

The work

London is a leading commodity trading centre through which raw materials are bought and sold. The principal markets are: London Futures and Option Exchange (coffee, cocoa, sugar) known as the London Fox (formerly London Commodity Exchange); London Metal Exchange (non-ferrous metals); International Petroleum Exchange (oil); Grain and Feed Trade Association (agricultural produce); Baltic International Freight Futures Exchange (shipping freight); London International Financial Futures Exchange (bonds and currencies). Firms act as brokers, matching producers who want to sell and consumers who want to buy. Only a small proportion of the actual goods traded are imported into the UK; most are passing between other countries. This is called the *physical* trade, because it concerns actual goods. Some commodities also have *futures* (or *terminal*) markets where standard 'lots' of a commodity can be bought or sold for delivery several months ahead. This helps both buyer and seller: a producer who has not yet harvested the crop is given a guaranteed price for it in advance, while the consumer/manufacturer can buy raw materials in advance at a known price. This method of reducing price risk is called 'hedging'. The 'futures' market is also used by speculators who neither produce nor use the commodity, but aim to make a profit by anticipating price fluctuations and buying and selling at what they hope is the right time. Increasing use of technology means physical trading is no longer carried out on the floor, but directly between offices. However, futures trading is still carried on by an 'open outcry' system between dealers on the market floor acting on their firms' instructions.

Jobs in the Commodity Markets

Numbers employed are small. Physical trading needs people with good knowledge of the particular commodity, finance, shipping, documentation and insurance. Staff tend to stay with one firm and either specialize in dealing or work their way up to more senior advisory posts. Futures dealing is more like the Stock Exchange or currency markets, where energy and flair are more important than background knowledge. *Futures dealers* are more likely to move from firm to firm for promotion. *Research staff* (like investment analysts) collect and analyse data with which to brief the brokers. They study information on climatic, political and economic conditions, gluts, shortages, price trends and market movements all over the world.

Training
Training is mainly on the job. There are no pre-entry training courses for the commodities markets. Internal training schemes are tailored to fit new entrants, who take one of the growing number of courses run by individual firms, trade associations and colleges. All staff, whether school leavers or graduates, spend time in different departments, for example shipping, insurance, financial control, before specializing.

Personal attributes
Mainly for dealing: entrepreneurial instinct and willingness to take risks; flair for figures; extrovert personality; ability to communicate easily on the telephone, personally and in writing; mental agility; quick-wittedness; high powers of concentration; exceptional self-confidence; memory for people and figures.

Late start
Only with professional qualifications in, for example, accountancy, economics, computing and general management.

Career-break
Would present problems in trading areas. Possible in research, analysis, computing and management areas.

Part time
Unlikely on trading side.

Position of women
The City may still seem a very male preserve, but opportunities are increasing for women willing to break down sex-barriers.

Further information
The Federation of Commodity Associations, 1 Commodity Quay, St Katherine's Dock, London E1 9AX

Related careers
STOCK EXCHANGE AND SECURITIES INDUSTRY

Computing/Information Technology (IT)

Entry qualifications

Nothing rigid: depends on job-type (see below). Ability to think logically and communicate effectively is more important than specific GCSEs and A-levels. For trainee programming jobs, in practice, at least 2 A-levels or degree (any subject); for software programming/engineer, usually computing science degree – computing science A-level not required for most of these courses. Sandwich computing science or IT degrees more helpful than full-time degrees.

The work

Wanting to work with computers is by no means a reason for choosing a computing career. In virtually any job, whether it is clerical, technical, professional; whether it is in banking, manufacturing, retailing or medicine, computers are used extensively. They are tools with which to process information, measure, assess, monitor facts, figures, progress, procedures. They are information-processing devices. The information or 'data' may be in the form of numbers, words or graphs. Strictly speaking, the term 'computer' is out of date. It was correct when, in the early days, computers merely performed complex arithmetical operations with phenomenal speed and complete accuracy – when they were merely 'number crunchers'. Now that their capacity and use have widened so dramatically, 'information technology' or IT is becoming the accepted term. IT describes the 'convergence' of office automation, telecommunications and computing. However, 'computing' and 'computer' have become part of the language, and the terms have stuck. For most major organizations computing has become an integral part of doing business. This has raised computing and IT to strategic importance as far as the business is concerned.

People usually want to work with computers because they are fascinated by their versatility, their capacity to cut out drudgery and to achieve results which in pre-computer days were either impossible to achieve, or took a vast amount of time and trouble. Thanks to microprocessors, robots now perform repetitive manufacturing tasks; while office automation systems have already transformed much of business practice. Word processors eliminate repetitive typing; databases help solicitors keep track of case-law without having to search through heavy tomes; management can gather information from various sources spread over various sites via communication networks to help it make decisions based on facts and figures rather than hunch. In all these spheres people who use computers need not understand any more about the working of the computing device than car drivers need to understand about engines – and they are no more computer professionals than car drivers are engineers. There is a vast and sometimes underrated difference between amateurs who program their computers and computer professionals.

To perform its information-processing tasks, the actual device, the 'hardware' (which is designed by engineers and computer scientists), relies entirely on 'software', the instructions or 'programs'. Hardware without software, computer people say, is as useless as a TV set without the programme companies' wares. It is the software which enables the computer to enter into a dialogue with the people who want to use it, and to respond to their needs. The versatility of the tasks which can be performed depends on the complexity and quality of the software, and on the size and sophistication of the computer. Many of today's micro- and minicomputers are approaching the power of yesterday's mainframes – and the power and complexity of the network to which they are commonly connected.

Software tools such as 4th generation languages (4GLs) greatly aid users, backed up by professionals, but the communication between user and professional will be vital.

Microcomputers have seen the growth of packaged software solutions to business problems, with spreadsheets, word processors and databases giving rise to many new support jobs within most organizations.

Computing Jobs

Computing and IT professionals comprise a range of highly skilled specialists who have to acquire their expertise just as any other professionals have to. The demarcation between the various computer specialisms is constantly changing, because devices are becoming ever more sophisticated, demanding new skills or newly combined skills. For example, a new growth area is computer-integrated manufacture, CIM, which brings together systems used for design, manufacture, marketing and finance. Teams of computer staff are headed by project leaders, who now have a well-defined planning and monitoring management role.

Systems Software Programmers/ Software Designers/Software Engineers
(titles are interchangeable)

These people produce the software which enables the otherwise inert hardware to provide the basic facilities – the 'controlling programs'. This has been likened to the electric power system into which users 'plug' various devices – it is the 'computer workhorse'. Whether it is a microcomputer, say a dedicated word processor, or a robot controller, or whether it is a system with 100 terminals, the controlling program, designed and developed by the *systems programmer*, makes the whole thing function. The work is a combination of applying *computer science* and *telecommunication* principles, creativity, high technology expertise and analytical reasoning. *Software programmers* work jointly with other highly trained professionals. They are the only computer people who (a) must have a technological/scientific background (a degree normally) and who (b) work almost entirely with other highly qualified experts and have little contact, at work, with non-computer people. Their work is basically Research and Design (see 'Design' and 'Research and Development', pp. 185, 186, under ENGINEERING).

Some develop existing operating systems, updating, extending, refining them; others work on software which will be ready for general use in the future. Theirs can be very much pushing-out-the-frontiers-of-science work. Most of the work requires high-calibre brains, but there is also scope for support staff (see 'Incorporated Engineers and Engineering Technicians', p. 197). *Systems programmers/software designers/software engineers* work mainly for computer manufacturers and software houses, but all companies which have large computer networks employ some systems programmers. Of all computing jobs, theirs is the most theoretical/academic, and a rapidly diminishing portion of the computer jobs market.

Network and telecommunications specialists

This growing group of specialists design and support the Local Area Networks (LANs) which allow computerized workstations to 'talk' to each other. Networking has become a means of integrating both computer applications and business functions.

Jobs in this area cover network design, implementation, support and management. This is one of the most rapidly growing areas of IT and suitable staff are in short supply.

Systems Analysts and/or Designers

They identify the problem and design the solution to it. There are three stages to the job. First, they investigate and analyse the existing system – or lack of it – in the organization which is intending to install a computer or system. In many organizations patterns of work have evolved haphazardly and, in the process, have become inefficient. For example, in a chain-store which has increased its volume considerably over the years, the method of recording sales, ticketing goods, making out bills, stock control and dealing with suppliers may be totally unsuited to the size of the organization today. The *systems analyst* spends several months getting to know the intricacies of the business, observing and talking to staff in all departments and at all levels – from junior clerk or packer to buyer or marketing and managing directors – to assess routines, bottlenecks, objectives. The work requires business acumen, knowledge of commercial practice and an ability to get people to talk freely about their work and to accept changes in old-established routines. When the old system has been translated into a logical sequence of procedures, the systems analyst writes a report on how computerization would affect the organization's staff, and how it would improve efficiency and profitability, and at what cost. If the report is accepted by the management, the systems analyst completes the analysis and design, using structured procedures, hands over the program specification to the programmers, and probably supervises the subsequent implementation, troubleshooting if necessary.

Analyst/Programmers

In commercial computing – the vast majority of jobs are in this field, rather than in science or engineering – the jobs of *analyst/ designers* and of *programmers* are normally merged into *analyst/ programmers*, who are currently much in demand. They see the whole project through, in teams, until it is completed and validated. The vast majority of analysts and designers work for computer users; 'in-house' analysis and design used to be more usual than having the work done by software houses, i.e. consultancies which provide professional services for a number of clients. However, computing and IT skill shortages have reversed this trend and many firms now employ consultants. Some analyst/ designers (with ample experience) work as freelances.

Analyst designers' work also covers advising employers, or clients, on what systems to buy; so they must be knowledgeable about and critical of the various systems available. They must be very good at explaining complicated matters to lay people – the computer users.

The attraction and challenge of this computing job is the mixture of tasks and of talents required: applying highly specialized technical knowledge; improving an organization's efficiency; assessing competing computer manufacturers' claims for new products. On top of applying technical know-how, systems analysts/designers must be very good at dealing with people: communication skills are vital. They must make the computer acceptable to staff; traditional working methods and hierarchies may have to change; re-training has to be arranged and accepted, and staff reductions may have to be faced.

Applications Programmers

There is a spectrum of *applications programmers*; some work to a 'loose specification', using great expertise and ingenuity; others work to a 'tight specification', need less expertise and have less scope for ingenuity. Most now become *analyst/programmers* (see above). The relationship between *systems analyst/design* and *applications programming* has been likened to that of architecture and building. Applications programmers work to 'program specifications' – a description of what the program is to achieve – provided by the systems analyst/designer.

Applications programming covers various stages. Applications programmers roughly assess the time needed to complete the program, break it down into separate components, and then break down each component into individual step-by-step sequences of instructions upon which the computer can act. All this needs logical, analytical reasoning, but not mathematical skills. Then comes the translation into an appropriate language, which is usually typed directly into a computer terminal. Applications programmers may produce programs to instruct particular machines to perform particular tasks: for example, to enable a chain of hotels to keep a constantly updated record of vacancies, or a hospital group to keep a constantly updated record of the lengths of waiting lists within the various specialities and the various hospitals within the hospital group. In large organizations teams of applications programmers would deal with a variety of programs – writing for new applications; updating existing programs. Applications programmers with considerable experience, working for software/systems houses, manufacturers, consultancies, users and, increasingly, as freelances, can also specialize in 'applications packages'. These are programs, or 'program systems' produced 'for stock', to be bought off-the-shelf by users with run-of-the-mill requirements: programs for stock control; payrolls; video games; office applications like word processing; spread-sheets and databases for personnel systems. As 'tailor-made' programs are very expensive – they take a long time to write – off-the-shelf programs are being produced in ever-growing numbers as more and more computers are being installed and therefore more users with similar requirements are catered for. Writing applications package programs requires special skills: the programs must be 'user-friendly' (easy for laypersons to understand), well documented and flexible enough to be adaptable to particular users' differing needs.

There is usually a hierarchy of programmers, from trainee right up to *project team leader*, and then on to various management jobs. Most work in mixed-project teams with systems designers and other specialists as required.

As virtually everybody in computing, however high up, has to have had some programming experience, programmers have a choice of ladders. Most large installations have two branches: one dealing with developing systems and with those in the planning stage, employing the above staff plus specialists, e.g. *database adminstrators*; and another one dealing with the actual functioning of the system in use.

Database Administration

Data is now viewed by most organizations as a valuable corporate resource. These organizations usually see data as a separate area for control and management. Database administration personnel/departments design, manage and maintain the company's data and control access to it. This is a highly specialized and technical area. Considerable experience of database systems and business needs are required.

Computer Engineers/Scientists and Information Technologists
(various disciplines)

They design and develop computers and related products ('peripherals') for computer manufacturers (see ENGINEERING, p. 191). Various specialists are involved, mainly but not only *electronic engineers, physicists, mathematicians. Information technologists* are emerging as specialists in their own right. At the moment titles of relevant degree courses vary (for example, IT or Computers and Communications); computing hardware professionals of the future must carefully study degree course syllabuses. Terminology of job-titles and specific functions vary, too. Hardware manufacture is an established industry, involving fast-moving research; in career terms it fits into high technology, highly competitive, high-risk manufacturing. (See ENGINEERING, p. 191.)

Some 'Spin-off' Jobs

With 'orthodox' (i.e. *applications* or *software programming, systems/software design/analysis*) qualifications and experience, there are a growing number of opportunities in rapidly changing and expanding computer careers, suiting individuals with various bents, abilities, expertise. *Information technology*, including as it does telecommunications (and office automation), is developing faster than any industry ever has done: new jobs are constantly emerging – but beware: the unskilled or semi-skilled ones may be short-lived: a few years ago there was a vast demand for computer operators and for so-called 'service engineers' who were often narrowly trained. Now, users themselves rather than specialist operators operate the majority of workstations; and some large computers can diagnose and rectify their own faults: *service engineers* now are thoroughly trained to cope only with serious faults (see 'Incorporated Engineers and Engineering Technicians', p. 197).

User Support Staff

As the users now include senior management, this is now a much more high-powered and expanding area than it was. Support staff provide a 'hand-holding' service to users who have bought a new system or updated and extended an existing one. Job content varies greatly. Support staff may be asked to provide training for everyone who will use or be affected by the new systems, from clerk to managing director; they may suggest additional or more efficient application of the system; or, if they work for manufacturers or software houses, they may visit at regular intervals to see all goes well – and possibly keep the customer informed of new equipment or software. The job combines ability to communicate and establish good relations with people at all levels in an organization, with technical expertise to keep up with technological developments.

Service Engineers

They work either for large users 'in-house' or for manufacturers, and visit customers – often irate and impatient – whose equipment has broken down (or apparently broken down: often it is simply wrongly used). Service engineers must thoroughly understand the complexities of hardware and software to be able to diagnose and rectify the trouble. Unlike engineers at the hardware/software production end, service engineers get out and about and meet the users (see 'Incorporated Engineers and Engineering Technicians', p. 197).

Sales and Marketing

For details of general *sales and marketing*, see p. 294. However, in the computer hardware and software area specialist knowledge is vital. Computing is not only technologically the most sophisticated industry, it is also a highly competitive, cut-throat industry. Sales people usually specialize in systems for specific markets – i.e. commercial, scientific or educational.

Knowledge Engineers

This is one of the newest and fastest-growing areas of work, involving the application of '*expert systems*' to commerce, industry and service industries. A knowledge engineer designs the computer system to perform tasks normally associated with a human expert, e.g. medical diagnosis or an oil rig's safety system.

Technical Writing

Writing manuals for – especially – mini- and microcomputer users is a growing job area. It requires the ability to put over complex information clearly, succinctly and unequivocally, and it requires thorough understanding of what the device described can and cannot do, and how it functions. Manual-writers have to know very much more about their subject than the people for whom they are writing. Existing manuals are often criticized; manufacturers say they have difficulty finding people who combine the necessary technological expertise with the necessary communication skills. Technical writers may be employed by manufacturers or by consultancies or work as freelance or 'in-house'. 'End-user documentation' production is becoming a sophisticated area. Writers have to produce material – both in print and 'screen dialogue' – which is 'user-friendly', i.e. easily understood by amateurs, as well as documentation for experts.

Consultants

Systems analysts and *designers* can ultimately become independent consultants – advising prospective users on whether a system would be of use to them and, if so, which one. Considerable experience of the computer-scene, plus specialist knowledge in a commercial, banking, retailing, etc., or industrial or educational area, is essential.

Training This is still evolving. Experience is, on the whole, more important than paper qualifications, but experience is often difficult to get without qualifications. It is still possible to start with a few good GCSEs as an operator and, with in-house training and preferably day-release, become an *applications programmer* and then a *systems analyst* – if the conditions and the personality and ability are right. Because of the quick expansion and rapid developments in the whole computer area, training is still disorganized and haphazard, with several overlapping types of qualifications. Many people at the top of the profession now have no formal computing qualifications, because when they started their careers there were no relevant qualifications. Others have got on without qualifications because of the shortage of computer staff, but new entrants must aim at a qualification (though the only work for which a degree is invariably demanded is *software/systems programming*). Training is also continuous, with the need for continuous updating. Yet still far too few IT employers are prepared to train staff.

Courses are at all levels from post-graduate to those for people with few educational qualifications. Non-degree qualifications are awarded by a number of different organizations, some specializing in a particular branch of the industry. The following are the main entry and training routes, but individuals should look very carefully at syllabuses to ensure that they choose a course to suit their particular interest and academic level. They need also to decide whether to take a full-time, part-time or distance-learning course (many can be taken by any of these methods).

1. Degree (full time or sandwich) in a computing subject (titles include computing science, software engineering, information engineering, business computing, information processing, computer systems). Science A-levels (physics and/or maths) are required for some, but not all, courses.

NOTE: see ENGINEERING, p. 196, for introductory/foundation courses for people with arts A-levels who want to take a degree normally requiring science A-levels.

2. Degree in business studies with a computing option.

3. Post-graduate or post-HND computing course.

4. BTEC/SCOTVEC (see pp. xxi, xxii) Higher National awards in computer studies, business information technology, software engineering, maths studies (with computing options).

5. British Computer Society: the main professional body; awards its own qualifications, from applications programming upwards. Candidates must have had at least 1 year in relevant employment. Part 1 is equivalent to an HND and Part 2 to an Honours degree. Degree and Higher National courses accredited by the BCS lead to exemptions from part or all of its examinations.

6. Institute of Data Processing Management (emphasis is on business applications): offers a Diploma qualification for people with 4 GCSEs or who have completed the IDPM Foundation course (no entry qualifications). There is also a Higher Diploma for those with *either* the Diploma *or* BTEC National in relevant subjects *or* 2 A-levels *or* 4 years' relevant experience if over 21. There is also a Graduate Diploma in Management Information Systems (various entry qualifications including degree and BCS Part 1).

7. BTEC/SCOTVEC National awards in computer studies.

8. City and Guilds (see p. xxiii) offers a flexible scheme covering most aspects of IT, from introduction to programming to advanced applications programming. There is also a scheme for microcomputer technology. Some parts of the scheme contribute towards NVQs (see p. xx).

9. The Royal Society of Arts (see p. xxiv) offers a Certificate, Diploma and Advanced Diploma in IT.

10. National Computing Centre: runs a government-sponsored 1-year Threshold Certificate scheme for school-leavers and adults, in several centres. This is a sandwich course, with a mix of college-based study and work placements. No educational requirements – entry is by aptitude tests. Threshold is accepted by BTEC as equivalent to a National Certificate.

11. Some employers take entrants with 2 A-levels or graduates (any subject) for in-house training; COSIT (Computer Service Industry Training Council) introduced systematic training for the software industry and has developed an Industry Standard Development Programme (ISDP). Training can be completed by most in 4 years (minimum 3); it may take longer. It is competence-based and combines a mix of formal and informal training and

work experience, leading to certificates. Two ISDP certificates currently lead to NVQs level 4: software systems design and software systems development.

NOTE: The IT Industry Training Organization (ITITO) has been set up to oversee future IT awards.

NOTE: Private schools' diplomas (full-time courses) vary enormously in value. Check with National Computing Centre or British Computer Society (see p. 155) before enrolling.

Computing is the fastest expanding career area. Old – in computing terms – job categories are breaking down, but for computing professionals who are flexible and prepared to continue learning new skills and for constant change and challenge, scope is immense. Computing is expanding in two dimensions: (1) It is penetrating ever more areas of activity, with more and more workplaces within each area installing or expanding systems; and (2) devices and systems are getting ever more sophisticated and versatile; for example, electronic mail and network services are widely used; voice input is in use in a number of specialized areas. As one generation of computers comes on to the market, the next one is in production, and the one after that on the drawing-board (or rather the researcher/designer's VDU). So computing professionals of all kinds have a promising future.

About 85–90% of computing professionals now work with users installing, programming, analysing/designing systems, controlling, managing, setting up project teams or computing departments, liaising with other staff, training existing staff to use systems. So *systems programmers, systems analysts/designers, analyst/programmers*, well-qualified *applications programmers, technical writers, user support staff* are all likely to be in demand for the rest of this century (see display advertisements in the press for variety of job-titles, tasks to be performed and levels of responsibility/expertise). But the demand for *operators* and for not-very-highly-skilled programmers is dwindling fast, as these tasks are increasingly performed by non-specialist staff – the users. Manufacturers and software houses employ the remaining 10–15%.

Broadly, then, prospects are excellent for highly skilled, highly trained people and for support staff – i.e. *technicians* (see 'Incorporated Engineers and Engineering Technicians', p. 197); but prospects are not so good for run-of-the-mill professionals who are lured into computing merely by the novelty of the work, and by the advertisements.

The prospects for people with engineering/science background plus computing experience/training are excellent. There is increasing scope for specializing within a work area: people with experience in, say, *retail, banking,* the *law* or *agriculture* may become computing professionals by grafting computing skills on to their particular expertise. (See 'Employment Training' and HTNT, pp. xxiv–xxv and 'Late start', below.)

Personal attributes

All professionals: Flexibility, willingness to adapt to new methodologies and to continue learning.

Systems analyst/designer: Well-above-average intelligence and powers of logical reasoning; numeracy; imagination to put themselves into the shoes of the people whose jobs they may be 'analysing away' or at least changing; tact and diplomacy; ability to get on well with people at all levels in an organization's hierarchy; a confidence-inspiring manner; curiosity; creativity to visualize how old-established methods might be changed; ability to explain complicated procedures in simple language; ability to listen; ability to take an overall view of a situation and yet see it in detail; business acumen, at least for many jobs.

Applications programmers/programmers/analysts: Powers of logical thinking; numeracy; powers of sustained concentration; great patience and willingness to pursue an elusive problem till solved; liking for concentrated desk-work; ability to communicate easily with people in computing as well as with lay people. Programmers who hope to progress to systems analysis should note the different personal qualities required.

Systems programmers/software engineers: Very high intellectual ability; originality; research-inclined mind; imagination; interest in high technology and its implications and rapid developments.

Operators: Practicality; liking for routine work; organizing/administrative ability for those wanting to get promotion.

Late start

Good opportunities, especially for people with business or related experience and for mature students, who may take full- or part-time degree or other relevant courses. Government-sponsored courses (see p. xxv) in various computing subjects may be available under HTNT. For graduates, there are standard post-graduate courses.

Career-break

See below.

Part time

See below.

Position of women

There are outstanding opportunities for women. The 85–90% + computing professionals who work with computer users (see above) are in 'dealing-with-people' jobs. Their computing expertise is the essential background for the job. So the vast majority of computer people are doing work which even the most traditionally minded would consider eminently suitable for women. It requires an interest in what makes people tick, to understand and know how to allay people's fear of new – and jargon-ridden – technologies. Women have shown that they appreciate employees' resistance to change and know how to work out changed working patterns which are both efficient and acceptable to staffs. In systems analysis/design women's knack of gaining staff's confidence at the investigation stage has proved particularly useful. One of the most prestigious and biggest software houses/consultancies is run and almost entirely staffed by women, many of them part-timers. So many women are freelance programmers working at home while raising a family that programming has been called the new cottage industry.

As the whole area is so new, there have been no traditional barriers to break down. Nevertheless, there is evidence now that a disproportionate number of senior project leader and other management jobs are being filled by men, and that women are 'dropping back'. A 1991 survey showed that women make up 3% of data processing managers compared with 32% of trainee systems analysts and 26% of trainee programmers. Of systems analysts, 28% are women, but only 20% of senior systems analysts and only 14% of project managers. Interestingly, the nearer the job to the user, the higher the proportion of women – rising to well over 50% on 'help desk' support. This pyramid structure could be due to senior managers' traditional attitudes to women in management jobs (see MANAGEMENT, p. 272). But there may be another reason: of the first generation of specially trained computing professionals, a sizeable proportion is at present either taking a child-rearing career-break, or experiencing the adverse effects of having taken such a break. In this fast-changing profession, it is essential to work continuously, or at least to keep one's hand in during the break. Women who take off more than a few months will inevitably be left behind. But as there are good opportunities for part-time or project-based work there is no need for a complete career-break.

So opportunities for women are excellent. But there are worrying signs that women are not making full use of these opportunities, and that computing is becoming a male-dominated area at an early stage. Parents are buying computers as toys for their young sons, not for their young daughters; in schools far more boys join computer clubs, and take (are persuaded to take?) computing at GCSE and A-level, although neither is generally required for degree courses. At degree level, the proportion of girls taking computing science is actually declining; it was 15% on university courses in 1984 and 13·6% in 1991 (polytechnic figures for 1990 at 22% were better). There is no simple explanation for girls' apparent decline of interest. One reason, computing professionals – both sexes – say, is that computer advertisers are projecting a false image. The main emphasis, as computing skills are needed in virtually every area of work, should be on communication skills, not just on mathematical/technological skills. There is no reason whatever why girls should not see computing as a 'fun subject', just as boys do, working with people in all kinds of job areas, and why women should not match men as computing professionals at all levels. The Women into Information Technology Foundation (WIT) is trying to encourage higher education institutions and employers to run events and take other initiatives to attract girls to this area. It also provides information on refresher training, useful for women returners.

Further information

National Computing Centre, Oxford Road, Manchester M1 7ED

British Computer Society, 13 Mansfield Street, London W1M 0BD

BTEC, Central House, Upper Woburn Place, London WC1H 0HH

Computing Services Industry Training Council (COSIT), 16 South Molton Street, London W1Y 1DE

Institute of Data Processing Management, IDPM House, Edgington Way, Ruxley Corner, Sidcup, Kent DA14 5HR

WIT Foundation, Concept 2000, 250 Farnborough Road, Farnborough, Hants. GU14 7LU

Related careers

ENGINEERING – MANAGEMENT SERVICES: *Operational Research* – SCIENCE

Dancing

Teaching and performing are two separate careers. There are two kinds of performer: (1) *ballet dancers* and (2) *modern stage dancers.*

Performing

Entry qualifications

No specific educational requirements, but a good general education is essential for ballet dancers.

Ballet Dancer

The work

Ballet dancers, whether they specialize in classical or contemporary dance, lead dedicated lives. Their days are spent practising, rehearsing and performing. They have little spare time and may not indulge in such activities as cycling, riding, etc., lest they develop the wrong muscles. They meet few people who are not in some way involved with ballet.

They are usually attached to one particular company and may be on tour for much of the year.

Ballet companies have only a few vacancies each year so opportunities are limited. Once a member of the *corps de ballet*, a talented dancer has a chance of rising to solo parts and understudying bigger roles, but it is rare indeed to rise to principal dancer status. Even a successful dancer's professional life is short; only the very exceptional still get engagements in their middle thirties. Dancers not suited to classical ballet may choose to join a contemporary dance company. There are some opportunities abroad – dance is a very international activity.

Training

Serious training must have started by the age of 11 with a professional teacher who prepares pupils systematically for one of the officially recognized major dancing examinations: e.g. those of the Royal Academy of Dancing, the Imperial Society of Teachers of Dancing, or the British Ballet Organization (RAD, ISTD, BBO).

The best training is given at professional schools which give general education for GCSEs and a thorough drama and dance training. It is advisable to apply only for courses accredited by the Council for Dance Education and Training (and for which most local education authorities will give discretionary grants). There is a degree in Contemporary Dance run by the London Contemporary Dance School and validated by Kent University.

Full-time professional training must start not later than at 16. It lasts for about 3 years.

There are ballet schools all over the country but pupils from the London ballet companies' schools have a far better chance of eventually finding a place in these companies, which recruit most of their *corps de ballet* from their own schools.

Ballet training includes national and character dancing, mime, history, art and literature, and usually French (most technical terms are in that language).

Before accepting a pupil, good schools insist on a thorough orthopaedic examination, which is repeated at regular intervals throughout training.

Personal attributes   Suitable physique, including strong back and feet; intelligence; intuition; emotional depth; musical talent; the ability to take criticism without resentment; a strong constitution; complete dedication; a distinct personality.

Modern Stage Dancer

The work   Modern stage dancers perform in musicals, pantomime, cabaret, on TV, and in light entertainment generally. They are not usually attached to a company, but appear in individual shows, usually with spells of unemployment in between. They do not have to work quite as hard as a ballet dancer – practising is not so all-important.

For the fully trained first-rate dancer (about 1 in 10) prospects are fair. But like other entertainers, a dancer must be prepared for months of 'resting', meanwhile earning a living in some other way yet being 'available to attend auditions. If lucky, they may get a long run in the West End, a tour, or a television series. Dancers must have made a name for themselves in their early twenties, or give up.

Training   3 years full time, preferably, but not necessarily, at one of the professional schools (see 'Ballet Dancer, Training'). At auditions, candidates must be able to demonstrate their ability to dance up to intermediate ballet exam level. The modern stage dancer should also have some training in voice production, drama and singing. The latest starting age for serious, but not necessarily professional, training is about 14.

Personal attributes   Attractive appearance, especially shapely legs; resilience; versatility; enterprise in tracking down jobs; sense of rhythm.

*

Teaching

Entry qualifications   Training for qualified teacher status (required for teaching in ordinary (i.e. not *dance*) schools): 2 A-levels and 3 GCSEs (A–C) (see TEACHING, p. 521). Very exceptionally, 1 A-level may be acceptable. Usually no set entry qualifications (except for dance proficiency examinations) for those wishing to train to teach in dance schools. (However, 5 GCSEs (A–C) are needed for Imperial Society of Teachers of Dancing Foundation Course.) Entry requirements may be waived for mature entrants.

The work   A dancing teacher may teach both children and adults, or may specialize in teaching one or the other. Adults are taught in private schools/classes or in local authority adult education centres.

Children are taught in ordinary schools; dancing schools; specialized professional schools.

Ordinary schools
Full-time or visiting part-time teachers teach dance to GCSE, mainly to improve children's poise and deportment.

Dancing schools
These are intended for children who don't have dancing lessons at school. They may be run by a teacher who hires a hall for the purpose, or they may be in a dancing school which caters for both children and adults.

Children are usually prepared for recognized dancing examinations (see 'Ballet Dancer, Training'). This ensures that children are being properly taught even though they do not intend to become professionals.

Professional schools
Dancing is an essential part of the curriculum in what is generally an arts-orientated private school; the teacher deals with specially talented children who hope to become professional dancers.

Job prospects are good for teaching adults and children. There are also good opportunities for teachers in Europe where non-professional dancing for children is now very popular. Royal Academy of Dancing and Imperial Society of Teachers of Dancing examiners often go abroad to organize, teach and examine.

Training

Leading to qualified teacher status

The Council for Dance Education and Training issues up-to-date lists of 'accredited' courses which would normally lead to teaching in *dancing* schools; these courses do not lead to 'qualified teacher status' (nor do they usually qualify for admission to post-graduate teacher training). To teach dancing in ordinary schools or in further education, training is *either* a 4-year course at one of the few dancing schools which have a link with a College or Department of Education; or a 3- or 4-year Bachelor of Education course which has a dance component – it is important to check prospectuses carefully before choosing such a course, as the 'dance component' varies from a few hours to a substantial proportion; *or* a degree in dance or in performing arts (titles and course content vary) followed by a 1-year post-graduate teacher training course.

Other courses

The following are also intended for performers, teachers and other professionals in dance, e.g. administrators and notators: the University of Surrey's Dance in Society degree; the London College of Dance/University of Buckingham degree; the BTEC HND in Dance at Coventry Centre for Performing Arts.

Personal attributes

The ability to explain and demonstrate steps and movements; a fine sense of rhythm and some proficiency at the piano; a liking for people of all ages; imagination; endless tact and patience; good appearance; graceful movements. (See also TEACHING, p. 521.)

Teaching Keep Fit and Exercise

This area has expanded rapidly in the last few years. Movement classes have mushroomed, changing their style frequently in order to follow the latest (often imported) fashion. Many people have cashed in on the dance/exercise craze without a proper knowledge of how the body works and what kind of movement is suitable for each type of student. The most suitable basic training for teachers in this area is either a proper dance course; or Physical Education teacher training; or a 2-year part-time course organized by the Keep Fit Association and run in conjunction with local education authorities.

Choreography

The work   The dancer who has exceptional imaginative powers and the ability to interpret music in terms of dancing may ultimately do choreography. This is dance composition: the grouping of dancers and sequence of dances which make up the entire ballet. In modern stage dancing, a choreographer may direct within a wide range from the production numbers on TV which involve scores of dancers, to the unexacting dances of a seaside concert party.

Choreography is not a career for which a novice can be trained unless there is a noticeable talent. Years of experience of ballet and a thorough musical training are needed (see MUSIC, p. 318). However, some dance courses now include choreography or offer it as an option.

Career-break   Many dancers take up teaching after a break from performing.

Part time   Good opportunities in teaching.

Position of women   *Performing*: 89% are women. More men are coming into the profession; but there is still a far greater shortage of *first-rate* male than of first-rate female dancers.

Teaching: This is still a predominantly female occupation (especially teaching children) but there is no reason why more men should not train for teaching.

Further information   Council for Dance Education and Training, Room 301, 5 Tavistock Place, London WC1H 9SS (for addresses of accredited ballet schools)

Imperial Society of Teachers of Dancing, Euston Hall, Birkenhead Street, London WC1H 8BE

Central Register and Clearing House (qualified teacher status B.Ed. and post-graduate courses), 3 Crawford Place, London W1H 2BN

The Keep Fit Association, 16 Upper Woburn Place, London WC1H 0QG

Related careers   DRAMA – MUSIC – TEACHING

Dentistry

Dental Surgeon

Entry qualifications

3 good A-levels (or equivalent) usually including at least 2 sciences (biology and chemistry are preferred). Chemistry, biology, physics and maths must usually be included at GCSE. Most dental schools accept 2 AS-levels in lieu of 1 A-level. (See 'Training' for arts A-level candidates.)

The work

Dentists (or dental surgeons) preserve teeth by filling, crowning and scaling. They extract teeth and design and fit artificial dentures. They also do surgical operations on the jaw, and orthodontics, which is the improvement of irregular teeth, mainly in children. The preventive aspects of dentistry are very important, involving regular teeth inspection for children. Prospects are good and qualifications are accepted in the EC.

General Practice

The majority of dentists are in general practice. Some treat National Health patients almost exclusively, some treat both private and NHS patients. Others treat only private patients.

Dentists in general practice have the best financial prospects and the greatest independence, but they are also likely to work the hardest. They may be in a partnership, or in practice on their own, working in their own premises with their own equipment, and employing their own dental surgery assistants (see p. 165).

It is usual to begin as an assistant or associate in a practice, with a view to becoming a partner later, but primarily to learn how a practice is run. This involves a good deal of organization, filling-in of forms, ordering stocks, and contact with technicians.

It is also possible to buy the 'goodwill' of a dentist who is retiring or moving away, or simply to put up a plate and wait for patients.

Community Dental Surgeon

The Community Dental Service is intended to foster the idea of dental care within the whole community through the dental inspection and treatment of priority groups such as school and pre-school children, expectant and nursing mothers and, increasingly, elderly and handicapped people.

Hospital and University Dental Surgeon

In hospitals, a dentist looks after sick patients whose teeth need urgent attention, and does jaw operations and complicated extractions. Outpatients may need only ordinary dental treatment.

Dental work in hospitals has the usual hospital advantages of life in a community, colleagues to discuss difficult cases with, and social and sports clubs. Dentists wishing to do university research and teaching usually combine this with some hospital work.

Training   5-year course at dental schools attached to universities. The dental course proper may be preceded by a 1-year preliminary science course (as for medical training). Students with A-level physics, chemistry, biology, zoology or maths are exempt from it.

Most dental schools have discontinued this course. Even when dental schools do accept students for a preliminary year, local authorities do not normally pay grants for what is in effect an A-level course.

Dental training lasts for 5 years. The syllabus covers anatomy and physiology, the uses of dental materials, design and fitting of dental appliances, pathology, some medicine, general as well as dental surgery, anaesthesia, orthodontics, children's and general preventive dentistry, radiology, dental ethics, and relevant law.

Practical work on 'phantom heads' normally begins in the second year, and work on actual patients during the second or third year of the dental course.

Personal attributes   Manual dexterity; a methodical and scientific approach; and good health. Left-handedness is not a disadvantage.

Dentist in general practice especially: The ability to establish easy relationships quickly with people, and give confidence to the nervous (the growth of the practice depends almost entirely on the patients' personal recommendations); organizing ability.

Community dental surgeon especially: The ability to get on with children.

Hospital dentist especially: The ability to work well as a member of a team.

General Dental Council, 37 Wimpole Street, London W1M 8DQ

Related careers   DENTISTRY: *Auxiliary Work* – MEDICINE

Auxiliary Work

For people interested in dentistry but without the necessary qualifications for dental training, there are four careers: *dental therapist, dental hygienist, dental surgery assistant* and *dental technician*.

Dental Therapist

Entry qualifications

Minimum age for training 18.

5 GCSEs (A–C), including English language, and a science subject, preferably biology, plus the Dental Surgery Assistants' National Certificate and minimum 1 year's experience in a dental surgery.

The work

Dental therapists do 'operative work'; they work in hospitals and community dental services, mainly helping dentists to give treatment to children and to teach them how to care for their teeth. They work under the direction of a dentist who prescribes the treatment to be given; this includes simple fillings, extraction of deciduous teeth, and cleaning, scaling and polishing teeth. Dental therapists always work under the direction and prescription of a registered dentist. Their responsibility is therefore limited. Many of the patients are very young – in welfare clinics under 5, in school clinics mostly under 11. Dental therapists do not work for dentists in general practice.

There is now intense competition for the very few training places per year.

Training

2 years full time, only in London. Practical training (on which more time is spent than on theory) is initially on phantom heads, so that students learn how to scale, polish, fill and extract teeth without worrying about hurting the patient; they also work on

patients, under supervision. Theoretical training includes anatomy, physiology of the teeth and jaw, some radiography, some dietetics – enough to understand why some foods are good and some bad for the development of children's teeth.

Personal attributes
Considerable manual dexterity; conscientiousness; some interest in science; good health; a way with children.

Further information
General Dental Council, 37 Wimpole Street, London W1M 8DQ

Dental Hygienist

Entry qualifications
Minimum age for training 17.

5 GCSEs (A–C), preferably including English language and a science subject. Candidates are given a manual dexterity test, and are expected to have had experience as a dental surgery assistant (see below).

The work
Dental hygienists also do 'operative work'. They do scaling and polishing under the supervision of dentists, but do not do any fillings etc. An important aspect of the work is preventive dentistry.

They work with adults as well as with children, in general practice as well as in community health clinics and hospitals.

More dentists in general practice, especially in partnership, now employ hygienists, but there are no promotion prospects.

Training
1 year full time at dental hospitals. Training is similar to that of therapists, but the extraction and filling of teeth are not included. Some time is spent in learning how to talk about oral hygiene to children and adults.

Personal attributes
As for therapists, plus the ability to express oneself lucidly.

Further information
General Dental Council, 37 Wimpole Street, London W1M 8DQ

Dental Surgery Assistant

Entry qualifications

None laid down, but most hospital training schools demand some GCSE passes, which should include English language and a science. None required for admission to the examination for the National Certificate of the Examining Board for Dental Surgery Assistants.

Minimum age for training usually 17.

The work

Surgery assistants do no 'operative work'. They act as the dentist's 'third hand', handing them the right instruments at the right time. They also look after the instruments, do sterilizing, get out patients' treatment cards, help with filling in forms and filing, do secretarial and reception work.

Surgery assistants work wherever dentists work, i.e. in general practice, in community dental clinics and in hospitals.

Training

Most dentists train their own assistants, but some prefer those who were trained at a dental hospital, for a period varying from 12 to 24 months. The type of training differs slightly from one hospital to another, but it is mainly practical, with some lectures and demonstrations.

The majority of dental surgery assistants, however, go straight from school or from secretarial college to a dentist's surgery and are trained on the job. They are advised to attend evening classes.

After the training they can take the examination for the National Certificate awarded by the Examining Board for Dental Surgery Assistants. The certificate is awarded after 2 years' work.

Personal attributes

A polite, friendly manner; some manual dexterity; a well-groomed, neat appearance; good health.

Further information

Association of British Dental Surgery Assistants, DSA House, 29 London Street, Fleetwood, Lancashire FY7 6JY

Dental Technician

Entry qualifications

For BTEC National Diploma in Science (Dental Technology): 4 GCSEs (A–C), including English, maths and 2 sciences. For SCOTVEC Diploma in Dental Technology, normally 4 O-grades including English and science subject.

The work

Dental technicians construct and repair dentures, crowns and other orthodontic appliances. They work either in commercial dental laboratories where work for individual dentists is carried out, or in hospital dental laboratories. It is highly skilled work and there is a great shortage of dental technicians.

Training   *Either* (in commercial laboratories or dental practices) a 5-year apprenticeship with day-release for BTEC National award; *or* (in dental hospitals and health authorities) a 3-year training scheme with block-release for the BTEC National award; *or* (less common) 3-year full-time course for BTEC/SCOTVEC National award plus 2 years' consolidation in an approved laboratory.

Approximately 10% of successful students take a 2-year part-time course for the BTEC Higher National certificate.

Personal   Great manual dexterity; patience; accuracy.
attributes

Further   General Dental Council, 37 Wimpole Street, London W1M 8DQ
informa-   Dental Technicians Education and Training Advisory Board,
tion   64 Wimpole Street, London W1M 8AL

Late start   1. *Dentists*: Unusual. Dental schools vary in their attitude to mature students and judge each case on its merits – acceptance depends largely on the number of years students would have after qualifying. There is, usually, no relaxation in entry requirements. Over-35s are unlikely to be offered a place. No employment problem once qualified.

2. *Auxiliary work*: Young students are given preference for training usually, but mature entrants are also considered.

Career-   No problem: for dentists there are refresher courses. The Dental
break   Retainer Scheme encourages women dentists to work at least 12 sessions and attend 7 education sessions a year, while paying reduced membership fees.

Part time   Good opportunities for employment, none for training. Job-sharing should be possible.

Position   1. *Dentists*
of   30% of practising dentists are women, but over 46% of students
women   are now female. Of all the top professions, dentistry is the most promising for women. They have truly equal chances of promotion in the health service; they are usually welcomed in private practice by partners and by patients; and it is a profession which can be carried on anywhere in the country.

2. *Dental therapists, hygienists and surgery assistants*
Predominantly female professions.

3. *Dental technicians*
Although most technicians are men, more women are now training
and their position is much as for other dental staff now.

**Related
careers**   MEDICINE – NURSING – SCIENCE

Dietetics

Entry qualifications

2 science A-levels, one of which must be chemistry; 3 GCSEs (A–C) which must normally include English and mathematics. See 'Training', below.

The work

Dietitians apply scientific principles of nutrition to normal and to therapeutic diets. Their functions have broadened in the last few years as healthy eating habits become recognized as a vital part of preventive medicine.

Dietitians' work divides broadly into *preventive* and *therapeutic* dietetics.

Preventive work, mainly in the community: As food becomes ever more expensive and as more 'convenience' and other processed foods come on the market it is becoming more and more important that shoppers should be able to assess the nutritional values of various foods, and the possible ill-effects on health. Preventive dietetics is part of health education. In preventive work dietitians try to get their message across to as many people as possible *before* they need therapeutic diets. To do this dietitians work 'through' other professionals – those who reach wider sections of the community than the dietitian could hope to reach. They endeavour to keep nurses, social workers, health visitors, midwives, teachers and GPs up to date on nutritional matters; they give talks in schools, to youth clubs, PTAs, Rotary Clubs, etc. There is an element of public relations work in preventive dietetics: dietitians have to make themselves and their work known and get themselves *asked* to speak to groups.

They also work out diets for special groups; for example cheap and simple-to-prepare meals for the elderly; for parents with large families, little time and little money; for people living alone; and for ethnic groups who have to observe certain dietary rules but cannot afford to buy their traditional foodstuffs here because they are too expensive.

Preventive dietetics overlaps with *therapeutic* work which involves advising individuals, mainly hospital in- and out-patients, on specific diets. For therapeutic work, dietitians use their expertise together with skill and imagination to make diets 'stickable-to' even when, for example, patients may have little understanding of the need to avoid certain ingredients in their diets while including others.

Dietitians do not do any cooking themselves; even direct supervision of diet-kitchens is now the exception rather than the rule. They act as consultants to catering managers in hospitals (or a group of hospitals) and other institutions. Most dietitians are employed by the National Health Service and are hospital-based. However, an increasing number are being employed in industry, for example in marketing (see p. 294) and public relations (see p. 409), as 'healthy eating' is now big business. At the top of the NHS dietetics tree are District Dietitians. They decide how to use staff to best advantage – e.g. whether to designate one dietitian to do the health education work in the community and let the rest work with patients in hospitals, or whether to let everybody do a bit of everything.

Some local authority social services employ dietitians entirely for community work; others employ them for work in the school meals and other institutional services.

Dietitians occasionally become catering managers in hospitals or other large organizations, because they prefer the possibly greater managerial content of large-scale catering management (see CATERING, p. 95) to dietetics. Some may work for contract catering firms (see p. 103) which supply hospital and/or school meals where these services have been privatized. Experienced dietitians may become lecturers and/or do research in industrial or public-sector jobs.

Experienced dietitians are usually in demand, but first jobs are not necessarily available where they are wanted. There are some openings in the developing countries and in the EC (for dietitians who speak the relevant languages). British qualifications are not automatically recognized in the USA, Canada and Australia but reciprocity of recognition may be obtained in the future.

Training   4-year degree course. Titles vary; some courses including the term 'nutrition' are recognized by the Dietitians Board as entitling holders to State Registration, and some are not. Registration is essential for dietitians wishing to work in the National Health Service or in other good jobs. Degree courses include at least 6 months' practical work. The syllabus includes physiology; biochemistry; microbiology; nutrition and food science; diet therapy; health education; large-scale catering systems and principles; economics of nutrition; sociology.

Graduates with relevant degrees (i.e. in nursing, or degrees which include human physiology and human biochemistry) may take a 2-year post-graduate Diploma.

Personal attributes *For all dietitians*: Interest in science as well as in food; curiosity about and sympathy with other people's ways of life and standards of food preparation; ability to get on well with people of all ages, temperaments, backgrounds in one-to-one consultations. *For dietitians who hope for promotion*: sufficient self-confidence, intellectual ability and communication skills to fulfil the dietitians' new role as health educator and consultant to other professionals.

Late start No age-bar in jobs, mature students welcome on degree courses. (See 'Access Courses', p. xxxi.)

Career-break Presents no problem; although there are no formal *refresher* courses, *ad hoc* arrangements are made by hospitals.

Part time Opportunities for part time and job-sharing at all levels of seniority. At present no part-time training opportunities, but modular courses which could be adapted to part-time training are being discussed.

Position of women About 90% a female profession, but the proportion of male students is increasing. Proportionately more men in lecturing and senior posts than among newly qualified dietitians.

Further information British Dietetic Association, 7th Floor, Elizabeth House, 22 Suffolk Street, Queensway, Birmingham B1 1LS (please send an s.a.e.)

Related careers CATERING – SCIENCE: *Food Science and Technology; Biochemist; Chemist* – HOME ECONOMICS – MEDICINE

Drama

Acting

No rigid requirements. See 'Training', below.

The work

A career only to be contemplated by those who feel they could not possibly be happy doing anything else. Complimentary notices for school or college plays are rarely pointers to professional success, because being the best of a group of local performers is irrelevant when competing with the best from all over the country. In addition, luck plays a large part: being in the right place at the right time is as important as being good at the job.

Entry to this overcrowded profession is extremely difficult. There are 'casting agreements' between theatrical, TV, film and commercials producers which control the employment of actors and virtually restrict employment to Equity members. Equity (the actors' trade union) in turn strictly controls the entry of new members.

Television

Provides well over half the total of acting jobs, but is not easy to get into: producers can pick and choose and tend to choose players who have had repertory experience or who have done exceptionally well at drama schools or in fringe theatre work. TV drama is recorded on video tape or film in short scenes or 'takes'. Each take rarely lasts for more than a couple of minutes. The actor may be asked to film scenes out of story order, which requires a high level of discipline. Rehearsal time is scarce; the technique now widely used is the rehearse/record method. The actors rehearse each scene on set, then record it immediately. Making TV drama can be very boring. At least two-thirds of an actor's time on set is spent sitting around waiting for technical problems to be sorted out. Added to this, actors have very little control over the finished product; the director, camera operator and editor have more control than they do. However, generally TV work pays better than theatre work and exposes the actor to a wider audience.

Theatre

Performers may give eight performances a week. In repertory, there are often rehearsals during the day as well, which leaves little free time. Reasonably priced digs near the theatre are rarely luxurious; theatre dressing-rooms tend to be cramped and uncomfortable.

No actor ever has a 'secure job' – contracts may be as short as 2 weeks; rarely longer than a year.

Apart from the conventional theatre, there has in recent years been a considerable growth in 'fringe theatre'. Companies are often set up by players working as co-operatives (for a very small wage), taking plays into small halls, pubs, schools, etc. This type of acting – without a proper stage – requires adaptability, devotion and special technique: it is not much easier to get into than conventional stage work.

Commercials

Work comes through casting agencies. Work is never regular; TV commercials' producers always look for fresh faces, and an actor or actress who is currently advertising, for instance, a baby food, is unlikely to be used for some time, either for a competitor's food or for, say, a sophisticated drinks or fashion advertisement. Once established, actors and actresses sometimes appear in commercials which are written to suit their particular style, or they do 'voice overs' – the speaking but not the visual part of the commercial. Commercials are not a way into acting, but useful bread-and-butter jobs.

Films

The film industry is very small. There is very little work; nobody can hope to be *only* a film actress or actor today. The decision whether to accept a tiny part in a TV soap-opera or wait for a hoped-for break in a film is always a difficult one. A performer who has accepted a part must stick to it and not let a producer down if something better turns up – this is essential to retain all-important agents' or casting directors' goodwill.

Acting is never easy, however good a player is. It gives great satisfaction, however, to people with stamina, real talent and lots of luck. At any one time over two-thirds of professional actors and actresses are out of work. An inquiry also showed that the chances of success are best for students who have attended one of the established schools (see 'Training', below) whose courses are accredited by the National Council for Drama Training. Another advantage of accredited schools is that their graduates who get jobs are automatically given the coveted Equity (provisional) card. Most of these belong to the Conference of Drama Schools. Those who have been to one of the lesser-known schools which are totally out of touch with the changing needs and techniques of the theatre and broadcasting, or those few who somehow slipped in without any systematic training at all, are much less likely to find work. Entry to good schools, however, is very competitive (RADA, for example, auditions over 1000 people a year for 25 places). 'Graduates' from established drama schools do not normally have great difficulty in getting their first job. They are usually fixed up within a few months of leaving drama school. It is the second step, into bigger and better repertory, or into TV, West End, etc., which is the problematical one – and which vast numbers never manage to take at all. It means coming to London, finding a good agent who will take a newcomer, and earning a living, yet being available if the hoped-for audition comes.

Entry requirements and training

No rigid academic requirements; acceptance at good drama schools depends on audition, but candidates considered suitable almost invariably have several GCSEs and often A-levels, especially in English language and/or literature. The average ratio of acceptance at good schools is about 12 to 1; for women candidates it is about 45 to 1.

About 85% of players who earn their living at acting have been to accredited schools. Although grants are not mandatory (i.e. automatic), an increasing number of local education authorities will give grants for NCDT accredited courses. Some run their own auditions before deciding.

Performers' courses last 2 or 3 years. Students unlikely to succeed are asked to leave, or leave of their own accord, well before the end of the course. Courses prepare students for all types of work, but individual schools' curricula vary considerably. All cover the three main aspects: *movement, voice production and acting studies*. All students do all types of parts, from musical to mime, Shakespeare to Stoppard. Courses include general stagecraft, play-construction, etc.

Drama can also be taken as part of a first degree course, but the primary purpose of nearly all these courses is the study of literary criticism, history and literature of the theatre; not vocational acting training. Graduates from these courses usually go into teaching or possibly into drama production (mainly TV); but there are far fewer such openings than there are drama degree students.

There are a very few degree and post-graduate courses for performers.

Post-graduate drama courses are usually academic, not vocational.

Personal attributes   Good health; well-cut features, but not necessarily beauty; the ability to learn lines quickly; a good memory; great self-confidence; imagination and sensitivity to interpret any part; resilience, to ignore or benefit from the constant and public criticism from teachers, producers, directors, colleagues and the critics; an iron constitution; a sense of rhythm, at least (preferably an aptitude for dancing and singing); outstanding acting talent and a 'stage personality'; grim determination.

Late start   Not impossible, but difficult owing to stiff competition for drama school places.

Career-break   Possible, provided contacts are kept up.

Part time   Only by the very nature of the work.

Position of women   Only about 1 woman applicant in 45 is accepted at drama school: the ratio of female to male students training is 3 to 1. Although there are far more parts for men than for women, more women graduate every year. In this profession it is of course not a question of discrimination at the employment stage, but entrenched tradition makes even women dramatists write more parts for men than for women. Actresses are therefore strongly advised to have a second string to their bow. Secretarial or word processing training is useful here, as 'temping' and part-time jobs enable an actress to be available for auditions while earning her living. Women directors still face a great deal of discrimination, especially in the established theatre. As a result of all this, some women-only drama groups and co-operatives have been set up to provide work for women directors and actors. A 1992 Equity survey showed that women were generally paid less than men for similar work.

Drama Therapy

Drama therapy aims to use various dramatic techniques (including mime and improvisation) to provide therapeutic experiences for mentally and physically handicapped and psychiatric patients. It is practised by both specialist drama therapists and other professional staff involved in the care and treatment of such patients.

Training   Either via part-time course while working in the health or community services (for details write to the British Association for Drama Therapists, 7 Hatfield Road, St Albans, Herts) or via the 1-year full-time course, Drama and Movement in Therapy, operated by Sesame (a charity) at Kingsway-Princeton College. Students should have had previous relevant experience, e.g. psychiatric nursing, teaching, social work or drama. For details write to the Department of Creative and Vocational Studies, Kingsway-Princeton College, Hugh Myddleton Centre, Sans Walk, Rosoman Street, London EC1R 0AS.

Stage Management

The work   Stage managers and their teams are responsible to the director, during rehearsals, for the implementation of her/his instructions. This usually includes such things as the recording of actors' moves and other stage directions in the prompt book; collecting props, sound effects, etc., for the director's approval; relaying the director's requirements to the scenic, costume and lighting departments; ensuring that the actors are in the right place at the right time for rehearsals, costume fittings, etc. During the run of the play stage managers are in charge of everything on stage and backstage, and are responsible for seeing that each performance keeps to the director's original intention. Stage managers may also conduct understudy rehearsals. They often work all day and are in the theatre until the lights go out. Stage managers are engaged by theatrical managements for one particular production, or for a repertory season, or occasionally on a more permanent basis.

There is a shortage of trained and experienced stage managers. Many directors start as stage managers. First jobs are the most difficult to find.

Training   Full-time stage management courses at drama schools for 2–3 years. Admission to the courses is by interview and only those who are interested in stage management for its own sake or as preparation for work as a producer or director, but not as a stepping-stone to acting, are accepted. As with acting, those who have attended courses accredited by the National Council for Drama Training have the best prospects.

The subjects studied include history of drama and theatrical presentation; literature; the elements of period styles; stage management organization and routine: play study; carpentry; stage lighting; voice; movement; make-up.

NOTE: Stage management training does not lead immediately to work in television and films, but, if supplemented with experience, it may do so.

NOTE: There are also a very few full-time courses for theatre *electricians* and *sound engineers*.

Personal attributes

Organizing ability; natural authority and tact for dealing with temperamental and anxious actors; a practical approach; ability to deal with emergencies from prop-making to mending electrical equipment; calmness during crises; interest in the literary and technical aspects of theatrical production; the ability to speak well – both lucidly and concisely; visual imagination; a genuine desire to do stage management in preference to acting: frustrated actors do not make good, or happy, stage managers.

Late start

Should be fair opportunities for people with amateur dramatic experience; maturity helps in a job which involves organizing others.

Career-break

Should be no problem if good experience before the break – and if willing to work all evening and often during the day.

Part time

Sporadic rather than part time.

Position of women

Proportions of men and women have always been fairly equal; women are welcome in this branch of the profession and do well in it.

Further information

National Council for Drama Training, 5 Tavistock Place, London WC1H 9SS (no reply without an s.a.e.)

Conference of Drama Schools (enclose s.a.e. for list of member schools), c/o Central School of Speech and Drama, 64 Eton Avenue, London NW3 3HY

Local theatre; drama schools

Related careers

LAW: *Barrister* – LEISURE/RECREATION MANAGEMENT – SPEECH AND LANGUAGE THERAPISTS – TELEVISION, FILM AND RADIO

Driving Instructor and Examiner

Driving Instructor

Entry qualifications

4 years' full (not provisional) car driving licence without disqualification: no minimum age but, in practice, registration rarely granted to anyone under 23.

The work

The majority of instructors work on their own. This is more lucrative, but also more precarious, than working for one of the big driving schools. Hours are irregular and long: far more pupils want lessons at lunch time, after work or at weekends than during normal working hours. Most instructors teach between 6 and 12 pupils a day.

Being a good driver is not the most important aspect of instructing: instructors must like teaching and have the natural ability to do so; they must be able to put themselves into the position of a nervous, possibly not very talented, learner. They usually drive all day and every day through the same streets, which can be dull. The attractions of the work are, largely, being one's own boss; developing learners' road sense and driving technique; talking, during lessons, to a variety of people.

Business depends on area: it is essential, before investing in a dual-control car, to find out whether or not the area is already saturated with instructors.

Personal attributes

Organizing ability, business acumen, ability to get on with all types of people and to put them at their ease; complete unflappability and fearlessness; some mechanical aptitude; teaching talent; endless patience; ability to criticize tactfully and explain lucidly.

Training

Instructors must pass the Department of Transport's 3-part examination: a written test (Part 1), a practical driving test (Part 2) and a test of instructing ability (Part 3). Parts 2 and 3 must be completed within 2 years of passing Part 1. The syllabus for Part 1 includes principles and applications of road safety, driving techniques, and theory and practice of learning, teaching and assessment. Part 2 is a stringent test at advanced level. In Part 3 the examiner plays the part first of a new learner and then of a pupil at about test standard. After passing Part 2, trainees are allowed to hold a 6-month training licence and charge for instruction, but they must pass Part 3 before being registered as an Approved Driving Instructor.

Driving Examiner and Traffic Examiner

Entry qualifications and training

Driving examiner
Minimum age 25, with experience of having worked with the public in a position of some authority; must have held a driving licence for 5 years without conviction for a serious motoring offence; wide experience of driving in the last 3 years; active interest in, and knowledge of, all motoring/road/traffic trends and problems; some mechanical knowledge of cars and other vehicles; preferably some experience of driving a variety of vehicles including motorcycles. Selection is based on driving experience, a special driving test and interview, followed by a 4-week course.

Traffic examiner
Minimum age 25 with some experience of law enforcement as it affects heavy goods vehicles. Selection is by interview.

The work

Driving examiners are Civil Servants. They work as members of a team under a senior examiner, attached to one of over 300 test centres throughout the country. They test learner drivers of cars and other vehicles to ensure that candidates are competent to drive without endangering other road-users and that they drive with due consideration for other drivers and pedestrians. To do this the examiner takes drivers over an approved route and asks them to carry out various exercises. While doing this the examiner must take notes without distracting the driver's concentration and must make a fair assessment. The work is highly concentrated and, for work as responsible as this, can be fairly repetitive.

Traffic examiners, also Civil Servants, investigate, by observation on the road, by inquiry of operators and by examination of drivers' records, whether laws concerning operation of vehicles (such as the hours a driver may be in charge of a vehicle without rest period) are being observed. Examiners do not have to examine vehicles' mechanical conditions.

Recruitment is only sporadic. For promotion, examiners may have to move to another area.

Personal attributes

Air of authority; friendliness; tact; ability to concentrate constantly; unflappability.

Late start   Most instructors and examiners have had some other job before; maturity is an asset.

Career-break   *Instructors*: There is a danger that, during the break, another instructor may set up in the area. Continued driving during the break would be essential.

Examiners: Too early to know what the opportunities for returners would be, but returners would be encouraged.

Part time   It is possible to have a small number of pupils, but it is never possible to work during school-hours only. Summer months are the busiest time. So far no part-time examiners, but part-time work and job-sharing is possible.

Position of women   *Driving instructors*: About 13% now are women. Women instructors have no special problem getting pupils.

Driving examiners: This is a relatively new career for women. They now form 10% of the total, up from just over 5% in 1987.

Further information   *Driving instructors and driving examiners*: Driving Standards Agency, Stanley House, Talbot Street, Nottingham NG1 5GU

Traffic examiners: Vehicle Inspectorate Executive Agency, Berkeley House, Croydon Street, Bristol BS5 0DA

Related careers   TEACHING

Economics

Entry qualifications

Degree in economics; A-level maths or statistics preferred, but not essential, for all courses.

The work

Economics is concerned with the organization, utilization and distribution of productive and financial resources, nationally and internationally. This includes the study of political, industrial and social relationships and interactions.

Economics comes under the Social Sciences umbrella, but it is not a science in the accepted sense. Economic theories are not 'correct' or 'incorrect'. Even if worked out on mathematical models and tested on the computer, premises are based on assumptions and imponderables rather than on unassailable facts and figures. Hence the variety of 'schools' of economists (e.g. Keynesian, monetarist), each with different answers to the same economic problems. Economics therefore involves making judgements, choosing to adhere to one set of principles rather than another.

Economists work in a wide variety of settings – in urban and regional planning, in industry, commerce, the City, the Civil Service (the largest employer), in financial and industrial journalism, as organizers or researchers in trade unions and in management consultancies and overseas in development programmes. They try (but do not often succeed) to identify the causes of problems like inflation and unemployment, and suggest courses of action which might solve or ease the problem. Some economists specialize in, for example, the economics of energy resources, the car industry, agriculture, transport.

Extent of specialization varies enormously. Some economists become very knowledgeable about a particular aspect or part of an industry; others in an area of economics. One assignment required an economist with a background in the catering industry to suggest sites for and types of new hotels which a major company wanted to build. Work involved research: what makes hotels successful at home and abroad? In what proportion do food, accommodation, hotel location, service, pricing, affect a hotel's profitability? What constitutes 'good' food, accommodation, etc.? The economist spent a year asking questions in hotels –

of guests and staff and management – analysing relevant companies' accounts, and then presented the report. Another economist
who specialized in 'agricultural economics' prepared a report on
measures to improve the productivity of an underdeveloped Third
World country. New specializations emerge as society's needs,
priorities and problems change. For example, economists in the
Civil Service are concerned with all aspects of our lives, from
energy conservation to services for the disabled, from monitoring
the performance of the higher education system to cost/benefit
analysis of a new motorway scheme.

Economists who take jobs as *economists* act as advisers, whatever type of employer they work for. They do not normally take
or implement decisions, and they have to be prepared for their
advice to be ignored. Economists who want to be involved more
directly with the work of the organization that employs them
would be wise to go into management in industry or commerce
(see MANAGEMENT, p. 272; BANKING, p. 69; ACCOUNTANCY,
p. 1).

An economics degree can be a general graduate qualification;
and it can be a 'specialist' qualification – for work in systems
analysis, statistics, market research, investment analysis, cybernetics, operational research (see under relevant headings).

Training   Most degree courses include as 'core' studies: micro- and macro-
economics, economic and political theory and economic history.
Specializations to choose from include agricultural economics,
monetary theory and policy, economics of under-developed countries, public sector management, econometrics, economic forecasting, economic geography, transport studies. Economics can be
combined with almost any other discipline including accountancy,
geography, computing, law, sociology, languages, maths, philosophy and a physical science. The content of individual courses and
the emphasis given to the many aspects of the subject vary greatly
from one to another, but quantitative methods are of increasing importance.

Personal   Numeracy; interest in political and social affairs; analytical
attributes powers. Resilience, to be able to persevere when events prove
research and theories wrong, and when suggestions are being
ignored; ability to explain complex research findings to lay
people.

Late start Should be no problem for people who have commercial, financial
or similar experience.

Career-break   It is essential to maintain contact through reading journals, going to meetings and reading reports, etc.

Part time   As freelance for established consultants. Job-sharing is possible, but not widely available as yet.

Position of women   Over a quarter of economics students are women; as maths A-level is by no means required for all economics degree courses, more women could read the subject. They do not seem to have any special difficulties getting jobs. A comparatively large proportion do well in financial journalism and in investment analysis. The subject is adaptable enough to enable women to work in some area at all stages of their career. Instead of part-time work they may do sporadic freelance work, if established and experienced.

Further information   No central organization.

Related careers   ACCOUNTANCY–COMPUTING / IT–INFORMATION WORK–JOURNALISM – MANAGEMENT – MANAGEMENT SERVICES : *Operational Research* – TOWN AND COUNTRY PLANNING

Engineering

Qualified engineers are divided into three sections on The Engineering Council's Register: *professional engineer*, *incorporated engineer* and *engineering technician*.

Chartered Engineers
(see p. 197 for Incorporated Engineers and Engineering Technicians)

Entry qualifica-tions

Degree: 2, often 3 A-levels, normally including maths and physics, and at least 3 GCSEs (A–C) which should include English language and often a foreign language and chemistry. Chemistry A-level is essential for chemical and, usually, agricultural engineering. BTEC / SCOTVEC National Certificates and Diplomas are accepted for many degrees if appropriate units were taken; their acceptance by universities is not automatic. (Introductory courses for people with the wrong A-levels are available at many institutions.)

The work

Engineering is not so much one career, more an expertise which opens doors into a vast range of jobs. Engineers probably have a wider choice of environment in which to work, and of type of job, than any other professionals.

The purpose of engineering is the design and manufacture of the 'hardware' of life. Engineers have a hand in the creation of anything in use anywhere – from chips (both kinds) to chairs; cable TV to toys; motorways to kidney-machines; robots to milk bottles. They are the wealth creators without whom the country's economy cannot improve, and they are also a twentieth-century type of missionary: by designing irrigation and similar schemes for the Third World they reduce famine and poverty. So engineering can be the right choice as much for the person who wants to improve the quality of life all round as for the person who wants a prestigious top managerial or professional job.

There is a range of engineering functions (see below), each appealing to different temperaments and talents. Engineers can concentrate on, for example, creative design; on developing ideas, seeing them translated into the end-product and sold at a profit; on managing people and/or resources and/or processes; on research into, say, laser beam applications or into robotics.

Apart from the many aspects of practical 'active' engineering, there is the vital commercial exploitation of ideas and products. Technical sales and marketing (see below) are now often considered the sharp end of the profession, and engineers do well in both these areas.

It is estimated that most engineers spend about one third of their time discussing work with colleagues, customers or clients, staff, bosses; but there are backroom jobs for loners.

An engineering qualification is much under-rated as a way into more glamorous-sounding and more difficult-to-get-into careers – e.g. marketing (see p. 294), industrial management (see p. 272), public relations (see p. 409), television (see p. 530) and other graduate employment. Engineering is, in fact, very much a 'transferable skill' – and that is immensely useful at a time when everybody is likely to change jobs several times in a working life.

Even non-engineering employers who recruit graduates often now prefer science and engineering to arts graduates. Their specific knowledge can be useful in an age when technology has a bearing on virtually any type of business; their analytical approach to problem-solving is invariably useful, even when the problem is not a technical one. So even young people who are not planning to spend their lives as engineers, but want to go into anything from merchant banking to journalism, might well consider taking an engineering degree as a stepping-stone. Engineering need no more be a vocational course than an arts degree (and engineering courses are much easier to get into than arts degree courses).

There are post-graduate courses in business management, systems analysis, transport, etc., which can be taken either immediately after qualifying or a few years later (after the *career-break*, p. 202). New-style courses in 'information engineering' (combining computing and electronic engineering) and 'mechatronics' (combining mechanical and electronic engineering) aim to train engineers to manage computer-based engineering systems.

Job prospects are good on the whole, because engineering is such an adaptable skill; the broader the areas of application of the discipline, the better the prospects; for example, mechanical and electronic engineers are needed in very many more areas of employment than are naval architects. Within electrical, electronic, mechanical and production engineering it is possible to switch from one branch to another. This usually requires taking a post-graduate course (possibly part time, while working). Many engineers, from any discipline, go into industrial and commercial management (see MANAGEMENT, p. 272) and into management consultancy (see p. 288). Others, especially electronics engineers, go into computing (see p. 142). Chartered engineers can become maths, physics and engineering science teachers. There are opportunities in the EC and elsewhere abroad. The new title 'European Engineer' (Eur. Ing.) will become a 'passport' enabling greater mobility and recognition for engineers working in Europe. To gain this title, professional engineers must show they have completed a package of degree, training and experience lasting not less than 7 years.

Engineers normally specialize in two dimensions: in one *branch* or *discipline*, and then, after training, in one *function*, or type of activity. The main functions within each branch are:

Design

This is the most creative of the engineering functions and is the core of the engineering process. Design engineers create or improve products which can be manufactured and maintained economically, perform satisfactorily, look good and satisfy proven demand. Looks matter more in consumer goods – microwave ovens, telephones – than, for example, in machine tools. Design engineers may also design a new, or improve an established, engineering process. Most designers work to a brief. For example, a car manufacturer's marketing department may request that next year's model within a given price range should incorporate fuel-saving and/or safety devices (which may have been perfected in Research or which Research may be asked to work on); and that the model should incorporate certain visual features which seemed to 'sell' a competitor's model; design engineers may add their own, totally new ideas.

Their job is to find efficient and economic solutions to a set of problems. They must investigate materials and processes to be used in the manufacture of the product, which means they have to consult experts from other disciplines; but it is the design engineer who specifies what goes into the manufacture of the product and what processes are to be used.

Because the work of design engineers varies so enormously, the job is impossible to define precisely. Designing an aircraft which is a team effort has little in common with adding a feature or two to an established type of machine tool or TV component. Most work is done in 'design offices', where several graduates assisted by technicians work under a *chief design engineer*. Some designing, in electronics for example, is done in the laboratory. CAD – computer-aided design – is now used extensively. An experienced design engineer can choose whether to be part of a team that designs, say, a whole new airport, or whether to work alone on simple, straightforward design.

Personal attributes High academic ability; an urge to put new technologies to practical use; creativity; imagination; ability to co-ordinate the work of others; interest in marketability of product; ability to work as one of a team or to lead it.

Research and Development (R and D)

In some organizations research and development are two separate departments; in some the two, plus design, go together. But most typically, research and development form one department, with design a separate, but very closely linked one.

R and D engineers investigate, improve and adapt established processes and products, and they may create new ones. The work is essentially experimental, laboratory-based, but the 'laboratory' could be a skid-pan on which new tyre-surfaces are tried out, or a wind-tunnel in which to experiment with aircraft models.

While there is some extending-the-frontiers-of-knowledge kind of research, most engineering research is 'applied', i.e. aimed at maximizing sales and profits; or at saving precious resources; or exploiting newly discovered materials or processes.

Work comes from several sources: *design engineers* may want to use a new material, but they need to know more about its 'behaviour' before using it; *production engineers* may ask R and D to investigate why there is a recurrent fault in a particular production process or product; the *marketing department* may complain that a particular aspect of a competitor's fridge or carphone makes the competitor's product sell better: R and D would investigate the better-selling product, and come up with suggestions. Research and development is very much team work.

Personal attributes Practical bent; high academic ability; imagination; perseverance in the face of disappointing research results; interest in following up ideas which have profitable application; ability to work well with colleagues from other departments; willingness to switch from one project to another if Marketing or Production have urgent problems.

Production

Confusingly, this is both a *branch* with its own degree and Chartered Institution, and a *function*. In addition, terminology is vague. People doing the work may be called *production planners* or *production managers*, or *production engineers*. Titles vary and may or may not denote different responsibilities or qualifications.

The production function broadly covers changing raw materials into all types of articles. This involves the selection of the most suitable material and the application of the manufacturing process and system in order to manufacture the products.

Products can range from pizzas to cars, CDs to beer cans. The production engineer must see that labour, equipment and materials are used efficiently and that the product is completed at the correct quality and cost, in the right quantity, at the right time. The work environment could be a huge (and noisy) heavy engineering plant; it can be a large, but very quiet, highly automated workshop.

In the past, production engineering was usually done by practical people with some knowledge of engineering processes. As manufacturing processes become ever more sophisticated, and as industry has begun to recognize the need for greater efficiency and streamlining, production engineering has grown in importance (and status). It is now an important equal of other engineering branches and functions.

Production managers' work has much in common with personnel management: smoothing out problems on the shop-floor before they flare up into disputes; dealing with unions and with staff problems which might affect the department's productivity.

Personal attributes
Organizing ability; practicality; ability to get on well with people of all types at all levels in the hierarchy – from operatives to heads of research and managing director; ability to keep calm under pressure and in inevitable crises; liking for being very much at the centre of action.

Technical Sales and Marketing

Sales engineers use engineering expertise in a commercial context. They spend most of their time away from the office, meeting people. Selling engineering products ('specialist selling'), which may be selling anything from machine tools to oil rigs, domestic freezers to road maintenance equipment and service, combines salesmanship with technical knowledge. Customers may be lay people to whom the virtues of a product have to be explained, or highly professionally qualified people (more so than the sales engineer, possibly) who ask searching questions about the product's performance and properties. Sales engineers also act as links between prospective customers and manufacturers, passing on criticism of and requests for products and changes. They must find out, for example, what features – design, after-sales service, cost – make a competitor's product sell better in other countries or at home. (See also MARKETING AND SELLING, p. 294.)

Searching out new customers is an important part of selling. Some sales may take months of meetings and negotiating. Sales engineers may travel abroad a good deal, or they may have their own 'territory' near home – it largely depends on the type of product.

Personal attributes   Outgoing personality; adaptability to use the right approach with different types of customers; perseverance, and indifference to the occasional rebuff; commercial acumen; interest in economic affairs; communication skills.

Consultancy

This function absorbs significant numbers only in civil and structural engineering, but numbers in other branches – notably mechanical, electronic and production engineering – are increasing. Consulting engineers work in partnerships in private practice, rather like accountants or solicitors. A few set up on their own. Firms vary in organization and extent of specialization. Basically, consultants provide specialist services for clients in charge of large projects who may be public authorities, architects, other engineers or quantity surveyors. Consultants advise, provide feasibility studies, design to a brief, and, sometimes, organize projects. They are not in the construction/manufacturing business but may be in charge of putting work out to contractors and, as their client's agent, may then be responsible for supervising contractors' work, including authorizing payment.

Consultants may specialize: for example, civil engineers may specialize in motorway or in oil rig design, or in traffic management; electronic engineers may specialize in telecommunications or in medical electronics or in instrumentation and systems. Consultants are usually *design engineers* (see above), but as they move up the ladder they spend more time dealing with clients and getting business – i.e. on the commercial side of the job. Some go into or specialize in *management consultancy* (see p. 288). Civil and structural consulting engineers work abroad a lot, especially in the Middle East, usually on contract for a fixed number of years.

Personal As for design engineers, plus a confidence-inspiring manner, per-
attributes suasive powers for dealing with clients and contractors; for senior
jobs: commercial sense.

Other functions

Apart from these specializations, there are many jobs which are,
usually, carried out within one of the main functions. Titles and
the work they describe vary. They include *maintenance* (work on
employer's premises) and *service* (work carried out on customer's
premises), *test, installation, quality assurance, systems, control*
engineers. These functions may be carried out by graduates early
in their career, they may be top jobs or they may be carried out
by technicians (see p. 197).

Considering the need for precision in engineering, job and
function titles are often surprisingly vague and can, therefore, be
misleading.

Engineering Disciplines

The main *branches* or *disciplines* are:

Mechanical Engineering

Mechanical engineers work in all branches and all functions; they
are concerned with the application of the principles of mechanics,
hydraulics, thermodynamics, to engineering processes. They have
a vast choice of end-product to work with and environment to
work in: literally no industry is closed to them; they work in
hospitals; in computer manufacture; robotics; all types of research
establishments. Engineers who want to help humanity as directly
as possible, who want to see the application of their efforts to the
alleviation of suffering and discomfort, can work in *medical
engineering* (see below); engineers who want to go into technical
sales or into marketing, or general management can take their
mechanical engineering training into anything from car manufacture to computers or North Sea oil extraction.

Environmental Engineering (Heating and Ventilating Engineering/Building Services Engineering)

Environmental engineers are concerned with heating, lighting, acoustics, ventilation, air conditioning, noise and air pollution and its control. They are called in as consultants by civil engineers and architects on building projects from hospital to airport, office block to housing estate, chain store to underground station. This branch straddles mechanical, electrical and structural engineering.

Civil Engineering

Civil engineering covers the design, planning, construction and maintenance of, firstly, the 'infrastructure': transport systems, water supplies and sewage plants; and, secondly, large-scale structures, ranging from oil platforms to power stations. Transport systems include roads, bridges, tunnels (including the vast Channel Tunnel project), ports and airports. Transport planning and management is another, growing, activity. Providing water supplies may involve building reservoirs; controlling the flow of rivers; ensuring safe drinking water and effective irrigation systems in developing countries; and the disposal and treatment of waste to prevent pollution.

Civil engineers work for local and central government, in industry and for international organizations. Many work as *consulting engineers*, called in by large organizations to design and carry out a project. Others work for civil engineering contractors supervising construction projects and dealing with building contractors; they may also do design work. Many British firms work on overseas contracts.

Structural Engineering

This is a specialized branch of civil engineering. Structural engineers are particularly skilled in non-traditional construction materials and techniques. Those working for civil engineering firms might design large-scale constructions such as grandstands and bridges. Those called in as consultants by architects might design the foundations and skeletal framework of large buildings such as skyscrapers and hospitals.

Electrical and Electronic Engineering

The two overlap. Broadly, *electrical engineering* is concerned with the use and generation of electricity to produce heat, light and mechanical power: electrical engineers work in generating stations, distribution systems and on the manufacture of all kinds of electrical machinery from tiny motors for powered invalid chairs to heavy motors for industrial plant. They are also concerned with research into the more efficient use of, and new sources of energy for, electrical power.

Electronics is mainly concerned with *computers, telecommunications, automation/instrumentation and control*.

(a) *Computers*: The electronic engineering industry is concerned with producing the machinery – the 'hardware' – which gives house-room to the software, i.e. the programs, and with producing the components and products which 'computer systems' need to perform their tasks. This includes microprocessors, visual display units, printers, mainframe and desktop computers. (For details of software/programming jobs see COMPUTING / INFORMATION TECH-NOLOGY, p. 142).

The proportion of design, research and development engineers is greater in electronics than in other branches. (Mechanical, electrical and chemical engineers, physicists, and computer scientists also work in computer manufacture.)

(b) *Telecommunications*: Include, for example, the extension of old-fashioned telephony into 'multi-facility' services such as 'conference calls': facilities for telephone conversations between several participants in different locations; and for 'confravision': centres in various towns equipped with closed-circuit television as well as with 'conference call' services are rented by the hour to business people who then 'hold meetings' with colleagues or customers without having to travel. Other telecommunications developments include optical fibre systems; the extension of radio networks; satellite and cable television.

Telecommunication technologies in offices include electronic mail – devices which enable keyed-in messages and reports to be transmitted instantly from one computer to another – fax machines and facilities like teletext.

(c) *Automation, instrumentation and control*: This is concerned with automatic control devices, from the operation of automatic flight control systems in aircraft to nearer-home gadgets such as automatic ovens and central-heating time-clocks, and robotics.

Then there is the vast area of computer-controlled equipment which has become possible as a result of the development of *microelectronics*: the design, development and production of scaled-down, minuscule electronic circuitry – the 'chip' – and with its application. The chip affects virtually every industrial, commercial, scientific and professional activity but it can do nothing by itself: electronics specialists develop its potential and 'program' (instruct) it to perform the precisely defined task for which it is intended.

Examples are hotel, aircraft and theatre seat reservations; supermarkets (bleeping checkouts that keep the warehouse management informed of the precise level of stock of every item in every store at any time); document storage and retrieval systems (see INFORMATION WORK, p. 229). In manufacturing, 'robotics' – assembly-line work done by programmed robots – is developing fast. Scientific applications include weather-forecasting; computer-aided design in civil and structural engineering; dating archaeological discoveries.

Medical or Biomedical Engineering

This is a combination of electronic, electrical and mechanical engineering and physics. Medical engineers at the moment usually take a degree in either mechanical, electronic or electrical engineering (but there are also medical engineering options in electronic and mechanical engineering degrees) and then either take a postgraduate course or join a team working on medical engineering projects. These are often carried out jointly with consultants in hospitals, who specify what they want any particular equipment to do. Kidney transplants, heart surgery, and many less spectacular procedures are only possible thanks to the imaginative co-operation of doctors and engineers.

Medical engineers also design aids for severely handicapped people – e.g. artificial, remarkably usable, replacement limbs or custom-built 'transport'.

Medical engineering is often overlooked as an alternative to medicine for people who want to be closely involved with alleviating disabilities.

Chemical Engineering

Chemical (or process) engineers are concerned with the design and development of laboratory processes, and with their translation into large-scale plant, for the production of chemicals, dyes, medicines, fertilizers, plastics, etc. Their expertise in designing and managing plant in which chemical processes take place is also used in food processing, brewing, paper, textile and other industries. Biochemical engineers specialize in the design and development of industrial plant in which biochemical processes can take place (see 'Biotechnology', p. 444), e.g. developing alternative sources of energy and converting noxious waste into useful by-products or at least into harmless substances. Chemical engineering has far wider application than is often believed: many chemical engineers do work in oil refineries and other heavy industry, but there is wide scope elsewhere, for example in textiles and electronics. 'Green' issues are of increasing importance.

Production Engineering
(see 'Production', p. 187)

Production engineering covers all aspects of manufacture. It embraces knowledge of many aspects of engineering and ensures that labour, equipment and materials are used efficiently.

The production engineer needs both technical and 'people management' skills, so that goods of the right quality are produced at the required time at the right price. The production engineer plans the production methods and systems (which nowadays often involve computer-controlled tools) and liaises with other departments such as design, R and D, purchasing and sales.

Naval Architecture

Despite the title, the work is engineering rather than architecture. It is concerned with the design, repair, construction and economic operation of craft which float on or under or hover just above the water. Craft can be of any size from sailing dinghy to supertanker, hydrofoil to oil rig. Naval architects work for the Services as well as for ship- and boat-building firms. A small branch.

Aeronautical/Aerospace Engineering

Concerned with aircraft design and construction and space and satellite research, as well as with planning, operation and maintenance of airlines' fleets of aircraft and aircraft components. They work for aircraft manufacturers, airlines and the Ministry of Defence. This is a small branch of engineering; a greater proportion work in R and D, fewer on production. People who want to work in this area can take electronics or physics degrees and leave more options open.

Agricultural Engineering
(see AGRICULTURE AND HORTICULTURE, p. 27)

Mining Engineering

Mining engineers' training is very much more vocational than that of other engineers. The majority of mining engineers (it is a small branch) in this country work in the coal industry; a few in quarrying, rock, salt, and potash mining. There are opportunities abroad in ore extraction and other types of mining and minerals processing, usually after some experience at home.

Other branches

Some engineering specializations described elsewhere (or advertised) have different titles from all those mentioned here. They may be small branches, or offshoots of, or options within, established engineering branches. Titles may describe jobs which can be done by people from various disciplines (e.g. in robotics). Or they may describe emerging new branches which are also still under the umbrella of an established branch.

Engineering can no longer be neatly categorized into the traditional disciplines. It is a fast-changing profession, developing as a result of scientific discovery (scientists discover; engineers exploit discoveries and make them work productively as well as in response to need). For example, new sources of energy will be needed next century: engineers are working on the development of wind, wave and solar energy – and become *energy engineers*. Technological tasks are so complex now that people from various disciplines have to pool their expertise: at the same time, some disciplines are becoming so unwieldy that they sub-divide. That applies specially in *electronics* and *mechanical engineering*. New titles do not have as precise meanings as have traditional engineering disciplines.

Here is a very brief (and superficial) guide to some of the current engineering job-titles and the – probable – umbrella discipline, or function, which should be the first port of call for information on what knowledge is required and what work involved:

Computer systems, control engineering: umbrella discipline – *Electronics*.

Offshore, oil, fuel, energy engineering: umbrella disciplines – *Mechanical*, *Electrical*, *Electronic* or *Chemical Engineering*.

(Energy engineering can also describe the energy-saving function in large organizations.)

Nuclear engineering: umbrella disciplines – *Physics* and *Electronics*.

Industrial engineering: umbrella discipline – *Production Engineering*, but can also be combination of *Management* and *Engineering*.

Manufacturing engineering: umbrella discipline – usually *Production Engineering*.

Process engineering: umbrella discipline – *Chemical Engineering*.

Plant, installation, test and commissioning engineering: umbrella disciplines – could be *Mechanical*, *Production* or *Chemical Engineering*, but also used for functions carried out by *Mechanical* or almost any other specialist engineer.

Training   Engineers who undergo 'accredited' training are registered in the appropriate category by The Engineering Council's Board for Engineers' Registration (BER).

Professional engineers are commonly called chartered engineers, although strictly speaking to use the title Chartered Engineer requires corporate membership of one of the chartered engineering institutions. However, they can be on the professional engineer section of the EC's Register (but without the designation C.Eng.) without joining an institution. The EC strongly advises people to register through membership of a chartered engineering institution.

One institution asks for a first- or second-class honours degree, which is a higher standard than that set by the EC. The situation is confusing, so anyone considering professional engineering should look carefully at each institution's requirements.

The EC recognizes several routes to qualification as a professional engineer:

1. The mainstream route: an honours degree in engineering jointly accredited by the EC and relevant engineering institution, leading to the award of Bachelor of Engineering (B.Eng.), not, as in the past, a B.Sc. (with a few exceptions). These 'enhanced' B.Eng. courses closely integrate theory and practice. In addition to the study of fundamental scientific principles, to be accredited they must include engineering applications such as design practice, production techniques, fabrication and financial applications.

They are normally 3 years full time, or 4 years sandwich. Some offer a general first year before specialization. A recent initiative has increased the number of courses specializing in, or offering options in, manufacturing systems engineering; these concentrate on the manufacturing process, its specification, design, maintenance, etc.

2. 'Extended' (plus enhanced) degree courses leading to Master of Engineering and lasting 4 years full time, 5 years sandwich. These cater for 'high-fliers' and are of three kinds, providing either study in greater depth than the B.Eng. of one branch of engineering or study of a range of engineering disciplines or engineering study plus a grounding in finance and management.

3. One of the new 'integrated' engineering degree programmes, leading to B.Eng. or M.Eng. The difference between these and (1) and (2) is that they emphasize the interdisciplinary nature of engineering. The syllabus may include civil, electrical, electronic, manufacturing and mechanical engineering, business and management studies, and, optionally, a foreign language. Their other feature is that they offer flexible entry requirements and are therefore suitable for people without A-level physics.

4. Other engineering courses – general or specialized – designed for people without maths and physics A-levels: these provide a foundation year after which students go on to take a 3- or 4-year degree course.

Candidates should always look carefully at different syllabuses and check whether courses have been accredited.

5. Students take a 'part-accredited' engineering or science honours degree and add sufficient 'bolt-on' modules to make good the academic gaps. This must not take longer than 1 academic year.

6. Graduates with an ordinary or unclassified engineering degree who first register as Incorporated engineers (see p. 197) can add modules as in (5).

7. Science or maths honours graduates who can satisfy the EC that their subsequent training and experience compensate for any deficiency in vocational background may register.

8. Technicians who follow the part-time BTEC route (p. 200) can take the EC's own 2-part examination leading to registration as chartered engineer.

Sandwich courses are particularly suitable for students wanting to enter industry, as they are able to sample the industrial scene. Many large companies sponsor students (i.e. pay them while they are studying), who thus gain work experience in that organization. College-based students work for a range of employers during their course. 'Thin' sandwich courses last 4–5 years, alternating 6 months' study with 6 months' work experience. 'Thick' sandwich courses last 5 years, with a year at the beginning and end spent with an employer and 3 years' full-time study in between.

Incorporated (formerly Technician) Engineers and Engineering Technicians

Entry qualifications

In practice normally 4 GCSEs (A–C) including maths and physics, but see 'Training', below, and BTEC/SCOTVEC (pp. xxi, xxii). Technicians can also start by training as craftsmen/women through Youth Training (see p. xxv).

The work

The technician scene is very confusing indeed to anyone outside the industry. There are, officially – that is according to the Board for Engineers Registration – two levels: *Incorporated engineers*, those whose work overlaps with graduates and whose breadth of knowledge enables them to take responsibility for a wide range of tasks; and *engineering technicians*, who take responsibility for jobs in a more narrowly defined area. In practice, however, the distinction is blurred. The term 'technician' is loosely used to cover a whole range of job levels. Very many 'technician' jobs are in fact done by graduates. Technicians become 'senior technicians' rather than 'Incorporated engineers' in some organizations. Some go on to qualify as Chartered Engineers (see 'Training', below). Manpower studies have shown that in electronics there are more technicians than professional engineers/scientists and probably four times as many civil engineering technicians as there are professional civil engineers.

Chartered and Incorporated engineers' work overlaps in all branches, but more in electrical, electronic, mechanical and production engineering than in the others. It also overlaps in all functions (see above) but much less in design and research where graduates' depth and breadth of training, and their creativity, are usually essential. After a few years' work, though, applicants' experience and ability rather than their qualifications count. At that stage, experienced technicians are on a par with *average* graduates (not with high-fliers). Degrees for chartered engineers became the normal qualifications about 20 years ago, when new technologies increased the complexities of engineering tasks (and as higher education became more accessible). But for every engineer who has the chance to make full use of degree-level knowledge – who is, say, responsible for the safe design of an oil rig or for a research project into the application of laser beams in surgery – there are hundreds of engineers whose jobs require sound professional expertise, but not the depth and breadth of knowledge needed for top jobs. Hence the increasing scope for technicians.

Incorporated engineers have never managed to put themselves

across as a professional entity, although in most branches they have their own professional institutions, and, within the engineering profession, they are fully recognized as vital experts in their field and essential colleagues. According to experience and training, they are either left to get on with tasks on their own, or are support staff with limited responsibility (both apply to average graduate engineers as well). Job titles such as, for example, *plant*, *project*, *production*, *commissioning*, *development* or *sales* engineer can describe *either* a Chartered *or* an Incorporated engineer. There is nothing precise about titles and demarcation by qualification in the engineering profession which depends so much on expertise and/or experience.

Work is as varied as that of chartered engineers.

Tasks include, for example:

In all branches: Draughtsmanship (usually computerized) which may be routine work, but may involve using initiative and special knowledge, and producing working drawings from designers' rough notes and/or instructions; or assisting professional engineers in research, design, development, perhaps building prototypes; *production* (see 'Production', p. 187); being responsible, for example, for one or several production lines or for continuity of supplies, or dispatch. *Estimating*: costing projects or parts of projects; supervision of installation of equipment on customer's premises or in firm's own factory; *repair and maintenance* in anything from garage to hotel, hospital to factory; *after-sales service* investigating complaints, for example. (Greatest scope in electrical and electronic engineering.)

Settings include:

Broadcasting (see p. 530).

British Telecom.

Newspaper production.

Hi-fi, television and video servicing.

Commercial recording studios – for example, as *balancing engineers* (who must be able to read music and have a good ear) are responsible for producing the required levels of sounds from various sources.

Civil and structural engineering sites: technicians help cost projects; supervise construction work; work out what equipment is required on bridge or road works; liaise with clients and, in municipal work, with local residents. In traffic management they may be in charge of compiling a 'street inventory' prior to the installation of traffic signals (finding out where gas and electricity mains are; what shops/schools and other 'traffic generators' there are) or organize traffic counts. They may also become *building control officers* for local authorities.

In *manufacturing* technicians work at all levels, from monitoring or servicing machinery to, jointly with personnel (see p. 365), working on job evaluation schemes. In *Marketing and sales* where (see above) engineering knowledge is only one of the necessary skills, experienced technicians do very well indeed and can rise to the top. Finally, experienced technicians can set up their own workshops/business (see WORKING FOR ONESELF, p. 557).

Prospects are good, especially for electronics, electrical and mechanical technicians. Even during recessions the demand for technicians often exceeds supply. Experienced technicians are also often able to get work *abroad*. Technician training is broadly based and, once trained, technicians can switch type of work.

Personal attributes

A practical and methodical approach and an interest in technology are needed in all technician jobs. There is room for backroom types who like to get on with their work on their own, for those who like to work in a team, those who like to work in a drawing office or laboratory, and for those who enjoy visiting clients and customers. For some jobs (the minority) manual dexterity. For others, ability to explain technical points in plain language and liking for meeting people.

Training

Training can be as a full-time student at college or part time while employed as a trainee technician.

Trainee technician route

Most employers follow training patterns recommended by the former Engineering Industry Training Board – now replaced by the Engineering Training Authority – EnTra – for technicians in manufacturing industry, or the Standing Joint Committee for the training of technicians in the civil engineering industry; these combine theory with planned practical experience.

The first year is spent 'off the job' on basic technician training. About a third of the time is spent at college learning the theory to go with the practical knowledge.

In the second year specialized training starts in the 6 main skills which are required in all technician jobs to a greater or lesser degree: choosing materials and components and understanding processing of materials; handling and using measuring tools or instruments; collecting and communicating information; understanding the manufacturing and commercial activities of the employer; planning and organizing one's own work as well as the work of others; diagnosing and solving problems and analysing faults.

The length of training varies, largely according to entrants' school qualifications and eventual aim, from 2 to 4 years. The normal pattern of training for all kinds of engineering technicians complements BTEC/SCOTVEC courses (see pp. xxi, xxii). BTEC/SCOTVEC National Certificate (2 years part time) or Diploma (3 years part time) with training and responsible experience leads to registration as Engineering Technician (Eng.Tech.). Technicians can then go on to take a BTEC/SCOTVEC Higher National Certificate (2 years part time) or Diploma (4 years part time) and with training and responsible experience become registered as Incorporated engineers (I. Eng.).

Technicians who complete recommended training and gain the National Certificate or Diploma are eligible for the award of an NVQ Level 3 (see p. xx). Those with HNC/D are eligible for an NVQ Level 4.

Full-time college route
Either a 2-year full-time or a 3-year sandwich BTEC National Diploma (or SCOTVEC equivalent). With training and responsible experience this leads to registration as Engineering Technician (as above).

Students can then take a 2-year full-time or 3-year sandwich course for a BTEC/SCOTVEC Higher National Diploma.

Entrants with at least 1 relevant A-level (usually maths or physics) and appropriate GCSEs (A–C) can go straight into a BTEC Higher award course.

Like part-time students those gaining National or Higher National awards are eligible for NVQs levels 3 or 4 once they have completed approved training.

Craft Level Entry

Entry qualifications

Average ability in maths, science (excluding biology), technical/practical subjects (excluding home economics). Employers normally test applicants' aptitudes. Many ask for GCSE pass in maths.

Maximum age: normally 17 (see TECs for adult training, p. xxv).

The work

Engineering craftsmen/women do skilled work and need sufficient theoretical knowledge to understand the principles behind the operations they carry out and to solve basic problems. They work in all branches and may be in charge of semi- and unskilled workers. Their work, and their scope, is changing as a result of new technologies. First of all, the distinction between craftspersons and technicians is narrowing, with craft-trained people becoming technicians more frequently than in the past; and second, as a result of automation in all engineering spheres, the distinction between the specialist trades is blurring. Traditional crafts or 'trades' continue to be practised, including:

Machine-shop Crafts

Toolmaking: The use of precision machinery and tools to make jigs, fixtures, gauges and other tools used in production work. Apprentices may start in the toolroom, or they are upgraded from other trades.

Toolsetting: Setting of automatic (such as computer/tape numerically controlled) or semi-automatic machines for use by machine operators in mass production.

Turning: Operating lathes which use fixed cutting tool(s) to remove metal/material from a rotating workpiece.

Milling: Operating milling machines where metal/material is removed from a fixed workpiece by rotating cutter(s).

Jig-boring: Highly skilled work in which very heavy articles are machined to a high degree of precision.

Grinding: Obtains a very accurate finish by removing small amounts of metal with rapidly revolving abrasive wheels. It is also used to sharpen tools.

Fitting

Fitters, whether working in mechanical, electrical or electronic engineering, combine the basic skills of the machine-shop craftsperson with the ability to use hand tools. In production work they may assemble cars, generators, TV sets, etc. They carry out maintenance and repair work on domestic appliances and office machinery either on customers' premises – private houses, factories, offices, etc. – or in workshops. Gas fitters install, service and repair gas-powered domestic appliances or industrial plant; marine engine fitters put together and repair ships' engines, etc.

Craftspeople may switch trades more easily than in the past, as well as learn new ones, but overall prospects are not as good as those for technicians.

Training   The Engineering Training Authority (EnTra – formerly the Engineering Industry Training Board) recommendations for Craft Training are:

    1-year ('Basic Engineering Training') 'off the job', i.e. in a

Training Centre, learning basic engineering skills. These include hand and machine skills, manipulation of sheet metal, welding and electrical/electronic skills.

2–4 years spent in the employing company on 'Module Segment' training – a package of skill training and experience 'on the job' to nationally agreed standards. A minimum of 6 Module segments must be completed for the training to be recognized for craftsmanship. A Certificate of Validated Achievement (CVA) is awarded after each stage showing what the individual trainee has achieved.

During both Basic Engineering and Module Segment Training trainees attend a College of Further Education by day- or block-release to learn relevant theory, working for City and Guilds or BTEC/SCOTVEC awards. Those who gain City and Guilds Part 2 or a National Certificate are eligible for an NVQ Level 3 for Craft Competencies.

This pattern of training can lead on to technician work and training (see above).

In civil engineering, craftsmen/women and operatives are employed by civil engineering contractors and follow the Civil Engineering Operative Training Scheme (CEOTS). Details from the Federation of Civil Engineering Contractors (see under 'Further Information', p. 205).

Late start (all levels)

Chartered engineers: Possible for technicians and people with related degrees or at least good, and recently acquired, science A-levels, or who have taken a foundation course (see p. 196).

Technicians: Good opportunities for people who have taken appropriate courses (see p. xxv for HTNT scheme), especially in electronics and related fields or such specialized areas as TV and other electronic equipment servicing.

Craft level: Not advisable.

Career-break

Because of the pace of technological change, a complete gap of even a few years would be difficult to bridge. But there are various schemes for enabling people on a domestic break (mainly women) to keep in touch. These include encouraging women to visit their former employers regularly during the break and, on their return, for them to have a 'mentor' or 'industrial tutor' who, in an informal way, helps them to catch up. During the break, women technicians and chartered engineers are encouraged to take the Open University (see p. xxxiv) 'Women in Technology' Associate Student programme. This has been specially designed for women who want to return to work after a child-rearing break. The 1985 Engineering Council report *Career breaks for women chartered and technician engineers* urged more engineering employers to adopt or develop retainer and refresher schemes: by attracting and retaining more highly skilled (female) staff in this way they would become more competitive. A further initiative is the Women's Fellowship Scheme aimed at providing part-time research posts for women scientists and engineers wanting to re-enter academic life after a break.

Part time   Few part-time jobs at present, but some opportunities for engineers who have specialized or can specialize in computing and related work. Others work on 'one-off' contracts. Job-sharing schemes do not seem to have been tried on any scale, but there is no reason why they should not work.

Position of women (all levels)   The proportion of women engineers is still woefully small. On average still less than 1% of the main chartered institutions' members are women (figures refer to 1991). Proportions vary according to age group: around 12% of student members are women; minute proportions of Fellows or equivalent. However, there is a significant increase in the proportion of female engineering students. They took up 14·7% of university (1991) and 12·5% of polytechnic (1990) first-year degree places. There are wide variations between different disciplines. In universities, 22% of chemical, 16% of general, 16% of civil, 10% of mechanical, 12% of electrical and 8% of electronic engineering students were women. The proportion of women electronic engineering students is especially disappointing. Yet electrical and electronic engineers are nearly always in demand and most work in clean, high-tech environments in which the dealing-with-people element is very great indeed.

The small proportion of women cannot be entirely explained by the still relatively small proportion who take A-level physics and maths (see p. xlv for GCSE and A-level male/female proportions); 54% of students accepted for ophthalmic optics in 1991 are women, and they normally also need A-level physics and maths (and ophthalmic optics courses are usually more difficult to get into than engineering courses). Yet engineering generally, and electrical engineering especially, leads to a far wider job choice and hence smaller risk of unemployment, than ophthalmic optics. Women's career-choices cannot be blamed just on poor careers information; it must also be due to the fact that women are still less long-term career-minded than men.

At technician level (see p. 197) the situation is even worse, with very few women, and not all trainees seem to be working for qualifications. However, BTEC has 9·6% of women on its HND engineering programme. The largest technician institution, many of whose members work in information technology, the Institution of Electrical and Electronics Incorporated Engineers, has 114 women among its 20,000 members. Yet the Institution has for many years now run an annual Young Woman Technician of the Year competition which always gets widely publicized and shows the wide range of jobs women do. (It is possible that women technicians are less willing to join institutions, but even allowing for that, the proportion is dismal indeed.) At craft level, women are very rare; good craftsmen/women get technician training so, as women who break into this male preserve are likely to be enterprising, they might as well go for technician training right away.

Women who have gone into engineering are doing well. Many have found that being female and therefore more noticeable may have helped in gaining sponsorship (for training) and jobs. Recruitment officers say they usually have 'more good and fewer average and plain hopeless' women than men applicants. They genuinely want more women Chartered and Incorporated engineers. The fact that a woman has the initiative to step off the tramlines and choose a non-traditional career shows she is more determined and interested than the average male who may have chosen engineering 'because it is there', and the obvious next step after school.

Promotion prospects, according to various surveys of women engineers, are reasonable in the early stages, but opportunities at management level, and for management training, could be better (see MANAGEMENT, p. 272, for hurdles in women's promotion paths). Nevertheless, the small but growing number of women in senior-middle and senior jobs (including non-technical work such as marketing) say that attitudes are changing and that opportunities *are* there – especially in the wide-ranging electronics area where 'people-related' skills are specially important.

Another good sign is that individual membership of the Women's Engineering Society has risen from 495 in 1984 to 750 in 1991.

There is no shortage of initiatives from industry, the Engineering Council, polytechnics and universities to attract more women. Conferences, seminars, residential weeks for sixth-formers, have all been running for several years and there are now many more young women engineers to act as 'role models'. The WISE (Women Into Science and Engineering) campaign has encouraged more girl pupils to consider engineering. TESS, a Technician Engineer Scholarship Scheme, gives suitably qualified women aged 18–25 scholarships to train as electronics technician engineers.

A booklet is available from The Engineering Council which gives details of awards, courses, visits and other initiatives designed to encourage girls and women to consider careers in science and engineering.

Further information

Engineering Careers Information Service, 54 Clarendon Road, Watford WD1 1LB (for manufacturing branches of engineering)

The Engineering Council (for list of individual Institutions as well as general information), 10 Maltravers Street, London WC2R 3ER

Civil Engineering Careers Service, 1–7 Great George Street, London SW1P 3AH

The Federation of Civil Engineering Contractors, 6 Portugal Street, London WC2A 2HH

For list of special courses (conversion and technician) for women: Engineering Council, or Careers Adviser (Women's Engineering Society), c/o Imperial College, Dept of Civil Engineering, Imperial College Road, London SW7 2BY

BTEC/SCOTVEC (see pp. xxi, xxii)

Related careers

AGRICULTURE AND HORTICULTURE – ART AND DESIGN – BUILD-ING: *Building Managers* – COMPUTING/IT – SCIENCE – SURVEYING

Environmental Health Officer

Entry require-ments
5 GCSEs (A–C) and 2 A-levels. Passes must include maths, English language and 2 sciences; one of the sciences must be at A-level. BTEC alternatives (plus English language) may be acceptable.

The work
Environmental health officers ensure that people are protected from a wide range of hazards in the environment in its widest sense – houses, shops, workplaces, leisure facilities, the air we breathe, our water supplies. Increasing public concern about the environment is reflected daily in the news: a leak of toxic chemicals; salmonella in eggs; contaminated water supplies; the effects of lead on children living near busy motorway junctions; an outbreak of legionnaire's disease; deaths from contaminated yoghurt; housing unfit through damp for human habitation. Environmental health officers deal with all these problems.

The majority of environmental health officers work in local authorities. Their role is both to advise on safety and hygiene and to enforce legislation. This involves visiting a great variety of sites; a high proportion of EHOs' time is spent out of the office.

EHOs ensure that safe and hygienic standards are met in the preparation, manufacture, transport and sale of *food*. This can mean visiting high-technology plants or market stalls, restaurants or slaughterhouses, to check on the cleanliness of equipment and staff, storage facilities and handling procedures. EHOs have powers to enter and inspect *housing* if they 'have reason to believe that the premises are not fit for human habitation' or they may be called in by the residents. They advise on repairs, improvements and sometimes demolition. Responsibility for *places of work* overlaps with that of factory inspectors (see p. 214). EHOs check on working conditions, for example sanitary arrangements, overcrowding, temperature, ventilation, lighting and hours of work for juveniles.

Noise, *pest control*, *water and waste*, *air pollution* and *communicable diseases* are also the responsibilities of EHOs. They may also deal with caravan and camping sites, houseboats and leisure boats, swimming pools and leisure centres, and some aspects of animal welfare.

Some EHOs have a general role covering a wide range of responsibilities; others specialize in, for example, food hygiene, housing or atmospheric pollution.

Some work in industry, e.g. food manufacturing.

Training

1. 3-year sandwich course leading to Diploma in Environmental Health.

2. 4-year sandwich degree course. Syllabus includes the basic sciences as applied to environmental health (control of infectious diseases and of vermin, for example); physical aspects of housing (dilapidations, unfitness); public cleansing; water supply; drainage, sewerage and sewage disposal; procedures under Housing Acts; hygiene of buildings (standards of heating, ventilation and lighting); food (hygiene and inspection), etc.

3. 2-year sandwich post-graduate course for graduates with appropriate degree.

All the above courses include a period of integrated professional training with a sponsoring local authority. An early choice of career is an advantage because it is easier to get financial support for (1) and (2) than for the post-graduate course.

4. *In Scotland.* 4-year degree in environmental health at Strathclyde University, in conjunction with 48 weeks' practical training in a local authority, followed by a Professional Interview for the Diploma in Environmental Health.

Personal attributes

Interest in people's living and working environment; ability to take decisions; sufficient self-confidence to go where one is not necessarily welcome; to be firm when necessary and to discuss complicated problems intelligently.

Late start

There is scope for late entry, though the older one is, the more difficult it could be to get the necessary practical training. Degree courses may relax the academic entry requirements for mature entrants; Diplomas do not.

Career-break

Should be no problem for those who keep in touch.

Part time

Should be possible to organize. EHOs' major employers, local authorities, have been among the most forward-looking on flexible working.

Position of women

Previously a male-dominated field, but more women are coming in. Entry is about 50/50 male/female. Those in senior positions are usually men, but there are few women of the right age and experience. In the past women were assumed not to be able or willing to do the rougher parts of the work in, for example, slaughterhouses or unfit-for-habitation dwellings, and so they did not get all-round experience. Now that there are more women, and changing attitudes and legislation enable them to broaden their experience, time will tell if they take their fair share of senior appointments in future.

Further informa- tion	The Institution of Environmental Health Officers, Chadwick House, Rushworth Street, London SE1 0QT The Royal Environmental Health Institute of Scotland, Virginia House, 62 Virginia Street, Glasgow G1 1TX

Related careers	SCIENCE: *Food Science and Technology* – HEALTH AND SAFETY INSPECTORS – HOUSING MANAGEMENT – TRADING STANDARDS OFFICER

Fashion and Clothing

The fashion and clothing industry is one of the largest in the country. Even at its highest fashion end it is concerned with business, not art. The vast majority of the industry is concerned with producing garments that large numbers of people want to wear, at a price they can afford. In the UK about three-quarters of production is for high street chain stores, with the retailers closely involved at all stages to ensure the right look and the right quality for their markets. Increasingly fashion and clothing is an international industry. Designs may be produced, patterns and lay plans developed, fabrics 'sourced', and garments made with each stage taking place in a different country; the finished garments may then be sold through shops in many parts of the world.

Entry qualifications

Vary according to level and type of training.

Main Sectors of the Industry

In *haute couture*, garments to an exclusive design are cut and made up for individual customers almost entirely by hand. *Up-market ready to wear* follows couture trends but makes more garments in more sizes for sale through exclusive shops. These are the glamour end of the market, but are extremely small. They are fairly insignificant in employment terms, though not in influence.

Most employment opportunities are in the mass-production sector. It covers a huge variety of garments for different markets and for a multitude of purposes: clothing is about far more than fashion.

Womenswear is the largest sector of the market, but *menswear* has become very much more fashion-conscious, as has *childrenswear*, a growing area with its own special demands from babywear to teenage fashion (and still including a significant amount of school uniform). *Leisurewear*, including dancewear, 'shell suits', sportswear and ski-wear, is a very lively market that has been enormously influenced by the development of special fabrics and finishes.

Workwear is a very varied sector of the market, ranging from simple overalls for canteen staff to heavy-duty specialist protective clothing, e.g. for the chemical industry and oil rig workers. The technical and design problems for specialist applications may be very complex and must usually take health and safety legislation into account. *Uniforms* (for the police, armed services and so on) are a specialized sector of workwear and range from dress uniforms to gas-tight suits. *Corporate wear* (e.g. for bank, airline and hotel staff) is a growing market.

The work

A very, very few *designers* become 'names' in *haute couture* or up-market ready to wear (or in 'diffusion ranges', which are good-quality wholesale production of designer name garments and have successfully brought good design down market in the last few years). Some young designers set up on their own, designing and making clothes for boutiques (sometimes their own), perhaps occasionally getting orders from store buyers. Most work in wholesale manufacturing, where high fashion is adapted for the high street.

Designers do not work in isolation but as members of a team with fabric designers or buyers, marketing specialists, production specialists, buyers from retail outlets. Very rarely is design an artistic 'gut feeling'. It is marketing-led, based on research. The designer almost always works within a trend (e.g. an ethnic influence) and within a firm's particular 'hand-writing', incorporating both into garments which will sell to a given type of market (for example, trendy, classic, young, elegant, country). The designer's skill is in adapting something for a new market, making it look fresh while retaining the features that made it popular. A recent example is the waxed jacket, taken from the country to the high street.

Different kinds of garments present different kinds of design challenges. For example, the designer of uniforms for paramedics is not concerned with high street trends but with considerations like how the garment will stand up to the weather, how to make sure it won't get in the way of the wearer's work, how to make it as hygienic as possible.

Some designers do their own pattern cutting, or it may be the job of a specialist *pattern cutter* or *technologist*. Pattern cutters cut an accurate pattern from which the 2-dimensional designer's sketch can be formed into a 3-dimensional sample garment.

Garment technologists are the bridge between design and manufacture. They take the sample and plan the way in which the garment will be made. They decide on, for example, what thread will be used, what seam and stitch types, what machinery will be needed, the costs at every stage. Sometimes a design proves too complicated or expensive, so the garment technologist will work with the designer to reach a compromise, perhaps changing some details in a way which will reduce the number and complexity of the manufacturing operations but still retain the designer's concept. Some garment technologists work for the large retailers, ensuring that the designs, quality and costs meet the retailer's specifications.

When the design is finalized, it returns to pattern cutters, who will return it to a 2-dimensional pattern suitable for mass production. A *pattern grader* then takes a standard size pattern and makes patterns to fit a range of different sizes. *Lay planners* work out how to place the pieces on the fabric in the most economical way. All these processes now make extensive use of computers.

The *production manager* is in charge of working out and managing production flow systems, ensuring that the manufacturing process, once it is broken down into a number of operations, will run smoothly, without bottlenecks, and keeping all the operators and equipment evenly busy.

The clothing industry invests very heavily in sophisticated machinery, so *engineers* are very important, ensuring that the machines are working effectively and advising on crucial investment decisions.

This industry is very varied. Job titles and functions are not clear-cut. People with different titles can be doing the same job and vice versa. People with different levels of qualifications can also be doing the same job. In smaller companies an individual may carry out several elements of the design/production process; in a larger company he or she may specialize in one particular function. There are also a number of liaison roles between retailers, designers and manufacturers.

Training   There is a very wide range of courses available at a number of levels. Titles include: textiles/fashion; fashion; clothing technology; fashion design with technology; design (fashion); fashion technology; knitwear design. Course title is little indication of course emphasis and content; for example, one BTEC HND in fashion/ fashion marketing focuses on the design and development of leisure and sportswear garments with career options ranging from creative design to fashion forecasting. Another, in clothing technology, offers work experience in local manufacturing companies *and* TV and theatre wardrobe departments. Basically, most courses will include elements of design, pattern technology, garment technology, production management, business studies and raw materials. The balance and emphasis will differ, but most lead to a range of overlapping jobs. Some graduates start work at a lower level than their qualifications would seem to warrant, but they should be able to find a way up with experience. People who start with modest qualifications can also work their way up; prospects are better on the production than on the creative side.

Courses available:

1. Post-graduate degrees and diplomas: 1–2 years, full time or sandwich; entry requirements – degree or equivalent.

2. Degrees: 3–4 years, full time or sandwich; entry requirements – 2 or 3 A-levels plus supporting GCSEs *or* BTEC/SCOTVEC National Diploma *or* foundation course.

3. Associateship of the Clothing and Footwear Institute (ACFI): a few colleges still run a 4-year sandwich course leading to this degree-equivalent qualification; entry requirements – 1 A-level and 5 GCSEs (A–C).

4. BTEC/SCOTVEC Higher awards: 3 years full time for the Diploma, 2 years part time for the Certificate (the SCOTVEC Certificate is 2 years full time); entry requirements – 1 A-level and 4 GCSEs (A–C) or National Diploma.

5. BTEC/SCOTVEC national awards: 2 years full time; entry requirements – 4 GCSEs (A–C) *or* BTEC First Certificate or Diploma.

6. Engineering: specialist degree and HND at Manchester Polytechnic. Other engineering qualifications suitable (see p. 183).

Local colleges may offer City and Guilds courses at craft and operative level. NVQs (see p. xx) are being developed in this area.

On behalf of the CAPITB Trust, EPR Ltd publishes *Fashion Course Selector*, a guide to higher-education courses. It covers 1–4 above with details of course structure and content, career options, student access to information technology and industrial liaison commitments. It also sets out to what extent particular courses develop competence in a range of fashion functions from identifying market demand to analysis of clothing materials for production. Available from ERP Ltd, 80 Richardshaw Lane, Pudsey, Leeds LS28 6BN, £6.99 (1992 price).

Personal attributes   Depends on particular job. *For top-level designers*, visual imagination, creative genius *and* exceptional business flair. *For others*, visual imagination and colour sense; adaptability; willingness to discipline creative flair to the technical and economic necessities of design for a popular market; self-confidence; some manual dexterity; ability to work as part of a team. *For production specialists*, interest in the technology of fashion; organizing ability; creative approach to problem-solving; eye for detail; ability to delegate and deal with people.

Late start   Depends on talent and drive. Competition from young college leavers is very stiff.

Career-   *Designers*: Depends on how established before break. *Production*:
break   Probably no problem for those who have had good experience before the break. Changing technologies can easily be coped with by well-trained production managers.

Part time   Not normally, except as freelance designer or, very occasionally, as relief (holiday) cutter, etc.

Position   Women can do well in this field. An increasing proportion of
of   designers are women. More would be welcome in production.
women

Further   CAPITB, 80 Richardshaw Lane, Pudsey, Leeds, LS28 6BN
informa-
tion

Related   ART AND DESIGN – JOURNALISM – PHOTOGRAPHY – PUBLIC
careers   RELATIONS – TELEVISION, FILM AND RADIO

Health and Safety Inspectors

Entry qualifications: For *factory* and *agricultural inspectors*, normally an honours degree in any subject; for agricultural work, a relevant subject may be preferred. GCSE (A–C) in maths and a driving licence essential. For *specialist inspectors*: normally a good degree, several years' industrial experience and a professional qualification where relevant (e.g. Chartered Engineer).

The work The Health and Safety Executive is concerned with minimizing death, injury and disease stemming from work activities. Inspectors, who are civil servants, are concerned with the health, safety and welfare not only of workers, but of any of the public who may be affected by their work. They have been closely involved investigating recent disasters such as those at the Hillsborough stadium, King's Cross station and the Piper Alpha oil rig, but most of their work deals with prevention. They act as advisers, investigators, enforcement officers and sometimes prosecutors, collecting evidence, preparing and presenting cases. They deal with everything from a small workshop where disabled people may make toys to huge projects like the Channel Tunnel.

The majority of inspectors are *factory inspectors*. They cover a large range of industries and workplaces, not only factories but, for example, hospitals, construction sites, shipyards, offices and shops. Depending on where they work, factory inspectors may deal with a limited number of industries or with a broad range. *Agricultural inspectors* are concerned with agricultural, horticultural and forestry establishments. There are also specialist inspectorates for railways, offshore safety, nuclear installations, mines and explosives.

Generally the work may be divided into 3 types or levels. Inspectors are the 'GPs' who carry out the day-to-day work, visiting sites across the whole range of industry to ensure that conditions, machinery and equipment, procedures and safeguards meet the requirements of legislation. For particular problems inspectors may call on the advice of specialists (analogous to consultants in medicine) who may be experts in very narrow areas. When required, the Research and Laboratory Services Division provides sophisticated research, investigation and analysis; for example, after the King's Cross fire one RLSD forensic lab constructed a 1/2-scale model of the escalator to investigate how the fire spread.

Inspectors are out of the office for as many as 3 days a week. They have considerable freedom to plan their work.

Training   *Factory* and *Agricultural Inspectors*: 2-year post-entry programme leading to the Health and Safety post-graduate qualification from Aston University. The programme covers legal, managerial and technical skills and consists of formal courses – including some residential ones – seminars, distance learning and on-the-job 'operational' training.

Specialist Inspectors: Receive on-the-job training, but do not take the post-graduate qualification.

Personal attributes   Self-reliance; interest in technical matters and in people; diplomacy; ability to get on well with all kinds of people at all levels in the work hierarchy; fitness; initiative; ability to take responsibility; ability to communicate easily; curiosity.

Late start   Very good opportunities. People with experience are needed, especially as the work is expanding. Track record may make up for lack of academic qualifications; each case is treated on its merit. Specialist inspectors always have previous experience.

Career-break   No problem. Inspectors are civil servants, see p. 125.

Part time   Again, as civil servants, prospects are good. Job-sharing, part-time, even term-time-only working are possible.

Position of women   In the Factory and Agricultural Inspectorate nearly 50% of entrants are female. In the specialist inspectorates, which people join in mid-career, there are very few women; women tend not to have the technical/scientific experience and qualifications needed.

Further information   Health and Safety Executive, St Hugh's House, Stanley Precinct, Bootle, Merseyside L20 3QY

Graduate and Schools Liaison Section, Room 1003, Office of the Civil Service Commissioners, Alencon Link, Basingstoke, Hants. RG21 1JB

The Private Sector

Many firms have their own safety officers whose job, broadly, is to ensure that all legal requirements are being met, and to advise management generally on all aspects of health and safety in the organization. There are no specific requirements for this work. Some practitioners are former health and safety inspectors or environmental health officers (see p. 206). The National Examination Board in Occupational Safety and Health offers certificates and diplomas leading to membership of the Institution of Occupational Safety and Health. Study is by part-time, block-release or distance-learning.

Further information Institution of Occupational Safety and Health, 222 Uppingham Road, Leicester LE5 0QG

Related careers ENGINEERING – ENVIRONMENTAL HEALTH OFFICER – SCIENCE

Health Services Management

The National Health Service is the largest employer in Europe with more than 1·2 million staff. It has been going through a period of unprecedented change, a key feature of which is the 'internal market'. This separates the Health Service into 'providers' and 'purchasers'. The providers, hospitals or other units, offer direct services to patients. The purchasers, district health authorities or fund-holding GPs (i.e. those who manage their own budgets), buy the services patients require from providers. The idea is that patients and those purchasing care on their behalf will have more choice, and thus the providers will be forced to be more efficient, cost-effective, and concerned for the needs of patients. Patients will no longer want to go to hospitals where, say, the food and cleaning are not up to scratch or where outpatients are never seen on time, while purchasers will not want to pay for inferior services.

It is too early to assess the full impact of these changes, but they are likely to affect the ethos and content of managers' jobs. They will need to develop an eye for value as well as service; they will need to calculate how much things actually cost and set up new monitoring systems; contracts negotiation and management will be important for both purchasers and providers; both sides will need new research on better services and ways of measuring and monitoring quality of service. Career patterns and the range of opportunities are also likely to change, with lateral moves becoming more common and varied.

Entry qualifications

Entry is at all educational levels. There are formal training schemes for those with A-levels or degrees. There is also direct entry with relevant professional qualifications and experience, and some managers move over from the clinical side.

The work

Health services managers provide the framework within which patients are treated by doctors and other clinical and paramedical staff. Their wide range of responsibilities includes strategic planning; financial and manpower planning; the maintenance of buildings; the purchase and control of supplies and equipment; personnel management; support services such as laundry, catering, domestic work, transport and other patient services.

Most jobs are with the 'providers' of health services, i.e. hospitals and other units, e.g. for the elderly or mentally ill. Work varies according to the size and structure of the unit as well as the individual manager's specific job. Thus one manager might be working on improving services to the ethnic community, arranging for translators and seeking advice on cultural expectations, while another works on the funding of a new consultant's position – what paramedical and other support staff will he or she need, when and where can an out-patient's clinic be fitted in, what about extra equipment? Increasingly managers work in interdisciplinary teams (including doctors and other professional staff) to plan and develop new services, implement change (which is caused not just by legislation and reorganization but by medical and technological advances, changing population and so on), and manage staff, budgets and facilities. Negotiating skills are essential since resources are finite and various interests often conflict; for example, the cost of advances in one clinical speciality might mean a reduced budget in another.

District health authorities' primary role will increasingly be as purchasers of health care. In the short term this is likely to result in fewer jobs at this level. The basic function of district managers is to assess the health needs of their population, identify ways of meeting those needs, enter into contracts with providers, and monitor the contracts and quality of provision. Regional health authorities have a strategic role. They are responsible for long-term financial and manpower planning and helping to develop the role of the other tiers of the structure. Traditionally, able, ambitious managers moved from unit to district to regional management, but the NHS changes might upset that pattern. For example, to head a large unit, possibly a self-governing trust, with the new management freedom and demands might offer a more attractive challenge. Family health services authorities, which have replaced family practitioner committees, are responsible for the family doctor, dental, pharmacy and optician services, and offer another career outlet for managers.

Training

Training for health services management is in a state of transition, as is the NHS itself. There is enormous flexibility and variety, but this can be confusing for prospective entrants. Training opportunities are both considerable in number and different in kind. They are multi-level and multi-mode. Schemes may be run nationally, regionally, by districts and possibly, in future, by larger units. Entry qualifications include degrees, A-levels and, for lower-level administrative work which can nevertheless lead to management, GCSEs. Trainees can work towards post-graduate qualifications (including MBA and DMS); relevant business/professional qualfications (e.g. in finance, personnel, purchasing); Institute of Health Services Management awards. Modes of study include full-time pre-entry courses, day-release, distance-learning and open learning. An individual's choice may be influenced not only by personal preferences and circumstances, but by what provision is available locally and the needs of a particular employer.

The National Management Training Scheme (NHS MTS) is intended to groom candidates for rapid promotion to senior management. Entrants must have a degree or acceptable professional qualification; in-service candidates may also apply. The Scheme, which normally takes 22 months (though there is flexibility), includes work attachments in a range of settings, formal management training, a real management post, projects and investigations which can take the trainee on a secondment into industry. Throughout, the trainee has as mentor a senior manager who helps him or her to plan development and assess progress. The training leads to a nationally recognized management qualification – there are various options.

In Scotland: Scotland has its own training schemes for health services managers. Major schemes for graduates and suitably qualfiied internal candidates are in general management, financial management, supplies management.

Because so many qualifications are appropriate and training opportunities exist at many levels, anyone interested should contact the regional or district health authority.

Personal attributes   Numeracy; flexibility; ability to discuss complex issues with specialists at all levels; organizing ability; ability to work as member of team; communication and negotiating skills.

Late start   Good opportunities for those with appropriate qualifications and experience – the NHS does recruit managers from outside. The flexible training opportunities, for example the MESOL (Management Education Syllabus and Open Learning) programme which offers three modes of study leading either to Open University or to IHSM qualfications, make the transition to or progress in health services management easier.

Career-break   Should be no problem, successful schemes have been running, but see 'Position of women', below.

Part time   Most part-time opportunities are at lower levels; some job-sharing has worked at higher levels, but see 'Position of women', below.

Position of women

The NHS is an enormous employer of women, but, according to an Equal Opportunities Commission survey published in 1991, it significantly fails to implement equal opportunity management practices, thus wasting the skills and training of a sizeable proportion of its workforce. 79% of NHS employees are women, but only 17% of unit general managers and 4% of district and regional general managers. Even though women have always been well represented on the 'fast stream' graduate training schemes, they are not getting through to the top jobs. At unit general manager level, women tend to end up in less glamorous, 'softer' jobs in, for example, non-acute, community and mental health units. It is a tradition, if not a rule, in the NHS that if you haven't managed an acute hospital you won't make it to the top.

Recent years have actually seen a *decrease* in the number of women at senior levels. One reason is that the number of provider units has been reduced; women managers are more prevalent in the smaller units, which are the ones which have tended to close or amalgamate. The reforms don't touch the male-dominated nature of the organization; if anything, they exacerbate it. The drive for efficiency, productivity and businesslike discipline and practice is based on a male model and has put great pressure on part-timers to work more. Senior contracts require that employees work the hours needed to do the job. How can a female manager say she wants to be home at 3.30 because of her children? Also under pressure are return-to-work schemes, job-sharing, crèche provision and so on. Yet how can it be efficient to waste the talent and potential of such a large proportion of your staff?

Further information

Regional health authorities
Institute of Health Services Management, 75 Portland Place, London W1N 4AN

Related careers

CHARTERED SECRETARY AND ADMINISTRATOR – CATERING: *Institutional Management* – MANAGEMENT

Home Economics

Entry qualifications   None laid down; depends on 'Training' (see below).

The work   Home economists act as a link between producers of household goods and services and their consumers. This covers a wide range of jobs. Within industry they also act as link between technologists who design and develop new products but often know little about consumer preferences and requirements, and marketing and general management staffs. So home economics, at least at senior level, requires communication skills as well as an understanding of technological and of social trends.

Home economists work in various settings: industry, social services, public relations, public utilities, consumer advice and protection, retailing, hotels and catering. Increasingly they are working in community care and in health and welfare fields. Home economics teachers are involved in health and design and technology education. There is nothing clear-cut about the professional home economist's work: people with related kinds of training may do the same, or similar, jobs; and qualified home economists branch off into related fields such as catering, marketing, consumer and trade magazines, and books.

The majority work in manufacturing industry on development, quality control, promotion and marketing of products, appliances and equipment used, or services provided in the home. Before new or improved food and washing products, dishwashers, cookers, central heating systems, etc. are put into production, home economists discuss details of design and performance with engineers, scientists, designers, marketing people. They put the customers' point of view; they test prototypes in the laboratory under 'ideal conditions', and they also use them in the same way as the customer might – being interrupted in their work and not always following the instructions as they should. For instance, they test whether a new type of butter-substitute creams easily, even if kept in the fridge too long and if clumsily handled; how a washing machine behaves if switches are turned on in the wrong order, or how easily a new cooker cleans when it is really dirty.

As a result of laboratory and 'user' tests, alterations are often made before a product is put into production. In the retail industry, home economists work in, or manage, food- and textile-testing laboratories, some become management trainees and then go into retail management (see RETAIL DISTRIBUTION, p. 428).

For gas, electricity and solid fuel suppliers they work as 'home service and energy advisers' (titles vary). They visit consumers in their own homes: this may be a straightforward 'after-sales service'; more often it is to investigate a complaint, maybe about a central heating installation which is not working properly. The home economist must be able to diagnose the fault and perhaps then to explain tactfully that the instructions have not been followed. Increasingly they are involved with educating the public in the need for, and methods of, energy conservation (for example, home insulation and other fuel-saving devices). The work combines dealing with lay people who have much less technical knowledge, and with experts who have very much more.

Under the heading *customer relations* or *marketing*, work involves writing clear, concise user-instructions for explanatory labels and leaflets which accompany fish-fingers, freezers, synthetic fibre carpets, babyfoods, etc., as well as dealing with inquiries and complaints correspondence.

Home economists also identify demand for new products or changes in existing ones. This may involve field work – interviewing potential customers in their homes (see 'Market Research', p. 16, and MARKETING AND SELLING, p. 294) and thinking up innovations which could be marketed profitably.

In the *media* home economists prepare features and programmes: they cook and cost elaborate as well as very cheap dishes, or arrange and cost domestic interiors which are then photographed and described, or demonstrated on TV. They also use their skills in assessing and reporting on equipment and on issues relevant to the consumer at home and at work.

In local authority *social services departments* home economists advise low-income families on budgeting and general household management; and they may run the home-help service and advise on the efficient running of the authority's residential homes. Those who have studied a housing option may work in local authority or private *housing management*. There are also openings in health education.

In *hospitals* home economists become domestic administrators at top management level.

They may also work in the *Trading Standards Department* (see p. 549) in consumer services.

Experienced home economists can work as freelance consultants: firms may wish to research and/or promote a new product and need a home economist for a particular project rather than permanently. For example, home economists work as freelances, writing explanatory leaflets, developing and checking recipes and equipment, etc. Some prepare food for magazine photography or TV commercials; some write books and articles for consumer magazines.

Job prospects are good, especially for graduates, although competition for top jobs (most are in cities) is keen. However, the combination of technical knowledge and understanding of family and consumer needs can be useful in a variety of jobs; home economists willing to be adaptable can find work in a wide range of organizations. Greatest scope in food and domestic appliance manufacturing, in retail, fuel and energy industries.

Training   No particular qualification leads to any particular type of job. It is possible for anyone with basic approved training or related training (see 'Institutional Management', under CATERING, p. 105) and the right experience and personality ultimately to do as well as a graduate. But the more thorough the training, the wider the scope of job.

1. *Degree*: Entry requirements: 2 A-levels and 3 GCSEs (A–C) (no specific A-levels but maths, English language and a science at least at GCSE level). Degree courses (usually at polytechnic or college of higher education) in Home Economics or related subject such as Food, Textiles and Consumer Studies; Home Economics and Resource Management; Applied Consumer Studies; B.Ed. (Home Economics) (see TEACHING, p. 521).

2. *BTEC/SCOTVEC Higher National awards in Home Economics*: Entry requirements: 1 A-level (preferably home economics) and 3 GCSEs to include English language, maths or a science. Diploma and degree courses include varying amounts of nutrition, food preparation and science; design and performance of equipment and materials, including textiles; business and marketing studies; consumer and social studies; communications and the media; information technology. Students can choose from a range of options, for example the carer in the community, ergonomics, housing and community health, product development, press and public relations.

3. *BTEC/SCOTVEC National awards in Home Economics*: Syllabus covers broadly the same subjects as HND but not in such depth; some courses concentrate more on practical skills such as cooking; home management; care of textiles, etc.

4. *City and Guilds*: For candidates without any or only a few GCSEs who prefer a course which concentrates entirely on practi-

cal skills: City and Guilds 2-year full-time course in Home Economics for Family and Community Care.

Not all types of courses are available in all areas.

Personal attributes
Practicality and organizing ability; interest in consumer affairs, ability to understand both consumers' and manufacturers' points of view; ability to communicate easily both with more highly qualified professional and with often poorly educated, possibly illiterate consumers; liking for people; humour.

Late start
Mature entrants are welcome on all courses.

Career-break
Should be no problem for people who keep up with developments.

Part time
Good opportunities; no reason why job-sharing should not be tried. Some part-time courses are being developed.

Position of women
This is a virtually 100% women's occupation, though there are now a few men in the profession. Industrial and media employers of home economists still tend to think of customers for whose benefit home economists work as housewives. Anyone who feels strongly about equality might not fit into many of the jobs done by home economists.

Further information
BTEC, Central House, Upper Woburn Place, London WC1H 0HH

City and Guilds of London Institute, 76 Portland Place, London W1N 4AA

Institute of Home Economics, Aldwych House, 71–91 Aldwych, London WC2B 4HN

National Association of Teachers of Home Economics Ltd, Hamilton House, Mabledon Place, London WC1H 9BJ

Related careers
CATERING – DIETETICS – PUBLIC RELATIONS – TEACHING – TRADING STANDARDS OFFICER

Housing Management

Entry qualifications   Various levels. Considerable graduate entry.

The work   Traditionally, housing managers are responsible for the administration, maintenance and allocation of accommodation let for rent. In recent years their scope has expanded enormously and it is still expanding. It now also includes, for example, the running of Housing Aid Centres; the administration of rent rebate, and rent allowance and housing benefit schemes; housing research and the formulation of housing policy. The majority of housing managers and housing assistants still work for local authorities, but as local authority housing stock has diminished (more council houses are sold than new ones built) and the number and scope of housing associations has increased, the proportion working for housing associations has grown. A small number work for building societies, property companies and voluntary bodies.

Day-to-day housing work adds up to an unusual combination of dealing with people, using technical knowledge and getting out and about. Duties may include interviewing applicants for homes; visiting prospective tenants in their homes to assess their housing needs; finding and monitoring bed and breakfast accommodation and trying as quickly as possible to move tenants into something more satisfactory; inspecting property at regular intervals and arranging, if necessary, for repairs to be carried out; dealing with tenants' complaints about anything from noisy neighbours and lack of play facilities for children to lack of maintenance. Rent collecting, which used to be the most important and time-consuming task, has all but died out: most tenants now take or send rent to the housing office.

Housing staff try to establish or maintain good tenant-landlord relationships and try to forge a conglomeration of dwellings into a community. To this end they may try to involve tenants in managing their block of flats or estate, or they may set up tenants' management committees. In Housing Aid Centres, housing staff advise on any problem related to housing, from how to cope with an eviction order or how to get a rent allowance, to where to apply for a mortgage.

At senior level, the work involves top-level general and financial management using modern management techniques; the purchase of properties; the allocation of accommodation (which is the most onerous task); research into housing needs and into such questions as 'How can we retain the neighbourliness of the slums in new developments?', 'What is a good environment?', etc.; advising architects and planners on social aspects of siting, design and lay-out of new developments.

The fact that there has been a considerable increase in owner-occupiers and a decrease in accommodation let for rent by local authorities has not diminished the importance of housing management, but it has changed its role. The social work element of the job is not as great as it was. The emphasis now is more on efficient management, and on exploring innovative ways of coping with housing need. New approaches to the problem include shared ownership; rent-into-mortgage schemes; leasing short-life property from private landlords; more cooperation between local authorities, housing associations, and building societies and private property companies. There is also now more movement between housing associations and local authorities than there used to be. It is still easier, though, to move from local authority to housing association than the other way around.

Many housing managers prefer to stick to day-to-day management throughout their careers, because they enjoy dealing with people. At senior level the jobs can be controversial. Directors of Housing may have to implement policies with which they do not agree, e.g. sale of council houses.

In local authority departments which administer thousands of dwellings, staff usually specialize in one aspect of the work at a time. In housing associations, which manage a smaller number, one housing assistant or housing manager may deal with everything concerning a number of tenancies. Housing associations increasingly provide facilities for special groups, e.g. for the elderly, single-parent families, the disabled. Some run hostels for such 'special needs' groups as ex-prisoners or people who have been psychiatric patients and still need support while adjusting to living in the community.

The profession is not expanding, but the proportion of graduates is increasing. Housing associations also often employ people without specific housing qualifications but other relevant ones, or simply with useful experience. This could be in general management, or accountancy, or with a degree in social science / administration or in surveying. As the stock of property increases, maintenance and conversion need more people with relevant knowledge. A new, as yet small, housing specialism is housing consultancy.

Consultants are people with housing experience who set up as freelances and advise on or help with state-of-the-art financial or general management, setting up rent-into-mortgage or other innovative schemes in which private and public sector organizations co-operate. They also help with in-house training.

Training

There are several routes to the professional qualification, the Institute of Housing's Professional Diploma (new in 1991):

1. The recommended route: Entry with at least 1 A-level and 4 GCSEs (A–C), for on-the-job training with day-release for the BTEC Higher National Certificate in Housing Studies. For candidates in whose area this fairly new HNC is not yet available there is a distance-learning package recognized by the Institute of Housing (also new in 1991). The HNC is followed by a further 2 years' part-time training for the Institute's Professional Diploma (this can be taken at a later stage, if preferred).

2. Candidates with 4 GCSEs (A–C) can first take the BTEC National Certificate in Housing Studies.

Training for full professional status thus takes 4 years for A-level entrants and 6 for GCSE entrants. Candidates who do not aim at senior management jobs can stop after taking the National Certificate. At that level there are several specialized courses in, for example, Repairs and Customer Relations; Caretaking and Estate Services; Finance; Tenant Participation; and Tenant Control.

3. Graduates, any discipline, either take the 2-year part-time course for the Professional Diploma, or they can take one of several full-time post-graduate courses, at university or polytechnic, in housing. Titles vary, and not all courses with 'housing' in the title are recognized by the Institute of Housing for at least partial exemption from the Professional Diploma exam.

4. A number of degrees in housing (titles vary) have been recognized by the Institute of Housing as leading to substantial exemption from the PD. (Even if the degree does not lead to such exemption, it may still be useful for housing association work.)

5. The Royal Institution of Chartered Surveyors (General Practice Division) qualification also leads to substantial exemption from the Professional Diploma.

The Institute's PD covers such varied areas of study as social policy; building construction and maintenance (to a standard which any interested person can cope with); law relating to housing; management studies; housing finance. Before finally qualifying for the award candidates must pass the Institute's Test of Professional Practice.

While housing associations often take graduates and do not expect them to train for the Professional Diploma, for career moves the PD is increasingly required.

NOTE: There are no BTEC Diploma (i.e. full-time) courses in Housing Studies.

Personal attributes   Getting on well with all types of people; an interest in social, practical and economic problems, and in planning; tolerance; ability to be firm; indifference to being out in bad weather; organizing ability and diplomacy for senior people.

Late start   Late entrants welcome in theory, but training vacancies are often difficult to find for mature entrants. More opportunities in housing associations where aptitude and relevant work, as well as 'life experience', are sometimes more important than qualifications.

Career-break   Returners are very welcome indeed. Short courses and workshops are arranged through HERA (see below) and by individual housing organizations. The Institute has reduced membership fees for the temporarily retired.

Part time   Excellent opportunities, especially, but not only, in housing associations, for part-time work and job-sharing.

Position of women   The proportion of women and men entering housing is fairly even, but *very* few local authority housing managers are women (see 'Position of women', under LOCAL GOVERNMENT, p. 271). There is no reason whatever why women should not do better. They do very well in housing associations.

Further information   The Institute of Housing, Octavia House, Westwood Business Park, Westwood Way, Coventry, Warwickshire CV4 8JP
National Federation of Housing Associations, 175 Grays Inn Road, London WC1X 8VP
HERA (Housing Employment and Advice), 2 Valentine Place, London SE1 8QH

Related careers   ENVIRONMENTAL HEALTH OFFICER − LOCAL GOVERNMENT − TOWN AND COUNTRY PLANNING

Information Work
(Librarianship/Information Science)

It has been said that we live in an information society. The sheer weight of information available increases all the time and impinges on every facet of modern life. We need information on which to base decisions on a whole range of issues. The fifth-former wants to find out where various A-level combinations could lead him or her. A doctor needs to know the possible side-effects of a new treatment. An investor might look into the performance of various shares. A marketing manager wants to keep abreast of what the competition is up to. Information is vital to our education, our work, our leisure, our health.

Developments in technology have had an enormous impact on the 'information industry'. Not only has technology led to new ways of collecting, organizing and retrieving information, but it has also led to more information! The information specialist has to deal with a range of sources far beyond books and other printed material.

Entry qualifications

For professional work, a degree; for paraprofessional work, nothing rigid, but 4 GCSE passes, including English, may be asked for.

The work

Distinctions between the librarian and the information scientist have blurred. Differences are often a matter of the emphasis of their work, rather than a fundamental difference of role or purpose. Job titles are not necessarily an indication of job content or emphasis. Information scientists may be chartered librarians; a librarian in a specialist library may work with highly technical information; some specialists have dual membership of the Library Association and the Institute of Information Scientists. Information officer and research officer are other titles that may crop up in job adverts.

The common basic purpose of the librarian/information specialist is to see that relevant information is available and used effectively. For whatever purpose, the job of the information specialist is to *acquire*, *organize* and *exploit* information. This covers a vast range of activity. *Acquiring* might range from maintaining as broad and balanced a collection as possible to cater for a wide range of general interests, within a given budget, to trawling the international market to build up a highly specialist collection of academic or technical interest. *Exploiting* might mean inviting a children's author to read his or her stories to pre-schoolers or preparing a newsletter to keep specialists aware of developments in their field.

The *public library* service is vast and provides a wide range of services to the public. Librarians are responsible for the selection, purchase, cataloguing and arrangement of a wide variety of materials – books and periodicals, videos, cassettes, records, slides, compact discs and information packs, for example. Many libraries run special services, such as 'books-on-wheels', children's activities, services to business or the ethnic community. All provide information, sometimes in specially produced packs, and answer inquiries. Many libraries have computerized information systems.

In a smaller library, and early stages of their careers, librarians' work may cover several functions, but many jobs involve some degree of specialization. More senior positions involve managing staff and resources. As in most jobs, routine work is inevitable, but many of the routine tasks associated with libraries – issuing books, filling and tidying shelves – are not done by professional librarians but by library assistants. Most public librarians will be chartered librarians (see below).

Academic libraries in universities, polytechnics and colleges offer a service to both staff and students, and sometimes to outsiders. In consultation with academic staff, librarians carefully select materials to support the teaching and learning going on in the institution. Many academic librarians are specialists in a particular subject area and often have a degree in that subject. Others may manage special collections, e.g. early printed books, manuscripts, music or computer software. Important aspects of the work in academic libraries are helping students to understand and use effectively the facilities available (including the latest technology) and helping academic staff to keep up to date with developments in their subjects. Many posts in academic libraries are open only to those who have a post-graduate qualification (see below).

Industry and commerce need good information to make good decisions. As in other areas, the information specialist is responsible for selecting material; this could demand considerable specialist knowledge of the organization's area of operations in, for example, science or engineering, as well as information skills. Computer technology has had an enormous impact on the storage and retrieval of information, as well as on the range available, and information specialists will be expected to exploit this to fulfil their company's needs, whether it involves designing and implementing a system to catalogue all the company's information resources, or buying in the latest database. The provision of information for specific purposes is an important task and might involve compiling a list (perhaps from a computerized system) of key references on a particular topic; exploiting a network of outside contacts, e.g. trade associations, learned societies, other company libraries; preparing summaries or abstracts of new information. A reading knowledge of a foreign language can be very useful.

Information specialists are also employed in government departments, museums, research and professional bodies, and the media. There are some opportunities to work as a freelance consultant.

In public and academic libraries, where services are affected by public-spending policies, openings are not increasing in numbers. In information departments and special libraries the number of jobs is increasing. Graduates in physics, chemistry, computer studies and related science/technology fields are keenly sought; there is also a need for specialists in accountancy, economics, finance, law and management. (However, any degree subject can lead to work in this field.)

Training   1. For membership of the Library Association (chartered librarians): a 3- or 4-year degree course in library/information studies *or* a degree in any subject followed by a 1-year full-time or 2-year part-time post-graduate course *plus* a minimum of 1 year's postcourse training. Most post-graduate courses prefer students to have had some experience as a trainee or assistant in a library before starting a course.

2. For membership of the Institute of Information Scientists: a degree in any subject plus a period of practical experience. An approved post-graduate qualification in library and information studies/information science/information management can reduce the period of qualifying experience by up to 3 years.

3. For library and information assistants: part-time courses leading to City and Guilds, BTEC and SCOTVEC National and Higher National Certificates in librarianship and information studies. There is also a 2-year full-time BTEC National Diploma course.

Employers' requirements and preferences can vary. For some jobs a relevant first degree can be more important than further qualifications. Some people take relevant post-graduate courses, but do not go on to professional membership. Others have dual membership of both professional bodies.

Personal attributes Good communication skills; curiosity; an interest in a variety of related topics without the desire to delve too deeply into any one; a methodical approach; a high degree of accuracy; organizing ability; a retentive memory; staying power for long, possibly fruitless search; resourcefulness; interest in electronic information systems; capacity to switch instantly from one topic to another; ability to cope with frequent interruptions when doing jobs requiring concentration; ability to anticipate users' needs. Because library and information work has so many different aspects, practitioners' relative strengths in these areas may vary.

Late start No upper age limit. Educational institutions may relax normal requirements for mature students, but finance is more difficult after 40 – part-time courses could help. Good prospects for unqualified assistants.

Career-break Should be no problem if well qualified and up to date. Short courses, can be used as refresher courses, though not intended as such. Formal schemes are increasing, particularly in the private sector.

Part time Reasonable opportunities at junior and up to middle-management level, but more difficult at senior levels.

Position of women A high proportion of library and information professionals are women. Previously women were not very successful in getting senior posts, but the position is radically changing. Increasingly women *are* now getting top jobs.

Further information Aslib (The Association of Information Management), 20–24 Old Street, London EC1V 9AP
The Library Association, 7 Ridgmount Street, London WC1E 7AE
The Institute of Information Scientists, 44–5 Museum Street, London WC1A 1LY

Related careers ARCHIVIST – BOOKSELLING – MUSEUMS AND ART GALLERIES – PUBLISHING

Insurance

Entry qualifications

For the qualifying exam of the Chartered Insurance Institute, *either* BTEC/SCOTVEC National award (see pp. xxi, xxii) *or* 2 A-levels and 2 GCSEs (A–C), including English at either level. Graduate entry is increasing, and some degrees give exemption from part of the CII exams. GCSE entrants with commitment and the willingness to study part-time (often with employer's help) can move up the ladder, but the best prospects are for people with A-levels, BTEC/SCOTVEC National, HND or degree.

Foreign languages are useful as insurance is an international activity and some jobs involve considerable travel.

The work

Insurance is a method of compensating for losses arising from all kinds of misfortunes, from the theft of a video to an airliner crash, from a holiday cancelled through illness to the abandonment of a major sporting event. It is based on the principle that many more people pay regularly into a common fund than ultimately draw from it, and thus the losses of the unlucky few may be made good. The organizers of the system are the *insurers*, i.e. the *insurance companies* or *Lloyd's underwriters*. Lloyd's itself is not an insurance company, but a society whose individual members are grouped together into syndicates to accept and underwrite 'risks'. Each syndicate is administered by an agency which employs a *professional underwriter* (see below) to carry out the business. Banks (see p. 69) and building societies (see p. 85) are also now moving into insurance. It is usual to specialize in one of the main branches of insurance: *marine and aviation*, *life and pensions*, *property*, *accident*, *motor and liability* and *reinsurance* (where very large risks are 'farmed out'), although transfers are possible. Occupational pension schemes are a growth area.

Underwriters are responsible for assessing risks, deciding whether they are insurable, and on what terms and conditions they can be accepted. Some underwriting decisions are routine and based on guidelines laid down by the company for dealing with standard cases (for example, ordinary motor insurance). Others are highly complex and/or unusual and demand specialized skill or judgement (for example, the Channel Tunnel or an art treasure on special exhibit).

In the case of buildings, industrial plant and other commercial operations, underwriters may call on the advice of *surveyors*. The surveyor prepares a factual report on any aspects that might affect the underwriter's assessment of the risks (e.g. fire protection or security arrangements). Some surveyors go into risk management, which is concerned with identifying, assessing and minimizing the risks a company may face in its day-to-day activities. Insurance surveyors are often selected from existing staff and trained internally; they are not necessarily chartered surveyors. When risks are very complex, science or technology graduates might be recruited for this work.

When a claim is received *claims staff* assess the loss and determine the amount to be paid. As with underwriting, some cases are straightforward (though you might be dealing with people whose loss demands your tact and sympathy), while others are complex and require technical, legal and medical knowledge. For large or disputed claims insurance companies may call in independent *loss adjusters* to examine the claim and help to reach a settlement. Some loss adjusters come from the claims department of an insurance company, but others have relevant qualifications, e.g. in law, surveying, accountancy, engineering.

Inspectors (or *sales agents*) have a good deal of independence. They are responsible for obtaining new business and ensuring that existing clients' cover is adequate as circumstances change. They may deal with 'agents' (e.g. brokers, solicitors, estate agents, building society managers) or direct with the public.

Insurance brokers act as intermediaries, bringing together the insurers and those who wish to be insured. Jobs include finding new business, looking after and advising existing clients, and placing the risks in the market (i.e. finding insurers to underwrite the policy). Brokers may be small High Street firms or international giants employing thousands of staff. Only accredited brokers ('Lloyd's brokers') are allowed to do business with Lloyd's underwriters.

Training   On the job, with day-release for 3 years (evening study is also necessary) for Associateship of Chartered Insurance Institute, followed by 2 years (approximately) for Fellowship of CII. A BTEC/SCOTVEC National award in Business Studies can lead to partial exemption from CII examinations, and leaves options open for work in other commercial fields. For some specializations, e.g. investment and pensions management, the CII exam is followed by Fellowship exams of a relevant institute. Graduate trainees may follow an accelerated training programme.

Loss adjusters may take the Chartered Institute of Loss Adjusters exams after insurance company experience (and often the CII exams), or as graduate trainees.

Personal attributes

Some mathematical ability; a liking for paperwork; ability to grasp the essentials of a problem; sound judgement; determination and a certain amount of push; tact; a persuasive, confidence-inspiring manner; ability to communicate with people, often in difficult circumstances. For brokers, extrovert manner and entrepreneurial flair.

Late start

Many employers are adopting a more relaxed attitude towards the age of recruits, but training vacancies can be more difficult to obtain after the age of 30. Mature entrants would be expected to follow the same training routes as young recruits, but the minimum academic requirements might be relaxed. In sales, maturity is an advantage.

Career-break

Employers are introducing schemes; details vary.

Part time

Part time, job-sharing, working from home are becoming more popular within the industry.

Position of women

The proportion of women members of the CII is rising. Though only 1 in 4 members is female, among the under-25s the proportion is nearly 50%.

Further information

The Careers Information Officer, The Chartered Insurance Institute, 7th Floor, 31 Hillcrest, London E18 2JP

The British Insurance and Investment Brokers' Association, BIIBA House, 14 Bevis Marks, London EC3A 7NT

Chartered Institute of Loss Adjusters, Manfield House, 376 The Strand, London WC2R 0LR

Related careers

ACCOUNTANCY – ACTUARY – BANKING – BUILDING SOCIETY WORK – COMPUTING/IT – STOCK EXCHANGE AND SECURITIES INDUSTRY

Journalism

<table>
<tr><td>Entry qualifica-tions</td><td>Newspapers: 5 GCSEs (A–C) including English language for traineeship, but nearly all school-leaver entrants have at least 2 A-levels. 55% of entrants are graduates. For pre-entry course: 2 A-levels.

Magazines: Depends on editor; for pre-entry course: 1 A-level, 4 GCSEs (A–C). About three-quarters of new entrants come from some kind of higher education course.</td></tr>
<tr><td>The work</td><td>Journalism covers a variety of jobs in a variety of settings (or 'media', which really should be 'media of communications'). Broadly, the main job groups are reporter; correspondent or specialist reporter; feature writer; news editor; editor; freelance. Division of duties depends on paper's size and organization.</td></tr>
</table>

Newspapers

Most newspapers now have computerized editorial systems, i.e. journalists input their copy through a keyboard directly into a computer. Virtually every journalist starts as trainee-reporter. Reporters cover any kind of event: from council or Women's Institute meeting to political demo, fire, or press conference for visiting film star or foreign statesman. Reporters 'get a story' by asking questions and listening to other journalists' questions and interviewees' answers at press conferences, or in one-to-one interviews with individuals. For such interviews, reporters have to do some preliminary 'homework' – to interview a trade union secretary or famous novelist, for example, requires some background knowledge.

Reporters must compose stories quickly and meet tight deadlines. Accuracy, brevity and speed are more important than writing perfect prose: reporting is a fact-gathering and fact-disseminating rather than a creative job.

Occasionally, reporters may be on a particular story for several weeks, researching the background and/or waiting for developments. They work irregular hours, including weekends.

Specialist Reporter or Correspondent

'Hard news' is broadcast more quickly than it can be printed; to fight TV and radio competition, newspapers have developed 'interpretative' or specialist reporting. Specialists' titles and precise responsibilities and scope vary; the aim always is to interpret and explain news, and to comment on events, trends, causes and news behind the news. The number (and the expert knowledge of) specialists varies according to the type and size of newspaper. On the whole, only the nationals have specialists who concentrate entirely on one speciality; on other papers and in news agencies, reporters with a special interest in a particular field (or several) may do specialist along with general reporting. The main specializations are: parliament and/or politics generally; industry; finance; education; foreign news; local government and/or planning; social services; sport; science and technology; agriculture and food; motoring; fashion, women's/home interests; theatre; films; broadcasting. Financial correspondents tend to be economics graduates, science correspondents are science graduates, but education correspondents are not normally teachers: there are no hard-and-fast rules about how specialists acquire their specialist knowledge (and how much they need).

News Editor

Journalists with organizing ability may become news editors, controlling reporting staffs, allocating stories to individual reporters and attending senior staff's daily editorial conferences. It is an office job and normally involves no writing. The title usually applies on daily papers; but titles and organization of work vary considerably from one paper to another.

Sub-editors

Sub-editors do the detailed editing of copy; they re-write stories to fit in with required length, re-write the beginning, and may 'slant' stories. They write headlines and, in consultation with the night or assistant editor, may do the layout of news pages. On large papers there are several specialist subs. Subbing is team-work and entirely desk-bound; it always has to be done in a hurry.

Feature Writers

Usually experienced journalists who can write lucidly and descriptively on any topic; but specialists may also write features. Reporters may combine reporting with feature writing.

Columnist

Like feature writing, a job for experienced journalists; there are specialists, for example financial or consumer affairs columnists, and general columnists. The work requires a wide range of interests and contacts.

Leader-writers

Leaders may be written by the editor, or specialist correspondent, or other experienced journalists.

Editor-in-chief, Assistant Editor, Deputy Editor

Editors (including departmental editors) are co-ordinators, policy-makers. The number of top jobs, and the amount of writing editors do, vary greatly: some editors write leaders on specific subjects, some write in crises only; some on a variety of subjects, others not at all.

The amount of freedom editors-in-chief have to run the paper in the way they want depends on the proprietor; policies vary enormously.

There is no set promotion structure on newspapers. Some journalists do all or several types of newspaper work in succession in preparation for senior editorial jobs (subbing is a vital step on the ladder), others become heads of departments (finance, fashion, home affairs, chief sub, etc.) fairly quickly. Many remain reporters.

Titles, functions and division of labour are not consistent throughout the industry and often change with a change of editor-in-chief or proprietor.

*

Freesheets

Locally distributed 'giveaway' papers are the fastest-growing advertising medium. Free newspapers vary enormously in the proportion and variety of their editorial content. A few are much like small local weekly papers; most carry very little editorial matter. Some are published by established newspaper houses, some by members of the Association of Free Newspapers, yet others are run individually from tiny offices by a man/woman and a boy/girl. Jobs on free newspapers with varied editorial content may be acceptable as traineeships (see below), but work on the majority is unlikely to lead to jobs on national or other prestigious local newspapers.

Magazines

Broadly there are two types:

1. Trade, technical, professional and business; and also 'house' journals, geared to a particular profession, trade or organization.

2. 'Consumer' magazines: they cater for all types of leisure interests and include women's, teenage and hobby magazines and comics.

On (1) journalists often work closely with experts in the particular field of which they must have/develop some understanding. They write features, report developments, and re-write experts' contributions. Magazine work, however specialized, can be a way into newspaper work – especially for graduates (particularly science or technology) with writing ability. It often requires broader skills than newspaper journalism: e.g. knowing about sub-editing and layout.

Consumer magazines employ feature writers, sub-editors and departmental editors more than reporters, but organization varies enormously. Consumer magazines use freelances more than do newspapers. Editors' work includes originating feature ideas and selecting and briefing outside contributors, both freelance journalists and specialists who are not journalists.

Freelance Journalism

Freelances are either 'generalists' – feature writers who write on any subject – or specialists. On the whole, only experienced journalists with staff experience, and particularly those with specialist knowledge which is in demand (technology, consumerism, child development, education, for example), succeed.

Specialists – teachers, engineers, lawyers, with writing ability and topical ideas – also do freelance journalism as a sideline, but this is becoming more difficult.

Training   *Newspapers*
Either:

1. *Direct entry traineeship*: 2 years, including 6 months' probation. Acceptance depends as much on paper's policy and candidate's suitability as on academic qualification. Candidates must apply direct to editors of provincial (including suburban) dailies and weeklies. The London-based nationals do not often take

trainees. (When applying for traineeship it is advisable to submit samples of work done: an article specially written for the particular paper, which shows the editor that the applicant has identified the paper's style, is better than work done for school or university paper, though that can be sent too.)

Trainees complete a distance-learning package during probation, and attend a 12-week block-release course later in their training. All trainees must pass qualifying examinations in law, public administration, newspaper journalism and shorthand. After a set period of work experience they then take the National Council for the Training of Journalists' National Certificate Examination. Subjects studied: English usage; relevant law; public administration; shorthand (which remains important despite new technologies: reporters may now feed copy directly into a central computer, but they still take notes in the traditional way, as well as using tape recorders); interpretative reporting (interviewing, fact-gathering methods, etc.); current affairs; sub-editing skills.

Practical training should cover work in all departments, including new technology production methods. Quality and thoroughness of training schemes vary, so it is essential to find out as much as possible about them before accepting a traineeship. 1 or 2 newspaper groups are now running their own training schemes, independently of the NCTJ.

2. *1-year full-time pre-entry courses*: 2 A-levels required. Over one-third of entrants to newspaper journalism now take such courses, at colleges of further education. Courses shorten subsequent apprenticeship by several months. A few candidates are sponsored by newspapers; the majority are accepted after having taken a written test and been interviewed by the NCTJ, to which applications must be made. Grants are not mandatory (see p. xxvi). Courses do not guarantee employment. Also *2-year Higher National Diploma course* at Napier Polytechnic, Edinburgh.

3. *Post-graduate course* at the Centre for Journalism Studies, University of Wales College of Cardiff, and at the City University, London. Graduates from these courses also have to start as trainees, but they take the NCTJ's National Certificate Examination after 18 months' training.

4. *One 20-week post-graduate course* at the South Glamorgan Institute of Higher Education. Graduates from this course can take the National Certificate Examination after 18 months.

5. *9-month post-graduate course* leading to Diploma in Journalism at the Scottish Centre for Journalism Studies. Accredited by the NCTJ, it also contains an option in broadcasting.

6. Some national newspapers are now taking on trainees without

previous experience. Sometimes this is done through the NCTJ's national training scheme.

NOTE: First degrees in journalism are being introduced (1991). Although these will be very attractive to school-leavers they are unlikely to give their graduates any real advantage over entry routes outlined above. Most editors currently prefer to take candidates who have shown breadth of interest by studying disciplines other than journalism/communications/media. Vocational training then follows the degree.

Magazines

Two courses at the London College of Printing: entry requirements for both: 1 A-level, 4 GCSEs (A–C) including English language or literature (the majority of successful candidates have higher qualifications):

1. *1-year pre-entry course* for periodical (any type) journalism.
2. *2-year BTEC* (see p. xxi) *HND Business Studies* with journalism option.

The London College of Fashion runs a BTEC Higher National Diploma in Fashion with a *fashion writing* option. The course is 2 years full time. Entry requirements are A-level English, 5 GCSEs (A–C) and a small art portfolio proving drawing ability. Entry is very competitive.

3. The post-graduate courses at City and Cardiff universities include a periodical journalism option.

4. An industry-wide Editorial Training Scheme administered by the Periodical Training Council is now standard in large (but not in small) publishing houses. This lasts 2–3 years and covers basic journalistic skills and knowledge. Trainees are issued with a training log to record their progress.

5. Twice yearly 17-week full-time pre-entry course run by Reed publishing group. Fee £2232 (1991) – no grants available. Successful students may be offered jobs within the group or in other publishing companies. 9-week post-graduate course run by PMA Training. Fee £1575 (1991). Both of these are approved by the Periodical Training Council.

Magazine journalism training is much less tightly structured than newspaper training and entry is still largely with specialist knowledge (especially scientific/technical/computing, but also other expertise, from drama to sport, education to law) and with writing/editing ability. Quite a few arts graduates are editing technical journals.

Competition for trainee posts in newspapers is fierce. Previous experience in student or freelance journalism is essential. Work on a journal dealing with one particular subject, whether electronics or municipal affairs, is good experience and can be a stepping stone to more general journalism. There is some scope in broadcasting (see p. 530) for experienced reporters. Science and engineering graduates have reasonable scope on the increasing number of publications which deal with various aspects of science and technology (especially information technology/computing) and which try to attract both specialist and lay readers.

Personal attributes

The different jobs demand different talents and temperaments, but all journalists need a feeling for words; the ability to express themselves lucidly and concisely; wide interests; an unbiased approach; a pleasant easy manner so that shy, inarticulate people will talk to them easily; a certain presence so that busy, important people do not feel they are wasting their time answering questions; powers of observation; ability to sift the relevant from the irrelevant; ability to absorb atmosphere and to sum up people and situations quickly; an inquiring mind; great curiosity; the ability to become temporarily interested in anything from apple-growing to Zen Buddhism; resourcefulness; resilience; tact; willingness to work very hard; punctuality; a fairly thick skin (interviewees can be rude). For *senior jobs*: organizing ability.

Late start

Newspapers: Late entrants account for 25% of the intake and follow the normal training programme (though this is not compulsory for those aged over 30).
  Magazines: Quite normal for specialists.

Career-break

Near-insurmountable problems as reporter on *newspapers*. Only well-above-average women who have proved their value to the paper before the break have much hope of returning after several years away. Many women turn to freelancing or edit, on a freelance basis, small organizations' or professional magazines: this is almost a cottage industry and badly paid. Fewer problems for feature writers, sub-editors.
  Few problems on *magazines*.

Part time

Mainly as freelance. Up to 80% of magazine copy may be written by freelances. Some job-sharing possibilities.

Position of women

Newspapers: A third of qualified journalists are women and the proportion of women trainees has increased considerably over the last few years to 50%. However, their share of senior jobs, though increasing, is still very little indeed; yet there is no shortage of applicants (as there is in some other careers where women do badly). Women have no more difficulty than men getting trainee-ships, but there seems to be discrimination at subsequent levels (on newspapers, not magazines). Women also still tend to have 'women's stories' allocated to them. They are not given the varied experience (city page writer; foreign correspondent; assistant to news editor; sub-editor, etc.) which is vital for top jobs. However, this is slowly changing; but women still have to be considerably better journalists, more determined and more undauntable than their male colleagues, to get beyond middle-level jobs.

Magazines: No problem. Approximately 55% of editorial staff and several editors are women.

Further information	National Council for the Training of Journalists, Carlton House, Hemnall Street, Epping, Essex CM16 4NL (for pre-entry courses only)
	Newspaper Society, Training Department, Bloomsbury House, Bloomsbury Square, 74–7 Great Russell Street, London WC1B 3DA
	Periodicals Training Council, Imperial House, 15–19 Kingsway, London WC2 6UN
	Scottish Centre for Journalism Studies, Dept of Communication, Glasgow College, 70 Cowcaddens Road, Glasgow G4 0BA
	Reed Business Publishing, Quadrant House, The Quadrant, Sutton, Surrey SM2 5AS
	PMA Training, The Old Anchor, Church Street, Hemingford Grey, Cambs. PE18 9DF

Related careers	ADVERTISING – INFORMATION WORK – PHOTOGRAPHY – PUBLIC RELATIONS – TELEVISION, FILM AND RADIO

Landscape Architecture and Design

Entry qualifications

Vary according to training, but for student membership of Landscape Institute: 3 GCSEs (A–C), 2 A-levels (or equivalent). Mix of science and arts subjects at both levels preferred. See 'Training', below, for graduate entry.

The work

Landscape architects plan and design the outdoor environment. Working with architects, civil engineers, planners or landscape contractors, they try to minimize the aesthetic damage done to the scenery by, for example, industrial development or new housing estates. In urban areas the work is mainly concerned with integrating the layouts of housing schemes, road works, parks and play areas into the environment and with general urban regeneration. It also includes planning of private and public gardens. In the countryside landscape architects plan industrial sites such as power stations and determine how best to blend new roads into their surroundings so that they are as unobtrusive as possible. They work on land reclamation, tree preservation and the control of mineral workings. They design layouts for open spaces, anything from spacious grounds for new hospitals to small private gardens, play – and recreation grounds. They may site and design picnic areas in country parks or lay-bys on motorways.

Once the design is agreed with the client, landscape architects invite tenders from contractors, arrange the contract and supervise the subsequent work, to ensure that it is carried out satisfactorily and within the budget. They are also responsible for specifying the right type of plants to achieve the desired appearance at all times of the year and at all stages of growth: this means balancing the amount of maintenance funds available in a public park, for example, with the amount of maintenance needed by the particular plant. Their knowledge of horticulture must be extensive.

Many landscape architects work in private practice, and a large proportion work in the public sector, mainly in local authorities. In public employment they are usually responsible to planning officers or architects, with less freedom than in private practice to carry out their own designs.

Prospects are good. The demand for qualified landscape architects is growing as the need to make the best of our remaining countryside is becoming more widely appreciated. Some opportunities in EC countries.

Training

The recommended route
Either: 4-year full-time course at a school of landscape architecture attached to a university or polytechnic plus 1 year's practical experience (which may come between years 3 and 4).

Or: Course in related subject, for example architecture, town planning or agriculture, followed by a university diploma or Master's course in landscape architecture, either 2 years full time or longer part time. Both these lead to graduate membership of the Landscape Institute.

Graduate members must gain 2 years' professional experience and pass the Institute's professional practice examination in order to become associate members.

Alternative method of entry
There is no technician grade or qualification in landscape architecture, but it is possible to get into this work by training in a variety of allied disciplines – for example, geography, geology, planning, soil science, plant sciences, rural environment studies, art and design, horticulture – and then learn on the job, working in a landscape architect's or developer's office. Initial training should preferably be at degree level, but there is always some limited scope for people with a flair for design and horticulture who are willing to combine some practical work with designing. This overlaps with gardening/garden design. (See 'Horticulture', p. 23). For membership of the Landscape Institute it is essential to take one of the Institute-recognized courses. Some private courses, which do not lead to membership of the Landscape Institute, are available.

Personal attributes

Visual imagination; flair for design; a keen interest in design and environment; a knowledge of how people live in town and countryside; ease of expression, both in drawing and writing; the ability to work well with other people; a good business head (for private practice).

Late start

As vacancies on landscape architecture courses are scarce, young applicants are given preference (but see alternative method of training). With the right initial qualifications it should be possible to make this a second career.

**Career-
break**   People who have kept up with developments should have no problems. Reduced subscription available for members temporarily unemployed.

Part time   Reasonable opportunities in employment; possibility of running small consultative practice – but part-time work likely to be sporadic rather than regular.

**Position
of
women**   Women were among founder members of the Institute. Now over 30% of qualified members and 44% of students are women. There has never been much discrimination in this career.

**Further
informa-
tion**   The Registrar, Landscape Institute, 6–7 Barnard Mews, London SW1 1QU

**Related
careers**   AGRICULTURE AND HORTICULTURE – ARCHITECTURE – ART AND DESIGN – ENGINEERING: *Civil Engineering* – TOWN AND COUNTRY PLANNING

Languages

The British notoriously lack foreign language competence and the implications are likely to grow more serious with increasing European integration. As we move into the single European market, British companies could be at a real disadvantage compared with European competitors with a polyglot workforce. As one European businessman put it, 'We are happy to sell to you in English, but we like to buy in our own language.' Individuals could also lose out as increased labour mobility within the European Community will favour those with language skills.

Nevertheless, it must still be emphasized that language skills on their own are of very little value. Saying that you can speak German or Italian is, on its own, about as useful to an employer as saying that you can speak English. What matters is the framework of technical, professional or practical skills within which you can apply your languages.

There are very few careers for which languages are the primary skill required, and even these require other skills and qualities. For a growing number of careers, however, languages are a useful, sometimes essential, secondary skill.

Languages as a Primary Skill

Interpreting

The work   *Conference interpreters*
At international conferences interpreters may do either 'simultaneous' (the main type) or 'consecutive' interpreting. They must be exceptionally proficient in at least 2 of the UN official languages, which are English, French, Spanish, Chinese and Russian; an additional knowledge of 1 or more of the less common languages is a help. *Simultaneous interpreters* relay the meaning of a speech, often on complicated subjects, almost instantaneously. The technique can be learned, but the talent and temperament are inborn. *Consecutive interpreters* relay a speech as a whole, or in

large chunks, after each speaker. This requires as much skill as simultaneous translating.

Conference interpreters invariably translate into their own language.

Some interpreters are employed by international agencies; others are freelances and are booked for a particular conference. Most of the year is spent travelling to and from New York, Geneva, Strasbourg, Brussels and London, living in hotels. The life may be luxurious, but it is extremely hectic, with very long irregular hours. Most conference interpreters now are specialists.

Conference interpreting is an extremely small profession. The professional association has only about 2000 members, in all languages, worldwide.

Business and specialist interpreters

Business organizations of many kinds may need interpreters, for example when receiving trade delegations, negotiating international contracts and at trade fairs. Some of these interpreters may need specialist knowledge (such as engineering, information technology, computing, physical science or economics). Translators, both staff and freelance, may undertake this type of work. There are also opportunities in the courts and for conference organizers.

Community interpreters

They speak one of the languages spoken by immigrants, such as Urdu, Hindi, Greek, etc., and are employed mainly by local authority social services departments to help members of ethnic communities whose first language is not English deal with officials in departments. For example, they help them to communicate with social security and housing officials, teachers and medical staff. Local authorities may train their own staff. Employment is usually part time.

General interpreters

Most of them take tourists around London. They are very few in number. Most of them are accredited guides (i.e. they need a considerable historical knowledge of London) and are on the books of hotels and travel agencies for occasional assignments. It is a pleasant sideline, but not a career in itself.

Interpreters in the last three groups use ad hoc or liaison interpreting, in which they interpret into and out of two languages, for example in a conversation between speakers of different languages.

Translating

The work Translators must be able to translate idiomatically and to write lucidly and concisely – being bilingual is not sufficient. They translate into their mother-tongue, so the prevalence of English has increased rather than reduced work for English translators.

They need a very good education and specialist knowledge of preferably a range of related subjects, though this may be acquired on the job. Most translations have some specialist content – contracts require some legal knowledge; scientific articles some understanding of the subject-matter; specifications (for construction work, of anything from ships to atomic power stations) need some technical knowledge. Translators often have to discuss phrases and technical jargon with engineers, scientists, lawyers, etc., to get the sense absolutely right; translating is therefore often team-work.

Government departments, and industrial, commercial and research organizations, often have translating departments which employ specialists in particular fields, and sometimes non-specialists, who have, for instance, Chinese or Arabic, as well as 1 or 2 of the more usual languages.

Translating agencies employ specialists, and people who have unusual languages, often on a freelance basis. They like to have on their books a large number of people with widely different specialities and languages, on whom they can call at a moment's notice. There is increasing scope in translating instruction manuals for consumer goods manufacturers.

Much is rushed deadline work, especially for freelances.

Training It is not necessary for interpreters and translators to have formal training and qualifications, but it is becoming much more common. The main courses and qualifications are:

1. Post-graduate courses, usually lasting 1 year, in technical and specialized translation/interpreting. Candidates must normally have a degree in 2 languages at the same level. Different courses offer different languages; Arabic, Czech, Slovak, Danish and Norwegian are among the more unusual options.

2. A few 4-year degree courses include emphasis on translating and interpreting skills.

3. The Institute of Linguists offers examinations (but not courses) leading to a Diploma in Translation. It is a post-graduate level qualification open to graduates and others who can demonstrate a high level of language competence (e.g. gained by living and working in a foreign country). They also offer a Certificate in Community Interpreting. A number of institutions offer courses;

distance-learning is available through the National Extension College.

4. The Institute of Translation and Interpreting offers practical exams leading to their Diplomas for those with at least 3 years' experience in translating or interpreting.

Personal attributes

An agile mind; interest in current affairs; a knowledge of cultural and social structures not only of their own country but of any country in whose language they specialize; ability to concentrate for long stretches and to work under pressure; ability to work well with others.

Conference interpreters need a calm temperament and the ability to snatch a few hours' sleep at any time.

Teaching
(see TEACHING, p. 521, for details)

Languages as a Secondary Skill

There are a number of areas in which a knowledge of a foreign language can be a requirement or an asset, though it is not the primary skill and may not be a day-to-day part of the work. They include broadcasting (see p. 530); bilingual secretarial work (see p. 462); librarianship and information work (see p. 229); the Diplomatic Service (see p. 131); travel and tourism (see p. 552); patent agents (see p. 361); banking (see p. 69); law (see p. 253). In industry and commerce languages are undoubtedly becoming more important, but it is impossible to generalize about the roles in which they are most useful. Export marketing is an obvious example, but engineers, computer staff, general managers could all, in some circumstances, need languages. Receptionists and switchboard operators are often the first point of contact with a foreign supplier or customer. You should not consider any of these careers simply as a way to 'use my languages'. Rather, you should recognize competence in a foreign language as a skill that can enhance almost any career, giving an entrée to more interesting prospects, at home and abroad.

General language training

There are many ways in which people may become proficient in a foreign language. Recent education initiatives aim to give more young people at least a starting-point at school. Under the National Curriculum all pupils will have to study a foreign language until the age of 16. GCSEs in languages concentrate much more on oral skills than previous courses did.

No matter which direction your education takes at this point, there will almost certainly be the chance to further develop language skills. Some people will go on to A-levels and then language degrees; the options include a traditional literature-based course, an 'applied' language course with emphasis on oral fluency and the economy, institutions and social climate of the relevant countries, or a degree combining languages with another subject such as law, engineering, business studies, marketing, computer studies and so on. There are also a number of college courses for A-level entrants which offer languages for business, as well as language options in Dip. H.E. and BTEC courses.

Examinations in languages at different levels, and for different purposes, are also offered by the Royal Society of Arts, the London Chamber of Commerce and the Institute of Linguists. Eventually these qualifications will be taken into the NVQ framework (see p. xx).

A spell abroad is an extremely useful way to refine language skills. Most schools run exchanges, and most language degree courses include a year abroad. There are also a number of European Community schemes to encourage young people to work or study in other member states. ERASMUS (a study scheme) and COMETT (a work scheme) are administered by universities and polytechnics for their students. Details on the Young Worker Exchange Programme, which organizes work placements, exchanges and language study for 18–28-year-olds (preferably those who have not had higher education), are available from the Central Bureau for Educational Visits and Exchanges, Seymour Mews House, Seymour Mews, London W1H 9PE.

Late start   Translating and teaching (see p. 521) possibly; interpreting unlikely.

Career-break   Unless very well established, return might be difficult for interpreters, as competition very keen.

Translating: No need to give up all contacts while raising family.

Part time   Theoretically there should be a good deal available as translating and interpreting are so often done by freelances. However, much of the work has to be done quickly – which means it is not regular part-time work, but a few days' or weeks' rushed full-time work every now and then.

**Position
of
women**

Rather more men than women are professional translators and interpreters, but women who do have the right knowledge and aptitude do well; women tend to be better than men at languages, but they fall down on the necessary specialist knowledge which sometimes requires long training.

**Further
informa-
tion**

Institute of Linguists, 24a Highbury Grove, London N5 2EA
Institute of Translation and Interpreting, 318a Finchley Road, London NW3 5HT

Law

Barrister (Advocate in Scotland)

Entry qualifications

First- or second-class honours degree (any subject).

The work

Barristers plead in courts and give advice on legal matters. They clarify points of law and use their critical judgement in deciding what legislation and what precedents are relevant in any particular case. Their expertise helps clients, but barristers are first and foremost concerned with points of law, not with helping individuals: their relation with clients is far more formal than that of solicitors.

Barristers are normally consulted by solicitors on behalf of their clients and do not normally see clients without a solicitor being present. In some instances barristers may be instructed by members of other professions, e.g. accountants, surveyors, architects and overseas lawyers.

Though it is no longer required, most barristers work from 'chambers', sharing overheads and administrative back-up with other barristers. However, each barrister is self-employed; they may not go into partnership or be employed by other barristers. Once in practice, a barrister must wait for briefs by *solicitors* or be given work by the *barristers' clerk* (see p. 257), who 'distributes' work which comes to the set of chambers rather than to a particular barrister in the chambers.

Barristers normally specialize either in *common law*, which includes criminal work (the greatest proportion: it covers any case of law-breaking, however minor the offence), divorce, family, planning, personal injuries litigation and commercial law; or in *chancery work*, a much smaller branch which covers conveyancing, trusts, estate duty, taxation, company law.

In common law the emphasis is on pleading in court ('advocacy'); in chancery on work in chambers, drafting 'opinions' and advising. Common law work appeals, therefore, more to people who enjoy verbal battles and the court's somewhat theatrical atmosphere; chancery work appeals to those who enjoy the challenge of intellectual problem-solving.

Common law barristers usually join one of the six 'circuits' into which England and Wales are divided for legal administration purposes; they may then plead in provincial courts as well as in London. About a third of barristers in independent practice work from provincial chambers.

Barristers earn very little at first and often supplement their income by coaching, or other work, unless they have enough money to live on for the first year or so. Many barristers never attempt to practise at the Bar (others try to, but cannot get into chambers or get work); instead they become legal advisers in industry, or in local or central government. Such work is usually more easily available. It is far less precarious than the Bar, and in industry and commerce can lead to board-level jobs, but the work is not as varied as, nor has it the glamour of, being at the Bar.

The *Civil Service* offers a variety of work (see p. 136). *Justices' Clerks* advise the lay justices (JPs) in magistrates' courts, and have close day-to-day contact with the public.

The *Crown Prosecution Service* is responsible for deciding whether or not to prosecute cases in the criminal court; where they decide to prosecute it is the solicitors and barristers employed at headquarters or in one of the 31 area offices who conduct the case, not, as previously, the police. In Scotland, *Procurators Fiscal*, assisted by Deputes, are the public prosecutors in the sheriff courts. Legal staff at the Crown office deal with more serious crimes.

Barristers, after at least 7 years' practice, are eligible for appointment (by the Lord Chancellor) as Chairpersons of Industrial Tribunals. These Tribunals deal with unfair dismissal, redundancy payments and other matters relating to employment generally. Under the Sex Discrimination Act they also hear complaints from individuals who believe they have been discriminated against in terms of equal pay, promotion, acceptance for a particular job and other employment matters. Other Tribunals involve mental health and social security. Chairpersons are appointed to regional panels and sit on Tribunals within a given area. Appointments can be full time or part time (i.e. some lawyers carry on with their practice as well).

It takes a good deal of determination, and sometimes good contacts, to succeed at the Bar. Now that solicitors have increased rights of advocacy, things could become more difficult for barristers.

Training

Training consists of an *Academic Stage*, a *Vocational Stage* and a *Practical Stage*.

1. The Academic Stage: Students take *either* a qualifying law

degree, which is basically one that covers the 6 'core' subjects (see 'Training', under 'Solicitor', p. 259), *or* a non-law degree followed by a 1-year course for the Common Professional Examination (the CPE) at an approved institution.

Law degree courses vary greatly in emphasis on particular aspects of law. Most include the core subjects, but these are not always compulsory, so students must make sure they take the appropriate subjects in order to fulfil the requirements of the Academic Stage. It is also important to relate content to one's interests and plans: for example some courses concentrate more on international and/or EC law; some on family and welfare law; some on tax and/or company law; some are geared more to private practice, some more to public service. Consult *CRAC Degree Course Guide*, see p. lvi.

2. The Vocational Stage: This consists of a 1-year Vocational Training Course at the Inns of Court School of Law. The emphasis is on the practical application of knowledge and advocacy skills. Students develop skills in, for example, negotiation, legal research, problem-solving, opinion-writing, drafting documents, oral and written communication, and presentation. Assessment is continuous and takes into account practical work, tests and examinations. On successful completion of this stage students are 'called to the Bar'.

3. The Practical Stage: Barristers wishing to practise at the Bar (or represent business employers in court) must serve 1 year's pupillage. During the first 6 months the pupil takes a background role, reading papers, drafting documents, attending court, helping to prepare cases, and becoming familiar with the rules of conduct and etiquette of the Bar. This period must be spent in chambers. During the second 6 months (which may be spent in commerce or government) a pupil may take cases on his or her own account. In the past the year of pupillage was often a time of financial hardship as pupils were not allowed to earn at all during the first 6 months. Now a guaranteed minimum income throughout pupillage is provided.

Before enrolling on the Vocational Course all Bar students must join one of the four Inns of Court and 'keep terms' by dining in the Hall of their Inn a certain number of times. The purpose of this is to make contacts with practising barristers and to be initiated into the traditional ways of the Bar.

Training (Scotland)

This is radically different. Scottish barristers, called advocates, must be members of the Faculty of Advocates in order to practise at the Bar. Candidates, known as 'intrants', qualify in 4 stages:

1. *Either* take a law degree from a Scottish university, giving

subject-for-subject exemptions from the Faculty examinations *or* (very unusually) take all the Faculty's own examinations. (Many intrants take 1 or 2 Faculty papers because it gives them greater freedom to choose other subjects in their degree courses.)

2. They then take a 1-year full-time course at a Scottish university for the Diploma in Legal Practice (in common with Scottish solicitors).

3. For those wishing to practise: 21 months' (reduced by 9 months in certain cases) traineeship in a solicitor's office, followed by 9 months' pupillage (known as 'devilling') with a member of the Bar. Solicitors with at least 5 years' experience need to serve only 6 months' pupillage.

4. Pass the Faculty examination in evidence, pleading, practice and professional conduct.

English barristers are exempt from paragraphs 2 and 3 if they have been in practice for at least 3 years.

Personal attributes
A confidence-inspiring personality; power of logical reasoning; gift of expression; a quick brain; capacity for very hard work; tremendous self-confidence; some acting ability, or at least a sense of drama and relish for verbal battles in front of critical audiences; physical stamina; a good voice; resilience.

Late start
Only for the very determined and able. *Exceptional* non-graduates over 25 may be accepted for a special CPE route (details from the Inns of Court School of Law at the Council of Legal Education address, below), but this is very rare. A law degree might be a better bet as it gives a degree more generally accepted in the jobs market. In Scotland, between 1984 and 1988, the average age of persons starting practice at the Bar was 32. About 60% of those admitted to the Faculty have at least 2 years' experience in another career, usually as solicitors.

Career-break
Opinions differ as to how easy this is. Certainly one must be very well established before any break. There is also evidence that a break may damage a woman's career prospects (but not a man's).

Part time
Barristers in practice at the Bar are self-employed practitioners and have some scope in arranging their workloads to suit themselves, but regular part-time work is impossible to arrange. Employed barristers may have more scope, especially in the Civil Service (see p. 136).

Position of women

This has traditionally been one of the most difficult fields for women to succeed in. It was only in the 1970s that women began entering the profession in any numbers at all. Since then the numbers have been rising quite dramatically. In 1969–70, 8% of those called to the Bar were women; in 1979–80, 28%; in 1990–91, 41%. However, 12% of male barristers are QCs (senior advocate and adviser), but less than 3% of women are. This can be important for judicial appointments, where women are also under-represented. Time out for domestic commitments is given as a reason why women take longer to reach senior appointments, but surveys have shown that most of the women who do reach them have *not* had time off; women seem simply to need more time and experience to reach the same levels as men.

Further information

General Council of the Bar, 11 South Street, Gray's Inn, London EC1R 5EL

Council of Legal Education, 39 Eagle Street, London WC1R 4AJ

Faculty of Advocates, Advocates Library, Parliament House, Edinburgh EH1 1RF

Related careers

ACCOUNTANCY – CIVIL SERVICE – *Legal Executive/Solicitor (see below)*

Barristers' Clerk (England and Wales only)

Entry qualifications

4 GCSEs (A–C), including English language and maths.

The work

This small profession has changed little over the past 100 years or so. Barristers' clerks 'manage' chambers and the barristers working in them (see Barrister, p. 253). The job of senior clerk (or Clerk to Chambers) is a unique mixture of power-behind-the-throne and humdrum clerking, involving negotiating fees and other matters relating to briefs coming to chambers with solicitors (from whom the briefs come). Clerks play a particularly important role in 'building up' young barristers: some briefs come to Chambers rather than to individual barristers and it is the senior clerk who decides which of the young barristers is to be given the brief.

Senior clerks usually have junior clerks who make tea, carry barristers' books and robes to court, type opinions and pleadings. There is no career structure and no hope whatever of progressing to becoming a barrister, but as senior clerks get a commission on all their Chamber's barristers' earnings they often earn more than some of the barristers for whom they are clerking.

Training   On the job, with lectures. Clerks now normally take the Institute of Barristers' Clerks examination, after 4 years' clerking.

Personal attributes   Very great self-confidence and presence; tact; willingness to tackle any kind of menial office job; respect for tradition and the established professional and social pecking order, in which barristers are a long way above clerks; interest in the law.

Late start   Upper age for starting is normally 20; people who worked as legal secretaries very occasionally switch to clerking at any age: i.e. barristers are not willing to train late entrants, secretaries would know what clerks' duties are.

Career-break   Return to work would be very difficult.

Part time   Limited opportunities, and none for senior clerk. (No logical reason for this.)

Position of women   About 25% of clerks are women. Very few women have become senior clerks.

Further information   Institute of Barristers' Clerks, 13 Old Square, Lincoln's Inn, London WC2A 3UA

Related careers   CIVIL SERVICE – *Legal Executive* – SECRETARIAL AND CLERICAL WORK

Solicitor

Entry qualifications   A degree *or* fellowship of the Institute of Legal Executives (see p. 261) (90% of entrants are graduates). In Scotland non-graduates need high grades in the SCE Highers, which must include English and either maths or science or foreign language.

The work   A solicitor is a confidential adviser to whom people turn for legal advice and information in a vast variety of personal and business matters. As everyday life becomes more complex, the solicitor is increasingly asked to help in matters where common sense, wisdom and an objective approach are as important as legal knowledge. Whenever possible solicitors try to settle matters out of court.

Solicitors have full rights to represent clients personally in magistrates' and county courts and a limited right to appear as advocates also in the Crown and High Courts (Scottish solicitors have somewhat greater rights in the equivalent courts). Increasing numbers of solicitors practise advocacy and their rights of audience will soon be further extended. When a barrister is briefed to appear for a client, the preparatory work and the liaison with the client is still undertaken by the solicitor.

The majority of solicitors work in private practices, ranging from large multi-partner departmentalized city firms to small general or even sole-practitioner firms. Work content, conditions and remuneration are correspondingly wide-ranging. A city solicitor will generally specialize immediately, working for corporate clients in mainly commercial fields such as banking, taxation, company law and property development. Solicitors in smaller practices tend to handle a wider range of tasks, usually for individual clients, but everywhere there is a trend to earlier and greater specialization. Typical areas of work in smaller firms are crime, family law, personal injuries, conveyancing, landlord and tenant matters, and smaller-scale commercial work. There are now several small firms which concentrate on providing an expert streamlined service in just 1 or 2 areas, for example medical negligence, entertainment law, immigration.

Most social welfare law, civil and human rights cases, and almost all legally aided cases are undertaken by smaller firms and to some extent by publicly funded law centres, usually in inner-city areas.

Relaxation of traditional rules has enabled solicitors to become involved also in financial services and estate agency and to advertise their services. Solicitors are now required to attend post-qualification continuous education courses.

A solicitor with 3 years' experience can establish a practice but will need capital and contacts to succeed. Securer employment opportunities are available at all levels in local government and the civil service. For those interested exclusively in criminal work there are opportunities in the Crown Prosecution Service. Many commercial, industrial and other organizations employ legal advisers where the nature of the work will depend on the activities of the employer.

After substantial experience solicitors can apply to become registrars, stipendiary magistrates, recorders or circuit judges. There are also opportunities for appointments to chair industrial and other tribunals.

Training   There are 3 routes to qualifying:

    1. The law degree route (about 75% of solicitors qualify this

way). After successfully completing a qualifying law degree (one covering the 6 'core' subjects – constitutional and administrative law, criminal law, contract, tort, trusts and land law) graduates go on to the new Legal Practice Course. This replaces the Law Society Finals Course in 1993, will last about 1 academic year, and will be more skills-based than the Finals course. Successful completion of the Legal Practice Course is then followed by a 2-year training contract ('articles'), which includes training in at least 3 different areas of law taken from a list of subjects laid down by the Law Society. There is a degree of specialization at this stage so it is important to choose carefully. Most people train in private practice, but there are some opportunities in the Civil Service, local government, the Crown Prosecution Service, the Magistrates' Courts Service, and industry and commerce.

2. The non-law degree route. Graduates take a 1-year course leading to the Common Professional Examination (CPE) before proceeding to the Legal Practice Course and articles as above. Qualifying therefore takes 1 year longer than for law graduates.

3. The non-graduate route. Candidates first become Fellows of the Institute of Legal Executives (see p. 261). They then *either* take the full-time Legal Practice Course *or* undertake 2 years' training while undertaking the Legal Practice Course on a part-time basis. (At the time of writing it is not known precisely how the part-time course will be structured; the pattern will possibly involve 2 weeks' full-time attendance in each year plus a series of weekends.)

Training (Scot-land)

Either a law degree at a Scottish university followed by 1-year full-time course for the Diploma in Legal Practice *or* a 3-year training contract with a firm of solicitors leading to the Law Society of Scotland's professional examinations, followed by the Diploma. The law degree route is the most popular. All 'intrants' undergo a 2-year post-Diploma practical training with a practising solicitor, either in private practice or a public service.

Personal attributes

Capacity for absorbing facts quickly; logical reasoning; ability to see implications which are not obvious; ability to come to grips with an intricate problem; a good memory for facts and faces; tact; patience; clear and concise expression in writing and in speech; sound judgement of character; an understanding of human behaviour; a personality that inspires confidence.

Late start

Mature entrants are advised to take the ILEX route or take a law degree (most academic institutions make concessions for mature students). It is easier than in the past for mature trainees to get articles, but not in prestigious City firms.

**Career-
break**

Some firms of solicitors are now instituting formal career break schemes. The Association of Women Solicitors runs courses for returners and is helping polytechnics and colleges to develop courses in this area.

Part time

Part-time opportunities are improving in private practice, the Civil Service and local government. The last two also offer job-sharing, but it is very rare in private practice, where part-time work is seen to be more acceptable.

**Position
of
women**

More than half of trainee solicitors are now women. Women's position within the profession has improved greatly in recent years as a result of market forces (i.e. a shortage of solicitors). Women do tend to become partners later than men, but to some extent this is probably correlated with their temporary absences. The City of London is perceived as having more liberal attitudes than some provincial firms.

**Further
informa-
tion**

The Law Society, Careers and Recruitment Service, 227–228 The Strand, London WC2R 1BA

Law Society of Scotland, 26 Drumsheugh Gardens, Edinburgh EH3 7YR

Legal Executive (England and Wales only)

**Entry
qualifica-
tions**

4 GCSEs (A–C). (A-level law shortens the training.)

The work

Legal executives work for a solicitor in much the same way as junior executives work for a managing director: they are responsible for a strictly limited section of work. Solicitors are in overall control, make contact with clients and lay down policy. Legal executives may specialize in one particular branch of the law – probate, conveyancing, litigation, company law, etc. – and work out the details as they apply in each particular case: looking up references in law books, preparing documents, interviewing witnesses and conferring with clients on points of detail. In small practices, or when managing a branch office, they may also be involved with the whole spectrum of work.

Although they cannot speak in open court, they appear before Registrars or Masters of the High Court or in the County Court on summonses in the course of proceedings. They may also appear before a Judge in chambers or before a magistrate.

Legal executives may become solicitors in 2 years after becoming Fellows (see p. 260).

Training	On the job, together with part-time training at day-release or evening classes, or by approved correspondence course, for the 2-part Institute of Legal Executives' Membership Examination. The syllabus includes general legal subjects and practice and procedure, and allows for specialization in one branch of the law. Training time varies from 2 to 4 years, but each part *normally* takes 2 years. There are a small number of full-time courses for Part 1. After 5 years' relevant employment (2 of which must follow Part 2) members can become Fellows.
Personal attributes	Sufficient powers of concentration to detect relevant details in a mass of complex documentation; patience and perseverance; self-confidence and ability to discuss matters with all types of people from criminals to judges.
Late start	Over-25s do not need specific educational qualifications: many decide to become legal executives only after having been legal secretaries for many years. It is possible to prepare for the Membership Examination without being in relevant employment.
Career-break	Should be no problem for people who keep up with legislative changes.
Part time	Some opportunities for jobs and also for training, but promotion is difficult. Job-sharing should be possible.
Position of women	This used to be an all-male profession; now over 60% of student members of the ILE are women and they hold about half of senior posts. Many women have taken the ILE examinations while being employed as clerk or secretary in the hope of getting a more responsible job once they have passed.
Further information	The Institute of Legal Executives, Kempston Manor, Kempston, Bedford MK 42 7AB

Related careers	*Barrister / Barristers' Clerk / Solicitor (see above) / Licensed Conveyancer* (see below) – CHARTERED SECRETARY

Licensed Conveyancers (England and Wales only)

Solicitors no longer have a monopoly in conveyancing property. Independent conveyancers may work on their own or in solicitors' or local government offices.

Entrants need to be at least 21 and have 4 GCSEs (A–C), including English. Training is in 2 parts:

1. Part-time or correspondence study for the Council for Licensed Conveyancers examinations Parts 1 and 2. Certain exemptions are available to those who have legal qualifications and experience in conveyancing.

2. 2 years' supervised full-time practical training (at least 1 of which must follow the examinations).

Further details, including information on approved courses and possible exemptions from Part 1, from The Secretary, Council for Licensed Conveyancers, Golden Cross House, Duncannon Street, London WC2N 4JF.

Leisure/Recreation Management

Though we may not have become the 'leisure society' as predicted some years ago, people are spending more time and money on leisure activities. The leisure industry is enormous. At its broadest it includes everything from hotels and catering to zoos and safari parks, taking in pubs, wine bars, cinemas, theme parks and heritage sites, sport and leisure centres, museums, art galleries and theatres, parks and playgrounds, even libraries. Though this may suit economists and industry analysts, it is not a practical starting-point for career-choosers. Running a pub is almost certainly not what someone turning to this chapter has in mind; nor is your average librarian likely to consider himself or herself as part of the leisure industry. Many people who will find themselves in this broad-sweep leisure industry are likely to have interests and motivations that lead them to other chapters in this book. Nevertheless, it is helpful for people who see leisure as primarily sport and physical recreation (as do most of those who contact the Institute of Leisure and Amenity Management) to recognize that the opportunities are very much wider than is commonly realized.

Entry qualifications

None specified. In practice professional qualification and/or administrative experience.

The work

The leisure industry has developed piecemeal, but it is characterized by growth, diversity and increasing integration. It is generally recognized that leisure and recreation are an important aspect of the well-being of both individuals and the community; it is also recognized that well-run leisure facilities can be profitable. So more facilities are being developed. They are increasingly sophisticated in response to market demand. Where once you had swimming pools you now have 'leisure pools' with waves, water slides, deck-chairs, even palm trees.

Integration occurs on several levels. Local authorities (who used to be the largest employers of leisure management staff, though they have now been outstripped by the private and voluntary sectors) have established integrated, multidisciplinary departments to cover indoor and outdoor sports, the arts, community and children's play facilities, municipal entertainments and libraries. Large-scale complexes are being developed where people can, for example, shop, eat, swim, bowl, or take in a film or concert. Increasingly leisure facilities are a partnership of public and private sectors with, for example, an authority providing finance for a development, while a private concern manages it on a contract basis. In addition to local authority facilities there are opportunities in, for example, company sports and social clubs, countryside and theme parks, the Sports Council and governing bodies of individual sports, arts centres, theatres and concert halls.

The work involved obviously varies a great deal and it is possible to give only a few examples. *Senior managers*, whatever their title, are responsible for financial management, marketing, promotion, and management and motivation of staff who might include administration, catering, maintenance and specialists, e.g. coaches or instructors. *Assistant managers* generally look after a particular function (bookings and administration, for example), a facility (e.g. the swimming pool and all associated activities) or a range of activities (e.g. all outdoor sports or entertainments in an authority's parks). *Supervisors* are concerned with the day-to-day running of activities and the work of staff such as poolside staff, gardeners or entertainment centre staff. There are variations on this pattern: in a smaller centre a manager will have to take on a broader range of responsibilities, while in a larger facility there may be more specialized roles. Depending on the size and nature of the organization there may also be central roles in policy formulation, budgeting and planning.

By definition 'leisure' is when you are not working, so leisure staff at operational levels must work when most other people are not working.

The leisure industry is a very broad-based pyramid with many more jobs at basic than at senior levels. Its relative lack of structure, however, makes it a fairly easy pyramid to climb for those with the right motivation and qualifications. On the other hand entrants often have to start at a level lower than their paper qualifications seem to warrant.

Some areas of this vast field are obviously more specialized. *Arts administration*, for example, has a particular character and appeal, especially for graduates. It entails enabling artistic events (plays, concerts, etc.) to take place. This may involve planning, publicity, engaging performers, booking venues, handling ticket sales, finance (often including negotiating grants and sponsorship), maintenance of buildings and general administration. The actual range of tasks will depend on the size and nature of the organization – in a small company managers might have to sell tickets at the door, at the Barbican they won't! There are a few relevant degrees and post-graduate courses, as well as options on more general leisure courses (see 'Training', below). There is still, however, a large foot-in-the-door element in this field and many people develop careers from spare-time activities and voluntary work.

Training   It is becoming increasingly necessary to have relevant educational or professional qualifications. Nevertheless, particularly in commercial leisure centres, successful managers may have few qualifications but lots of flair and entrepreneurial skills. Generally speaking, however, and certainly for local authority posts, systematic training is advisable.

Relevant courses and qualifications

1. ILAM (Institute of Leisure and Amenity Management) Certificate and Diploma. Entry qualifications are 1 A-level and 4 GCSEs including English language and maths, *or* relevant BTEC/SCOTVEC, City and Guilds or management qualification. Candidates are normally expected to have a minimum of 2 years' experience in the industry. People normally achieve the *Certificate* through the BTEC Continuing Education Certificate (Leisure Management) which gives exemption from all but one of the ILAM Certificate examinations. Part-time modular courses, normally lasting 2 years, are offered at a number of colleges; individual modules may also be undertaken. It is possible to prepare for the ILAM examinations by 'self-study', but the BTEC route is highly recommended.

For the *Diploma*, 2 specialist Diploma in Management Studies (DMS) courses incorporating leisure and recreation give exemption from all papers except a compulsory Diploma Case Study. Other courses under (2), (3), (4) and (5) below may also give some exemptions.

2. With a degree (any discipline) and, usually, relevant experience: post-graduate award in recreation management or similar area of study.

3. With a degree, or several years' relevant experience: Diploma in Management Studies (see 'Training', under MANAGEMENT, p. 276) with recreation management option or BTEC Certificate in Management Studies.

4. With 2 A-levels: B.Sc. in physical education, sports science and recreation management or BA combined studies with recreation option.

5. With 1 A-level (in practice usually 1 passed and another at least studied, if not passed): BTEC/SCOTVEC Higher National award in Leisure Studies.

6. With 4 GCSEs (A–C): BTEC/SCOTVEC National award in Leisure Studies.

7. With no set qualifications: City and Guilds Certificate 481 or BTEC First Certificate in Recreation and Leisure Industries.

8. Other courses: *Horticultural, landscape architecture* and some *agriculture college* qualifications (see relevant sections) also include aspects of recreation management.

NOTE: NVQs (see p. xx) are being developed in this area.

Personal attributes	Good organizing ability; practicality; ability to make different specialists work as a team; interest in the needs of all sections of the community; confidence in dealing with members of the public (even when they are impatient or boisterous).
Late start	No reason why not.
Career-break	Should be possible, but keen competition for jobs.
Part time	Should be possible – also job-sharing – as there is considerable shift-work in some jobs.
Position of women	As there are few traditions, there are no barriers against the promotion of women to be broken down. There are, though, still comparatively few women managers.
Further information	ILAM, Lower Basildon, Reading, Berks. RG8 9NE Institute of Baths and Recreation Management, 36/38 Sherrard St, Melton Mowbray, Leicestershire LE13 1XJ Sports Council, 16 Upper Woburn Place, London WC1H 0QP (for list of courses) Scottish Sports Council, Caledonia House, South Gyle, Edinburgh, EH12 9DQ BTEC, SCOTVEC, City and Guilds (see pp. xxi–xxiii)
Related careers	AGRICULTURE AND HORTICULTURE – LOCAL GOVERNMENT – MUSEUMS AND ART GALLERIES – PUBLIC RELATIONS – SPORT – TEACHING

Local Government

Local government is not a career but an employer. More precisely it is more than 500 employers throughout England, Scotland and Wales. Together they employ about 2¾ million people and spend more than £30 billion every year providing services, many of which are required by law, to the local communities.

Most local authorities are organized into 2 tiers, counties and districts (regions and districts in Scotland). In general county councils provide larger-scale, more strategic services such as education, social services, highways and refuse disposal, while district councils are responsible for more local services such as housing, refuse collection, and leisure and recreation. Additionally there are the London borough councils and the metropolitan district councils, which are single tier and provide the full range of services. At the time of writing, the structure of local government was again under review.

In recent years there have been great changes in the way local services are managed. Increasingly services are put out to competitive tender with the council's own workforce in many instances competing with outside firms. Some council departments are run as external consultancies, selling their services to other departments. The idea is that the providers of the service will have to improve efficiency, while the 'purchasers' will develop a keener eye for quality of service and value for money, both of which local residents and businesses are entitled as Council Tax payers to expect. As in other public-sector areas, new management skills are required of those responsible for bringing a more businesslike approach to the provision of public services, e.g. contract management and quality assurance.

Entry qualifications

Entremely varied; entry is at all educational levels.

The work

This varies enormously. Local government is enabled or required by law to provide a wide range of services. Among the most important are: education, which includes schools, colleges, the youth service and the careers service; social services; public protection, which includes the work of the police and fire services, consumer protection and environmental health; leisure services, which can include sports and community facilities, libraries, museums, theatres and the promotion of tourism; highways, housing, buildings and planning, which ranges from strategic planning to provision and maintenance of a range of community buildings. Obviously the scope of such activities involves a large number and wide range of people doing different things!

Among the scores of careers in local government are a number which can be pursued both inside and outside of local government. These include accountancy, law, engineering, computer work, librarianship, public relations and human resources management. Local government is one option within these career areas. For another group of careers local authorities are the exclusive or major employers. These include teaching, social work, town planning, careers advisory work, environmental health and trading standards (consumer protection). Another large group is involved in general administration, advising on policy formulation and procedures and co-ordinating the implementation of policies agreed by the elected councillors. Their work may include servicing committees, research and report-writing, as well as the day-to-day administration ensuring the smooth running of departments and services.

Many of the professionals employed by local authorities provide services directly to the public, e.g. teachers and librarians. Others, however, are part of the vast, essential support structure. Legal services and computing, for example, are not services which are offered direct to the local community, but they are essential to the provision of education and social services. In fact departments and services are not self-contained and projects usually involve multidisciplinary teams. For example, the building of a new school would involve not only the education department, but architects and surveyors, lawyers, planners, finance, possibly the fire services, even the leisure department if, say, it were intended that the school's sports facilities be used by the community outside school hours.

People may be promoted within a department and authority, but it is common to move among employing authorities, and bring willing and able to move can aid rapid progress. It is also becoming increasingly easy, especially for those with good management skills, to move across departments.

Training　　Local authorities provide extensive training for all levels of staff, with opportunities to study for appropriate qualifications in a range of areas. The entry point, length and structure of training may vary. In some cases local authorities offer graduate entrants the opportunity to gain the practical training and experience necessary for professional qualification; in others they offer A-level (or equivalent) entrants sponsorship on an appropriate degree course. Other entrants may be sponsored for day-release for relevant qualifications. Among the fields in which training schemes are offered are: personnel (human resources management), computers, environmental health, town planning, trading standards, accountancy, engineering, surveying, careers work, social work, leisure management, architecture, housing management, law.

For individual professions: see individual entries. (Some professionals train with local authorities; others join after qualifying.)

For general administration: entry qualifications vary. An increasing number of administrative officers are *graduates*, with many authorities running special graduate-training schemes. The professional qualification for senior administrators is membership of the Institute of Chartered Secretaries and Administrators, for which day-release may be available. *A-level entrants* may also study for this qualification or for a BTEC Higher award in public administration. Those with *4 GCSEs (A–C)* can begin work and study for BTEC National awards in public administration; those who are motivated and able can continue on to a related BTEC Higher award, a degree and/or ICSA membership. (It is probably best for those who are ambitious to aim for educational qualifications that will take them to the highest entry point possible for them.)

It is difficult to draw lines about who is an administrator and who is not. Many of the professionals mentioned above are part of the administrative structure (for example, personnel), and many qualifications can lead to senior management. In some departments it is very common for the senior management to have grass-roots experience; for example, senior education administrators commonly have teaching experience.

Personal attributes
Depends on the particular type of work. *For all jobs*, interest in local affairs. *For administrative work*, ability to deal with people; capacity for picking out the relevant facts from a mass of detail; organizing ability; ability to work as one of a team. *For senior management*, willingness to carry into effect decisions taken by councillors, whether or not one agrees with them.

Late start
Good for those with relevant experience and, as seen above, so much is relevant. However, in times of financial restraint competition for jobs increases and young entrants may be preferred. Authorities' policies and practices vary.

Career-break Should be possible. Local authorities have been among the most forward-looking employers on flexible working arrangements. Arrangements vary from authority to authority.

Part time Over the last few years local authorities have made a virtue of necessity and been among the first to implement job-sharing and other flexible work patterns on a wide scale. Opportunities vary somewhat with type and level of work, but individuals have been known to sell their own personal scheme to bosses.

Position of women In spite of large numbers of women employed, relatively enlightened policies on recruitment, retention and flexible working, very few women have made it to the top in local government. One factor may well be that fewer women are willing or able to move to different authorities to get the breadth of experience required for top jobs. Yet there are doubtless other less obvious barriers, the so-called 'glass ceilings'. METRA (the Metropolitan Authorities Recruitment Agency, a consortium of metropolitan and a few other authorities) has established a national working group to identify the real barriers and promote the extension of good practice including courses for returners, work-shadowing, refresher courses, support networks, childcare provision and assertiveness courses for women.

Further information Local Government Management Board, Arndale House, Arndale Centre, Luton LU1 2TS

METRA, P O Box 1540, Homer Road, Solihull, West Midlands B91 3QB

Related careers CIVIL SERVICE

Management

Entry qualifications

Nothing specific (see 'The work' and 'Training', below), but a degree or professional qualification is advisable.

The work

Management is a vast and confusing field, with vague terminology. It is not so much one structured career as an activity, the purpose of which is to make the best use of available resources – human, money, material, equipment, time – in order to achieve a given objective. It is becoming much more professionalized, with specific, though varied, theories, techniques and training leading to various qualifications (or none). It is also a 'transferable skill': managers now often take their expertise from one type of organization – say manufacturing industry – to another, say tourism. Any system which provides a product, or a service, has to be managed – i.e. controlled by a hierarchy of managers who are sandwiched between the policy-makers at board or equivalent level, and the 'doers'. At all levels, managers must enthuse their subordinates into doing things as efficiently as they – the managers – would wish to have done them themselves.

One of the most important aspects which applies to all types and levels is, therefore, communication: managers spend between 70% and 90% of their time talking to people – in conference, on the phone, in one-to-one discussion. That applies whether a manager manages a whole or part of a supermarket; an international sales force; a large export department or a small section of one; an engineering workshop; a manufacturing company.

There are basically two ways into management: *either* by first becoming a specialist in something, *or* by starting as 'management trainee' in an organization with a management training scheme. But trainee schemes which give broad-based, systematic training are not easy to get for people without qualification, so pre-entry training for a qualification is advisable (see 'Training', below).

Levels of management: There is no clear-cut distinction between junior, middle and senior management. Designations vary between organizations. Rising from one level to another does not necessarily depend on gaining further qualifications. However, qualifications are very useful and may be essential, especially when changing employers.

Most people who choose a management career think of senior, and general, managers – but they are the smallest management section.

Junior managers are the easiest to define. They are usually responsible for controlling the work of a number of people who are all doing the same work – usually work in which the junior managers are trained (or at least which they are able to do) themselves. For example a supervisor fitter is a skilled fitter; a word processing supervisor is a word processor operator or secretary (see p. 462), though he/she is now often a graduate management trainee; a factory production line supervisor has worked on the production line (though possibly as a graduate engineer gaining experience). Junior managers organize the flow of work, and sort out minor problems (often including subordinates' personal ones). In the office of, say, an export department, a junior manager might be responsible for ensuring that documentation relating to goods for one or two countries is dealt with correctly; on the shop-floor junior managers might be responsible for one or two production lines, which could mean about 100 people. Junior managers are also the link with middle management.

Middle managers co-ordinate and implement policies. This level of management spans a wide range of jobs and levels of responsibility. The step from junior to middle management is the most crucial on the management ladder: while junior managers are usually responsible for people all doing the same kind of work, middle managers are responsible either for the work of a number of junior managers who are all doing different jobs, or for a larger group of people in the same field. Junior managers who want promotion must therefore broaden their experience and 'move sideways' before moving up. This experience-broadening is part of 'management development' (see PERSONNEL ... MANAGEMENT p. 365) and should be built into managers' training, but in very many firms young managers have to plan their own career-paths rather than rely on personnel managers to do it for them. This is partly what makes 'management' such a difficult career to plan and to describe. It is not so much qualifications as varied experience, luck, drive and initiative, which matter.

The majority of managers remain middle managers always, gradually taking responsibility for a wider range of activities or for bigger departments. For example a sales manager in charge of a regional sales force is a middle manager and remains so even when responsibility covers a larger sales force, or becomes more important in cash-terms or regions. A manager in charge of a mail order firm's dispatch department, responsible for a large sum of money and for the firm's reputation for reliability, is a middle manager, and might still be a middle manager when, say, also overseeing the dispatch and the packing departments. However, in another firm the job might be designated 'senior manager': it depends on a firm's organization, and their interpretation of what senior management is.

A vital and growing 'senior-middle management' area is *management of change*. Managers must be aware of the organizational and technical as well as the human aspects of automation. Introduction of new technologies – whether robots in a factory or desk-top computers in an office – is a 'socio-technical' problem. There is as yet no single tried and tested way of tackling this development and its implications. In some companies consultants in 'organizational change' or 'organizational behaviour' (usual backgrounds: social or behavioural science degree plus/or extensive business experience) may be called in to advise; more often managers (departmental, office, production, personnel – it varies enormously) have to cope. These managers may have to deal with employees' fears of new and unknown working practices; with the 'de-skilling' of some jobs and retraining staff for others; with 'slimming down' the workforce and with the search and training for new job opportunities for redundant employees. 'Planning for change' is evolving into a management specialism or at least a new management task (see MANAGEMENT CONSULTANCY, p. 288). It involves analysing where, how, when, why and whether new technologies should be introduced and, if so, what preparation for a smooth transition from old to new working patterns must be made and whether to call in outside advice. No one person is likely to know enough about the various types of machines and systems on the market to choose the equipment most suitable for each particular purpose. *'Planning for change'* involves close co-operation with computer and other specialists.

Senior managers innovate and lead. They may plan far ahead and base planning and policy decisions on information and advice from specialist managers. The higher up the ladder, the more creativity, imagination and understanding of economic and social trends and the environment in which an organization operates is required. Senior managers also initiate changes in both the structure and the direction of an organization, and they are responsible for establishing effective lines of communication to ensure that policies are known and understood (and discussed) right down the line. They must also ensure that the effects of policy-implementation are monitored.

There is, however, no strict dividing line between middle and senior managers. Anyone responsible to the board is definitely a senior manager. That usually includes heads of departments – personnel, production, finance, marketing, etc. And 'general managers', who do the co-ordinating, are usually considered senior managers.

Some terms used in management jargon

Line management: A line manager is the manager in charge of whatever the organization's principal activity and main purpose is. In a manufacturing industry it is the production manager; in retail it is the store manager; in an air freight charter company it is the person selling aircraft space. (The term 'line' is apparently derived from 'being in the firing line' – the line manager is the one who tends to get shot at when things go wrong.)

General management: General managers co-ordinate the work of several specialist departments (or functions), for example personnel, production, accountancy, etc. By training they are usually specialists in one of the functions for which they are responsible, which one is immaterial.

Executives and managers: The distinction is vague. Broadly, managers are responsible for controlling other people's work, whereas executives are not necessarily: for example, a legal adviser is a senior executive, but not a manager. But middle or senior managers may also be called executives.

Managers and administrators: Again the distinction is vague. What is called management in industry is often called administration in the public sector. The terms are often interchangeable (in terms of activity), but 'administrators' are more likely to be concerned with the smooth running of a department or organization without making any changes; whereas 'managers' are expected to choose the most efficient (or 'cost-effective') of various alternative routes to achieve an objective. Management implies more decision-making. But as in the whole of the management field, different people mean different things by the same terms.

Management covers such a vast range of jobs that it is impossible to generalize about prospects. However, there is a serious shortage of good managers (especially with a technical background). Nevertheless, entry to management trainee jobs is very competitive. Graduate and HND candidates on the whole stand a better chance than others. Over one-third of vacancies are for 'any discipline' graduates; where the discipline is specified, engineering/technological degrees are most in demand with computing subjects and then business/management studies next. First jobs are often in large firms' *production* (see p. 187), *marketing and sales* (see p. 294), *purchasing and supply* (see p. 417) departments, and in small and medium firms where specialisms are not so clearly defined. There are numerically more openings in small and medium-sized firms than in the large, household name 'first choice' companies and all-round experience in small firms can be very good training.

Employers prefer management trainee applicants who have had some work-experience – if not on a sandwich placement, then in holiday or temporary employment. Having worked abroad – in whatever capacity – can also be an advantage. It follows that it may be advisable to take almost any job even if it is not a 'management' one, to gain experience of the 'real world' work environment.

Training Paths into management and progress once in are nothing like as clear-cut as they are in established professions – because of the diversity of management tasks, environment and objectives; of levels of responsibility and of 'management styles' (and because there is no precise, universally agreed definition of 'management'). What has become clear over the last few years is that getting *in* requires a very different combination of qualities and qualifications than getting *on* afterwards. That makes description and definition of training rather difficult. However, here are some guidelines and trends:

There has been a 'qualification inflation': jobs once done by people with O-levels now tend to be done by people with A-levels; jobs once done by people with A-levels now tend to go to graduates or HND holders (though there are some exceptions: in some cases employers are switching back and are now asking for A-level leavers for jobs for which a few years ago they wanted graduates).

To be considered for a management trainee job, qualifications certainly matter in the majority of cases, but they must be accompanied by the right personal qualities (which vary from one employer to another – for broad guidelines see 'Personal attributes', below). Later, the balance and combination of requirements are different. For promotion, paper qualifications are less important; track record is more important. For example, a person with a degree but unimpressive work experience has fewer promotion/job-change chances than a person who proved managerial ability in a previous job, and somehow acquired the necessary theoretical knowledge. But the relatively few organizations with elaborate management training schemes cannot train all the managers required; so for the majority of potential managers these are the usual ways of qualifying for management in industry, commerce and elsewhere:

Senior management
1. Degree in business or management studies (titles vary). Courses usually include practical experience in industry or commerce (or

public authority) which gives students an insight into the real world of work. This enables those who do not enjoy the atmosphere, or find the pace too exacting, to change to some other graduate career. Employers welcome business/management studies graduates because they have had work experience, know what to expect, and have a basic understanding of business. All polytechnics and many universities and colleges of higher education run business/management degrees. All polytechnic courses are 4-year sandwich degrees. They come in 2 versions: 'thick sandwich' students normally spend 2 years at college, then 1 year in paid and supervised work experience, with a final year at college (but some students start with a year's practical work). 'Thick sandwich' students are usually sponsored. They spend their work experience period with their sponsor and normally get a job with their sponsor after graduating. 'Thin sandwich' students usually divide their first 3 years between college and work experience and spend the whole final year at college. They are not sponsored and spend work experience periods in a variety of work environments. They gain a wider range of experience, but do not acquire so much indepth knowledge of any particular aspect of business. Neither type of sandwich course is 'better' than the other, though people who know exactly what kind of work they want to do eventually may prefer the sponsored 'thick sandwich'. Institutions normally run *either* 'thick' *or* 'thin' sandwich courses – rarely both kinds. There are also part-time business/management degrees, mainly for people in relevant employment, though people who have had previous relevant experience may be accepted. These courses are useful for people who want to return to work after a break or want to switch to a business career while still in other employment. Some 'mixed mode' courses enable students to combine 1 or 2 years' full-time study with 2 or 3 years' part-time study.

Syllabuses vary. Titles vary too, and do not necessarily indicate any specific content or structure. 'Management Science' does not involve more management science than does 'Business Studies', for example. All courses contain a systematic introduction to management theories and techniques and to the various business functions; most courses specialize and many offer options in a particular branch or management function – for example, marketing or international marketing; industrial relations; export management; manpower planning; finance; organizational behaviour, etc. Some courses are more suitable for people interested in, for example, 'human resources management'; others for those interested in business economics/finance; or in transport or distribution or engineering management.

Students should study the CRAC *Degree Course Guide*, *Which*

Degree, the relevant handbooks and individual course prospectuses.

Entry requirements: Normally any 2 – or now often 3 – A-levels and 3 GCSEs (A–C), including English and maths. Only a few courses require A-level maths; and a few (those which specialize in international marketing or European business administration) a modern language. Most courses accept good BTEC/ SCOTVEC National awards (see pp. xxi–xxii) in lieu of A-levels. Mature candidates are often accepted with experience in lieu of qualifications.

2. A degree in any discipline or specialist qualification (see 'The work', above), e.g. in accountancy (p. 1), engineering (p. 183), work study (see MANAGEMENT SERVICES, p. 291).

3. *Post-graduate or post-experience training* (includes post-relevant professional qualification and post-BTEC Higher National award – see below). Courses fall into two main groups: (i) courses in general management; and (ii) courses leading to specialist qualifications such as personnel management, international marketing, transport, production, export management, etc. Both types of courses can be either full time, part time while in relevant employment, or, possibly, while preparing to go back to work after a break. The best-known courses are at the graduate business schools in London, Cranfield and Manchester, but there are a great number of others. Most courses last 1 or 2 years full time or 2–4 years part time. Many are suitable also for people who have been working for a few years but have no academic or professional qualifications, and for people who have been out of employment for some time (women who raised families mainly) as well as for mid-career changers.

Courses may lead to higher degrees (Master of Business Administration – MBA, M.Sc. or M.Phil.) in management sciences, administrative management, industrial management, international management, etc. Titles vary and do not necessarily indicate a particular emphasis or content. Prospective students should look at graduate study guides and carefully study course prospectuses. MBAs especially have proliferated recently.

Another type of course is the Diploma in Management Studies (DMS), currently awarded by CNAA (but see p. xxx); it is the largest single management training scheme. Courses are available at about 90 higher education establishments. The course structure is very flexible. The DMS can take 9 months full time; but most are of 2 or 3 years' day- or block-release or evening study. (A few DMS courses are organized to suit people with children to look after, with 10 to 3 attendance. Inquire at local polytechnic about existing or planned short-day courses.) The scheme is intended primarily for people with at least 2 years' middle-management experience. Entry qualifications are *either* HND/C, degree, equivalent professional qualifications; and, often, minimum age 23, *or* minimum age 27 with, usually, at least 4 years' relevant experience in lieu of academic qualifications.

DMS courses update students' knowledge of management techniques and aim to improve their management skills. Most courses also specialize either in a 'management function', for example, personnel; export marketing; production management; or in an 'operational area', for example, recreation/leisure management; transport management; public administration; education administration. Like other vocational training (rather than academic education) courses, DMS course content is constantly changing to meet employers' and students' requirements.

Some business degrees, post-graduate and post-experience courses offer options in 'small business' management, mainly for people who want to set up and run their own small show (see WORKING FOR ONESELF, p. 557) and for those who particularly want to work in small firms.

Below degree-level training

BTEC/SCOTVEC (see pp. xxi, xxii), Higher National Diplomas and Certificates. Higher National Diploma courses are usually 2 years full time or 3 years sandwich. Higher National Certificates are usually taken by day- or block-release while in appropriate employment (see Employers' Training Schemes, below). *Entry qualifications*: see p. xxii.

All BTEC courses cover what are called 'central themes': (i) money – basically financial consequences and implications of decisions taken; (ii) people – how to get on with and manage them; (iii) communication – overlaps with (ii) and broadly means making sure everybody in an organization understands what others are doing and why. It involves explaining actions and proposals clearly, in writing and verbally; (iv) numeracy and application of new technology to problem solving. This involves learning how to 'quantify' plans, problems and situations, and developing an analytical approach. BTEC's 'central themes' approach should enable students to be flexible and adapt to the different kinds of jobs everyone is likely to be doing throughout their working lives.

On top of the 'central themes', BTEC students specialize in a career group. Each group has 'core modules', plus 'option modules' to suit each student's (and local employment) requirements.

The 3 BTEC business-related groups are:

1. *Business and Finance*: Covers non-specialized work in a wide range of commercial, manufacturing, service and financial organi-

zations. Options include personnel; stock control; data processing; transport management; purchasing; insurance; banking; building societies. This group is also a suitable choice for students who want to go into small or medium-sized organizations, where functions are not as specialized as in large ones; for those who are not sure yet exactly where their interests lie; or for those who know they want to specialize in finance.

2. *Distribution* (wholesale, retail (see p. 428), mail-order): travel and tourism (see p. 552); also hotels and catering (see p. 95): Most courses are part time for people in relevant employment. If not locally available, students take the Business and Finance Studies course and add Distribution, etc. options.

3. *Public Administration*: For students who want to work in local and central government; public utilities (electricity, water authorities, etc.); health service management; police. (For the vague distinction between management and administration, see p. 275 above.)

SCOTVEC (see p. xxii) qualifications are awarded in 'occupational areas'. The business-related areas are 'public sector administration', business studies and 'business administration'. Modules can be chosen to suit students' needs and, for students in or expecting to go into management in industry, cover much the same ground as BTEC students' core and option modules in the three business-related groups.

BTEC/SCOTVEC Higher National awards may lead to complete, and certainly lead to partial, exemption from relevant professional bodies' 'intermediate' examinations; for example, BTEC Business and Finance HND leads to the Chartered Institute of Bankers' and Chartered Institute of Insurance's final examinations. Increasingly, professional bodies in the commercial field accept, or require, BTEC Higher National awards instead of their own 'Stage 1' or 'intermediate' examinations. The advantage from the students' point of view is that they can postpone narrow specialization till they know more about all the related specializations, and that they can more easily switch specializations in mid-career. (For range of BTEC HND specializations see *Compendium of Advanced Courses in Colleges of Further and Higher Education*.) For SCOTVEC Higher award options and specific HNCs and HNDs, write to SCOTVEC for list of higher awards.

Qualifications leading to junior management which can be stepping stones to middle management:
(i) BTEC National Diploma or BTEC National Certificate.
(ii) BTEC Certificate in Management Studies (CMS). A 1-year part-time course for managers and potential managers. Minimum

age usually 21, but most students are older; candidates normally have either 5 GCSEs (A–C) or a BTEC National Award, or extensive experience. (Candidates over 25 who have had at least 3 years' supervisory or management experience may be admitted without academic qualifications.) Most courses are 'generalist' – but there are some specialist ones, e.g. National Health Service, Local Government, Recreation/Leisure Management. The course is intended for people who want to progress up the management ladder and have to acquire specific knowledge as well as general education/training to be able to analyse and understand changing management processes and practices.

Employers' training schemes: Many firms (mainly large ones) and nationalized industries run training schemes. Entry is at various levels either for training, with day-release, for a professional qualification, or, for professionally qualified people – in whatever subject, but specially business/management, accountancy or engineering – as 'graduate trainee' or 'management trainee'. Schemes vary enormously in content, quality and usefulness to the trainee. In some firms, trainees learn only how to be of use to that particular organization – and thus their future job choice is more limited; in others they get a thorough management training. Detailed research before accepting management trainee jobs is essential. Large organizations often take only, or mainly, graduates for training schemes likely to lead to senior or even senior/middle management. Some organizations consider HND and degree holders on an equal footing. Some large companies – sometimes as part of a consortium – run in-house MBA programmes tailored to their particular needs.

Open or distance-learning (see p. xxxvi) – primarily intended for people at work, but useful also for career-changers and returners: BTEC offers Continuing Education study units in business administration, intended for people over 21 with at least 3 years' work experience (not necessarily immediately preceding the course) who want to update rusty skills or learn new ones. Units include *managing the office, information technology for managers, industrial relations.*

Units can be built up into a Certificate (CBA). Time to complete a unit varies from one person to another, but on average a unit is expected to take 90 hours' private study. Tuition material includes video and audio cassettes as well as printed texts. Students can study entirely on their own as on traditional correspondence courses, but links with local colleges are encouraged, so that students have some face-to-face contact and can use libraries. SCOTVEC arrangements are similar.

The Open Business School, part of the Open University (see

p. xxxiv), works on similar lines. Courses include tutorials, weekend schools and are at 3 levels: Professional Certificate in Management, Professional Diploma in Management and MBA. The first two, which can each be completed in a minimum of 1 year, have no entry requirements. The Certificate includes compulsory courses *accounting and the PC for managers* and *managing customer and client relations*, plus either *the effective manager* or *managing health services* or *managing voluntary and non-profit enterprises*.

To gain the Diploma, Certificate holders choose a number of courses from a range that includes *personnel selection and interviewing*, *managing design*, *managing people* and *international marketing* and complete a project.

The MBA is in 2 parts: part 1 consists of either the Certificate and Diploma or, for managers aged 27 plus with an honours degree or equivalent, a 9-month foundation course for *the competent manager*. Henley Management College and some other establishments are also running, or planning, distance-learning schemes.

The Management Charter Initiative (MCI): Concern among employers about Britain's poor record in management training (over 90% have no management qualification and have had very little in-service training or development) and the damaging effect this has on the country's international competitiveness led to the setting up of a National Forum for Management Education and Development. This aims to attract employers, individual managers and colleges keen to improve the quantity and quality of management training, with the emphasis on what managers actually do rather than on academic study. The Forum set up the MCI in 1990: employers who belong sign a commitment to a 10-point code of good management development practice. MCI publicity aimed at new graduates suggests questions they need to ask potential employers about the management training and development they offer. The MCI is also creating a framework of qualifications, nationally recognized and based on competence in the workplace, at 4 levels, from supervisory to senior management. To help experienced managers assess their own training needs, a system of accreditation of prior learning (APL, see p. xxxiii) is being piloted by which they can match what they know and can do with a set of competencies recognized by MCI and leading eventually to NVQs (see p. xx).

Personal attributes   Numeracy, business acumen, the ability to get on well with and be respected by people at all levels in the hierarchy, natural authority, willingness to take the blame for subordinates' mis-

deeds, self-confidence, unflappability in crises, organizing ability.
For senior management: an analytical brain; creativity and imagination; ability to see implications and consequences of decisions and
actions taken; ability to sift relevant facts from a mass of irrelevant
information; enjoyment of power and responsibility; a fairly thick
skin to cope with unavoidable clashes of temperament and opinion; resilience, courage, entrepreneurial flair; boundless ambition;
ability to take snap-decisions without worrying about them afterwards; physical and mental energy.

Late start See above for post-graduate courses, DMS and Open Learning.

A few companies, so far mainly in retail and in catering, are
encouraging women of 30+ to become management trainees.
Candidates are expected to have a degree, or professional qualification, or relevant experience which is usually selling or secretarial;
but a few companies realize that women who have managed a
home, family, voluntary work and/or hobbies of some kind have
in fact been 'project managers', i.e. they know how to bring
different strands together.

**Career-
break** See below.

Part time Few opportunities at present; there could be more in future,
if women present their own proposals for job-shares or other
arrangements.

**Position
of
women** Women should have a great future in management, but they are
actually faring worse in industrial/commercial management than
in the professions. Only 5% of the British Institute of Management's members are women. (However, of the 1991 intake 13%
were women!) BIM members are middle and senior managers
and normally must have degrees or professional qualifications to
be eligible for membership. (This figure is a far better indicator of
women's share of responsible management positions than census
and labour force survey figures which give women's share of
management jobs variously as between 6% and 22%. These
figures include supervisory and junior management jobs.) The
majority of women managers – all levels – are in service industries
like retail or catering rather than in wealth-creating manufacturing, and in personnel rather than in 'sharp end' functions like
production or financial management. Yet manufacturing industry
is desperately short of *good* managers, and for today's 'participa-
tive' management style establishing and maintaining good personal relationships with a wide variety of types of people is

considered one of the most important management qualities. Women are supposed to be 'good with people', so it is illogical that so few are managers. As industry now realizes that it cannot afford to waste half the nation's management potential simply because it happens to be held by females, several research projects (and many conferences) have been funded in recent years by government and industry to find out (a) why women are making such slow progress in industry (it is not just discrimination; it is clearly more complicated than that), and (b) what can be done to get more women managers.

Various research projects have identified (or, perhaps, confirmed?) that there are three basic and interrelated reasons why women do badly in this traditionally male area:

1. *Organizational causes*: Traditional career paths were designed for men, and have not been sufficiently adapted to take account of the fact that most women want to have children and a career.

2. *Assumptions* which do not stand up when tested: for example it is still widely believed that women management trainees/managers leave their first employer sooner than their male colleagues, and before they have 'paid off' the money invested in their training. But this is not so. Statistics show that women leave to have babies after 5 to 7 years; men switch employers after 5–7 years. Many women who leave cite poor career prospects as the reason.

Another false assumption is women's alleged worse absentee record. Women employees *as a whole* take more time off, it is true. But, for all employees, the lower the level of responsibility, the higher the level of absenteeism: *far* more women have lowly jobs, so far more take time off. What the statistic obscures is that at middle and senior management level, women's record equals men's. Other assumptions which research has disproved include: women are more emotional at work; men do not want to work for women. Broadly, research has proved that discrimination, founded on false assumptions, persists, but is *very* slowly diminishing. (A 1987 BIM survey found that 55% of companies surveyed then had one or more women executives compared with 49% a year earlier, and that women occupied 5·5% of 'executive positions' compared with 4% the previous year. However, a more recent survey showed women accounted for only 1–2% of senior executives.)

3. The third and most intractable reason why women do badly in management lies in *women themselves*: their attitudes, aspirations, qualifications. Women lack confidence and hence ambition; they need to do more strategic career-planning than men and in fact they do less. This ties up closely with (1) above: career

structures are planned for men: in most companies young men are *assumed* to want to go up the ladder – their careers are almost automatically 'developed'; they are sent on courses and given broadening experience which fits them for promotion. Women have to *ask* for 'career development', to be sent on courses and given broadening experience (this applies at all levels of management, but especially junior management). Women therefore have to be much more highly motivated in order to get as far as men do automatically.

Women find themselves in two kinds of chicken-and-egg situations: (a) If they push themselves forward, they are dubbed aggressive – and that is unacceptable in women managers. If they do not push themselves forward, they are far less likely than men to be noticed and given the training/experience essential for promotion. (b) Women have few 'role models'. As so few women are in top jobs, few girls know, or know of, anyone with whom they can identify, whom they can emulate. They feel they will not be promoted anyway; so they do not try. They do not try, so they do not get promoted.

Women are also less likely than men to have the kind of qualifications which help to get on the management ladder. Fewer women than men have technology- or business-based qualifications. Lower down the ladder fewer girls than boys have the sort of qualifications which enable them to start as technicians and get day-release for technical qualifications which can then lead to supervisory work and junior management.

Research has also found that women's careers 'take off' later than men's. Only when the employer *and the woman herself* seem sure that she takes her career seriously is she considered for appropriate 'career development'. Generally, women's careers lag behind those of men shortly after graduation, long before childbearing becomes an issue. Despite many years of equal opportunities legislation and pressure groups' efforts, women are still less likely to apply for promotion or training than men with equal qualifications and/or experience. There is evidence that recruitment ratios now reflect application ratios. Again, lack of self-confidence and of role-models means that women need stronger personalities or more ambition (and push) than their male colleagues to do equally well.

The most important, though not startling, proposal for attracting more women into industry and commerce is that career structures must take account of women's 'broken career-pattern'. Maternity leave provisions have not solved the problems of combining career and family responsibilities. Fewer women than expected want to return to full-time work after the statutory maternity leave. Many are returning to jobs below their qualification and pre-break status because these are the only jobs they can do part time, or as job-shares (see p. xxix). An increasing number (though still few) employers now want to minimize this 'waste of human resource' – especially where they have invested heavily in the training of highly qualified women. A number of schemes to encourage and enable women managers to return to work at a level commensurate with their experience have, therefore, emerged. Two types, or levels, of arrangements are being made: (a) Women are encouraged to keep in touch during the *career-break* by, for example, working a few weeks a year, or a day or half day a week. (b) Returners are allowed to work part time (often called 'less than full time') for a few years after the break. This may take the form of, for example, working half a week, or fewer weeks a year than normal (perhaps during term-time only). In as yet a *very* few cases women are connected to the office by computer – not to do computing work but using the computer merely as a communication tool – and visit the office only occasionally. Such schemes may well become more numerous (for both men and women, incidentally).

No blueprint for action has been produced, but, for women with relevant qualifications or with ambition and self-confidence, prospects are now good. Employers like to be seen to be complying with equal opportunities legislation and they also realize that women, as they still have to prove themselves, tend to work harder and be more committed to succeeding than men of comparable ability. The – regrettably few – women who go into the 'sharp end' business functions such as finance or production do particularly well, probably because only women with above-average self-confidence and ability take up jobs in areas which are still very much male preserves.

At present, women are more likely to do well in large than in medium-sized and small companies, and they do well in managing their own business (see WORKING FOR ONESELF, p. 557).

To help women gain the confidence and the social skills needed to progress, many kinds of courses for women have been set up. Some are short day or weekend courses/seminars organized by the Industrial Society and other, smaller organizations. Course titles vary from 'Putting Yourself Across' to 'Getting Going' or 'Assertiveness Training'. All courses stress the need for women to learn how to be assertive without being aggressive, and they explain the vital difference between being aggressive which is a Bad Thing for women in business and being assertive (broadly, confident and polite yet firm) which is a Good Thing. Courses include role-playing and workshops. Then there are longer general management courses, some of which offer special bursaries to women; some are specially for women. Some companies sponsor women to attend. The women's training scene is changing constantly. Some of the post-graduate and post-experience (including post-senior secretarial experience) courses (see 'Training', above) give special scholarships to women and want to attract more women students. Post-graduate and post-experience courses are useful for potential returners and usually accept women who have been away from their jobs for some time: returners' maturity, life-experience and having managed home, family (and especially voluntary work) are recognized as being valuable in management jobs. The Diploma in Management Studies (see 'Training') can be particularly useful for returners.

The Open University runs an 8-week course 'Women into Management' (see also 'Open Learning', p. xxxvi). Post-graduate and post-experience courses still have few women applicants. For example in 1991 only 25% of applicants for the London Business School's part-time Master's Programme were women. Approximately 20% of the Association of MBA's members are women (and membership ensures that graduates can keep in touch with developments in business). So while at present a career-break still hinders women's promotion prospects considerably, women do not seem to do as much as they could to ease their return.

Further information
No one specific information point; see specific careers; higher education prospectuses; CRAC Degree Course Guides: BTEC; SCOTVEC

Institute of Management, Management House, Cottingham Road, Corby, Northants. NN17 1TT (can supply members with list of management courses, including those specifically for women)

1993 NOTE: The British Institute of Management and the Institute of Industrial Managers have amalgamated to form the Institute of Management.

Related careers
Virtually every career offers management opportunities

Management Consultancy

Entry qualifications

Degree and/or professional qualification and, usually, management experience. This is essentially a *'second career'*.

The work

The term 'management consultant' is often used rather loosely. Some self-styled management consultants do not satisfy established practitioners' or the professional organization's standards. The Institute of Management Consultants – the professional body to which most practitioners belong though they do not have to – defines management consulting as 'the service provided to business, public or other undertakings by an independent and qualified person or persons in identifying and investigating problems concerned with policy, organization, procedures and methods; recommending appropriate action and helping to implement those recommendations'. To be accepted for membership, practitioners are expected to have relevant qualifications and experience.

Management consultants need to be seen as, basically, troubleshooters (increasingly organizations call them in before trouble has arisen). They are called upon to improve organizations' effectiveness, diagnose faults and suggest remedies. They may, for example, be called in by a food manufacturer to investigate reasons for the company's declining market-share. Before producing a plan of action to improve matters, they thoroughly research the firm's organization, its potential, and the competition. They might then suggest the company should widen, or narrow, or completely change, its product-range; or they might recommend changes in the company's marketing strategy, its management structure, its industrial relations policy, the introduction of new technology – or a combination of any of these and perhaps other strategies. But work is by no means confined to industry. Consultants are increasingly called in by, for example, charities and public authorities. A particular growth area is 'managing change' in any type of organization – i.e. helping to implement smooth transition from traditional to new working patterns – not only new technology-based ones but also such innovations as job-sharing.

Because the field is so wide and requires so many varieties of expertise, consultants tend to specialize. They may specialize in an aspect of management – for example in financial, distribution, marketing, human resources (see PERSONNEL ... MANAGEMENT p. 365), or information management. They may also specialize in working with one type of organization – local authorities; charities; manufacturing industry or even one type of manufacturing such as light engineering, or one type of service industry such as catering or retail. Others specialize as consultants in 'change management'.

There is a growing demand for management consultants. But because of that and because there is no clear-cut qualification structure, unqualified 'consultants' have jumped on the bandwagon and, after a few years, have to give up for lack of clients. So, prospects are very good – for suitably experienced experts. Membership of the Institute is increasingly seen as proof of high standards.

Training/ experience

A few management consultancies recruit new graduates – usually people with technical or business/management degrees – and train them by giving them background research to do. But the vast majority of recruits have a few years' post-graduate or post-professional qualification/experience. Many have an MBA. Consultancy firms may then provide in-house training and/or send staff on external courses. Large consultancies are often offshoots or departments of large accountancy firms, but other specialist skills, especially in the information technology and related areas, are equally in demand.

Personal attributes

Ability to work as one of a team as well as independently; ability to cope with possibly hostile attitudes on the part of staff whose work is being scrutinized; adaptability to working in different environments; great diplomatic skill to deal with people at all levels and persuade them to change their ways; self-confidence and a confidence-inspiring manner; an analytical mind; an open mind to approach each new set of circumstances on its merits; curiosity; patience; willingness to work long hours; ability to put complex matters concisely and simply.

Late start

Maturity and experience are an asset.

Career-break

It is essential to keep up with developments and to keep the break short.

Part time

Theoretically possible by having small work loads or job-sharing (see p. xxix) but so far few women consultants have felt established enough to try unconventional, i.e. less than full-time, work.

Position of women

The proportion of women is still small, but it is increasing as more women have had the opportunity to acquire the essential management experience. Their share of Institute membership is 15–20% and growing. Women have tended to specialize in service industries consultancy and in recruitment/human resources management, though they too cover the whole range, from economists to agriculturalists to IT specialists. Recently, some have set up as specialist consultants in introducing equal opportunities programmes, and in change-to-new-technology management in office work.

Further information

Institute of Management Consultants, 5th Floor, 32–3 Hatton Garden, London EC1N 8DL

Related careers

ACCOUNTANCY – COMPUTING/IT – MANAGEMENT – PERSONNEL/HUMAN RESOURCES MANAGEMENT – MANAGEMENT SERVICES

Management Services

Entry qualifications

For *work study* and *organization and methods*, nothing rigid, just appropriate work experience. For *operational research*, a degree, normally in a subject requiring numeracy.

The work

'Management services' is the collective term for a number of functions concerned with the application of analytical techniques to problems concerning the efficient use of manpower, machinery or systems. They provide objective information and analysis for improved management decision-making. The 3 core management services are work study, organization and methods (O & M) and operational research (OR), but some management services departments include other specialists such as economists (see p. 180), statisticians (see p. 448), or systems analysts (see p. 145), while some work study or O & M work might come under another department, for example human resources.

Work Study and Organization and Methods

Work study had its origins in production, and organization and methods in the office, but the aims and principles are basically the same. There are 2 main aspects of the work: method study and work measurement. Method study is the analysis of how operations are carried out and how they might be improved. Work measurement means using specific techniques to measure the time and human effort involved in specific tasks so that standards of performance can be established for planning, control, payment systems and the introduction of new technologies, for example.

In addition to identifying problems, collecting the necessary data, evaluating and proposing solutions, work study and O & M practitioners often get involved in implementing the solutions, for example by training line managers or helping to design a new office layout or select new equipment. Tact, sensitivity and good communication skills are needed at every stage. People at all levels can be reluctant to admit there is a problem and can feel resentful at being 'measured' or threatened by the thought of change. Your solutions may have to be 'sold' to a range of interested parties.

Operational Research

Whereas work study and organization and methods are concerned with the detail of systems in the workplace, operational research applies scientific method to complex organizational and management problems at a broader policy or strategic level. The aim is to improve existing systems and methods of decision-making. Many opportunities are with large concerns with extremely complex problems. For example, OR is used by the coal industry to develop strategies which will stand up to a range of possible future prices for coal; factors taken into account are estimates of future demand, availability, and production and freight costs. At the other end of the scale OR has been instrumental in the development of computer packages which enable schools to design a timetable which satisfies the choices of as many pupils as possible.

A key tool of OR is the 'model', a computer simulation of the system to be improved. All sorts of variable factors can be incorporated to see what would happen in given situations if different courses of action were taken. The implications of alternative decisions can then be compared. The operational researcher needs good technical and analytical skills to find the right model, method or technique to suit the problem. He or she also needs good communication skills to help define the problem in consultation with management, gather the necessary information, explain the progress, often to a non-technical audience, and promote the solution at senior levels. Numeracy is important but, unlike in OR's early days when it was very 'hard' or quantitative, there has been an increasing realization that problems often have a large non-quantitative element. When the problems are 'messy', OR needs to be 'soft'.

Most operational researchers are young; OR is a good springboard to general management and to related areas such as corporate planning, marketing, finance, distribution and production.

Training   For work study and O & M, largely on the job as an assistant. Distance, day-release, evening and a few full-time courses are available for the Certificate and Diploma of the Institute of Management Services. It usually takes 3 years of part-time study to reach the Diploma via the Certificate.

For operational research a post-graduate degree may be an advantage. Employers may sponsor students on these courses. On-the-job training is also provided, often supplemented by in-house or outside short courses.

Personal attributes Numeracy; ability to get on with people at all levels in an organization; good communication skills; methodical approach; analytical mind; tact. *For work study and O & M*, common sense and imagination. *For OR*, ability to understand and explain complicated matters clearly.

Late start Prospects are good in work study and O & M, which are very much 'second careers'; most people entering have some previous work experience. In OR a late start is possible only for those with suitable degree and industrial experience. As mentioned above, OR is largely a young person's field; it is estimated that some three-quarters of practitioners are under 40.

Career-break Should be no problem for those who keep in touch. Diversity of settings makes it difficult to be definite.

Part time Part-time work is rare and likely to take the form of project or consultancy work rather than reduced hours in a regular job. Opinions differ on how job-sharing might work; keeping in touch would be vital and home computer links could help. Given the problem-solving nature of the work, the 'two minds' argument seems persuasive.

Position of women Only about 8% of members of the Institute of Management Services are women, but at a recent Young OR Conference (for the under-30s) about 50% of the delegates were women. Women who identify these careers and enter them do well. The move from 'hard' to 'soft' OR has probably helped, but more women should recognize how much work study and O & M depend on common sense, organizing ability and establishing good relations with people.

Further information Institute of Management Services, 1 Cecil Court, London Road, Enfield, Middlesex EN2 6DD
Operational Research Society, Neville House, Waterloo Street, Birmingham B2 5TX

Related careers ACTUARY – COMPUTING/IT – ENGINEERING – HEALTH AND SAFETY INSPECTORS – MANAGEMENT – SCIENCE: *Mathematical Sciences*

Marketing and Selling

Entry qualifications

Nothing specific; for *Chartered Institute of Marketing's Certificates*: *either* 1 A-level, 4 GCSEs (A–C) including English *or* 5 GCSEs (A–C) plus 1 year's marketing experience *or* BTEC/SCOTVEC National *or*, if aged over 21, 3 years' experience. For *Diploma*: *either* the Certificate *or* relevant degree *or* Higher National award. Considerable graduate entry.

The work

Effective marketing is the key to profitability and essential for Britain's trading position in the world economy. Marketing goods and services is as skilled an occupation, and as important, as producing them. But marketing is a rather vague term, often used loosely to cover a range of activities. Different establishments interpret the term differently, and titles include brand manager; product manager; development manager; marketing executive; marketing manager; export manufacturing manager, etc. Titles do not necessarily indicate any particular level of responsibility or scope.

The Chartered Institute of Marketing defines the purpose of marketing as follows: 'Marketing is the management process responsible for identifying, anticipating and satisfying customer requirements profitably' – at home and, vitally important, abroad.

Marketing people (sometimes called 'marketers') find out what customers want or, more important, can be persuaded to want, at what price, and then relate potential demand to the company's ability to produce whatever it is, get it to the 'point of sale', and do all that profitably.

Marketing involves researching the market and analysing research results – which involves devising and organizing surveys and interpreting the results; discussing results with accountants, production, distribution and advertising people. Marketers may suggest the company adapt its existing products to cope with the competition's better products, or with changes in buying habits, or they may think up a totally new product and help to develop and launch it, or they may introduce a better after-sales service.

All these activities have always been carried out in business, but as business has become more complex and professionalized, with decisions being based on researched facts and, above all, figures rather than guesswork and experience, the 'marketing function' has become a 'business profession' and even a degree subject. Its importance in business has grown enormously in recent years. Poor marketing in the past is blamed for poor business performance. This applies particularly to *international marketing*. As exporting is becoming more and more essential for economic survival, international marketing is becoming a vital function in many more businesses. Marketing people have good prospects of going to the top in general management.

Marketing is often split into *consumer goods and services marketing*; *industrial marketing*; and *international marketing* (which could refer to either, and is part of the export business).

In all these activities, marketing involves several types of work: detailed research to establish customers', and potential customers', needs and potential needs: what type of customers, where, might buy at what price, with how effective an after-sales service, etc. Whether it is yet another washing powder or, in industrial marketing, a new piece of office machinery or computer, a new magazine or a food product, the procedure is basically the same. In *industrial marketing*, an engineering or science background is useful, but people switch from one area of marketing to another. In *international marketing*, a thorough understanding of other nations' cultural as well as social and economic set-up is vital (and of course speaking the relevant language). Perhaps the most crucial among several other marketing activities is *sales forecasting*. How many cars with what particular features will country X be willing to buy in 2, 5, 10 years' time?

Marketing people must always base their conclusions on researched social and economic trends, which include statistics. Marketing has a glamorous image, but the basis of it is the correct interpretation of statistics.

Though the majority of marketing people work in large, often multinational, companies, increasingly medium and small companies are separating 'the marketing function' from general business management.

Selling is both a career in itself, and an essential part of (and the best way into) marketing. The two are closely linked: *marketing* finds out what customers want and helps to put the goods/ services on the market; *selling* is concerned with finding and dealing with customers for the product/service.

There are different kinds of selling – and various ways of categorizing sales staff. A useful division is between *consumer goods selling* and *specialized selling*. In consumer goods selling (this totally excludes retail and door-to-door selling), sales representatives, or reps, sell to wholesalers and/or, more usually, to retailers. Selling to retailers involves 'merchandising', which means helping the retailer to maximize sales, by promotion campaigns, suggesting ideas for improving shop display, etc. Reps may also advise retailers on new sales techniques, shop display, etc. There is a hierarchy in consumer goods selling, with the *field sales supervisors* and *area sales managers* in charge of reps, and *sales managers* and *sales directors* at head office directing the whole sales operation.

Speciality or *technical* or *industrial selling* is usually done by staff with technical background and perhaps production management experience (see p. 187). An engineering background is particularly useful (see ENGINEERING, p. 183). The speciality selling process differs totally from consumer goods selling: purchasing decisions are made not by shopkeepers or store buyers, but by technical and financial experts. To effect one sale may take months of negotiations, and extensive after-sales service. Speciality sales staff do not necessarily sell only standard products – whether they are large pieces of machinery or machine tools – they may agree for their company to modify a product or produce a 'one-off' piece of equipment.

Sales reps may form part of a team, or be the only rep in the firm. They may have a 'territory' in this country which may require them to be away from home for several days most weeks, or it may be a territory near home – it depends on the kind of product and on how many potential buyers there are within an area. *Export sales executives* of course travel extensively.

Training

There are various ways into marketing – the most usual way to start is as sales rep. *Production* (see ENGINEERING, pp. 187, 193) people often move into marketing (which is sometimes better paid). Many graduates go straight into marketing as assistants.

While working as trainee or whatever the title, marketing staff can take part-time courses for the Chartered Institute of Marketing's examinations. These are at 2 levels:

1. 2-year part-time course leading to either the Certificate in Marketing or the Certificate in Sales Management. Both syllabuses include fundamentals of marketing and selling, economics, statistics, business law and accounting. (In some subjects there is a common syllabus with the Institute of Chartered Secretaries, see p. 110, and the Institute of Purchasing and Supply, see p. 417.)

2. 1-year part-time course for the Diploma in Marketing. Subjects include international marketing, marketing planning and control, marketing communications, and marketing analysis and decision-making. The Diploma is now accepted by some higher

education institutions as an entry qualification for post-graduate study.

For *export marketing* some trainees work for the Institute of Export's examination (see p. 477), by day-release or correspondence study. The syllabus adds export procedure and principles of export management to marketing methods, principles and procedures.

Pre-entry training for marketing is either by business studies degree with marketing option or by specialized marketing degree. These degrees either link marketing to a specific area such as chemicals or textiles or engineering; or concentrate on international marketing and export. An engineering or science degree is a good way into speciality selling.

There are also BTEC/SCOTVEC Higher awards (see pp. xxi, xxii) with marketing export options, and distribution options.

Personal attributes
Marketing: A high degree of business acumen and of numeracy; a little risk-taking instinct; self-confidence; ability to assess the effects of economic, social or political events; ability to stand perhaps unjustified criticism when forecasts turn out wrong, due to unforeseeable causes; social awareness and interest in social and economic trends; ability to communicate easily with colleagues and clients, whatever their temperament and their degree of expertise.

Selling: Numeracy; extrovert personality; ability to establish instant rapport with people; judgement; sensitivity for gauging right approach to customers; indifference to the occasional rebuff; enjoying being alone when travelling; willingness to be away from home a lot.

Late start
People with technological or business qualifications can switch to marketing.

Career-break
It is not likely that in this competitive field it will be easy for any but the best and most determined women to return to what is essentially still a young person's and a man's career. Women with technological or science degrees or experience stand the best chances in industrial marketing.

Part time
Only in backroom research – very few openings indeed.

Position of women
This is an area in which personality counts more than qualifications. Women have good prospects if they fit the employer's idea of what the 'right type' for any particular job is. In *export marketing* their scope is limited because employers often claim

that in many countries saleswomen and women negotiators are not acceptable. Graduate women stand much better chances than school-leavers, who tend to be offered secretarial jobs 'with a view to progressing in marketing', and then do *not* progress. Female graduate sales reps who are good at their job say they are at an advantage: they tend to be noticed and 'trained up'. So far, however, there are very few women sales directors (except in cosmetics etc.). Potentially it could be a promising area. Especially in *specialized selling*, more women would be genuinely welcome in many organizations. Companies say that not enough women graduates apply. The proportion of female graduates *accepted* is slightly higher than that of males accepted. Probably women who do apply are more highly motivated. It is too early to say, however, what women's promotion prospects to senior sales management positions are. Only about 1 in 20 qualified CIM members, but a third of CIM students and half of Institute of Export students, are women.

Further information	Chartered Institute of Marketing, Moor Hall, Cookham, Maidenhead, Berks. SL6 9QH
	Institute of Export, Export House, 64 Clifton Street, London EC2A 4HB
	Market Research Society, 175 Oxford Street, London W1R 1TA

Related careers	ADVERTISING – MANAGEMENT – PUBLIC RELATIONS – RETAIL DISTRIBUTION – SHIPBROKING . . . EXPORTING

Medicine

Entry qualifications

3 good A-levels (or Scottish equivalent) or 2 A-levels and 2 AS-levels are normally required for entry to medical school. Chemistry is invariably required with other subjects commonly chosen from biology, maths and physics, though an increasing number of medical schools are happy to consider candidates whose third A-level (or ASs) are in non-science subjects. A small number of medical schools run a 1-year pre-medical course for candidates without the usual science A-level background (good sciences at GCSE would normally be expected).

General Practice (Family Doctor)

The work

About half of doctors qualifying go into general practice. Family doctors are in the front-line of primary health care. As self-employed practitioners GPs have considerable autonomy in deciding how best to provide the services to patients required under their NHS contracts. Under the recent NHS reforms some practices have become 'fundholders', permitted to purchase services for their patients from hospitals.

All family doctors are involved in: acute disease management, i.e. diagnosing, treating or referring for specialist treatment a range of ailments presented by patients; preventive medicine, helping patients to understand how to prevent, look for and deal with problems; counselling, i.e. dealing with patients' fears and feelings, both those that have a medical basis and those that lead to physical symptoms. General practitioners might also get involved in other work in the community, e.g. in old people's welfare, the Red Cross, nursing homes, schools and businesses. Some do sessional work in hospital out-patient clinics. There is also liaison with other sectors of the NHS, for example hospitals, on the provision of health care.

Most family doctors work in partnership with other doctors. Some practices organize themselves along specialist lines with, perhaps, one partner particularly experienced in obstetrics and gynaecology, while another may have a special interest in stress and another in heart disease.

A typical family doctor's day might consist of a morning

surgery from, say, 8.30 until 11.00 a.m.; routine office work, dealing with telephone inquiries, signing prescriptions, reading the post, dealing with letters to and from hospital consultants; home visits; lunch; visits or clinics (e.g. antenatal, minor operations, diabetic, child development); more office work; evening surgery. Doctors within a practice or several practices normally get together to provide a night and weekend emergency call rota. The larger the rota the less often any one doctor is on duty, but the busier he or she is likely to be when on call.

Recent years have seen enormous changes in general practice. New drugs are continually available; practices have direct access to investigation facilities and new equipment enabling them to provide care over a more interesting range of conditions; practice nurses handle routine procedures and extend health education and preventive work. Computerization is used for repeat prescription control, for the maintenance of registers (e.g. of all women due for cervical screening, or all under-5s due for immunization) and for the compilation of data that enables the doctors to measure and assess what they are doing for their patients as a whole. However, all these developments are merely aids to improve and monitor service. They do not replace the family doctor's traditional role of caring for patients largely by listening to and talking with them.

Hospital Service

The work *All* doctors start their careers in hospitals, though eventually only about half as many stay there as enter general practice. Doctors who remain in hospital medicine become specialists. There are more than 50 specialities. General medicine group and surgical group are the largest; within each are many sub-specialities ranging from the substantial general medicine and general surgery to very small fields like audiological medicine, palliative medicine or paediatric surgery. Other major specialities are accident and emergency, obstetrics and gynaecology, anaesthetics, radiology group, pathology group and psychiatry group.

Both the nature and pattern of work in different fields can vary considerably. For example, general medicine and surgery and obstetrics have far more emergency work than psychiatry or dermatology, while pathology has very little. The nature of the round-the-clock demands on anaesthetists means they have evolved a more predictable shift system than other doctors.

For many years of hospital doctors' careers they are, though fully registered and in paid employment, technically in training posts. As they progress through jobs as house officer, senior house officer, registrar, senior registrar, they take on more and more responsibility under the supervision and guidance of more senior doctors. The most junior doctors take responsibility for practical, routine day-to-day care and administration (keeping records, communicating with families and other members of the medical team), progressing to more advisory work and greater clinical responsibility. Junior doctors' hours are long and irregular; the more senior doctors become, the less they are likely to be called from their beds to an emergency, but the more complex the decision or procedure when they are.

At the head of hospital teams are consultants, who have continuing responsibility for patient care. It can take from 8 to 12 years of specialist training to reach this level.

Doctors' choices of speciality are determined not only by interest and inclination, but often by opportunity. Some fields are very much more popular and competitive than others, and it can take some time and experience before a final choice is made.

Public Health Medicine and Community Health

The work   Public health medicine is concerned with the promotion of the health of a whole community rather than of specific individuals. It is primarily about preventive medicine and there is no direct clinical contact with patients.

Most public health doctors are employed in regional or district health authorities. Their work includes the overall administration, planning and development of the 3 branches of the health service (environmental health, personal health, community care); the development of comprehensive information; and health education services. Community physicians also act as advisers to local authorities, which retain responsibility for running school, environmental and some personal health services.

Environmental health covers infectious disease control and prevention (regular immunization and special immunization campaigns); food and other hygiene inspection; prevention of insanitary conditions in restaurants, shops, housing (including overcrowding); control of noise nuisance and air pollution. The day-to-day work is carried out by environmental health officers (see p. 206).

Personal health services cover provision of antenatal, postnatal and child health clinics; midwifery; district nursing services (see separate entries); care of handicapped children.

Community care covers provision for the care of the mentally ill and handicapped who increasingly live at home or in hostels;

support in the home given by social workers; day centres and social clubs for the elderly and handicapped; hostel accommodation and organization; co-operation with local voluntary organizations in the mental health field. (See District and Psychiatric Community Nursing for increase in numbers of patients cared for in the community.)

There are also opportunities for public health doctors in: the four government health departments (England, Scotland, Wales and Northern Ireland); the Public Health Laboratory Service and Communicable Disease Surveillance Centre; medical schools; international agencies such as the World Health Organization; and abroad, especially in developing countries. This is a growth area and there are more training vacancies than can be filled.

Community health clinics are not staffed by public health specialists, but by community medical officers (who probably have a Diploma in Community Health) or by GPs or by those with post-graduate training in obstetrics, paediatrics, geriatrics, etc. Community health offers opportunities for part-time sessional clinic work and mature entrants (returners) are very welcome.

Occupational Health or Occupational Medicine

The work Occupational medical officers give medical check-ups to employees and work with personnel departments. They also do research into occupational health, studying the effects of diverse environmental conditions on health and efficiency of the staff. The scope of their work is very wide. For example, it might include studying the effects of new technology, chemical processes and underground working on employees. It also requires knowledge of conditions such as occupational asthma, dermatitis and alcoholism and how they affect workers' efficiency. They work closely with trade union representatives and may make suggestions to management about ways to improve employees' health at work.

Research and Teaching

The work Research into new forms of treatments and new drugs and their effects is done in hospitals, research establishments and drug firms. Doctors can, and usually do, combine clinical and scientific work, but there are also research appointments, often including some teaching, for those who are interested in the scientific side of medicine rather than 'patient contact' (see SCIENCE, p. 435).

Training (all doctors)

This is in 2 parts: pre-registration and post-registration. Doctors must obtain a 'registrable qualification'. There are several, each signified by different initials; all are essentially of equal value.

The undergraduate course takes 5 or 6 years. It usually falls into 2 parts. The first is the *pre-clinical* course, which lasts 2 years and includes anatomy, physiology and biochemistry. The work consists of lectures, laboratory work and a great deal of reading. The *clinical* course lasts 3 years. Students are attached to a succession of consultants in different specialities ('firms'). They have contact with patients, take case histories and, under supervision, make diagnoses and prescribe treatments. The clinical course is extremely hard work, with little spare time.

It is vital to look closely at courses since they vary greatly in organization, teaching methods and emphasis. Some include study for a B.Sc. degree, while for others this is optional. Before students get their registrable qualification they must spend a 'pre-registration year' as full-time resident junior house officer in hospital. (At this stage they start earning.)

Post-registration training is essential, very hard work, and rather haphazard. In some areas junior doctors have to arrange their own succession of hospital 'training posts', but many others have rotational training schemes which doctors slot into. Each training post has to be educationally approved by the relevant Royal College (for example, in England and Wales a training post in surgery has to be approved by the Royal College of Surgeons). Post-registration training in a succession of approved training posts as senior house officer, registrar, senior registrar can take from 8 to over 12 years before becoming a consultant (it depends mainly on the specialty chosen). During this period of full-time work, doctors study for specialist qualifications (and many fail the exams the first time).

Doctors wishing to become *general practitioners* must take a 3-year post-graduate training, consisting of 2 years in a choice of specified full-time hospital (and, sometimes, community medicine) posts, and 1 year as a full-time trainee in general practice (or the equivalent on a part-time basis).

Doctors wishing to become *public health doctors* take the examinations of the Faculty of Public Health: subjects include epidemiology, statistics, aspects of the social services, the principles of administration and management.

Doctors wishing to specialize in *occupational health* or *medicine* take the examinations of the Faculty of Occupational Medicine.

Personal attributes

The ability to take responsibility and to make vital decisions after weighing up all the relevant factors; self-confidence; conscientiousness; resourcefulness; the energy and stamina to work hard for long and often irregular periods; great powers of concentration; above-average intelligence; good health.

Especially for general practitioners and the hospital service: Patience with people unable to express themselves clearly; sympathy without emotional involvement; understanding of and liking for all types of people and tolerance with human weaknesses.

For consultants: Competitiveness and willingness to put work before social life.

For research: Patience for long-term projects and an inquiring mind.

Late start

Medical schools vary in their policies on accepting mature candidates, so one has to inquire from several before giving up – if determined to start; it becomes very difficult if over 30. Most schools require an upper second honours degree in a related subject, for example biochemistry, or equivalent qualification (including nursing). However, length of training is not reduced even for qualified nurses or people with other related qualifications.

Career-break

Very few doctors take a complete break during their careers. It is not advised for those aiming to become consultants. It is essential to keep in touch, otherwise the continuous changes make it difficult to slot back in. Since 1972 there has been a Doctors' Retainer Scheme to enable doctors to maintain a foothold in medicine during periods when domestic commitments prevent full- or part-time work. The Scheme gives the opportunity to do a small number of specially arranged clinical sessions and attend some post-graduate medical education sessions. The doctors are paid a retainer and are required to keep up to date. The Retainer Scheme is not recognized for training purposes and doctors are advised not to remain on the Scheme longer than necessary.

Position of women

In general practice 24·8% of doctors are women: 22·8% of principals, 48·5% of trainees, 63·3% of assistants.

In public health medicine and community health 60·9% of doctors are women.

In 1991 women accounted for about 50% of medical school entrants. Studies have found that, in general, female medical students are more strongly motivated than men, do better in medical school, and progress more quickly through the early stages of their careers, up to SHO level. However, at registrar

Women in various branches of hospital medicine

	Proportion of women overall, %	Proportion of consultants who are women, %
General medicine	27·8	12·8
Surgical group	15·0	3·0
Obstetrics and gynaecology	34·2	11·6
Anaesthetics	27·7	19·7
Radiology group	24·3	20·8
Pathology group	32·7	22·9
Psychiatry group	34·7	25·6

level and above, women doctors progress far more slowly than men, especially at consultant level. Women doctors are consistently under-represented at levels from registrar upwards and consistently over-represented in the lower grades. (These studies compared actual with expected achievement and are therefore not distorted by age and the lower expectations and smaller numbers of girls entering in the past.)

Some women complain of discriminatory attitudes in the health service, and there is no question that indirect discrimination is built into the traditional training and employment pyramid. The long training and arduous work conditions of junior hospital doctors disproportionately affect womens' progress. Domestic responsibilities do not fit in easily with the long hours of work and study; part-time training is not widespread; and there is a feeling that the doctors who have spent longer than the norm in reaching particular grades, who have had unconventional career patterns, and who are older are regarded less favourably by appointments committees.

In 1991 the Department of Health published *Women Doctors and their Careers*, the report of a working party convened to look into the waste of the talents of women in medicine. As women form a higher proportion of entrants, the implications of failing to pay sufficient attention to their needs are considerable. Among the recommendations of the working party were: increased opportunities for part-time training (for which the Medical Women's Federation has fought for years) at all levels; more flexibility in the way the Royal Colleges assess whether candidates meet their requirements; more part-time career posts; and more flexible working arrangements, including job-sharing and shift work, which would make even full-time working more predictable.

In general practice women wishing to work part time have had relatively few problems. However, the Medical Women's Federation fears that the new NHS contract for GPs could have an adverse effect on women. By affecting the way in which part-timers are paid, practices may be reluctant to take on part-time partners.

Further information

British Medical Association, BMA House, Tavistock Square, London WC1H 9JP

Medical Women's Federation, Tavistock House North, Tavistock Square, London WC1H 9HX

Studies have commented that prospective doctors, particularly women, need more and better careers advice, especially during training. We recommend: for those considering a career in medicine, *Learning Medicine*, by Peter Richards, published annually by the BMA, £3.95 (1991 edition); for medical students, *Living Medicine – Planning a Career, Choosing a Speciality*, by Peter Richards, published by Cambridge University Press, £8.95 (1991 edition).

Related careers

ANIMALS: *Veterinary Surgeon* – DENTISTRY – ENGINEERING: *Medical or Biomedical Engineering* – NURSING – OCCUPATIONAL THERAPY – OPTICAL WORK: *Optometrist* – ORTHOPTICS – OSTEOPATHY – PHARMACY – PHYSIOTHERAPY – SCIENCE – SOCIAL WORK

NOTE ON COMPLEMENTARY MEDICINE: Complementary medicine is the general name for a number of therapeutic techniques which include acupuncture, osteopathy (see p. 359) and chiropractic, herbal medicine, homeopathy and naturopathy. In recent years interest has been growing in this style of medical practice, which regards health and disease in terms of the whole person. A demand for more treatment is bound to lead to a demand for more practitioners.

Because there is no statutory regulation for complementary medicine, training has been a minefield. Courses range from those for qualified doctors only, through 4-year degree courses, to those lasting only a few days, with, in many fields, little objective guidance as to the reputableness or otherwise of courses. 'Buyer beware' has been the rule for both prospective entrants and clients/patients. The situation is rapidly changing, however. With government approval, the Institute for Complementary Medicine has set up the British Register of Complementary Medicine. To be admitted to the Register practitioners must meet standards set by scrutiny panels. Though registration is voluntary, it is beginning to have an effect; for example, some magazines accept advertisements only from registered practitioners. Having established standards of practice, the Institute can then look to those training establishments which turn out practitioners to those standards.

A further potential benefit to the prospective student is proposed legislation which will put on the purveyors of services (e.g. training) the responsibility for ensuring that all aspects within their control are 'proper, safe and fit for the purpose'. It is also being considered whether complementary medicine might be taken within the NVQ framework (see p. xx).

Further information is available from the Institute for Complementary Medicine, PO Box 194, London SE16 1QZ. Send a large s.a.e. (plus 3 loose first-class stamps), together with details of your interests and qualifications, for lists of training courses.

Merchant Navy

Entry qualifications

Engineer, Deck and Radio Officers: normally 4 GCSEs (A–C) including maths, English and physical science. *Catering Officers*: BTEC/SCOTVEC Hotel, Catering and Institutional Operations (but see 'Training', below).

The work

Although Britain's merchant navy fleet is much smaller than it used to be, there are still opportunities for those wanting to go to sea and recruitment has picked up after some years of decline. There are very few cruise ships; most of the fleet consists of cargo vessels, tankers and ferries.

Over half of these vessels are less than 5 years old, and living conditions for crews are far better than they used to be (and still are on passenger liners). Everything is being done to minimize boredom and irritation which tends to arise when groups of people live and work together in a close community. Vessels now often have single or double cabin accommodation, TV rooms, spacious lounges. Life at sea in modern ships is a mixture of modern technology and traditional hierarchy. Modern vessels have family accomodation so that officers can bring their wives.

Engineer Officers

They are responsible for ships' engines including heating, pumps, etc. They ensure that the ship sails smoothly and efficiently; supervise repairs at sea and overhauls in port. When on watch, the engineer monitors the engines, now usually done with computerized equipment. Modern ships' engine-rooms are clean, airy and contain a mass of electronic equipment. They have nothing in common with old-fashioned boiler rooms, although the work is still very practical.

Engineer Officers are in charge of and responsible for the work of engine-room staff; so managing people is part of the job, as with all ships' officers.

Deck (Navigating) Officers

They navigate the ship. In port they are responsible for efficient loading and unloading, which involves both mathematical and common-sense problem-solving, especially in ships which carry a variety of cargo, simultaneously or in succession. They are responsible for controlling large numbers of seamen; in port they may negotiate with stevedores and others concerned with loading and unloading.

Deck Officer is a step on the ladder to becoming Captain or Master.

Radio/Electro-technical Officer

Increasing numbers of ships are allowed to sail without a radio officer, as automated equipment means other members of the crew can handle everyday communications between ship and shore. As the equipment becomes more and more complex, however, radio officers are needed to cope with regular maintenance and with breakdowns. They may be called radio or electronics or electro-technical officers.

Catering Officers (called Purser or Hotel Manager on cruise liners; sometimes Chief Steward on tankers, etc.)

Responsible for purchase, storage, preparation (supervision) of food, meal service, maintenance of accommodation. On liners, they are also responsible for passengers' banking, information and entertainment services.

Training

Engineering Cadets (trainee officers employed by shipping company)
1. With minimum 4 GCSEs (A–C), including maths, physical science and English, 4-year course for BTEC/SCOTVEC Higher National Diploma in Marine Engineering.
  2. With A-level maths and physics studied and a pass in one of them: 3-year course for HND as above. All courses include periods of practical training at sea. All cadets take the Department of Transport Class 4 Certificate of Competency examination.
  3. With A-level maths and physics: B.Sc. in Marine Engineering.

Deck Cadets (trainee officers employed by shipping company)
1. With 4 GCSEs (A–C) including maths, physics and English: 3–4 years for BTEC/SCOTVEC National Diploma in Nautical Science, leading to Department of Transport Certificates of Competency.

2. With A-level (subjects as above); or degree: 3-year 'accelerated cadetship'.

3. With 2 or 3 A-levels (1 in physics or maths) and 3 GCSEs (A–C): full-time or sandwich course for B.Sc. Nautical Science.

There are some openings with the Small Ships Training Group for cadets with slightly lower entry qualifications.

Radio Officers (employed normally by radio companies)

Unlike cadets they must get their qualifications, the Radio-communications General Certificate and the Electronic Navigational Equipment Maintenance Certificate, before going to sea. They need 4 GCSEs (A–C) including maths, English and preferably physics, and then take a 3-year full-time course for BTEC/ SCOTVEC National Diploma in Telecommunications and Higher National Certificate in Electronic and Communications Engineering (or SCOTVEC HNC in Electrical and Electronic Engineering, Radio and Radar). After a period of sea-going experience radio officers may be sponsored for Higher National Diploma.

Catering Officers

Entry is normally as Catering Rating, though a small number start higher up the ladder with Hotel, Catering and Institutional Operations BTEC/SCOTVEC award (see p. 106).

Other opportunities at sea (very limited)

Assistant Purser: Must be over 21, have good secretarial skills, a foreign language, 4 GCSEs (A–C).

Children's hostess: Must be RGN/RSCN (i.e. have combined general and sick children's nurse training, see pp. 330, 332) or teacher.

Nurse: Must be experienced RGN (see p. 330) and over 26.

Steward and stewardess on ferries and passenger liners: Employment largely seasonal, experience of domestic work in hotels and a foreign language useful. Not a career with prospects.

Ship's doctor: Newly qualified doctors may work as ship's doctors for a few months.

Personal attributes   Practicality; resourcefulness; ability to supervise and control people at work; gregariousness; willingness to take orders and accept one's place in the hierarchy, coupled with ability to take responsibility and make instant decisions. *For women*: also self-sufficiency, as being the only woman, or 1 of 2 or 3 women among large groups of men, can be lonely; indifference to standing out in a crowd and therefore being constantly 'on show'.

**Position
of
women**

Women officers and cadets sail on modern ships described above. There are some female *ratings*, but as most *deck* and *catering ratings* are trained initially at the Sea Training College, where there are residential facilities for only a few girls, their chances of being accepted are very small. However, girls are being recruited as *Deck Officer Cadets* by a number of companies and are eligible for training as *Engineer Cadets*. There have been women *Radio Officers* for some years. More women would be welcomed as Deck, Engineer and Radio Officers. Catering Officers have rather less scope, mainly because the majority of Catering Officers come up through the ranks, after training at the Sea Training College.

So far very few women are ship's doctors, but on vessels with adequate accommodation theoretically no bar.

**Further
informa-
tion**

Individual shipping companies
The Co-ordinating Agent, General Council of British Shipping, 30–32 St Mary Axe, London EC3A 8ET

**Related
careers**

ARMED FORCES – SHIPBROKING . . . EXPORTING

Meteorology

Entry qualifications
Scientific Officers: A degree in maths, physics, meteorology, computer science or a BTEC/SCOTVEC Higher award (see pp. xxi, xxii) in a scientific or mathematical subject.

Assistant Scientific Officers: At least 4 GCSEs (A–C) including English language, maths and physics or double award science. Many have better qualifications.

The work
The Meteorological Office is part of the Ministry of Defence. It is responsible for weather forecasts for the Forces, Civil Aviation, the Merchant Navy and government departments, public corporations, local authorities, industry and the media, as well as the general public. It also does a considerable amount of research. (NB: Radio and TV forecasts form a very small part of the work.)

Scientific Officers

Entrants with good honours degrees normally do research and are concerned with climate changes due to the greenhouse effect and changes in the ozone layer; others become forecasters or support scientists (see 'Science Technician', p. 452). Shift work may be necessary.

Assistant Scientific Officers

They do a variety of jobs. At airfields they make and record weather observations and pass them on to air traffic control (see p. 115) and other collecting centres. The information is then transmitted nationally and internationally through an exchange system. They plot weather maps and graphs, answer telephone inquiries and generally assist forecasters in preparing weather information. This might be routine information for use by aircraft pilots, or warnings of impending bad weather for local authorities and others who need such information. At headquarters in Bracknell ASOs also do statistical and computational work and help on research. Some are trained as computer programmers. They must be prepared to work anywhere in the United Kingdom, and move when required. They may be required to do shift work.

Competition for vacancies is very keen. Once in, there are reasonable prospects for promotion if a higher qualification in a relevant subject is gained. (Day-release may be granted.) There are also a few opportunities for experienced meteorologists outside the Civil Service, to supply oil rigs with forecasts, for example.

Training
Initial training at residential Meteorological Office College lasts 8 weeks for Assistant Scientific Officers and up to 5 months for Scientific Officers, followed by on-the-job training.

Personal attributes
Self-sufficiency; the ability to work in a team; interest in science.

Late start
There are no age limits, but for ASOs entrants aged about 18 are preferred.

Career-break
Women are eligible for reinstatement (see CIVIL SERVICE, p. 138), though need for mobility and to work unsocial hours deters many mothers from returning. Continual changes in all aspects of meteorology make it hard for potential returners to keep up to date, which is essential for resuming work.

Part time
Limited opportunities, mostly at headquarters.

Position of women
At the moment the ratio of men to women is 9 to 1; among new entrants it can be less than 3 to 1, but about half of graduates appointed are women. No women above Principal Scientific Officer at present.

Further information
Meteorological Office, Recruitment, London Road, Bracknell, Berks. RG12 2SZ

Related careers   SCIENCE

Museums and Art Galleries

Entry qualifications
Various (see 'Training', below); for curator-level jobs, in theory 4 GCSEs, in practice degree or equivalent.

The work
The scope of museum work has widened greatly in recent years. Established museums and art galleries have shed their image of solemn shrines devoted to earnest study of art, artefact and history; they have become more user-friendly, wanting to entertain as well as inform and thus attract a wider public. The term 'museum' is now used rather loosely and covers a more varied range of establishments than it used to. Museum and heritage sector establishments overlap in terms of the work, which is basically selecting and organizing exhibits and attracting and organizing visitors.

Over half of Britain's roughly 3000 museums were started in the last 20 years, and it is these museums which have transformed the museums scene. Museums fall into 3 main groups:

1. 19 national museums: the large and prestiguous ones like the British Museum and the National Gallery. These establishments offer the greatest scope to the traditional academic specialist type of curators who chose the job because of their interest in pursuing their specialism. These curators may or may not combine collection management with general departmental management: there is a move to divide these 2 management functions. National museum curators are normally graduates in subjects relevant to the department concerned. They usually start as assistant curators. Science/technology graduates are as likely to get a job as arts graduates. Competition is very keen indeed.

2. About 1000 local authority-run museums and art galleries. They include a few large and prestigious ones and hundreds of small local museums of local history or industry. Employment prospects vary; few jobs are research-based; most involve coping with everything. Entry is usually with a degree or comparable qualification (which could be non-specific management experience).

3. The largest and fastest-growing group: the 'independents'. They are either funded by sponsors and entry fees or entirely by

entry fees. They are 'market-led'. Their success depends on a commercially viable idea, and management, marketing and communication skills. The group includes sophisticated tourist attractions like the Yorvik Viking Centre in York and the Museum of the Moving Image in London, as well as hundreds of small special-interest ones like the Silk Museum in Macclesfield and the Freud Museum in London. Jobs go to applicants with commercial and communication skills; academic qualifications are not required, but as competition is very keen, academic qualifications in addition to the required skills help.

Both local authority and independent museums use volunteer labour fairly extensively; such volunteer experience is very useful when applying for 'real' jobs. As there are always more applicants than vacancies, only applicants with volunteer experience stand much chance of acceptance.

Apart from traditional curators, who are concerned with collection management and research, there are many other museums jobs, including a few 'museum-specific' ones:

Exhibition designers. A growing number of museums are appointing in-house designers, but the majority are self-employed or work for exhibition design consultancies; their expertise is 'bought in' by museums. The work now often includes using audio-visual and interactive video equipment (the National Gallery extension which opened in July 1991 has 'work stations' with touch-sensitive screens where visitors can 'research' pictures and artists in a computerized encyclopaedia). Designers work closely with *interpreters.* Interpretation means showing objects in their context and imaginative presentation. It overlaps with *education officers* and may involve role-playing: perhaps dressing up as a 1920s chauffeur when showing transport from that period, or as a Roman shopkeeper when interpreting shopping in ancient Rome. Interpreters also help visitors use the high-tech equipment. The National Curriculum's emphasis on hands-on experience has increased the scope for museum–school collaboration. Education officers may also give lectures which are targeted at specific audiences, from tourists to groups of scholars.

Designers usually have an art-training background at BTEC Higher award or degree level; *interpreters* and *education officers* are usually graduates (no particular discipline), and may or may not have teaching experience.

There is now some movement between independent and other staff; experience in an independent museum may lead to work in a traditional one. Work in a heritage sector establishment or even a pure tourist attraction is useful experience in exhibit and visitor management. (A former theme park director was recently appointed development manager of a national museum.)

Other museum work, not museum-specific, includes marketing, public relations, shop management.

Conservation is a profession in its own right and is a growth area. The national and a few local authority museums and art galleries use in-house conservators, but most are self-employed or work for private firms and collectors as well as for museums and art galleries. They don't by any means deal only with paintings or other traditional exhibits; anything from agricultural machinery to dresses or first-generation computers needs conserving. Conservators see their job in three stages: examination to assess the object's properties and need for repair; preservation to arrest or prevent deterioration; and restoration. Most conservators specialize by material and/or type of object: textiles, paintings, machinery, furniture, etc.

Training

This is becoming much more flexible, to take account of changes in the work. The Museum Association's Diploma, which was the professional qualification for curatorial jobs, is being phased out. The Museum Training Institute, set up in 1989, is administering the Diploma until 1994, when the last exams will be held. The MTI is then replacing the Diploma with its own system of qualifications which will be based on NVQs (see p. xx). Certificates of Competence in various areas of work will be awarded at levels 1–5.

The main centre for museum studies for curatorial jobs will continue to be Leicester University. 'Any-discipline' post-graduate Diploma courses take 12 months full time. Part-time students must complete the course, which is taken in separate chunks, within 21 months. There is also a Master's degree which takes a little longer, both full and part time. Manchester University and University College London run similar post-graduate courses; several other higher education establishments run courses with museum studies elements; yet others provide heritage management courses: the MTI is interpreting the term 'museum' broadly, to include heritage sector management. The MTI is preparing a database of all courses which it will accredit under its Accreditation of Prior Learning/NVQ system of awarding Certificates of Competence.

Personal attributes

Intellectual ability; a love of knowledge for its own sake; visual imagination; a lively curiosity; organizing ability; an understanding of laypeople's interests and tastes; communication skills; patience for waiting for the right job and for promotion.

Late start   No objection in theory, but competition from young post-graduate candidates very strong.

Career-break   In national and local authority museums Civil Service (see p. 125) and Local Government (see p. 268) conditions apply; in independent museums and the heritage sector the situation varies greatly.

Part time and job-sharing   These are beginning to be widely accepted.

Position of women   The ratio of men to women is about even up to senior/middle level, but so far there are very few women directors of museums, etc.

Further information   Museum Training Institute, Kershaw House, 55 Well Street, Bradford BD1 5PS

Association of Independent Museums, c/o Weald and Downland Open Air Museum, Singleton, Chichester, W. Sussex PO18 0EU

Conservation Unit, Museums & Galleries Commission, 16 Queen Anne's Gate, London SW1H 9AA

Related careers   ARCHAEOLOGY – ARCHIVIST – ART AND DESIGN – INFORMATION WORK

Music

Entry qualifications

Acceptance at music colleges depends on performance at audition. For most performers, except for singers, intensive musical training must have started by their teens at the latest.

For teaching, see p. 521. For degree courses, at least 2 A-levels and 3 GCSEs (A–C) with, usually, A-level music.

The work

Work with music covers a very wide field: performing, composing, recording, video-making, administration, teaching, criticism and journalism. Some of the traditional boundaries between what are loosely called 'serious' and 'pop' music and musicians are breaking down and fashions come and go as in any arts or entertainment area. In 'pop' and other 'non-traditional' music it is possible to reach the top without a proper musical training; success depends on many other factors. This section is concerned only with those parts of the profession that need formal training.

Performing

Some symphony orchestras, smaller ensembles and opera houses employ orchestral players on a full-time basis. Others are made up largely of regular but freelance musicians who may, or may not, work for other orchestras as well. Singers may be salaried members of a chorus or freelance.

Most freelance musicians, however devoted to serious music, are glad to work as 'session players' on TV commercials, film background music and other light music recording sessions, etc. A violinist may play in a concert at the Barbican on one evening and the following day in a TV jingle recording session.

A freelance musician has to fit in work as it comes. The work may fluctuate from 3 daily sessions (3 hours each) over a long period, to no work for many weeks. Long practice at home is always necessary. TV, radio, live concerts or recording sessions are arranged well in advance, and accepting bookings requires careful judgement. Once a date is booked, it is unwise to break it, even if a better engagement is offered.

The musician's work is physically exhausting, and may include travel over long distances, combined with rehearsals and nightly performances, often in cold or overheated halls. An engagement for a season with a ballet or opera company may involve 5 performances a week with as many rehearsals, and practice at home. The atmosphere amongst musicians is usually friendly, although the competition is keen.

Part-time teaching, either privately or in schools, gives many freelance musicians a supplementary income. However, it is often difficult to fit in performing engagements with teaching.

Prospects in music have never been good and have been made harder recently with cutbacks in state and local authority funding. It is estimated that only about 1 in 10 of music students who finish their full training (itself restricted to the good students) eventually makes a living as a performer. Only 1 in as many hundreds becomes a soloist. Good luck is almost as important as talent.

Teaching

As the main job this is quite a different career. Teachers are employed in primary and secondary schools. They teach music either full time in one school, possibly with a second subject, or part time in various schools and/or youth clubs and evening institutes run by the local education authority.

There is scope for imagination and initiative. Music teachers' main job is to promote interest and enthusiasm, as only a few pupils take music examinations. They may start an orchestra, or record evenings; organize record libraries, visits to concerts, etc.

There is currently a shortage of music teachers.

Sound Engineering and Instrument Technology

For broadcast sound engineering see TELEVISION, FILM AND RADIO (p. 530). Sound engineers (not to be confused with professional engineers) in recording studios are responsible for the overall recording quality and for interpreting the producer's ideas. They need a grasp of basic physics and electronics in order to understand how to work their equipment, but they do not need great technical knowledge to start with (most enter as tape operators or assistant engineers). Some highly qualified and experienced sound engineers may be called *music technologists*. They apply advanced technology to the creation and reproduction of sound. They work on the design and manufacture of equipment, as well as in recording studios and broadcasting.

It is difficult to enter this area; really good engineers, however, are always in demand and a few become producers. Limited openings as yet for music technologists as this is still a relatively 'new breed'.

There is some limited scope in musical-instrument technology, which means making or repairing musical instruments – anything from harpsichords to clarinets, organs to synthesizers. The electronics side, involving the manufacture and repair of musical equipment, probably offers the best prospects. There is a steady demand for piano-tuners.

Training

Normally, *either*: 3–4 year full-time course at a college of music. Students usually choose *either* the teaching *or* the performing course after the first year, but it is sometimes possible to switch from one to the other later in the course. Some lead to graduate status, others to a licentiateship.

The syllabus normally includes a principal subject and a second study subject. Instrumentalists play two instruments. Singers may either take an instrument as a second study or they may take speech and drama. Other subjects included are music appreciation, theory and history of music, aural training, choral and opera study, orchestra practice, and often a language. A handful of courses specialize in pop music, jazz, contemporary music and recording.

Or: a BA in music. Most degree courses are largely academic and theoretical. At some universities music can be taken as a subject in a general or performing arts degree. Some post-graduate performers' courses are also available.

To teach music in schools, courses must be followed by 1-year course of professional teacher training (see TEACHING, p. 521). In some B.Ed. courses music can be taken as a main subject. Instrument teachers do not necessarily need professional teacher training.

Sound engineers learn on the job and via in-service courses. A few are given day-release for a part-time course in Sound Studies. *Music technologists* need a degree in physics, electronics or a combined music/physics degree. *Musical instrument technologists* can take courses leading to City and Guilds, SCOTVEC National Certificate or college certificate (usually 2 years full time); or BTEC National/Higher National Diploma or SCOTVEC HND; or a degree.

Piano-tuners can study full time as above or by day- or block-release.

Personal attributes

For performers: Apart from outstanding talent, perseverance, resilience, courage, and indifference to setbacks; the ability to work as one of a team; a pleasant manner; good health; very wide musical interest; good sight-reading speed; willingness to work outside the musical field between engagements. *For teachers*: as for teaching (p. 527), plus creative imagination and initiative.

Music Therapy

This is a small but growing field. Music therapists work with physically or mentally handicapped children and adults. They work in the fields of mental illness and mental handicap in both the health and the education services. Music can contribute to the development and treatment of handicapped and maladjusted people in various ways as a medium of non-verbal communication – by helping to relax their bodies and minds, as a mental stimulus, and as an emotional outlet. Autistic children, for example, and severely withdrawn adults, who do not respond to any other form of activity and cannot form relationships, often benefit greatly from listening to, and making, music.

There are 3 1-year full-time post-graduate courses in music therapy. Candidates must have had at least a 3-year full-time musical education. Some work full time in one hospital, some do 'sessions' in several centres. The work needs maturity and sensitivity.

Career-break
It is unlikely that performers can resume orchestral playing after a long gap unless they kept up with serious daily practice; but there should be no problem returning to teaching.

Part time
Performing: work as freelance is possible in many areas – but work tends to be sporadic rather than regular part time. *Teaching and music therapy*: part time or job-sharing should be possible, but not necessarily exactly where one wants it.

Position of women
Women are still under-represented in large professional orchestras, considering that they make up around half of music students. There are still only a few women conductors. Women still appear to be discriminated against, though it is probably impossible to prove this.

Further information
For early training: Local education authority music adviser.
For music colleges: Incorporated Society of Musicians, 10 Stratford Place, London W1N 9PE and *The NATFHE Handbook* (p. lv)
City and Guilds Institute (see p. xxiii)
BTEC and SCOTVEC (see pp. xxi, xxii)
For music therapy: British Society for Music Therapy, 69 Avondale Avenue, East Barnet, Herts. EN4 8NB

For musical instrument technology: London College of Furniture,
41 Commercial Road, London E1 and other individual colleges

Related   DANCING – LEISURE/RECREATION MANAGEMENT – TEACHING –
careers   TELEVISION, FILM AND RADIO

Nursery Nurse/Nursery Officer/ Nanny

Entry qualifica-tions

None laid down, but most colleges demand at least 2 GCSEs (A–C); many entrants have more; a few have A-levels. Private training colleges demand at least 3 GCSEs (A–C).

The work

Nursery nurses look after children 7 years and under (8 in Scotland). They are primarily concerned with healthy children (they are now often called nursery officers), but, strangely, in this context 'healthy' may include children with problems and also the physically and mentally disabled.

Nursery nurses' roles cover very much more than physical care and supervision of young children. Young children learn through play and through communicating with other children and with adults; they need adequate stimuli and individual attention to ensure their healthy intellectual, emotional and social development. When nursery nurses read to children, talk to them individually, discuss, say, their painting efforts, and generally help them to enjoy nursery activities they are, in effect, teaching.

Nursery nurses work in various settings:

1. Nursery classes and schools (for 3–5s) and infant schools (5–7s), run by local education authorities (LEAs). Nursery nurses help organize play activities, read to and play with children. Usually 1 nursery nurse is responsible for a small group of children. A qualified nursery or infant teacher (see p. 522) is normally in charge.

2. Day nurseries and family centres, run by social services departments for under-5s (mainly 3–5s) who are at risk socially, physically or emotionally; and for children where both parents have to go out to work or for other reasons cannot satisfactorily look after them during the day. There are now very few places for children whose parents merely think that nursery is a Good Thing. A proportion of children in day nurseries have special needs, so work can be very demanding. Occasionally staff involve parents in the nursery's activities – largely to help parents understand the children's needs and development. Staff may also do unofficial 'casework' (see SOCIAL WORK, p. 480).

3. Private day nurseries, workplace nurseries and crèches: there is an increasing number of these, catering for parents who want their children to have the benefits of nursery experience, especially in areas where there are few LEA-run nursery places. Most cater for working parents by being open all day, and some are, in fact, attached to one or more companies and open only to their staff.

4. In hospital, nursery nurses help to look after babies in maternity wards, and on children's wards they play with and care for children. Actual nursing is done by registered nurses (see p. 332).

5. The largest single group work in private families, as 'nannies', mainly these days in homes where both parents go out to work. Unlike in the past, most nannies expect to share the care of the children with the parents.

There is a variety of working patterns: some live-in nannies take charge of a young child or 2 or 3 children all day; in addition, in between the end of the school day and a parent's return from work (and perhaps during the school holidays), they may look after several schoolchildren whose parents share the nanny's salary. Other nannies work 2 days for one family, 3 days for another if the mothers concerned are themselves part-timers and need only part-week nannies. Work in a family differs from that outside the home in that nannies are on their own: nobody to ask for help in emergencies, and much of the time no other adult to talk to. The work is both more responsible and lonelier; it may also be less rigorous. Most nannies do some housework or at least cook for the children while the parents are at work.

6. A very small proportion work in hotels and holiday camps as children's hostesses.

Of NNEB (see below) students qualifying in 1990 35% went to work for private families, 20% for LEAs, 15% for private organizations, 7% for social services and 2% for health authorities. Opportunities are increasing in the private sector, but are less good in local authority day nurseries and also in hospitals, where nurses have taken over some of the tasks previously performed by nursery nurses. Experienced nannies can get jobs abroad.

Nursery nurses who take the post-Diploma courses have fair promotion prospects and may become officers in charge of nurseries of all kinds, at home and abroad. However, the ratio of senior to junior jobs is low.

Training   1. The usual method: minimum age 16. A 2-year full-time or longer part-time course at a college of further education. Students spend three-fifths of their time at college, two-fifths on 'placements' working with children. Most placements are in public sector nurseries, etc., but colleges often include days-only placements in private families considered suitable for training purposes. Students do not normally have sole charge of children or get experience of 24-hour care, and do not get the 'feel' of being a nanny where both parents work.

The syllabus includes the social, emotional, physical and intellectual development of children from 0 to 7 or 8; children's social, emotional and physical needs to ensure normal development; children with all kinds of special needs, including physical and mental disabilities; importance and significance of play, companionship, communication; promotion and maintenance of health (including nutrition and prevention and control of infection); organizing play activities (which includes things like making toys from egg-boxes, etc.); patterns of family life and social institutions – and changes in both; the nanny in a private family; how the social services work; arts and crafts; social and complementary subjects to help students develop their own personality and interests.

In England and Wales courses lead to the Diploma (formerly Certificate) of the National Nursery Examination Board. Courses are becoming modular, starting with a pilot scheme in 1992.

In Scotland courses comprise SCOTVEC National Certificate modules and lead to registration by the Scottish Nursery Nurses' Board. This programme will be changed in due course with the introduction of NVQs/SVQs (see below).

The NNEB Diploma can be followed after 2 years' work experience by a modular course lasting about 2 years, leading to an NNEB Diploma in Post-Qualifying Studies. Students have to complete 6 modules or units, and can specialize in special groups, such as handicapped or disturbed children, or ethnic minorities, or in nursery management. Different modules are offered by different colleges and students study by day- or block-release.

In Scotland there is a 1-year day-release Post Certificate course, but this is soon likely to be replaced in most regions by SCOTVEC HNCs and HNDs.

There is also a 1-year full-time course leading to an NNEB Certificate in Playskills for those wishing to work with the under-5s. This can give entry on to the second year of the Diploma course.

2. 18–24-month courses at the 3 private Association of Nursery Training colleges. Students must be at least 18; to make sure they like the work, most look after children privately, in between school and college. Private colleges prepare students for the NNEB examinations and for their own diplomas.

3. The National Association for Maternal and Child Welfare

runs Diploma courses which, though not recognized as a qualification for public sector work except in a handful of local authorities, lead to work as mothers' (or parents') help and nanny. Course structure, length and content varies.

NOTE: NVQs/SVQs (see p. xx) in Child Care and Education at levels 2 and 3 are being introduced throughout the UK. For the time-being NNEB awards are likely to keep their existing titles. Students completing courses leading to recognition by the NNEB and SNNB should, generally, be eligible for an NVQ 3.

Personal attributes A way with young children; patience; imagination; willingness to take responsibility and to work hard at routine chores; ability to work well in a team; interest in mental, social and physical development of children.

Late start There are now 35 part-time courses in England and Wales and some offer Accreditation of Prior Learning (see p. xxxiii), enabling suitable students to gain the Diploma in under 2 years. The main obstacle for mature students is getting a grant. In 1990 about 30% of NNEB students were over 18.

Career-break Should be no problem.

Part time Little opportunity at present in social services department nurseries and in infant nursery schools and classes, but growing opportunities as daily nanny – working for women who are themselves working part time.

Position of women Under 1% of students are men; no reason at all why this should remain so – men welcome on courses and in jobs.

Further information National Nursery Examination Board, 8 Chequer Street, St Albans, Herts. AL1 3XZ (enclose s.a.e.)

Scottish Nursery Nurses' Board, 6 Kilnford Crescent, Dundonald, Kilmarnock, Ayrshire KA2 9DW (enclose s.a.e.)

National Association for Maternal and Child Welfare (NAMCW), Strode House, 46–8 Osnaburgh Street, London NW1 3ND (enclose s.a.e.)

Local authority education or social services departments

**Related
careers**   NURSING – SOCIAL WORK – TEACHING

Nursing

This section covers *hospital* and *community nurses, health visitors* and *midwives*, as well as traditional and 'Project 2000' (p. 335) training. Nursing, especially nurse training, has changed dramatically in recent years and is still changing. After decades of discussions and reports a blueprint for nursing in the nineties and beyond was finally agreed by the Royal College of Nursing (the professional body), the United Kingdom Central Council for Nursing, Midwifery and Health Visiting (UKCC, the statutory body) and the government. Reforms are now being implemented. This is important to know for persons who are interested in nursing but put off by what they have heard about training and working conditions.

Among the reasons why changes had to come:

1. More than any other profession, nursing has been affected by women's wider career choices. It now has to compete with jobs for which training is less stressful, and in which pay and promotion prospects are better, and which *also* provide job satisfaction.

2. Numbers of 18-year-olds in the population are dropping. Nursing is not attracting the proportion of the age group with the necessary academic qualifications which it needs.

3. At present, of every 100 recruits, only 65 finally qualify, and an uneconomically high proportion of qualified nurses leave after a few years.

4. Changes in health care and nursing philosophy affect nursing tasks. For example: increasing emphasis is put on health promotion and prevention of disease; patients are now discharged from hospital much more quickly than used to be the case. Though at home, many patients still need nursing care. More nurses are therefore needed to work in the community, away from the hospital (where there is always someone senior to ask for advice). At the same time, a far greater proportion of patients in hospital (acute/general or psychiatric) need highly skilled and time-consuming nursing care. In other words, the quicker 'patient throughput' in acute hospitals, and the trend for people with psychiatric problems/mental handicap to live in the community, have changed the nature of nursing in hospital, and changed the balance between hospital and community nurse requirements (just as it has changed

the balance between near-convalescents and seriously ill patients *in* hospital).

Some changes, less easily definable than those in education, training and nursing structure, have already taken place. For example, the doctor/nurse relationship has changed. There is generally today much more joint decision-making, and more mutual respect for the other's function. The patient/nurse relationship has changed too: nurses no longer 'nanny' patients; instead the emphasis is, at least in theory, on 'consultation between equals'.

To attract more mature candidates and returners, and to retain more nurses with children, both training and work have been made more flexible. Part-time and job-sharing opportunities are moving higher up the ladder, and nurses with post-Registration qualifications (see p. 345) now have wider choices and better promotion prospects. All these changes are beginning to attract more men into the profession.

'Nursing' covers a range of jobs which vary widely in terms of levels of functions, of responsibility, professional qualifications required, environment worked in. There is therefore scope for people with widely differing aims, interests, abilities. Some nurses, for example, concentrate entirely on practical bedside nursing; others manage whole hospital groups' nursing services (jobs which equal top executives' in industry in terms of power and responsibility). Then there is scope for people interested in the impact of new technologies on nursing procedures; for those interested in psychiatry, in the sociological and psychological aspect of patient-care, in preventive medicine and increasingly in nursing in the community, outside the hospital. Nurse-training can also lead to jobs not directly concerned with the care of the sick, both in and outside the hospital (e.g. specialist publishing and health service management).

Nursing is *not* a second-choice career for people unable to get into medical schools (or put off medicine by the long training). The two professions are complementary and suit people with very different aims and personalities. A vital difference is that the doctor's contact with the patient is fleeting and episodic, while the hospital nurse must establish and keep up a relationship with the patient (this applies even to most of those nurses who after a few years' ward-nursing opt for other specializations).

Nurses' work is much more difficult to define than other professionals' because there are so many, and some contradictory, facets to it. For example, nurses must be able to establish relationships with their patients, they must be prepared to do basic bedside nursing chores, and they are highly trained professionals, who take vital decisions and use highly sophisticated equipment.

Entry requirements (all registered nurses)

Minimum age UK except Scotland: 17½; Scotland: 17. 5 GCSEs (A–C) (Scotland 5 O- or S-Grades 1–3) or equivalent, which normally includes BTEC National or equivalent SCOTVEC awards. Applicants with lower qualifications may be able to sit an entry test which assesses their potential, motivation and 'track record' (work/life experience). However, colleges of nursing often set their own entry requirements at a higher than minimum standard. Many want candidates to have at least studied (not necessarily passed) a science; most teaching hospitals (i.e. those where medical students are trained) ask for A-levels or Higher grades.

NOTE ON TITLES: Project 2000-trained nurses' titles have been changed (see pp. 335–6). The jobs described here refer to both traditionally and Project 2000-trained nurses.

Nursing in Hospital

Registered General Nurse/Adult Branch

The work

Whenever possible, nurses now apply what is called 'the nursing process': they have got away from the image of nursing as a collection of separate tasks – from giving out bedpans to doing the round with the consultant. Instead, 'patient care' now comprises assessing, discussing and planning for individual patients' needs, putting the plan into operation, and then monitoring and, if necessary, changing it. Normally, every nurse is, on each duty round, allocated a number of patients to look after. That involves, for example, being present when consultants visit 'their' patients, talking to relatives, as well as ensuring that the patients are washed, sent for treatment, etc. Detailed notes have to be kept to assure continuity as colleagues often have to take over when a patient's 'own' nurse is not on duty. To carry out the 'nursing process', nurses need extensive knowledge for a variety of highly complex, responsible tasks. These include: administering a vast array of drugs in the right dosages and understanding what side effects to watch out for; using highly sophisticated machines in coronary and other intensive care units; keeping records on patients and knowing at all times what changes if any have occurred in their patients' condition; organizing the ward team; discussing patients' conditions with relatives and doctors; helping distressed patients to come to terms with their situation; trying to allay anxious patients' fears. A nurse may have to decide whether a patient's condition warrants sending out an emergency call for the doctor, or whether to suggest in discussion with the doctor that the social worker (see p. 480) should come and help sort out a patient's domestic problems. Qualified nurses also help with the teaching of nurses in training.

However, staffing levels are at present often too low to give nurses as much time with 'their' patients as the nursing process demands. Coming changes should improve staffing levels.

The majority of staff nurses (first post-Registration job) now take one of the large variety of post-Registration courses (see p. 345). They can become clinical specialists in, for example, theatre work, intensive care, geriatric or coronary care, and eventually be 'team leaders', or be in charge of a number of wards or units within a hospital or hospital group, and act as consultant to colleagues from other specialties as well as to junior staff. They can go into teaching where innovative methods and structures of courses are changing traditional teaching methods; or they can go into management.

Nurse-managers are not as much directly concerned with patient-care as with the smooth and efficient running of a complex organization. The work resembles management in commerce and industry; a large number of people carry out a variety of vital, interrelated activities which have to be co-ordinated. These 'managers' may have greater job-satisfaction than managers at that level in industry, because the end-product is the well-being of patients. Nurse-managers normally take a succession of management courses, often at business schools together with senior managers from industry; the principles of management are the same, whatever the organization to be managed (see also HEALTH SERVICES MANAGEMENT, p. 217).

Opportunities for nurses to work in the community rather than in hospitals have increased enormously in recent years and are still increasing (see below for the various kinds of community nurses). Then there are opportunities in the prison service, in the services, in the private sector – both in private hospitals and in patients' homes – and in agency nursing: many nurses do agency work a year or two after qualifying (or later, as returners), either because they prefer occasional days or nights to a regular job, or because of the variety that agency work offers. As many hospitals depend fairly regularly on agency nurses to fill gaps, agency nurses can often arrange to work for a time in nursing areas of their choice, e.g. on surgical or orthopaedic wards. In that way they widen their experience and can make an informed choice before deciding on any particular post-Registration course.

**Personal
attributes**
Common sense; practical bent; sympathy for the sick and the old without sentimentality; an interest in medicine without morbid curiosity about illness; sensitivity coupled with a certain amount of toughness so as not to get too emotionally involved; organizing ability; patience; a sense of humour to put up with the inevitable occasional short tempers and difficult people; ability to know when to be firm – and how to be firm but not rude; powers of observation; initiative; ability to take responsibility one moment and to do exactly as told the next; good health.

Registered Sick Children's Nurse/Child Branch

The work
This is much the same as for RGN plus keeping children amused, and dealing with relatives rather more. Nursing sick children can be both more rewarding and more arduous than nursing adults. Many children stay only for a very short time; others stay for longer because they are very seriously ill and/or suffer from a rare condition which has to be assessed. Increasingly, paediatrics is very concerned with detection and follow-up of physical and mental handicap. Some paediatric nursing is highly specialized, with nurses having taken post-Registration specialized training.

Children's wards are run to resemble home conditions as much as possible. Visiting is now normally allowed at all times; rigid tidiness and regimentation is frowned upon. Mothers or fathers often stay in hospital with their young children and/or help to bath, feed and generally look after their children.

Jobs for children's nurses are not as readily available everywhere as they used to be or as jobs for RGNs. There are now only very few jobs in hotels, boarding schools, with airlines, etc., but more as nannies at home and abroad, and as school nurses.

**Personal
attributes**
The same as for the general nurse; plus extra patience and a way with children. A sick children's nurse must be able to talk to children on their own level. Many of the best children's nurses come from big families. Good powers of observation are essential, as small children cannot explain their ailments.

Psychiatric Nurse

Two branches: Registered Mental Nurse/Mental Health Branch and Registered Nurse for the Mentally Handicapped/Mental Handicap Branch'
1. Nursing the mentally ill
1 adult in 8 in this country at some time in his or her life needs

help because of some form of mental illness. The majority don't need hospitalization, and even most of those who do stay for only a short time, probably a few weeks, and possibly return for further brief spells in hospital in between leading normal lives. Only a minority are long-stay patients. The term mental illness covers a wide spectrum. In mild cases (the majority) it can be difficult to decide whether a person is over-excited or eccentric or is actually mentally ill. In severe cases sufferers may be unable to separate fantasy from reality and react to people and situations in unreasonable, even alarming, ways. 2 groups of patients have increased in recent years: (1) people of all ages who cannot cope with the stresses and strains of modern life; (2) old people who suffer from senile dementia.

Over 90% of patients are 'voluntary' or 'informal'. Many of them are able to go out to shop or visit friends or relatives, and when in hospital busy themselves in the hospital's workshops, recreation rooms or gardens. For most patients a vital part of their treatment is the contact with a friendly nurse; the inability to communicate with other people is part of most mental illness; nurses help a great deal towards patients' recovery by talking to them and, above all, listening sympathetically.

In most psychiatric hospitals the atmosphere is relaxed and informal. Patients and staff live in a friendly so-called 'therapeutic' community. Patients are encouraged to share with the staff responsibility for running wards and for the active social life of the hospital. The aim is always to minimize the institutional atmosphere.

At informal meetings with staff the patients are encouraged to discuss and even criticize treatment, to talk about their difficulties and to help each other with their problems. At staff-only meetings, after ward meetings with the patients, even the most junior nurse has a chance to discuss patients, treatments and new methods with consultants and senior staff.

Psychiatric nursing can of course sometimes be harrowing. Nurses must always remember that their patients' selfishness or childishness is a symptom of their illness. Teamwork among the staff helps a great deal, and during their training nurses learn to recognize and handle the emotional aspect of their work.

There are an increasing number of day-hospitals for patients well enough to live at home (see 'Community Psychiatric Nurse', p. 340) but still in need of contact with nurses, occupational therapy and perhaps psychiatric treatment.

Personal attributes   Curiosity about what makes people behave as they do; emotional stability; patience and perseverance; the ability to listen well and to be genuinely concerned without becoming emotionally involved; interest in outside work to keep a sense of proportion; a sense of humour; a gregarious nature; good physical and mental health.

2. Nursing the mentally handicapped

People with learning difficulties are immature: their mental development usually stopped before birth or sometimes later, through severe illness or accident. Unlike mental illness, this condition is not normally curable, and some patients stay in hospital all their lives. However, the tendency today is to enable as many patients as at all possible to live in the community (see 'Community Mental Handicap Nurse', below). This means that patients *in* hospital tend to be severely handicapped, often both physically and mentally. Nurses help patients develop their potential as far as it is possible to do so. The extent of the disability in each patient determines the degree of independence that can be achieved. It takes very great patience and perseverance sometimes to enable a patient even to dress or feed him/herself. However, once the patient has taken even one small step towards independence, both patient and nurse feel they have achieved something. Some patients are prepared for life outside the sheltered hospital atmosphere and learn to shop, use money, etc. This type of nursing is always a mixture of teaching, showing understanding, and establishing relationships of trust with patients. Nurses work in teams with doctors, psychologists, occupational therapists and physiotherapists. Like other psychiatric nurses, these nurses attend meetings with other professionals to discuss patients and problems.

Personal attributes

Affectionate nature; a practical approach; teaching ability; patience; gentleness; interests unconnected with the work; ability to be genuinely concerned without becoming emotionally involved. Those who like looking after small children often enjoy this work.

Training (all registered nurses)

Training for Registration is in the throes of revolutionary changes. 200 or so schools of nursing have been reduced to about 90; small ones which were not able to give students the breadth of experience required either closed or amalgamated. Schools are now called 'colleges' of nursing. Most importantly, the structure of training is changing:

Traditional training

Nurses learn the apprenticeship way. They decide before starting their 3-year training whether to become a Registered General Nurse, Registered Mental Nurse, Registered Mental Handicap

Nurse or Registered Sick Children's Nurse (but prospective children's nurses normally first take an RGN training and then add a further year's course to qualify as RSCN).

After several weeks in the classroom on the course for their chosen branch, practice largely takes over from theory. Students still have lectures, study days and homework, but throughout the course they learn mainly by doing, observing and being observed, and taught, by qualified nurses and nurse tutors. Student nurses are salaried employees without whom the hospital could not function. Third year students' work is often similar to that of staff (i.e. Registered) nurses. At the end of their course, students take their Finals and become Registered in their chosen branch.

New training

The new system, known as *Project 2000* (or P2000), is what is called 'education led'. It leads to a dual qualification: Registration as nurse in 1 of the 4 branches and the Diploma in Higher Education, which is an academic qualification.

Dip. H.E. holders are eligible for acceptance into the third year of a nursing degree course (see below). Once they have got their degree they can apply for that large proportion of graduate jobs which are open to 'graduates in any discipline'. The status of nursing is thus raised, and nurses' options are increased. This, it is expected, will reduce the drop-out rate from training and, together with improved pay, encourage more men to take up nursing. From 1992 all courses in Scotland, Wales and Northern Ireland are of the P2000 type; in England about 75% of courses will have changed over by the end of 1992, with the remaining courses expected to change soon after.

P2000 students *are* students, not salaried employees. They are 'supernumerary' for all but about 20% of their course. Courses are at colleges of nursing which have links with a higher education establishment. Nursing students may share some lectures, and college facilities, with students on other higher education courses. However, the extent of integration of college of nursing/HE establishment varies, and is still developing as the system is so new.

The structure of P2000 courses differs fundamentally from the traditional pattern. All students, whichever branch of nursing they have chosen, start with an 18-month Common Foundation Programme – or CFP (this has applied in Scotland for several years). The second 18 months are devoted to the student's chosen branch. There may, at that stage, be a chance to change from the originally chosen branch if during the CFP the student changed his/her mind. Titles of branches have changed: they are now

Adult Branch, *Mental Health Branch*, *Mental Handicap Branch*, *Child Branch* (the latter is now also a straight 3-year course).

Course content has been updated to take account of changes in society and in the thinking about health and disease. Much of the course content is the same as before, covering nursing practice and theory in the relevant areas, but there is now much more emphasis on the healthy individual, and on health promotion and preventive care. More time is spent studying the social and biological sciences. Teaching is more 'student-centred', with more time for discussion of issues between students and staff. About 50% of course time is spent on practical work on the wards, or in community settings. Students spend considerably more time learning about and working in the community, to prepare them for the increasing work outside the hospital – but note that P2000 nurses are *not* qualified as community nurses (see below for community nurse work and training).

P2000 students receive non-means-tested bursaries rather than a salary. Bursaries are a little larger than student grants – nursing students work harder and have less holiday. All P2000 courses comply with EC directives so Registered nurses (who have the necessary language skills) can work in EC countries.

It is too early to know whether P2000 nurses will go up the career ladder more quickly than traditionally trained ones. The former will have had less hands-on experience and may be expected to stay staff nurse (first rung on the qualified ladder) a little longer before taking post-Registration courses (p. 345). It seems inevitable that for the first few years of the new system, nurses with either type of training will be a little suspicious of nurses who learnt by the other system.

As before, it is important for candidates to choose their course carefully, looking not only at the *Applicants' Handbook* but also studying individual colleges' prospectuses. The emphasis on different aspects of nursing varies between courses, and so do the facilities and the extent of integration with the relevant higher education establishment. (Continuous assessment and project work are part of every course.)

Part-time training: There are expected to be more opportunities for part-time training under P2000. Each college makes its own arrangements, but there seems to be general agreement that the CFP part can be arranged on a 'short day' basis, and that individual branch programmes can be lengthened on 'an individually negotiated basis'. However, some colleges are much more willing to make such arrangements than others.

Nursing at degree level
There is a growing number of degrees which lead to Registration. Organization and emphasis varies from one course to another

and has little to do with the course title: 2 degrees in 'Nursing Studies', for example, may have less in common than 2 degrees of which one is in 'Nursing', the other in 'Nursing Studies'. So it is essential to look at prospectuses. All degrees in Nursing and Nursing Studies lead to Registration, normally in one branch of nursing.

Most degree courses started before P2000 began to replace traditional training; they are likely to adapt as necessary to comply with P2000 guidelines. Some newer degrees, notably those at the universities of Wales and Birmingham and at Oxford Polytechnic, were planned on P2000 principles (CFP, community nursing emphasis, etc.).

Degree courses originally started to attract students who were interested in nursing but also wanted – and were qualified for – a higher education qualification. As P2000 courses now lead to an HE qualification as well as Registration, the difference between degree and non-degree nursing courses is not as great as it was. Nevertheless, prospective nurses with degree course qualifications probably will still want to take a degree rather than a Dip. H.E. Nursing degrees usually lead to Registration in one branch of nursing (mainly General/Adult branch), but a few lead to Registration in more than one branch. There are also a few shortened degree courses for applicants with 'relevant' degrees, as well as a few part-time degrees for Registered nurses.

Nursing in the Community

Nurses who work outside the hospital, where there is always someone more highly qualified to discuss problems with, have much more independence in terms of decision-making and organizing their working days. *District nurses, health visitors, community psychiatric nurses, school nurses, practice nurses* and *community midwives* all come under what is now often loosely called the 'community nursing' umbrella. They are part of the multi-professional community care team, working closely with GPs, social workers and other colleagues from related professions. The proportion of community nurses is growing, as more and more patients, especially those with learning difficulties (what used to be called mentally handicapped), live in the community but still need nursing care and support. It is expected that many community nurses will soon have limited prescription rights, which underlines the responsibility they have. Few community nurses wear uniform.

District Nurse

Entry qualifications
Registered general nurse/registered nurse.

The work
District nurses undertake skilled nursing duties for patients not ill enough to be in hospital but needing nursing care. They visit acute and chronically ill patients as necessary and elderly people at regular intervals to keep an eye on them. They may also help permanently disabled patients to learn to use new aids, and help relatives to learn to carry out routine nursing tasks. When necessary they put people in touch with social workers or with other members of the health care team. District nurses work closely with local general practitioners, who advise on whom to visit and, often, the treatment required, and with hospitals. As there is a tendency for patients to be discharged from hospital as early as possible, district nurses are undertaking more and more technical nursing procedures, such as changing dressings for post-operative patients, taking out stitches, observing and reporting on patients' progress. They also give moral support, helping patients and their relatives to come to terms with their situation, etc.

Experienced nurses often lead teams which include several district nurses and nursing auxiliaries. To provide a 24-hour service, nurses work shifts. Because of the close co-operation between hospital and community services, district nurses may often also do some clinic sessions in hospital. This means they have both independence of community nursing and the companionship and chance to talk shop. Some district nurses specialize, e.g. in work with diabetics, the disabled, the elderly, terminal care.

Training
At present: 1 academic year for the Certificate in District Nursing, at a higher education establishment. The course includes learning how to adapt hospital nursing procedures to nursing under often less than ideal home conditions; teaching home nursing to patients' relatives; the organization, scope and availability of the social services; counselling (see 'Counselling', p. 407). There is also a nursing degree course which includes district nursing. But see changes in post-Registration training, p. 345.

Personal attributes
As for general nursing, plus organizing ability. District nurses must wish to work independently and to use their experience and ability in the community rather than in the sheltered atmosphere of the hospital. They should be resourceful, friendly and good listeners. They need a wide interest in the community in which

they live and work, and tolerance of other people's way of life. They should know when to be critical and when to accept patients' own standards of cleanliness, etc.

Health Visitor

Entry qualifications   Registered general nurse/registered nurse.

The work   Health visitors are professionals in their own right. They organize their own work.

The important difference between health visitors on the one hand and nurses and social workers on the other is that the latter usually meet clients when something has gone wrong. The purpose of health visiting is the promotion of health and the prevention and early detection of physical and mental ill health. Health visitors give health care advice, identify the need for and if necessary mobilize other sources of help.

They are responsible for monitoring children's health from the time midwifery care ceases (a few weeks after birth usually) until the school nurse (see p. 343) takes over checking children's development. They advise mothers on childcare, health hazards and health care both by regular home visits and in clinics. Routine home visits may act as an 'early warning system', and health visitors often notice signs of stress or disorder before these develop into problems. For example, a young mother who gave up the companionship at work just before the child was born may feel lonely, and guilty for not being a radiant mother; the health visitor helps by discussing her feelings and by suggesting ways of coping with the problem. Other matters which might develop into problems but for the health visitor's early advice are older children's health or behaviour, or marital difficulties.

Health visitors' work may overlap with that of district and community psychiatric nurses. They may visit patients recently discharged from hospital; mentally ill or handicapped people who are cared for at home; the elderly; anyone who may be referred to them by social workers, doctors, a neighbour even. They are very much involved with health education and may lecture in schools, etc.

When visiting, health visitors are concerned with the family as a whole, not only the ill or disturbed member of the family. They may be based in doctors' practices, or work from health centres.

Training   At present: 1 academic year at a higher education establishment.

Subjects studied include: social aspects of health and disease and preventive medicine theories and practice; social studies with special reference to the family as a social institution; health education; organization, scope and availability of social services; counselling (see 'Counselling', p. 407). There is also a degree in Nursing Studies and a health visiting qualification. But see changes in post-Registration training, p. 345.

Personal attributes

Interest and belief in preventive medicine and social advice; understanding and sympathy with social pressures and with people, whatever their temperament, background, life style, competence; desire and ability to use expertise in the community; tolerance; patience.

Community Psychiatric Nurse

Entry qualifications

Registered mental nurse/mental health branch.

The work

Community psychiatric nurses are sometimes (unofficially) referred to as 'district nurses for people with psychiatric problems'. But community psychiatric nursing is much less clearly definable than district nursing. As a post-Registration profession in its own right, it is still evolving – there is no one way of operating – different health/social services authorities organize the work in different ways. CPNs have, therefore, great scope to develop their own ideas and initiatives. It is very much a growth area within nursing because of the accelerating trend for psychiatric patients to live 'in the community' rather than go into or stay in hospital. Very broadly, CPNs combine 3 main, overlapping, functions.

1. They give practical help and counselling support (see 'Counselling', p. 407) to patients discharged from hospital and now having to adjust to living with their families, in hostels or on their own; also, to patients who right from the start of their illness are treated as out-patients and/or attend day hospitals.

2. CPNs provide a preventive service: they see people who may be referred by GPs, social workers, district nurses, health visitors, even relatives or neighbours, or they could be 'self-referred': i.e. people who realize they have problems which they cannot cope with.

3. CPNs help to 'educate' the community to understand the nature of mental illness; they also help families and foster-families (even landlords) – anyone who has a patient living in their home –

to cope with disturbed people's behaviour. Supporting patients' families, etc. is a *very* important part of community psychiatric nursing.

CNPs may also run clinics, do group-work (see 'Psychotherapy', p. 405) with patients and/or their families, and help run day centres. Because of the increasing numbers of patients with psychiatric problems cared for in the community, the profession is expanding greatly.

Training   At present: 9-month course, usually at polytechnic or other higher education establishment. Training is not yet mandatory: because of the shortage of specially trained CPNs, some are accepted without having taken the course. However, training is likely to become mandatory, at least for senior posts. Part-time day-release courses may become available. There is not yet a statutory post-Registration qualification. But see changes in post-Registration training, p. 345.

Personal attributes   As for psychiatric nurses (mental health), plus the desire to work independently and to help expand and consolidate community care.

Community Mental Handicap Nurse

Entry qualifications   Registered nurse for the mentally handicapped/mental handicap branch

The work   They are responsible for the care of persons with learning difficulties (the term now used in preference to 'mental handicap') who live in the community. Over 60% of persons diagnosed as suffering from this disability now do live with their families, on their own, in shared accommodation or in hostels. Their need for continued care vary enormously from the occasional chat to regular care. A client – the term now preferred to 'patient' – may, for example, have 'an eating problem': a GP or social worker may have alerted the nurse who will then visit and teach the client to use a spoon, etc., and probably also try and persuade the client's family to encourage their client to be more independent. The nurse may find that the extent of the client's learning difficulty is much smaller than the parents assumed. Teaching relatives how to care for clients is an important part of the nurse's work. Some clients, perhaps those only recently discharged from hospital but able to live in a shared flat, may merely have to be encouraged to increase their independence: to learn such social skills as saying 'hello' to neighbours, and such 'living skills' as paying the milk-man or using public transport. The aim of nurses is always to develop clients' potential as fully as their disability allows.

Nurses also hold 'information sessions' to help other community care and health professionals, as well as the community at large, understand developments and changes in the treatment of people with learning difficulties.

There is at present much discussion (and some disagreement) on the most effective way of organizing community care. One point everybody agrees on: it is an expanding area.

Training   At present: 1 academic year at a higher education establishment, but the training is not yet obligatory. Course content much like that for CPNs above. See changes in post-Registration training on p. 345.

Personal attributes   As for mental handicap nurses, plus desire to work independently and organizing ability.

Occupational Health Nurse

Entry qualifica-tions   Registered general nurse/adult branch.

The work   Occupational health nurses work in factories, stores and wherever else there is a large number of employees, with the aim of promoting health in the work place. The work is partly preventive, advising on diets, keeping an eye on the disabled, discussing worries with individuals. Occupational health nurses also deal with accidents and sudden illness and give minor treatments, such as injections, changing dressings. They advise both on health problems generally and on those peculiar to a particular industry, e.g. skin or respiratory diseases caused by certain types of work. They are now very much involved, at least in most large and/or progressive organizations, with research into the effects of the introduction of new technologies and/or working patterns on employees' health and on their job-satisfaction. This may involve discussing the arrangements of desks in word processing stations, or checking noise levels in tool shops, as well as shift and night work arrangements and canteen facilities. An important aspect of their work is the identification of health hazards, and initiating whatever measures are necessary to eliminate or minimize such hazards. They work closely with factory inspectors (see p. 214).

They work closely with occupational health doctors (see p.

302). They usually keep medical records of all employees and assist at the medical examination of prospective employees. They often arrange for such ancillary services as chiropody, eye-testing, physiotherapy. They discuss health and safety measures on the shop-floor and in the office with management, shop steward and factory inspector (see p. 214) and work closely with the personnel department. For example, if an employee's work is deteriorating, OHNs help to find the psychological or physical cause. OHNs also help to find suitable jobs for the disabled and may discuss with management measures which should be taken in special cases.

In large concerns there may be a medical department; more often there is one occupational health nurse working for the personnel director and/or the visiting medical officer.

Unlike other nursing jobs, normal office hours usually apply.

Training   At present: 1-year full-time or 2-year part-time (day-release usually) course for the Occupational Health Nursing Certificate, normally at a higher education establishment. The syllabus includes industrial organization, factory and allied legislation; toxic hazards; effects of and coping with technological and organizational change. But see changes in post-Registration training on p. 345.

Personal   As for general nursing, with a special interest in industrial health,
attributes   new technologies and changing patterns of work, safety problems, and human relationships at work. The ability to work independently and to discuss matters easily both with workforce and management is essential.

School Nurse

Entry   Registered general nurse/registered nurse.
qualifica-
tions

The work   School nurses take over the monitoring of children's development where health visitors' work stops, i.e. when children reach school age. They work in the school health service and regularly visit a number of schools. Their routine checking of vision, hearing, growth, etc. is a preventive service: they hope to detect minor problems before they develop into serious ones. Teachers and parents ask school nurses' advice when a child shows signs of not being quite 'up to scratch', physically or mentally. The school nurse may contact parents when that seems advisable.

School nursing varies very much from one area to another, according to local organization; how many schools one school nurse is responsible for; and also according to individual school nurses' initiative and interpretation of their role.

School nurses are also very much involved in health education. Again, the extent of involvement varies: in some areas health education officers (usually health visitors by qualification) are appointed and school nurses would work with them; in other areas health education is left to health visitors and/or school nurses. Increasingly, school nurses take part in a programme of lectures/talks both to schoolchildren and at parents' evenings/meetings, on such issues as drug abuse, AIDS, etc.

In some areas school nurses hold a kind of 'surgery' at certain days in 'their' schools, when parents, children and teachers can come and discuss any problem that bothers them. School nursing is very much less structured in terms of specific duties than most other nursing specializations.

Although school rolls are falling, the need for monitoring and for health education is rising; so opportunities for school nurses may be increasing. Most school nurses are part-timers.

Training   At present: 12-week course at a higher education establishment. The course covers child development; social and physiological influences on health and disease; health education and disease prevention. See changes in post-Registration training on p. 345.

Personal   As for health visitors, with particular interest in working with
attributes   children and adolescents.

Practice Nurse

Entry   Registered general nurse/registered nurse.
qualifica-
tions

The work   Practice nurses have worked in GPs' practices for some time, carrying out such routine procedures as taking blood samples, changing dressings, etc. However, recent NHS changes greatly increased the range of tasks GPs or their support staff are asked to undertake; practice nurses' numbers and their importance have therefore increased greatly. Exactly what they may and may not do is still a 'grey area'. Their duties are not as clearly defined as those of other specialist nurses, and their work varies according to their GP employers' views and their own experience. Most practice nurses now undertake such non-routine tasks as setting up and running health promotion clinics (e.g. well-women, asthma and hypertension, and baby clinics), and they may also do some screening: i.e. check patients' health. All new patients who register with a GP must be offered screening, and all over-75s at least once a year (the latter). Practice nurses may do this screening and decide whether the patient needs to see the doctor. In the case of elderly patients this may involve home visits. It is expected that practice nurses, like health visitors and district nurses, may soon have (strictly limited) prescription rights.

Training   Training is not yet obligatory but it is strongly recommended. Courses take about a month, plus day seminars on an on-going basis.

Post-Registration Courses

Post-Registration training is also changing. Both structure and content are being updated to take account of changes from traditional to P2000 pre-Registration courses, and also of changes in patients' needs and expectations.

Structural change means that most courses in future will be 'modular'. They will consist of 'shared' or 'common core' modules plus specialist modules. The extent of shared modules in the various training programmes will vary, and is probably greatest on courses for community-based nurses: health visitors, district nurses, community psychiatric nurses, etc. all have to acquire the skills which enable them to work independently. They must learn how to relate to individuals and groups in the community and understand what makes communities tick and where and how they themselves fit in. Courses for community nurses may be shorter in future as P2000-trained nurses will have learnt more about working in the community than traditionally trained nurses did.

Post-Registration courses will still vary greatly in length and objective, from those taking a few days to others taking a year and leading to another qualification. Courses for clinical specialists, teachers and managers all will be rejigged. It is hoped that in future most nurses will feel that Registration is only the first step on a ladder of opportunities, rather than an end in itself. However, as before, a Registered nurse is a fully qualified professional.

In Scotland and Wales most courses have changed; in England changes are going to be implemented soon.

The English National Board also launched a new Higher Award at the end of 1991. It is intended for nurses who do not want to take further exams. Colleges of nursing will 'assess candidates' effectiveness'. The emphasis is on individuals' professional development, competence and expertise. Preparation for the award can be by various modes: short or longer courses, open learning, private study, or simply going on working. Individuals' learning needs will vary; for example, a returner will need more structured learning and more support than someone who has worked continuously. The new award is expected to contribute to solving the nurse retention problem (see above) as practitioners will have something to aim for without having to take further exams.

Midwife

Entry qualifications   As for registered nurses, see p. 330.

The work   Midwives look after mother and child from early pregnancy until about 4 weeks after the birth of the child (when health visitors take over). They give ante- and post-natal advice, support and instruction, and take full responsibility during the birth in straightforward cases and call a doctor in case of complications which they are trained to spot at an early stage. They run hospitals' baby units including those for premature and sick babies. They are trained to a high professional standard and work closely with doctors. They also run clinics for pregnant women as well as training sessions for expectant fathers and mothers. As mothers' stay in hospital is often very short, midwives' home visits are vitally important. These may involve counselling women who suffer from post-natal depression, or who need advice on coping with a new-born baby without neglecting their other children. It also often involves family planning advice.

Midwifery is a unique combination of applying complex practical and high-tech skills, teaching parentcraft and counselling.

There is today much more emphasis on the psychological aspects of childbirth and its effects on the rest of the family than there used to be. The majority of births take place in hospital, but midwives are very much involved with the home-versus-hospital birth debate. To ensure continuity of care from early pregnancy until the health visitor takes over care of mother and child, the emphasis is on an integrated hospital and community midwifery service, with individual midwives working in both home and hospital. But there are also opportunities for midwives to work *only* in hospital or *only* in the community. A small number of midwives work in the private sector. There is at present a shortage of midwives.

Training   Until recently most midwives had to be registered nurses and then take an 18-month post-Registration course: only very few midwives were able to take 'direct entry' courses. This is changing. The majority of courses are now 3-year pre-Registration courses at colleges of nursing and midwifery. A few courses also lead to a Diploma in Higher Education (in Scotland *all* midwifery courses now do) and a few lead also to a degree. All courses include a period of working in the community, learning how to adapt sometimes unsatisfactory home conditions for safe delivery.

Like nurses, midwives can take various post-Registration courses. Unlike nurses, midwives are *obliged* to take a refresher course every 5 years. This emphasizes the fact that midwives are independent practitioners with high responsibility.

Personal attributes   As for district nurses (see p. 338), plus of course special interest in babies and the self-confidence needed particularly when persuading fathers to get involved in the preparation for the birth.

Late start (all above professions and specializations)   Excellent opportunities. Mature entrants of both sexes are very welcome because their drop-out rates are lower and their stay in the profession is longer than young entrants'. Special tests assess mature entrants' potential rather than their 'school knowledge'. Work/life experience is considered more important than academic achievement. If necessary, mature entrants are advised to take an Access course (see p. xxxi).

Career-break   Returners are very welcome indeed; Return to Nursing courses are available in most districts and can be tailored to suit individuals' needs. Enrolled nurses may be able to take conversion courses, or they take returners' courses. There are 'refreshers' for all community nurses, specialists, managers and teachers.

Promotion prospects for returners are good.

Part time   Opportunities for flexible work patterns are now available much higher up the promotion ladder than they used to be. Part time is encouraged at virtually all levels, and job-sharing is also encouraged (but the initiative still often has to come from individuals).

Part-time training is also becoming more widely available, especially under the P2000 system of training.

Position of women   Still only about 10% of men in the profession, but it seems to be increasing. Men still hold far more than their share of top jobs (especially in management and teaching) but that is probably due to the fact that until recently so many women dropped out when they had families or returned part time, and promotion for part-timers above Sister is still fairly new. So women's share of top jobs is likely to increase considerably in the next few years.

Further information

From appropriate National Boards:

English National Board for Nursing Midwifery and Health Visitors: PO Box 356, Sheffield S8 0SJ

Scottish National Board: 22 Queen Street, Edinburgh EH2 1JX

Welsh National Board: 13th Floor, Pearl Assurance House, Greyfriars Road, Cardiff CF1 3AG

Northern Ireland Board: RAC House, 79 Chichester Street, Belfast BT1 4JR

Royal College of Nursing, 20 Cavendish Square, London W1M 0AB

Related careers

MEDICINE – NURSERY NURSE – OCCUPATIONAL THERAPY – PHYSIOTHERAPY – SOCIAL WORK

NOTE: *Enrolled nurse training* is being phased out. If you do not have the entry qualifications required for registered nurse training and in any case want to stick to practical bedside nursing rather than take responsibility for complex procedures, you should now go into a hospital where *health care assistants* are given training. At present, health care assistant is not a 'protected title', and support staff may be called HCA but not get any training. The Department of Health wants HCAs to be given on-the-job training so that they qualify for an NVQ (see p. xx) at level 1 or 2. You will have to shop around for a suitable hospital; it is more likely that hospitals where the new P2000 training has started also train HCAs than hospitals which still do traditional training. At present there is no 'bridge' from HCA to professional nurse training but an NVQ level 3 should be 'on stream' soon, and that will probably be considered as an equivalent to orthodox entry qualification. In any case it should enable candidates to take the registered nurse training entry test (see p. 330).

Open learning: Various open- and distance-learning packages are available. They are intended mainly for returners and for nurses who want to take further examinations. Information is available from the National Boards and from the Royal College of Nursing.

1993 NOTE: Private nursing homes, community care establishments, occupational health departments, etc. may also enable health care assistants to qualify for NVQs. It is entirely up to the individual employer.

Occupational Therapy

Entry qualifications

3 GCSE (A–C) passes and 2 A-levels (or equivalent, including Scottish Highers) in different subjects. At least 1 science is required; biology is useful and is required for some courses. Alternative qualifications (for example, BTEC National Diploma in appropriate subject) may be acceptable. Courses may ask for more than the minimum. English is commonly required.

The work

Occupational therapists are concerned with helping people with physical and mental disorders to live as full a life as possible by overcoming as much as possible the effects of their disability. This covers a very wide range of activities concerned with physical, psychological, social and economic well-being. Some occupational therapists feel that the title conjures up out-of-date images of patients weaving baskets or doing jigsaws during long days of convalescence, and that 'rehabilitation therapist' would better convey the essence of their work. Others feel the title is fair enough, given that they are concerned with all the things that 'occupy' patients day-in, day-out – basic everyday care, work, leisure, social interaction. The work covers a spectrum that borders physiotherapy at one end and social work at the other.

Occupational therapists work with people of all ages and various kinds of problems. *Physical disability* may be the result of accident, illness or old age. It may be the kind of problem that gets better – or one that gets progressively worse. It may be part of a complex combination of multiple handicaps. Together with other members of the health care team, the occupational therapist assesses the problem and devises a programme of treatment to help the patient regain as much independence as possible. The emphasis is on patients' ability, not disability. Treatment might involve strengthening exercises – or shopping expeditions. Occupational therapists devise new ways for patients to perform old tasks, e.g. cooking from a wheelchair, dressing, getting in and out of bed and bath. They may take patients on a trial visit home from hospital so they can advise on how the environment may need to be adapted. The solution is sometimes as simple as rearranging a room, or as complicated as building an extension. Sometimes there is no solution but rehousing, so the occupational therapist may have to liaise with the housing department. They also provide patients with various kinds of aids and equipment, from those which open jars to sophisticated hoists.

The problems of people with *mental disabilities* are very different, but the aim is the same – to give them the confidence and ability to live as independent a life as possible. The work varies and might include just visiting and talking with acutely ill patients who are too ill to join a structured programme; devising games and exercises to improve, for example, concentration or memory; art or dance therapy to help patients become aware of their immediate environment and express themselves; planning 'paired' or group activities to encourage patients to socialize. Interests and hobbies are encouraged so that patients will be able to use their leisure and reduce isolation. The practical skills that they will need for living in the community are taught and practised – daily care and personal hygiene, cooking, shopping, using public transport, budgeting. Occupational therapists also help patients rediscover and practise the skills they need for their jobs. This may involve liaison with employers.

Occupational therapists treat patients in hospitals, special centres, schools and in their homes. The main employers are the National Health Service and local authority social services departments. There is a growing emphasis on community care as the number of elderly people in the population increases and patients are discharged earlier from hospital. There are also opportunities in prisons, industry (where OTs might deal with stress management and relaxation techniques) and private practice.

Courses are broad-based, but after qualification occupational therapists may specialize in work with particular groups, e.g. children, orthopaedic patients, stroke patients, alcoholics, drug addicts.

Occupational therapists are important members of the health team. They are practical problem-solvers and have enormous involvement in people's lives at a critical time. The success of their work depends on winning people's confidence, establishing a relationship, being able to work as part of a team but also independently. There is a shortage of occupational therapists and increasing demands with limited time and resources can lead to frustrations.

OT helpers help in hospitals and social services departments. They can specialize in work with the handicapped, with long-stay patients in hospital and, above all, in work with the elderly, who account for an increasingly large proportion of OT patients. OT helpers do not usually get systematic training, but may be taken into the NVQ framework (see p. xx). They also have the possibility of in-service training leading to full professional qualification (see 'Training', below).

Training   1. 3-year full-time course leading to a degree. About 1 year is spent working in different types of OT settings. The syllabus includes anatomy, physiology, psychology, medicine, surgery (theoretical only), psychiatry and the theory and underlying principles of occupational therapy for physical and mental disabilities. Under 'occupational techniques' comes practical work such as 'self-help', which is concerned with helping disabled or sick patients back to independence in everyday life. Many schools have or are developing international links and student exchanges.

2. 2-year accelerated Diploma courses for graduates.

3. 4-year part-time in-service Diploma courses for mature entrants already working in OT. These may become degrees in future.

Personal attributes   Organizing ability; the ability to explain things clearly to all types of patient; adaptability and judgement to find the right approach to psychiatric patients; resourcefulness, patience, cheerfulness, good powers of observation; some dexterity; an interest in practical work; and a fairly strong scientific bent.

Late start   Good opportunities – about 30% of students are mature entrants. Applicants must check individual schools' requirements. Mature students may be accepted without the normal academic qualifications, but they are normally expected either to have considerable work experience or to show evidence of recent academic study (e.g. an A-level, Open University Foundation Course (see p. xxxiv) or Access course, see p. xxxi). There are also special courses – see (3) under 'Training', above.

Career-break   No problem. Refresher courses available.

Part time   Good opportunities for basic-grade jobs, but promotion prospects poor. Job-sharing is likely to provide better prospects. Both depend on employer requirements.

Position of women   Traditionally an all-female profession, but the proportion of men is increasing – 16% in the 1990 intake, compared with 5% overall.

Further information College of Occupational Therapists, 6–8 Marshalsea Road, Southwark, London SE1 1HL

Related careers PHYSIOTHERAPY – NURSING: *Psychiatric Nurse*

Optical Work

All practising opticians must be registered with the General Optical Council. There are two kinds of careers for opticians:

1. *Dispensing opticians*, who, working to a prescription, supply spectacles, contact lenses and other optical appliances;

2. *Optometrists/ophthalmic opticians*, who test eyesight and prescribe (and may also supply) whatever spectacles or contact lenses are necessary to correct defects.

Dispensing Optician

Entry qualifications

5 GCSEs (A–C) including maths or physics, English, plus 1 other science subject.

The work

Dispensing opticians do not do any sight-testing or other eye-examination. They interpret the prescription of the ophthalmic surgeon or ophthalmic optician using complex apparatus to measure for, fit and supply spectacles, contact lenses and artificial eyes. All such work requires calculations of distance and angles, etc. Equally important are the selling and 'cosmetic' aspects of the work. Dispensing opticians discuss with patients (a term opticians use in preference to customers) which type of frame is the most flattering in each case.

Most dispensing opticians also deal with other types of optical instruments, supplying apparatus to ophthalmic surgeons, opticians and laboratories, and selling sunglasses, opera glasses, microscopes, etc. to the general public.

Dispensing opticians can also get managerial jobs in 'prescription houses' (firms which make lenses to prescription) and in firms of dispensing opticians which manufacture optical instruments.

Dispensing opticians usually start as assistants but later may manage a shop, or practice, in which optometrists or surgeons do the eye-testing.

They have at least as great a variety of jobs and settings to choose from as optometrists. In relation to their educational qualifications and the length of their respective trainings, they do better financially – a dispensing optician manager may in fact earn more than a practising optometrist.

Training   *Either* (and recommended): a 2-year full-time course at a technical college, plus 1 year's practical experience; *or*: 3 years' work as a trainee with a dispensing optician, plus theoretical instruction, either by day-release or by correspondence course (which must be approved by the General Optical Council) with some attendance at a college.

All methods of training lead to the qualifying examinations for Fellowship of the Association of British Dispensing Opticians.

The syllabus covers optical physics, the anatomy and physiology of the eye, the interpretation of ophthalmic prescriptions, the necessary measurements and adjustments for frames, and the recording of facial measurements. The full-time course also includes business practice.

Personal attributes   Some manual dexterity; interest in salesmanship and in fashion; ability and enjoyment in dealing with flow of people.

Late start   No special problems, except for competition from young entrants. Science graduates may be exempt from part of the course.

Career-break   No problem: *refresher* courses exist and may increase.

Part time   Good opportunities also for job-sharing at all levels up to managing a high street shop.

Position of women   Steady increase of women entrants over last few years; now women account for about half of practitioners and many are in senior management jobs.

Optometrist (Ophthalmic Optician)

Entry qualifications   2, or more often 3, science A-levels plus 3 GCSEs (A–C) which must include English and physics or physics with chemistry and a biological subject if physics and biology respectively are not offered at A-level. Most degree courses insist on A-level physics.

The work   The main duties of an optometrist are examining eyes; measuring vision defects with the help of optical instruments; and working out lens-prescriptions for short- or far-sightedness and astigmatism.

Some optometrists now test sight with computerized equipment instead of using the traditional methods. They are also trained to dispense ophthalmic prescriptions. Optometrists do not treat patients with diseased eyes. If they find any abnormality or signs of disease in the eye they refer the patient to an *ophthalmic surgeon*. They are concerned with optics, not with medicine; their work is essentially scientific, not medical, but they should see the patient as a human being, not simply a pair of eyes. The work combines dealing with people and applied science.

Optometrists work either in general practice, doing mainly sight-testing, or in hospital, where they see more intricate eye conditions and assist ophthalmic surgeons with investigations and treatment of eye disease, and with research.

General practice may mean seeing patients in 'rooms' – possibly in the optician's own home; it may mean managing and/or owning an optician's practice and doing all the dispensing work as well; frequently it means doing the ophthalmic work in a shop managed and/or owned by a firm of ophthalmic or dispensing opticians which owns several practices.

There is a steady demand for optometrists.

Training   3 years for a B.Sc. degree (in Scotland 4 years) plus 1 year's clinical experience in paid employment. The syllabus includes physical optics, optical instruments, anatomy and physiology, abnormal and pathological conditions of the eye, refraction. The British College of Optometrists is the examining body for ophthalmic optics. After passing the College's Professional Qualifying Examination and completing a pre-Registration year, students apply for Registration with the General Optical Council. Registration is obligatory for practitioners.

Personal attributes   An interest in physics and maths; patience; manual dexterity; a liking for briefly meeting a flow of new people; a confident manner especially with old people and children; business ability.

Late start   This is a long training and courses are oversubscribed, therefore only applicants with up-to-date knowledge of science likely to be accepted. Approximately 7% of entrants are over 30. Once trained there should be no problem getting jobs.

Career-break   If one has kept up with developments, no problem. *Refresher* courses available for all optometrists.

Part time   Good opportunities at all levels. Job-sharing possible.

**Position
of
women**
Women have been accepted for a long time and have no problems getting good jobs. The proportion of registered practitioners is about 30%. However, in 1991 56% of home students accepted for optometry degree courses at university were women. Thus the proportion of women students choosing optics is larger than the proportion of men doing so. Optics is probably the easiest profession in which to work successfully part time. Women optometrists have also found it relatively easy to return to full-time work after a spell of part-time work.

**Further
informa-
tion**
The Association of British Dispensing Opticians, 22 Nottingham Place, London W1M 4AT

The British College of Optometrists, 10 Knaresborough Place, London SW5 0TG

**Related
careers**
ORTHOPTICS

Orthoptics

Entry qualifications   5 GCSEs (A–C) including English language, maths and a science subject, and 2 A-levels, preferably including a science subject.

The work   Orthoptists work with ophthalmic surgeons. They are responsible for the diagnosis, investigation, treatment and progress-monitoring of patients who have defects of binocular vision, e.g. squint, double vision or related vision conditions. The orthoptist's role is expanding. The importance of early diagnosis and treatment of children is increasingly recognized. Orthoptists therefore work on screening programmes for pre-school-age children. Special equipment and special skills enable orthoptists to assess the visual abilities of even very young children – some patients are under a year old. Orthoptists also deal with children who have reading difficulties. They must be able to build up relationships with children of all ages and with their parents.

Other patient-groups include the physically and mentally handicapped; people who have had accidents or strokes; multiple sclerosis sufferers; and the elderly who can be helped to achieve their maximum visual potential, for example in glaucoma clinics. The latter client group is increasing in size as the proportion of elderly people in the population is increasing.

Orthoptists thus deal with a very wide age-range; with a wide range of conditions, and in a range of settings – in hospitals, in paediatrics, school, geriatric and neurological clinics or departments. Patients are referred by ophthalmic surgeons, neurologists, general physicians, paediatricians, and other specialists.

Equipment used for diagnosis and treatment is highly sophisticated. Its use requires great technical knowledge and skill. The need for getting clients of all ages to co-operate and do exercises – both in the clinic and at home – requires orthoptists to understand and communicate well with people of all ages and temperaments.

There are opportunities for experienced orthoptists to become clinical teachers of orthoptics, and to work in private practice. British qualifications are accepted in most countries and there is scope for orthoptists in the EC if they speak the relevant language.

Training This has changed (1992) to a 3-year degree course. Syllabus includes general anatomy and physiology; child development; anatomy and physiology of eye and brain; optics; diseases of the eye and the principles of eye surgery; practice of orthoptics.

Students gradually gain clinical experience working with patients of all ages.

Personal attributes A scientific bent; powers of observation, deduction and persuasion; understanding of people of all ages and temperaments; ability to work as one of a team, and also independently; communication skills.

Late start The orthoptists insist on normal entry qualifications and schools tend to prefer school-leavers; however, determined candidates in their 20s or 30s may be admitted for training especially if they have had experience of dealing with children. Approximately 5% of entrants are mature (see 'Access courses', p. xxxi).

Career-break Depends on (a) whether orthoptist kept up with developments, and (b) on level of vacancies. Young entrants tend to be given preference. Short 'up-dating' *refresher* courses are available.

Part time Fair opportunities; promotion to head of department possible; job-sharing schemes can be arranged by enterprising practitioners.

Position of women This is still a virtually all-female profession, but no reason why it should remain so. About 5% of orthoptists are male.

Further information British Orthoptic Society, Tavistock House North, Tavistock Square, London WC1H 0HX

Related careers OPTICAL WORK: *Dispensing Optician; Optometrist (Ophthalmic Optician)*

Osteopathy

Entry qualifications

See 'Training', below.

The work

An osteopath uses manipulative methods of treatment for the correction of derangements of the bony and muscular structures of the body, and makes a special study of the spine in relation to health and disease. Osteopathy does not include the curing of organic disease but it covers the treatment of some organic functional disorders. The majority of patients need treatment because of stiff joints, slipped discs, etc. Patients are often referred to osteopaths by GPs who recognize the value of osteopathic treatment for certain disorders, but the majority of patients come through personal recommendation.

Osteopaths are not recognized by the National Health Service, because they do not need to have orthodox medical qualifications, though some do. The normal procedure after qualifying is first to obtain experience as an assistant to an osteopath or at a clinic, then to start one's own part-time practice in addition, and perhaps finally to concentrate entirely on one's own practice.

This is a small profession, but interest in osteopathy is growing steadily.

Training

There are 3 main training schools, all offering 4-year courses:

1. *The British School of Osteopathy* offers a B.Sc. degree course in Osteopathy. Graduates are eligible to apply for membership of the General Council and Register of Osteopaths. Entry requirements: 2 science A-levels, preferably biology and chemistry, and 5 GCSEs. There are special provisions for mature students (i.e. Access, previous relevant experience in lieu of A-levels).

2. *European School of Osteopathy*: Entry requirements and training as in (1); leads to Diploma of Osteopathy and eligibility for membership of the Register.

3. *British College of Naturopathy and Osteopathy*: Entry requirements are A-levels as above, plus GCSE (A–C) passes in at least 2 of the following: English, maths and physics. This course also leads to a Diploma and eligibility for membership as in (1).

The syllabus for all courses includes anatomy; physiology; osteopathic theory, practice and technique; diagnosis; pathology; applied anatomy; applied physiology; preventive medicine; biochemistry; dietetics; bacteriology.

There are other, smaller, training organizations. There is also a move within the profession to agree standards so that osteopaths can seek recognition in the EC.

Personal attributes Confidence-inspiring manner; skilful, gentle, yet strong hands; good health; patience; interest in people's lifestyles.

Late start Some relaxation of entry requirements if candidates considered suitable; shortened courses for people with relevant qualifications (e.g. physiotherapy, medicine). Late entrants have no difficulty getting patients once trained. About 20% of students are mature entrants.

Career-break The vast majority of women osteopaths continue working part time from home throughout their career. Post-graduate *refresher* seminars available.

Part time Very good opportunities.

Position of women About 40% of osteopaths are women, and so are about 50% of osteopathy students. Experienced osteopaths say that it is not a job for frail women: they would find some of the work physically impossible. But on the whole women osteopaths have no problem getting patients.

Further information British School of Osteopathy, 1–4 Suffolk Street, London SW1Y 4HG

General Council and Register of Osteopaths, 56 London Street, Reading, Berks. RG1 4SQ

European School of Osteopathy, 104 Tonbridge Road, Maidstone, Kent ME16 8SL

British College of Naturopathy and Osteopathy, Frazer House, Netherhall Gardens, London NW3 5RR

Related careers MEDICINE – PHYSIOTHERAPY

Patent Agent (Chartered) and Patent Examiner

Entry qualifications	Minimum 2 A-levels for Foundation exam, but in practice a science or engineering degree; working knowledge of French and German very desirable.

Patent Agent

The work	Patent agents work in the field of intellectual property. Put very simply, a patent is the right to stop a product, process, trademark, design or written material that has been invented or originated by one person from being copied or developed by another for a certain number of years. It is a mixture of legal and scientific/technological work. A patent agent advises inventors, and others concerned with inventions, on the validity and infringement of patents at home and abroad. Until recently only patent agents registered with the Chartered Institute of Patent Agents had the right to submit patents. A change in the law means that now anyone can do the work of a patent agent but cannot be called a 'patent agent' unless registered. (They may be called 'consultants'.)

Patent agents make 'searches' for clients to ensure that their inventions really are new, and prepare detailed specifications, descriptions and formulations of claims which 'cover' the invention. They file and negotiate the application for patents on behalf of their clients at the Patent Office. Having assisted in the creation of a patent, they may deal with its commercial application. They deal not only with patents for processes and products, but also with 'Registered Designs', 'Registered Trade Marks' and Industrial Copyright.

The majority of agents specialize in a particular type of work, e.g. in chemical or mechanical inventions, or in electronics – a very important area – or in designs and trade marks. Most firms of patent agents are trademark agents, but there are also independent trade mark agents.

Patent agents work in private practice or for industrial organizations. It is usual to start as an assistant doing searches in the Patent Office and other libraries.

Patent agents' work has increased in scope and complexity since the coming into force of the European Patent Convention. In addition to preparing and processing patent applications in this country and corresponding with patent agents abroad to obtain similar protection for clients' inventions there, patent agents who are suitably qualified draft patent applications for submission to the European Patent Office in Munich. There are reasonable opportunities for travel to Europe and other countries.

Although this is a small profession there is increasing scope.

Training

The Chartered Institute of Patent Agents introduced new training regulations in 1991. There is now a Foundation and an Advanced level, with separate exams for the Patent Agents and Trade Marks Registers.

There is no longer a minimum training period before passing the exams, but trainees must have 2 years' professional experience after passing the exams before being registered. Most are expected to go on to take the exams of the European Patent Institute in order to qualify as European Patent Attorneys, eligible to submit patents to the European Patent Office.

Preparation for examinations is mainly by private study; some firms sponsor trainees on a 3-month full-time course for the Foundation Stage. The Chartered Institute arranges lectures and tutorials. Some technical assistants never qualify yet nevertheless do very well, but they cannot become partners in private practice firms.

Personal attributes

Curiosity; an analytical mind; a good memory; a scientific bent; the ability to assimilate facts quickly and to reason and speak clearly; ability to write clearly and unambiguously; liking for concentrated desk work.

Late start

Entrance requirements may be waived for people with relevant experience, but there are difficulties getting training vacancies.

Career-break

Return possible only for those who have kept up with legal and technological changes/developments.

Part time

Some opportunities; it is also possible for experienced patent agents with good contacts to run a small private practice from home. Job-sharing should be possible.

Position of women

Women make up 10% of Institute members. Nearly 7% of Chartered patent agents and 29% of students are women, so numbers are increasing. Few women tried to enter this profession until recently; there is no discrimination.

Further information

Chartered Institute of Patent Agents, Staple Inn Buildings, London WC1V 7PZ

Patent Examiner

Entry qualifications

First- or second-class honours degree in a scientific, engineering or mathematical subject; ability to read French and German is very important.

The work

Patent examiners work in the Patent Office in London, and examine applications for patents. They are civil servants (see p. 125). An examiner's work involves detailed examination of the description of an invention; making a search through earlier specifications to ascertain the novelty of the invention; classifying and indexing the features of the invention; writing a report embodying the findings; and, if necessary, interviewing the inventor or the inventor's agent to discuss any problems. The work requires an analytical and critical mind. Each examiner works in a specialized field. Training is on the job. Vacancies arise very rarely.

Personal attributes

As for Patent Agent.

Late start

Possible for people with relevant (technological) degrees and experience.

Career-break

Presents problems – few vacancies; need to keep up with developments; competition from new graduates.

Part time

Not at present. No reason why job-sharing should not work. (See CIVIL SERVICE, p. 138.)

Position of women

10% of senior staff and about 50% of entrants are women.

Further information

The Patent Office, Concept House, Cardiff Road, Newport, Gwent NP9 1RA

Related careers	CIVIL SERVICE – ENGINEERING – SCIENCE

Personnel/Human Resources Management

Entry qualifications

For Institute of Personnel Management's Professional Education Scheme: *either* 2 A-levels and 3 GCSEs (A–C) and minimum age 21; *or* at least 2 years' relevant work experience. About half of all entrants are *graduates* and many have BTEC HND Business Studies (see p. xxi). See 'Training', below, for alternative method of entry.

The work

Personnel officers are part of the management team. Titles vary and are not necessarily any indication of scope and level of responsibility. The term 'human resources manager' is now often used. Their primary aim is always the efficient use and development of people's talents. The Institute of Personnel Management says that personnel management is not a job for people who merely want to 'work with people'. Personnel managers' main job is 'to provide the specialist knowledge or service that can assist other members of the management-team to make the most effective use of the human resources – people – of the organization'.

Personnel management used to be considered an offshoot of social work; it is certainly that no longer. The average personnel officer does not necessarily spend more time in one-to-one discussions with individuals who need advice than do, for example, solicitors or accountants. 'Personnel' is a 'management function', like buying, marketing and production. Its challenge is to interpret conflicting views and objectives to people at various levels in an organization, some of whom have divergent interests.

Personnel officers are employed not only in industry, but also in hospitals, local and central government: the efficient use of human resources is equally vital to profit-making and to non-profit-making organizations. The range of jobs is very great indeed. In a large organization, employing say 70,000 people at several sites, a personnel director may have a staff of 70, some of whom specialize in one aspect of the work; in a small organization 1 or 2 people might do everything.

Main (overlapping) personnel specializations:

Recruitment, training and management-development: Devising, monitoring and applying selection procedures, possibly selecting the most suitable of various psychological testing and assessment methods for all levels of staff; identifying individuals' potential and planning their education, training and career development. This involves reconciling individuals' needs and aims with the employer's requirements for staff with specific skills at specific levels of responsibility. It is a very important specialization now because of the emphasis in the last few years on the need for a more highly skilled workforce at all levels from operatives to management. This department may include the formation and implementation of equal opportunities policies.

Management of change: Personnel people may or may not be responsible for masterminding this – see MANAGEMENT, p. 274 – but they are invariably involved. During the introduction of new technologies or structures personnel people work closely with systems analysts/designers, with, perhaps, technologists, occupational psychologists and other specialists and with union officials, ironing out problems arising when changes in traditional working patterns are proposed and implemented. This requires personnel people to have thorough understanding of individuals' present tasks, of their place in the hierarchy, and of how proposed changes will affect individuals' jobs.

Compensation and benefits: Covers job evaluation and equal pay for equal work administration. It involves systematic study of the tasks that make up individual jobs within the organization, in order to establish their gradings. 'Compensation and benefits' sounds misleadingly like a desk-bound routine job, but it can be one of the most non-routine and controversial specializations.

Employee relations: Establishing and maintaining lines of communication between an organization's various interest groups. It involves discussing, with shop stewards and management, 'worker participation' schemes; implication of new legislation (of which there is a constant flow); mergers; implementation of new technologies; dealing with consequent redundancies, and planning reallocation of tasks and retraining schemes.

Health and safety, sometimes called employee services, covers all welfare aspects. It may include personal counselling services (see 'Counselling', p. 407); responsibility for canteens, etc., as well as sophisticated job satisfaction improvement schemes and co-operation with manpower planning, training and other personnel specialists.

Not all personnel departments divide personnel functions in the same way; there are many variations on the 'effective use of human resources' theme.

Personnel workers who get to the top normally have had

experience in several specialist fields, but there are few hard and fast rules. A specialist training officer in a large and/or progressive organization may have greater scope, responsibility and status (and salary) than a personnel director in charge of all specialist functions in another organization. It is impossible to generalize about career-paths, but it is probably best for those aiming at top jobs to get experience in large organizations, where they have the chance of working on a wide range of problems using a variety of personnel techniques.

Many organizations with establishments in different towns expect personnel officers to move around the country. It is quite usual to move from one employer to another, not necessarily remaining in the same type of organization, for example from factory to hospital, store to local government, etc. However, with the introduction of new technologies more personnel people stay either in manufacturing or in service industries.

Training   The Institute's Professional Education Scheme is divided into Stage 1 (Professional Management Foundation Programme) and Stage 2 and leads to graduateship of the Institute. Students take a 1-year full-time, or a 2–3-year part-time course, normally while in relevant employment (but see 'Position of women', below).

BTEC/SCOTVEC Higher National award holders (see pp. xxi, xxii) and graduates may qualify for partial or total exemption from Stage 1, depending on the relevance of the subject studied for the previous qualification.

It is possible to prepare for IPM exams by correspondence course, preferably, but not necessarily, while in relevant employment. The Institute offers its own flexible learning version of Stage 1, and a flexible learning scheme for Stage 2 will be available from September 1992.

Those not qualified or experienced enough to follow the Professional Education Scheme may take a Certificate in Personnel Practice. Study is part time and is suitable for students from a variety of backgrounds, including clerical, secretarial and line management, who will acquire practical personnel skills to help them in their job.

Graduates with a business studies or social/behavioural science degree or post-graduate qualification may get on well without IPM qualifications if they have acquired the necessary knowledge (legislation, training techniques, industrial relations procedures, etc.). Some employers do not mind whether staff have IPM qualifications or not. In fact, some heads of department positively prefer graduates, preferably with social/behavioural science degrees *and/or* with relevant experience acquired in *any* capacity –

as secretary, technician, junior manager/supervisor, etc. – who do *not* have IPM qualifications. However, qualifications *are* increasingly required by many employers, and they are valuable for women who want to return to work after the child-rearing gap.

Personal attributes A flair for seeing all sides of a problem and interpreting each side's point of view to the other; a good memory for names and faces; at least an absence of dislike for figure-work, preferably a liking for it; interest in profitable management and in change; lack of prejudice; tact; detachment; an understanding of people of all types, age, race and background, and the ability to gain their confidence and respect; organizing ability.

Late start Some opportunities for mature entrants who have had relevant experience.

Career-break Personnel workers are able to return to the work if they have kept up with legislation and other personnel developments. They can take part-time or correspondence *refresher* courses (see 'Training', above) to update their knowledge. The IPM is preparing a career break information pack.

Part time Very few opportunities, but recently some determined returners have convinced employers that part time works. Job-sharing (see p. xxix) is possible with more progressive employers.

Position of women There were proportionately far more women personnel managers in the past, when personnel work was largely concerned with welfare. As emphasis changed from 'dealing with people' to improving the efficient working of an organization, men took over top jobs and it became customary for women simply to look after women personnel, i.e. women only remained in top jobs, if at all, in stores and other places where most of the staff were female. Statistics are misleading because job titles give little indication of level of responsibility, but women are now known to be in the minority at head of department level. However, many do well as specialists in training and management development and in management of change. They also have good scope in small and medium-sized organizations where there is little personnel-function specialization. There are very few women with industrial relations experience, which is essential for most senior jobs in large organizations. Women who have got to the top of the profession say that the opportunities are there – it is the lack of role models, and women's lack of confidence to apply for senior posts, which is keeping numbers in senior jobs so low. Over half the qualified members but only a quarter of student IPM members are men.

Further information   Institute of Personnel Management, 35 Camp Road, London SW19 4UX

Related careers   CAREERS WORK – HEALTH AND SAFETY INSPECTORS – MANAGEMENT – RETAIL DISTRIBUTION

Pharmacy

Pharmacist

Entry qualifications

3 A-levels including chemistry and 2 chosen from a mathematical subject, physics and a biological science. The subject not offered at A-level should be offered at GCSE. In practice, an English GCSE (A–C) is essential. Some pharmacy schools will accept BTEC awards (see p. xxi) in place of A-levels.

The work

Pharmacists work in 3 distinct fields: *community*, *hospital* and *industry*. Students do not need to decide which branch of pharmacy they want to go into until after qualifying.

Community Pharmacists (usually called 'chemists' – a title pharmacists discourage)

Pharmacists dispense or supervise the dispensing of prescriptions. They act as a link between doctors and their patients, by explaining the effects and the correct use of medicines.

Most medicines are now available ready-made but pharmacists still make up the occasional prescription in the dispensary. They are also responsible for the safe and correct storage of a variety of medicines and some chemical substances. They are legally required to keep records such as the 'controlled drug' registers.

Pharmacists may also deal with the buying and selling of cosmetics, toiletries, etc., and the training of shop staff. In larger pharmacies, and particularly in chains of pharmacies, the pharmacist has the choice of remaining involved with the dispensing and sale of medicines, or of becoming more involved with the commercial side.

The role of pharmacists is changing. As more and more new drugs come on the market, both doctors and patients are making more use of pharmacists' thorough knowledge of the composition, action and interaction of new drugs. Many doctors ask pharmacists' advice – or at least their views – on the best way to use new drugs for particular conditions. Pharmacists have more time to keep up with pharmaceutical developments than doctors. Also, patients increasingly ask pharmacists' advice for minor ailments and their opinion on whether they should consult their doctor. Pharmacists are well qualified to know when medical advice must be sought and when a simple remedy (which may be cheaper than one on prescription) is all that the patient needs.

Because pharmacists are becoming more involved with community health care (they may, for example, visit residential homes) their professional association is now trying to change the traditional term 'chemist' to 'community pharmacist'.

Pharmacists are now more often managers of pharmacies or of dispensing departments than owners of their own business.

Abroad: Qualified pharmacists can practise and get jobs fairly easily in some countries of the Commonwealth; harmonization of qualifications within EC countries has been agreed.

Hospital Pharmacists

The work   Particularly suitable for those interested in the science of pharmacy. Hospital pharmacists dispense – and supervise the dispensing of – prescriptions for out-patients; they advise patients on the proper use of their medicines; they issue medicines for use within the hospital and they work closely with doctors and nurses to ensure that medicines are used safely, correctly and economically. They advise on doses and side-effects of drugs and are often involved in clinical trial work on new drugs. Most medicines used in hospital are ready-made, but some preparations are made up in the hospital pharmacy. They also have a teaching role – they assist with the training of student pharmacists and student pharmacy technicians; and they lecture to doctors and nurses.

Some hospitals offer a 24-hour pharmacy service, provided by pharmacists who live in when on duty.

Hospital pharmacists' role is also changing. Pharmacists may accompany consultants on ward rounds and may be consulted on the best drug to use in any particular case. Young doctors often ask pharmacists' advice and pharmacists may be asked to check patients' drug-charts to look for adverse reactions if patients take several different kinds of drugs; so there is more patient-contact than in the past.

Hospital pharmacists have a definite career structure. There is work which involves contact with people, and backroom work. Hospital pharmacists work in a community, with the opportunity of meeting people in similar jobs.

Industrial Pharmacists

The work They work in laboratories of pharmaceutical and related firms and on the production and development of new drugs and the improvement and quality control of existing drugs. As in other scientific work (see p. 435), pharmacists work in teams, often together with scientists from other disciplines. Some jobs involve mainly desk-work such as providing information to doctors and the preparation of data on new products for the Licensing Authority. Those with a bent for salesmanship can become representatives, visiting doctors in their surgeries and in hospital, providing information on their companies' products (and they may become marketing executives, an expanding area).

There is therefore scope for the quiet backroom type content with semi-routine work, for the team leader with a bent for pursuing new lines of thought and for those who want to go into general management, marketing and pharmaceutical sales.

Training 3-year degree course. The syllabus includes *pharmaceutical chemistry* – the origin and chemistry of drugs; *pharmaceutics* – the preparation of medicines; *pharmacology* – the action and uses of drugs and medicines in living systems; *pharmacy practice* – dispensing and counselling skills, pharmacy law and ethics.

After graduating, students must obtain 1 year's pre-registration experience in pharmacy, which must include at least 6 months in community or hospital practice, and pass the professional examination, before they are eligible to apply for registration as pharmaceutical chemists.

Personal attributes *For all pharmacists*: A strong scientific bent; meticulous accuracy; a strong sense of responsibility; a calm, logical mind; ability to concentrate; organizing ability.

For retail and industrial pharmacists: A flair for business; ability to deal with semi- and untrained staff; a liking for people.

For industrial pharmacists: An inquiring mind; ability to work as one of a team; infinite patience.

Late start No upper age limit for training or jobs, but there is no relaxation of entry requirements.

Career-break Should be no problem. Several schools of pharmacy run short *refresher* courses to help returners update their knowledge and dispensing skills. In some cases the Department of Health will even pay costs of refresher courses. Some large multiple pharmacy groups also offer re-training. There are also some distance-learning courses.

Part time   Good opportunities (although in hospital promotion prospects poorer than for full-timers). Job-sharing is becoming accepted in hospital and in community work.

Position of women   This is a very promising career for women; 42% of registered pharmacists are women and 65% of students starting university pharmacy degrees in 1991 were women. Proportionately more women work in hospitals than in community and in industry. But that is by choice: they are welcome as community pharmacy managers (the majority of clients are women) and also in sales and marketing and have equal promotion chances. The National Association of Women Pharmacists sends useful free pack, *Women in Pharmacy*, on request.

Further information   Royal Pharmaceutical Society of Great Britain, 1 Lambeth High Street, London SE1 7JN *or* 36 York Place, Edinburgh EH1 3HU

National Association of Women Pharmacists, c/o Office Manager, Royal Pharmaceutical Society, London address

---

Related careers   MEDICINE – *Pharmacy Technician (see below)* – SCIENCE: *Chemistry; Biochemistry . . .*

---

*

Pharmacy Technician

Entry qualifications   Depend on type of work and employer, see 'Training', below.

The work   This varies according to whether the job is in *retail (community)* pharmacy, *industry* or the *NHS*. In *retail*, technicians tend to spend most of their time on the selling side, although they also assist the pharmacist with dispensing (but work always under the supervision of qualified pharmacists who must check prescriptions, etc.). In *hospitals* and *industry*, technicians have more chance to do responsible and varied work. They assist with experiments, with interviewing patients, and they may liaise with other departments, etc. The role of the technician in the NHS and in industry is changing: as in other science-based jobs (see SCIENCE, p. 435) technicians now often do jobs which overlap with graduates', but there will always be a considerable difference between the project-leader type and level of work, and that of technicians who implement proven techniques. While using their judgement and expertise, they do not take ultimate responsibility or do original research.

There is only a limited demand for pharmacy technicians.

Training   *For NHS and most industry jobs*: BTEC/SCOTVEC National Certificate in Pharmaceutical Sciences. Entry requirements: 4 GCSEs (A–C) including a science, or BTEC First Certificate (see p. xxi) in Science. SCOTVEC requires 3 S grades including chemistry. The 2-year day-release National Certificate course is for people in relevant employment and subjects include broad, basic sciences, human physiology, action and uses of drugs, and quality control.

Community pharmacy technicians, for whom the BTEC course is unnecessarily academic and comprehensive, take *either* companies' own training scheme *or* the National Pharmaceutical Association's correspondence course. Most employers allow students up to 5 hours a week for study. There are no rigid entry requirements, but students without a GCSE in a biological science will find the course difficult. The NPA course, and company training schemes, prepare students for the Society of Apothecaries' Dispensing Technicians examination. This qualification does not carry much weight in the Health Service or in industry. Technicians who may want to switch from community to another type of employer should, therefore, *try* to get a job with day-release to take the BTEC course (for which they need higher entry qualifications).

Personal attributes   Meticulous accuracy; a scientific bent but not necessarily great academic ability.

Late start   Depends on local supply and demand position. Entrance requirements may be waived; but school-leavers may be given preference.

Career-break   Returners' opportunities depend on supply and demand position.

Part time   Fair opportunities.

Position of women   The vast majority of technicians are women.

Further information   Society of Apothecaries, Blackfriars Lane, London EC4V 6EJ
National Pharmaceutical Association, Mallinson House, 40–42 St Peter's Street, St Albans, Herts. AL1 3NP

BTEC, Central House, Upper Woburn Place, London WC1H 0HH

Related careers   RETAIL DISTRIBUTION – SCIENCE: *Science Technician*

Photography

Photographer

Entry qualifications
No definite educational requirements for photography as such, but see individual course requirements under 'Training', below.

Photography covers over 30 specializations, but many photographers combine several of these. London photographers tend to be more specialized than those in the provinces. Many freelance photographers take on any work which is offered, in order to earn a living. 'Bread and butter' jobs can help pay for more creative, but less well-paid, assignments.

Creative Photography

The work *General practice*
Approximately half of all photographers work in general photographic studios. The bulk of their work consists of portraiture, group photographs and commercial services. Portrait subjects include, increasingly, pets; some photographers specialize in children.

Photographers prefer their subjects to come to the studio to be photographed, because it is easier to arrange the lighting there. However, there is an increasing demand for portraits in the home, garden or workplace, especially in the case of children's portraits. The 'natural' portrait is much more popular today than the formal one. To produce not just a good likeness, but a characteristic portrait, photographers must have considerable understanding of, and insight into, human nature; they must be able to put sitters at ease so that their expression is natural.

Weddings and other group photographs (e.g. sports and social clubs) form another important part of the work. Wedding photography now offers more scope for 'creative' pictures in a less formal style than it used to. Commercial work is mainly for publicity purposes – for local companies, estate agencies, architects, etc. who do not have enough work to employ a staff photographer.

Opportunities are reasonable. One way in for the keen amat_ur is to help a busy studio with Saturday weddings.

Advertising

Very varied. Although advertising photographers are often given exact instructions about what to photograph and what effect to aim at, they are also expected to suggest their own ideas for new angles. Many advertisements are records of everyday life – whether it is of a child eating breakfast, or a woman getting out of a car – and involve both work with models, and persuading ordinary people to agree to be photographed.

Advertising photographs are taken either by the photographic departments of advertising agencies, by photographic studios (i.e. several photographers working as partners, sharing darkroom and office facilities, or salaried photographers and assistants working for an employer), or by freelance photographers. Most do some catalogue work; some studios specialize in *mail-order* photography (and may be owned by the mail-order company).

This is the best paid and hence a very competitive branch; success depends entirely on ability, efficiency and the right personality.

Fashion

Although advertising includes fashion photography, some photographers specialize in fashion. Most fashion photography is done by specialist studios or freelances who are commissioned by editors, fashion houses or advertising agencies; they usually work under the direction of a fashion expert.

This is the most sought-after branch and hence *very* difficult to enter.

Photo-journalism (feature photography), press and editorial photography

Photo-journalism is, essentially, telling a story in pictures, and therefore a journalistic sense is needed. *Feature photographers* may work with reporters as a team; they may be freelances, or work for studios. Only a tiny minority are on editorial staffs. It is very varied work, and leads to assignments at any time and in any place – photographing VIPs at home, or life in foreign parts, or schools at work – anything that makes a story. Hours are irregular.

There is more hard, hurried work than glamour in *press photography*, which consists almost entirely of single news pictures. Press photographers must be versatile in taking all kinds of subjects.

They must know what makes a good news picture; be able to write accurate captions; work well with reporters; be very quick and often work under difficult conditions. Hours are irregular.

Editorial photographers work mainly for magazines, nearly always as freelances. Work can be very varied, depending on the article or report which needs illustrating. It varies from shots of a TV star at home with children/pets to a travel feature; from contestants in a cookery competition to action shots of a parachute jump.

Prospects are fair, but competition is stiff. The market for photo-journalists is small. Most work as freelances and may specialize, e.g. in travel. For press photography there are always more candidates than jobs. Some possibilities for photographers in other branches to sell work to newspapers or press agencies. Editorial photography depends on building up good contacts and a reputation for reliability.

Industrial and Scientific Photography

The work   This is the most varied branch of photography and has the most openings. Clients include manufacturing companies, research organizations, government departments, higher education establishments, the police and HM Forces. Examples of the work: making photographic progress reports in laboratories; recording the various stages of manufacturing processes; photographing building sites. Industrial photographers also take pictures for house magazines, exhibition stands and instructional purposes. Most of these photographers are salaried employees; some work as freelances or for studios (see 'General practice', above, p. 376).

Medical Photography

The work   Most teaching hospitals and medical research institutions employ medical photographers, sometimes as part of a medical illustration team with medical artists and audio-visual technicians. They make still and cine records of work done in operating theatres and research laboratories, and of particular cases among patients. They also illustrate health care guides for patients and teaching material for student nurses and doctors. Medical photographers must not be squeamish.

Of all careers in photography this is the least hectic, least tough, most companionable and worst paid. There is some demand for medical photographers.

Training   *All photography*
Study can be part time, while working as a junior in a studio, or, increasingly, full time. The main courses recognized by the British Institute of Professional Photography are:

1. With, preferably, GCSEs (A–C) in English and maths: 2 years full time or 3 years part time for City and Guilds Photography scheme. Students are sometimes encouraged to study full time for the first year, then to work for a photographer for a year and return to college as either a full-time or a part-time student. The City and Guilds course will eventually be replaced by a new scheme leading to an NVQ (see p. xx).

2. With 4 GCSEs (A–C), normally including English language, maths and/or a science: a full-time 2-year course for BTEC National Diploma in Design (Photography), *or* 3-year part-time course for BTEC National Certificate (or SCOTVEC equivalent).

3. With 1 or 2 A-levels, *or* BTEC/SCOTVEC National award, *or*, in some cases, City and Guilds certificates: 2-year full-time course for BTEC/SCOTVEC Higher National award.

This can be followed by a further year leading to the BIPP's *Professional Qualifying Examination (PQE)*.

There are a few part-time courses leading to BTEC/SCOTVEC National Certificate and Higher National Certificate.

4. With 2 A-levels and 3 GCSEs (A–C), or for some courses an art and design Foundation Course: a degree in photography or photography, film and television or photographic science and technology. Several art and design degrees (see ART AND DESIGN, p. 55) have photography options.

Press photography
Either: 1-year pre-entry course organized by National Council for Training of Journalists (see JOURNALISM, p. 236): Entry requirements: 4 GCSEs (A–C) plus 1 A-level, including English.

Or the NCTJ's traineeship (see JOURNALISM, p. 236): Entry requirements: *either* 5 GCSEs (A–C) *or* 4 GCSEs (A–C) plus 1 A-level, *or* 2 GCSEs plus 2 A-levels, *or* recognized photography course, *or* 2 years' substantial photographic experience.

Medical photography
With GCSEs or preferably A-levels, or after general photography course, entry as trainee in a hospital medical photography department. Then *either* private study for BIPP Basic and Higher Medical Photography certificates *or* part time or block-release for the Primary Certificate of Institute of Medical and Biological Illustration, leading to the Diploma in Medical Illustration.

Photographic Technician

The work The processing and printing of films is an extremely important aspect of photography and one in which backroom types are happiest. They may work in 'photofinishing' companies which process film taken by amateurs (e.g. holiday snapshots) or in laboratories which service professional photographers. Most work nowadays is in colour and is increasingly automated. The work requires considerable concentration and technical knowledge, especially of the complex chemistry of colour film; without these skills a photographer's assignment worth hundreds or even thousands of pounds could be ruined. Technicians may take turns at all the jobs: processing, transparency-making, enlarging, printing and mounting, or may stick to one or two. Experienced technicians can learn more specialized skills, e.g. retouching or making duplicate transparencies.

There is a shortage of good technicians; there is a greater demand for technicians than for photographers. Photofinishing offers most openings to school-leavers.

Training Usually starting as a junior or trainee in a photographic laboratory, and studying by day-release and/or evening classes for City and Guilds examinations (see p. xxiii). Also, some in-service courses provided by laboratories and manufacturers of photographic materials.

Personal attributes *Needed by all photographers in varying degrees*: Visual imagination; eye for detail and composition; patience; perfect colour vision; artistic sensitivity; creativeness; trust in their own judgement (photographers, unlike other craftspeople and artists, do not usually know whether they have done a good job or not until it is too late); good powers of observation; ability to work quickly, under pressure, surrounded by crowds – in all kinds of unfavourable circumstances; ability to work well with others while keeping to their own individual style; originality; unusual inventiveness (for advertising and fashion photography); business sense (for arranging appointments, sending out bills etc.), as very few can afford secretaries; willingness to 'sell' themselves; a manner which encourages people to co-operate.

Press photographers: News sense; ability to remain calm and unmoved, however tragic or unpleasant the circumstances.

Medical photographers: A scientific bent; tactful and reassuring manner; total lack of squeamishness.

Technicians: A scientific bent; manual skill; an eye for detail; patience.

Late start   Press photography: upper age 24. A number of photographers have worked in other fields before taking up photography. Some colleges waive entry requirements for mature students. The main drawbacks are intense competition from college-leavers and poor salaries of trainee or assistant photographers.

Career-break   Depends on stage reached before the break and type of work done. Possibly difficult to return to best-paid and most competitive fields, but it should be possible to return to some kind of photography and/or to do some freelance work even while raising a family. The BIPP may offer reduced subscriptions for women on a maternity break.

Part time   Fair opportunities, especially as freelances.

Position of women   Only 9% of BIPP members are women, but about 40% of college applicants are women. There are now a fair number of well-known women photographers, although very few have reached the top in the advertising field. Women still have a little more difficulty than men getting in, especially to press photography.

Further information   British Institute of Professional Photography, Amwell End, Ware, Herts. SG12 9HN
City and Guilds of London Institute, 46 Britannia Street, London WC1X 9RG
BTEC, Central House, Upper Woburn Place, London WC1H 0HH
Institute of Medical and Biological Illustration (IMBI), 27 Craven Street, London WC2 5NX

Related careers   ART AND DESIGN – FASHION AND CLOTHING – JOURNALISM – TELEVISION, FILM AND RADIO

Physiotherapy

Entry qualifications

5 GCSEs (A–C) including an English and 2 science subjects and 2 A-levels or 3 Scottish Higher Grades in academic subjects, preferably including a biological science. Alternative qualifications such as BTEC may be acceptable; individual courses may also set their own entry requirements – many ask for 2 science A-levels.

The work

Physiotherapists use exercises and movement, electrotherapy – the use of heat, high frequency currents and ultrasonics – manipulation and massage to treat the injured, disabled, sick and convalescents of all ages for a large variety of conditions. They are responsible for assessing and analysing patients' conditions and for planning their treatment. Most patients are referred by doctors who give physiotherapists the information they need to devise suitable treatment, but physiotherapists in private practice also treat self-referred patients.

Patients too ill to be moved are treated in bed; others, such as post-operative patients, may have to be helped to walk properly again. Stroke patients are taught to make their healthy limbs or muscles do the work, as far as possible, of paralysed ones, and how to use paralysed limbs.

Some patients do exercises in water and the physiotherapist works with them in heated swimming pools.

Some patients are treated in groups, but most individually. In all cases, physiotherapists must use their judgement. They must know how far to coax a patient into doing an uncomfortable exercise, and must adapt treatment to suit each patient. They use tact and encouragement together with specialist knowledge when, for example, explaining to a patient why it is important that exercises are done regularly at home, or when persuading children to co-operate; or when allaying patients' fear of electrical treatment.

The work can be physically strenuous as it involves lifting and supporting patients, but physiotherapists learn to lift heavy weights without strain. ('Lifting' is one of the things they teach: patients needing treatment for strained backs are taught to lift correctly.)

The vast majority work in hospitals. After usually about 2

years' work, gaining all-round experience, they may specialize, for example in work with the elderly; in orthopaedic, chest or neurological conditions; and, increasingly, in work with mentally ill or handicapped children and/or adults. Work outside the hospital in the community is increasing. This may be giving treatments or preventive health education work; advising in factories, hospitals etc. on how to deal with carrying heavy weights etc. Physiotherapists also work with expectant mothers in clinics. There is also room for physiotherapists who want to do only preventive work: sports clubs employ physiotherapists (often part time) to keep their members fit, and to treat minor injuries; large industrial and commercial organizations employ physiotherapists to see that office desks are the right height for comfort, health and therefore efficiency; to show staff how to sit without strain; to teach sales assistants to relax while standing; to teach porters to carry without strain, and so on. Health farms and, sometimes, keep fit classes also employ physiotherapists.

There is a world shortage of physiotherapists, and of physiotherapy teachers and specialists, but promotion prospects vary. Increasingly experienced physiotherapists set up in private practice, treating patients either in their own treatment rooms or in patients' homes. But this needs good contacts with local doctors and capital to buy equipment and see them over the first few months. Qualifications are recognized in the EC and in many countries abroad, but in the USA and some other countries physiotherapists may have to take additional examinations.

Training

Until recently most courses led to a diploma. Now all but one lead to a degree. Courses are at polytechnics or universities working closely with hospitals. Both diploma and degree holders are eligible for membership of the Chartered Society of Physiotherapy, and for State Registration which is essential for work in the National Health Service, as well as for most other jobs.

The syllabus of both types of courses covers much the same ground (with the honours degree course covering subjects in more depth and breadth). The first year is always pre-clinical (theoretical); subjects studied include anatomy, physiology, physics, behavioural sciences, pathology and technical treatment skills. From the second year theory is combined with working with patients.

In job-getting terms there is no difference between diploma and degree courses. An important difference between diploma and degree students is that the latter have the opportunity to mix with students from other disciplines (also, as graduates, they are later eligible for the large numbers of jobs open to graduates of any discipline).

Post-graduate courses in specialties and in teaching are open equally to degree and diploma holders.

The North London School of Physiotherapy trains blind and partially sighted people to become fully qualified physiotherapists.

Personal attributes
Enough interest in science and medicine to keep up to date with new developments; a sympathetic yet objective approach to the sick and disabled; ability to work as one of a team and to take responsibility; good health.

Late start
Most colleges now welcome mature students up to about 35. Entry qualifications are not rigidly enforced; applicants' work and life experience are taken into account; but for those who do not have the usual qualifications, evidence of ability to cope with degree-level study (including science) is required. An Open University credit or similar post-school study is useful. (Applicants may be advised to take an A-level science or Access course, see p. xxxi, and reapply later.) See *Guidelines for Mature Entrants*, below.

Career-break
Returners are welcome; *refresher* training arranged by hospitals or health authorities; it is essential after a break of more than 2 or 3 years.

Part time
Excellent opportunities, increasingly even in senior jobs. Job-sharing is encouraged.

Position of women
The vast majority (86%) are women. Women head most schools of physiotherapy, which used not to be the case. A growing proportion of entrants are men.

Further information
Chartered Society of Physiotherapy, 14 Bedford Row, London WC1R 4ED (*Guidelines for Mature Entrants* available free)

Related careers
OCCUPATIONAL THERAPY – SPEECH AND LANGUAGE THERAPISTS – TEACHING

1993 NOTE: All courses now lead to a degree.

Police

Entry require- ments

Vary slightly from force to force. In general, candidates must be at least 18½ and have good health and eyesight. *All* entrants sit an initial recruitment test. There are also nationality restrictions. (In Scotland, age and height restrictions may still apply.) There is also graduate entry.

The work

The primary purpose of the police is to protect life and property and enforce law and order. Notions of how best to serve that purpose change from time to time as society becomes more complex and its demands change. The emphasis today is on community policing, responding to the demands of the public. Surveys have shown that the public want to see their police and expect them not just to solve crime, but to prevent it. On one level this is reflected in the traditional role of the PC on the beat, getting to know the community, keeping an eye out not only for trouble but for potential sources of trouble. But there are also broader initiatives through which the police forge links with and respond to the community. Community liaison officers, for example, might work with a range of community groups from schools to old age pensioners.

The 43 police forces in England and Wales and 8 in Scotland are run independently and their organization will vary. Within a force, too, different areas will have different policing needs. The problems of the inner city are not the same as those of a rural area or middle-class suburb. Whatever the situation, the police need to establish channels of communication so that problems can be evaluated and means established to reduce and prevent crime. A serious drugs problem might involve links with the local youth and community workers, while tackling car theft and vandalism in a town centre car park involves liaison with town planners and other local authority officers.

Within a typical large station you might find: the uniformed officers who patrol the community, some on foot, some in ordinary cars, some in fast cars; crime prevention officers, who, for example, advise individuals on safeguarding their homes and property; community liaison officers; juvenile liaison officers, who enforce the policy on dealing with juveniles; the custody officer, responsible for ensuring that arrests are lawful; CID, who work together with uniformed officers on the detection of crime. In the control room, staff are responsible for the operation of the computerized command and control systems, sending the right officers to the right jobs. Increased flexibility and improved shift working patterns enable the police to respond better to the community's needs, which are obviously not the same at 11 a.m., 11 p.m. and 4 a.m.

Other areas of specialization are *traffic*, with responsibilities ranging from planning and operating large-scale traffic control systems to dealing with major accidents, and *mounted*, *dog-handling* and *river* police, all very small. Within the CID, specializations can include fraud, special branch and serious crime. Police do not specialize permanently; promotion often involves a move to a new area of specialization and/or a new force.

Promotion is through the ranks. Everyone starts out as a PC, gaining experience in various areas of police work, from communicating with the public to dealing with a traffic accident, from sorting out a domestic disturbance to dealing with a riot. Even those on accelerated programmes (see 'Training', below) spend at least two years in this rank. Those promoted, after a qualifying exam and further assessment, to Sergeant take on a more supervisory role with responsibility for a team of PCs. An Inspector's time is divided between operational and managerial roles. Chief Inspectors, Superintendents, Chief Superintendents, and Assistant and Deputy Chief Constables take on progressively more managerial responsibility and become more involved in strategic and policy issues. The Chief Constable's responsibilities include financial planning and budgetary control, training and recruitment policy, and development of the force within the community. Some constables choose not to go in for promotion because they enjoy grass-roots uniformed police work and the contact with the public which it involves.

Training   1. *Probationer training* for all new recruits is provided partly at seven regional centres and partly in-force. (The Metropolitan Police runs its own recruit training at Hendon Training School.) Subjects covered include law, liaison with social services, courts and policing procedures, and crime prevention. Role-playing exercises are carried out to teach, for example, how to deal with traffic accidents, street fights, domestic disputes, hooliganism, self-awareness, interviewing skills (e.g. how to take statements from shocked suspects or rape victims). Courses also include some sociology, psychology and training in community relations to enable officers to understand the underlying causes of contemporary problems, such as racial tension and vandalism and how to deal with them. Self-defence and physical education also play an important part in training. *Further training* is organized by forces and includes a wide range of courses on specialist subjects, management development and local procedures.

2. Officers with ambition, ability and the potential to achieve high rank may be sent on the *Special Course* at the Police Staff College. At present this consists of a 3-month residential course followed by 1 or 2 years in-service 'developmental' training, then a further 4 months at the College. Promotion to at least Chief Inspector eventually is more or less guaranteed.

NOTE: It is proposed to replace the Special Course with a modular Accelerated Promotion Course which will be more closely integrated with career development in forces. It will consist of shorter residential modules at the College alternating with longer developmental periods spent in forces. The new course will be introduced gradually in 1992–3.

3. *The Accelerated Promotion Scheme* (formerly the Graduate Entry Scheme) is designed to seek out the most capable graduate entrants, give them a thorough grounding in the basics of police work and promote them quickly to the higher ranks. It includes attendance on the Special Course (Accelerated Promotion Course), usually after 3–4 years' service. Graduate entrants can reach Chief Inspector within 7 years of joining, and promotion prospects after that are very good. Some graduates are selected for APS on entry; others join the fast stream after standard entry.

Personal attributes   Maturity; honesty; courage, both physical and moral; sense of humour; flexibility; reliability; real desire to help people; resilience; an observant eye and a cool head; understanding of and sympathy with human weakness; ability to accept both authority and discipline and a high degree of personal responsibility; good health.

Late start   No upper age limit (within reason), except for the graduates' Accelerated Promotion Scheme, for which the limit is 30.

Career-break   Some forces now allow career-breaks and run 'keep in touch' schemes.

Part time   There are plans to pilot part-time schemes in several forces.

Position of women

Women account for 1 in 8 police officers, but a substantially higher proportion of new recruits. Theoretically women enter and compete for promotion on exactly the same terms as men, and the abolition of the minimum height and maximum age rules is of clear benefit to women. So are moves towards more flexible working arrangements. However, a recent collaborative exercise by the Metropolitan Police and the Equal Opportunities Commission uncovered a number of practices which are detrimental to women's prospects, though the report points out that such indirect discrimination is not always 'overt, intentional, or vindictive'. A key problem for women, the study found, has been the stereotyped deployment of officers in stations, with men allocated to, for example, driving, public order and outside duties, and women to communications, work with women, children and young people, and inside duties. While many women may enjoy and be good at some of these social work aspects of policing, the effect can be to limit their experience and thus their access to specialist branches like CID and their promotion prospects. There is no reason to suppose that these problems should have been unique to the Metropolitan Police. Women considering a police career should ensure that they are aware of some of the issues which have been identified – and test the awareness of various forces before making a choice. In 1989 the government issued guidelines on equal opportunities in the police service, the implementation of which is supposed to be regularly monitored.

Further information

Any police force recruiting department

Police Department, Room 624, Home Office, Queen Anne's Gate, London SW1H 9AT

Graduate Liaison Officer, Room 553, Home Office, Queen Anne's Gate, London SW1H 9AT

Police Division, Scottish Home and Health Department, St Andrew's House, St James Centre, Edinburgh EH1 3DE

Related careers

ENVIRONMENTAL HEALTH OFFICER – HEALTH AND SAFETY INSPECTORS – PRISON SERVICE – SOCIAL WORK

Politics

This is not a career in the usual sense; with some notable exceptions prospective politicians must usually first prove their ability in some other area before they stand any chance of attracting votes. Politics is included here simply because so many young people want to know how to get into it.

Entry qualifications

An interest in people's problems and in forming legislation. It helps to have been politically active, e.g. doing part-time voluntary work in constituency parties or serving on local councils (see 'Training', below).

Member of Parliament

The work

There are 650 MPs. The House of Commons sits in the afternoon and evening for an average of 35–40 weeks a year. Sessions often last late into the night. MPs spends much of their time listening to and, if they wish, participating in debate. Mornings are spent in committee (where much of the most important parliamentary work is done), answering constituents' letters, seeing visitors, researching. If at all possible, MPs spend a day (usually Fridays) a week or frequent weekends in their constituencies, holding 'surgeries', arranging and holding meetings. They must find time to attend social functions, open bazaars, be interviewed by the press, TV, radio, and attend weekend meetings.

Many MPs carry on with some kind of job which can be fitted in with their busy parliamentary schedule; many are journalists, some lawyers, trade union officials, business people. MPs have very little free time indeed. Though vacations are long, they have to attend to constituency matters all the year round.

Prospects are impossible to predict. There are usually far more candidates than constituency vacancies. When elected in a marginal constituency, an MP is very insecure; even in a safe seat the unexpected can happen at the next election; MPs may also fail to be re-adopted by their constituencies. Most MPs hope to hold ministerial office eventually, but only a small proportion ever do so. It depends partly on their ability and hard work, but also on luck – mainly whether their party is in office, and whether their views on particular issues are acceptable to the party leader.

Selection and training

Candidates must normally have been members of their party for at least 2 years. Many learn the business of politics – debating, dealing with constituents' problems, canvassing, collecting relevant facts, making speeches – by being (unpaid) local councillors. Prospective Labour candidates must be members of an appropriate trade union, if eligible. Some start their political life in their party administration or research departments. A background in student politics is also helpful.

The methods of selection are, with minor variations, basically the same for the 3 main parties. In general, candidates must first be approved by the central or regional party organization. All candidates submit their applications and credentials to the selecting constituency. If successful they are called to interview and, if approved, put on a shortlist of, normally, 3, from which the candidate is selected.

First-time candidates tend to be given hopeless seats to fight, so that they gain experience and prove that they have the enthusiasm needed to campaign successfully.

Personal attributes

Strong political faith and convictions; self-confidence; resilience; considerable public speaking skills; great physical stamina; willingness to work unsocial and long hours and to give politics priority over other interests/activities; thick skin to cope with personal attacks.

Late start

Politics is really a second career and maturity is an asset, but a *woman* candidate of 40 who competes for adoption with a man of 30 is probably at a disadvantage.

Position of women

Nothing like as many women as men put themselves forward as candidates, even though women are very active as voluntary party workers. Women MPs numbered between 20 and 30 for many years. However, in the 1987 election there were many more women candidates than ever before, and 41 were elected. In the 1992 election 59 women were elected and 2 women joined the Cabinet. The SDP has a constitutional provision requiring it to include women in short-lists and this move has resulted in the other parties looking to see how they could encourage more women to put themselves forward.

The long hours, the need to be absent from home and the lack of creche facilities make politics a difficult career for women with children and/or with husbands who are not equally committed to politics or at least to running home and family in their wives' absence. It is in any case harder for women to be adopted in the first place: a woman candidate has to be of better calibre than a man to stand equal chance of adoption. There is no indication that women candidates fare worse than men in parliamentary elections (which may of course be due to the fact that women candidates generally are of above-average ability). All parties genuinely want more women MPs – as long as they are exceptionally good. Once in Parliament, women are very successful in terms of holding office in relation to their numbers, and they are very active on committees.

Proportions of women in politics have not changed much over the years. Still only 9% of MPs are women; 22% of local councillors are women; 14% of European Parliament Members. The 300 Group (formed in 1980) is trying hard to persuade more women to enter politics (its name was chosen to indicate that at least 300 MPs ought to be women). The Group is supported by all parties and by prominent men and women in public and professional life who are not politicians but see advantages to be gained by everyone if more women were in decision-making positions. The Group runs seminars, provides speakers for schools, clubs and associations, and individual advice, also by letter, to anyone (also men) who wants to get into politics at any level, in any party.

Constituency Agent

The work
Agents are paid or unpaid constituency officials (not all constituencies have agents). They are responsible for efficient constituency organization, for checking electoral registers, for membership and fund-raising drives, for organizing meetings and MPs' visits and general local party matters. They normally have mainly voluntary helpers.

Selection and training
Potential full-time agents must have worked for the party for at least 2 years. Before being eligible for appointment, Labour Party workers take a correspondence course and an examination for the Diploma in Electoral Law and Party Organization. Tory workers have a minimum of 15 months' training working with a qualified agent while taking the examinations for the Associate Membership of the National Society of Conservative and Unionist Agents. Liberal Democrat Party training is less formal, but their agents also have to learn relevant law and organization during a residential crash course.

There are not many posts, but all parties welcome more applicants. Promotion can be either to a key constituency, or to a regional or central office post. Agents' work is grist to the mill for anyone wanting to become an MP eventually, but a certain period of time has to elapse before agents may stand as candidates in constituencies in which they were agents.

Personal attributes	Much as for MPs, plus considerable organizing ability, and ability to make volunteers work hard.
Late start	No problem.
Part time	Possibe in theory; in practice part-time agents tend to be volunteers.
Position of women	In the Liberal Democrat party, about half the agents are women, rather fewer in the Labour and Tory parties, but this is entirely due to the proportion applying. There is no discrimination in this (usually badly paid or voluntary) work.
Further information	Local or central party organizations The 300 Group, 36–7 Charterhouse Square, London EC1M 6EA

Related careers	DRAMA – ECONOMICS – JOURNALISM – LAW

NOTE: *On the fringes of politics*: *Researchers* in political parties and trades unions are recruited from graduates, mainly in relevant disciplines, such as economics, politics, sociology. All but the Conservative party have very small research staffs.

Trades union organizers are mainly recruited from unpaid union officials; but occasionally graduates are taken on.

Reporters and *transcribers* record the proceeding of both Houses of Parliament, as well as the various Standing Committees. Competition for traineeships is very stiff and preference is given to candidates with good shorthand speeds. Most, but by no means all, are graduates.

Printing

Entry qualifications

See 'Training', below

The work

Printing has been called the 'meeting place of art and science', but above all it is an industry. It uses a variety of technological processes to create a product of visual impact; it is always a form of communication. The product may be books, newspapers, theatre tickets, posters, packaging, stamps, circuit boards, manuals, record sleeves, credit cards, or reproductions of old masters. The printed materials include paper, card, plastic, metal, textiles. Some printing processes are centuries old, but printing technology has changed enormously in the last few years and continues to change. For example, traditional letterpress is much less common than it was, having been largely replaced by lithography, especially offset litho. Screenprinting is widely used for non-paper materials. Most text is produced by computer-aided typesetting, and special typesetting programmes can 'convert' different sorts of disks used by the growing number of writers using word processors so they are ready for typesetting. Electronic scanners are used in the production of both black and white and coloured illustrations; and holograms can be printed on credit and identity cards.

Office printing can now be done 'in house' by using computers with special graphics and typesetting programmes together with laser printers. For smallish quantities it is now almost as simple to print as to photocopy – *desk-top printing* is now a reality. Transmission of text and illustrations by satellite for printing in another continent is now common.

There are several main types of printing organizations: apart from *newspaper printing* (which is the most visible, but least typical kind), there are large and small *general commercial printers*, *specialist packaging printers*, high quality *book printers* and the High Street *instant print* shops. The *production manager* (or *planner*) decides with the client on the most advantageous and economic method of production for each item; this means weighing up factors such as efficient use of materials, speed, cost, quality, eventual use and appearance.

Apart from working in printing production, technicians and technologists also work in research and development of printed products and on new machinery, paper, inks.

In most areas of printing prospects are reasonable for trained people at all levels (except during recession) and there is a move to increase the number of graduates entering the industry. Newspapers now form a very small part of the industry, as changing technology has reduced the numbers of jobs.

Training

Craft: Trainees learn one of the following recognized skilled occupations: origination (preparation for print, which includes typesetting and platemaking); machine printing; print finishing (includes operating cutting and folding machines); bookbinding; carton manufacture; or manufacturing stationery. There is no set training period, but trainees work for the nationally recognized Certificate for Skilled Production Workers. Trainees under 18 also work for the City and Guilds Graphic Communications Certificate.

NVQs (see p. xx) are being introduced.

Technician: While increased technology in some parts of the industry has led to the loss of some jobs, in others it has meant greater demand for highly skilled workers. Entry qualifications for craft and technician training overlap and promotion from craft to technician level is encouraged. Most common routes are:

1. With good standard of education, but no specific examination passes: 2-year full-time course for London College of Printing Diploma in Graphic Communications.

· 2. With 4 relevant GCSEs 2-year full-time course for BTEC National Diploma in Printing (or SCOTVEC equivalent, see pp. xxi, xxii).

3. 3-year (2 for City and Guilds certificate holders) part-time course for BTEC/SCOTVEC National Certificate.

4. With A-level mathematics, physics or chemistry or BTEC/SCOTVEC National award: part-time or sandwich study (2–3 years) for BTEC/SCOTVEC Higher National award.

5. With 2 or 3 A-levels including at least 1 science (preferably chemistry): 4-year honours degree in Printing Technology or 3-year B.Sc. in Printing and Photographic Technology.

6. Art-school training (see ART AND DESIGN, p. 55), with specialization in *Graphic Design* or *Typography*, can also lead to printing jobs.

Instant print and small printing units (for example, in-house) train mainly on the job, but may give day-release for the City and Guilds certificate in Reprographic Techniques. Most recruit experienced people.

Personal attributes Depends on type and level of work, but generally some visual imagination; interest in machinery; practicality; some dexterity.
For managerial jobs: organizing ability; ability to work under pressure; being a self-starter.

Late start About 20% are late entrants. Credit given for prior learning (see APL, p. xxxiii) and shorter training possible.

Career-break Return to work is likely to be difficult because of technological changes and shortage of jobs. A few retraining courses exist.

Part time Few opportunities in printing: possibly as freelance typographer.

Position of women Once one of the most traditional industries, printing now employs increasing numbers of women in skilled occupations; the number of women becoming skilled has doubled since 1984. Currently 23% of those employed on production are women. However, employers would like to see many more women coming into the industry, particularly as the flexibility of the new training scheme and changes brought about by new technology have improved women's prospects. At the technology level there is no valid reason whatever why women should not succeed; they have no difficulty getting on to degree or HND courses. Art-school-trained women are doing well in typography and production/design. There are now national agreements between employers and printing unions containing provisions for women's rights and equal opportunities.

Further information British Printing Industries Federation, 11 Bedford Row, London WC1R 4DX
Institute of Printing, 8 Lonsdale Gardens, Tunbridge Wells, Kent TN1 1NU

Related careers ART AND DESIGN – ENGINEERING – PUBLISHING – SCIENCE

Prison Service

Entry qualifications

Minimum age 20. Minimum height for men, 5ft 6in. (167·7 cm) (in Scotland, 5ft 7in. (170 cm)); for women, 5ft 3in. (160 cm). No specific academic requirements. Selection is by aptitude test and interview. Also graduate entry to Accelerated Promotion Scheme.

The work

The work of a prison officer goes far beyond locking and unlocking cells and patrolling corridors. One of the responsibilities of the prison service as set out by the Prison Board is 'to provide for prisoners as full a life as possible, to care for physical and mental health, advise and help with personal problems, work, education and training, physical exercise and recreation, and an opportunity to practise their religion'. What this means in practice is maintaining a community where prisoners eat, sleep, work, train, learn, play and so on. Prison officers are concerned with care as well as control, well-being as well as security. They are also concerned at senior levels with the management of staff and resources.

Prison officers supervise inmates in the activities mentioned above, escort them to and from courts and hospitals, accompany visitors to the visiting room, receive new prisoners. Whatever tasks they are involved in, they must try to work through co-operation with prisoners. An important part of their role is rehabilitation, helping to prepare prisoners to return to the outside community as law-abiding citizens. This involves helping them to develop skills, confidence and self-respect. Partly this is done through activities, but also through building up a relationship. Prison officers can be involved in motivating prisoners to improve their education, whether it be learning to read or studying for an Open University degree; providing a shoulder to cry on when someone gets a 'Dear John' letter; reasoning with someone threatening violence. They must recognize and know how to deal with prisoners who are having to cope with feelings of anger, anxiety or shame, with those who are troublesome and those who are extremely worried or depressed. It may be important to know how physically to restrain a violent and abusive inmate, but it is equally important to understand how such situations arise and how to re-establish communication and co-operation.

Many prisons are old and over-crowded; prisoners' frustrations can lead to tensions that sometimes explode in violence. Most prisoners reoffend. Many are unappreciative, some abusive. Prison work can be frustrating, even depressing, but it offers more scope for personal initiative, individual responsibility and the development of interpersonal skills than is commonly realized. Like social work, it can be very rewarding and is a vital service to the community.

The demands and routines of prison work will vary according to the type and size of institution. These include remand centres, which are mainly for young offenders and those awaiting trial; prisons where high-security prisoners are dispersed; open prisons for those requiring a lesser degree of security; Young Offender Institutions, which place a great emphasis on teaching inmates useful skills; local prisons, which are often multi-purpose with separate sections for different categories of prisoner. Prison officers must be prepared to serve in any kind of institution, in any part of the country, though preferences are taken into account whenever possible. 'Opposite-sex posting' (i.e. female officers in men's prisons and vice versa) is possible, though voluntary, but most officers will for the time being continue to serve in same-sex postings.

All prison officers begin 'on the landings' (the equivalent to 'on the beat' for police constables) as part of a team. On promotion, for which it is often necessary to move, officers take on increased responsibility – for a team, a wing, a function or service (e.g. inmate activities, staff training), ultimately a whole establishment. There is an accelerated promotion scheme (see 'Training', below) for experienced officers and graduate entrants with top management potential. There are also opportunities, after basic experience, to specialize as, for example, a hospital officer, a physical education officer or a trades officer (teaching a skill or trade).

Training

1. After 2 weeks' pre-training experience (paid) at a prison near their homes, recruits attend a 9-week course at a Prison Service College. Through instruction and role-play they learn practical skills such as body and cell searching, radio skills, physical restraint techniques, prison routines and court duties, as well as communication skills, professional conduct and teamwork. This is followed by a posting as a basic grade officer, under the supervision of a more senior officer, for the remaining 9-month probationary period.

2. The *Accelerated Promotion Scheme* begins with a 1-week induction course at the Prison Service College followed by a 2-week attachment at a prison near the trainee's home. They then move on to a 9-week course at the Officer Training College where

they learn practical and social skills and discuss issues such as race relations and leadership. A series of graded postings, starting with 2 years 'on the landings' as a Grade 8 officer, together with further management training, are designed for rapid promotion to senior positions (a governor of an establishment would normally be at least a Grade 3).

Personal attributes

Leadership; a sense of right and wrong, without being censorious; a genuine desire to help people in trouble and the ability to understand and sympathize with people's failings without necessarily condoning them; the ability to find the right approach to all types of people; immense patience with people at their most unbearable; interests entirely outside prison work to help keep a sense of proportion; a friendly, naturally happy disposition; sense of humour.

Late start

Entry up to 49½ (normally under 42 in Scotland).

Career-break

No problem (if there is a local prison).

Part time

Virtually none.

Position of women

As there are relatively few women's prisons, the development of 'opposite-sex posting' should open up more promotion prospects for women.

Further information

Home Office, Freepost, London SW1E 5BX

Scotland: Scottish Prison Service Recruitment, Calton House, 5 Redheughs Rigg, Edinburgh EH12 9HW

Related careers

PERSONNEL/HUMAN RESOURCES MANAGEMENT – POLICE – SOCIAL WORK

Psychology

Entry qualifications

2 or 3 A-levels, plus maths and English at GCSE (A–C) if not at A-level. Requirements may vary according to whether the course leads to a B.Sc. or BA; a few courses require A-level sciences or maths.

The work

Psychology is the scientific study of human and animal mental processes, behaviour and experience. Psychologists study individuals' development and how individuals interact with one another. They use observation and experimental and other methods (e.g. surveys, intelligence tests) to assess and measure all kinds of cognitive (mental) processes, attitudes and emotions. (They must not be confused with psychiatrists, who are *medically qualified* specialists who give treatment to the mentally sick and disturbed.) Psychologists must understand the difference between 'normal' and 'abnormal' behaviour and use their knowledge and skills to solve (or alleviate) a wide range of problems. Although psychology is a science, it is a young science and still offers few cut-and-dried answers to the questions it poses.

The British Psychological Society recently set up a Register of Chartered Psychologists; people wanting to be Chartered Psychologists and who are eligible (i.e. have taken training approved by the BPS) can belong to one of the following specialist psychology divisions: clinical; educational and child; occupational; criminological and legal. Psychologists involved wholly in teaching and/ or research can also belong.

There is a small but steady demand for psychologists (see 'Training', below, for need for post-graduate training for specializations). Although only a small proportion of psychology graduates become practising psychologists, a psychology degree is a useful preparation for employee relations and other personnel functions, for social work, and generally for jobs in organizations where 'dealing with people' is important.

Clinical Psychology

Clinical psychologists help people to come to terms with various kinds of problems. Therapeutic work is carried out with children and adults, in individual counselling sessions and in groups in hospitals (see 'Psychotherapy', p. 405); in therapeutic communities (see 'Psychiatric Nurse', p. 332); at day-centres (see SOCIAL WORK, p. 480); and in family groups. The wide range of problems treated includes physical and mental handicap; phobias (including children's inability to face school); neurological and obsessional disorders; brain damage; sexual difficulties; reading and writing difficulties.

Clinical psychologists organize, co-ordinate and co-operate in vocational guidance for the handicapped, rehabilitation, training and retraining programmes for patients with physical handicaps or learning difficulties. They set up systems for job analysis, assess and evaluate the work potential and the progress of patients. The broad types of therapeutic work undertaken are behaviour therapy, psychotherapy and counselling (see PSYCHO-THERAPY AND COUNSELLING, p. 405), rehabilitation and training. Most clinical psychologists work in hospitals, some in child guidance clinics. They work in close collaboration with neurologists, psychiatrists and other specialists. There is a new specialization, health psychology, which involves working in general hospitals with patients undergoing stressful procedures, e.g. surgery or AIDS screening.

Some clinical psychologists spend most of their time on individual case work, while others are more involved in teaching other professional groups, e.g. nurses. The great majority work in the Health Service, but there are opportunities also in private practice and as consultants, e.g. to private clinics.

Educational and Child Psychology

Educational psychologists advise teachers, parents, doctors and social workers on children's and young people's adjustment and learning problems. They are responsible for making formal recommendations (Records or Statements of Special Educational Needs) for the education of children with learning difficulties. Assessment involves sessions with the 'problem' child as well as, usually, its parents and teachers, and a thorough study of the individual's background and environment. Various established techniques, such as ability tests and 'personality schedules' are used. Treatment (called 'intervention') may include individual counselling sessions with child and/or parents and advice to parents and teachers on the 'management' of the problem. Apart from helping individuals when problems have arisen, educational psychologists work with 'systems' or organizations: whole schools, families, groups of teachers or social workers, school classes, youth clubs.

Running in-service courses for different groups is an important part of their work. They are employed by local education authorities and work in school/county psychological services and child guidance clinics. They have considerable autonomy right from the start.

Occupational Psychology

Occupational psychologists deal with people as workers. They advise on how people can both enjoy and be efficient in their work by giving vocational guidance to both children and adults. They set up selection procedures for employers and develop training schemes; they help in the organizing of work itself by devising new methods of doing jobs; and they advise on the design of tools and machines so that they are easy to use ('ergonomics'). They also research into and advise on psychological implications of organizational structures and proposed changes, aiming at improving both job satisfaction and the organization's effectiveness.

Occupational psychologists have developed techniques for collecting information from people about what they like doing and what they are good at, as well as what they find difficult and unpleasant. They match this information against that collected by detailed studies of the actual work involved in the jobs concerned. They are very much involved with 'managing change' of working practices in offices and manufacturing, e.g. when new technologies are introduced (see MANAGEMENT, p. 274).

Other occupational/social psychology specializations are concerned with retirement: pre-retirement counselling and training and generally looking into problems connected with the growing proportion of retired people in the community; with mid-career changes necessitated by changes in job opportunities; with problems connected with women's changing career patterns and aspirations; with stress management.

The main employer of occupational psychologists is the Civil Service, mainly in the Home Office (Prison Department), Ministry of Defence and Department of Employment. Opportunities are increasing in industry and commerce, especially in personnel/human resources departments.

Criminological and Legal Psychology

Psychologists are employed in the Prison Department or by Regional Health Authorities to work both with prisoners and with those who look after them. They work in all kinds of prisons, including institutions for mentally abnormal offenders and in regional secure units. They may run training courses for prison officers and therapy sessions for prisoners and their families, as well as carrying out case work with individuals and preparing psychological reports to help judges decide on sentencing.

Other Opportunities

Some psychologists teach in further and higher education; a few are involved solely in research, but most research is carried out by lecturers as part of their work. For research it is usually necessary to take a Ph.D. in a specialist subject. Research may be commissioned by government departments, the police, industrial organizations, research institutes. Research fields vary widely; as well as the mainstream areas – clinical, educational, etc. – there are other specializations; for example:

Social psychology
Concerned with the attitudes and interaction of individuals and groups: what causes whom to behave in what manner; what effect do events, media presentation, individuals' and groups' actions have on other individuals and other groups within the community? They investigate, for example, the causes of, and possible cures for, football hooliganism; or the voting behaviour of individuals and groups. They look into the effect of television on different groups in the community, and they may look into the problems of integration of ethnic minorities into the community, and into the attitudes to, and effect of, class differences among adults and among children.

Neuropsychology or physiological psychology
Concerned with trying to discover the relationship between biological processes and behaviour. For example, how do drugs affect memory and personality? What area of the brain controls speech?

Experimental psychology
Research psychologists who specialize in experimental psychology work in most psychological disciplines to help solve a wide range of problems. They use special experimental methods that have been developed to study human and animal behaviour. They may be given a particular problem to solve: they would then plan the experiment, collect and analyse information, and draw conclusions to enable someone to make decisions. In addition experimental psychologists are always trying to extend the scope of psychology

by carrying out experiments to find out more about people and how the human brain works. They may work with animals. Experimental psychologists usually work in teams with other scientists, mainly in government and university research, often on short-term contracts.

Training   3-year (sometimes 4-year) degree course. The composition of the courses varies: some lead to BA, some to B.Sc. Topics usually covered include: experimental study of such cognitive processes as thinking, memorizing, learning and perceiving; biological basis of behaviour; animal behaviour; development of children; social relationships and their effects on personality; mental disorders; abnormal development; applications of psychology to the study of society, industry and education; techniques of testing and experiment; counselling skills. There is considerable emphasis on statistics and, increasingly, computers are used.

There is no need to decide which branch of psychology to specialize in till after the course. Post-graduate courses are essential:

Clinical psychologists take either a 2–3 year Master's degree course or a 3-year in-service Diploma training course.

Educational psychologists must first take a postgraduate certificate in education (PGCE) and gain at least 2 years' teaching experience (not a requirement in Scotland); they then take a Master's degree course normally lasting 1 year (2 in Scotland). Southampton University offers a combined PGCE and Master's course. Alternatively, qualified teachers can become educational psychologists by taking a psychology degree followed by the specialist Master's degree.

Occupational psychologists may take a degree in their specialization and go straight into a job, or take a more general psychology degree followed by a 2-year full- or part-time Master's degree or Diploma course. (This may be done after several years' work experience, except in the case of ergonomists, who need specialized training immediately after graduating.)

Criminological and *legal psychologists*: some go straight into the Prison Department after a first degree, others first train in a specialization such as clinical or occupational psychology, or take a (new) Master's degree in applied criminological psychology.

Personal attributes   A detached interest in individuals' and communities' behaviour rather than personal involvement; an interest in scientific method; the ability to work well on one's own, but also to work as part of a team and to co-operate with people from different backgrounds; patience; numeracy. For most jobs, especially in education, a warm and easy manner.

Late start   No problem for qualified late entrants to degree courses; maturity and relevant work experience can be an asset. Owing to competition, and the length of training, mature applicants without normal entry requirements may have difficulty finding a place. Proof of an adequate knowledge of maths at least is essential. An Open University degree in psychology may be the best bet.

Career-break   Depends on competition from newly qualified people (particularly for academic posts). Most psychologists manage to work full or part time while raising a family.

Part time   Some opportunities; and job-sharing exists.

Position of women   Over 50% of British Psychological Society members and approximately 75% of psychology undergraduates are women. Women have no more difficulties in getting jobs than men.

Further information   The Hon. General Secretary, The British Psychological Society, St Andrew's House, 48 Princess Road, Leicester LE1 7DR

Related careers   PERSONNEL/HUMAN RESOURCES MANAGEMENT – NURSING: *Psychiatric N.* – SOCIAL WORK – SOCIOLOGY – TEACHING

Psychotherapy and Counselling

Psychotherapy and counselling are included in this guide because of the interest in and confusion about these occupational areas. The explanations given do not fit into the format used in the rest of the guide.

Psychotherapy

The term *psychotherapy* has two meanings: it is an umbrella term for various forms of treatment of patients with emotional or psychological problems through dialogue with a skilled practitioner. Its aim is to help patients change the way they manage their problems. In this context, psychotherapy covers several methods which differ in intensity and underlying philosophy. The term *psychotherapy* is also used to define an occupation, but one without agreed entry requirements, qualifications or career structure (except for *child psychotherapy*, see below). It is *never* a career option for school or college leavers but invariably a 'second' or 'late start' career for people with relevant qualifications, work and life experience.

Persons with a range of qualifications (or none) practise psychotherapy:

1. *Psychiatrists*: They are medically qualified doctors (see MEDICINE, p. 299) who have subsequently qualified for membership of the Royal College of Psychiatrists. Psychotherapy is only one of a range of treatments they use (drug therapy is another). Most psychiatrists work in the NHS, some work partly or entirely in private practice.

2. *Psychoanalysts*: They normally have a medical degree or comparable qualification (some are also qualified psychiatrists); they have undergone lengthy personal analysis and then taken an approximately 4-year (part-time but very time-consuming) training in Jungian, Freudian or similar psychoanalytical method. Although not a registrable profession, it is generally agreed that in this country only people who have qualified for membership of the Society of Analytical Psychology or the British Psychoanalytical Society are entitled to call themselves psychoanalysts or analysts. *Very* few analysts work in the NHS; most are in private

practice with, possibly, some sessional work for voluntary advice centres.

Psychiatrists who practise psychotherapy, analysts and those clinical psychologists (see 'Clinical Psychology', p. 399) who do some psychotherapeutical work are all sometimes called psychotherapists – which is the reason for the confusion surrounding the term.

3. *Psychotherapists*: At present anyone, whatever their qualification (if any), may use the title 'psychotherapist', a fact which rigorously trained psychotherapists very much regret. But there are too many psychotherapy organizations and philosophies for them to agree on a common training or accreditation scheme (although a Standing Conference on Psychotherapy is currently looking into accreditation of training because of the need for mutual recognition of qualifications in post-1992 Europe). The mainstream organizations, however, base their treatment on psychoanalytical methods. Their professional bodies accept for training only candidates with relevant degree or comparable qualifications and experience; require them to undergo lengthy personal analysis or therapy and then train them much as do psychoanalytical organizations. Courses last a minimum of 3 years part time. In fact psychoanalysts' and psychotherapists' training and work shade into each other (though psychotherapists more often than analysts also treat people in groups – families, couples, fellow-sufferers such as addicts, phobics, etc.).

There are virtually no jobs for *psychotherapists* in the NHS (except for *child psychotherapists*, see below); they rely on private patients and – very few – voluntary organizations' clinic sessions.

Because there is a growing demand for help from people with problems, a vast number of self-styled psychotherapy organizations have sprung up over the last few years. Some are experimenting with new methods of 'alternative psychotherapy' in good faith, but the methods and the credentials of some organizations are dubious. Before signing up for training (often expensive, and/or too short and not rigorous enough to be of any value) potential psychotherapists must thoroughly check organizations' claims.

The above refers to what is called 'adult psychotherapy'. *Child psychotherapy* is a recognized profession (though a very small one). Child psychotherapists treat children for psychological disturbances of behaviour, thinking and feeling. The work is focused on the relationship established between the psychotherapist and the child, through which insight into the problem is gained. Children, adolescents and parents are seen, usually individually, sometimes in groups. Child psychotherapists work in child guidance clinics, young people's advice and treatment clinics, and in private practice. To be accepted for training with one of the four accredited organizations, candidates must have a psychology degree or comparable qualification and experience of work with normal children. Training, a mixture of theory and practice and including extensive observation of young children, takes 4–5 years. There is a growing demand for child psychotherapists in the National Health Service, especially outside London, e.g. in the Midlands, the South-West and Scotland. Full-time and sessional work is available.

Counselling

This is a much over-used and therefore vague term. It is best defined as the skill of helping normal people, through discussion, to decide how best to cope in specific situations. By listening attentively and without passing judgement the counsellor gives clients the opportunity to explore, discover and clarify how and why they feel as they do; they (the clients, not the counsellors) may then be able to make choices and decisions about their situation which they were incapable of making before.

While psychotherapists may try to change patients' personalities, or at least their attitudes, sometimes over a long period, counsellors tend to deal with immediate, often practical problems, e.g. redundancy or alcohol addiction. Yet psychotherapists' and counsellors' work may overlap, as they use similar methods. Psychotherapists more often deal with severe psychological disorders, especially if working in hospitals, but in private practice both may see patients with similar problems.

Counsellors work in many settings – schools, colleges, GP practices, clinics, counselling centres, staff welfare departments, as well as in private practice. There are counselling services that specialize in particular groups, e.g. young people or ethnic minorities, or in specific problems, such as drug addiction or AIDS. The number of full-time posts is increasing, but there are more trained counsellors than there are jobs. Many combine part-time work with social work, welfare rights work and administration.

There are a few full-time training courses for teachers, social workers and others working in the field. There are many more part-time courses leading to a certificate or diploma. These mostly expect people to have a degree or a professional qualification. For people hoping to do counselling as volunteers and not looking for a vocational qualification there are part-time introductory courses, courses in counselling skills, and specialist courses in bereavement, cancer, child abuse, etc., counselling.

Although there is no legal requirement for counsellors to be properly trained, people interested in the work are advised to contact the British Association for Counselling for advice (address below).

Further information

British Association of Psychotherapists, 121 Hendon Lane, London N3 3PR

London Centre for Psychotherapy, 19 Fitzjohns Avenue, London NW3 5JY

Tavistock Clinic, Belsize Lane, London NW3 5BA

Association of Child Psychotherapists, Burgh House, New End, London NW3 1LT

British Association for Counselling, 37A Sheep Street, Rugby, Warwickshire CV21 3BX

The British Psycho-analytical Society, Mansfield House, 63 New Cavendish Street, London W1M 7RD

The Society of Analytical Psychology, 1 Daleham Gardens, London NW3 5BY

1993 NOTE: A voluntary register of psychotherapy organizations has now been set up as a precursor to statutory registration. Prospective psychotherapy students are strongly advised to ask any organization they intend to train with whether satisfactory completion of training leads to eligibility for admission to the register.

Public Relations

Entry qualifications

95% of new entrants to the Institute of Public Relations are now graduates.

The work

Public relations officers (now often called 'public affairs' officers or executives) advise on ways to develop relationships with sections of the public whose support and goodwill is essential for the success of an enterprise. It is often part of the marketing process. Public relations is more than a publicity tool – it is an essential part of successful management in an increasingly competitive environment. Public relations officers provide factual stories about clients or their product to newspapers, magazines and television, thus keeping the product or the service in the news and creating a 'favourable climate or image'. They answer journalists' questions about their client's product, views or services, and may take journalists to see the client's product or service. They arrange receptions, exhibitions and other projects to 'put over' a client or promote a cause, and give talks to interested groups – schools, women's organizations, etc. They deal with inquiries (and also complaints) from the public.

Public relations officers work either in public relations consultancies (several partners each with their own accounts and a shared office and staff), or in public relations departments of advertising agencies, or in separate press and public relations departments of individual organizations – from stores to charities and government departments. This last type of work is increasing. (The title here may be Information Officer.) More and more organizations employ PR specialists to advise on and put into action ways of communicating the organization's functions and activities to relevant groups. Today, local authorities, trade unions, employers' federations, charities and professional organizations such as the British Medical Association employ public relations or information officers. An important area now is financial PR; some sporting and TV personalities also use public relations officers to help further their careers.

Entry into PR is highly competitive; far more people want to do this sort of work than there are opportunities, although really talented people are sought after. There has been a growth in the number of small, independent consultancies in the last few years.

Training

Competition for jobs is such that it is now very difficult to get into PR by working oneself up from a junior position, such as secretary. The following are all possible entry routes:

1. A sideways move with a degree and work experience in a relevant discipline or industry (e.g. engineering or science). Traditionally many PR people moved sideways from journalism and this is still a possible route.

2. As a trainee with a PR firm or in a PR department with a non-specialist degree. Useful degree subjects are business studies, economics, languages, communication, but employers will take promising people from any discipline.

3. With one of the new (very few) degree or post-graduate degree courses in PR.

Training is usually on the job with part-time study for the examinations set by CAM (Communication, Advertising and Marketing Education Foundation). Study can be full time, part time, by correspondence or private. There is now a 2-week intensive introductory course for trainees run by the Public Relations Consultants Association.

Entry requirements for CAM Certificate: 3 GCSEs and 2 A-levels (including English language); or BTEC or SCOTVEC Higher National award (see pp. xxi, xxii); or London Chamber of Commerce and Industry Third Group Diploma in Marketing or Public Relations; or 1 year in full-time employment in the communication business and 5 GCSEs (A–C) or equivalent, including English language.

The Certificate covers marketing; advertising; public relations; media; sales promotion and direct marketing; research and behavioural studies; communication practice; business and economic environment. It normally takes about 2 years' study, usually at evening classes, occasionally by day-release or distance-learning.

Certificate-holders can go on to take the CAM Diploma and specialize in a specific aspect of the communication business.

Partial exemption may be granted on a subject-for-subject basis from the Certificate stage to holders of related awards, e.g. certain BTEC awards (see p. xxi), or degrees in Business Studies or Communication Studies.

NOTE: from 1992 people wanting to join the Institute of Public Relations must hold the CAM Diploma in PR.

Personal attributes

Ability to get on exceptionally well with people of all kinds, whether hard-hitting journalists or less confident members of the public; enterprise and initiative; good news sense; sense of salesmanship; a calm temperament; analytical powers; ability to write and speak well and persuasively; imagination; tact; ability to keep polite under provocation and/or pressure.

Late start

Only advisable for people with special expertise/experience. Approximately a quarter of CAM students are aged 30+.

Career-break

No problem for women who were firmly established before the break. Many work from home, perhaps having only one client for a year or so, then gradually increasing their workload.

Part time

Fair opportunities, especially working from home or for small, non-commercial (i.e. usually voluntary) organizations.

Position of women

Women do very well in PR; 60% of practitioners are women and they hold some of the top jobs. But, while women account executives outnumber men 2 to 1, only one-third of directors are women. Starting as a secretary used to be a useful way in, but this is no longer advisable.

Further information

Institute of Public Relations, The Old Trading House, 15 Northburgh Street, London EC1V 0PR

CAM Education Foundation, Abford House, 15 Wilton Road, London SW1V INJ

Public Relations Consultants Association, 1st Floor, Willow House, Willow Place, London SW1P 1JH

Scottish Public Relations Consultants Association, Campsie House, 17 Park Circus Place, Glasgow G3 6AH

Related careers

ADVERTISING – FASHION AND CLOTHING – CIVIL SERVICE: *Information Officer* – JOURNALISM – MARKETING AND SELLING – SECRETARIAL AND CLERICAL WORK

Publishing

Entry qualifications

In practice a degree or comparable qualification and/or specialist knowledge/experience; art school training for some aspects of production. In specialist publishing, such as educational, scientific or art, editorial assistants normally have a degree in a relevant subject. In general publishing, the degree subject is normally irrelevant.

The work

Book publishing is an industry (one of the smallest in the country), not a profession. It requires business acumen and an interest in *marketing* (see p. 294) as much as creativity and literary flair. The function of publishing has been described as extending the author's idea into a finished book and getting it into readers' hands – in other words publishing involves the organization of production, marketing and distribution as much as (and in many cases more than) literary effort.

Publishing houses vary greatly in size, from large ones with overseas branches and several 'imprints', producing hundreds of titles a year, to those run on a shoe-string with a handful of employees and a small yearly output. The trend is towards 'conglomerates' with large houses buying up smaller ones, but keeping their identities fairly separate. Some publishers specialize in educational, scientific, art books, or paperbacks. Desk-top publishing, in which one person can edit, design, lay out and typeset copy on a personal computer, is increasingly used to produce magazines, booklets, etc. for organizations' own use and also for books which have very limited sales.

Publishers select and commission manuscripts, design the appearance of the books, have them printed and bound, and promote and sell the finished copies, but the internal organization of 'houses' varies. The process is usually divided into 3 main departments (apart from the usual commercial ones such as accounts). The division of work is more rigid in some houses than others; in small houses everybody may have to do anything that needs doing (a good way of learning).

The 3 main publishing departments or 'functions' are:

Editorial

Main duties are selecting and commissioning manuscripts; getting outside specialist readers' opinions; preparing typescripts (or disks) for the printer; liaising with authors, possibly suggesting changes; dealing with contracts, copyright, subsidiary rights (these may be separate departments). Editorial departments also deal with new editions of existing books.

An editorial director or chief editor (titles and responsibilities involved vary greatly in different houses) is usually in charge. Individual editors may each be responsible for books on a special subject, or for a range of subjects. They may initiate a book on a special subject, select the author and deal with the project right through. The number of books one editor deals with at any particular moment varies according to type of firm and type of book, and so does the amount of contact the editor has with the author.

Editorial assistants or 'copy-editors' deal with 'copy preparation'; checking facts and references, spelling, punctuation, and possibly doing some rewriting, proof-reading and correcting. Again, responsibilities and duties vary greatly.

Production

The production department receives the edited manuscript (or disk) and decides, in consultation with the editor, on the appearance of the book, on the shape, typeface, paper, illustrations, etc.; and it deals with printers, paper merchants, binders, etc. Production staff must understand something of costing and marketing and of the various types of illustration and typography. But above all they must understand the new printing and production technologies which are drastically changing established production methods. Technical and textbook publishers may employ their own illustrators, but most artwork is commissioned from freelances and outside studios.

Marketing (includes Sales)

In some ways the most important publishing activity, marketing or 'promotion' is responsible for planning, researching for and preparing review lists, sales campaigns, writing 'blurbs', and for the representatives who call on bookshops, schools, libraries, etc. to give information on forthcoming books and to collect orders. In addition, marketing people in many houses now often initiate projects, based on feed-back gained by the sales representatives when they visit bookshops. On the basis of a 'feasibility study' –

mainly researching the market and costing – it is decided whether to go ahead and, jointly with editorial, get the book commissioned, or whether to abandon the idea. This is a good department in which to learn how publishing works.

There are many more posts in non-editorial than editorial departments.

Other kinds of publishing

Book Packaging

A small, but growing development outside traditional publishing is book 'packaging'. Packagers are *marketing* people. They find an idea which is likely to be profitable, commission an author and artwork and produce a dummy-copy of the book. They then offer it to publishers, usually in several countries. 'Packages' are usually highly illustrated; a 'bank' of pictures is printed separately and then overprinted with the translated text with the minimum production expense. Promotion, selling and distribution are done by the publishers who buy the packaged book.

Packagers' overheads are lower than traditional publishers' and it is therefore easier to start up as a packager than as a publisher. But good contacts, publishing experience and ideas are essential.

Electronic publishing

This has much more in common with *information technology* (see p. 142) and with information work (see p. 229) than with 'literary' publishing – at least for the present. It provides databases or 'on-line information services' and is in fact sometimes called 'database publishing'. It produces such services as Prestel and Ceefax and individual organizations' and professions' computerized research bases/libraries. *Computer specialists*, *information scientists* and *librarians*, as well as experts in the appropriate field (i.e. anyone from accountant to zoologist), might work in electronic publishing, but it is at present a very small job area.

Magazine publishing

This is quite different from book publishing. *Feature editors* need to be able to write original copy; *editorial assistants* must be able to 'sub' (reword, shorten, etc.) other people's writing. They all need to know something about layout and production, as well as to understand the business side of magazines (including advertising). Some editors started as secretaries, others as freelance or staff journalists (see JOURNALISM, p. 236). Most magazines have a 'publisher' responsible for the business side: the usual background is in advertisement selling, but some publishers are ex-editorial staff.

*

There are very limited opportunities on the editorial side of publishing, which attracts the most applicants, especially in general publishing; more scope in technical, scientific, educational. First editorial job is usually as editorial assistant ('assistant editor' may mean the same thing). Opportunities are slightly better in other departments, especially in sales and marketing and production.

Training Nothing specific; degree in any subject advisable. See 'The work', above.

There are a small number of pre-entry courses, some of which are for graduates, and there are 2 degree courses in publishing. There are training courses in book production and design, and some art and design courses include book design and production (see ART AND DESIGN, p. 55). Pre-entry training is recommended especially for these departments. A few firms run their own training schemes, but most rely on short in-service courses provided by, for example, the Book House Training Centre.

Previous bookselling or other sales experience is useful.

In the past many editors came up the secretarial ladder; this still occasionally happens, but there are far more graduate secretaries working for publishers and hoping to make the break than there are editorial jobs.

Personal attributes Creative ability; interest in social and economic as well as literary trends; ability to see books as a marketable commodity; some writing ability; critical judgement; common sense; resilience; good business sense; willingness to take responsibility and make decisions; ability to get on well with a wide variety of types of people.

Late start Difficult because of the competition from young graduates, but possible in technical and educational publishing for people with technical/scientific background.

Career-break	It should be possible (and it is advisable) not to give up completely, even temporarily.
Part time	Experienced proof-readers, copy-editors, editors may be able to do sporadic freelance work.
Position of women	*Book publishing*: There are far more male than female editorial directors and publishing house board members, but a handful of women have now reached the top. Many women have done well in 'senior middle' jobs, especially in marketing, also as children's and educational book editors. Among copy-editors and editorial assistants women greatly outnumber men. Many women go into publishing as secretaries hoping to become editors; some do, although far more remain in junior editorial jobs. *Magazines*: Women have little problem reaching senior positions.
Further information	Publishers' Association, 19 Bedford Square, London WC1B 3HJ Scottish Publishers' Association, 137 Dundee Street, Edinburgh EH11 1BG Individual publishing houses
Related careers	ART AND DESIGN – BOOKSELLING – INFORMATION WORK – JOURNALISM – PRINTING

Purchasing and Supply

Entry qualifications

For professional qualification: 2 A-levels, 3 GCSEs (A–C), including English language and a quantitative subject; or BTEC/ SCOTVEC National award. Also *graduate* entry. No specific qualifications for mature entrants with relevant work experience (see also 'Late start') but see 'Training', below.

The work

Purchasing and supply is a broad-based function covering the whole business of 'managing materials'. Purchasing and supply officers work in private industry – manufacturing, retailing, distribution – and in the public sector. They are responsible for ensuring regular supplies of materials, tools, components, equipment – anything other departments in the organization may require to function efficiently. This can range from raw materials, office equipment and machine components to medical supplies and disposable towels for hospitals and audio-visual equipment for schools. They work closely with the 'consumers' – for example production managers, medical staff, education officers – who specify exactly what is required. They then search out the most suitable supplies and negotiate terms and delivery dates. They may have to decide, at times, when to agree to pay more than budgeted for in order to get supplies which are in short supply; this would probably be decided jointly with production manager and accountant. They are a vital link between the various departments which need supplies, and the suppliers – their success depends largely on maintaining good relationships with suppliers and on negotiating advantageous contracts.

Some purchasing and supply staff travel all over the world and should be able to speak foreign languages; they must be aware of technological, social, economic and political developments which might affect price levels and availability of supplies.

They can switch from one type of buying to another: commodity knowledge is not vital as specialists give purchasing officers detailed specifications; for example, machine tools or electronic equipment can be bought by a purchasing officer who previously bought raw materials for a food manufacturer. However, a technical background (engineering for example) is useful in many jobs.

Once supplies have been bought, purchasing managers, in

charge of departments, are responsible for stores management and inventory control. Deciding how much stock to hold and how far to let it run down before re-ordering can greatly improve (or reduce) an organization's efficiency and/or profitability. They need to know how far forward supplies can be bought in, weighing up price rises and possible future shortage against possible spoilage and storage costs. They must be conversant with contract and negotiation procedures in this country and abroad.

Purchasing and supply staff must also ensure that the goods ordered actually reach the right department as quickly as possible, so that production/the service is not held up. They may also be responsible for the disposal of waste materials.

Opportunities have increased as medium-sized organizations where buying used not to be a specialist function now often employ purchasing specialists; purchasing is one of the functions which can lead into *general management* (see p. 272).

Training

The Institute of Purchasing and Supply's Professional Examinations Scheme is in 2 parts – the Foundation and the Professional stages. Courses are mainly part time (day or evening) or correspondence, but there are a few full-time courses. Most Foundation stage students qualify via BTEC/SCOTVEC courses (see pp. xxi, xxii). Holders of business studies degrees and BTEC Higher awards are eligible for exemption from the Foundation examination. (There is a common syllabus for 3 Foundation subjects with the *Institute of Marketing* and the *Institute of Chartered Secretaries and Administrators* and for 1 subject with the *Institute of Personnel Management.*) The syllabus includes business procedures, buying methods, economics. For the Professional stage examination which is set by the IPS students may specialize in marketing; structure, planning and control of public sector work; commercial procedures and techniques; materials and production planning and control. All take general purchasing subjects.

There is a 'second-tier' qualification, for school-leavers with 4 GCSEs (A–C) and mature entrants with at least 2 years' experience in purchasing and/or stores work. Study, by day-release, leads to the Certificates of the Association of Supervisors and in Purchasing and Supply. These Certificates qualify holders to enter the IPS Foundation examination training.

Personal attributes

Numeracy; organizing ability; practical approach to problem-solving; considerable business acumen and some gambling spirit; ability to establish friendly relationships quickly; judgement to gauge the right approach to individual suppliers; awareness of technological changes and their implications for purchasing.

Late start   Good opportunities. 30% of IPS students are over 30 (but not all are new entrants). People with previous work experience are welcome. Graduates and others with relevant experience are granted substantial exemption from IPS exams, and GCSE requirements for those over 26 are waived. IPS courses are open to those not yet in relevant employment.

Career-break   Should not present problems, but keeping in touch with world economic conditions and commercial law is vital. Short Institute courses can be used as *refreshers*. Temporarily retired women pay reduced Institute subscriptions.

Part time   Good opportunities. Job-sharing is possible.

Position of women   At the moment there are very few women indeed, but there is no logical reason for this – women have long been established as buyers for retail stores, which is similar work. Women represent only 4% of qualified IPS membership, but 16% of student membership. Women who have gone into purchasing are doing well – a number are in engineering purchasing. The main reason why there are so few women in this field is because they don't know about it or imagine they need specialist knowledge.

Further information   Institute of Purchasing and Supply, Easton House, Easton on the Hill, Stamford, Lincs. PE9 3NZ

Related careers   COMMODITY MARKETS – MANAGEMENT – RETAIL DISTRIBUTION – SHIPBROKING . . . EXPORTING – SURVEYING: *Quantity Surveyor*

Radiography

Entry qualifications

Degree course requirements. 1 or even 2 sciences, at either level, may be required; BTEC/SCOTVEC awards may be accepted in lieu. It is essential to check with individual courses.

See 'Late start', below, for mature students' entry.

The work

Radiography has 2 branches: *diagnostic* and *therapeutic*.

Diagnostic Radiographers

They work with medically qualified radiologists and take X-ray photographs to assist doctors in diagnosing diseases and injuries. They also operate ultrasound 'imaging' and other high-tech equipment. Doctors normally give only brief instructions: the radiographer is expected to know exactly how to use the X-ray apparatus, to understand the theory behind imaging, and how best to radiograph the relevant part of the patient's body. Radiographers, therefore, need a considerable knowledge of anatomy, physiology and physics.

Normally they work in X-ray departments, but occasionally they take X-rays during an operation, when it is particularly important to take quick, accurate pictures. They also work on the wards using mobile equipment.

Diagnostic radiographers normally see each patient only once or twice and will meet a large number of people on a rather fleeting basis.

Therapeutic Radiographers

They give treatment, usually for malignant disease, by means of, for example, ionizing radiations under the direction of a medically qualified radiologist. The latest advances of science are used to help cure disease, and the work involves using new and powerful substances and methods.

Treatment is given to seriously ill and worried patients, possibly over a long period of time. Therapeutic radiographers' duties are therefore twofold: first the actual treatment, and second establishing a friendly relationship with patients to give them confidence.

The effect of radiotherapy is permanent: once given, it cannot be undone; therapeutic radiographers' responsibility is heavy. They need extensive knowledge of human anatomy and physiology and of radiation physics. Because of constant changes, therapeutic radiographers frequently take short updating courses.

Exposure to X-rays can be dangerous, but X-ray departments are equipped with safeguards which ensure that operators are not harmed in any way. Protective clothing is worn and operators are never within reach of the actual X-ray beams. The controls are operated from outside the treatment rooms so that the radiographer is never exposed to radiation; treatment rooms are lined with material which the X-rays cannot penetrate.

There is a shortage of radiographers, especially therapy specialists. The majority work in hospital. There are a few posts with specialists in private practice; these may be better paid, but the work is lonelier than in hospital. There are also some openings with mobile X-ray units. For both these jobs previous hospital experience is necessary. Radiographers can earn their living in most countries of the world, provided they speak the appropriate language. The College of Radiographers runs specialist post-Diploma courses in the newer techniques of medical ultra-sound, radio-nuclide and magnetic resonance imaging, which are concerned with diagnostic and treatment methods for various diseases.

Training

This is changing. The Diploma of the College of Radiographers is being phased out and replaced by a 3- or 4-year degree at university or polytechnic. But about 60% of the course is spent on 'clinical education'. This covers all those competencies which can be learnt only in the hospital environment.

Qualified radiographers can go on to take the College's Higher Diploma, Management Diploma or Teachers' Diploma.

Personal attributes

A strong scientific bent; a steady hand and a sharp observant eye; a genuine liking for people and a desire to help the sick; a cheerful, confident manner; patience; calmness; firmness; ability to take responsibility and to work well with others; good health.

Late start

Upper age limit for training is 50. Mature applicants are increasing. Entry requirements are relaxed. See also 'Access courses', p. xxxi.

Career-break

No problem, but retraining essential – extent depends on length of break (changes in procedures and equipment are drastic and rapid). *Refresher* courses are available.

Part time   No part-time training. At the moment part-time job opportunities are still limited, but there is no reason why work should not be organized on a part-time or job-sharing basis (see p. xxix), as it is in similar professions.

Position of women   Until recently about 90% of radiographers were women; there are still only around 12% men. Men have a disproportionate share of top jobs.

Further information   College of Radiographers, 14 Upper Wimpole Street, London W1M 8BN

Related careers   PHOTOGRAPHY – SCIENCE: *Scientist*; *Science Technician*

Religious Ministry:
Main Religions in Britain

Entry qualifications
Normally 3 GCSEs (A–C) and 2 A-levels. Provisions for those who lack these qualifications, especially mature entrants (see 'Training', below), but must show evidence of ability to undertake academic study.

The work
Ordained ministry: Many duties are common to all denominations and include: holding services, preaching, conducting marriages and funerals. Less formal but equally important is 'pastoral care', such as visiting the sick, comforting the bereaved and helping individuals with their religious and personal problems. Like family doctors, priests receive many confidences and try to help their parishioners come to terms with their weaknesses and circumstances. They must also find time for solitary prayer and study. Rabbis in addition play a large social and sometimes political role in their communities.

Traditionally, ministers have been appointed to one congregation. Nowadays many work in team ministries, particularly in inner cities, within which individuals may specialize, e.g. in youth and community work. Many serve as hospital chaplains and some are responsible for the administration of schools. Others become chaplains in colleges, the Forces, industry, prisons.

The Roman Catholic and Anglican churches have *religious communities*; in some members are committed to a life of prayer and contemplation, in others they help to run schools, hospitals or residential homes.

Lay ministry: Many churches train and employ lay workers, both stipendiary and non-stipendiary (paid and unpaid). They assist ordained ministers in services and pastoral work and may also be responsible for particular branches of the ministry, such as teaching or counselling.

Training
All candidates have to go through a rigorous selection process to assess their 'calling' and suitability. Training is followed by a probationary period and does not lead automatically to ordination.

Church of England (Ordained Ministry)

Graduates under 30: With theology degree, 2 years full time at theological college; with degree in any other subject, 3 years and may include theology degree.

Non-graduates under 30: 3 years full time at theological college, sometimes preceded by 2-year part-time training scheme (the Aston Training Scheme).

Graduates and non-graduates over 30: 2 years full time or a 3-year part-time course.

Stipendiary lay ministry: As for ordained ministry, except for the Church Army, which runs its own 3-year course for trainee officers.

Roman Catholic Church

6-year full-time course of academic study combined with pastoral training. May include theology degree. Course length may be reduced for graduates and mature entrants.

In the Church of England and the Roman Catholic church *religious orders* carry out their own training.

Church of Scotland (Ordained Ministry)

Under 23: With Scottish university entrance qualifications *either* 4-year degree course in divinity plus 2 years' further study *or* degree in any subject followed by 3-year course leading to degree in theology.

Aged 23–40: 5-year training incorporating degree or licentiateship depending on academic qualifications.

Aged 40+: 2- or 3-year course for graduates, 3 years for non-graduates.

Lay ministry
Aged 18–23: With minimum 3 Ordinary and 2 Higher Grades (SCE), 2-year foundation course plus specialist training.

Over 23: Individual training programme.

Methodist Church

Ordained ministry
Under 30: With minimum 4 GCSEs (A–C) and Accredited Local Preacher qualifications, 3-year full-time course. Those with university entrance requirements may take degree.

Aged 30+: 2-year full-time or (if married) 3-year part-time course.

Ministers in local appointments
As above, but MLAs are normally aged over 30 and remain in their own occupation, carying out ordained ministry in their leisure time.

Lay ministry
Qualifications for *deacons* (men and women) similar to ordained ministry, but applicants need not be accredited local preachers.
   Lay workers – no minimum qualifications.

Baptist Union

Minimum qualifications: Cambridge Diploma/Certificate in Religious Studies and at least 3 GCSEs (A–C), including English. Details of entrance requirements for various courses of ministerial training from Baptist Union affiliated colleges.

United Reformed Church

Graduates under 30: 4-year full-time course.
   Graduates over 30: 3-year full-time course.
   Non-graduates aged 21–30: With good academic qualifications, 4-year full-time course which may include degree.
   Non-graduates over 30: 3- or 4-year full-time course.
   Aged 55: Shortened training available.

Jewish Faith

Orthodox
Either 3–4-year post-A-level course at Talmudical college, followed by rabbinical training, *or* (more commonly) 3-year degree course at Jews College followed by 3–5 years' rabbinical training.
   Other training courses: B.Ed. in Jewish Studies for intending teachers; Cantorial course for conductors of services.

Progressive (Reform and Liberal)
A degree in any subject followed by 5-year full-time course for rabbinical ordination at Leo Baeck college.
   A 4-term part-time teacher training course exists for those wishing to teach at religion school. There is a 1-year part-time course for kindergarten teachers.

Personal attributes Total sense of vocation and conviction that no other kind of work will give personal satisfaction. Desire to share faith with others; good intellect; ability to relate to all members of the church however well or poorly educated. Good health and stamina, mental and physical; open-mindedness and genuine desire to serve others without discrimination; willingness to be continually 'available'; self-discipline and self-sufficiency – although at the centre of the church ministers are always slightly 'set apart'. Emotional stability. Ability to work on own and as part of a team. Administrative skills.

Late start All denominations make provision for mature entrants (see 'Training', above).

Part time Some opportunities.

Position of women The status of women varies widely between denominations. The Roman Catholic and Orthodox Jewish faiths exclude women from ordination. The Progressive Jews ordained the first woman rabbi in 1976. The Church of England now ordains women as deacons, but not as priests, but there is a strong pro-ordination movement within the church. The Church of Scotland and the Free Churches have traditionally allowed women to be ordained, although some still feel that they have to be intellectually better qualified than men to receive the same acceptance by the congregations. Many women seek ordination later in life.

Further information *Church of England*: Advisory Board of Ministry, Church House, Great Smith Street, London SW1P 3NZ

Roman Catholic: Fr Michael Johnston, Vocations Director, Allen Hall, 28 Beaufort Street, London SW3 5AA

Church of Scotland: Church of Scotland Department of Education, 121 George Street, Edinburgh EH2 4YN

Methodist Church: The Candidates Secretary (Division of Ministries), 25 Marylebone Road, London NW1 5JR

Baptist Union: The Ministry Office, Baptist Union of GB, P.O. Box 44, Baptist House, 129 Broadway, Didcot, Oxon. OX11 8RT

United Reformed: The General Secretary, The United Reformed Church, 86 Tavistock Place, London WC1H 9RT

Jewish Religion: Orthodox: London Board of Jewish Religious Education, Woburn House, Upper Woburn Place, London WC1H 0EP; *Progressive*: Leo Baeck College, The Manor House, 80 East End Road, London N3 2SY

**Related
careers**   SOCIAL WORK – TEACHING

Retail Distribution

Entry qualifications   Nothing rigid; all educational levels, but considerable and growing *graduate* entry (see 'Training', p. 431).

The work   Retailing is one of the largest industries in the country and one of the few career areas where getting on does not necessarily depend on passing examinations.

The industry is constantly adapting to changing life styles and new technologies. For example, shopping hours are lengthening in many shops because more women go out to work and cannot shop during the traditional working day; computerization and 'rationalization' (less personal service; more part-timers for peak-hour work; fewer leisure periods for full-timers) has led to a reduced total workforce but, proportionately, more management opportunities.

No industry-wide career-structure exists. Titles, and responsibilities attached to titles, vary from one company to another, and so do recruiting and promotion procedures. The main types of 'retail outlet' are *hyper- and supermarkets*; *department stores*; *chain stores*; *co-operatives*; *independents*. The categories are not as clear-cut as they used to be. Supermarkets and multiples have 'diversified', i.e. sell more than one type of merchandise; some department stores give houseroom to specialist shops – for example, photographic equipment; some independents have joined together for bulk-buying purposes; out-of-town hypermarkets, like traditional department stores but looking like giant supermarkets, offer 'one-stop shopping' – everything under one roof, but at rock-bottom prices, cash-and-carry only and the emphasis on fast turnover rather than on attracting regular customers as in department stores; some out-of-town centres combine retailing, entertainment and leisure facilities.

A growing type of retailing is '*franchising*': a group of outlets – at present mainly food and fashion – is centrally controlled and sells to 'franchisees' the right to use its name and image, and to sell its centrally bought merchandise. Within certain guidelines, franchisees then run their own shows. *Mail order* is a growth area, mainly but not only, in fashion and household goods. It divides into two kinds: the traditional 'catalogue companies' which sell through part-time agents; and the more up-market 'direct mail', 'direct response' or 'direct marketing' companies. These sell through advertising in the press and/or through catalogues sent to likely customers. This is a sophisticated, high-risk business, more a marketing operation (see MARKETING AND SELLING, p. 294) than traditional retailing. Success depends on selecting a few sure-fire items for sale, the right advertising media and the right people to send catalogues to.

In traditional retailing, buying and selling organization varies from one company to another. For chain stores, hyper- and supermarkets buying is usually done centrally: identical merchandise is allocated to stores which are also given display and promotion guidelines. In department store groups, buying is also done centrally, but individual outlets still have their own distinctive character and do not necessarily all sell the same merchandise; they target specific customer groups, e.g. sophisticated in Knightsbridge, London, down to earth in small northern town.

Many people go into retailing because they want to be buyers, but nearly everybody starts, and most stay, in selling and store management. Specialists, such as *fashion graduates* (see p. 209), *food technologists* (see p. 459) and *electronics experts* (see ENGINEERING, p. 183) are sometimes recruited as trainee-buyers.

Starting on the shopfloor – the 'sharp end' – is essential to learn about customer-relations and trading principles. There are varying hierarchies from sales assistant, shelf-filler, checkout operator, warehouse clerk, via section, department, specialist (transport, staff, distribution, etc.), deputy to store manager, and after that perhaps area manager. Job titles, and job functions, vary from one retail concern to another. At any time after the first few weeks or months (it varies), individuals may be offered a buying or other management traineeship. Speed, and likelihood of promotion, varies from company to company, and according to age and ability.

Store managers co-ordinate the various retailing functions: stock control; security; staff deployment; maximizing profit per square metre of premises; dealing with customers' complaints and queries; liaising with head office, etc. Supermarket and department store work differ greatly; supermarkets are much more hectic places with emphasis on fast-moving goods; managers must make their own, quick decisions, whether they are dealing with a staff, delivery or customer problem. In department stores, managers have such 'support services' as personnel, distribution and complaints departments on the premises and there is more emphasis on personal service. Hypermarkets and chain stores again make different demands. Ideally, prospective retailers should decide which type of atmosphere and work is right for them. In practice, there may not be much job choice, but one can switch from one type of retailing to another: basic retail expertise is a 'transferable skill', although it is easier to switch from supermarkets to chain stores than the other way around.

Staff management and training may have its own hierarchy, parallel with store management, and it may be a step on the store management ladder (see PERSONNEL . . . MANAGEMENT, p. 365).

Buying is very different from its image of spending other people's money on items one likes. It consists of selecting from suppliers' existing lines and also, jointly with manufacturers, developing new ideas, and adapting existing lines and prototypes bought or seen abroad or at a competitor's at home. Developing 'own brand' lines is expanding. Buyers work closely with marketing and production specialists and with store managers. Buying policies are based on methodical analysis and interpretation of past sales figures, on economic forecasts, on demographic trends (the present ageing population and the reduction in the number of late-teenagers have important implications for buyers); on lifestyle changes (the trend for more casual than formal clothing; the fashion to drink out of mugs rather than cups; the increase in foreign travel and resultant interest in foreign food and drinks, etc.). Buying is a commercial activity and requires communication and negotiating expertise and number-crunching, as well as flair for guessing next year's preferences. It involves complex decision-making. For example, a buyer may find a very efficient and inexpensive spindryer with an unsatisfactory after-sales service. 'Does good performance and competitive pricing outweigh less-than-perfect after-sales service?' is the kind of decision buyers have to take – and be able to justify later, if customers complain.

Merchandising can be a step above buying. But, confusingly, the term means different things in different companies. It is usually a senior head office job with responsibility for setting selling targets and for ensuring that the right range of merchandise is available at the right time in the right place. But it can also describe people employed by wholesalers or manufacturers who ensure that their employer's products are adequately displayed in retail outlets. And it can describe persons who, working closely with display specialists, are responsible for the display of goods in a store.

Commodity knowledge – expertise in one type of merchandise – used to be all-important; then managerial and commercial expertise determined promotion and buyers easily switched from buying one type of merchandise to another. Now, commodity knowledge, at least in 'high-tech' consumer goods, textiles and food, again seems to matter more; but it varies from company to company.

Head office jobs include *general management* (see MANAGE-MENT, p. 272); *marketing* (see p. 294); *design* (see p. 55); *food and other technologies* (see p. 459); *personnel* (see p. 365); *store planning*; and *retail analysis*: what type of shop/shopping centre is likely to be profitable in the year 2000 – where, and why? How will European competition affect our stores once we are in the integrated European market, and what can we do to remain competitive once European retailers set up their shops in this country in greater numbers? As retailing is becoming ever more sophisticated and professionalized, new specialisms emerge, or traditional jobs are being fined down into separate functions. For example, 'transport management' may be divided into 'vehicle and depot management' and 'operations management' with responsibility for the movement of goods from supplier or port of entry to depot or store. These planning/forecasting jobs involve a mixture of crystal-ball gazing, statistics, technological and economic forecasting, psychology and sociology (and are very much a growth area for graduates from any discipline).

Retailing also offers good opportunities to systems analysts and other computer experts (see COMPUTING, p. 142) as more companies adopt computerized 'point of sale' stock-control and 'electronic fund transfer' systems and prepare for computer-based armchair shopping.

Fashion retailing is a specialized job for people with experience of fashion (see p. 209) as well as of general retailing. Boutiques are a growth area but also (together with builders) a 'high risk' business.

A knowledge of a foreign (European) language, together with an understanding of the relevant country's culture, will be a great advantage for retailers from now on.

Food retailing has been called 'recession-proof'. It did well even during the 1990s recession.

Training   Training is patchy and haphazard. There is no industry-wide qualification system. Some employers – including most but not all of the well-known chain and department stores – train staff systematically, using outside courses and/or their own in-house training schemes, to produce 'retail professionals' with transferable skills (i.e. trainees who can later use their training in all kinds of retail companies). Other companies give little career training, but teach people to perform specific jobs in their organization. While promotion up the retail hierarchy does not depend on having paper qualifications, the importance of expertise is growing enormously, as technological and management systems are becoming ever more sophisticated; such expertise can, in practice, only be acquired by systematic training. However, there are many ways of training. It is generally agreed that the best way of becoming a retail professional is to learn on the job, with additional off-the-job training. That means finding a job with day-release or similar facilities for taking courses.

The alternatives to a job-with-training are (a) taking any job in retailing and learning by experience and possibly taking a relevant distance-learning course or evening classes or (b) to take a pre-entry course (see below).

Individual companies' training schemes vary greatly. All retailers stress the flexibility of their training schemes and emphasize that no specific qualification or training scheme automatically leads to any specific point on the retail job ladder. Individual patterns vary not only from one company to another, but also from one year to another according to company plans for expansion or consolidation/contraction or change of emphasis, and also according to current views on which type of training (length, outside or in-house course, theory-and-practice mix) is the most cost-effective. Candidates are strongly advised to look at several companies' recruitment literature, to read the small print and, at interviews, ask questions about promotion prospects, etc.

For 16–17-year-olds with fewer than 4 GCSEs there are 1- as well as 2-year training schemes. These may and may not include day-release for BTEC First Certificate (or SCOTVEC equivalent) (see pp. xxi, xxii). In some companies trainees are now assessed for the work-based NVQ/SVQ (see p. xx) levels I and II, which lead to the Retail Certificate (Certificate in Retail Distribution in Scotland). Levels III and IV are being developed and may lead to supervisor and departmental manager level jobs. The qualifications are awarded jointly by the Retail Training Council and the NCVQ/SCOTVEC (see pp. xx, xxii).

Candidates with at least 4 GCSEs or the Scottish equivalent, including usually maths and a subject proving competence in English, *or* with a few years' retail experience as untrained shop assistant, are eligible for 2-year training schemes with day-release for the BTEC National Certificate in Distribution (or Scottish equivalent); or they may get comparable in-house training.

GCSE entrants with only good Saturday/holiday retail experience may be eligible for 2-year training schemes planned for A-level entrants, which may lead to the BTEC Higher National Certificate or Scottish equivalent. Equally, A-level entrants with some work experience may be eligible for graduate training schemes. Graduates are expected to be ready for their first junior management job in 9–15 months; A-level entrants and others with good hands-on experience are expected to take 15–24 months. Degree subject is immaterial, and Higher National Diplomas (BTEC or Scottish equivalent) are usually considered as of equal value to degrees. Training patterns are as varied, and as confusing, as this.

Once NVQs/SVQs have become generally accepted, retail training and qualifications may become streamlined. However, company training policies and candidates' personal qualities are likely to remain more important than paper qualifications. A 16-year-old without any GCSEs but with potential (including the potential to make supervisors notice it!) can catch up with a 21-year-old graduate entrant: when the graduate starts training, the school-leaver has had 5 years' practical experience and is eligible for management training along with the graduate.

For persons who prefer full-time pre-entry training (and those who cannot get a job with training) there are BTEC full-time diplomas in Distribution.

As stated above, degrees and HNDs in any subject can lead to management training schemes. But for entrants who are certain they want a retail career, there are now specialist degrees in retailing (titles vary and so does emphasis on certain aspects of retailing). These courses are intended to produce 'fast track' trainees who will become senior managers and specialists in retail planning, analysis, marketing and distribution, able to cope with the complexities of international retail organization in an integrated EC market.

Personal attributes   Numeracy; an outgoing personality; an interest in both people and things; organizing ability; communication skills; commercial sense. For *store management*: leadership qualities; ability to delegate and take decisions quickly and to keep calm in crises; physical stamina. For *buyers*: interest in social and economic trends; negotiating skills; objectivity to be able to judge the relevance of one's own taste and gauge that of customers.

Late start   Good opportunities. Most companies positively welcome people who have had work experience, and will train people of up to about 35 for management. BTEC/SCOTVEC courses also welcome mature students and distance-learning courses are available.

Career-break   Most companies encourage returners and provide refresher training.

Part time   Ample opportunities up to supervisor level, and increasingly also at management levels. With lengthening shopping hours, several managers share store management anyway, so it is quite possible to organize part time and job-sharing at management levels. Head office jobs, including buying and merchandising, can also be done at 'less than full time'. So far, job-sharing and part-time work at senior head office levels seem to have been started only when enterprising individuals have taken the initiative.

Position of women

Considering that the vast majority of sales assistants, and of customers, are women, surprisingly few women are in senior management. But the situation has improved in recent years; more women are moving up the ladder faster. In chain store management – until fairly recently a male preserve – women are now doing quite well, and they are also doing well in department stores.

Women *buyers* are no longer confined to fashion and similar areas. There are still very few women in supermarket management. The reason given is that managers may have to help humping heavy goods; however, it is unlikely that there is much work which is too hard for any but the most delicate females. Because retailing is such a diffuse industry, women in retail have no forum as have, for example, women in banking or medicine.

Further information

National Retail Training Council, Bedford House, 69–79 Fulham High Street, London SW6 3JW
Individual retailing concerns

Related careers

CATERING: *Hotels* – MANAGEMENT – PERSONNEL/HUMAN RESOURCES MANAGEMENT

Science

Scientist

Main functions or activities: Research and development; analysis and investigation; production; technical sales and service; technical writing.

Main branches: Physics; chemistry; biological sciences; environmental sciences and conservation; cybernetics; mathematical sciences; materials science.

Entry qualifications

Scientists and technologists normally need a degree, but the borderline between scientist, technologist and senior technician – BTEC/SCOTVEC Higher award holder (see pp. xxi, xxii) – is often blurred; many of the latter have degrees.

Precise degree course requirements vary from one course to another. In general:

For *physics, cybernetics and applied sciences* degrees, A-levels must include physics and mathematics.

For *some mathematics* degrees, A-levels must include pure and applied maths.

For *chemistry* degrees, chemistry and physics and/or mathematics A-levels are preferred, but other combinations may be acceptable.

For *biological sciences*, biology, a physical science – preferably chemistry – and mathematics are ideal; other combinations may be acceptable.

For *some* science degrees biology may only be accepted as a third A-level: if only 2 A-levels are offered they must both be in sciences more relevant to the degree subject.

In general – though there are exceptions – polytechnics and other colleges are more likely than universities to accept applicants with only 2 A-levels.

For *BTEC/SCOTVEC Higher National Diploma*: 1 relevant A-level passed and another studied at A-level (or 2 Highers); for *BTEC/SCOTVEC Higher National Certificate*: *either* BTEC/SCOTVEC National award or 2 relevant A-levels passed (but for individual subject Certificate courses requirements may vary).

The work   All jobs are based directly or indirectly on scientific or technological developments. More to the point, all jobs are likely to be
affected by today's or tomorrow's scientific developments or their
exploitation. 'Scientific literacy' – an understanding of what
science is about and how it affects virtually every aspect of
industrial society – is an advantage in most jobs, and is essential
in many, however remote from schoolroom science.

A science qualification is, of course, often a vocational qualification, but it need not be by any means. The image of the white-
coated, lab-based scientist as the only, or even the main kind of,
science professional, is quite out of date.

Science practitioners

Scientists can choose: they can become 'science practitioners' or
'practical scientists' and use their scientific training and education
in all kinds of science jobs. In research, they can push out the
frontiers of knowledge even further – in space and astronomical
investigations; interaction of energy and matter in lasers; optical
fibres; bioengineering, etc., there is a vast variety of research
areas. Then there is work for scientists who want to solve problems
thrown up by scientific developments: advances in medical science
have led to over-population and food-shortages; excessive use of
energy requires alternative sources; chemical industries have led
to pollution of the environment. Biotechnologists, chemists and
other specialists investigate and try to alleviate undesirable but
inevitable side-effects of innovation. And then there is of course
the vast, mainly physics-based, information technology industry
and its spin-offs, to give just a few examples.

The nature of practising scientists' work ranges from
laboratory-centred 'boffin' research to 'people-centred' activities
like technical selling (see p. 440) or people-and-technology-
centred work in production (see p. 440) or profit-centred work in
marketing and other commercial functions. (See below for details
of the various 'functions', and of the main science specialisms or
'branches'.)

The outlook for scientists varies considerably from one branch
to another and may change from one year to the next. Physicists
are in greatest demand (mainly in the electronics industry, see p.
191), but mathematicians, cyberneticians and some applied scientists (e.g. materials and polymer specialists) are also in demand,
followed by chemists, biochemists and microbiologists. Botanists,
zoologists and environmental science graduates are least in
demand. However, scientists can often switch to another, related
field (this may involve a post-graduate course).

Prospects in the various types of work or *functions* vary mainly according to economic climate. In research and development, cutbacks tend to bite much earlier than in production and analysis and investigation. Technical writing and technical sales are expanding functions. However, scientists only specialize in a function *after* graduation. (But some degree subjects are more likely to lead to one function, some to another: for example *applied* scientists are much more likely to be in demand in production than, for example, botanists, and a broad-based integrated course is not likely to lead to research.)

Scientists often start in laboratory work (*research and development, analysis, investigation*) and then move into *production, technical sales and service*, or *writing*; or they may use their science background in *marketing* (see p. 294); in *information work* (p. 229) or in *patent agency* (p. 361) or *operational research* (p. 291). *Teachers* of mathematics and most sciences are much in demand in schools (but higher education teaching prospects are bleak).

Career prospects are generally much better for graduates who have at least a reading knowledge of a foreign language (at the moment especially German or Russian). Anyone who wants to work in EC countries must be fluent in the relevant language and/or have specific experience. Short-term contracts possible in developing countries.

Science as a tool

Scientists can equally choose not to practise as scientists, but to use their understanding of science as a tool with which to do other kinds of jobs – in commerce, industry, the public service – more effectively. People who have scientific curiosity but are not sure whether they want to be scientists, can choose a science qualification confident in the knowledge that their scientific background will be a door-opener into a variety of jobs in many different settings. For example, a scientist who goes into stockbroking or merchant banking is better able to assess a new high-technology company's chances of success, or the advantages or disadvantages of a merger between two science-based companies, than someone without a scientific background who has to go by hunch, or someone else's advice. A senior Civil Servant is better at advising ministers on, for example, the implications of rapidly changing technology when discussing the future of, say, transport, or the health service, or defence expenditure, than someone without a scientific background. (The Civil Service very much wants to attract more scientists as Administration Trainees (see p. 126) – the potential high-flyers in the Civil Service – and into the Science Management Training Scheme.) In publishing, to choose a very different example, a scientist will be at an advantage over a nonscientist when judging the implications of electronic publishing – and the speed with which electronics might severely affect traditional 'print' publishing. There are dozens of similar examples.

In industrial and commercial management (see p. 272) and in marketing (see p. 294), science graduates are welcome. About a third of all employers' vacancies for graduates are open to graduates from any discipline: the employers buy graduates' 'trained minds' rather than their specific knowledge. Increasingly, when recruiting any-discipline graduates, employers tend to prefer science or technology to arts graduates. The former's scientific literacy is useful at a time when science and technology impinge on so many aspects of every organization. Scientists' analytical approach to problem-solving is invariably useful even when the problem is not a scientific one. Scientists with communication skills are above all badly needed to close the communication gap: to explain basic relevant scientific facts, trends and implications to their scientifically illiterate colleagues (many of them in very high places). Information work (see p. 229) has good openings for scientists. Finally, for people who want to set up in business on their own (see WORKING FOR ONESELF, p. 557), a science background is extremely useful (though it will have to be complemented with business knowhow).

Practising scientists' work can be divided in two ways: by the types of activities or 'functions' and by the various 'branches' or science-specializations:

The Main Functions

Research and Development

Research is the lifeblood of science, enlarging existing knowledge and stimulating the growth of new branches. *Development* translates research findings into new – or improved – products and processes. The two overlap.

The terms 'pure' and 'applied' are often used to describe the type of research undertaken. In this context 'pure' research means increasing knowledge for its own sake and 'applied' research is 'goal-orientated' – directed towards solving technical problems, improving national defence or prestige – or 'wealth creating'. Science research is very expensive to carry out, much of it is sponsored, by industry or government, and is goal-orientated. Some university departments may fund 'pure' research from their resources or through research studentships which lead to higher research degrees (M. Phil. or Ph. D.).

Most research is teamwork, with several scientists, often from several disciplines, and technicians, working under a team-leader. The work may be divided into projects; several scientists are then responsible for their own project within the overall framework.

Personal attributes   Above-average intelligence; enthusiasm; willingness to work patiently for long hours (or even months) and persevere with tricky problems; creativity; ability to work in a team and to take decisions and stand up for them if things go wrong; ability to communicate findings effectively; great powers of concentration; stubborn persistence in the face of disappointing research results. Industrial researchers must be willing to change direction – at however interesting a point in their research – in the interests of the company's profitability.

Analysis and Investigation

Routine tests and investigations are carried out in all fields of science. In chemical research, for example, analysis of intermediate compounds enables scientists to keep track of chemical changes that are taking place. In manufacturing industry, the composition of both raw materials and products is monitored by analysing samples in *quality control* laboratories. In the food industry, regular checks are made on biological and chemical purity of foodstuffs. In pharmaceuticals the safety of drugs, beauty preparations and food additives is investigated. Before such products can be marketed, substances are tried out on experimental animals to see whether there are any toxic side-effects. In the agrochemical industry, new fertilizers and pesticides are given field trials; the chemicals are used on experimental plots in various parts of the country – and sometimes overseas – so that scientists can determine how performance is affected by different soils and climates.

Many analytical techniques are automated; most routine testing is carried out by technicians (see p. 452). The professional scientist trains and supervises technicians, initiates, organizes and oversees projects and researches into new experimental methods.

Personal attributes   Interest in applied science; methodical approach; patience; ability to organize other people and their work; ability to communicate effectively with highly specialized colleagues and with trainee technicians; observation to recognize the unexpected.

Production
(see also ENGINEERING, pp. 187, 193)

The central activity in industry is organizing production. That involves supervising the people who operate the industrial plant. Production managers (titles vary) are a vital link in the chain of command from chargehand to production director, and between production and other departments. Their main function is to see that production runs smoothly and is as efficient as possible. That means they must keep up with technological developments and arrange for and supervise the installation of new equipment as necessary. Hours can be long and irregular, and may include some shift-work – but this is by no means so in all plants. Production managers usually have a small office, but they spend little time in it. The work involves daily contact with other professionals and managers from other departments as well as with shop stewards, etc.

Production professionals are equally concerned with managing people and with the exploitation of new technologies. The largest opportunities are for chemists. Production managers, or whatever the title of persons in charge, are normally graduates; technicians work under them. Production specialists can switch from one type of plant to another; and they can later go into *marketing* or *general management*.

Personal attributes
Willingness to accept responsibility and take decisions; ability to keep calm in a crisis; leadership skills to motivate and organize plant operatives; practicality; ability to get on well with people at all levels in the industrial hierarchy; interest in the commercial application of science.

Technical Sales and Service

Two closely related activities: selling a science-based product and providing a technical back-up service for the customer. The product might be a sophisticated scientific instrument, an industrial chemical, a drug or a pesticide. The customer could be a research scientist, an industrial manager of a tiny or a large concern, a pharmacist or a farmer, i.e. a person with a lot of or no scientific knowledge. The technical sales executive or 'rep' needs a thorough knowledge of the product, its uses and limitations. The kind of technical service a company provides depends on the nature of its products. A technical service scientist representing a plastics manufacturer deals mainly with customers who mould plastics into containers and would investigate complaints and answer technical queries (and perhaps suggest new ways of using the material). It is part of the job to act as a link between the research laboratories and the sales staff.

Representatives for pharmaceutical firms visit doctors and pharmacists and inform them about new drugs and also provide feedback to the company on doctors' opinions of its products. In agricultural service industries reps may sell fertilizers, pesticides and animal health products to farmers and give advice about how they should be used (see AGRICULTURE AND HORTICULTURE, p. 22). Reps are usually given a 'territory'; its size depends on what they sell and whether it is a country area or town: some reps may be away from home all week; others come home every night. Many work from home and only go to the office occasionally.

Personal attributes Outgoing personality; liking for meeting a succession of people; a thick skin for the occasional rude customer; sensitivity to gauge the right approach (long-winded, brief, aloof, friendly, etc.); ability to communicate facts effectively to customers who may be much more, and may be much less, knowledgeable than the reps themselves; self-sufficiency for possibly long hours of lone travelling.

Technical Writing

A technical writer assembles a package of scientific or technical information for a particular readership. The work is often done on a contract basis; specialist firms hire out technical writers to client companies for the duration of a particular writing project. This may concern, for example, a set of handbooks and instruction manuals to accompany a complex piece of electronic equipment which is being marketed by an electronics manufacturer. Two 'packages' may have to be written: one in simple language for operatives or chargehands who have only to know how to operate the equipment; and another package aimed at technical managers who want to know more technical details and may need to be able to repair or adjust the equipment. In the pharmaceutical industry, writers prepare 'case histories' of new drugs (experiments done, etc.) for submission to the Committee on Safety of Medicines.

Technical copywriters (see ADVERTISING, p. 16) may write promotional material for science-based products. This is an expanding field, particularly in electronics, engineering generally and pharmaceuticals.

Personal attributes Wide scientific/technological interests and knowledge; an inquiring mind; ability to search out information and sift the relevant –

for the particular purpose – from the irrelevant; ability to explain complex matters lucidly and concisely; a scientific grasshopper mind, to switch from one type of subject to another; liking for desk-work.

The Main Branches of Science

The classification of science into content areas is constantly changing. Most people are familiar with physics, chemistry and biology but as scientific investigation gets more complex, or is applied for different purposes, so different classifications may arise: a 'subset' of one of the main disciplines may be identified for more detailed study (e.g. astronomy – the study of extra-terrestrial systems – or virology – the study of viruses). An overlapping area of two main disciplines may emerge as worth studying in its own right (e.g. biophysics, biochemistry) or an interdisciplinary area may be identified, usually problem-orientated (practical rather than academic) and develop its own concepts and methods of study (e.g. cybernetics, environmental sciences, materials science, biotechnology).

Physics

Physics – the study of matter and energy – lies at the heart of science. It is closely related to mathematics and also quite closely to chemistry; *chemical physics* – the study of materials and molecules – is a subject in its own right. *Biophysics* – the physical properties of living matter – has assumed greater importance as biological knowledge has grown. Many aspects of *engineering* and *materials science* are 'applied' aspects of physics. So the physicist, who always has a sound mathematical background, has a wide choice of occupations and settings in which to work.

Most industrial openings occur in engineering and related industries – especially in electronics, telecommunications, computing and transport; other opportunities exist in chemical and energy industries, e.g. oil, gas, electricity. In the Civil Service physicists work on problems ranging from research into navigation to recycling industrial waste. (See also 'Medical or Biomedical Engineering', p. 192)

The work of medical physicists is increasingly important to medicine. They form part of a team of specialists concerned with the diagnosis and treatment of disease, using radiotherapy and diagnostic radiology, radio-isotopes, ultrasonics and many other physical methods to help doctors cure patients. In *occupational hygiene*, physicists help prevent damage to people's health by monitoring potential hazards from radiation, noise, dust and other sources in working environments. (See also 'Environmental Sciences and Conservation', especially *geophysics* and *meteorology*, below.) There are very limited opportunities for physicists (who may or may not have taken a degree in astronomy or astrophysics) and for mathematicians to branch out into *astronomy*. Research into such aspects of astronomy as satellite communications systems or the structure of the universe is done at government, university, and some commercial telecommunications (i.e. electronics) research laboratories. In *computer* design and manufacture, physicists play an important part.

Chemistry

Chemistry – the study of the composition of materials, their properties and how they change and react with other materials – occupies a central position in the sciences. It forms the basis of, for example, the manufacture of metals, pharmaceuticals, fertilizers, paints, synthetic fabrics, dyestuffs, plastics, paper, cosmetics, herbicides, pesticides and many other products.

It has links with all the other sciences, such as physics, biology and geology and contributes to 'applied' science areas such as *food science*, *forensic science*, *materials science*, *pharmacology* and *pharmacy* and *textile technology*. So someone with an interest in chemistry has a wide choice of employment. The big chemical manufacturers, oil, drug and cosmetic companies are the biggest employers of chemists. In the Civil Service, chemists in the Science Group work on road-surfaces, building materials, nutrition, pollution, and other research; others are employed as forensic scientists (see p. 133); in the general Civil Service they are welcome as Administration Trainees (see CIVIL SERVICE, p. 126), using their expertise in an advisory capacity and as background knowledge. Others work in the public health field, e.g. analysing drinking water, food and drugs, and in hospital laboratories. A few chemists work on restoration and research in museums. (See also 'Biochemistry, microbiology and biotechnology', below.)

Biological Sciences

Biology can be subdivided into 4 major disciplines – the study of: plants (*botany*); animals (*zoology*); micro-organisms (*microbiology*); chemistry of living matter (*biochemistry*). However, as the interdependence of plants and animals is increasingly recognized, more emphasis is being placed on biology as an integration of botany and zoology, e.g. *ecology*. More specialized biological sciences deal with particular groups of living organisms – viruses (*virology*) and insects (*entomology*) for instance – and with particular biological processes such as the functioning of the body's organs (*physiology*) or the mechanisms of heredity and variation (*genetics*).

Botany and zoology

Most opportunities occur in the public sector – mainly in the Civil Service Science Group, agricultural (e.g. animal and plant breeding) and medical research, and conservation. For example, the Ministry of Agriculture, Fisheries and Food employs marine biologists to monitor fish stocks and pollution levels. A small number of biologists work in the Health Service, for water authorities and museums. In industry there are limited opportunities in pharmaceuticals and agrochemicals.

The most marketable aspects of botany and zoology are those related either to medical and pharmaceutical research (such as parasitology and physiology), or to agriculture and horticulture (such as plant pathology and entomology). Opportunities in *marine* and *freshwater biology* and *general ecology* are very limited. However, concern for the environment has meant an increase in jobs in industry for 'environmental' biologists.

Biochemistry, microbiology and biotechnology

Biochemists and microbiologists have much better career prospects than botanists or zoologists; there is a steady demand from industry (mainly food, drink, pharmaceuticals and agriculture), from medical research and hospital laboratories, specialist research organizations and, to a lesser extent, the Civil Service Science Group.

A *biochemist* working for a pharmaceutical company might study the mechanism of a new drug or (helped by a microbiologist) investigate biochemical aspects of the production of antibiotics by fermentation. *Hospital biochemists* work alongside medical colleagues and technicians as members of a team: they supervise routine biochemical testing (see 'medical laboratory scientists', p. 455), do research into, for example, the function of hormones or the body's defence mechanisms, and may also teach clinical biochemistry to doctors and nurses. Some use biochemical analysis in clinical diagnosis or in forensic laboratories (e.g. for genetic fingerprinting).

Microbiologists often specialize in bacteriology and virology and become experts in plant or animal diseases. In the food industry and in environmental health laboratories they check samples for pathogenic microbes and investigate spoilage. In oil companies they explore ways of producing synthetic protein by feeding bacteria with the by-products of petroleum refining.

Biotechnology is fairly new as an academic discipline but covers processes which use multi-disciplinary approaches to problem-solving in science-based industries. It is, very broadly, the use of living organisms to perform a useful task. The main uses are in manufacturing industry – particularly brewing and the food, fertilizer, animal feedstuffs and pharmaceutical industries – medicine, agriculture and horticulture. It has also been described as 'factory farming of bugs' or microbes – the smallest living organisms – which are then put to industrial uses.

Biotechnologists work in a vast variety of science-based jobs, for example on the development of synthetic proteins; of new strains of wheat; of hormones and drugs. They also work on pollution control (e.g. with biodegradable waste products), and on the generation of new sources of energy from such varied natural materials as plant tissue and animal waste products. The usual way into biotechnology is via a science degree – preferably chemistry, biochemistry or microbiology – followed by post-graduate study, or a biotechnology degree. Genetic engineering – the manipulation, using scientific techniques, of genes – is one aspect of biotechnology. It is increasingly used to produce varieties of crops which are especially resistant to disease or tolerant of poor weather. *Molecular biology* – the understanding of how genetic information is stored and passed on – has opened up vast new areas of research.

Environmental Sciences and Conservation

The environmental sciences are fashionable. Concern with pollution, dwindling natural resources and threatened plant and animal species has given a fresh impetus to the scientific study of the environment. *Conservation* and *ecology* (the study of how plants and animals interact with their natural surroundings), together with *meteorology*, *oceanography*, *geology* and *geophysics*, are important environmental subjects.

Environmental science is often (and best) a *post-graduate* specialization: scientists take a first degree in a traditional subject and then either graft on an appropriate post-graduate course or get trained by employers in environmental aspects of their subject. *Meteorologists* and *physical oceanographers* usually have degrees in physics or maths; biologists normally take a specialist course (for example, in ecology or marine biology) before becoming conservationists. *Geology* graduates are the exception: they can go straight into geological work without further training. *Geophysicists* usually build their specialist knowledge on a foundation of physics, geology or engineering. But there is an increasing number of first degree courses in environmental subjects – either joint honours (such as physics and meteorology) or broad-based integrated courses in environmental sciences.

Conservation

Nature conservation used to mean protecting unusual plants and animals and their habitats. Now, many human activities have a wider environmental impact. Crop protection chemicals, for example, can upset the balance of ecological systems. If herbicides are used to control aquatic weeds, dead plants consume oxygen while decaying. As a result, fish and other organisms may die through lack of oxygen. A pipeline laid across country may disturb plant and animal life around it; an open-cast mine may leave a permanent scar on the countryside. Modern conservationists, recognizing the importance of protecting flora and fauna, are concerned with the wider problems of preserving the countryside as a whole.

The Nature Conservancy Council – responsible for conserving the wildlife and physiographical features of Great Britain – was superseded in 1991 by separate conservancy bodies for England, Scotland and Wales. Between them, they manage over 100 National Nature Reserves and several thousand Sites of Special Scientific Interest, and advise farmers, landowners, local authorities, industrialists and others on conservation matters. Scientists (mainly biologists, botanists, zoologists, geologists and geographers) are employed as Assistant Regional Officers. The Nature Reserves are run by Wardens (often non-graduates) who are experienced conservationists. Environmental research covering land, ocean and fresh water is carried out by the many institutes which come under the aegis of the Natural Environment Research Council (NERC).

Geology and Geophysics

Geology is the study of the structure and history of the earth; *geophysics* is concerned with its physical properties and, in particular, with the application of physical techniques to solve geological problems. Geologists locate, and then extract, oil, natural gas, minerals, useful rocks and underground water in the earth's crust. The first stage of exploration often entails making a geological map of a region and then following this up with an aerial survey to provide greater detail of the terrain.

Geophysical techniques are widely used in geological exploration. In *seismic surveying*, for example, shock waves from a small underground explosion set off by geophysicists bounce off the rock layers and are recorded by instruments. By analysing the data with a computer, geophysicists can unravel the underlying geological structure.

Geologists and geophysicists are employed by commercial organizations such as oil companies, the mining industry, civil engineering firms concerned with roads, reservoirs, dams and site construction, water authorities, quarrying firms and specialist consultants. There are some openings in the Natural Environment Research Council (which administers the British Geological Survey), museums, the national nature conservancy councils, and in research and teaching.

Meteorology and Oceanography (see also METEOROLOGY, p. 312)

Meteorology and oceanography – concerned with the atmosphere and the oceans – are closely related. The physics and dynamics of atmospheric and oceanographic processes have much in common; the oceans exert a powerful influence on the weather. At honours degree level, *meteorology* and *physical oceanography* are highly mathematical; numerical methods are widely used in modern weather forecasting.

The Meteorological Office also carries out research into such topics as the physics of cloud formation and energy exchange between atmosphere and oceans. Scientists are usually involved either in *forecasting* or in *research*.

Research in physical oceanography is undertaken at the Institute of Oceanographic Sciences (part of the Natural Environment Research Council – NERC). Topics include studies of waves, tides, currents and general circulation of ocean water. NERC also investigates the ecology of deep-water organisms, the composition of the sea-floor, *marine biology* subjects. Oceanographic work is done partly in the laboratory and partly at sea.

Cybernetics

The original definition of cybernetics as 'control and communication in the animal and the machine' now extends to activities as different as landing a man on the moon, and using 'natural enemies' to kill pests. In a cybernetic system – such as a thermostat keeping a room at constant temperature – one thing controls another which reacts on the first to form a feedback loop. Since feedback processes operate in man-made control systems as well as in economics and biological systems, the term cybernetics is interpreted differently by people in different scientific spheres.

Cybernetics courses with a strong technological slant – containing such topics as feedback control theory and computer technology and application – are particularly suitable for a career in computer-based automatic systems (those used in navigation and air traffic control, for instance). Courses with a strong theoretical element – including the mathematical theory of cybernetics, artificial intelligence, biological and human cybernetics, for example – could lead to a career in computer design, systems analysis, operational research or planning.

The cybernetic aspects of industry, such as computer technology and applications, are expanding.

See also COMPUTING/INFORMATION TECHNOLOGY (p. 142).

Mathematical Sciences

Mathematicians – pure and applied – are much in demand. They work in commerce, e.g. in finance and in actuarial work (see ACTUARY, p. 11), in science-based activities and in computers (see p. 142). They frequently work in teams with scientists and engineers. For example, in science-based industries they may analyse data produced by scientists. In manufacturing industry and in the Civil Service they may work on translating problems into mathematical terms (making 'models'), working out solutions and then expressing the results in non-mathematical form. They make calculations which enable *control engineers* (see p. 191) to make adjustments to the manufacturing process. Sometimes the mathematical models are so complex that a special technique called *numerical analysis* is used to solve them. Some mathematicians specialize in numerical analysis; others become expert in *operational research* (see p. 291).

Statisticians – including mathematicians who have specialized in statistics – work in industry, medical, social and agricultural research, and in the Civil Service (Central Statistical Office and all the departments with a statistics division). They are concerned with the design of experiments, questionnaires and surveys and with the collection, analysis and interpretation of results. In a government department they provide information on which policies can be based; for example they predict the effect of changes in the tax system or the likely demand for energy. Wherever computers are used – and that, see COMPUTING/INFORMATION TECHNOLOGY (p. 142), is in virtually every field of activity – statisticians process and interpret data and help design and improve systems. There is also scope for statisticians in marketing and market research where they design surveys to establish demand for goods and services. The majority of statisticians need a scientific background; some need social science expertise (it is easier to switch with a science background to statistics in social sciences than to switch with a social science background to statistics in science).

Materials Science

Materials science is an umbrella term for sciences concerned with a variety of metallic and non-metallic materials (including *polymers*, *rubber*, *paper*, *ceramics*, *glass* and *textiles*). *Metallurgists* work on the extraction, refining and fabrication of ferrous and non-ferrous metals used in products ranging from aircraft bodies to electronic components. *Textile* technologists work with domestic materials, such as clothing and furnishing fabrics, and with industrial products used for a wide variety of purposes, e.g. insulation, road reinforcement and even the manufacture of artificial veins. *Polymer* scientists and technologists work on all kinds of plastics and other polymeric materials used in products ranging from picnic plates and computer keyboards to gas pipes and gear components.

It is possible to specialize early on in metallurgy, polymers, textiles or one of the other non-metallic materials, but most entrants to these industries have followed a broader course in materials science. There are good opportunities for materials scientists to use their interdisciplinary approach in these industries, as well as in the newer ones concerned with composite materials: polymers reinforced with glass or carbon fibre, for example, and others still in the experimental stage. Physics, chemistry and engineering graduates are also recruited.

Training   Normally a degree. Science courses usually consist either of a detailed study of a single subject, with supporting ancillary subjects, or of a study of 2 distinct disciplines in a joint honours course, or of a cluster of several related disciplines, such as biological sciences. The question of whether a broad-based or a specialized degree leads to better prospects is impossible to answer in a general way: it depends on an individual's adaptability, motivation, specialization, on changing economic circumstances and on technological developments. There is a continuing need for specialists, but a 'generalist' scientific education possibly leads to a wider choice of jobs especially for 'non-practising' scientists; its built-in flexibility enables the scientist to change direction if, for example, that should be desirable or necessary after a career- break, or because supply and demand in a specialization have changed.

For *research* a first or upper second honours degree is usually required but research assistants who work part time for a Ph.D. are often taken on with a 2.2. A first degree may have to be followed by a career-orientated post-graduate course. First-degree course emphasis varies greatly. Some courses are very much more practical and vocational in approach and structure than others, and prospective students need to do careful research in publications like *Which Degree*, *CRAC Degree Course Guides*, course prospectuses.

Many CNAA and some university degrees are 4-year sandwich courses, with a year spent at work. This may be an advantage to people who want to go into industry: their experience of the work situation during their training reassures employers that the applicant at least knows what a working environment is like.

BTEC/SCOTVEC Higher awards (see pp. xxi, xxii) or Dip. H.E.s normally lead to senior technicians', not to professional scientists' jobs, but the distinction between scientist and technician is often blurred. Technologists may have an applied science degree or BTEC/SCOTVEC Higher award.

BTEC/SCOTVEC Higher award students can complete their professional training by taking a further 1-year full-time or 2-year part-time (day-release) course leading to the graduate membership examinations of one of the relevant scientific institutes, e.g. the Royal Society of Chemistry.

Once in a job, training, or at least learning, continues. This may or may not lead to a further qualification.

Late start   Degree course requirements in terms of GCSEs and A-levels may be relaxed, but candidates' knowledge of maths and science has to be up to date; many late entrants first take evening classes or other preparatory courses to freshen up their school sciences, etc. Opportunities limited.

Career-break   Return only possible if one has kept up with developments, and even then some areas, such as research and development, would probably be difficult to get back to. But it is possible to use a science degree to switch to technical writing (see p. 441) or information work (see p. 229) or teaching (science teachers are in great demand). A few firms now provide opportunities for women who want to keep in touch, by arranging regular visits to labs, home-based projects or part-time work. But such schemes are still very few. Individuals can ask for arrangements to be made. Another way of keeping up with developments is by taking a short Open University course (see p. xxiv). Most professional institutions offer reduced subscriptions for people on a career-break.

Part time   Not many opportunities at the moment, except in technical writing (and then it is spasmodic rather than part time) and in science and mathematics teaching (see p. 521), but job-sharing should be possible in many types of work.

Position of women   The number of women scientists remains relatively small and there are few in the top jobs in most disciplines. This is mainly due to the fact that fewer girls than boys have been taking science GCSE and A-levels (except in biology). In 1990, 8% of girls getting A-levels passed physics, compared with 26% of boys. 13% passed chemistry (21% of boys), 18% passed maths (32% of boys), but 18% passed biology (only 12% of boys). Under the National Curriculum girls will not be able to drop sciences at GCSE, so A-level entries should increase.

The proportion of women taking science degrees is rising even more slowly. In 1991 17% of university students accepted for physics courses, 35% for chemistry, and 34% for maths were women. A much larger proportion of women started biology and botany degrees (57% and 52%) which carry much less weight on the job market. When choosing science-based courses women do not assess their chances in the job market as realistically as do men. For example, women made 50·6% of the applications for medicine in 1991, entry for which, like veterinary science, is one of the most competitive. The ratio of applications to acceptances for medicine was over 9:1. Similarly, women made 56% of biological science degree applications, where the ratio was 8·2:1. Other university science courses are not as over-subscribed. For example, the ratio was 5·4:1 for physics (but only 18·2% of applications were from women), 5·6:1 for chemistry (35% from women), 6·4:1 for mathematical sciences (24% from women) and 6·2:1 for engineering and technology (12·9% from women). Industry would welcome more women scientists in research, as well as in technical sales, marketing and production. However, a survey by the Institute of Physics revealed that women physicists tended to hold less well-paid and prestigious jobs in industry than their male colleagues.

A few universities and polytechnics now arrange 'conversion' courses, allowing entrants with good science GCSEs but without the usually required A-levels, to prepare for science degrees.

Further information   Biochemical Society, 59 Portland Place, London W1N 3AJ

Royal Society of Chemistry, Burlington House, Piccadilly, London W1V 0BN

Institute of Biology, 20 Queensberry Place, London SW7 2DZ

Institute of Mathematics and its Applications, Maitland House, Warrior Square, Southend-on-Sea, Essex SS1 2JY

Institute of Statisticians, 43 St Peter's Square, Preston, Lancs. PR1 7BX

Institute of Physics, 47 Belgrave Square, London SW1X 8QX

Institution of Geologists, Burlington House, Piccadilly, London W1V 9AG

Civil Service Commission, Alencon Link, Basingstoke, Hants. RG21 1JB

English Nature, Northminster House, Peterborough, PE1 1UA

Nature Conservancy Council for Scotland, 12 Hope Terrace, Edinburgh EH9 2AS

Countryside Council for Wales, Plas Penrhos, Ffordd Penrhos, Bangor, Gwynedd LL57 2LQ

Natural Environment Research Council, Polaris House, North Star Avenue, Swindon, Wilts. SN2 1EU

BTEC and SCOTVEC (see pp. xxi, xxii)

Science Technician

Entry qualifications

Nothing rigid. They vary according to the job's and to colleges' requirements; from a few lower grade GCSEs with at least 1 science to 2 science A-levels or even a degree. (The Civil Service requires 4 GCSEs (A–C) including a science, maths and English language.) For BTEC National awards the minimum entry qualifications are 4 GCSEs (A–C) in appropriate subjects or a BTEC First Certificate (see p. xxi). See also SCOTVEC National Certificate, p. xxii.

The work

Laboratory technician, assistant, technical assistant, research assistant, scientific assistant, technical officer, assistant scientific officer are all titles used to describe people who perform science-related procedures and techniques under the overall supervision of scientists. As scientific investigations become more complex technicians become more important and the variety of jobs is growing. They are essential team-members, not unskilled bottle-washers: there is a growing need for them to be able to use new technologies and analytical methods, rather than rely on practical skills. Their tasks range from mundane routine to work which overlaps very much with that of professional scientists.

They may work in any of the functions and branches described under 'Scientist' (see above).

Training – general (see also under different branches)

This can be full or part time.

Full time: normally 2-year full-time or 3-year sandwich courses, leading to BTEC National Diploma (or 2 years full time for SCOTVEC equivalent, see p. xxii). Entry requirements for these courses are, in most colleges, 4 GCSEs (A–C), including a relevant science, maths and an English subject. There may be full-time 'catching up' opportunities for students who want to become science technicians but lack appropriate GCSEs. (See BTEC First awards p. xxii.)

Part time: on the job with day- or block-release for BTEC National award (see p. xxii) in the biological sciences, physics or chemistry with specialist options to fit in with their work. Technicians can switch specialization by adding option modules to basic Certificates. There is a great variety of options. Not all specialist subjects are available at all colleges – it depends largely on local job opportunities.

Students without the entry requirements for BTEC National can work for a BTEC First certificate or City and Guilds Science Laboratory Assistant (or Technician, the latter is slightly more theoretical in content) Certificate by part-time study while in relevant employment. With experience, they may then be able to go on to BTEC National Certificate training.

In Scotland students take appropriate modules for the SCOTVEC National Certificate (see p. xxiii).

Higher or *senior technician training*: Students with BTEC National Certificates containing sufficient units (see p. xxii) or BTEC National Diplomas can take a BTEC Higher National Certificate (part time) or BTEC Higher National Diploma (full time or sandwich). Again, there are a great many specializations.

Direct entry requirements to Higher National Certificates and Diplomas vary according to main subjects. For example, for the Applied Biology Higher National awards the following requirements now normally apply: A-level study in biology and chemistry or physics and a pass in one of these. For Chemistry Higher National awards: A-level in chemistry plus 2 sciences studied beyond GCSE (normally maths and physics). For Physics Higher National awards: A-level in physics, GCSEs (A–C) in maths and English subject plus maths studied beyond GCSE. (Maths must of course always be offered at GCSE (A–C) if not included in A-levels.) For SCOTVEC Higher National awards entry is at the discretion of colleges, but normal requirements are 5 SCEs (including 2 at 'H' grade) including maths and 2 relevant sciences or appropriate National Certificate modules.

There are 4 main settings: hospitals, industry, education, Civil Service.

Hospitals

Technicians

There is a wide variety of technician jobs in hospitals. Some are physics-based, others require a good knowledge of biology and chemistry. Some consist almost entirely of laboratory work, others involve occasional or regular patient-contact. Most technicians are now called Medical Technical Officers. The main groups are: *medical physics technicians* and *physiological measurement technicians*.

Medical physics technicians: Broadly deal with 'imaging' equipment – X-ray machines; scanners; ultrasound; isotopes and similar matters, and with medical electronics generally. They may administer tests, i.e. have some patient-contact; or they may be wholly or largely concerned with the checking, recalibrating, maintenance, development and modification of equipment from lasers to renal dialysis machines – i.e. no or very little patient-contact. The very expensive and advanced imaging equipment is available only in teaching and large district hospitals, hence few medical physics jobs. In some hospitals radiographers have taken over the radioisotopes part of the technicians' work and the maintenance side may be carried out by staff from the works department (see ENGINEERING, pp. 192 and 198).

Physiological measurement technicians: Administer a variety of diagnostic tests (i.e. it is work with constant patient-contact) and it is normal to specialize in one type of work. *Audiology* technicians test the hearing and balance of adults and children, using special instruments, and select, fit and adjust hearing aids; *neurophysiological* technicians are concerned mainly with using EEG (electroencephalography) to record the electrical activity of a patient's brain. *Cardiology* technicians measure heart function and electrical activity, using cardiograms (ECGs) and monitor pacemakers. *Respiratory* technicians administer tests on lung function to help in diagnosis and treatment of lung disease.

Other technicians There are also some types of work which do not really fit into the above categories. *Perfusionists* work in cardiac departments, using an artificial circulatory system to re-route the blood around a particular organ in order to isolate it (necessary for bypass operations). *Anaesthetic* technicians are involved mainly in laboratory research work. *Operating department practitioners* help prepare patients for operations and help look after supplies and equipment in the operating theatre. *Pathology* technicians assist pathologists in examining bodies to establish cause of death and deal with members of the public who come to the mortuary.

Training   Students may be recruited into a particular department and train from the start in, for example, audiology or ECG; or they may be recruited on to a general training scheme which gives them a chance to look at different specializations before making up their minds. Nationally agreed schemes last for 2 years with day- or block-release. Further education is mainly based on the BTEC/SCOTVEC National Certificate in sciences or electronics with relevant options. Students can then go on to take a BTEC/SCOTVEC Higher National Certificate, specializing in medical physics or physiological measurement. Some technician associations run their own education scheme which may or may not be linked with BTEC/SCOTVEC. Pathology technicians work for a Royal Institute of Public Health and Hygiene certificate. Operating Department Practitioners work for an NVQ (see p. xx); NVQs are due to be introduced for other technicians.

Although in theory trainee technicians require only the entry qualifications for BTEC/SCOTVEC courses (see pp. xxi, xxii), in practice they need 2/3 A-levels or a BTEC/SCOTVEC Higher National award to get a hospital job. Many new entrants, especially in medical physics, have physics degrees. At present, non-graduates who want hospital technician jobs have more scope in biology/chemistry-based medical laboratory work (see below) than in the fast-changing and developing physics-based area. There are some jobs for assistant technical officers (ATOs) who help MTOs and can apply to join MTO training schemes after gaining experience.

Medical laboratory scientists: Most work in the National Health Service, where they are officially known as Medical Laboratory Scientific Officers (MLSOs). Some are *biochemists*. They are concerned with laboratory investigations for diagnosis and treatment of disease, and research into its causes and cure. Trainees work under the overall direction of senior staff who have specialized in the application of their particular discipline to medicine. Work is done in hospitals, universities, blood transfusion centres, public health laboratories, veterinary establishments and pharmaceutical firms. In hospitals, there may be some contact with patients, depending on the specialization. Qualified staff may supervise medical laboratory assistants.

The main specializations are: *clinical chemistry*: the analysis of blood and other biological materials; *medical microbiology*: the isolation and identification of bacteria and viruses from patients with infections, or in water and foodstuffs; *haematology and serology*: the study of blood; *histopathology and cytology*: the study of tissues removed during surgical operations and at post-mortem examinations, and in investigations for the early detection of cancer.

Prospective entrants should aim for a degree, although in theory it is possible to start with GCSEs (A–C) in biology or human biology, chemistry, physics and maths and an English subject. Entrants take a 2–3-year day- or block-release course while in relevant employment for the BTEC National Certificate in Science. They can then go on to the BTEC Higher National Certificate in Medical Laboratory Sciences. They may then apply for Associate membership of the Institute of Medical Laboratory Sciences and, after a period of approved practical training, can become state registered (essential for NHS jobs). Alternatively, students can take a full-time BTEC National Diploma in Science (Medical Laboratory Sciences), followed by a BTEC Higher National Diploma in Medical Laboratory Sciences, and then apply for a job. Applicants with A-levels in chemistry and biology can go straight on to a BTEC Higher National course. In Scotland trainees take equivalent SCOTVEC awards.

In practice it is hightly unlikely that anyone with fewer than 2 science A-levels (one of which should be chemistry) and good supporting GCSEs will get a training vacancy which will lead to membership of the IMLS. Many entrants are graduates and the IMLS supports all-graduate entry to the profession. For *biochemists*, degrees are mandatory. Relevant degree disciplines are *chemistry*, *microbiology*, *biological sciences*, *physics*, and *biochemistry*. There are also some IMLS-accredited *vocational degrees* in medical laboratory sciences and in bio-medical sciences, but these limit graduates' job-choice more than do other, less vocationally orientated, science degrees. Graduate IMLS students normally are eligible for IMLS membership after 1 year's practical experience. For promotion to senior posts MLSOs usually need to study for the Fellowship examination of the IMLS (certain IMLS accredited higher degrees exempt students from further study).

Industry

Very varied work most of which falls into two broad categories: *quality control*, and *research and development*.

In *quality control* ('QC'), during the production of chemicals, detergents, plastics, cosmetics and other manufactured goods and in the food processing industry, technicians test, for example, the purity and/or nutritional value of foodstuffs. In the pharmaceutical industry they help with tests on drugs and medicines. In electronics, technicians may test computer circuitry or the quality of television and radio components (their work overlaps with that of engineering technicians, see p. 197).

In *research and development* technicians assist scientists with all types of research (see p. 438). They may use new equipment and help modify it and they adapt standard procedures to suit particular experimental work.

Education Establishments

Technicians help researchers, teachers and lecturers. They work in science faculties, in research institutes and medical schools, secondary schools and colleges. They prepare work for lectures; and they help generally in the department. Technicians may prepare specimens for lectures in microbiology, histology, zoology, botany or geology, using for example techniques for culturing bacteria, or prepare thin sections or rocks or fossils for microscopical study, etc. In a chemistry faculty technicians are concerned with the assembly, care and maintenance of apparatus, and the preparation of bench reagents used for demonstration and experiment. They may, in research, use such techniques as flame photometry, spectro-photometry, chromatography, or use radio-isotopes.

The job of the school or college lab technician used to be rather menial, but conditions and prospects have now improved considerably. The work combines science with dealing with children and young people; it covers preparing, setting out and maintaining demonstration materials and apparatus as well as helping students and pupils in the classroom. In smaller establishments there may only be one technician; in one day the technician could then help in and prepare for classes in physics, chemistry and biology. In large establishments several technicians work under the direction of a chief technician, and there are opportunities for progress, with training, to a more senior post, and to specialize in either biology, chemistry or physics.

Science Group of the Civil Service
(see CIVIL SERVICE, p. 125)

Technicians are called Assistant Scientific Officers. They are part of a team led by a scientist engaged in research in any of the scientific disciplines.

In laboratories scientists carry out fundamental research, investigate new techniques and equipment, ensure that standards of safety are maintained. Technicians provide support to research and project teams. Their work includes making observations of experiments, logging data, summarizing results for interpretation. For example, they may measure jet-pipe temperatures of a helicopter engine; determine the nitrogen content of animal fodder; test for drugs for police investigations; make weather observations at an airport.

Openings vary according to changing situations, geographic area, area of specialization, level of qualification. Best prospects probably for well-qualified physics-based technicians, e.g. in the information technology 'hardware' industries as well as elsewhere. For biology/chemistry-based technicians, fair prospects in pharmaceuticals, agricultural chemicals and similar industries and hospital medical research. People with low school-leaving qualifications but interested in the job should try and improve their qualifications if they cannot get student-technician jobs. On the whole there is a growing range of jobs which are loosely called 'science technican'.

Personal attributes generally

Manipulative skill; patience; scrupulous attention to detail; a sense of responsibility; willingness to take orders; ability to work both independently and as one of a team.

Late start

Not much scope in most branches, school-leavers tend to be given preference. But adults can take full-time BTEC/SCOTVEC science courses, and there are a reasonable number of late entrants to hospital technician work (e.g. see 'Physiological measurement technicians', p. 454).

Career-break

As this is a rapidly changing area, only technicians who systematically keep up with developments can return, but there are updating opportunities, partly through the Open University (see p. xxxiv). The Department of Health is encouraging health authorities to offer retainer schemes to all their staff. The Institute of Medical Laboratory Sciences has special membership for non-working members.

Part time and job-sharing

Fair opportunities at all levels.

Position of women

There are about equal numbers of males and females, but far more men are senior technicians mainly because fewer women have physics at A-level. As a result more women go into dead-end low-level technician jobs where they do not get – and often do not ask for – day-release for further qualifications. Women with physics GCSE and A-levels do as well as men.

Further	City and Guilds of London Institute, 46 Britannia Street, London
informa-	WC1X 9RG
tion	BTEC, Central House, Upper Woburn Place, London WC1H
	0HH

Further information

City and Guilds of London Institute, 46 Britannia Street, London
WC1X 9RG

BTEC, Central House, Upper Woburn Place, London WC1H
0HH

SCOTVEC, Hanover House, 24 Douglas Street, Glasgow G2 7NQ

Institute of Medical Laboratory Sciences, 12 Queen Anne Street,
London W1M 0AU

Regional Health Authorities for information on Medical Technical
Officers

The Institute of Science Technology, Mansell House, 22 Bore
Street, Lichfield, Staff. WS13 6LP (This runs mainly work-
based courses, including one for its own Higher Diploma)

Related careers

ENGINEERING: *Engineering Technician* – MEDICINE – OPTICAL
WORK – ORTHOPTICS – PHARMACY – PHYSIOTHERAPY – RADI-
OGRAPHY

Food Science and Technology

All educational levels, see 'Training'.

The work

Food science is concerned with the chemical and biological nature of
food and its behaviour under natural conditions, during processing
and during storage. *Food technology* is the application of relevant
sciences, including engineering, to the processing, preservation
and development of raw materials and manufactured foods. Food
scientists and technologists work in quality control, product development and production departments (see p. 440) of food companies which make anything from fish fingers to fruit cake or
canned soup. They also work for equipment manufacturers, flavour makers, public analysts and in research centres where experiments with new food products using unorthodox materials (such
as seaweed or plankton) may be carried out. Some work in
research and development on 'fast foods' and 'systems catering'
(see CATERING, p. 95), monitoring the behaviour of foods as new
technologies are used. Some work together with *biotechnologists*
(see p. 444). Some research jobs are for food *scientists*; production
jobs tend to be held by *technologists*; but there is no clear-cut
division between the two and both types of specialists are found
in most job areas. There are jobs for technicians and for professional scientists and technologists: the division between senior
technician and scientist/technologist is often blurred.

The industry is less affected than many by economic slumps. Its diversity provides opportunities to specialize. The broad-based training allows for flexibility. As in other industries, technologists now often move into top general management (see 'Line management', p. 275).

Training   *Technician level*: with 4 GCSEs (A–C) including a science, maths and a subject testing use of English, BTEC award in Food Science/Food Technology with various options. Courses can be part-time day-release (2 years), full time (2 years); or sandwich (3 years).

With 1 science A-level passed and another studied to A-level (more often 2 passed, in practice), one of which should be chemistry and the other either physics, maths or biology, and GCSE (A–C) in maths, or BTEC National, BTEC Higher award in Food Technology (part time, full time or sandwich). For equivalent SCOTVEC awards, see p. xxii.

Graduate level: with 2, or sometimes 3, science A-levels which must include chemistry (precise requirements vary), degrees in various aspects of food science. Degrees vary in title, emphasis and content, so candidates need to study different syllabuses carefully. Some are more commercially orientated (combining food science and marketing for example); some are more science-based; others put more emphasis on relevant technologies; yet others on management.

While food science and technology degrees are strictly vocationally orientated, *science* and *engineering* graduates (see pp. 435 and 183) can also get into the food industries and then take post-graduate qualifications, either by part-time or full-time study. There are post-graduate courses in food science; food analysis and composition; food and management science; food microbiology; food engineering; biotechnology.

Personal attributes   A meticulous approach to technical problems plus an interest in people as consumers and changing tastes and eating habits. For many jobs a real interest in food is desirable, as is the ability to work as part of a team. For *management careers*, ability to organize people and work, to work under pressure and to take decisions.

Late start   The proportion of late entrants – 10–20% – is fairly high. Recent study of chemistry is an advantage.

Career-break   Provided people stay in touch through professional institutes there should be no problem. There are a few short *refresher* courses.

Part time Few opportunities at present, but job-sharing of certain posts should be possible.

Position of women There are more women than men entering this field. They have little difficulty entering all areas.

Further information Institute of Food Science and Technology, 5 Cambridge Court, 210 Shepherds Bush Road, London W6 7NL

Related careers ENGINEERING: *Engineering Technician* – OPTICAL WORK – PHARMACY – RADIOGRAPHY

Secretarial and Clerical Work

Entry qualifications	Various educational levels: minimum usually 4 GCSEs (A–C), including English language; but see 'Training', below.
The work	Office work consists largely of handling information – searching for, producing, passing on (verbally or in print) facts and figures, questions and answers, messages and instructions. 'Information technology' (IT) which broadly describes the equipment and systems used to process, transmit, file or otherwise handle information electronically, has changed the nature of office work. But fear of the unknown has tended to exaggerate IT's effect. The 'paperless office' is not about to take over overnight. The workforce is shrinking – especially at the lower, unskilled end where automation is drastically reducing the scope. But secretaries and people who produce and handle text will still be needed even when all managers have their own desk-top computers on which they can call up information and which they can use to communicate with each other, customers, clients, etc. IT also creates some new jobs.

The main jobs:

Secretary

Titles have no precise meaning: executive secretary, private secretary, personal assistant are used indiscriminately. Some of the most high-powered secretaries prefer to call themselves merely 'secretary'; some 'personal assistants' just do junior executives' typing and telephoning.

The confusion over titles arose because traditionally there was no promotion ladder and career-structure, and no precise definition of the secretary's work nor of the differences between *personal assistant*, *secretary*, *shorthand- or audio-typist*, or *word-processor operator* and *clerk*. Differences between these jobs are considerable, but in employers' and employees' minds they are blurred, which leads to disappointment and frustration on both sides of the desk. However, with the wider choice of career opportunities for women, fewer able women are now willing to stay in jobs without prospects of advancement (and there are still *very* few male secretaries). Mainly for that reason some organizations are now introducing something resembling career-structures (see below). For example, the difference between 'personal assistant' and 'secretary' is now often being taken seriously. Secretaries follow their boss's instructions; when they fully understand the department's work, they become a 'personal assistant' and in that capacity make their own decisions. For example, a sales manager's secretary would, if a sales representative falls ill, ask the boss to whom the sick person's work should be allocated. A personal assistant would simply reallocate the work, without asking the boss.

Another development which is changing the secretarial scene is 'team secretaries' (in another office, they might be called 'administrative assistants'). They 'manage' a group of, say, several junior architects in an architectural partnership, or overseas marketing people in an export department. They organize appointments, travel schedules, etc. and keep track of the department's various projects and assignments. If the head of the department or partnership wants to know where X is, or how project Y is progressing, the team secretary knows the situation.

Both personal assistant and team secretary are in fact junior/middle management jobs but they are not necessarily recognized as such (see MANAGEMENT, p. 272 and 'Position of women', p. 473).

The traditional secretary usually still works for one person or, increasingly, more than one. (This is of course the 'office' secretary, not the administrator in charge of an institution, learned society or similar organization (see CHARTERED SECRETARY, p. 110). It is the secretary's task to husband the boss's time and energy so that he or she can concentrate on whatever the job is at that moment.

Secretaries act as buffer between the boss and callers and phone calls, and take minor decisions on her/his behalf. They must understand their boss's work well enough to know when to act on their own initiative and when to ask for instructions. This is one of the most challenging secretarial skills. Secretarial duties may also involve:

1. Acting as link between individuals and various sections in an organization; this could be departments in a university, company or store, or individuals in a management-team, and may involve writing memos, ringing people up, going to see them.

2. Collecting information from a variety of printed and personal sources – this involves knowing where to go for whatever the information required, perhaps telephoning trade associations or government departments.

3. Preparing agendas for meetings and collecting documents supporting the various items, distributing the papers at the right time to the right people; taking minutes at meetings, editing them and writing them up.

4. Looking through the day's mail and deciding which letters the boss has to deal with personally and which ones to cope with independently; summarizing lengthy letters and documents; drafting replies to some letters and presenting them to the boss for approval and signature.

5. Making travel arrangements and arranging meetings, at home or abroad, for several busy people: this is a time-consuming task which requires meticulous attention to detail and may involve international trunk calls and lengthy correspondence until finally a time and place suitable to everyone has been agreed upon.

The amount of typing or word-processing secretaries do varies. In large offices they may deal only with their boss's confidential correspondence, other matters being dealt with by a 'junior secretary' or someone from the typing-pool or word-processing unit. Secretaries may be in charge of one or several juniors, or cope single-handedly.

The extent of automation still varies from one office to another, but it is increasing everywhere. The new technologies mean that secretaries and bosses both have access to numerous types of computerized equipment. As well as enabling bosses to do *their* job more effectively, secretaries are able to perform many administrative tasks more effectively than hitherto. They are also able to relieve their bosses of administrative tasks, and possibly take over part of the boss's main task. The availability of data-processing equipment – and opportunities to use it – should, in theory, enable capable secretaries to take part in executives' decision-making tasks, e.g. financial forecasting and analysis and production progress charting; or assessing customer response. The *potential* for merging the two roles – that of the manager/executive and the secretary – now exists. How much, in practice, the secretary will be able to exploit the potential depends on the boss's willingness to let go of responsibilities, the secretary's initiative, and a host of imponderables.

Traditional secretarial tasks which are, increasingly, computerized, include arranging meetings; booking conference rooms; recording and instant dispatch of voice and text messages; maintenance of lists, e.g. personal addresses, business contacts (with background information), internal telephone directories; 'unstructured information', e.g. product descriptions; training records; filing and retrieval; travel arrangements.

Invariably, being a secretary is a self-effacing job. Good secretaries rarely get the kudos they deserve when, thanks to their efficiency, crises are avoided, but they are likely to be blamed if things go wrong – if they forget to remind their boss of an appointment which she/he too had forgotten and which is written down in the appointments diary.

There are good opportunities for 'real' secretaries. They can pick and choose the environment they want to work in, whether the City, a public institution or a professional office – say, accountants' or solicitors'. There are some possibilities in fashion, in travel, employment and estate agents – in areas where specialist training is not expected – for going up the management ladder. *Very* few secretaries in television manage to jump the abyss between secretarial and creative work.

Secretarial work used to be the best way into management generally, but there are much better ways now (see MANAGEMENT, p. 272). The vast majority of secretaries remain secretaries throughout their working lives. Promotion usually still means becoming secretary to someone higher up in the hierarchy – e.g. from secretary to sales manager to secretary to finance director to secretary to managing director to secretary to chairman. In this promotion system, expertise gained in one job tends to be fairly useless in the next, therefore the opportunities for independent work, for becoming PA (or acting as PA at least) or executive, tend to be less in the new job than they were in the previous one. Many secretaries find that the higher up in the hierarchy their boss, the less the boss is likely to delegate. So secretaries who want a career and not a job need to find out far more details about what an advertised job involves than do people who go into structured careers with accepted work-content, qualifications, promotion prospects, etc.

Secretaries who have word processing experience can become *supervisors/co-ordinators/trainers*. They are the buffer between the users ('text originators') and the operators; they schedule work as it comes in and they appease users whose text cannot be dealt with instantly. They may also diagnose and possibly deal with minor equipment faults and deal with the equipment suppliers if things go seriously wrong. This job can lead to, or be combined with, 'in-house training' – work which involves training new word processor operators and persuading managers to learn what the equipment can and cannot do; writing manuals; advising office managers by evaluating the many different types of machines when new ones are to be bought. This type of job is still evolving. It always involves contact with a large variety of people; its exact content varies according to size, type and ideas of the employing organization.

Secretaries who want to get out of the office atmosphere and yet use their work experience can become *customer support representatives* with manufacturers. They demonstrate equipment to prospective clients and later provide a 'hand-holding' and trouble-shooting service for companies which have bought their equipment. This work, in turn, can lead to selling and marketing (see p. 294) for word-processing equipment manufacturers. (See also WORKING FOR ONESELF, p. 557.)

Specialist Secretary

Though there is no need to decide on any specialization before training, there are 3 specializations for which special training is useful but not essential.

1. *Medical secretaries*: They work in hospital, for one or several consultants; in consultants' private consulting rooms; or for general practitioners. They require knowledge of medical terminology and of health and social services organization. In hospital, secretaries have less contact with patients than in consulting rooms and general practice, but they have more companionship. In GPs' group practices the work involves organizing/administration.

2. *Farm or agricultural secretaries*: They deal with the paperwork which modern farming entails. They fill in forms, keep accounts, keep and analyse records, and deal with correspondence, often on their own initiative. Only very big farms employ fulltimers; most need part-time help. So farm secretaries either work as freelances, spending a number of days a month on different farms, or they are employed by farm-secretarial agencies and are sent out to different farms. The work is varied, as it involves working on different types of farm; and it requires experience and self-confidence because farmers, unlike other employers, usually know less about the work to be done (accounts, filling in VAT and other forms) than their secretaries. Specialist training is a great advantage.

Both medical and farm secretaries now often use computers; doctors' secretaries to keep patients' records; farm secretaries to record, for example, cows' milk yield in relation to expenditure on various foodstuffs.

3. *Bi- or multilingual secretaries*: They translate incoming mail; they may compose their own letters in a foreign language from notes dictated in English, but most outgoing mail is written in English. They sometimes read foreign journals and search for and translate or summarize relevant articles. Occasionally they may act as interpreter. Their scope varies: some secretaries hardly use their languages at all; others are relied upon totally by their

mono-lingual bosses. Foreign Office secretaries must be proficient in 1 language but many never use that knowledge even when working in embassies abroad. There are commercial opportunities abroad for truly bilingual secretaries with, occasionally, the relevant shorthand. International organizations usually require previous senior secretarial experience. Overall, the greatest demand is for French/English, German/English and French/German/English, mainly in international marketing and in export. There is a small, steady demand for Spanish, for other European languages, and for Russian and a growing demand for Japanese and Arabic.

At home, foreign shorthand is rarely required; in order to master it, it is essential to be *absolutely fluent* in the language(s) concerned. For most linguist-secretary jobs a grasp of the relevant country's economic and social set-up is far more important than shorthand and 100% speaking and writing fluency.

They get jobs easily, but not necessarily with much scope for using their language proficiency. Graduates are often overqualified. GCSE or A-level language plus knowing how to use a dictionary is often all that is needed, even when the job was advertised as for a linguist. There are more secretaries who want to work abroad than there are jobs available. However, good linguists with about 3 years' secretarial experience can get jobs in EC countries and elsewhere, mainly in British or multinational companies' offices.

Shorthand- and Audio-Typist/Word-Processor Operator

Many so-called secretaries are really typists or word-processor operators. They work for a number of people, often in a typing-pool or central word-processing unit or 'station', and not for individuals as secretaries do. Their job is far more impersonal, concerned with producing texts efficiently and economically rather than dealing with people and all the various jobs the secretaries cope with. It is work for people who like getting on with the job without having to talk much to their bosses; but it can be a step to secretarial work too.

The demand for *shorthand*-writers is still great though diminishing. There are still many executives who insist on dictating to an individual rather than into a machine.

Copy-typists have virtually disappeared. Offices now either use photocopying or similar machines or word processors (WPs).

A word processor basically consists of a typewriter-like keyboard connected to a visual display unit (VDU) which looks like a TV screen, and to a computer with a 'memory' in which previously 'keyed-in' texts are stored, coded, filed ready for 're-trieval', i.e. for future use either in further printed texts, or for 'call up' on VDU screens. The WP keyboard is usually connected to a printer; it may be connected to other WPs, either in an office next door, or in one, or several, offices hundreds of miles away. An operator or indeed a manager/executive could be transmitting a message instantly to other VDUs as well as producing the text in printed form. (Word processors may also be linked to other data-processing equipment, see COMPUTING, p. 142.)

Briefly, the word processor's main advantages over typewriters are these:

1. It enables the operator to correct mistakes easily and quickly.

2. It can produce any number of perfect 'top-copies' instantly.

3. It can automatically file, code, sort and have ready for future use not only whole printed texts but individual paragraphs or sentences or lists of names and/or addresses.

4. It can combine individual sections with new texts and/or with lists of addresses, or with other sections of text stored in the 'memory'.

Clerk

This may involve some typing and/or word processing and/or using computers (see COMPUTING, p. 142). Clerks' work varies even more than secretarial work. Some clerks work on their own all day; others are in constant contact with colleagues and/or the public. Clerks in travel agencies may send out brochures to customers or hand them out over the counter; in a mail order firm, however computerized the system, they may check incoming orders to see whether the right postal orders are enclosed; in a hospital or commercial office a junior may do nothing but photo-copy. Clerks may work in post-rooms, collecting and distributing mail from and to various departments and individuals. In person-nel departments, they may work on computerized staff records, entering details about absence, wage increases, etc. In large organi-zations, whether town hall, store or manufacturing company, there is often a computerized filing system. In a small office a clerk may still do 'old-fashioned' filing, answer the telephone, make the tea and do some typing/word processing. The extent to which clerks' work has been affected by the introduction of computerized equipment varies enormously but job opportunities have lessened. At the moment, many offices still rely largely on the old-fashioned methods of entering and updating facts and figures, transmitting messages, collecting and distributing information. But this is changing. For example in insurance offices, when updating clients' policies, clerks first had to look for the file, then re-type part of the policy and file it again. With computerized equipment however, the clerk keys in the reference code, the policy is 'called up' (appears on) the video display unit, the clerk keys in the necessary amendments and, at the press of a few buttons, the policy is amended as required, printed, and stored in the equipment's memory – the electronic file. Any telephone inquiry dealt with by clerks, whether from a supplier in a manufacturing industry or an airline customer, is dealt with now by keying in the question and getting the answer instantly on the VDU.

Clerks may also become telephonists or receptionists. The receptionist's job may be rather more complex than it appears – receptionists are expected to have a good knowledge of who does what in the organization so that they can direct callers to the right person or department. Hotel receptionists (see CATERING, p. 98) may do behind-the-scenes accounts work as well as dealing face-to-face with clients and staff.

Training   No set pattern. Secretaries should still learn shorthand, at least at 90–100 words per minute (and transcribe it adequately), and audio-type at 50 words per minute. They must be able to spell. They must know how to use, and where to find, sources of reference. They need a good grasp of who does what in the commercial world, in the community, in government. They must be able to draft and summarize letters, reports, etc. – both verbally and in writing.

Where, and how, they acquire the 'secretarial core skills' is totally immaterial. Certificates and Diplomas awarded by colleges, the Royal Society of Arts, the London Chamber of Commerce and Industry, Pitman's, for example, and specialist ones by the Association of Medical Secretaries, are useful when there are more applicants than vacancies. Qualifications secure a first interview, but they count for far less than impression made at interview.

A sixth-form education, A-levels in such subjects as geography, English, economics, and intensive courses in shorthand, typing and then word processing, are far more useful than leaving school at 16 and taking a 2-year secretarial course. GCSE (A–C) English language is essential: a degree is rarely an advantage. Even when an employer specifies 'graduate secretary', an intelligent, well-informed sixth-form leaver is usually acceptable. There are so many graduate secretaries simply because some arts graduates cannot think of anything else to do – not because many secretarial jobs are so intellectually demanding that only graduates could fill them. Graduate secretaries do not even have significantly greater chances of getting into management than sixth-form leavers.

There is a tremendous variety of secretarial courses, but there is no pecking order, no 'best buy'. Much education and training for secretarial/general office work and word processing is sadly disorganized and out of date, with several overlapping qualifications. Certain qualifications, such as the Royal Society of Arts', are well known and carry considerable weight, but individual colleges, teaching methods and equipment vary enormously. At this stage in the 'office revolution', when new office equipment and routines are being widely introduced, a course for a good qualification at a college with antiquated equipment, and teachers who know little of present-day office practice, may be less useful than a course in a college which arranges visits to modern offices, and which has teachers who understand 1990s office technology, even if the college only awards its own diploma.

One cannot even judge the usefulness of secretarial courses by their entry requirements. There are some courses which only accept entrants with at least 2 A-levels (some even insist on a degree) which may lead fairly quickly to senior secretarial jobs. But it is quite likely that students who take these courses would have got equally far, equally quickly, if they had merely taken a short sharp typing/word processing-only course. However, NVQs (see p. xx) are now in place at levels 1 and 2 which makes it possible to equate the standards of different organizations' certificates and diplomas. Higher-level NVQs are in the pipeline.

Courses fall into broad categories, each with many variations; and often with various optional subjects:

1. Courses for students with 2 A-levels or with degrees or comparable qualifications, lasting between 3 and 9 months; a 3 months' crash course, learning the core skills, should be sufficient.

2. 6-month to 2-year courses for students with 4 or 5 GCSEs (A–C). Unless 2-year courses include something like medical, legal, farm or linguist secretarial work, or A-level study, 2 years is unnecessarily long.

3. 1- or 2-year courses for students with 3 to 5 GCSEs (A–C). They often include GCSE (or A-level) study. Courses are likely to lead to clerical rather than secretarial jobs in the first instance.

4. Courses for students with 'a good general education' (no specific passes). These are not strictly speaking *secretarial* courses (whatever their title). They should last 2 years and include general educational subjects if they are eventually to lead to secretarial work.

5. 1-year courses in English, shorthand, typing, word processing, office routine, lead to *clerks'* and *typists'* or *word processors'* jobs (also applies to commercial courses at school).

6. BTEC (see p. xxi) courses, part time or full time. Broadly, First awards lead to *clerical* work; National awards lead to *secretarial* work. First awards should include Introduction to Keyboarding and its Application options, and National awards should include word/information processing options. For SCOTVEC equivalents see p. xxii.

However, adequate word processing is not available at all colleges. Many lack up-to-date equipment or have too little of it. Applicants with good typing skills can still get jobs: they may then be given in-house word processing training. However, as employers are often in a buyers' market now, applicants who are familiar with word processors are at a distinct advantage in the job market. For that reason, private word processing schools have proliferated over the last few years. Their courses vary enormously in quality; some use out-of-date equipment and/or provide insufficient 'hands on' WP experience and/or are unnecessarily long. Most good courses normally last only about 1 week full time (or longer part time/evenings only) *and they only accept students who can type.* So before signing on for a private school WP course, it is essential to make sure that it is a good one. On the whole, courses attached to well-known secretarial agencies are a wise choice. Most of them have been started to ensure the agency has a pool of well-qualified people on its books rather than to make a profit; they are run 'at cost'. Courses normally teach on the two or three types of machines in widest use. Word processor operators who then get jobs where they have to use a different type of machine, get short 'conversion training' on the job. In any case on-the-job training goes on for some time: it takes quite a few months for a word processor operator to be really proficient at the job.

Specialist training

Bi- or multilingual secretary: Entry requirements from 'good GCSE pass' or 'A-level standard' in the relevant language to language degree. Most courses last 2 years. Prospective secretary-linguists who intend to take a language degree should look out for degree courses including 'area studies' – which means the course covers the relevant country's history and social and economic institutions, etc. That type of knowledge is also very important for getting jobs abroad with commercial firms and international agencies.

Medical secretary: With 4 GCSEs (A–C) including English

language, 2-year full-time course; with 1 A-level, 1-year full-time course for *Diploma for Medical Secretaries*. With two GCSEs (A–C) one of which must be English language: 1-year full-time (or longer part-time) course for *Certificate in Medical Reception*. This can be converted into Medical Secretaries' Diploma by taking part-time day-release or evening courses. Home-study for the 2 qualifications is possible, if there is no course available locally.

Part-time courses leading to the *Diploma in Practice Administration* (approved by the British Medical Association and the Royal College of General Practitioners) are available for persons holding the Certificate in Medical Reception plus at least 1 year's experience; for those holding the Diploma; and for experienced secretaries who have not taken the Certificate or Diploma examination but have several years' experience of the work and hold a 'Letter of Recognition' (from the Association of Medical Secretaries).

Details from Association of Medical Secretaries, Tavistock House North, Tavistock Square, London WC1H 9LN.

Farm secretary: National Certificate or BTEC National Diploma courses for farm secretaries are run at some agricultural colleges.

Personal attributes

Secretaries who hope (probably in vain) to become executives: exceptional organizing ability, self-confidence, determination and ambition, a logical brain, business acumen, willingness to take responsibility and willingness to take orders; ability to communicate easily with people at all levels of education and status in the organization; willingness to work long hours.

Personal assistants: The above qualities without the ambition and business acumen; willingness to take responsibility must be coupled with willingness to remain in a supportive role; a sympathetic manner, a desire to be of use to others; ability to ignore getting undeserved blame when things go wrong and not getting well-deserved praise; indifference to seeing less able 'executives' have higher status and pay, and more responsibility.

Typists/word processor operators: Wanting to get on with one's work without involvement with people and in the organization's business; accuracy.

Clerks: depends on type of job – some require a liking for quiet backroom work dealing with paperwork; others a liking for dealing with people; most require attention to detail and willingness to do as told.

Late start

Secretarial work is easy to start late. While there are some employers who will not consider anyone over 35, there is a growing number of employers who prefer the over 35s. Some

courses geared to mature students are available under Employment Training (see p. xxiv) (including specialist secretary's
courses).

**Career-
break**

Should be no problem for secretaries with word processor operating experience. Post-experience BTEC/SCOTVEC (see pp. xxi,
xxii) units on Using Word Processors and Supervising Word
Processing have been introduced as *refresher* courses. These will
be useful for people returning after a gap.

Part time

Good opportunities for word processor operators. Not quite as
good for secretaries, who are expected to be available whenever
the boss wants them. However, even here part-time work and job-
sharing is gradually becoming accepted, but part-timers are never
likely to have as wide a choice of jobs as full-timers. The fewer
the hours they are willing to work, the more restricted the choice
of job.

Part time can be anything from 6 hours a week, to 4 full days; 2
or 3 full, or 3 or 4 half days are the most usual. A flexible number
of hours, to suit both secretary and employers and varying week
by week, is sometimes possible. There are a few jobs which can be
done in term-time only, leaving mothers free during the children's
holidays; and occasionally some 1 week (or fortnight) on, 1 week
(or fortnight) off jobs.

'*Temping*' is a kind of part-time work. It is particularly suitable
for actors, artists, models, etc., people who have to 'fill in' while
waiting for their own kind of work; for mothers who cannot get a
term-time-only job, and for secretaries, WP operators and typists
who prefer a frequent change of environment to getting involved
with one set of people and one type of work. Temps normally
work for agencies who send them to employers on a weekly or
daily basis; only those with very good contacts and experience can
work as freelances.

**Position
of
women**

This is still almost 100% women's work, but some men have
become secretaries. Some word-processing unit supervisors and
customer support representatives are male graduates who come
into the organization with computing experience or as management trainees.

**Further
informa-
tion**

No central organization. Local education authority for lists of
local courses (and see 'Medical secretaries', p. 471).

Related careers	CIVIL SERVICE – CATERING: *Hotel Reception* – COMPUTING/IT – HEALTH SERVICES MANAGEMENT – LANGUAGES – MANAGEMENT – PERSONNEL/HUMAN RESOURCES MANAGEMENT – PUBLIC RELATIONS – WORKING FOR ONESELF

Shipbroking, Airbroking, Freight Forwarding and Exporting

Entry qualifications
All educational levels; in practice at least 4 GCSEs (A–C). Also *graduate* entry. Fluency in at least 1 foreign language is a great advantage.

The work
Shipbrokers, airbrokers and freight forwarders are concerned with the efficient and economical movement of goods from one part of the world to another. The shipbroker uses only ships, the airbroker only aircraft, the freight forwarder uses any means of transport. The work is a vital part of world trade and at the centre of the country's commercial activities. Work in shipping and forwarding offices can lead to export management (see MARKETING AND SELLING, p. 294).

Shipbrokers

They match up empty ships with cargoes and negotiate terms on behalf of their clients. This process is known as 'fixing', and is rather like solving a giant jigsaw puzzle. Shipbrokers may use a regular cargo run or charter a ship for a single voyage or a series of voyages, or a part of a ship's freight space. They also act as agents for shipowners when their ships are in port and deal with customs formalities, loading documentation, arrangements for the crew and any problems that may crop up. Shipbrokers also buy and sell ships for their clients. Some specialize in one activity, others are involved in several.

Shipbrokers often work long and irregular hours, as they have to be in telephone contact with people all over the world during their working hours.

The Baltic Exchange in the City of London is the world's only shipping exchange. The 700-odd members comprise shipbrokers, grain traders, and others concerned with shipbroking. They meet 'on the floor of the Exchange' to trade (see also COMMODITY MARKETS, p. 140) and exchange mutually useful shipping information.

Airbrokers

They also match cargoes (and people) and carriers from and to all parts of the world. Air-chartering is done mainly by telephone; airbrokers rarely meet each other or see the aircraft they are chartering or the people whose goods or clients they are carrying. They may also buy and sell aircraft and equipment for their 'principals'. Work can be very hectic, as charters may be arranged only a day or so before take-off. However, most of the work is carefully planned ahead. The variety of aircraft for charter is much smaller than the variety of ships; the variety of cargo carried is growing steadily. The bulk of air-chartering is still concerned with two types of cargo: (1) people – aircraft are chartered 'on time charter' to tour operators or, for example, construction firms which transport personnel to and from the Middle East; and (2) perishable foods. Airbroking is still evolving, with airbrokers constantly looking for new business – especially to and from and in the Middle East, Far East and Africa. Opportunities are limited in what is a precarious industry.

Freight Forwarders

They arrange transport of all types of freight to and from any-where in the world. They search out the most efficient method or combination of methods of transport in each particular case, evaluating respectively the need for speed, security, refrigeration, the fragility of the goods, etc. Goods may be sent by traditional methods such as rail, or something more modern such as container ship or jumbo jet, or by a combination of several modes of transport. Freight forwarders must be well acquainted with the advantages and disadvantages of the various methods of transport (which they are likely to learn by experience and from colleagues rather than from the transporters themselves), and with the intrica-cies of freight handling and storage and the different techniques and arrangements in the various ports and airports all over the world. They must make it their business to find out routes which, though possibly longer in mileage, may be more efficient because turn-round arrangements in some ports and airports are quicker than in others.

They are also responsible for documentation, such as Bills of Lading, import and export licences, and for specialized packing and warehousing.

Some freight forwarders specialize in certain commodities or geographical areas; others in certain methods of transport and/or types of packing or warehousing.

Exporters

A wide range of companies have export departments and some
staff move into the export function from another department,
most obviously from sales within the UK. However, companies
frequently recruit staff from outside who have particular experience and expertise in dealing with overseas markets. Job titles and
functions vary, but examples are:

Export clerk in manufacturing company: checks and acknowl-
edges orders; liaises with production and packing departments;
lets customers know of any delays; organizes necessary paperwork.

Export sales correspondent: prepares quotations, tenders and
delivery schedules for customers, often within a geographical area
or product range; supervises the work of the export clerk; takes
part in sales promotions and deals with overseas agents.

Export area sales or *product manager*: responsible for reaching
sales targets within a market or product area; visits and looks
after existing customers and agents and researches openings for
new business; arranges overseas promotions/exhibitions; negotiates new contracts.

Export manager/director: in charge of all aspects of export
function; visits customers and agents in all the company's markets
and product areas; appoints new staff; sets sales targets; liaises
with UK sales and production managers.

Prospects depend largely on world trade conditions: both ship-
and airbroking were affected by the recent recession. London is
one of the world's largest shipping, air chartering and freight
forwarding centres and specialized freight forwarding is an expanding industry. There are some opportunities for experienced shipbrokers and for freight forwarders to work abroad for a spell.

Training   On the job: experience is the most important part of training and
there are no full-time training courses. There are specific institutes
for each of these specializations which set their own examinations;
these are studied for part time or by correspondence courses. In
some cases exemptions from the examinations or certain papers
may be given to holders of degrees or post-graduate awards in
transport/export management or similar or BTEC/SCOTVEC
Higher National awards with a transport or overseas trade option.
A few companies take graduate and occasionally A-level trainees
and pay for examinations.

The *Advanced Certificate in International Trade* (formerly
the *Foundation Course for Overseas Trade*) is jointly run as a

first-stage professional examination by the *Institute of Export* and the *Institute of Freight Forwarders*. Students then go on to take part 2 of the institutes' professional exams. (People working in export departments may take the Institute of Export's Certificate in Export Office Practice before the Advanced Certificate.)

Trainee shipbrokers take the Foundation Diploma in Shipping (including one of these specialist subjects: dry cargo chartering, ship management, ship sale and purchase, tanker chartering, liner trades or port agency) and then take the remaining qualifying examinations for membership of the Institute of Chartered Shipbrokers.

Personal attributes   Interest in commercial geography and world trade; a practical approach; a liking for paperwork, a good telephone manner; *especially for ship- and airbroking*: an entrepreneurial spirit and ability to win people's confidence.

Late start   Unusual, but should be possible for people with related industrial, transport or commercial experience (correspondence courses available).

Career-break   Might not present any problems for experienced shipbrokers/freight forwarders – except that methods of transport change rather rapidly and competition from young people is very keen.

Part time   Not at the moment – no reason why it should not be possible.

Position of women   In the past firms have been reluctant to appoint women to responsible positions because, they say, *shipbrokers* and *freight forwarders* deal with countries in which women are not at all equal, and a woman negotiator might therefore lose the firm some business. However, the position is changing and there is no reason why women should not succeed in this field – practicality and getting on with people easily are important ingredients, and women are supposed to be good at both. In *airbroking*, which is a newer career area where there were no traditions to break down, the number of women has increased and they have done well.

Further information   Institute of Chartered Shipbrokers, 24 St Mary Axe, London EC3A 8DE

Baltic Air Charter Association, The Baltic Exchange, St Mary Axe, London EC3A 8BU

Institute of Freight Forwarders Ltd, Redfern House, Browells Lane, Feltham, Middx. TW13 7EP

Institute of Export, 64 Clifton Street, London EC2A 4HB

| Related careers | MANAGEMENT – MARKETING AND SELLING – PURCHASING AND SUPPLY – STOCK EXCHANGE AND SECURITIES INDUSTRY – TRAVEL AGENT/TOUR OPERATOR |

Social Work

Entry qualifications

For entrants under 21, 2 A-levels and 3 GCSEs (A–C) in different subjects *or* 5 passes in the SCE, including 3 at Higher level, *or* approved alternative. For entrants over 21, evidence of ability to cope with course. For post-graduate courses, a degree.

The work

Social workers help people to overcome or adjust to a wide variety of social or personal problems. They work in a variety of settings: in local authority social services departments, dealing with the problems of families and children, the elderly, those with physical and mental disabilities and the homeless; in hospitals and other health settings, dealing with those who are ill and their families; in probation and after-care, dealing with offenders, prisoners, ex-prisoners and their families; in education departments, with children who are having problems which affect their education; in voluntary agencies which supplement the work of statutory services, sometimes with particular groups, e.g. the elderly or disadvantaged children.

The training of social workers is 'generic', i.e. it equips them to deal with all kinds of social problems, in various settings, with all age and client groups. Nevertheless there is scope to specialize in work with particular client groups, e.g. children or the elderly.

Field work

Field social workers work with people who live in their own homes, as opposed to in residential care. Most local authorities' social services departments (social work departments in Scotland) organize their field workers into area teams, providing a full range of services across the spectrum of client groups in a given geographical area. Within the area team there may be specialist workers or teams dealing with particular groups. Organization and balance between 'generic' workers and specialists vary. Some generic workers become virtual specialists simply by the balance of their case allocation. The nature of the area also affects social workers' caseloads; problems occur in some areas (e.g. a large refugee population) which are non-existent in others.

The work is a mixture of counselling, liaison, mediating, monitoring and practical problem-solving. Some people who turn to social services for help have immediate problems which can be sorted out fairly quickly. For example, a family with a young baby might need a social worker to negotiate on their behalf with British Gas so that their supplies are not cut off. Other problems require a longer-term relationship in which the social worker provides both practical assistance and counselling, helping individuals or families to identify both their problems, which are often complex and interrelated, and ways in which they might cope with them. The problems are very varied, from the stresses and problems of intractable poverty or long-term ill-health to the strains of caring for elderly relatives or handicapped children.

Social work is very much more complex than simply offering a sympathetic ear and practical help. There is a great deal of legislation which gives social workers both responsibility and powers to act in cases where people are at risk. The most obvious example is child protection, which is a top priority at present and which can take up a large proportion of a social worker's time. Social workers must assess and monitor families at risk of neglecting or abusing their children, visiting regularly and giving support, keeping an eye on how they handle their children, perhaps referring them to a family centre to learn childcare skills and discuss their problems. Sometimes, of course, social workers decide that it is not in the children's best interests to remain with their families and must take the necessary action and provide the proper supervision. The mentally ill are another group over whom social workers have powers of removal if they become a nuisance or a danger to others or to themselves.

Social workers do not just sort out problems: they try to prevent their getting worse or leading to other problems. For example, the isolation and poverty of young mothers can lead to child abuse. Social workers' preventive work can take the form of individual counselling and support, work with whole families or group work, where people with similar problems are brought together for mutual support.

The day-to-day work of a field social worker is very varied. Much time is spent visiting clients, listening to their problems, offering support and encouragement and monitoring those at risk. Most team members will have a day as duty officer, seeing clients who come into the office (e.g. seeking advice on benefits or without money to pay overdue bills) and taking calls (e.g. from a neighbour or teacher concerned about a child with unusual bruising). Time is also spent on paperwork, keeping detailed case notes, and writing reports, e.g. on a juvenile offender or for an adoption hearing. Liaison with other professionals or organizations is very important and time-consuming. For example, a social worker might have to arrange for an elderly client to have a home help, find residential accommodation for someone unable to cope alone, or track down additional complementary support from a voluntary agency.

Some field social workers within area teams specialize in, for example, adoption or child abuse cases. Others do more specialized work in a variety of other settings. *Social workers in hospitals* help with the problems that can arise through illness. For example, children might need to be looked after while their mother is in hospital; a family might need advice on financial assistance when the main breadwinner is unable to work; a pregnant teenager might need support and advice before, during and after the birth of her baby. Some social workers are attached to special units, such as clinics for the treatment of those dependent on drugs or alcohol, and some work in general practices or health centres alongside the family doctor, nurse, health visitor, community midwife and district nurse.

Social workers also work in day centres, adult training centres, social education centres, child guidance clinics and intermediate treatment, which involves working in the community with young people at risk. *Community social workers* (there is debate about to what extent they are a part of mainstream social work) work in the community to help people identify their common problems and work together to solve them, e.g. by setting up a mother and toddler group or establishing a community social centre. (With cutbacks in public expenditure this type of work has virtually disappeared in some areas.)

Education Welfare Work

Education welfare officers or *education social workers* deal with the problems which prevent children benefiting fully from their education. The problems can be very wide-ranging, from inadequate transport in a country area to complex family problems leading to truancy or behaviour problems, to material or emotional deprivation. The social workers work with schools to identify the problems, establish links with the home and devise ways of overcoming the problems. Most education welfare officers are employed by local education authorities, but some are with the social services department.

Probation Service

In England and Wales the probation service is organized into 56 areas responsible to the Home Office; in Scotland probation is part of local authority social work departments.

Like other social workers, probation officers have a dual role of care and control. It is their job to supervise offenders in the community and to 'advise, assist and befriend' them. The involvement begins before sentencing when the probation officer may be asked to prepare a social inquiry report to be taken into account when deciding on a suitable penalty. The probation officer develops a picture of the offender through interviews with him or her, the family, employers and so on, and tries to establish any circumstances relevant to the offence and whether it might happen again. A recommendation is then made to the court about suitable penalties.

Offenders may be released into the community on probation orders, community service orders or suspended sentence orders. The probation officer supervises them, making sure they understand the nature of the order and comply with any conditions.

Probation officers try to help offenders develop self-knowledge and self-discipline and regain self-respect. They might help with accommodation, work, developing skills, getting treatment for a psychiatric problem or social adjustment. Some offenders welcome the sympathy, interest and assistance offered by probation officers, but others are hostile to any figure of authority. Probation officers have to find the right way of gaining cooperation, but can always ultimately refer back to the courts.

Residential Care

Some people have problems that cannot adequately be dealt with in their homes with their families, even with the other help available. These people may need residential care on a long-term or temporary basis. Residential homes vary in size, purpose and client group. They may be run by local authorities or by voluntary agencies. They may cater for the elderly, the physically or mentally handicapped, ex-prisoners, single mothers or children.

The work varies greatly according to the type of home and client group. It can range from complex assessment and care in conjunction with other professionals to arranging birthday and other celebrations, to helping with basic day-to-day tasks such as dressing, feeding, shopping and so on. Counselling is also part of the job and may arise from many everyday occurrences. The aim is to help the residents to as much stability and independence as possible, whether they return to their own homes or remain in care. Good residential care depends on developing good relationships with residents and effective team-work with colleagues.

Residential care workers do not necessarily need to live in, but may be required to do so on a shift basis. Even those who live on site are not required to be on call all the time. A high proportion of workers in residential care are not qualified social workers. There are NVQs (see p. xx) available for care assistants.

Training

The new professional qualification for social workers is the Diploma in Social Work. Programmes leading to the qualification last at least 2 years (many are longer) and are planned and run by educational institutions and social work agencies working together as programme providers. The Dip.S.W. is a generic qualification but students have the opportunity for an extended placement and associated study in one particular practice setting. Students may begin courses at 18, but the Dip.S.W. is not awarded until the candidate is 22. (Most entrants are older.)

Programme content includes: knowledge and understanding of human growth and behaviour and of a range of human needs; the process of observation and assessment; transcultural factors; aims, methods and theories; social work settings; administrative and legal systems which provide the framework for social work practice. Students also learn about the rights of clients and examine the ethical issues which confront social workers, as well as developing skills in, for example, making decisions, using resources and compiling social histories.

Programme structures vary to meet the needs of those entering at different points. Most programmes lead to an academic award (e.g. Dip.H.E., degree, post-graduate degree or diploma) as well as the Dip.S.W. Some students are employment-based; others are college-based. (Employment-based students are already employed in the personal social services, are admitted to a programme with the agreement of their employers, keep their jobs and continue to be paid a salary.) College-based students are often required to have had relevant paid or voluntary experience.

The main patterns of training are:

1. Non-graduate route: 2-year full-time courses leading to Dip.S.W.; many courses also award Dip.H.E.; some 3- or 4-year part-time courses available.

2. Degree route: 3- and 4-year full-time courses leading to Dip.S.W. and degree in relevant subject.

3. Post-graduate route. 2-year full-time courses leading to Dip.S.W. and a relevant post-graduate degree or diploma.

Personal attributes

The desire to help people irrespective of one's own personal likes and dislikes; the ability to communicate with every level of intelligence, cultural or social background or emotional state; perseverance in the face of apparent failure when clients/groups show no sign of improvement or appreciation of efforts made for or on behalf of them; stability; a ready understanding of other people's way of life and point of view; sympathy and tolerance of human failings; belief in individual's potential to do better; good verbal and written skills to record and report; the ability to take an interest in other people's problems without becoming emotionally involved; a sense of humour; wide interests unconnected with social work (to keep a sense of proportion); patience and empathy.

Late start Maturity is essential. Over 90% of students on Dip.S.W. programmes are over 25; 40% are between 35 and 44. Some programmes are specially designed for those with family commitments.

Career-break Returners are welcomed back. Some authorities may have formal schemes.

Part time Part time and job-sharing available.

Position of women About three-quarters of social workers are women. A much smaller proportion of senior jobs is filled by women, but their position is improving. 21 Directors of Social Services are now women (out of 132).

Further information CCETSW Information Services: Derbyshire House, St Chad's Street, London WC1H 8AD; 78–80 George Street, Edinburgh EH2 3BU; 6 Malone Road, Belfast BT9 5BN; St David's House, Wood Street, Cardiff CF1 1ES

Related careers CAREERS WORK – NURSERY NURSE – NURSING – POLICE – PRISON SERVICE – TEACHING – YOUTH AND COMMUNITY WORK

Sociology

Entry qualifications   2, or more often 3, A-levels and 3 GCSEs (A–C); usually maths or statistics and English at either level.

The work   Sociology is sometimes confused with social work, but there is a vast difference between the two. Social workers deal with individuals with problems (see SOCIAL WORK, p. 480); sociologists try to examine the way society functions: they study the conditions under which problems arise to understand why they do so. Sociologists research and develop theories and 'concepts', and try and find solutions or at least ameliorations to problems. Social workers need some understanding of sociology; but sociologists do not need the professional social workers' skills of coping with individuals' problems.

Sociologists research and develop theories about the social relationships that make up society and how these change or remain constant over time. They look at the interactions between individuals, between groups, and within and between whole communities. For example, sociologists who study schools may investigate what happens when teachers and pupils meet in different institutional settings – in class, on the sports field, in the street. From such investigations theories about the structure of school life, its importance to society and the problems that arise during education can be constructed.

Sociology covers every area of human social activity, e.g. race relations, interaction between the sexes, union–management disputes, the doctor–patient relationship, problems caused by homelessness, poverty and unemployment. Sociologists examine the institutions which make up society's legal, political and economic systems, the workplace, the family, and both urban and rural communities.

Virtually every aspect of modern life is of interest to sociologists. They are usually concerned with highly topical issues. In recent years these have included the impact of technological advance; the sociology of science and medicine; child sexual abuse and its detection; the treatment of people suffering from AIDS and understanding the social factors involved in stopping its spread.

Sociologists hope that by understanding the complexities of society they can avert some problems. An example is where new technology innovations change the nature of available jobs in a city and older male workers find themselves out of a job. Sociologists recognize that for some men unemployment can strain relations between them and their families, leading to potential domestic violence or suicide. Because sociology has devoted much research to the key concepts of class and gender, it can suggest which groups might find the strain greatest. Therefore advice can then be offered to employers, councils and government on the consequences of changing employment patterns.

Sociologists collect information in a variety of ways, mainly by the fieldwork techniques of observation and interviewing. Observation may involve participating in the work of an institution or an organization such as a factory or a youth club, or it may mean moving into an urban or rural community and joining in the life of that community. A particular study may take months or years. Interviewing can sometimes be combined with observation, but is often carried out independently using systematically prepared sets of questions. Different kinds of research call for different styles of survey. Apart from this fieldwork, there is the collation, analysis, interpretation and presentation of the information collected. Statistics and computers are used extensively. For some sociologists the important part of their job is the development of theory and concepts which can then be used as starting-points for new investigations.

Sociology is closely allied to and overlaps with other social sciences, especially social anthropology, social psychology (p. 402) and economics (p. 180).

There are far more sociology graduates than jobs/training as sociologists. Careers in research and higher education have become very scarce. While a sociology degree is never a vocational qualification, it can be the basis for further specific training and for many kinds of jobs with on-the-job training. There are reasonable opportunities within health and social services and with voluntary agencies for jobs involving a substantial amount of applied research. Now, more sociologists go into industry, to work in *industrial relations* or other *personnel specializations* (see p. 365) and generally on questions related to organizational and technological change. There are some opportunities in *market research* (see p. 16) and *marketing* (see p. 294). The *police* (see p. 385) welcome sociologists' understanding of human behaviour.

Training   Honours degree in sociology or a combination of social sciences. There are also some courses which combine sociology with arts or with modern languages. On some business studies degrees sociology is a major option. There are also a few courses where sociology can be combined with physics and/or maths, engineering, education, management studies, computer studies.

The choice of the right course is important, and complicated: the wording used to describe courses varies, and the combination of subjects covered and the emphasis given to the different aspects of sociology cannot necessarily be deduced from the title given to a particular course. It is essential to study up-to-date prospectuses, and to consult the *CRAC Degree Course Guide* before choosing a course. It is not wise to go by the experience of people who read sociology even recently, because of the many changes and innovations in this field.

During their first year, students study the rudiments of the social sciences generally: economics, politics, social institutions, social and/or economic history, psychology, statistics, geography. During the second and third years they concentrate entirely on sociology or choose 2, occasionally 3, subjects from among: sociology, economics, geography, social administration, politics, philosophy, and statistics.

Personal attributes   A deep but detached interest in how people live, think and behave; a rigorous scientific approach to contemporary social problems rather than emotional responses; the ability to get on well with all kinds of people at all levels of intelligence, at least sufficiently well to interview them successfully; ability to recognize one's own biases; an analytical, logical brain; the ability to discuss and write lucidly, and some mathematical ability.

Late start   Many mature students study sociology. Maturity helps in work which centres around understanding human behaviour, but as jobs are scarce young graduates tend to be given preference.

Career-break   Should not cause any problems as long as people keep up with developments. Reduced fees for British Sociological Association.

Part time   Occasional research assignments. Job-sharing possible.

Position of women   Depends entirely on type of job: on the whole women sociology graduates do not encounter special problems. As the degree is a preparation for a wide variety of jobs, it could be a useful preparation for women who intend to return to work after a break and who are not quite sure what they want to do eventually. More women than men take sociology degrees.

Further information	British Sociological Association, Room 701, 7th floor, Columbia House, 69 Aldwych, London WC2B 4DX (send s.a.e.)

Related careers	ADVERTISING: *Market Research* – ECONOMICS – MANAGEMENT SERVICES: *Work Study* – NURSING: *Health Visitor* – PERSONNEL/HUMAN RESOURCES MANAGEMENT – POLICE – PSYCHOLOGY – SOCIAL WORK

Speech and Language Therapists

Entry qualifications

Degree course requirements. Subjects should normally include English, a science subject, maths, a foreign language. Some courses specify certain sciences at A-level.

The work

Speech therapy is concerned with communication difficulties. Recent advances in the field mean that speech therapists can assess and treat successfully all kinds of voice, speech and language defects. Children may have an articulation problem or be excessively slow in learning to talk. Stammering can afflict people of all ages. In hospital clinics therapists work with children and adults who may have lost the ability to speak through brain damage (e.g. a stroke) or disease. Patients who have had their larynx or voice box removed have to be taught an alternative method of sound production.

Every patient needs a different approach – in helping each case, therapists must apply their knowledge of phonetics, psychology, anatomy and physiology, neurology and acoustics, and their common sense.

Speech therapists work in clinics, special schools or in hospitals. Some patients are treated in groups, most individually. Most speech therapists work on their own, some as members of a team. In rural areas considerable travelling may be necessary.

A speech therapist meets a great many people – teachers, social workers, doctors, psychologists, as well as patients. The work is very demanding and responsible.

There is a steady demand for therapists, but jobs are not necessarily available just where they are wanted. There are some opportunities in the Commonwealth and other English-speaking countries.

Training

This is now an all-graduate profession.

3- or 4-year degree course syllabus includes: speech pathology and therapeutics; phonetics; linguistics; anatomy and physiology; psychology; neurology. Students are given an insight into related fields, such as physics of sound; paediatrics; the social services;

plastic surgery in relation to speech therapy; audiology; diseases of the ear, nose and throat. During practical work in hospital and in school clinics students first observe then assist with treatments.

There are 2-year post-graduate Diploma courses for graduates in psychology, linguistics or other relevant subjects. Both methods are equal in job-getting terms.

Personal attributes Understanding of people, whatever their age, temperament, background, and mood of the moment; desire to help; ability to detect personal problems which may have a bearing on the cause and treatment of the defect; tact; unlimited patience. Because much of the work is with children, and sometimes with emotionally disturbed ones at that, the knack of gaining children's confidence; a pleasant voice – young patients are apt to imitate; a sensitive ear to detect slight sound differences; a calm manner and stable temperament; good command of concise written English for reports and notes to guide parents. *For senior posts*: organizing ability.

Late start Possible: over-25s may be accepted with slightly lower than normal entrance qualifications. Jobs should be no more difficult than for the young entrant.

Career-break Should be no problem. *Refresher courses* available.

Part time Some opportunities, but not usually for head of department jobs. Job-sharing is increasing, even at senior level.

Position of women This used to be an all-female job, but now an increasing number of men are entering the profession. They now account for about 10%.

Further information College of Speech and Language Therapists, 6 Lechmere Road, London NW2 5BU

Related careers DRAMA – SOCIAL WORK – TEACHING: *Special Needs Education*

Sport

Entry qualifications   No formal educational qualifications. For degree courses in sport or recreation studies: 2–3 A-levels.
NOTE: an A-level in Sport Studies is now widely available.

The work   Sport can be divided into 3 main career areas, although many people combine 2 or more:

1. *Players* or *participants* who are paid professionals. This guide is concerned only with those sports in which it is possible to earn a living, but the professional/amateur distinction is frequently blurred or has disappeared altogether.

2. *Teaching* or *coaching* children or adults.

3. *Administration* (which overlaps with LEISURE/RECREATION MANAGEMENT, see p. 264).

Professional Players

In most cases those with sufficient talent will have been spotted well before they leave school. People whose job it is to find and nurture talent will have discovered potential players through schools, youth clubs, local and county teams. In general it is too late to start serious training for a sporting career after leaving school (exceptions are horse and motor racing which cannot be started while at school). For most people sport has to remain a recreation.

Training   *Football (boys only)*
The traditional method of entering football, the club apprenticeship, has been replaced by the 2-year YT for 16/17 year olds. The first year of the scheme is broad-based: on-the-job training includes football training and coaching, work experience in various aspects of running and maintaining the club. Trainees follow a day-release course at college, working towards City and Guilds certificates (including Recreation and Leisure), life saving and sports leaders' awards and following an Information Technology course or BTEC National Certificate (Leisure option). After the first year they are assessed: the majority stay on at the football club and continue their football training and day-release course.

Others may choose to concentrate on another area of work within the club or transfer to a more appropriate YT. At the end of the 2 years, the club decides whether or not to offer a professional contract: the majority are not good enough and leave the game by their early 20s.

Cricket (boys only)
Most county cricketers are recruited straight from school, having already played trial matches. For a few seasons they play in club and second XI matches. If they are considered to have first team potential they may be offered a contract by the county: they agree to play exclusively for the club. About 50 county players each year find cricket jobs overseas during our winter, playing cricket or coaching. The rest have to find other employment in the close season (a few play professional football). Most have stopped playing by the age of 40, although top players may stay in the game as coaches, umpires or managers.

Tennis (boys and girls)
The most promising players follow a national training scheme run by the Lawn Tennis Association. Most will have started playing at age 8 or 9 (usually short tennis at school). They start by playing in local club tournaments and may be selected for county training. The best county players are then selected for regional training, at around 10 years old. The best of these players are then sent for weekend courses to the Lawn Tennis Association Rover School at Bisham Abbey, Bucks. The LTA organizes and helps finance national and international tournaments, as well as local training, for them. Some become full-time players by age 16–17. It is often clear by the age of 19 if they are good enough to make it their career. In any one year, only around a dozen men and women make a full-time living and only a handful earn very large sums (and only provided they are ranked in the top 50 internationally). A few gain scholarships to the United States at 18/19 years.

Golf (boys and girls)
There are 2 distinct kinds of golfing professional: (1) the *club professional* (belonging to the Professional Golfers' Association) and (2) the *tournament player* (since 1985, belonging to the PGA European Tour and, for women, the WPG European Tour). In the whole of Europe there are fewer than 250 tournament players and fewer than 3,000 PGA club professionals. Although some professional golfers have become successful in both areas, this is not recommended for newcomers, since intense competition within each branch requires single-minded dedication to one only.

1. *Club professionals*: Work at a club, running the shop, repairing equipment and giving lessons. The job requires a high level of playing ability (they have their own tournaments organized by the PGA), business flair and organizing ability. In golf there is a very clear distinction between amateur and professional status and aspiring club pros should first seek advice from the PGA before taking the plunge and forfeiting their amateur status. Before being registered as trainees, potential professionals (men and women) must first spend a minimum 6-month probationary period with a PGA approved training establishment. During this they retain their amateur status and aim to reduce their handicap to 5 or less. They then take the PGA entrance examination (unless they have GCSEs A–C in English and maths), sign a contract and become professional. They follow a 3–4 year planned programme of work (covering all aspects of the business) with on- and off-the-job instruction (including residential courses), leading to a final exam. They must be prepared to work long hours, perform menial tasks and earn very little while learning. Since September 1991 there is a BTEC Higher National Diploma (sandwich course) in Golf Studies for amateurs. During the second, work experience, year they are expected to turn professional. This course is also available to qualified professionals as a distance-learning package.

All potential pros must have a single-figure handicap before starting; all the first intake on to the HND had a handicap of 4 or less.

2. *Tournament players*: aspiring professional men players have to qualify the first season for 1 of the 50 available Player's Cards by competing in a pre-qualifying school (tournament), then in the qualifying school held in Europe. To retain their Card they need to finish in the top 125 in the European tournaments that season. Only a handful of tournament players are successful enough to earn large sums through winnings and commercial sponsorship.

Women's golf is a growth area (there are around 250 tournament players) and women have their own association. Applicants for probationary membership of the WPG European Tour must be aged 18 or over and, if amateur, have a current handicap of 1 (without star). Existing professionals may also apply, provided they are members of a recognized Ladies' Professional Golf Association/Tour. All applicants must be proposed and seconded by members of the Tour.

Horse racing (*boys and girls*)

There are 2 kinds of races – flat and National Hunt (over jumps). Increasingly, training of stable staff for both kinds of racing stables is carried out by the British Racing School, Newmarket, rather than by trainers themselves. School leavers can either apply direct to the BRS or to individual trainers who will then send them to the School after some practical experience in the stables. Pupils must be 16/17, around 9 stone or under. Previous riding experience is not essential but helps.

Basic courses at the British Racing School, Newmarket, last 9 weeks, those at the Northern Racing School 12 weeks. Boys and girls are then placed with trainers or thoroughbred stud owners as stable 'lads'. Courses cover riding, grooming, mucking out and basic care of horses, plus lectures on racing topics. The training is for stable staff, not jockeys. Trainees work towards a vocational qualification in Racehorse Care and Management. NVQs (see p. xx) levels 1 and 2 are in the process of being accredited. (The awarding body is the Racing and Thoroughbred Breeding Training Board.) A tiny minority become apprentice jockeys – the great majority remain as stable 'lads' (there are 50 'lads' for every jockey). National Hunt 'lads' are heavier (up to 9/10 stone); they need to gain experience first with a National Hunt trainer, who will send them to the British Racing School if they think they are suitable (in which case the weight restrictions are waived). A very small number become 'conditional' jockeys (the National Hunt equivalent to apprentice jockeys). There is a clear distinction between *amateur* and *professional jockeys*, with many more races for professionals.

Women have done well over jumps and on the flat but their racing history is comparatively short. They have only been allowed to ride as professionals on the flat since 1975 and over jumps since 1976. The problem is that only those considered likely to ride winners are given rides; so until they have had success and proved themselves, they are unlikely to be chosen, which makes it hard for them to get started.

Teaching, Coaching/Instructing

For *PE teaching*, see TEACHING, p. 521.

Coaches and instructors in individual sports work at varying levels and in different settings, from national teams to youth clubs, from private sports clubs to local authority leisure centres. A great many coach part time and/or voluntarily, while following another paid occupation. Full-time paid coaches are nearly all ex-professionals or leading amateurs. Some combine playing with coaching. As well as having great technical expertise they need the ability to get the best from players, to know when to sympathize and when to put on pressure. The relationship between player and coach is crucial to success. All the sports' governing bodies run courses for coaches and instructors, e.g. the LTA Training of Coaches Scheme.

Sports Administration
(excluding Leisure/Recreation Management
– see p. 264)

Most sports governing bodies have a very small paid staff. Apart
from the usual secretarial and clerical posts, the administration of
organizations such as the FA or Lawn Tennis Association is
carried out by people with relevant expertise, either as former
players or managers, or in business or public relations which
could help to bring in sponsorship. There are occasional openings
for people with degrees in sports science or recreation management. (The LTA runs a Diploma in Tennis Management.)

Active sports careers are necessarily short. After this a minority
manage to find work in some way connected with their sport
(coaching, managing, promoting products), while the majority
have to look elsewhere for employment. Therefore it is essential
that those considering a sporting career should look ahead and
reach as high a standard academically as possible while at school
or college to enable them to take up another training later. This
may mean combining a course of further or higher education with
part-time playing (e.g. as some cricketers do).

Personal   Total dedication and single-mindedness; strong competitive urge
attributes   and will to win; high level of physical fitness and mental and
physical stamina; ability to respond positively to criticism; resilience and will-power to cope with injuries and setbacks.

Position   Sport is different from any other work area. Private clubs are
of   excluded from the Sex Discrimination Act altogether and, as most
women   sport is organized by clubs, those who choose to can refuse
women as members; also sporting competition may be confined
to one sex where the 'average' woman is at a physical disadvantage
to the 'average' man (i.e. in football, not darts or horse racing).
Even the outstanding girl or woman who is good enough to merit
a place in a male team and who may be the best available player
can be barred and so is unable to experience the highest level of
competition. All too often girls who are good at sport at school
are considered rather unfeminine, while boys who are good at it
are highly valued. Girls are often automatically assumed to be
worse at sport whereas certainly at primary school sex differences
are negligible (and it is at this age that serious interest and
training in most sports needs to start). Men's events are generally
more prestigious, better sponsored and carry higher prize money

than women's. Very importantly, the media takes very little notice of women's sporting achievements, whether amateur or professional. However, the situation is improving little by little and no potentially outstanding sportswoman should be put off. In certain sports the gap is narrowing between male and female achievements and each year sees a new 'first' for a woman.

Further information

The Sports Council, 16 Upper Woburn Place, London WC1H 0QP

The Central Council of Physical Recreation, Francis House, Francis Street, London SW1P 1DE (for list of courses)

The Footballers' Further Education and Vocational Training Society Ltd, 2 Oxford Court, Bishopsgate, Manchester M2 3WQ

Test and County Cricket Board, Lord's Ground, London NW8 8QN

The Lawn Tennis Association Trust, The Queen's Club, West Kensington, London W14 9EG

Professional Golfers' Association, National Headquarters, Apollo House, The Belfry, Sutton Coldfield, West Midlands B76 9PT

The PGA European Tour, The Wentworth Club, Virginia Water, Surrey GU25 4LS

Women Professional Golfers' European Tour, The Tytherington Club, Macclesfield, Cheshire SK10 2JP

British Racing School, Snailwell Road, Newmarket, Suffolk CB8 7NU

Northern Racing School, The Stables, Rossington Hall, Doncaster, South Yorks. DN11 0HN

Related careers

LEISURE/RECREATION MANAGEMENT – TEACHING

Stock Exchange and Securities Industry

The London Stock Exchange is the central market place through which investors, both individuals and institutions, buy and sell securities, i.e. stocks and shares. These securities are a means by which companies and government raise finance. As well as the Official List of securities quoted on the Exchange, there are also: an Unlisted Securities Market, which deals in smaller, less well-established companies; the 'Third Market' for new companies; and the London Traded Options Market – an option is the right but not the obligation to buy or sell a set amount of security, at a set price, within a set period of time; it is also a 'contract' which can itself be traded.

Recent years have seen enormous changes in the operations of the London Stock Exchange. Trading on the market floor has been replaced by the computer screen and telephone. (Options are still traded on the floor but this is due to change.) Rules governing membership of the Exchange were changed and securities dealing now takes place in merchant banks, clearing banks and investment banks, as well as the old stockbroking firms. The term 'securities house' is frequently used.

Though London and its London Stock Exchange are a major world centre for the trading of domestic and international securities, the securities industry is truly international, with trading a 24-hour activity.

Following the changes known collectively as 'Big Bang' in 1986 and the resultant explosion in securities trading activity, it became clear that the financial rewards could be extremely high. More recent years have made equally clear that the risks are high as firms have cut down or pulled out of trading activities – and got rid of large numbers of highly paid staff.

Entry qualifications Nothing rigidly laid down, but at least GCSE (A–C) maths and English normally expected. Most employers have substantial *graduate* recruitment. Most analysts/researchers will be graduates.

The work Since 'Big Bang' did away with the separate and distinct functions of the stockbroker and jobber and established broker/dealers, some of the terms have come to be used loosely. A broker/dealer may be a firm or an individual; an individual may be just a broker or just a dealer, or combine both roles; some firms specialize in one or other activity or segment of the market, others offer a complete service.

Researchers, or *analysts*, provide the information on which to base advice to clients. They usually specialize in a particular industrial sector or group of companies. They develop a thorough understanding of their area by studying company reports, meeting managers, seeking out any information of relevance to the industry and keeping up to date on any news likely to affect it, analysing past, present and future indicators and forecasting future performance.

Brokers, or *salesmen/women*, take the results of the research and try to persuade their clients to buy or sell shares. Some deal with institutional clients, developing long-term relationships with their fund managers. Brokers dealing with private clients may have to deal with many more clients and many more securities, since small investors may be interested in a range of companies too small to be considered by the institutional investors. Some clients follow the market themselves and require only an execution service. Others require advice on investment and brokers or salesmen/women must thoroughly understand their clients' circumstances in order to give appropriate advice.

Dealers, or *traders*, carry out the technical side of deals. They may act for brokers and their clients, negotiating the deal with other 'market-makers' (who are specialized dealers) or a third party, or they may act on their own account as principals, seeking to make a profit out of buying low and selling high. (Strict regulations ensure that clients get the best price available.)

Settlement staff process the transactions arranged by the dealers. Routine work is done by computer; the rest is highly specialized and involves the preparation of documents and calculating and arranging payment of commission and taxes. (The Exchange is now working to introduce a computerized automatic execution system for the transaction of smaller orders, as well as a method of 'paperless transfer'.) Settlement staff with the right skills can move into sales or dealing.

Training   On-the-job training has always been a feature of Stock Exchange work and continues to be. This, however, can mean a very sophisticated graduate training programme. While training, perhaps by a 'Cook's Tour' of several back-room departments, recruits who plan to deal in securities or give investment advice normally study for the exams of the Securities and Futures Authority Limited. These must be passed before one can become a *registered trader* or *registered representative*, which is mandatory for those who trade or advise. Study may be by evening classes, distance learning or in-company tuition.

These exams are tests of basic knowledge; there are more specialized exams leading to the Securities Industry Diploma.

Administration of the London Stock Exchange: the Exchange itself employs staff in a variety of roles. Many of the vacancies are for computer-trained staff to help in the design, development and running of the various automated systems. People with accountancy, legal, company secretary and general management skills are also recruited. Each year the Exchange takes a number of graduates with good honours degrees and management potential on to the Graduate Training and Development Scheme.

The Exchange also manages a YT scheme: trainees may work in the Exchange or in member firms, and there is a very high success rate in permanent placements for those completing the scheme.

A large number of staff are employed in general clerical and administrative work and there is good scope for promotion from within the organization.

Personal attributes
For *researchers/analysts* – numeracy, ability to assess long-term trends, analytical skills; for *brokers/salesmen/women* – affability, the ability to develop good relationships with clients and inspire confidence; for *dealers* – stamina, willingness to take risks, ability to make quick decisions, high powers of concentration, exceptional self-confidence, memory for people and figures.

Late start
Opportunities mainly for those with professional qualifications in, for example, accountancy, economics, computing, general management. Analysts often have previous experience in industry. Dealing is a young person's job.

Career-break
Possible in research, analysis, computing and management areas.

Part time
Rare. Possible in administrative areas.

Position of women
Opportunities are increasing for women willing to break down traditional barriers. Proportions of women at junior levels and among graduates in research and analysis are growing.

Further information   Public Affairs Department, the London Stock Exchange, London EC2N 1HP

Related careers   ACCOUNTANCY – BANKING – BUILDING SOCIETY WORK – ECONOMICS – INSURANCE

Surveying

Surveyor

Entry qualifications

For membership of the Royal Institution of Chartered Surveyors: 2 A-levels (or 3 Scottish Highers), 3 GCSEs (A–C) or equivalent; maths and an English subject to be included, at either level. For many degree courses, specific A-levels or A-levels from a group of subjects are required. For example maths, or geography or economic geography or a physical science may be asked for.

For membership of the Incorporated Society of Valuers and Auctioneers: 5 GCSEs (A–C) or equivalent, including English language and maths.

The work

The work is not *necessarily* mainly technical: in many surveyors' jobs the commercial element is greater than the technical; but technical expertise is essential background knowledge. The variety of jobs is very great.

Surveying is an umbrella term for jobs which are, in varying degrees and in varying proportion, concerned with, to quote the RICS, 'the measurement, management, development and valuation' of virtually anything: oceans, rivers, harbours, earth's surface, all land, and anything that is in or on land or water, whether natural or man-made. Many surveying jobs are also concerned with protecting or improving the urban and rural environment and the efficient use of resources. However, most surveying is a commercial activity rather than an environmental subject.

The various surveying branches each involve a different mix of technical, commercial, practical and academic ingredients, and different amounts of time spent on dealing with clients, dealing with other professionals, and on office and outdoor work. Each branch, therefore, suits people with different temperaments, interests, aptitudes. For example, the urban estate agent-surveyor has little in common with the hydrographic surveyor charting oceanic depth, or with the planning surveyor doing research into shopping centres.

The professional surveying specializations are grouped into 'Divisions' by the Royal Institution of Chartered Surveyors. These are, in order of size: general practice which covers valuation, estate agency, auctioneering and urban estate/housing management; quantity surveying; building surveying; land agency and agricultural surveying; planning and development; land and hydrographic surveying; mineral surveying.

The Incorporated Society of Valuers and Auctioneers' qualification covers much the same ground as the RICS's General Practice Division *except* housing management. (See also HOUSING MANAGEMENT, p. 225). The ISVA divisions also include fine arts and chattels, agricultural practice and plant and machinery.

The main surveying branches:

General Practice Surveyors

Valuation surveyors (also called valuers, or simply surveyors)
They assess the value of any type of property at any particular time. It may be in connection with rating, insurance, death duty purposes, as well as for general commercial and, these days, for investment purposes. Some specialize as *investment surveyors*. There are various valuation methods; the most commonly used is the 'comparison' method. This is an intricate mixture of basing judgement on ascertainable facts – value of property in the neighbourhood or other similar property; quality, etc. – as well as on 'getting the feel'. When assessing the value of residential property, or a row of shops, for example, factors taken into account include possible future development in the area (motorways, one-way traffic schemes, housing estates, parking restrictions); amenities (open spaces; swimming baths; entertainment facilities generally); proximity to schools, shops, transport; noise; as well as type of neighbourhood and informed guesswork as to whether the area is likely to go down/come up or whether it has any feeling of community (which might affect quality of school or be of interest to the elderly, etc.).

Valuers also assess contents of houses. Though they are expected to be able to tell a Rembrandt from an amateur's efforts, valuers do not normally assess the value of works of art but call on an expert in that field as necessary (who may be a colleague qualified in the chattels section of the RICS General Division or the ISVA's Fine Arts and Chattels Division). If working for a property developer or local authority they may value land. They may inspect, for example, a plot of land which is up for sale, assess its potential in terms of houses, shops, flats, etc. to be built there, and do a rough 'costing' of whatever type of building is being considered. They also value all kinds of plants and machinery.

Apart from working for estate agents, local authorities, property developers and other commercial concerns, valuation surveyors also set up in private professional practice. Work for property developers requires a certain amount of gambling instinct and very pronounced business acumen; local authority valuers' work is more concerned with valuing according to laid-down criteria.

Estate agents

Valuation surveyors (as described above) may be estate agents, but estate agents are not necessarily valuation surveyors. Within surveying, estate agency is the most commercially and least technically oriented specialization and probably the largest in terms of opportunities. There is at the moment no need for estate agents to have particular qualifications (but this may soon change). However, most firms of estate agents have at least one RICS-, ISVA- or NAEA- (see p. 509) qualified partner. Estate agents negotiate the sale, purchase, leasing of property – not only of houses but also of industrial and commercial premises, agricultural and other land. They arrange and advise on mortgages and on implications of rent acts, and on relevant law generally. As *managing agents* they manage property for clients, which involves drawing up leases, collecting rents, responsibility for maintenance, etc.

Estate agents' clients may be property managers of vast commercial empires, or first-time house purchasers who need to be guided through the complexities of making the most expensive purchase of their lives. Estate agents may specialize in one type of property (residential, or commercial or industrial), or they may deal with a mixture of types of properties. *Negotiators*, who deal with clients, often specialize in dealing with one type of client, for example with house purchasers, helping them to sort out priorities: few can afford their dream house, i.e. what they want exactly where they want. Negotiators help weigh up advantages of, say, sunny garden or 'good neighbourhood'; solidly built but no garage; not-so-solid but near shops/school/transport/parks, etc. Or they specialize in dealing with industrial property: are there goods transport/loading facilities; planning restrictions? Is there a supply of skilled labour?

Estate agents advise vendors on the price to ask, so they have to understand something about valuation, even if they are not professionally qualified valuers. The work involves a lot of client-contact, of getting about and getting to know an area and being aware of changes in type of locality and its effect on property values.

Auctioneers

Most estate agents are also auctioneers. (Normally estate agents employ different people as negotiators and as auctioneers, but in small firms everybody might do everything.) Some firms specialize in auctioning commercial, industrial, residential or agricultural property; others specialize in furniture, machinery, works of art. (The few well-known auction rooms where paintings etc. are auctioned are staffed by art specialists who have learnt about auctioneering as well as by the estate agent-valuer-auctioneer.) An auctioneer outside London may well auction the contents of a house one day, cattle in the local market-place the next, and a row of shops the day after that. Work varies according to whether done in country town or big city. The actual auctioneering is only part of the work: it also involves assessing value and advising vendors on 'reserve price', and it involves detailed 'lotting up' and cataloguing items to be sold.

While some firms of auctioneers, especially in the country, engage people specially for auctioneering and teach them the necessary skills and techniques, it is advisable to train as valuer (see above) as well.

Quantity Surveyors

Quantity surveyors are also called 'building economists', 'construction cost consultants', 'building accountants'. Quantity surveyors are essential members of the design team on building projects of any size. They translate architects' or civil engineers' designs into detailed costs – of labour, materials, overheads; and they break down all materials and processes to be used into detailed quantities and timing. They evaluate alternative processes and materials and may suggest alternative design technologies and materials to those suggested on the original design. Their thorough and up-to-date knowledge of new construction technologies and materials enables them to find ways of getting work carried out in the most speedy, economical and efficient way, without impairing the design. Calculations involved may be very complex – for example, future maintenance costs have to be considered when evaluating the use of alternative materials and processes. Calculations are usually done with computers.

Quantity surveyors are normally appointed by the designer of the project, i.e. the architect or civil engineer. Because of soaring costs and constantly changing technologies, the quantity surveyor's status in the design team has risen enormously in the last few years. Although the architect/civil engineer still has the last word, the quantity surveyor's suggestions for modifications are taken very seriously indeed.

Quantity surveyors are responsible for cost control during the whole project. They advise on cost implications of any proposed variations to the design, make interim valuations of completed work, check contractors' interim accounts and settle final accounts. They are also involved with financial administration of contracts for mechanical and electrical engineering and similar services and may be responsible for overall project management.

Quantity surveyors' work is a combination of straightforward figure work, complex calculations and negotiating skills. They must be able to deal with colleagues from other disciplines, contractors, clients. They spend more time at their desks doing calculations or writing reports and at negotiations than on the building site, but the time spent on the various ingredients of the job varies from project to project, and according to the type of employer and method of working.

About 60% of quantity surveyors are in private professional practice; others work for contractors, consultant engineers, in government departments, local authorities, commercial and industrial firms.

Building Surveyors

Building surveyors make structural surveys of and diagnose defects of buildings of all types, for prospective purchasers, vendors, owners, building societies. They assess maintenance costs and control maintenance programmes; they prepare plans for conversion and improvements. They draw up plans and specifications, go out to tender, and may supervise contractors' work and check accounts. They advise on building, planning, health and safety regulations, and they may also be involved with restoration or maintenance of ancient monuments and historic buildings. They spend a good deal of time clambering about on buildings to check roofs, lofts, drains, fire escapes and general structural soundness, so their work requires agility.

Many work in private professional practice; others are employed by any type of organization which owns, sells, buys, builds, manages property. This includes housing associations, building societies, all types of industrial and commercial firms, local authorities and central government. This is the most practical specialization, with the least office work.

Rural Practice Surveyors (formerly Land Agent/Agricultural Surveyors)

Terms are confusing as they have changed in recent years. Traditionally, land agents (called factors in Scotland) were (usually resident) managers of farms or other rural properties. More usually now their work is done by firms of agricultural surveyors (now called by the RICS rural practice surveyors), who manage a number of farms and estates on a contract basis. They do much the same work in rural areas as general practice surveyors do in towns. They may do valuation (including livestock and agricultural plant), estate agency, auctioneering, or they may concentrate on farm management (see AGRICULTURE AND HORTICULTURE, p. 21). Increasingly they also advise on alternative uses of land, for recreational purposes such as country parks, caravanning and camping sites, country trails, long-distance footpaths, nature reserves. They would then also implement changes.

Rural practice surveyors may also conduct sales and auctions of country properties, contents of country houses, livestock, agricultural machinery, plant, forests and forest products.

Many are in private professional practice. According to the size of the practice, other specialist surveyors (valuers, building surveyors) may be employed. Rural practice surveyors sometimes now do farm business management as well, perhaps employing specialists to advise on mechanization, diversification (see alternative land use above) and other ways of improving farm profits. They are also often involved with conservation issues, trying to reconcile landowners' and conservationists' sometimes conflicting interests.

They also work for MAFF (see AGRICULTURE AND HORTICULTURE, p. 22), local government, the National Trust and other bodies which own/manage land.

Rural practice surveying is an unusual combination of business, technical, environmental and agricultural work, and is one of the few professional jobs which include getting about the countryside.

Planning and Development Surveyors

The work overlaps with TOWN AND COUNTRY PLANNING (see p. 545).

Planning surveyors are concerned with the efficient allocation of resources in planning and with planning economics and planning law. The work is largely desk research (including statistics) and communicating with other specialists concerned with planning. A planning surveyor, for example, investigates the economics of a proposed shopping area. That would involve collecting facts and figures from various sources, assessing their implications and writing up the findings. Another project might mean having to find a suitable site for an industrial plant which has to be somewhere within a given area, must be near an inland waterway, near transport and must not be within an area of scenic value. That would not necessarily involve travelling, but consulting maps and relevant organizations.

The planning surveyor also advises clients on planning implications or proposals to buy and develop a property. This could involve visiting the site, taking photographs, and then appraising the proposal from a civic design point of view. They are also involved in marketing completed properties.

Planning and development surveyors work for planning consultants, local and central government, or as specialists in general practice surveying firms.

Land and Hydrographic Surveyors

Land surveyors are surveyors in the strict sense of the word and must not be confused with land agents/agricultural surveyors. They use sophisticated technologies (including satellite positioning systems and laser alignment devices) to measure and plot the precise shape and position of natural and man-made features on land for the purpose of map-making, including large-scale maps which are used for engineering constructions. (Before motorways can be sited, for example, or bridges built, the minutest physical details of the area have to be plotted and mapped. Their expertise was essential in planning the Channel Tunnel.)

Land surveyors do not draw maps; that is done by cartographers (see p. 92). Land surveyors work in private practice, or for the government (Ordnance Survey, Ministry of Defence mainly), or for consulting engineers and big contractors. Some work for the Directorate of Overseas Surveys which sends (experienced) surveyors to the developing – and other – countries to survey land, some of which has never been surveyed and mapped before. Some go into Archaeological Surveying (see ARCHAEOLOGY, p. 39).

Hydrographic surveyors are the smallest and most scientific branch, although the recent growth of off-shore oil and gas industries has widened their scope. They survey oceans, waterways, harbours and ports for purposes of producing nautical charts which show the precise shape, size, location of physical features of the sea bed, etc. and hazards, currents, tides, sunken wrecks. They supervise the dredging of ports and channels. The information sent by hydrographic survey ships operating in most parts of the world to the Navy's Hydrographic Department is being continuously revised. Collecting and interpreting information is done with highly sophisticated electronic equipment. British Admiralty Charts are used by seafarers all over the world, and by North Sea oil and gas engineers.

Many hydrographic surveyors are also naval officers. This is fairly tough outdoor work, combined with high technology.

Minerals or Mining Surveyors

This is the smallest specialization. Mining surveyors are responsible for mine safety and for mapping mineral deposits, and are involved with the potential use, value, properties, management and exploitation of mineral deposits, which means combining technical, scientific, managerial and commercial aspects. They are also responsible for minimizing environmental damage to the countryside where mineral deposits are mined.

In this country, mining surveyors are concerned mainly with coal mining, but minerals surveying overseas covers a variety of other minerals.

Prospects for chartered surveyors of all kinds vary according to economic conditions, but are mostly reasonable, especially as a wider range of organizations now employ surveyors, for example financial institutions; best opportunities are for general practice, quantity, and building surveyors. Some opportunities in EC countries (for those who speak the relevant language fluently), especially for quantity surveyors, who are also in demand in Africa and the Middle East.

Training   For membership of the Royal Institution of Chartered Surveyors (any surveying specialization) about 70% take 3-year full-time (or 4-year sandwich) degrees or diplomas in surveying which lead to full or partial exemption from RICS Membership examinations; others study while in appropriate employment, which takes 5 to 6 years of part-time study (or 4 years for the new 'distance-learning' diploma course run by the College of Estate Management). Day-release is often granted in public sector employment. In the private sector, students usually have to study in their own time by correspondence course and evening classes. Quantity surveying students may find it much easier than others to be given day-release.

Choosing a course needs careful research. Some courses allow students to choose between several allied specializations during the second year, but for complete exemption from RICS examinations in certain divisions, such as land or quantity surveying, the decision has to be made before starting a course. It is essential to study the RICS and ISVA up-to-date lists of exempting degrees and diploma courses in each division. Course titles, especially for general practice, vary and are often misleading. For example there are several different titles for courses leading to General Practice Division exemptions; nor are the titles necessarily an indication of course emphasis.

Though it is usual to work initially in the specialization in which one qualified, it is quite possible to switch specializations later. In practice some specializations (such as, for example, building and quantity surveying) are more easily interchangeable than, for example, general practice and hydrographic.

General practice surveyors (i.e. valuers, estate agents, auctioneers) can train *either* for the RICS General Practice Division, as above, *or* for membership of the Incorporated Society of Valuers and Auctioneers (see 'Entry qualifications', above). ISVA training is *either* by 3-year full-time course (courses only at a few colleges); *or* by day-release; *or* (the most common method) by correspondence course, taking 4 to 6 years, while in approved employment.

Graduates from any discipline may take a post-graduate conversion course or study for the RICS or ISVA Graduate Entry Scheme examination by part-time study or correspondence course, while in appropriate employment. Study takes about 18 months to 3 years. Alternatively, they may take the 'distance-learning' diploma course (see above). Though theoretically an arts graduate could qualify in any of the specializations, most opt for the General Practice Division. Science/engineering graduates might opt for Building or Quantity Surveying RICS divisions. History of art graduates might choose the Fine Arts and Chattels division of the ISVA. Graduates with related degrees, for example in building or planning, qualify for partial exemption if they opt for the Building or the Planning and Development Divisions. There is 1 3-year Diploma in Fine Arts and Chattels Valuation for people with 2 A-levels or experience in valuation.

Personal attributes
Practical approach to problem-solving; ability to inspire confidence in clients; ability to take complex decisions on own initiative and work as one of a team as well; for some jobs ability to handle labour. For *consultancy* and *estate agency*: business acumen; liking for being out of doors.

Late start
Possible, but requires very strong motivation. No problem getting training, but first job may be difficult for over-30s. Depends on previous experience. Those over 24 with relevant experience and, normally, 1 A-level may be partially exempted from normal RICS requirements. Normal entry requirements may be waived by ISVA.

Career-break
Should not be difficult in, for example, general practice surveying; possibly more difficult in areas where technologies change rapidly, but here keeping up with developments by reading journals and attending meetings should help. No *refresher* courses so far. Reduced membership fees of ISVA.

Part time   Not very common, but the profession is looking at ways to promote it. No reason why established surveyors should not suggest to their employers that part time with flexible hours or job-sharing should work well.

Position of women   There is no logical reason whatever why there should be so few women surveyors. Just under 7% of qualified RICS members are women, and even of its student members only 16% are women. The ISVA has about 4% qualified and 15% student women members.

The few women in the profession are doing well, although some have changed employers rather often because promotion was blocked for them. The majority have gone into general practice, fine arts and chattels, and management or teaching (one polytechnic has a woman as head of the surveying department); fewer choose quantity or building surveying.

Only mining and hydrographic surveying should present any problems. However, the first woman chartered minerals surveyor qualified in 1986. Mining surveyors during training must visit mines (women have only recently been allowed to work as miners) and hydrographic surveyors are trained, partly, by the Navy, on naval vessels. These two are, in any case, a tiny minority of surveyors. No other surveying makes demands on physical strength or presents any hazards with which most women, however traditional in outlook, cannot cope as well as men. (Building surveyors go up scaffolding, but women have no worse heads for heights than men.)

In fact, much surveying work is concerned with improving the environment and generally the quality of life, and much of it involves dealing with people: even the most traditional-minded women should find something to their liking in surveying. It is lack of knowledge of what surveyors actually do which keeps women from entering this many-sided profession in greater numbers.

Further information   Royal Institution of Chartered Surveyors, Education Department, Surveyor Court, Westwood Way, Coventry CV4 8JE

Incorporated Society of Valuers and Auctioneers, 3 Cadogan Gate, London SW1X 0AS

College of Estate Management, Whiteknights, Reading RG6 2AW

Related careers   AGRICULTURE AND HORTICULTURE – ARCHITECTURE – CARTOGRAPHY – ENGINEERING – HOUSING MANAGEMENT – SURVEYING: *Technician* – TOWN AND COUNTRY PLANNING

Surveying Technicians

(includes managerial jobs in the construction industry; see BUILDING, p. 80)

Entry qualifications

Either 4 GCSEs (A–C) including maths, a science and a subject proving competence in the use of English for BTEC National awards (see p. xxi); *or* 1 A-level passed and another one studied for direct entry to BTEC Higher National awards. For SCOTVEC equivalents see p. xxii.

The work

Most specializations overlap very much with supervisory and management jobs in the building industry (see p. 80). Titles vary: the term 'technician' may not be used, even when the qualification required is a technician qualification.

Individual technicians' work varies enormously: some are desk-bound draughtspersons, some are out and about; all now use computerized procedures and equipment. Some have a great deal of client-contact, some have none. Almost invariably they are part of a team.

The majority work under the overall direction of chartered surveyors, architects, civil engineers or planners. Some of their work is indistinguishable from that done by chartered surveyors: until some years ago, chartered surveyors qualified almost exclusively by on-the-job plus part-time training, and they had only slightly higher entry qualifications than technicians often have now. While chartered surveyors' training is certainly much more demanding academically than technicians', many tasks are still the same as they always were and do not require the chartered surveyors' in-depth training. Technician-level qualifications are sufficient for the majority of those 'surveyors' who, while wanting responsibility and professional training, do not aspire to initiate and take charge of complex projects.

Surveying technician specializations:

Building Surveying Technicians
(see 'Building Surveyors', p. 506 and 'Building Managers', p. 81)

Sub-divisions cover construction and assessment of structures; administration of building regulations; preparations of plans; specification for and organization of work to be carried out by contractors; estimates of cost before projects start; dealing with tenders and contracts and checking and passing contractors' accounts; advising lay public on soundness of construction of property they consider buying (while ultimate responsibility for such advice lies with the employing chartered surveyor, the actual surveying on which surveyors' reports to clients are based is often carried out by technicians – the customer is not necessarily aware of this); advice to property owners on maintenance and repair. This may include drawing up schedules for redecoration, advice on eradication of damp, dry rot, etc.

Building surveying technicians work in a great variety of settings – and under a great variety of titles (for example *building manager*, *building surveyor*, *building inspector*). They are employed by virtually any type of organization which owns or is responsible for the building and/or maintenance of property, and by firms of consultants. When they work for building contractors, they may also be called *planning* or *contracts manager*, or *contracts surveyor*. Their work may be mainly organizational – ensuring that manpower and equipment are used efficiently; this means planning all the operations which are involved in completing a contract to build whatever it is. For example, if a firm of building contractors is engaged simultaneously on converting several houses into flats and building office blocks, the contracts planner or manager has to estimate for how long how many workers and which equipment will be required on each job and when the various specialists, such as heating engineers, plasterers, electricians, should be where.

While in the past only very large contractors had contract planners, now middle-sized firms often engage such staff (under various titles, and not necessarily only engaged on this type of planning).

Another job for building surveying technicians is as *site managers*. They are responsible for organization of the sequence and smooth working of operations on site.

Technicians who prefer desk-bound work can become draughtspersons and eventually be in charge of a drawing office. But drawing offices now have fewer vacancies as so much work is computerized and completed more quickly. Many work for estate agents, where they meet the general public (see p. 504).

Quantity Surveying Technicians
(see 'Quantity Surveying', p. 505)

They form part of the surveying team concerned with the costing and financial management of all types of building work. They may use computers and word processors. There are three main, but inter-related sub-divisions (with rather quaint traditional titles).

1. *Takers off*: They abstract and measure from architect's, surveyor's or engineer's drawings every item of labour and materials to be used on a project, and list them in recognized terms. The information is needed to produce a 'cost plan' or Bill of Quantities. The job is usually office-based, and involves liaison with architects and other specialists, often as part of a technician team.

2. *Workers up*: They work out volumes, quantities and areas of all the items which have been measured by the taker off, and record them in a way which can be understood by all construction workers. These are then presented on the Bill of Quantities used by the quantity surveyor (see p. 505) in deciding the most economical means of construction. Workers up are entirely office-based; they may be responsible for a part or whole of a project.

3. *Post-contract surveyors* and *site measurers*: They divide their time between office and site. Work includes monitoring work done so that interim payments can be made to contractors. They may discuss the implications of variations on the plans with sub-contractors employed on the site and must understand contracts. Post-contract surveyors may be physically measuring work on site one day, attending a site meeting with a number of colleagues from different building-work spheres the same afternoon, and negotiating final payment with a sub-contractor the next day. Usually they will have been workers up and takers off before becoming post-contract surveyors. Their job overlaps very much with that of chartered quantity surveyors.

General Practice Technicians
(see 'General Practice Surveyors', p. 503)

This division covers the work done by chartered general practice and planning surveyors. (At chartered level, there is a separate Planning and Development division.)

General practice technicians may specialize in valuation, estate agency, estate and property management, housing management, town and country planning (see p. 545). Openings are the most varied, ranging from suburban estate agency's or international property company's *negotiator* (see p. 504) to Inland Revenue or insurance company's valuation technician. This specialization offers scope both to those who are mainly interested in meeting members of the public and to those who want to do mainly drawing or other office work and are interested in combining technical and commercial work.

Land Surveying Technicians
(see 'Land and Hydrographic Surveyors', p. 508)

These work with chartered land surveyors. The work has changed considerably in the last 10 years with the use of electronic distance-measuring equipment and digital coding and modelling of land shapes. There are also opportunities in photographing and tracking man-made satellites, and in aerial photography.

This is one of the most adventurous of technician specializations, with work for oil companies and air survey companies at home or abroad, including Third World countries.

Minerals Surveying Technicians
(see 'Minerals or Mining Surveyors', p. 509)

This is a small division and involves the preparation of accurate plans in connection with safety, operation and development of mines, and geological formations in connection with mineral deposits. Much of the work is underground.

Hydrographic Surveying Technicians
(see 'Land and Hydrographic Surveyors', p. 508)

Making and up-dating charts of seas and coastlines, and profiles of sea beds; 'sign posting', on charts, of shipping lanes. This can be arduous outdoor work on survey ships and requires practical seamanship; only few draughtsmanship, office-based jobs.

Agricultural Surveying Technicians
(see 'Rural Practice Surveyors', p. 506)

This work overlaps with agriculture (see p. 21) and land agency. Main employers are local authorities and public bodies such as gas and electricity boards.

Surveying technicians generally are in demand but especially in quantity, general practice, land surveying and building surveying where their work often overlaps with that of chartered surveyors. In these specializations there are often more opportunities for technicians than for chartered surveyors. Experienced technicians have some opportunities in EC countries if they speak the relevant language fluently.

There is a 'bridging arrangement' which enables qualified technicians to take RICS examinations and become chartered surveyors (but few want to).

Training (all technicians)   Students choose courses according to the type of work they are in or want to do. However, BTEC/SCOTVEC courses are flexible and, within related areas, it is usually possible to switch from one specialization or division (see p. 502) to another; possibly adding course units.

The main surveying divisions are now covered by two 'generic' course categories:

1. *Building Studies*: This covers *building surveying* and *quantity surveying*.

2. *Land Administration*: This covers *general practice surveying* (incorporating valuation and property management/estate agency); *land surveying* (incorporating land, sea and air surveying; cartography); *planning* (incorporating town and country and regional planning).

Then there are specialized courses: *minerals surveying* technicians take *mine and mining surveying* courses; *hydrographic surveying* technicians train either at the Royal Navy Hydrographic School, Plymouth (residential) or take special options in BTEC *land surveying* courses. There are few training vacancies (and jobs) for mining and hydrographic surveying technicians. *Agricultural surveying* technicians normally take the National Diploma in Agriculture (see AGRICULTURE AND HORTICULTURE, p. 25).

BTEC Courses are normally taken *either* by day- or block-release, and last 2 years for the BTEC National Certificate and a further 2 years for the Higher National Certificate, *or* they are taken by 2-year full-time study for the BTEC National Diploma, followed by a further 2 years' full-time or 3 years' sandwich study for the Higher National Diploma. It is possible to switch from part-time National to full-time/sandwich Higher National and vice versa. (And there are plenty of opportunities, for the less ambitious, with National rather than Higher National awards.) Entrants with 1 relevant A-level and another subject studied at A-level can go straight into the Higher National Diploma course or into the second year of the National Certificate course. In Scotland, students take relevant SCOTVEC National Certificate modules (see p. xxii) and then take the Higher National award. They can then take the Joint Test of Competence run by the RICS and SST.

For the majority of jobs, Higher National awards are as marketable as degrees. For some jobs in the building industry they are in fact preferred because of their practical content and approach.

The Chartered Surveyors Youth Training Trust runs a technician training scheme for school-leavers in the London area and West Midlands. Trainees are placed with employers and study part time for the BTEC National Certificate.

The National Association of Estate Agents offers a correspondence course leading to a Certificate in Residential Estate Agency. It has recently launched a Certificate of Practice in Estate Agency intended for branch managers.

Personal attributes   Some mathematical ability; interest in finding practical solutions to technical problems; liking for outdoor work; ability to work as one of a team and also to take responsibility, coupled with willingness to work for people more highly qualified than oneself; meticulous accuracy; ability to supervise building site workers.

Late start   There is no reason why people should not start in their twenties or thirties, especially if they have had some related experience or training, e.g. a geography degree or work experience in estate agency, on a building site, with computers.

Career-break   It is too early to know how returners would fare but, if they have kept up with developments, there is no reason why experienced technicians should not return to work. It would probably be easier in general practice and quantity surveying than, say, in agricultural surveying.

Part time   Not at the moment, except, perhaps, in quantity surveying but no reason why experienced technicians should not try and make their own part-time or job-share arrangements, especially in estate agency work.

Position of women   The proportion of women members of the Society of Surveying Technicians is minute (though there have been draughtswomen for a long time), well below 1%. However, especially in planning, estate agency (general practice) and quantity surveying, there are good opportunities for women, but very few are applying for training or jobs. Only tradition is keeping this area of employment virtually a male preserve.

In some offices women may still be unwelcome, but there are many more where they are welcome. Training courses invariably welcome women students. (However, women may have problems if they want to train for mineral and hydrographic surveying because of the practical work down the mines and on survey ships.) Women do very well in estate agency as negotiators.

Further information

Society of Surveying Technicians, Surveyor Court, Westwood Way, Coventry CV4 8JE

BTEC and SCOTVEC (see pp. xxi, xxii)

The Chartered Surveyors Youth Training Trust, c/o Sweby Cowan, 9 Cavendish Square, London W1M 0BB

National Association of Estate Agents, Arbon House, 21 Jury Street, Warwick CV34 4EH

Related careers

ARCHITECTURE: *Architectural Technician* – BUILDING – *Chartered Surveyor (above)* – HOUSING MANAGEMENT

Tax Inspector

Entry qualifications	First- or second-class honours or post-graduate degree in any subject or equivalent. (Opportunities also for those starting as Tax Officer, see 'Executive Officers', p. 128).
The work	Tax Inspectors work in the Inland Revenue department of the Civil Service. Their main duty is to investigate the accounts of business concerns in order to agree the amount of profits for taxation purposes. By examining accounts and interviewing individuals they aim to spot any cases of tax evasion or fraud. They also advise taxpayers on tax and business law. Their work brings them into contact with the whole range of Britain's industry and commerce in their own district.

They deal with many kinds of people – accountants, lawyers, industrialists, farmers, small shopkeepers – by personal interview as well as by correspondence. They also represent the Crown before an independent tribunal when they and the taxpayer concerned cannot agree on the tax assessment.

There are District Offices in all areas. Promotion prospects are best for people willing to move to where there happens to be a vacancy. Opportunities also exist outside the Civil Service as tax advisers to companies and individuals.

Training	On the job. During the 3 years' initial training inspectors take part-time and residential courses to a professional standard and have to pass examinations which qualify for promotion.
Personal attributes	Common sense; judgement; administrative ability; keen intellect; the ability to sum up people and situations; impartiality; equanimity; enjoyment of responsibility.
Career-break	See CIVIL SERVICE, p. 138.
Late start	See CIVIL SERVICE, p. 138.
Part time	Some opportunities. See CIVIL SERVICE, p. 138.

**Position
of
women**   See CIVIL SERVICE, p. 138.

**Further
informa-
tion**   Civil Service Commission, Alencon Link, Basingstoke, Hampshire
                 RG21 1JB

**Related
careers**   ACCOUNTANCY – ACTUARY – BANKING – INSURANCE – CIVIL
                 SERVICE

Teaching

The image of teaching has suffered in recent years. Though there sometimes seems little consensus about what schools are actually for, they are blamed for failing to deliver. Constant change and criticism have undoubtedly taken their toll. Teachers admit to feeling over-stressed, underpaid and undervalued. They are charged with falling standards of achievement and discipline. Some of the continuous changes they are required to implement they disagree with; others they support but are forced to carry out without adequate time, support or resources.

Yet there are still plenty of people who can make a good case for teaching as a career. Two points are clear: good teachers are the key to any worthwhile educational reform and national prosperity, and for many teachers their rewards stand up to comparison with many more glamorous, less beleaguered professions.

It is vital overall that first-class teachers be recruited and retained, but supply and demand does vary from subject to subject. There is great competition to recruit graduates with backgrounds in maths, science, technological subjects and modern languages. The requirements of the National Curriculum will exacerbate many of these shortages as children who would have dropped subjects are compelled to carry on with them. Currently, to combat shortages, bursaries (in addition to the usual grants) are available to those doing PGCEs (see 'Training', below) in maths, technology, craft design and technology, chemistry, biology, balanced science, modern foreign languages, Welsh and physics. The demand for primary teachers is increasing and many parts of the country are particularly short of 'early years' teachers. Primary teachers with special knowledge and skills in areas of the National Curriculum such as science and technology are likely to have excellent prospects.

Entry qualifications

A degree plus GCSE A–C (or equivalent) in maths and English language.

Primary Schools
(including Nursery)

The work   Primary schools are generally organized in two broad categories, infant and junior or first and middle. The age ranges vary slightly; sometimes the break is made at 7, sometimes at 8. Most children go on to secondary school at 11, but some remain at their primary/middle school until 12 or 13. Sometimes the younger and older primary children go to separate schools; in other cases a single school deals with the whole primary range. Some schools have attached nursery units, taking children at 3 or 4. (N.B. To teach in a state-maintained nursery school you must be a qualified teacher, though there may be unqualified assistants.)

The precise organization of primary education varies from one local education authority to another. Schools also vary greatly in size, location and catchment area. Some schools will have as few as 2 teachers, others as many as 30. In the former case each teacher will teach several age groups; in the latter several teachers will share responsibility for an age group, sometimes through 'team teaching'.

Nursery and lower primary children learn largely through play and activity, which are planned and supervised by the teacher to achieve certain goals. So a bright child might be 'playing' in such a way that will develop manipulative skills which lag behind his or her reading, while a listening game might be devised for those children who have poor concentration. The teacher is observing all the time to recognize which areas need working on for each child. Children of this age are extremely demanding, able to work independently for only very short periods of time, demanding attention and cuddles and asking endless questions of the person who is usually next to Mummy and Daddy in importance in their lives. (And of course some children don't have a Mummy and/or Daddy.)

Formal teaching in the primary school is introduced gradually. Much work remains individual. The teacher fosters the growing ability of the children to work independently, both as individuals and in groups. Much work is integrated into multi-disciplinary topics or projects with the emphasis on stimulating children's natural curiosity and enthusiasm and widening their experience. The teacher has to plan the topic, relating it to the age group; make sure all the necessary resources are to hand; check that it meets the National Curriculum attainment targets in the appropriate subjects and record them; see in which areas of the curriculum the topic isn't working and go back to those subjects.

One of the primary teacher's most important skills is classroom management. It includes timetabling, the grouping of children and the organization of the classroom. Learning time is wasted if the most boisterous child sits with those of his or her peers least able to cope, or if children involved in a messy activity have constantly to move among children quietly engaged to get to their materials.

Primary teachers normally take their classes for all subjects, all day. The demands of the National Curriculum and the introduction of new subjects have led many teachers to take additional in-service specialist training to enable them to act as advisers or co-ordinators for a particular subject within their schools. Primary teachers do not have as much marking as the teachers of older children, but lesson preparation can take up a good deal of time. Time is also spent on assessment and recording, organizing displays, extra-curricular activities and maintaining good relationships with parents.

Secondary Schools

The work Commonly at the age of 11, but sometimes at 12 or 13, children transfer to secondary school. Most children go to comprehensive schools, which cater for the whole range of ability. Some authorities, however, have retained a selective system with the more academically able children going to grammar schools. In some authorities children remaining in full-time education at 16+ go to sixth-form colleges, some of which offer a traditional sixth-form curriculum, while others offer a more diverse range of courses.

Unlike primary teachers, secondary teachers teach a limited number of, usually, closely related subjects to many different age and ability groups throughout the day and week. Within the framework of their specialist knowledge, they need the teaching skills to establish working relationships with, for example, the unmotivated, the slow learners, the young pupils who look to the teacher for everything, and the sixth-formers who test them with profound questions. They must try to stimulate the interest of all pupils and help them to achieve the best they can, whether it be 2 hard-earned GCSEs or 3 top grade A-levels. This demands enthusiasm and flexibility.

Secondary teachers obviously need a good grounding in their subjects, but they do not need to know it all. Modern education is about learning how to learn, handling data, developing thinking and problem-solving skills. These are skills and challenges for teachers as well as pupils.

Secondary teachers spend a good deal of time (much of it out of school hours) on preparation and marking. They must be clear what they are going to achieve in each lesson, following the scheme of work as planned in the syllabus, and have the necessary material ready at each point, in each lesson, every day of the week. Good organization is vital. Formal assessment and recording have, in recent years, involved teachers in a good deal of additional administrative work, but much assessment is intuitive and goes on all the time with teachers watching to see if their pupils are keen, interested, responsive and so on.

Most teachers have responsibilities in addition to their subject teaching. Personal and social education, for example, is often a shared responsibility. Time is taken up in registration, form time, assemblies, administration, departmental and other meetings with colleagues, contact with parents. Many teachers get involved in a range of extra-curricular activities, from sport to drama, to chess or other special interest clubs, which can take up considerable time. Some plan and accompany children on trips. In addition, everyone on the staff shares responsibility for standards and so is effectively 'on duty' throughout the day, watching out for, preventing and dealing with problems.

It is a fallacy that, once established, a teacher can do the same things year after year. New subjects are introduced; old subjects develop and are approached in new ways; teaching and examining methods change; each class is different. Good teachers need to update and evaluate their work constantly, deciding what to change, what to repeat, finding the right method for a particular pupil or group.

Special Needs Education

Children may have special educational needs for a variety of reasons ranging from emotional or behavioural disturbance, through specific learning difficulties, to complex multiple physical and/or mental handicaps. Increasingly, such children are, whenever possible, educated in ordinary schools. Depending on circumstances the child might be integrated into an ordinary class but have special help or be in a special unit or class attached to an ordinary school. Some children still need to go to special schools, sometimes for the whole of their schooling, sometimes only for short periods.

The work is emotionally and physically demanding. The teacher is involved not only in teaching academic subjects but also has to help pupils to overcome problems in a range of day-to-day activities, such as eating or playing. The teacher needs to build up a good relationship with the child, but also with the others concerned with the child's welfare and development, e.g. doctors, social workers, speech and language therapists, physiotherapists, psychologists.

Apart from teachers of the blind, deaf and partially hearing, special needs teachers do not need special qualifications. It is usual to gain teaching qualifications (see below) and experience of teaching 'normal' children before moving into special needs work and taking in-service training courses.

Independent Schools

Independent education covers a very wide range of institutions, from the renowned public schools to Montessori nursery schools. Some are based on a traditional academic approach while others are very 'progressive'. Many have outstanding records in preparing their pupils for external examinations and higher education, while others compare unfavourably with good state schools. Some pay their teachers considerably more than the scale for teachers in the maintained sector while others fall far short.

Teachers in independent schools do not need to be professionally qualified. A good honours degree is usually the required qualification. However, many independent school teachers do have a professional teaching qualification which enhances their flexibility in the jobs market. There are courses and qualifications of interest to particular sectors of independent education (e.g. Montessori and Rudolf Steiner), but these do not qualify one to teach in state schools.

Further Education

Many of the courses offered in the further education sector have a vocational bias. Some colleges are devoted to one particular field, e.g. agriculture. However, colleges also offer a broad range of other courses, from GCSEs and A-levels (which many students take in conjunction with vocational studies) to leisure interests such as painting, foreign languages and keep fit. Increasing numbers of school-leavers are continuing their education in FE colleges and some local education authorities are making them the focus of 16+ provision.

You do not need a professional teaching qualification (see below) to teach in further education. What is important is experience and/or qualifications in the field you wish to teach. However, a few colleges offer training for FE teachers, and other qualified teachers do compete for jobs. What precisely is required is likely to depend on supply and demand and the subjects involved. For example, a PGCE (see below) is likely to be more of an advantage for a teacher of a GCSE course than for someone teaching a BTEC in engineering.

Higher Education

In higher education, a higher degree is normally required for teaching. One's academic qualifications are far more important than teaching skills. The role of higher education institutions is not merely to pass on knowledge, but to extend it, so research is an important element of work in this sector. Administration is another key task. Higher education is facing a period of growth and diversification; some institutions may specialize while others may disappear or amalgamate.

Training

There are 2 main methods of initial teacher training leading to Qualified Teacher Status (QTS):

1. Bachelor of Education degree (B.Ed.). Entry qualifications are 3 GCSEs (A–C) or equivalent, including English language and maths, plus 2 A-levels or equivalent. Courses normally last 4 years and include classroom work, professional practice (theory of education, child development, etc.) and subject study. Students normally specialize in the teaching of certain age ranges and subjects, but they are not restricted to those in their subsequent careers. Most primary teachers qualify by this route. Not all secondary subjects are available on B.Ed. courses, so most secondary teachers qualify by method (2) below.

2. Post-graduate Certificate of Education (PGCE). Entry qualifications are an appropriate degree plus GCSE (A–C) in English language and maths. Courses normally last 1 year and do not concentrate on subject knowledge but on professional skills. Course structures vary, but all must include 15 weeks (out of 36) in schools. By September 1994 all secondary PGCEs must be 60% school-based.

A number of variations on the PGCE theme are evolving. There is a small but growing number of *2-year part-time PGCE courses* in certain subjects. There are also *2-year conversion PGCE* for graduates wishing to teach a subject which was not the subject of their first degree; subjects available include maths, physics, chemistry, modern languages, CDT (craft, design and technology) and music. *Articled teachers* (primary only) are graduates on a 2-year school-based PGCE who spend 80% of their time in schools. From 1993 there will be an *Open University PGCE course*, which will last 19 months and combine distance-learning and teaching practice under the guidance of a local tutor.

There are a number of other 4-year degree courses which lead concurrently to a teaching qualification. For additional schemes aimed mainly at mature entrants, see 'Late entry', below.

1993 NOTE: The pattern of primary teacher training is under review.

NOTES ON THE SCOTTISH SYSTEM

To be eligible for permanent teaching appointments in maintained schools in Scotland, teachers must be registered with the General Teaching Council for Scotland. To be eligible to register one must hold a Teaching Qualification, in either Primary Education, Secondary Education or Further Education.

The patterns of qualification are similar to those in England. Unlike in England, however, one is registered to teach a particular age range and, in the case of secondary education, a particular subject or subjects. *Primary teachers* may take *either* a 4-year B.Ed., for which the normal entry requirements are 3 SCE Higher passes and 2 Standard or O-Grade passes (English must be passed at H-grade, maths at either grade), *or* a 1-year postgraduate course for which a UK degree plus H-grade English and Standard or O-grade maths are required. *Secondary teachers* usually take a 1-year post-graduate course in specific subjects following first degrees with sufficient specified achievement in the relevant subjects. There are secondary B.Ed.s in physical education, music and technology.

As in England, alternative equivalent qualifications may be acceptable for entry. Mature students may get some concessions, but the requirement for maths and English must be met. Teachers who have trained outside Scotland and who have suitable qualifications may be admitted to the register, in some cases after additional training.

Teachers in further education do not need to be registered. The course for registration is open only to serving teachers seconded by their authority.

Personal attributes   Liking for children and young people; patience; sense of humour; enthusiasm; flexibility; fairness and consistency; confidence; optimism; organizing ability; sensitivity; good communication skills; ability to work on one's own and as part of a team.

Late start   There are good prospects. In 1989 more than 1 in 4 of all students on initial teacher training courses were mature students. There are a number of initiatives for such students:

1. Shortened B.Ed. In a number of subjects (maths, chemistry,

physics, modern languages, music, business studies and CDT) there are shortened 2-year B.Ed. courses for those who already have appropriate technical or professional qualifications and experience.

2. Licensed teacher scheme. LEAs have discretion to take on suitably qualified candidates who are employed as classroom teachers and trained on the job. The period of training normally lasts 2 years, but may be shorter for those with some teaching experience. Licensed teachers must be at least 26 (at the time of writing it was being proposed that this be reduced to 24), have GCSE A–C or equivalent in English language and maths, and have successfully completed at least 2 years' full-time (or part-time equivalent) higher education.

3. Teacher training colleges may be able to offer alternative tests or recommend 'access' (see p. xxxi) courses for those who do not have the specified formal qualifications for entry to an appropriate course.

Career-break

The education authorities are keen to attract teachers back from the 'PIT' (pool of inactive teachers). Initiatives include induction courses being adapted for returners, the encouragement of flexible working arrangements such as supply work, part-time work and job-sharing, and the provision of childcare to ease teachers' return to work. The TASC (Teaching as a Career) Unit also recommends authorities to provide counselling and advice before the career-break and regular communication with teachers during any break to keep them up to date with developments. Teachers who return on a regular full- or part-time basis are entitled to be paid at a point on the standard national scale no lower than the point on which they were last regularly paid. Employers can take into account any experience or qualifications gained during the break in deciding whether to appoint at a higher point.

Part time

Depends on local situation, subjects offered and so on. Supply work, part time and job-sharing are all possibilities.

Position of women

Teaching offers many women something they want: the opportunity to do a professional job but work school hours and term-time only. A career-break can be relatively easily fitted in as well. Of course, that is only part of the story. While a woman teacher can certainly be home during the school holidays, the normal workload extends far beyond the formal end of the school day. Women's inability or unwillingness to take on additional responsibility because of family commitments and the time and experience lost during a career-break are two factors in women's underrepresentation at the higher levels of the profession. The male-dominated education establishment and indirect discrimination are claimed to be other factors. In 1991 the *Times Educational Supplement* reported the picture as follows: 16 out of 108 chief education officers in England are women; in primary schools, though about 80% of teachers are women, only one in 14 is a head, compared to 1 in 3 men; in secondary schools, 60% of teachers are women, but fewer than 1 in 100 female teachers is a head, compared with more than 3 in 100 of males; in further education, 32% of the Lecturer 1 scale are women, but only 4% of the Principal's scale; in universities only 3% of professors are women at a time when the proportion of female students is approaching 50%.

Further information TASC Publicity Unit, Department for Education, Sanctuary Building, Great Smith Street, London SW1P 3BT

The Advisory Service on Entry to Teaching in Scotland, 5 Royal Terrace, Edinburgh EH7 5AF

Related careers CAREERS WORK – NURSERY NURSE – PERSONNEL/HUMAN RESOURCES MANAGEMENT – SOCIAL WORK – YOUTH AND COMMUNITY WORK

Television, Film and Radio

Entry qualifications

Very varied.

This whole area is going through a period of unprecedented change, both technological and organizational. The ultimate impact on career and training opportunities is difficult to forecast. In the period surriounding the awarding of the ITV franchises, large numbers of staff (probably around 25%) had been shed, and recruitment and training were at a virtual standstill. Increasingly some of the franchise winners will buy in, rather than originate, programmes and so have no permanent production staff or facilities. The BBC has been less affected, but they too have been cutting back on staff, recruitment and training, and, in common with ITV companies, will be required to commission 25% of their output from independent companies. It is in the independent, non-broadcast sector that there is likely to be most growth, but they rely very heavily on freelances.

TV, Film and Video

The industry consists mainly of the 'terrestrial' (as opposed to satellite) broadcasting companies and independent companies producing for broadcast, the corporate sector (e.g. training and corporate image promotional film and videos), commercials, music promotion and feature films. There are also production facilities in educational establishments and community-based units. (Satellite broadcasting buys in rather than makes programmes apart from news and is likely to offer job opportunities mainly in sales and marketing.) The boundaries between the sectors of the industry are becoming increasingly blurred. Independents commonly work in more than one sector, e.g. both making programmes for broadcast and doing corporate work. The broadcast companies are also diversifying into, for example, corporate work or making programmes for satellite and cable.

A wide range of jobs is involved. In 1989 the Institute of Manpower Studies undertook a study into the industry. They identified more than 100 jobs in the different sectors, but the terminology and job content can vary considerably. Job titles are not clear-cut. In addition, there is an industry-wide trend towards 'multi-skilling'. Sometimes this is the result of technical development when, for example, 1 piece of equipment and operator can do what previously took 2 pieces and 2 operators. Another impetus is the need for a more flexible workforce; film editors learn video editing in order to survive.

Nevertheless, the IMS team identified 9 'key grade' groups: camera, light, sound, production, post-production, engineering, make-up, wardrobe and journalists. Below are some of the programme-making jobs involved in broadcast TV. They are based on the BBC, but similar jobs are needed elsewhere in programme production, including the growing independent sector. Indications of the kind of qualifications and training normally needed are given but see 'Note on entry and training', p. 541.

Production Staff

Producers/directors

The work Exact functions vary. Producers are usually responsible for initiating, budgeting, casting, and the shape or 'treatment' of programmes. Directors are responsible for interpreting the idea and actually making the programme. These top jobs are very responsible and are done by specialists in particular fields, such as current affairs, drama, education, science or technology, who have long, often technical experience in the medium. Many work on contracts for particular projects.

The BBC runs a highly competitive production training scheme for graduates and/or experienced journalists. Courses last 2 years, after which trainees compete for contracts as either *assistant producers* or *researchers*. (The BBC will use more independent producers in future – this is likely to affect the numbers of in-house production staff.)

Production assistants

They provide organizational support to a programme. They may do some research, make bookings, arrange meetings, sit with the producer in the gallery checking on timing, cue the inserts of film or tape and are normally responsible for continuity. They have considerable contact with people both inside and outside TV. Where there is no production secretary in a department they perform any necessary secretarial duties. They are normally recruited from among *production secretaries*.

Production secretaries

Entrants who start as secretaries may become secretary to a producer, if they are lucky and very good. They see to it that the right instructions about make-up, costumes, sets, rehearsal times and studio bookings go to the right people. They type (and often re-type) the shooting script. Not all programmes (e.g. drama) have a secretary.

Floor managers (known as 'stage managers' in outside broadcasts)

They may be involved at the planning stage in advising on design, sound and props. During recording they control the studio floor. They are responsible for discipline on the floor and for safety of staff and artists. Duties include relaying the producer's/director's instructions to actors and presenters, using headphones to keep in touch with the gallery. They are responsible for cueing the actors, which can be a complicated task as they are often working on different sets and cannot see each other. The floor manager has to move around the sets while keeping out of camera shot. A diplomatic, pleasant personality is essential. In outside broadcasts they have to liaise with the general public.

Entry   Nearly all from the ranks of assistant floor managers or other production posts.

Assistant floor manager

Similar to assistant stage manager in the theatre. Work varies according to size and type of production, but usually includes making sure that all the props are available, taking charge of the prompt book and mark-ups during rehearsals. Assistant floor managers usually start their on-the-job training with the easier talks and discussion programmes before going on to drama series etc.

Entry   Candidates are expected to have experience in professional stage management, in theatre, film or TV.

Researchers

Research may be anything from looking through newspaper cuttings and finding a suitable person to be interviewed – not by researcher but by interviewer/presenter – on a news programme, to spending several months researching the background for a documentary or drama series. Researchers must be good all-round-ers, able to pick out relevant facts from a mass of material. They usually write 'briefs', which may range from a few questions which an interviewer is to ask on a programme, to exhaustive background material for a documentary scriptwriter. Researchers in current affairs must also be able to think up programme ideas and to work under tremendous pressure. Specialist researchers, for example for scientific or medical programmes, are often freelances.

Entry   Usually graduates and/or ex-journalists, or by promotion from within.

News staff, presenters, interviewers

Newsroom staff compile and write scripts for the *presenters*; *reporters* and *correspondents* 'get the stories' and present some themselves. The essence of broadcast news is brevity. *TV and radio journalists* must be instant fact-selectors and decision-makers. They may be sent anywhere at any time. *Editors* are senior staff responsible for piecing a programme together.

Entry   The BBC runs a training scheme (about 2 years' duration) for news trainees (television and radio). It is intensely competitive. Entrants are almost invariably graduates (any subject) with keen interest in current affairs, but 'general education' plus proven journalistic ability (i.e. good job on a good paper) are also acceptable.

Other routes into presenting are radio interviewing, journalism (reporters on provincial papers are occasionally given a try-out) and, occasionally, acting.

Design

Set designers

They are responsible for designing the sets down to the smallest accessories in accordance with the producer's concept. The producer calls in the designer when the idea is beginning to take shape. The designers' interpretation of the atmosphere the producer has in mind and their own suggestions are vitally important to the success of the production. They must have a good grasp of the technicalities of production.

Design assistants work with the designer on the technical, rather than creative, tasks. They draw ground plans and make working drawings; draw up specifications; make models of sets; and make or search for props.

Graphic designers and their *assistants* create credit titles, 'linking material', captions, maps and general illustrations. This is now frequently done using computers, but nevertheless it is still essentially creative work.

Scenic artists and *assistants* paint backcloths and decorative features such as curtains, carpets and portraits.

In the BBC (which has the only permanent special effects department in the world) *visual effects designers* and *assistants* devise, make and operate a wide variety of visual effects and 'illusions'.

Entry   Whatever the level of entry qualifications, all first appointments are to the post of assistant. Generally speaking, promotion to designer is from design assistant. All design assistants need degree level qualification in relevant art discipline. Additionally, graphic design assistants normally need commercial art experience (e.g advertising) following a degree or diploma; scenic artists need wide knowledge of painting, history of art and architecture and interior design; visual effects staff need to be able to work in all kinds of materials, make models and have a basic grasp of physics.

Costume designers (also called 'wardrobe')
They are in charge of hiring, designing and adapting up-to-date and period costumes. They are called in on new productions at an early stage to discuss the costumes and to advise on whether to hire, make or adapt, and to arrange for this to be done. Later they liaise with other designers and make-up staff. They need a thorough knowledge of period styles, but further research is often needed to make certain of representing the exact year or season. Assistants help designers in all aspects of their work and may stand in for them, e.g. when filming on location.

Entry   Preferably with a theatre or textile design degree and considerable experience in theatre or film costume. All entrants start at assistant level, from which designers are promoted. Assistants must be at least 19 with an A-level standard of education and a good knowledge of costume design and history (a degree or diploma is essential for promotion to designer).

Dressmakers make up costumes under the supervision of designers and make alterations to costumes which are hired or from stock.

Entry   With BTEC/SCOTVEC Higher National Diploma in Fashion and a minimum of 2 years' experience in the theatre or with a theatrical costumier. Knowledge of history of costume an advantage.

Dressers work on last-minute ironing and maintenance of costumes and help actors to dress for performance.

Make-up artists/designers

Television make-up is highly skilled. It requires the ability to understand and defeat the camera's often unkind effects on faces. It also requires a thorough knowledge of period hairstyles. An experienced senior assistant is usually in charge of each dramatic production and makes up the star actors. Juniors see to the rest of the cast and also look after the simpler make-up required for non-dramatic productions. Tact and diplomacy are essential.

Entry and training   Qualifications sought are A-level standard (preferred subjects: art, history, English) plus beauty therapy/hairdressing/art school training. Minimum age $20\frac{1}{2}$–21. Experience in make-up in amateur theatre very useful. Training courses last 16 months. Basic training is followed by carrying out practical duties under supervision, starting with simpler make-up and hairdressing and gradually learning more intricate techniques, such as creating 'scars' or 'wounds'.

Technical Operations

These concern the technical interpretation of the director's instructions and producing the required sound and vision effects which are finally seen and heard. Most TV programmes are pre-recorded. When recording a programme as well as during 'live' transmission, previously recorded and/or filmed material may be slotted in. The operational and technical sides of creating programmes and getting them on to TV screens are highly complex and require creativity, technical expertise and an unflappable temperament.

Camera operators help in setting up and operating electronic cameras and associated equipment in studios and on outside broadcasts. Promotion is to assistant and later cameraman/woman, vision supervisor, vision controller and ultimately possibly to technical manager responsible for lighting (various titles).

Sound assistants help in setting up and operating sound recording and reproduction equipment; they 'collect sound effects', and may eventually become sound supervisors responsible for control and balance of the various sound sources which are combined for final transmission. They are London-based in the BBC.

Audio assistants do similar work to sound assistants but they work in the regional (smaller) centres, and are also involved in the operation of radio sound equipment in joint radio/TV centres.

Recording operators control the increasingly sophisticated video-tape and telecine (the film equivalent) equipment. They set up and run the recorders and must respond instantly to the producer's requirements. Recordings may be for instant replay or later transmission.

Entry and training　Minimum age 18. GCSEs (A–C) in English language, maths and physics. Applicants must also have a keen interest in, and some 'hobby experience' of, hi-fidelity reproduction, tape-recording music, colour photography or lighting for amateur dramatics, and, for sound operators, ability to read a musical score. A strong interest in current affairs is also very useful. Acceptance depends very much on interview. Training normally starts with an approximately 3-month course, and continues on the job with further full-time courses for 2–3 years. Promotion is on a competitive basis and not *guaranteed* even when the training has been successfully completed, but BBC technical training is highly valued by all sound and vision recording studios outside the BBC.

Vision-mixer
Up to 6 cameras may be in operation during a production. The producer in the control room decides which camera's picture to send out to the audience, and tells the vision-mixer, who switches to the selected camera as the order is given. This needs concentration and quick reflexes.

Training　Mostly on the job for existing TV staff.

Engineering

Some TV engineers work in studios, outside broadcasting, coping with emergency repairs and sudden equipment failure, generally acting as technical 'back-up'. Others are responsible for operation and maintenance of equipment used to route, control and distribute signals from various sound and vision programme sources. All this work can be hectic and needs quick decision-making and a cool head. Other departments are concerned with research, development, planning, installation of a variety of complex equipment (see ENGINEERING, p. 183, for engineering functions). In a time of changing technology they must be prepared to update their knowledge and assimilate new ideas quickly.

Trainee engineers, or *technicians*, are the professional engineers' support force (see 'Engineering Technician', p. 197) and may assist in any of the engineering departments.

Entry and training   Minimum age 18. *For BBC trainee engineers*: GCSEs (A–C) in English language, maths and physics and A-level study of physics and maths.

BTEC/SCOTVEC National Diploma in electrical engineering, electronics or applied physics plus GCSE (A–C) English language are acceptable. Acceptance depends very much on interview. Trainee engineers must show that they understand the basic principles of electricity and magnetism and have a good grasp of their practical application. 'Hobby experience' as for technical operations trainees.

Training starts with a 3-month, BBC-run course and continues on the job with further courses for about 2½ years. After satisfactorily completing training, trainee engineers are eligible for promotion to BBC engineer posts.

The majority of engineers enter as graduates with degrees in electrical or electronic engineering, applied physics or other relevant science subjects, or with BTEC/SCOTVEC Higher National awards in electronics or telecommunications. For posts in BBC Research and Design (the same as 'Design' in ENGINEER-ING, p. 185) minimum entry qualification is now a first or second class honours degree. There is also scope for engineers with higher degrees. The BBC also recruits some non-electronics graduates and 'converts' them into engineers via an 'in-house' training scheme.

Filming for TV

Film camera and sound staff are quite distinct from TV camera and sound staff. A considerable amount of television material is filmed (although most is on videotape); whole programmes are filmed, e.g. schools broadcasts, documentaries; film is also used as an important ingredient in all kinds of programmes – light entertainment, current affairs, children's programmes, plays and series. Camera crews travel a lot and at short notice. There are three basic jobs: *editing*, *camera*, *sound* (titles may vary).

Film editors work entirely in the cutting-room, 'editing down' material shot in the studio or on location. A great deal of their work is done on their own initiative, as directors do not have time to be with editors all day. The job is highly creative as it is the editor who shapes and fashions the final programme which audiences see. Editing can lead to directing.

Assistant film editors look after the practical side of running the cutting-room. They do the 'joins', log film on its way out of and back into the studio and laboratories. They learn by watching, and often cut sequences under the editor's supervision.

Cutting-room work is almost invariably done under great pressure.

Film camera crews usually consist of 2–4 people. The head of the camera crew is in charge of lighting; works in close co-operation with the director; knows the script thoroughly and arranges the all-important lighting and camera angles for each individual shot, so as to achieve the atmosphere the director wants. Lighting cameraman/woman can be an important step to directing film.

Assistant camera crews load and change magazines, make sure the right equipment is available at the right time and place and in working order, and they learn how to operate cameras and lighting equipment. Promotion is pretty slow – it takes about 10 years to reach lighting cameraman/woman status.

Rostrum camera crew record on film and tape the artwork produced by the *graphic designers* (see p. 533).

Film sound recordists/sound technicians are concerned with dubbing, sound-transfer and above all with mixing sound from various sources. This may include location recordings on tape, and sounds produced by effects machines. Achieving the correct balance, controlling the 'input' from various sources, is a highly skilled job, requiring great technical skill and musical creativity.

Assistants manipulate microphones and other recording equipment and learn by watching. Far fewer apply for sound than vision jobs so chances of acceptance are better.

Projectionists (or *film assistants*) operate projection equipment and may also work on dubbing.

Entry qualifications and training (TV film)

Interest and 'hobby experience' are crucial. There are a number of film/TV courses at art schools, either as part of an art and design degree course, or 2–3 year BTEC/SCOTVEC Diploma courses, or at post-graduate level. Course emphasis (and entry requirements) vary enormously: for example on closed circuit educational television films; on feature or instructional films; with technical or creative bias, etc.

Equally useful in later job-opportunity terms, but more difficult to get into (several hundred applicants for every training vacancy) is the *BBC film training scheme* (1 year approximately; age 18–25). No specific GCSE requirements, but several GCSEs (A–C) are in practice essential; above all, candidates must show 'evidence of lively interest in film-making techniques' and know enough about cinematography principles to absorb advanced film training; they also need 'special knowledge of some of the following: photography, the cinema, music, magnetic sound recording, sport, news, current affairs'.

Film and Video Industry

Feature film making has for several years been a depressed part of the industry in Britain. The future demands of cable TV and the home video market should provide greater opportunities than the recent past. However, entry into cinema film making will remain very highly competitive. The only real job prospects lie with the growing number of often very small production companies which combine TV film making and, very occasionally, cinema, with the whole range of other productions, e.g. training and advertising films.

Video recorders, while not offering the same 'creative' scope as film cameras, have very wide and growing applications: sales promotions (e.g. for pop records and at 'point of sale' in shops), training of all kinds, recording ballets for a dance company's repertoire, monitoring the performance of racehorses during meetings. Many companies use only freelance staff as and when they need them and many of these specialize, e.g. in making wildlife or travel films. Studio facilities and sophisticated equipment are often hired from 'facility houses' which do not themselves make programmes.

Entry and training

There is no essential difference between filming for TV and making non-broadcast films. Similarly, people employed in video production do much the same work as those in films.

There are no jobs which can be done straight from school. Entry is normally via one of the following:

1. TV training and experience.

2. An appropriate diploma, degree or post-graduate course at film school or art college (titles and content vary, so it is essential to study prospectuses carefully).

3. An electronic engineering course (all levels) plus in-service training.

4. The JOBFIT scheme (supported by all sides of the film and TV industry) which started in 1985 to co-ordinate new entrant training in the *freelance film industry*. Candidates are considered not only on the basis of academic qualifications, but also on a proven commitment to the industry (i.e. through amateur film and video-making). The scheme lasts 2 years. Year 1 is general, with attachments to editing, camera, sound or art departments. Trainees then choose their specialization and spend the second year in their chosen area.

5. Specialized knowledge leading to making videos on a particular topic.

6. Very occasionally, extensive amateur experience.

There is more scope for versatility in video than in film making: people can – and with changes in industry may have to – move from one type of work to another fairly easily. Technicians need to be able to work in both film and television. There is always room in this expanding industry for really good technical people.

Radio

Entry routes differ between BBC network, BBC local and independent local radio. Once trained it is possible to move from one to another. Below are some examples from network radio.

Production

Producers are responsible for initiating and developing programme ideas. They need an interest in the creative use of radio, a journalistic approach, and some experience in relevant subject areas, e.g. the arts, science, medicine, social issues, drama, comedy, popular music, etc. Producers are recruited from within the BBC – from local radio, researchers, studio managers, and radio production assistants, for example; by direct advertising in the press; via the radio production trainee scheme.

Radio production assistants help producers by providing all-round administrative back-up for a programme, varying from typing scripts to helping in the studio. They are recruited from secretarial and clerical staff within the BBC or direct from outside.

Researchers work on individual programme strands. They will have specialist knowledge and skills and be recruited from within the BBC or by direct advertising in the press.

Continuity announcers/newsreaders are recruited from existing broadcasters in local radio or from other employees with good, clear voices. Occasionally jobs will be advertised in the press; previous broadcasting is generally required.

Sports assistants and correspondents often come from local radio, or have experience as sports journalists on newspapers. They need a good broadcasting style, an all-round knowledge of sport and more detailed commitment to one or more sports.

Reporters who work on all the main 'magazine' programmes from *Woman's Hour* to *Kaleidoscope* are freelances who generally started their careers on local or independent radio.

Technical and Engineering Services

The *studio manager* works with a whole range of professional broadcasters, newsreaders, actors and musicians, as well as with those who have never been in a studio before, under the direction of a producer. His or her job is to pull together their creative efforts into technical output for the listeners. They use microphones, complex sound-mixer desks, tape machines, disc players and professional CD players. The job can involve anything: rattling nappy pins for a drama serial, recording interviews and editing tapes for a magazine programme, or playing in jingles for Radio 1. Studio managers are recruited from within or outside the BBC. Applicants for training will generally be in their twenties. They will need wide interests; some experience in sound or radio, however amateur, will be valuable.

Engineering staff are recruited with degrees or diplomas in relevant disciplines.

NOTES ON ENTRY AND TRAINING (TO THE INDUSTRY GENERALLY)

The uncertainty in the industry at the present time means that training schemes in independent television have virtually ceased. The BBC continues to run many of its training schemes, but they are likely to take fewer people and run not on an annual basis but according to operational need. These schemes are an excellent way into the industry but they are intensely competitive. As far as the numbers entering are concerned, they have only ever been the tip of the iceberg. For example, in 1990 the BBC recruited about 3,500 permanent staff (i.e. those not on short-term contracts). Only 6% of those – about 200 people – were trainees (across the board in all areas). 31% were secretarial/clerical staff. The remainder covered all other areas, including finance, law and personnel.

Some of those secretaries will make it to production (many will not) because this is still a foot-in-the-door industry. The IMS survey (see p. 530) looked at first jobs in the broadcast TV industry and where they led. More than two-thirds of employees had started in one of 7 first jobs: engineering technician, technical assistant, secretarial/administration, sound assistant/trainee, camera assistant, trainee editor and assistant floor manager. Many of these led to a diverse range of careers. For example, nearly half the technical assistants had become engineers, but more than half were in sound, camera, light, post-production, production and producer/director jobs. Looking back to first jobs, 158 producers/directors reported 27 different first jobs: 13% had started as production assistants, 12% in secretarial/admin work. Though

53% of those in camera grades had started as camera assistants, 6% had started in secretarial/administration.

Clearly, the 'take-any-job-do-anything' strategy can work. But it is not easy to get these first jobs. On the operational side you need to get skills and that means you need to be enterprising. Hospital and local radio often need volunteers and can offer 'hands-on' experience. Get involved in amateur theatre or make your own videos or recordings. Watch television and become aware of companies' output.

Independent production and facilities companies, corporate in-house production units, major educational and franchise work-shops are likely to be growth sectors and can provide experience that can take you into the broadcast companies as permanent staff or on a freelance basis (*all* sectors are going to make increasing use of freelances). They are also career outlets in themselves. Most are very new (formed since 1981) and very small. Probably about three-quarters of them have 10 or fewer employees. Recruitment and training patterns are haphazard, but a small organization can often offer all-round experience. Corporate in-house production units offer employment to only a very few people, but they often have state-of-the-art equipment. Try knocking on doors – people have been known to get jobs this way, turning up just as someone was needed, or trying again and again and again *until* someone was needed. Consider taking a job as a 'runner' – the person who makes the tea, does deliveries, deals with the post and answers the phone can really find out how the industry works and who does what, which is vital. Trade directories like the *BFI* (*British Film Institute*) *Directory* can be very useful sources of information.

Many people entering the industry, especially on the production side, are graduates. Relevant degrees in, for example, film and media studies are very popular, but they do not give candidates a head-start. What employers are looking for is a lively interest in current affairs and broadcasting, and evidence that you have got practically involved in a way to complement your interests. Before taking any 'relevant' course, question in what ways it will stretch your mind and help you to develop wide interests – and ask to see details of what previous graduates have done.

Once in, most people develop their own careers. They may pick up new skills informally, by following around someone more experienced or experienced in a different area, or formally, as through the BBC's system of 'attachments' whereby staff can try out other jobs. The industry recognizes the need for more struc-tured training, especially as the need for freelances increases, and is developing NVQs (see p. xx).

Even when particular training is useful or essential, getting that training doesn't guarantee a job. Much depends on being the right person in the right place at the right time. The more you know about the industry, the nearer you are to being the right person – and the better able to find the right place.

Personal attributes   Creative imagination; wide interests generally, a special interest in a particular subject; a clear, quick, logical mind; appreciation of what audiences want; a strong constitution; the ability to work as one of a team and to take responsibility; a sociable nature; a fairly thick skin; tact; calmness in crises; speed of action; self-confidence; determination and persistence; desire to communicate ideas; ability to take criticism.

Late start   Scope mainly for people with relevant experience and qualifications, especially for experienced journalists and engineers.

Career-break   Depends on how well established before, but in some areas return presents problems. Companies are generous over maternity leave but it is essential to get back to work as soon as possible as there is so much competition. The National Film and Television School runs courses to update skills in the light of new technology.

Part time   The BBC is encouraging flexible working arrangements, including job-sharing. Many staff in the industry are freelance and work on short-term contracts.

Position of women   In general, on the programme production side women do reasonably well up to about middle-level jobs (nearly half are women). Although there are still very few women indeed in policy/decision-making jobs, opportunities generally for women are increasing, so their chances of reaching the top have never been better. However, they need the commitment to be willing to work long and irregular hours and to be mobile when necessary.

On the vast technical side there is only a small proportion of women. This is only because not enough women have taken science or technical subjects at school, or had the relevant 'hobby experience' which is so useful. Any woman who really wants to get into broadcasting should consider getting in via an engineering degree or technician qualification. She would stand out and be noticed and, generally, receive plenty of encouragement. She might later be able to transfer to programme production.

In the BBC women-only management courses have been running very successfully. 'Operational Awareness' courses for women are being tried out in various technical areas, with the aim of making it possible for some existing staff to undertake technical/engineering training. There are also some workplace crèches.

Further information
BBC Corporate Recruitment Services, Broadcasting House, London W1A 1AA

BBC Engineering and Technical Operations Recruitment, Broadcasting House, London W1A 1AA

ITV Association, Knighton House, 56 Mortimer Street, London W1 8AN

Related careers
ADVERTISING – ART AND DESIGN – DRAMA – JOURNALISM – MUSIC – PHOTOGRAPHY

Town and Country Planning

Degree or post-graduate qualification accredited by the Royal Town Planning Institute (see also 'Training', below).

Town Planners

The work Planners aim to reconcile the community's desire for a high standard of environment for work, home and leisure with the conflicting demands for land from industry, traffic, etc. They are concerned, in broad terms, with civic design, urban renewal, land-use and transportation systems. The majority work in local authorities, some in the Civil Service and some in private consultancy firms. In recent years planning emphasis has changed. Planners have learnt from past experiments; for example instead of large-scale slum-clearance schemes which dispersed long-established communities, planners now recommend rehabilitation of existing houses, to keep 'urban villages' intact; or help revitalization of inner-city areas: as factories and inhabitants move out, small workshops are being created out of derelict warehouses and factories to attract light industry and create local jobs. Altogether, the social and economic consequences of planning are researched and considered much more thoroughly now than they were only a few years ago.

The planning process may be broadly broken down into two separate but interrelated functions:

Survey, analysis, and research
Involves devising and conducting surveys of the structure, functioning, wishes and needs of communities and assessing problems and aims of urban and regional development. This is social research (see SOCIOLOGY, p. 486). Physical planners' final plans are based on the outcome of these findings.

Physical planning
Drawing up development plans and implementing them. When, for example, a twilight area is redeveloped, planners draw up plans for new road networks, for shopping precincts, leisure and

recreation facilities, the number and types of schools likely to be needed, etc.

Each county (see LOCAL GOVERNMENT, p. 268) is covered by a *Structure Plan* which outlines planning policy for that area in relation to neighbouring counties' Structure Plans. This is 'regional planning'. A county council planner might collate and analyse information in order to predict, for example, likely levels of need for transport, leisure facilities, schools, if plan 'A', proposing plans for increased industrial development, is implemented.

Structure Plans are mainly written policy statements. District planning authorities draw up *Local Plans*. These fit into a Structure Plan, and go into much more detail. They consist largely of maps and drawn plans. A Local Plan would show, for example, streets which are designated conservation areas; or a plan for small workshops and a shopping precinct. Local planners are also concerned with development control – dealing with planning applications from the public. Very broadly, there is more scope for improving the environment at Structure Plan-level planning; but more contact with the general public and such immediate environmental matters as closing roads and rerouting traffic, rehabilitating old houses rather than pulling them down, at Local Plan level.

Jobs are very dependent on public authority spending levels, although there are increasing opportunities in the private sector. There are occasional openings for experienced planners in developing countries, mainly on a short-contract basis.

Training   *Either*: 4-year full-time, 6-year part-time or 5-year sandwich degree recognized by the Royal Town Planning Institute; *or*: a degree in any subject followed by a 2-year full-time or 3-year part-time course recognized by the RTPI. A few schools of planning offer preparatory courses for people without the normal degree or professional qualifications (e.g. some BTEC Higher National award holders) which then give entry on to their accredited post-graduate courses.

After 2 years' practical planning experience, candidates who have fulfilled the academic requirements of the RTPI qualify for election to membership as Chartered Town Planners.

Sociologists, geographers, economists, architects, landscape architects and other specialists concerned with the various aspects of planning also work in planning departments, particularly in counties and big cities. For work concerned with overall strategic planning problems and policy, i.e. for senior posts, however, a planning qualification is essential.

See also ARCHITECTURE, 'Training' (p. 44).

Personal attributes

A keen interest in other people's priorities and way of life; powers of observation; creative imagination; patience for painstaking research; the ability to work as one of a team as well as to take responsibility; interest in social, economic and environmental developments.

Late start

Graduates with relevant degrees (geography, social science, engineering) could start post-graduate training. There is no specific upper age limit. An RPTI 'distance-learning' course is available for people (graduates or non-graduates) who want to switch to planning from related careers (architects, geographers, engineers, etc.) in mid-career. It should also be useful for people returning after a *career-break*.

Career-break

Planning priorities and legislation change constantly, so planners must keep up with developments. There are 'mid-career' updating courses and seminars for all planners, which could be useful as *refresher* courses (see 'Late start', above). Returners can also take additional courses, for example in traffic engineering/planning at the returning stage. Reduced RTPI subscriptions available.

Part time

Experienced planners increasingly do freelance work. Some local authorities have job-sharing schemes. Part-time courses available (see above).

Position of women

About 15% of qualified and 35% of student members of the RTPI are women. Women do well up to middle-level jobs; very few are Chief Officers in local government planning departments.

Further information

The Royal Town Planning Institute, 26 Portland Place, London W1N 4BE

Planning Technicians

They are the support staff, carrying out various technical and practical tasks. These include drawing up of plans; preparing maps and diagrams; conducting surveys and interpreting results; dealing with enquiries from the public. They use computers for the various activities and may be in charge of a department's computer system.

Entry qualifications

4 GCSEs (A–C) including maths and a subject involving written English.

Prospects are not good at the moment as much technician work is done by graduates who cannot get higher level jobs, especially in the public sector.

Training   On the job with day-release for the BTEC National Certificate in Land Administration (or SCOTVEC Certificate in Planning) (see pp. xxi, xxii), which takes 2 years, with a further 2 years for the BTEC/SCOTVEC Higher National award. It is possible, but not usually recommended, to cross over to professional membership of the RTPI by taking a town planning degree after the BTEC National Certificate.

Late start   Few opportunities

Career-break   Could be difficult as no *refresher* training.

Part time   Very limited, but job-sharing should be possible.

Position of women   A growing number – 26% – of Society of Planning Technicians are women.

Further information   Society of Planning Technicians, 26 Portland Place, London W1N 4BE

Related careers   ARCHITECTURE: *Architectural Technician* – CARTOGRAPHY – ECONOMICS – ENGINEERING – HOUSING MANAGEMENT – LANDSCAPE ARCHITECTURE AND DESIGN – LOCAL GOVERNMENT – SURVEYING: *Auctioneers*

Trading Standards Officer

Entry qualifications
For the Diploma in Trading Standards: 2 A-levels, 3 GCSEs (A–C), including English, maths and physics at either level. *Graduate* entry: about 60%. For the Diploma in Consumer Affairs: 5 GCSEs, including English language, or relevant experience.

The work
Trading standards officers are employed by local authorities to ensure a fair system of trading between consumers and traders, and between traders themselves. They are responsible for the enforcement of consumer protection legislation, such as the Trade Descriptions Act, Food Act, consumer credit, and food and drugs legislation. Complaints and investigations may concern, for example: a holiday brochure which misled travellers into expecting a luxury hotel on the beach when in fact they bought a holiday in a guest-house in a back-street; a 'showerproof' coat which does not withstand the briefest of showers; a 'pre-shrunk' shirt which is two sizes smaller after the first wash. Officers ascertain facts, which involves getting expert opinion and/or having articles examined in a testing laboratory, and get matters put right. If necessary, they take offenders to court. They may also investigate complaints from the public about unscrupulous phoney companies offering products like double glazing, loft insulation, etc.

They also check the accuracy of weighing and measuring equipment – from the nip used to sell whisky in a pub to the weighbridge which weighs lorry-loads in the docks (the Trading Standards Administration developed out of the Weights and Measures Department). They use elaborate electronic equipment to check quantities in, for example, prepacked goods; they use straightforward methods to check that, for example, petrol pumps dispense correct amounts.

Britain's entry into the EC has greatly affected and expanded the trading standards officer's work, as British quantity and quality control methods have had to be brought into line with Continental practice.

Officers divide their time between dealing with traders and with individuals who have complaints and/or queries; inspection; report writing. The higher up the hierarchy, the greater the management content of the job, the smaller the checking of equipment and quantities element. TSOs meet a great variety of people and have much scope for decision-making.

This is an expanding area but opportunities depend on local authority spending priorities. It may be necessary to move to get a job and even more often to obtain promotion.

Training   On the job with block-/day-release and home study for *either* the Diploma in Trading Standards (takes normally 3 years) *or* the Diploma in Consumer Affairs (normally 2 years).

The DTS is a statutory requirement for Trading Standards Officers responsible for overseeing weighing and measuring legislation, but not for those involved in enforcing other consumer legislation. A department is likely to employ more staff holding the DCA than the DTS.

The syllabus for the DTS includes relevant legislation, science of materials and principles of measurement, economic and commercial practice, statistics and quality control, enforcement and advice. The syllabus for the DCA comprises compulsory papers in law and constitution, structure of trade and the consumer movement, plus options in, for example, animal health, consumer credit, consumer safety, practical consumer advice and money advice.

1 or 2 degree courses leading to exemptions from the professional exams are being developed.

Personal   Good communication skills, written and verbal; objectivity; scru-
attributes   pulous attention to detail; self-confidence; ability to work on one's own and to explain technical points to traders and consumers; some persuasive powers.

Late start   People with business or other experience of dealing with people or with the law (police officers, for example) should have reasonable chances. In theory, this is a good 'second career'; in practice young entrants may be given preference when there are more applicants than vacancies.

Career-   Too early to say whether return to work will be easy; there should
break   be no difficulty in theory if those in temporary retirement keep up with legislation and other developments.

Part time   Not at the moment – not enough people have asked for it. Job-sharing should be possible.

Position of women

It used to be an all-male preserve, mainly because trading standards officers' predecessors, weights and measures inspectors, were required to lift heavy sacks, etc. for weighing. This is no longer a requirement and the work should appeal to women, as so much of the work is concerned with women shoppers' complaints. This seems to be happening: while only about 9% of total members of the Institute of Trading Standards Administration are women, they now make up over half the student members.

Further information

Institute of Trading Standards Administration, 4–5 Hadleigh Business Centre, 351 London Road, Hadleigh, Essex SS7 2BT

Related careers

ENVIRONMENTAL HEALTH OFFICER – HEALTH AND SAFETY INSPECTORS – HOME ECONOMICS – LAW

Travel Agent/Tour Operator

Entry qualifications

None specified, but entrants to travel agencies usually have several GCSEs. Also increasing *graduate* entry (mainly tour operators). Foreign languages especially useful for incoming tourism.

Travel and tourism form the UK's biggest growth industry, employing 1·5 million people. It overlaps with the growing leisure industry and is essentially concerned with providing services for people who are away from home, on business or on holiday. These may be UK residents travelling within Britain or going abroad or 'incoming' tourists who make a substantial contribution to the UK economy. Both business and leisure travellers increasingly seek a broader range of services and more sophisticated or unusual ways of spending their time and money. The business traveller may want sports facilities and saunas. The holiday-maker may want to try hang-gliding, hill-walking, wine-tasting, bird-watching or painting.

Many jobs in tourism are concerned with providing accomodation and food – whether for farm-based holidays or international conferences. Other jobs are in transport operations – from hire car fleets to coach companies, airline operators to Caribbean cruise ships. Others are in entertainment and visitors' attractions, tourist information services and – increasingly important – marketing and promotions. Tourist information is both general and specific, ranging from selling Britain to potential visitors all over the world to helping a family find bed-and-breakfast accommodation in Northumbria.

As the industry becomes more complex and competitive, so it needs better-trained people who are adaptable, creative and thoroughly professional.

This section deals with 2 distinct sections of the industry: travel agencies and tour operators. A few large companies own both agencies and operators.

Travel agents are the retailers. They sell tour operators' holidays, plan trips for people within the UK and abroad, and sell tickets for rail, air, ferry and coach travel. Some specialize in business travel, arranging travel and accommodation for company executives. *Tour operators* usually specialize in either incoming or outgoing operations. They put together and organize package holidays – anything from self-catering cabins in the Scottish Highlands to trekking in the Himalayas. Tour operators concentrate on planning – and selling – their holidays, with such subdivisions as British and foreign, summer and winter; business and holiday; party and individual packages. Although the bulk of the package holiday business is controlled by a few huge operators, there has been a growth in small companies catering for special interest holidays, for example cycling and art history tours.

Travel Agents

The work   *Counter work*
This is essentially selling. Clients (never called customers) may know what they want and simply buy a ticket for a train journey, or book a world tour, or want some travel literature. But most have no idea of what they want. Their leisure-time tastes must be summed up, and 'channelled' into what the counter-clerk thinks is the holiday they will most enjoy in a price range they can afford.

Counter-clerks usually have not been to the places they suggest – but they should know, from travel literature or from colleagues, as much about the holidays they recommend as possible. They must take trouble with each client; their responsibility is far greater than that of most other sales assistants. Most people 'buy' only one holiday a year, and if this one is not a success, they will go to another agency next year.

Business house clerks deal with companies, mainly over the telephone, making travel arrangements for their staff. In smaller agencies staff may share all the tasks.

All clerks perform a range of tasks behind the scenes and may spend many hours on the telephone. They keep elaborate filing systems with cross-references; every member of staff must be able to find quickly details about block and individual bookings. Much of this is now computerized. Each booking involves filling in forms, sending them out, filing, checking and possibly dealing with detailed correspondence. Itineraries and currency-conversion have to be worked out; timetables checked. Minor clerical errors can have disastrous consequences for clients' holidays and trips. Nearly all agents now use Prestel.

Managers co-ordinate the work of clerks and select those tour operators' brochures which they think will offer their clients what they want. As their profit is made from selling packages, travel agents must have good knowledge of tourist areas and also know how to advertise and promote their services to existing and potential clients.

Opportunities in travel agencies have decreased in recent years as many smaller retailers have gone out of business. There is a high proportion of junior to senior staff, so promotion prospects are not very good.

Tour Operators

Planning
This is done by directors and 'travel technicians' (i.e. experienced clerks). 'Planning trips' last from 1 to 8 weeks twice a year and are exhausting. 2 or 3 resorts and perhaps 12 hotels may be investigated in a day. Local transport, garage facilities, food, amusements, beaches will be checked and local tourist officials consulted. Planning of the tour later involves checking timetables and maps, costing, and conferring with transport and accommodation services suppliers. Costing is crucial and the success of operators depends largely on ability to negotiate discounted prices with hotels, villa companies, airlines, etc. All this has to be done up to 2 years in advance, which adds to the difficulties.

Sales
Sales people visit travel agents to make sure brochures are on display. Those companies specializing in school parties (for example to ski resorts) have a sales team which visits schools to try to win their custom.

Reservations
Reservations staff take bookings from individuals and travel agents. However, increased use of computerized reservations systems is reducing the size of these departments.

Representatives or couriers
Many are freelance and are employed for the summer or winter season (occasionally both) by individual companies. The majority work with incoming tours, i.e. with overseas visitors to Britain. A minority work overseas, either travelling with groups from Britain to their holiday destination or based at a resort. Some may do secretarial work and/or planning off-season. This is not a career as such but rather a pleasant change for competent secretaries/ linguists or simply good organizers. Training is mainly provided by the company (although 1 or 2 private organizations run short courses for people hoping to become couriers).

Most travel staff work long hours and most Saturday mornings.

Training   NVQs (see p. xx) are already in place.

Training can be full or part time or by distance-learning.

1. Part-time/distance-learning courses validated jointly by ABTA and City and Guilds (see p. xxiii). (See also 'Late start', below.)

COTAC (Certificate of Travel Agency Competence) levels 1 and 2. Each comprises 2 written tests, plus work-based assessment of practical skills: travel agency tasks at level 1, supervisory skills at level 2. COTOP (Certificate of Tour Operating Practice) levels 1 and 2, also comprising 2 written tests.

Level 1 COTAC or COTOP normally takes 18 months' part-time study and leads to the *Certificate in Travel Skills* (NVQ 2). Level 2 takes a further year and leads to the *Diploma in Travel Skills* (NVQ 3).

People aiming at management can then study for the *Certificate in Travel Agency Management*. This is turn leads to the *Diploma in Advanced Travel Skills* (NVQ 4).

New courses (1991) are the *Certificate for Overseas Resort Representatives* (2 written tests and assessment as in COTAC) and the *Certificate in UK Tourism*, for staff working in travel agencies or other parts of the tourist industry.

ABTA Youth Training is the main way into travel work for school-leavers. There are no set entry requirements, but in practice many trainees have 3–4 GCSEs. Most openings are in travel agencies, but there are also a few in business houses, with tour operators and airlines. Trainees are expected to reach NVQ levels 2 and 3.

There is also an ABTA Employment Training scheme (see p. xxv), which takes adult entrants up to NVQ level 2.

2. 1-year full-time (occasionally part-time) course for ABTA/ City and Guilds *Certificate in Travel Studies*; this incorporates the 'technical' knowledge of COTAC level 1.

3. BTEC National award (see p. xxi) in Travel and Tourism or in Leisure with tourism option (or SCOTVEC equivalent). It is important to check that courses have the ABTA 'seal of approval'.

4. BTEC/SCOTVEC Higher National award in Business and Finance, Leisure or (in Scotland) Tourism.

There are some *post-graduate* courses; which may also accept BTEC/SCOTVEC Higher National award holders. At graduate and post-graduate level, *tourism* and *catering* training and work overlap. *Graduate* entry is mainly with relevant degree or HND or with *marketing*, *accounting* or similar qualifications.

The Institute of Travel and Tourism no longer runs its own examinations for new entrants. Instead it accepts for the appropriate membership grade holders of approved ABTA or BTEC/SCOTVEC awards. Experienced staff over 21 without these awards can take the Institute's own examination.

Personal attributes Aptitude for figure work; good judgement of people; a friendly manner; accuracy; organizing ability; common sense; a good memory.

Late start Little opportunity in travel agencies, as most posts filled by school- and college-leavers. Some opportunities with tour operators. It is possible to prepare for entry, or to update skills or retrain, by using ABTA's Self-Study training packages.

Career-break Opportunities for returners depend on contacts, on having kept up with changes in the industry. See Self-Study packages under 'Late start'. Suitable updating courses also available.

Part time Normally only seasonal.

Position of women Although more women than men are employed in travel agencies, only about 1 manager in 8 is a woman. In large tour operating companies, women are beginning to do well, though they have to have more paper qualifications (and languages) than the men with whom they compete.

Further information ABTA National Training Board, Waterloo House, 11–17 Chertsey Road, Woking, Surrey GU21 5AL (enclose s.a.e.)
Institute of Travel and Tourism, 113 Victoria Street, St Albans, Herts. AL1 3TJ (enclose s.a.e.)

Related careers CATERING: *Hotels* – CIVIL AVIATION: *Cabin Crew*; *Ground Staff* – LANGUAGES – LEISURE/RECREATION MANAGEMENT –SECRETARIAL AND CLERICAL WORK

Working for Oneself:
Mini-Entrepreneurship

Creating one's own job has now established itself as an 'alternative career'. Potential mini-entrepreneurs can get encouragement, advice, and sometimes financial help, from various sources, but their business plan has to stand up to severe scrutiny.

Entry qualifications

See 'Personal attributes' and 'Training', below.

The work

The variety of self-generated work is unlimited. It can be broadly divided into three overlapping types of activity: *providing a service*; *selling*; *making*. Most enterprises combine two activities, one of which is usually the crucial one. Deciding which type of enterprise to choose requires a great deal of research, because setting up a business is an uncharted area in conventional career terms. First impressions of what is involved in, say, running a sandwich delivery or motorbike messenger service, or a musical instrument repair or manufacturing workshop, tend to be misleading. They conceal any number of pitfalls – the need for unexpected areas of expertise, or for much more capital than bargained for, for example.

Providing a Service

This requires least capital, involves least risk, covers a vast range, e.g. babysitting, window or office cleaning, running a bicycle delivery service – activities based on using one's time, basic skills and possibly basic equipment; or repairing videos or motor-bikes, cooking directors' lunches in offices, running a word-processing or computer programming service, i.e. using specific skills plus equipment and, possibly, premises – kitchen, garden shed, living-room.

Networking is a fairly new high-tech, home-based service enterprise. Professionals – in law, accountancy, systems analysis, etc. – with considerable experience, set up their own computerized service and sell their expertise to companies for specific projects. This is still very much in its infancy but is likely to be a growth area. It enables professionals to be their own boss, working from home, while retaining links with previous employers and at the same time also working for new clients. Companies like it because having work done by 'tele-commuters' saves overheads.

Selling

This usually overlaps with *providing a service* or with *making*, or it depends on 'buying-in' goods to sell (or collecting them from friends, etc.). It includes, for example, making sandwiches at home and delivering them to regular customers, running a second-hand clothes or clutter stall, selling 'bought-in' groceries from a mobile shop (probably a battered old van). This kind of selling could be a run-up to opening a shop, restaurant, mail-order business. Selling involves more initial organization and business know-how, capital and risk than *providing a service*.

Making

This usually overlaps with *selling* and covers anything from making children's clothes to assembling car roof-racks to manufacturing high tech components for the computer industry or electric guitars. It ranges from using talent plus basic skills to using sophisticated skills acquired by a range of levels of training, from YT to degree and post-graduate course, plus equipment. It requires some capital and probably premises. But if the idea is viable (see below) and the skills are there, finance and other help is available (see below).

*

The Law

Far fewer formalities have to be complied with than would-be entrepreneurs tend to fear. Mini-entrepreneurship is fashionable and a Good Thing in bureaucracy's eyes. The spirit rather than the letter of by-laws has to be observed. It is not permissible to run a saw-mill in one's garden because the noise would annoy the neighbours. It is unlikely that the Environmental Health Officer (from the Town Hall) would forbid sandwiches for sale being prepared in one's kitchen as long as that is clean. Local authorities must be consulted about planning and other regulations, but permission to go ahead is rarely 'unreasonably withheld' in the present climate of encouragement for so called 'start-ups' – small businesses. Even the Inspector of Taxes and the departments of Health and Social Security, which have to be told, advise, inform and encourage rather than hinder. (Many people, for example, fear they will have to cope with VAT if they want to set up in business. In fact few people will reach the annual turnover limit necessary for registration in the first year or two.)

Business Format

Far fewer formalities have to be observed in the initial stages than generally believed. The basic formats are (a) *Sole trader*: The Income Tax and DSS merely have to be informed that the business exists; (b) *Partnership*: If two or more people set up a business jointly, a solicitor draws up a straightforward agreement. Both sole traders and partnerships are liable for all the debts they incur should the business fail; (c) *Limited company*: Requires slightly more formalities, but once set up persons involved are only liable for the money they put into the business should things go wrong; (d) *Co-operatives*: Various types; to set one up, solicitors' or special agencies' advice is essential (see 'Further information', below).

Training

No formal training structure as for conventional careers exists, but for most businesses mini-entrepreneurs need special skills. Welders, beauty therapists, typographers, software engineers, electronics engineers (technicians and graduates) or whatever, must first acquire the skill they intend to 'sell', i.e. which they want to use as the basis for their business. (See under individual career headings how to acquire such skills.) But to survive in the tough business world, basic business know-how is absolutely essential, too. The meaning of such terms as cash-flow, balance sheets, mark-up and, say, the difference between marketing and market research must be understood. The overall failure rate of new mini-ventures is fairly high. However, the failure rate can be linked closely to the level of research done and specialist advice/training taken prior to starting up. Statistics are misleading because there are so many variables which affect success or failure, but there is general agreement among experts that successful entrepreneurship requires several indispensable ingredients:

1. *A marketable idea*: No idea is good in a vacuum. It must fill a gap in a given market. A bike repair service in a seaside suburb mainly inhabited by retired people would fail; one on a new housing estate some miles from shops and offices, etc. stands a good chance (as long as there is no efficient competition or, if

there is, the competition has more work than it can cope with and/or the local market is expanding); a mobile grocery-van on that housing estate where few shops have yet been opened sounds a good idea; a mobile grocery-van near a large shopping centre does not; a small-van removal service might flourish in bedsitter-land; it would not in a large-one-family-houses suburb. Research-ing the market and making a marketing plan are probably the most essential tasks when preparing to go it alone.

2. *Motivation and commitment*: Mini-entrepreneurs have to be willing to work harder, and more irregular hours, than employees (see 'Personal attributes', below).

3. *Resources*: If the idea fills a gap in the market and the commitment is there, advice, possibly financial assistance and help with finding premises (if kitchen/garden shed/living-room are insufficient/unsuitable) are available.

Because the powers-that-be agree that in business small is beautiful (at least to start with) and that an increase in self-generated jobs will reduce unemployment, a plethora of agencies to help 'start-ups' have sprung up over the last few years. Many of these have since disappeared, but there are still several sources of help, advice and training which can help those starting a new business to avoid some of the more obvious pitfalls and to maximize their chances of success. The main change has been the replacement of national schemes by more locally based initiatives (see 'Training', below).

The 2 main points of contact for new entrepreneurs are:

1. *Training and Enterprise Councils* (TECs) in England and Wales and *Local Enterprise Companies* (lecs) in Scotland. These receive money from central government to fund local services and it is they who decide who should get what. Under their operating agreements with the Department of Employment they are required to provide a business information advisory and counselling service; in most cases this should include help for people wanting to start businesses. (They have taken over responsi-bility for this aspect from the national Small Firms Service – the SFS was at the time of writing still operating in London and the South East, but its future is uncertain.) There are local variations: for example, some TECs will make an initial training course a condition of financial help, while others will make it voluntary. Some TECs provide a range of training sessions on various aspects of running a business and some place considerable empha-sis on helping people for a period after they have actually started their business. TEC advisers explain what training and financial/ business support schemes are available, and for what, in their area. These take into account local needs and possible gaps in the

market. Potential business start-ups will be very closely scrutinized – a proper business plan is essential – and backing only given where the TEC think there is a good chance of success. TECs also administer financial schemes such as Enterprise Allowance (formerly the Enterprise Allowance Scheme). The local Jobcentre can give the address of the nearest TEC or lec.

2. *Local Enterprise Agencies* (Enterprise Trusts in Scotland): there are several hundreds of these, privately run, and many work closely with TECs. They help with information on the local business scene, with forming a business plan and with business counselling generally. They can give advice on tax, marketing, law, etc. The London Enterprise Agency (LEntA) runs 1-day sessions for anyone thinking of starting up their own business, and similar introductory courses may be available in some other areas. *Business in the Community* is the umbrella organization for these agencies and keeps an up-to-date list.

At the time of writing most of these services are free. Other useful organizations are:

3. The *Scottish Business Shop* provides a range of advisory services to small businesses throughout Scotland, including an information pack, a database of factual information and 3 free counselling sessions.

4. The *Rural Development Commission* (formerly CoSIRA) gives advice and help to people intending to set up in business in rural areas.

5. The *Crafts Council* will advise people thinking of setting up a pottery, weaving or similar crafts workshop.

6. The *Prince's Youth Business Trust* and *Livewire* advise and help young people (under-25s usually) who choose the self-employment option.

7. *Graduate Enterprise*: Intended to persuade more new graduates (in any discipline) to opt for self-employment. Consists of briefing sessions and in some areas 2-day workshops.

8. *Design Business Enterprise Programme*: Series of workshops available only in London for art and design graduates with viable business ideas but lacking in commercial know-how.

Details of 7. and 8. available from graduate careers advisory services.

9. Some business studies degrees, post-graduate courses, BTEC and SCOTVEC awards (including BTEC Continuing Education units) have self-employment options.

10. *Open University* (p. xxxiv) *Start Up Your Own Business course*: It includes tuition by correspondence material (cassettes, work assignments, etc.) as well as support from an adviser with business experience for up to 9 months.

11. The *Open College* (p. xxxviii) has courses for people considering self-employment.

12. *Local education authorities* run courses which, though not necessarily planned for potential entrepreneurs, are very useful – e.g. in book-keeping, marketing, basic computer application. Some are evening classes, others are day-time courses organized under the '21 hours rule' which means unemployed people can draw benefit while attending college for a maximum of 21 hours a week.

Personal attributes   Unquenchable resilience; tenacity; decisiveness; organizing ability; being a bit bossy; exceptional stamina; business acumen; enjoying risk-taking – being a bit of a gambler; ability to put up with temporary hardship; resourcefulness; self-confidence bordering on conceit; true enjoyment of hard work; ability to get on well with other people however unreasonable their requests/criticisms/impatience; imagination; ability to work under pressure; interest in economic and social trends. (Extent of these qualities depends on extent of venturesomeness of enterprise contemplated.)

Late start   Age is a positive advantage in this 'alternative' career. Anyone who has had experience of the world of work scores over school/college-leavers when it comes to applying to banks, etc. for funds or to other agencies for premises or other help. Career-changers and returners are welcome on courses.

Career-break   Might present problems. It is too early to say at what stage in this particular work area a complete break would be least harmful. Most women entrepreneurs at present have either not yet reached the career-break stage, or they started their enterprise when there was no longer any need for a career-break.

Part time   Only possible by running small home-based businesses, or by being part of a well-organized co-operative.

Position of women   Women were slower than men to start choosing the self-employment option (24% of self-employed people in 1991 were women) but they are catching up fast. But figures are misleading because more women than men run small-scale enterprises from home – anything from catering to word-processing and cosmetics manufacturing – which do not necessarily show up in the statistics. The failure-rate among women entrepreneurs is believed to be smaller than that among their male counterparts – probably because to get bank loans women have to produce a more thoroughly researched business plan than men. Bank managers realize that women are less likely than men to have the unpaid 'back-up' help which male entrepreneurs tend to get from wives, and that women have more difficulty than men persuading suppliers that they are creditworthy. So the women who have managed to get the necessary start-up finance tend to succeed.

Self-employment can be the answer both for women who want to combine work with looking after a family by running small-scale enterprises from home, and for women with managerial ability who feel thwarted in the male-dominated business world. However, many women lack the necessary self-confidence to start. The Women's Enterprise Development Agency (Aston Science Park, Love Lane, Aston Triangle, Birmingham B7 4BJ) will advise low-income women.

Further information	Local TEC or lec (ask at Jobcentre or look in telephone directory)
	Rural Development Commission, 4 Castle Street, Salisbury, Wiltshire SP1 3TP (England and Wales only)
	Scottish Business Shop, 120 Bothwell Street, Glasgow G2 7JP
	Crafts Council, 44A Pentonville Road, London N1 9BY
	London Enterprise Agency, 4 Snow Hill, London EC1A 2DL (write for useful booklet, 'Getting Started')
	Business in the Community (for addresses of local enterprise agencies), 227A City Road, London EC1V 1JU (for England and Wales); 25 St Andrews Square, Edinburgh EH2 1AF (for Scotland)
	Livewire: Freepost Livewire, Newcastle upon Tyne, NE1 1BR
	The Prince's Youth Business Trust, 5 Cleveland Place, London SW1Y 6JJ
	Several high street banks have useful booklets on running your own business
	Women into Business, 46 Westminster Palace Garden, Artillery Row, London SW1P 1RR does not provide advice to individuals but is an advisory group concerned with promoting women entrepreneurs

Related careers	MANAGEMENT

Youth and Community Work

Entry qualifications

Depend on age and experience. See 'Training', below.

The work

Youth and community work has elements in common with education and social work. A primary concern is the social education of young people, helping them to explore their strengths and weaknesses, develop physical, intellectual, moral, social and emotional resources, and facilitate their growth from childhood to adulthood. Recent years have seen increased 'targeting' of disadvantaged groups, but current debate sets that against the need for more mainstream work. Many young people stay at home these days in rooms full of TVs, videos, stereos and computers – all essentially passive entertainments – and miss many opportunities for social development.

Job titles vary. People with different titles can be doing substantially the same work, while the work of people with the same title can vary greatly. *Youth workers* or *youth and community workers* may be club- or centre-based, 'detached' or community-based. In a club or centre the youth worker plans activities to appeal to a wide range of ages and tastes. They give young people the means to mix socially and organize themselves, to develop confidence and skills, both practical (e.g. in sport or drama) and social (e.g. co-operating as part of a team), to channel their energies in a constructive way. Forming relationships with young people is a very important part of the work and may involve the youth worker in counselling or unofficial social work. For example, the youth worker may be the first person to recognize signs of drug abuse or the bottled-up effects of a family break-up.

In some centres activities are organized for other groups within the community, e.g. mother-and-toddler groups, pre-school playgroups, leisure interest classes, literacy classes or English for immigrants. Sometimes the youth and community worker is responsible for such activities; sometimes the role is one of liaison with other groups. The balance between 'youth' and 'community' varies greatly; in some areas local authority services that changed their name from Youth Service to Youth and Community Service are now changing back.

Many youth and community workers are 'detached', i.e. they do not work from a fixed base. Some go out into the community to make contact with young people who do not come to clubs to identify their needs and help develop community solutions. Others do project work on, for example, drug abuse, unemployment or health education. Some youth workers are attached to schools (they usually need teaching qualifications) and a number work in social services departments with 'at risk' young people.

Youth work is very dependent on part-time, often voluntary workers. Even in a large centre there may be only 1 qualified worker, and, increasingly, qualified workers are given area responsibility for a number of clubs or centres. This means that qualified youth and community workers have less face-to-face contact with young people. Their job includes lots of administration, organizing of events and activities, recruitment, training and support of part-time workers, management of budgets and premises, liaison with the management committee and other groups, and seeking grants, sponsorship and other material support.

Youth and community workers are employed by local authorities (the Youth or Youth and Community Service is usually part of the education department, but sometimes comes under the leisure department), or by voluntary groups; it is estimated that 80% of youth work is provided by the voluntary groups (e.g. churches and organizations like Guides and Scouts). There is, however, a great deal of co-operation between the statutory and voluntary sectors.

Training   This is flexible and ensures that suitable people, whatever their age and educational qualifications, have a chance of qualifying. Though applicants for courses are normally expected to have 5 GCSEs (A–C) plus experience of voluntary or paid (for example, *playleader*) work with young people and/or other community work, applicants whose practical work experience has shown that they are suitable for the work may be accepted with lower educational qualifications. Minimum entry age varies from one course to another and again depends on individuals' experience and maturity.

Types of courses

1. 2-year full-time course leading to qualified youth and community worker status. Minimum age usually 23, occasionally younger.

2. 3-year part-time course.

3. Apprenticeship schemes for those with experience. No formal qualifications required; they may make you ineligible.

4. Full-time or part-time post-graduate course. Any degree subject acceptable; previous experience required.

5. Degree course in community studies, youth studies, or youth and community work. 2 A-levels required. Practical experience may be required.

6. *In Scotland* 3-year full-time course; may be reduced to 2 years for mature entrants with appropriate experience. Graduates and those with certain appropriate professional qualifications take a 1-year course.

Personal attributes An outgoing personality; ability to communicate easily with people who may need 'drawing out'; patience; imagination to put oneself into the shoes of people who feel alienated from society; wide interests in current social and economic trends and problems; organizing ability; feeling at ease with people of all ages; creativity to think up activities (see also SOCIAL WORK, 'Personal attributes', p. 484).

Late start Mature candidates are welcome on courses. This can be a suitable 'second career' for people changing direction in their twenties or thirties, if they have relevant experience.

Career-break Should not present any problems.

Part time Ample opportunity in youth work. Job-sharing is beginning to appear.

Position of women There is no reason why women should not do well in this career and the number of women on courses has risen.

Further information National Youth Agency, 17–23 Albion Street, Leicester LE1 6GD
Scottish Community Education Council, West Coates House, 90 Haymarket Terrace, Edinburgh EH12 5LQ

Related careers LEISURE/RECREATION MANAGEMENT – SOCIAL WORK – SPORT – TEACHING

Index

Bold type denotes main section.

READ MORE IN PENGUIN

In every corner of the world, on every subject under the sun, Penguin represents quality and variety – the very best in publishing today.

For complete information about books available from Penguin – including Puffins, Penguin Classics and Arkana – and how to order them, write to us at the appropriate address below. Please note that for copyright reasons the selection of books varies from country to country.

In the United Kingdom: Please write to *Dept. JC, Penguin Books Ltd, FREEPOST, West Drayton, Middlesex UB7 0BR*

If you have any difficulty in obtaining a title, please send your order with the correct money, plus ten per cent for postage and packaging, to *PO Box No. 11, West Drayton, Middlesex UB7 0BR*

In the United States: Please write to *Penguin USA Inc., 375 Hudson Street, New York, NY 10014*

In Canada: Please write to *Penguin Books Canada Ltd, 10 Alcorn Avenue, Suite 300, Toronto, Ontario M4V 3B2*

In Australia: Please write to *Penguin Books Australia Ltd, 487 Maroondah Highway, Ringwood, Victoria 3134*

In New Zealand: Please write to *Penguin Books (NZ) Ltd,182–190 Wairau Road, Private Bag, Takapuna, Auckland 9*

In India: Please write to *Penguin Books India Pvt Ltd, 706 Eros Apartments, 56 Nehru Place, New Delhi 110 019*

In the Netherlands: Please write to *Penguin Books Netherlands B.V., Keizersgracht 231 NL–1016 DV Amsterdam*

In Germany: Please write to *Penguin Books Deutschland GmbH, Friedrichstrasse 10–12, W–6000 Frankfurt/Main 1*

In Spain: Please write to *Penguin Books S. A., C. San Bernardo 117–6⁰ E–28015 Madrid*

In Italy: Please write to *Penguin Italia s.r.l., Via Felice Casati 20, I–20124 Milano*

In France: Please write to *Penguin France S. A., 17 rue Lejeune, F–31000 Toulouse*

In Japan: Please write to *Penguin Books Japan, Ishikiribashi Building, 2–5–4, Suido, Tokyo 112*

In Greece: Please write to *Penguin Hellas Ltd, Dimocritou 3, GR–106 71 Athens*

In South Africa: Please write to *Longman Penguin Southern Africa (Pty) Ltd, Private Bag X08, Bertsham 2013*

READ MORE IN PENGUIN

REFERENCE

The Penguin Dictionary of Literary Terms and Literary Theory
J. A. Cuddon

'Scholarly, succinct, comprehensive and entertaining, this is an important book, an indispensable work of reference. It draws on the literature of many languages and quotes aptly and freshly from our own' – *The Times Educational Supplement*

The Penguin Spelling Dictionary

What are the plurals of *octopus* and *rhinoceros*? What is the difference between *stationery* and *stationary*? And how about *annex* and *annexe*, *agape* and *Agape*? This comprehensive new book, the fullest spelling dictionary now available, provides the answers.

The Roget's Thesaurus of English Words and Phrases
Betty Kirkpatrick (ed.)

This new edition of Roget's classic work, now brought up to date for the nineties, will increase anyone's command of the English language. Fully cross-referenced, it includes synonyms of every kind (formal or colloquial, idiomatic and figurative) for almost 900 headings. It is a must for writers and utterly fascinating for any English speaker.

The Penguin Dictionary of English Idioms
Daphne M. Gulland and David G. Hinds-Howell

The English language is full of pitfalls for the foreign student – but the most common problem lies in understanding and using the vast array of idioms. *The Penguin Dictionary of English Idioms* is uniquely designed to stimulate understanding and familiarity by explaining the meanings and origins of idioms and giving examples of typical usage.

The Penguin Wordmaster Dictionary
Martin H. Manser and Nigel D. Turton

This dictionary puts the pleasure back into word-seeking. Every time you look at a page you get a bonus – a panel telling you everything about a particular word or expression. It is, therefore, a dictionary to be read as well as used for its concise and up-to-date definitions.

READ MORE IN PENGUIN

REFERENCE

Medicines: A Guide for Everybody Peter Parish

Now in its seventh edition and completely revised and updated, this bestselling guide is written in ordinary language for the ordinary reader yet will prove indispensable to anyone involved in health care – nurses, pharmacists, opticians, social workers and doctors.

Media Law Geoffrey Robertson, QC, and Andrew Nichol

Crisp and authoritative surveys explain the up-to-date position on defamation, obscenity, official secrecy, copyright and confidentiality, contempt of court, the protection of privacy and much more.

The Slang Thesaurus

Do you make the public bar sound like a gentleman's club? The miraculous *Slang Thesaurus* will liven up your language in no time. You won't Adam and Eve it! A mine of funny, witty, acid and vulgar synonyms for the words you use every day.

The Penguin Dictionary of Troublesome Words Bill Bryson

Why should you avoid discussing the *weather conditions*? Can a married woman be celibate? Why is it eccentric to talk about the aroma of a cowshed? A straightforward guide to the pitfalls and hotly disputed issues in standard written English.

The Penguin Dictionary of Musical Performers Arthur Jacobs

In this invaluable companion volume to *The Penguin Dictionary of Music* Arthur Jacobs has brought together the names of over 2,500 performers. Music is written by composers, yet it is the interpreters who bring it to life; in this comprehensive book they are at last given their due.

The Penguin Dictionary of Physical Geography John Whittow

'Dr Whittow and Penguin Reference Books have put serious students of the subject in their debt, by combining the terminology of the traditional geomorphology with that of the quantitative revolution and defining both in one large and comprehensive dictionary of physical geography ... clear and succinct' – *The Times Educational Supplement*

READ MORE IN PENGUIN

DICTIONARIES

READ MORE IN PENGUIN

BUSINESS

Management and Motivation	Victor H. Vroom and Edward L. Deci
The Art of Japanese Management	Richard Tanner Pascale and Anthony Athos
The Penguin Management Handbook	Thomas Kempner (ed.)
Introducing Management	Peter Lawrence and Ken Elliott (ed.)
The Entrepreneurial Manager	A. L. Minkes
An Insight into Management Accounting	John Sizer
Understanding Company Financial Statements	R. H. Parker
Successful Interviewing	Jack Gratus
Working in Organizations	Andrew Kakabudse, Ron Ludlow and Susan Vinnicombe
Offensive Marketing	J. H. Davidson
Corporate Recovery	Stuart Slatter
Corporate Strategy	Igor Ansoff

READ MORE IN PENGUIN

BUSINESS AND ECONOMICS

From Boom to Bust David Smith

When Margaret Thatcher took office for the third time in 1987 her monetarist experiment had been replaced by more pragmatic policies, inflation and unemployment were both low, and there was even talk of an 'economic miracle'. By 1991 this short-lived boom was just a distant memory.

Atlas of Management Thinking Edward de Bono

This fascinating book provides a vital repertoire of non-verbal images that will help activate the right side of any manager's brain.

Almost Everyone's Guide to Economics
 J. K. Galbraith and Nicole Salinger

This instructive and entertaining dialogue provides a step-by-step explanation of 'the state of economics in general and the reasons for its present failure in particular, in simple, accurate language that everyone could understand and that a perverse few might conceivably enjoy'.

The Economist Economics Rupert Pennant-Rea and Clive Crook

Based on a series of 'briefs' published in *The Economist* , this is a clear and accessible guide to the key issues of today's economics for the general reader.

The Rise and Fall of Monetarism David Smith

Now that even Conservatives have consigned monetarism to the scrap heap of history, David Smith draws out the unhappy lessons of a fundamentally flawed economic experiment, driven by a doctrine that for years had been regarded as outmoded and irrelevant.

Understanding Organizations Charles B. Handy

Of practical as well as theoretical interest, this book shows how general concepts can help solve specific organizational problems.